FALSE PROFITS

Beware of false prophets which come to you in sheep's clothing, but inwardly they are ravening wolves.

— Matthew 7:15

The false gods they used to invoke will leave them in the lurch, and they will perceive that they have no way of escape.

— Qu'ran XLI, verse 48

FALSE PROFITS

The Inside Story of BCCI,
the World's Most Corrupt
Financial Empire

PETER TRUELL
AND
LARRY GURWIN

HOUGHTON MIFFLIN COMPANY

Boston and New York

1992

Library of Congress Cataloging-in-Publication Data

Truell, Peter.
False profits : the inside story of BCCI, the world's most
corrupt financial empire / Peter Truell and Larry Gurwin.
p. cm.
Includes bibliographical references and index.
ISBN 0-395-62339-1
1. Bank of Credit and Commerce International — Corrupt practices.
2. International finance — Corrupt practices. 3. Bank failures.
I. Gurwin, Larry. II. Title.
HG1978.T78 1992
364.1'68 — dc20   92-37248
                                          CIP

Printed in the United States of America

AGM 10 9 8 7 6 5 4 3 2 1

To the memory of my parents,
Margaret and Michael Truell

— P.T.

To my wife, Jacqueline

— L.G.

CONTENTS

Contents

A Cast of Characters and Companies

Many of the Arabic and Pakistani names in this book can be spelled in different ways. Sheikh Zayed's family name, for example, can be spelled al-Nahyan or al-Nahayan. The authors have attempted to follow the preferences of the people mentioned.

After Financial General Bankshares was acquired in 1982, it was renamed First American Bankshares, as noted in Chapter 3. In subsequent chapters, the First American name is generally used, even in discussions of events that occurred before the name change.

Abedi, Agha Hasan. This charismatic Pakistani financier founded and led BCCI.

Abu Dhabi Investment Authority. A government agency controlled by Sheikh Zayed, it manages a large portion of Abu Dhabi's oil wealth.

Adham, Kamal. The former head of Saudi Arabia's intelligence agency, Adham is a brother-in-law of the late King Faisal and still advises the ruling family. He was listed as a shareholder in Attock Oil, BCCI, Capcom, and First American Bankshares.

Akbar, Syed Ziauddin Ali. Akbar headed BCCI's treasury division until 1986, when he became managing director of Capcom. He presided over much of the looting of BCCI.

Altman, Robert A. A law partner and protégé of Clark Clifford, Altman served as an attorney for BCCI and First American and assisted Clifford in the running of First American.

Attock Oil. A company in London connected to BCCI. The shareholders included Adham and Pharaon.

Awan, Amjad. This BCCI banker handled Manuel Antonio Noriega's personal financial needs.

Bank of America. Based in San Francisco, the huge international bank was one of BCCI's biggest shareholders from its founding in 1972 until 1980.

BCCI Holdings (Luxembourg) S.A. The holding company for Abedi's far-flung banking empire, it controlled two main subsidiaries — Bank of Credit and Commerce International S.A. in Luxembourg and Bank of Credit and Commerce International (Overseas) Ltd. in the Cayman Islands, a Caribbean tax haven.

Bin Mahfouz, Khalid. The head of National Commercial Bank, the largest bank in Saudi Arabia, which is controlled by his family, Bin Mahfouz was a big shareholder in BCCI and First American.

Blum, Jack A. This lawyer investigated BCCI for Senator John Kerry's subcommittee on terrorism and drugs. He then blew the whistle on BCCI.

Bush, George W. The president's eldest son, he is a part owner and a board member of Harken Energy, which got an unusually advantageous oil concession with the help of several people connected to BCCI.

Capcom Financial Services Ltd. A commodity futures trading company in London, it was linked to BCCI and helped it to "lose" hundreds of millions of dollars.

Carter, Jimmy. A former president who became close to Abedi after leaving the White House. BCCI contributed millions of dollars to his pet projects. Carter helped BCCI project a respectable image.

Casey, William J. A fervent anticommunist, Casey headed the CIA during most of Reagan's presidency. The agency's relationship with BCCI flourished during that period.

CenTrust Savings Bank. Until its collapse in 1990, this institution based in Miami was the largest S&L in the Southeast. Through Pharaon, it was connected to BCCI.

Clifford, Clark M. BCCI's man in Washington and an adviser to every Democratic president since 1945, Clifford was also a preeminent Washington power broker. He served as chairman of First American Bankshares and legal counsel to both BCCI and First American.

First American Bankshares, Inc. Formerly known as Financial General Bankshares, it was taken over by BCCI clients in 1982 and renamed. It soon became the biggest bank holding company in Washington, D.C. First American owned banks in the District of Columbia, Florida, Georgia, Maryland, New York, Tennessee, and Virginia.

Gauhar, Altaf. With BCCI's financial backing, he launched the Third World Foundation and *South* magazine.

George, Eddie. The deputy governor of the Bank of England, he decided that BCCI had to be shut down.

Gokal brothers. Abbas, Murtaza, and Mustapha Gokal ran the Gulf Group, an international conglomerate of shipping and commodities companies. The Gulf Group was BCCI's biggest borrower.

Hatch, Orrin. A Republican senator from Utah, Hatch came to BCCI's aid when the bank was under pressure on Capitol Hill.

ICIC. A company in the Cayman Islands controlled by BCCI, it was used to appropriate deposits, massage BCCI's accounts, and serve as a dumping ground for bad loans.

Independence Bank. A small bank in the Encino section of Los Angeles connected to BCCI through Ghaith Pharaon.

Jackowski, Mark V. An assistant U.S. attorney in Tampa, Florida, he was the lead prosecutor in the first criminal case brought against BCCI in the United States.

Kerry, John F. A Democratic senator from Massachusetts, Kerry played an important role in exposing BCCI.

Khalil, Abdul-Raouf. A Saudi communications and intelligence maven, Khalil was also a shareholder in BCCI, Capcom, and First American.

Lance, T. Bertram ("Bert"). A folksy Georgia banker and best friend of Jimmy Carter, Lance was forced to resign from the Carter administration in disgrace. He went on to help BCCI penetrate the U.S. market and introduced Abedi to Stephens and Carter.

Magness, Bob. The founder and chairman of Tele-Communications Inc. (TCI). He and his protégé, Larry Romrell, owned stock in Capcom and served on its board.

Mazrui, Ghanem Faris al. The head of Sheikh Zayed's Department of Personal Affairs, Mazrui was a senior man at the Abu Dhabi Investment Authority and a BCCI board member.

Mazur, Robert (aka Robert Musella). An undercover agent with the U.S. Customs Service, Mazur headed a sting operation that snared BCCI.

Morgenthau, Robert M. The Manhattan district attorney and a former U.S. attorney in Manhattan, Morgenthau pursued and eventually cracked the BCCI case.

Moscow, John W. An assistant district attorney in Morgenthau's office, Moscow directed the probe of BCCI.

Naqvi, Swaleh. Abedi's faithful deputy, Naqvi succeeded him as chief executive of BCCI.

National Bank of Georgia. Based in Atlanta, it was controlled by Bert Lance until 1978, when Pharaon stepped in. First American bought it in 1987.

Paul, David L. The chairman of Miami's CenTrust Savings Bank and a friend and business partner of Pharaon's, Paul was a major donor to political candidates.

Pharaon, Ghaith Rashad. A flamboyant Saudi tycoon and a frequent front man for BCCI, Pharaon was also a shareholder in BCCI and several companies close to it, including Attock Oil, CenTrust, Independence Bank, and National Bank of Georgia.

Price Waterhouse. An international accounting firm that audited BCCI's Cayman Islands units and later most of the BCCI group.

Rahman, Masihur. BCCI's chief financial officer, Rahman provided prosecutors with important information about the bank.

Romrell, Larry. A top official of Tele-Communications Inc. (TCI), the

huge cable television company that bailed out Ted Turner, Romrell
served as chairman of Capcom. Romrell and TCI's chairman, Bob
Magness, were also major shareholders in Capcom.

Stephens, Jackson. An investment banker from Little Rock, Arkansas,
and a generous political donor to presidential candidates, he runs
Stephens Inc., one of the country's biggest brokerages. He helped
BCCI penetrate the United States.

Zayed bin Sultan al-Nahyan. The multibillionaire ruler of Abu Dhabi and
president of the United Arab Emirates, Zayed was Abedi's most important patron and the controlling shareholder of BCCI.

PROLOGUE

AFTER LINING UP on the sidewalk for as much as an hour in the summer sun, the press was impatient and ill-tempered. It was stiflingly hot in New York that day — Wednesday, July 29, 1992 — and the Manhattan district attorney's office was jammed with photographers, reporters, sound technicians, lighting crews, and all the paraphernalia of the modern media. Cameramen shoved one another to try to win a better spot for their equipment; secretaries struggled to push open the office's windows to let in more air. The room, festooned with pictures of the Kennedy family and other souvenirs of a life in public service, reeked of the D.A.'s cheap cigars.

At 11:13 A.M., Robert M. Morgenthau walked through the back door of his office, followed by several staff members and representatives of the U.S. Justice Department and the Federal Reserve, to face the waiting crowd. Uncharacteristically, the district attorney was several minutes late. The seventy-two-year-old prosecutor stood behind a wooden lectern as his colleagues arranged themselves behind him. Some reporters stood on leather chairs to get a good view; others squatted on any spare piece of floor space.

The slim, white-haired D.A. read in a quiet, halting voice from his prepared text: "A New York County grand jury has returned two indictments, charging six individuals, including Clark M. Clifford and Robert A. Altman, for criminal conduct arising out of the operation of the Bank of Credit and Commerce International — BCCI." This bank, Morgenthau said, was "a criminal enterprise" that had "bribed central bankers, government officials, and others worldwide to gain power and money." Among those bribed, the indictment alleged, were Clif-

ford and Altman; the grand jury accused them of receiving tens of
millions of dollars from the corrupt bank for their part in its illegal
schemes.

These were shocking charges. Clark Clifford had been one of the
most powerful and admired men in the nation's capital since the
1940s. An elder statesman of the Democratic party, he had advised
every Democratic president from Harry Truman to Jimmy Carter and
had served as Lyndon Johnson's secretary of defense. After years
of cultivating a reputation as a man of integrity, Clifford now faced
charges that carried a maximum penalty of eight years in prison
and $80 million in fines. Altman, his forty-five-year-old protégé,
could be sentenced to twenty years' imprisonment and $80 million in
fines.

In addition to the indictments, Morgenthau outlined a plea bargain
his office had negotiated with Kamal Adham, the former intelligence
chief of Saudi Arabia and an adviser to that country's King Fahd.
Adham admitted to helping BCCI in its crimes in the United States and
agreed to pay a $105 million fine. He also pledged complete coopera-
tion with the Manhattan district attorney and other U.S. authorities,
raising the possibility that someone from the bank's inner circle would
testify against Clifford, Altman, and other defendants.

After reading his prepared statement, Morgenthau took questions.
When one reporter tried to bait him by asking about future indictments and other sensitive issues, the seasoned prosecutor said, "You
know better than to ask me that." There were also provocative questions about the strength of the evidence his office had gathered. In
some instances, he conceded, his investigators had found witnesses but
no supporting documentation; in others, they had documents but no
witnesses. Within forty-five minutes, the press conference was over.
News agency reporters hurried off to find telephones to start filing
their stories.

The indictment of Clifford and Altman was a milestone for Robert
Morgenthau. For more than three years he had struggled to piece
together the secret history of BCCI and bring some of the culprits to
justice. It had been an extraordinarily challenging task, partly because
of BCCI's political clout. It had pitted Morgenthau's prosecutors and
detectives against much of the Washington establishment, in which
BCCI and its associates seemed to have an unlimited number of friends
and allies. Morgenthau and his investigators were also challenged by
the vast scope and complexity of the bank's criminality. In his long

career in law enforcement, the New York prosecutor had never encountered anything like BCCI.

For Morgenthau, the affair had begun in the spring of 1989 when a former U.S. Senate investigator had turned up at his office with a string of allegations about BCCI's involvement in drug money laundering and other crimes. The Manhattan district attorney, long known for his passion for attacking white-collar crime, started a small investigation under one of his most trusted lieutenants, Assistant District Attorney John W. Moscow, a streetwise New Yorker famed for his one-liners. Gradually Morgenthau's office built a picture of a rogue bank that seemed to break laws regularly and with impunity. Several former BCCI officials provided evidence about BCCI's modus operandi. As other government investigators in the United States and overseas ignored BCCI or failed to press ahead with probes, Morgenthau's office persevered, undeterred by the many roadblocks thrown in its path by the bank and its powerful friends. By the spring of 1991, the D.A. was able to empanel a grand jury to hear the mounting evidence his office had collected against the bank and its principals.

Government officials in many countries had known for years that BCCI was a corrupt bank, but none of them had taken serious action until they were forced to do so by Morgenthau's probe. The Federal Reserve and the Department of Justice as well as investigators in Britain and continental Europe waited anxiously to see what Morgenthau would do. When it became clear that he was prepared to bring serious criminal charges against BCCI, bank regulators in London, New York, and other financial centers seized the corrupt institution on July 5, 1991, and put it out of business.

Just over three weeks later, Morgenthau announced the first major indictment of BCCI. A New York grand jury charged the bank and its founder, the Pakistani financier Agha Hasan Abedi, and his deputy, Swaleh Naqvi, with perpetrating what Morgenthau called "the largest bank fraud in world financial history."

In the months following, Morgenthau focused his attention on other alleged culprits, including Clifford and Altman. In the D.A.'s view, the two lawyers had played a critical role in the BCCI affair. Clifford had used his considerable prestige and political influence to help the bank expand its empire and protect itself from government investigators. Morgenthau felt he could prove that Clifford and Altman had helped BCCI carry out a secret and illegal scheme to acquire control of First American Bankshares, the biggest banking company in Washington.

Clifford had been chairman of First American, Altman its de facto chief executive. As the scandal spread, Clifford and Altman steadfastly maintained that they — like the nation's top regulators and politicians — had been deceived by BCCI.

Now, in the summer of 1992, the Manhattan district attorney was investigating BCCI's political allies in Washington and in the capitals of Europe and the Arabian peninsula.

Clifford and Altman were booked at Manhattan's huge and grimy central criminal courts building the same morning that Morgenthau announced the charges against them. They were spared the rigors of "central booking," a humiliating routine in which groups of defendants are processed in assembly-line fashion. "It is the normal courtesy extended to an eighty-five-year-old defendant with no prior record and a recent history of heart trouble," John Moscow told reporters as he stood by the elevators after Morgenthau's press conference. Nevertheless, both men were fingerprinted, and they were scheduled to come back the following week for mug shots.

Shortly after two o'clock, the two lawyers returned to the courts building for their arraignment before Judge John A. K. Bradley, a short, rumpled man wearing black-rimmed spectacles. Bradley, who often tried complex financial cases, would hear Clifford's and Altman's pleas and later set a date for trial. A tremendous clacking of camera shutters announced the arrival of the two men outside the building. When they entered the courtroom, however, no photographer awaited them; they had exercised their right to ban cameras from the room.

Inside, Altman strode to take his place at the defendants' table. The white-haired Clifford moved slowly up the aisle, his hallmark gray fedora in hand. He was as elegant as ever, wearing a double-breasted pinstripe suit and a white shirt with French cuffs. Carl Rauh, a defense lawyer for the two men, carried Clifford's briefcase, a gesture that underscored his client's frailty.

Courtrooms and legal proceedings were familiar to Clifford. After all, he had been an attorney for most of his life, having begun the practice of law more than six decades earlier. But this was the first time that he had attended court as a defendant in a criminal case. He took his seat beside Altman, a man who was much more than his law partner. They had such a strong personal bond that several friends described Altman as the son Clifford never had. For more than two decades Clifford had groomed Altman, turning him into a consummate Washington power broker. Like his mentor, Altman was a friend of some of the most powerful people in town, including influential members of Congress and senior officials of the Bush administration.

The court clerk asked the two defendants to stand while he read part of the indictment. When asked for their pleas, Clifford and Altman answered in unison: "I plead not guilty." Judge Bradley released them on their own recognizance. They left the courthouse by a side door, ignoring the shouted questions of reporters as they climbed into a chauffeur-driven Cadillac.

The indictment of Clifford dealt with only one aspect of the BCCI affair, which by the summer of 1992 had become a vast and complicated scandal embracing a multitude of individuals and institutions around the world. Before its closure, BCCI had operated in seventy-three countries and had been a major force in such financial centers as New York, London, Geneva, Paris, and Hong Kong and in the capitals of the Persian Gulf, where many of BCCI's sponsors lived.

Among the most important of BCCI's patrons was Sheikh Zayed bin Sultan al-Nahyan, the aging ruler of the Arab emirate of Abu Dhabi. Zayed cuts a medieval figure in a modern world; he visits his countless palaces and mansions — from Pakistan to Spain's Costa del Sol — accompanied by a court jester and a huge entourage of relatives and retainers. Transformed from desert Bedouin to petrobillionaire in the space of a few years, Zayed once spent millions on a wedding for a son he sired with one of his harem of more than a dozen wives.

Despite such unorthodox backers, BCCI had outwardly seemed like a normal financial institution, with attractively designed branch offices, its own traveler's check business, and a reputation for financing international trade. But behind this convincing façade, BCCI was a criminal enterprise that catered to some of the most notorious villains of the late twentieth century, including Saddam Hussein, the bloodthirsty ruler of Iraq; leaders of the Medellín drug cartel, which controls the bulk of the world's cocaine trade; Khun Sa, the warlord who dominates heroin trafficking in Asia's Golden Triangle; Abu Nidal, the head of one of the world's leading terrorist organizations; and Manuel Antonio Noriega, the drug-dealing former dictator of Panama. BCCI not only assisted others in committing crimes, the institution was itself a fraud. The men who ran the bank collected billions of dollars in deposits and then systematically looted it. BCCI insiders had also plundered other financial institutions — in Europe, the Middle East, and the United States.

This criminal rampage lasted for nearly two decades. Rarely was BCCI hindered by bank regulators, law enforcement authorities, or politicians, in part because it had bought off many of the people who should have been policing it. Its political reach was awesome: the BCCI network was connected to some of the most powerful people in the world, including Middle Eastern potentates, Asian strong men, and political leaders in Europe and the United States. The bank and its allies even had personal and financial ties to people in the inner circles of President George Bush and the man who was aiming to unseat him, Governor Bill Clinton of Arkansas.

BCCI officials used a panoply of techniques to cultivate powerful people. Some were bought off with banknotes in a briefcase. Others were provided with prostitutes, or "dancing girls," as Abedi's Pakistani colleagues preferred to call them. Abdur Sakhia, a veteran BCCI official, has said that payoffs to VIPs were made "in the form of cash or the hiring of their relatives, contributions to their favorite charities, payment for their medical bills." In other cases, "charities were funded, their projects were financed at favorable rates, loans [were granted] at favorable rates. So it took various shapes and forms." No matter what the method, the purpose was always "to buy influence." BCCI used this influence to protect itself from its enemies; equally important, the bank was actively involved in promoting the political agendas of its backers, especially the rulers of Arab nations in the Persian Gulf.

BCCI's ability to operate with impunity for so long may also have had something to do with its connections to the murky world of intelligence. It had generated tremendous goodwill at the CIA by assisting in a series of sensitive covert operations. BCCI's relationship with U.S. intelligence was so close that questions have been raised about whether the CIA was one of the original sponsors of BCCI — and even one of the beneficiaries of its larceny.

The political and intelligence dimensions of the affair make it far more than a financial scandal. Some pundits have labeled it an "international Watergate." Others have called it "the mother of all scandals." It is a tale of intrigue and political corruption on a worldwide scale with an amazing cast of characters. The most remarkable of all is the founder and guiding force of BCCI, Agha Hasan Abedi. It was his vision, charisma, and hunger for power that propelled BCCI and inspired the almost religious devotion of his staff. Alberto Calvo, who helped to establish BCCI's network of offices in Latin America, describes Abedi as "intelligent, brilliant, lucid and shady; prophetic; angel and devil; generous to the point of absurdity; a megalomaniac; a manipulator."

So successful was Abedi that one observer called him the "Moriarty of finance," an allusion to Sherlock Holmes's nemesis who was blamed for half the crime in London. In Abedi's case, it would eventually seem as if he had a hand in half the crime in the world.

FALSE PROFITS

1

THE COURTIER AND
THE SHEIKH

IN EARLY AUTUMN, Abu Dhabi can seem cool at night after the daytime's dizzying heat. One evening in September 1972, a fashionably dressed Pakistani businessman walked quickly from his limousine to a suburban villa, and anyone who saw him might have assumed that he was eager to escape the chill air. But Agha Hasan Abedi had another reason to hurry: he had just received good news and wanted very much to share it with Majid Ali, his friend and confidant.

The fifty-year-old Abedi strode through the hallway into Ali's living room, smiling at his host's family and the half dozen or so friends who were visiting. After politely but hastily greeting each person in turn, Abedi took Ali by the arm and led him from the room, whispering excitedly with each step.

For months, the two men had been secretly discussing Abedi's plan to secure the backing of Sheikh Zayed bin Sultan al-Nahyan for a new international banking venture. Zayed was the fantastically wealthy ruler of Abu Dhabi as well as president of the United Arab Emirates, of which Abu Dhabi was the most important part. Abedi had spent the past six years and more cultivating the sheikh from his base in Karachi, Pakistan. It was there that Abedi ran United Bank, which he had founded thirteen years earlier with money provided by his patrons, the Saigols, a family of shipping and textile magnates. But Abedi's ambitions had always ranged beyond Pakistan, and in his old friend Ali, a financial adviser to the sheikh, Abedi saw an opportunity. A fellow Pakistani, Ali did all he could to secure the backing of the ruler and other sheikhs for a new enterprise.

Within minutes of leaving the room, Abedi and Ali returned arm in arm, beaming at the assembled company. "You are among close friends here and you should share the good news with them, too," Ali said to Abedi, nodding to his wife and their guests. Standing in the middle of the room with his muttonchop sideburns and carefully coiffed mane of black hair, Abedi looked every bit the nineteenth-century preacher addressing his flock. "It is truly by the grace of God," he said, "that the sheikhs have been kind enough to give me their trust and support the new bank that we are creating."

It had been a harried few months for Abedi, who had shuttled between Pakistan, Abu Dhabi, Britain, and the United States to line up support for the new bank. Wooing Sheikh Zayed and other Arab leaders in the Persian Gulf at the same time as he courted San Francisco's Bank of America — then the largest bank in the world — was a challenge, even for such a charming and persuasive man.

The new institution, Abedi told his audience in Ali's living room, would enable him and his colleagues from United Bank to recover from the incredible turmoil of the past few years. Pakistan had been torn apart in 1971 when East Pakistan broke away to form the nation of Bangladesh. Many United Bank employees in the east had been displaced. What is more, Pakistan's leader, Zulfikar Ali Bhutto, had instituted radical economic policies, including the nationalization of several industries, one of which was banking. When United Bank was taken over by the government, Abedi was one of several bankers placed under house arrest by Bhutto; they were suspected of having helped the previous military regime.

Now, Abedi told his approving listeners, Providence had intervened to provide a secure future for the employees of United Bank. Their new haven would be in Europe. Abedi's bank would be incorporated in Luxembourg but would have offices throughout the world. In choosing a name, Abedi signaled the scope of his ambition. He called it the Bank of Credit and Commerce International.

Abedi's description of the role played by Divine Providence was not quite accurate. The Pakistani banker had given Providence a great deal of help in his courting of Sheikh Zayed and other local potentates. Abedi owed much of his success to his origins. For more than a century, his family had learned how to cultivate powerful men in their role as courtiers to the Shi'ite Muslim rajahs of the city of Mahmudabad, in what is now the northern Indian province of Uttar Pradesh.

The Shi'ites, who derive their name from the Arabic term *Shiat Ali* (party of Ali), form the main minority sect of Islam. Their tradition dates from the earliest days of Islam, for they believe that the authority of the Prophet Muhammad was passed to his son-in-law Ali. In contrast, the Sunni sect, whose name comes from *Sunnat Allah* (way of God), maintains that authority was passed on to a series of caliphs chosen from Muhammad's followers. In the wars that followed the Prophet's death, the Sunnis triumphed, establishing themselves as the dominant sect.

Nevertheless, strong Shia communities prospered, particularly in Iran and Iraq as well as Mahmudabad. The cities of Mahmudabad and Lucknow were the center of the once-great Mughal Empire. According to local legend, Abedi is directly descended from a participant in a largely Muslim rebellion against the British in 1857. His forebear, the story goes, was exhibited in a cage in the streets of Lucknow once the colonialists reasserted control.

Abedi was born in Lucknow on May 14, 1922, and "grew up moored to a rich Muslim tradition, including the sense that patronage and power are the essence of empire," in the words of Najam Sethi, a Pakistani journalist. "Abedi's philanthropy and his fondness for perfume, gourmet cuisine, fine clothing, art and the color white for its purity can all be attributed to his Lucknavi Muslim heritage."

The young Abedi enjoyed the privileged education of a courtier's son. "I had a master's degree in English literature in 1945 and my law degree in 1946," he told American lawyers several years later. He neglected to mention that both qualifications were from Lucknow University, an institution not likely to impress the attorneys. In 1946, the rajah of Mahmudabad recommended Abedi for a job with Habib Bank in Bombay. After all, the Abedis were loyal confidants who helped the rajahs live regally while most of their subjects toiled in rural poverty.

Abedi's banking career began just as the colonial era was coming to an end in India. In 1947, British India split into independent states dominated by either Muslim or Hindu. The predominantly Muslim territories to the northwest and the northeast became Pakistan, leaving the rest of India to the majority Hindu population. Chaos and sectarian fighting left hundreds of thousands dead as Muslims struggled to reach the new state of Pakistan and Hindus rushed to India. Like many Muslim businesses in India, Habib Bank decided to move its headquarters to Pakistan at the time of the partition, and the twenty-five-year-old Abedi went with it. The new state offered great opportunities for an aspiring banker, particularly because it had to start its financial institutions from scratch.

Like many young Muslims from India, Abedi found the move a traumatic experience that bred a lifelong sense of insecurity. His background had made him a would-be aristocrat in British India, but he was a double outsider in Pakistan: a Muslim immigrant from India and a Shi'ite in a largely Sunni country. At the same time, the migration to Pakistan fostered a clannishness within the community of former Indian Muslims. Throughout his career, Abedi would choose his closest associates from the Shi'ite Muslim oligarchy that once prospered in Uttar Pradesh. The experience also gave him an appreciation and affinity for minority and immigrant societies, particularly Pakistani communities around the world.

Abedi's career at Habib Bank flourished in Pakistan, but the young man was eager to run his own organization. That chance came after he helped the powerful Saigol family by arranging financing for a textile plant in the poor northern Pakistani town of Quetta. In the late 1950s, the Saigols put up the money for a new institution — United Bank — and named Abedi chief executive. Abedi was anxious to project a prestigious image. He was concerned about "the high quality of appearance of the offices," according to a former colleague, and he recruited a former prime minister, I. I. Chundrigar, to serve as chairman of the board.

Every major success that Abedi had achieved up to this point had come about with the aid of powerful patrons. The rajah of Mahmudabad had helped him find a job at Habib Bank. The Saigols had put him in charge of United Bank. Although he was now an important financier, Abedi continued to seek new patrons and allies. He forged ties with the Pakistani military, which wielded considerable influence in the country's politics. Through the Saigols, Abedi met other important businessmen in Pakistan and in the Arab world. It was in the Middle East, in fact, that he would find the most important patron of his life, Sheikh Zayed of Abu Dhabi. At the time, Zayed was an obscure Bedouin chieftain, but he would become one of the richest men in the world.

When the Middle East was carved up during the Age of Imperialism, the dominant powers in the region were Britain, France, and the Ottoman Empire. In the early part of this century, new nations began to achieve independence. Saudi Arabia and Iraq were among the first.

Others followed over the years, including Jordan, Israel, and Lebanon. One of the last places to become independent was a territory on the Persian Gulf east of Saudi Arabia. A British protectorate, it consisted of seven sheikhdoms called the Trucial States: Abu Dhabi, Dubai, Ajman, Fujeirah, Ras al-Khaimah, Sharjah, and Umm al-Qaiwan.

The Trucial States were sparsely populated, desolate, and extremely backward. The largest, Abu Dhabi, had just 46,000 inhabitants in 1968. All of the rest combined had another 134,000. The biggest "city" in Zayed's emirate — Abu Dhabi town — was a sleepy and dusty place with a few hundred buildings at most. It suffers from stifling humidity and temperatures of well over 100 degrees Fahrenheit in the summer months. Smaller fishing communities were scattered along the emirate's desert coastline, and a few Bedouin tribes were clustered around the occasional oasis in the desert interior, which extended a hundred miles and more to the mountains of Muscat and Oman in the south.

Dubai, the second most important sheikhdom, was more cosmopolitan. With its unmatched natural harbor, it served as a port and entrepôt for all the sheikhdoms. It also played an important role in trade with nearby India, and many emigrants from the Indian subcontinent settled there. Unlike Abu Dhabi, Dubai had a strong commercial tradition. There were fishermen, pearl divers, and smugglers. Gold concealed in boats from Dubai was taken across the Arabian Sea and sold to Indian hoarders.

The Trucial States hardly seemed like a promising place to find a patron, but Abedi must have sensed that it would not be a backwater forever. Like other parts of the British Empire, it was destined to become independent. Furthermore, the Trucial States might even be rich one day, for they were endowed with large quantities of oil, the vast majority of it in Abu Dhabi. Neighboring countries had already enjoyed an economic boom after oil was developed. The major Western oil companies had been drilling in the northern Gulf — Iraq, Iran, Kuwait, and Saudi Arabia — for several years, but it was only in 1960 that oil was discovered in Abu Dhabi, and it was first pumped in commercial quantities two years after that.

In the mid-1960s, Abedi began to court the desert potentates, concentrating on Abu Dhabi.

Abu Dhabi had been dominated by the al-Nahyan family for generations and, since 1928, ruled by Sheikh Shakhbut bin Sultan al-Nahyan.

The second most powerful figure in the family was his brother Zayed, who was born about a decade before Shakhbut became ruler.

Zayed lived in the town of al-Ain, about a hundred miles south of Abu Dhabi town, in a clay fort surrounded by red sand dunes. As governor of Abu Dhabi's southeastern province, he typically spent his days mediating between tribesmen over camel rustling and negotiating with the neighboring rulers, the sultan of Muscat and the governor of the neighboring Saudi Arabian province.

He had all the traits that Bedouin expected in a leader. When the British explorer Wilfred Thesiger met him at the Buraimi oasis near al-Ain in 1948 and 1949, he was impressed by the young Arab chieftain, characterizing him as "a powerfully built man of about 30 with a brown beard." Zayed, said the Englishman, had "a strong intelligent face, with steady observant eyes." Zayed wore a dagger and a cartridge belt and carried a rifle. A wily leader, he seemed to command the admiration of others. The Bedu tribesmen liked him for "his easy informal ways and his friendliness, and they respected his force of character, his shrewdness and his physical strength," according to Thesiger's account. "Zayed is a Bedu," the tribesmen would say. "He knows about camels, can ride like one of us, can shoot, and knows how to fight." Skirmishes with other tribes and rival camel rustlers were common. Zayed, of course, had his own share of ruffians and outlaws in his entourage, for as a crafty tribal leader he clearly preferred to have them with him rather than in some rival sheikh's fort.

In the foothills of the mountains, Zayed was able to indulge his great loves, reciting and composing poetry and hunting with falcons and salukis. He would take trips of several weeks to catch *houbara*, as that turkey hen–size bird, the McQueen's bustard, is known locally. Desert hares and antelope were other favored quarry.

Zayed was highly regarded by the British, who considered him more progressive than his brother. Shakhbut was so out of step with the times, he once argued that the oil companies had more use for money than he did. He had increasingly frustrated both the British and his tribal subjects by refusing to push Abu Dhabi's development or to distribute the growing revenues derived from oil exports.

By contrast, Zayed was eager to develop the desert sheikhdom. As governor of the southeastern province, he had pressed Shakhbut to finance a simple development plan for the Buraimi oasis and brought in an agricultural expert to argue his case. Shakhbut would have none of it, and there was a showdown between the brothers. "My people know more about agriculture in their own land than you can tell them," the sheikh told the agricultural expert with a sneer. As for spending money on an agricultural development plan, "The budget is a pure waste of money," Shakhbut said. "We don't want it and we won't have it. What can you tell us that we don't know?"

Zayed was terribly disappointed but nevertheless retained the agricultural specialist, a Pakistani named A. H. Khan, paying him out of his own pocket. "The most disheartening feature of all was Shakhbut's simple refusal to give his own people, a pastoral, agricultural and fishing society, the easy assistance which his growing wealth could provide," said the political agent Colonel Hugh Boustead, reflecting the prevailing British wisdom on Shakhbut.

With encouragement and help from the British, Sheikh Zayed left his wild frontier life to depose his elder brother in a bloodless coup d'état — the first time in generations that a coup had been accomplished in Abu Dhabi without murder. The history of the Nahyan family was beset with fratricide, but the mother of Zayed, Shakhbut, and their two brothers made them, as youths, swear that they would never do violence to one another. Thus spared by Zayed, Shakhbut spent a few years' exile in France, eventually returning to live out his life quietly in Abu Dhabi.

Although the British had installed Zayed, they did not treat him especially well. They practically forced him to yield to Saudi Arabia's demands for additional territory and an oil field to settle a festering border dispute. Earlier, the British had steadfastly backed Zayed's legitimate claims; now they merely wanted the dispute settled, even if it meant yielding to the weaker claims of the stronger party.

Despite this and other periodic frictions, Zayed became aligned with Saudi Arabia. In an increasingly democratic world, absolute rulers like the king of Saudi Arabia and the sheikh of Abu Dhabi had to stick together, for they faced similar threats. In the 1960s and 1970s these came mainly from radicals, communists, and others, supported by Egypt and the Soviet Union. The Saudis had aided royalist Yemeni forces through much of the 1960s against their republican opponents, who were backed by Egypt.

Zayed was popular in Abu Dhabi — and certainly more progressive than his brother — but he had some obvious limitations. One was his lack of education, particularly in financial matters. For a time after his ascension, Zayed's monies and gold bars mostly remained where Shakhbut had kept them: in a storeroom of the traditional clay fort in

Abu Dhabi. Rats had eaten into the notes there, some of which dated from Queen Victoria's time, or so the story goes.

With great reluctance, Zayed finally agreed to have his funds removed from the palace in Land Rovers and taken to a branch of the British Bank of the Middle East (virtually the only bank in the country) with a musket-toting tribesman riding on top of each vehicle. To the consternation of the bank's staff, Zayed appeared several days later, unannounced, demanding to see his money. Apparently it took a couple of days and an emergency flight from Bahrain to assemble sufficient funds.

Zayed's ignorance of finance was certainly no drawback in Abedi's eyes. The Pakistani banker would be more than willing to assist the ruler.

Abedi's courtship of Sheikh Zayed began around the same time that the ruler came to power. Abedi also began cultivating key figures in neighboring sheikhdoms, including Dubai's Sheikh Rashid bin Said al-Maktoum, a wily merchant who was suspicious of outsiders. The banker also developed close ties to members of the rulers' families.

In the mid-1960s, Abedi and an assistant flew to Abu Dhabi in a two-seat aircraft, according to Najam Sethi, bearing "an exquisite hand-knotted carpet under his arm." After an audience with the sheikh, Abedi was granted permission to open a branch of United Bank in Abu Dhabi. Zayed would also deposit money in the Pakistani bank. Abedi is said to have advised the manager of the new branch: "Hang on to the sheikh's coattails."

Zayed became a frequent visitor to Pakistan, and Abedi treated him as if he were the head of state of a major industrial country. The banker would arrange for hotels as well as travel and entertainment for Zayed and his entourage of relatives, servants, and retainers. Abedi also arranged hunting excursions for the sheikh. Abdullah Darwaish, an adviser of Zayed's who later ran the ruler's personal office and served as ambassador to Pakistan, said that when he first met Abedi in 1969 he could see that Zayed and the banker were friends. Abedi's efforts to cultivate Zayed and the other rulers were soon rewarded, for these obscure potentates soon became leaders of an independent country — a very rich one.

Britain, beset by economic malaise at home, decided to withdraw from the Trucial States and hastily arranged a partnership of the seven emirates. One day in December 1971 the British flag was lowered and an independent country was born, the United Arab Emirates (UAE). One historian described it as "the fig leaf with which the British government hoped to conceal its diminished parts from the quizzical gaze of the outside world."

The British refused to leave any troops in the UAE. Eager to ensure continued British protection from Iranian and Saudi Arabian expansionism, the rulers of Abu Dhabi and its neighbors had even offered to pay for a continued British military presence. But the British pulled their last remaining troops, a battalion of the Royal Irish Rangers, from the emirate of Sharjah that same December.

Inevitably, the UAE was dominated by Sheikh Zayed, who ruled what was by far the largest component, with as much as 85 percent of the federation's land area and the vast majority of its oil. Four of the other six emirates — Ajman, Fujeirah, Ras al-Khaimah, and Umm al-Qaiwan — have virtually no oil or gas reserves; the remaining two, Dubai and Sharjah, have only modest energy resources. Abu Dhabi is the prize, with oil reserves that are estimated to total as much as 10 percent of the world's known resources — a stunning amount of wealth for a country with only a few hundred thousand people.

As ruler of Abu Dhabi, Sheikh Zayed has absolute control over this wealth, as one of his lawyers later explained. "All the natural resources of the states," he said, "are also regarded as the personal property of the ruler and his heirs, who enjoy complete authority to utilize them as they see fit."

The value of that oil soon became apparent to the world. Oil prices began to rise in 1970 and 1971, thanks in large part to aggressive bargaining by Libya's leader, Moammar Qaddafi. The oil shock was just around the corner, and it would bring incalculable wealth to Sheikh Zayed and the other oil potentates in the region — as well as incalculable opportunity for Agha Hasan Abedi.

Zayed and his country were not prepared for the economic tumult and development that the Gulf would see in the 1970s after oil prices soared. Abu Dhabi not only had few people, it lacked the skills necessary to develop a modern state. Labor and technical help increasingly had to come from overseas.

There was no shortage of candidates to fill this void, which had only been enlarged by the hastiness of Britain's departure. Businessmen from Europe, the United States, and Japan, workers from poorer Arab lands like Yemen, Egypt, and the Sudan, and servants and professionals from India and Pakistan rushed to earn higher wages in Abu Dhabi. To be sure, many of those who flocked to the Gulf were opportunists and con men. "Zayed's court is packed with a host of impostors, intriguers, sycophants and flaneurs (most of them northern Arabs), who ceaselessly jostle with one another for his attention and favour," wrote J. B. Kelly, a British academician who was an adviser to Zayed. "Flattering, wheedling, shamelessly soliciting for personal ends, they swarm about the person of the ruler like so many flies."

Zayed and his family already had a special affinity for Pakistan, a few hundred miles across the Arabian Sea. It was Muslim, and it was near enough for easy access from Abu Dhabi but not so close as to be threatening. The sheikhs admired the Pakistanis, especially those in the military and from the northern tribal homelands, for their courage and martial skills. These fellow Muslims had other needed abilities, too, as Khan, the agricultural expert, had shown by helping Zayed develop the Buraimi oasis. A few members of the UAE's ruling families went to college in Pakistan in the 1960s. With a vastly greater population and an established educational system, Pakistan could provide many of the skills that the sheikhdoms lacked.

Strategically positioned between South Asia and the Middle East, the Pakistanis were experienced in international politics and had for more than a century witnessed and even participated in the Great Game of wrestling among the world's foremost powers of that era — Britain, Germany, Russia, and the Ottoman Empire — for control of the northwest frontier passes that lead to Central Asia. These people had been actors on a critical international stage. Such worldliness impressed the sheikhs of the Gulf, who in the 1970s were struggling to come to terms with their significantly greater international role.

Pakistan could also provide the desired military assistance. Its officers gradually replaced the British as instructors for the sheikhdoms' fledgling defense forces. Pakistan and Abu Dhabi had also shared some important experience. As part of British India, Pakistan too had experienced colonial rule.

These were exciting times for everyone in Abu Dhabi, and especially for the members of the educated Pakistani elite who had come to work for Sheikh Zayed. Many, like Abedi, believed that the opportunities in their own country were narrowing. Bhutto was intent on rapidly introducing a new brand of socialism to Pakistan. Abedi, as we have seen, was detained because of his ties to the previous regime.

When the time came to establish BCCI, it was relatively easy for Abedi to secure the backing of Sheikh Zayed and other UAE rulers.

His relationship with Zayed was so close that one former colleague of the banker's, Abdur Sakhia, even ascribed to Abedi a role in the founding of the federation. "Abedi created the UAE," said Sakhia. "He planted the idea of the UAE as a federation to Sheikh Zayed." These personal relationships counted for a great deal, as did Zayed's need for foreign expertise to handle his mounting oil revenues. Ever intent on discretion, Zayed was also secure in the knowledge that Abedi would disguise his degree of ownership. His new bank was a convenient vehicle for other sheikhs in the region as well. By lending their names to the venture, they could make good money.

Abedi's developing friendships with other powerful Arab figures would prove useful. Kamal Adham, a top foreign policy adviser to Saudi Arabia's King Faisal and the country's intelligence chief, and Ghaith Pharaon, the son of another adviser to the king, would both become important shareholders in BCCI and other ventures of Abedi's. The bigger challenge was to bring in a Western partner.

At a meeting early in 1972, Abedi explained to Swaleh Naqvi, his loyal deputy from United Bank, and Masihur Rahman, BCCI's future chief financial officer, his dream for a new bank — "a world bank, a global bank for the Third World," as he put it. When Rahman expressed incredulity, Abedi said, "Rahman, in ten years' time you'll see, we will all be millionaires." Abedi, said Rahman, "had lined up backing from Sheikh Zayed. All that was left was to find a big international bank to provide the instant prestige to break out of the confines of the Third World."

Abedi searched tirelessly for a powerful Western partner in the first half of 1972. In February — just weeks after his release from house arrest — he flew to New York, where he met with Bank of America's Roy P. M. Carlson, the head of the bank's Mideast-Africa region, at the Waldorf-Astoria Hotel on Park Avenue.

There were some ironic parallels between the two banks. Bank of America, founded by A. P. Giannini in the early years of this century, was originally very much an ethnic bank; its early customers were largely Italian immigrants. Similarly, Abedi's new bank would base its rapid growth on the Pakistani and Muslim Indian émigré communities around the world.

As it happened, Abedi and Bank of America had reciprocal needs. The Pakistani banker, eager to build a new type of international institution with a focus on developing countries, needed a prestigious partner to win credibility in the most important world financial markets — New York, London, Hong Kong, and Tokyo. Meanwhile, at Bank of America, Carlson and his colleague Samuel Armacost, who would later become B of A's president, were eager to build up their bank's operations in the Middle East. Its large rivals, like Citibank and Chase Manhattan, had stolen a march by opening branches there in the 1950s and 1960s. Armacost, a Lebanese American, hoped to establish ties in the Middle East and prosper from the oil boom. Abedi, who claimed to have the backing of Zayed and other wealthy potentates, could provide an entrée to the region.

What Abedi described to Carlson at the Waldorf was a truly international bank, founded with Arab and American capital, with a multinational staff that would be managed by Abedi and his lieutenants from United Bank, with some guidance from Bank of America. As any big institution might, Bank of America took some months to decide, but it finally accepted Abedi's terms. It was so desperate to expand in the Middle East that it even allowed Abedi to have complete control over the operations and administration of BCCI and permitted him to use its logo on the bank's letterhead. Abedi flew to San Francisco for a celebratory lunch at B of A's headquarters.

The initial capital was a modest $2.5 million, so Bank of America had to invest just $625,000 for its 25 percent stake. With its shareholding, it won access to Sheikh Zayed and several other sheikhs — as well as access to some of the region's oil wealth.

Abedi was a man in a hurry, the finance director, Masihur Rahman, has recalled. "He was already an older man when he began BCCI, and he was determined not to waste time in taking his vision and turning it into something very big." Initially, the head office was in Abu Dhabi. Within months, Abedi and his coterie, many of them veterans of United Bank, moved the headquarters to London, the leading international banking center. But BCCI was not really a British bank. It had been incorporated in the Grand Duchy of Luxembourg, a tiny country that was eager to launch itself as a financial center. Later, Abedi set up a separate holding company in the Cayman Islands, a British colony in the Caribbean.

Abedi had timed the founding of BCCI to perfection. Oil prices had already begun to ratchet up. But the events of the next two years would send them to unprecedented levels, producing a torrent of money for · the Arab oil-producing states. Most of it, of course, would have to be deposited in banks.

2

THE NETWORK

ON DECEMBER 22, 1973, the petroleum ministers of six Middle Eastern countries gathered in Tehran. Their host was Mohammad Reza Pahlavi, the shah of Iran. A large contingent of reporters watched the delegates arrive in their limousines. Until a few months earlier, few people had heard of the Organization of Petroleum Exporting Countries. Now the cartel was the focus of international attention: the fate of the world's economy was in its hands. During the two months before this meeting, OPEC had doubled the price of oil, to $5.12 a barrel. Another price hike seemed likely, but no one knew how big it would be.

On the morning of December 23, the shah called a press conference and broke the suspense. The price of oil would double once again, to $11.65. He added, in the manner of a stern father lecturing a spendthrift teenager, that it would be a good idea for people in oil-importing countries to live a bit more frugally.

OPEC's quadrupling of oil prices caused one of the biggest transfers of wealth in human history. Hundreds of billions of dollars flowed into the coffers of oil-producing states from oil-importing nations in both the industrial and developing worlds. Commentators reached back in time to find parallels — to Croesus or to the Spaniards' plundering of gold from the New World. Henry Kissinger called the price hike "one of the pivotal events in the history of this century."

It was far more than an economic event, for it was fraught with political consequences. Middle Eastern potentates who had once been ignored — or scorned — in the West were now avidly courted. Former colonial powers like Britain and France were humbled, forced to beg for loans and investments from the people they had once ruled. The Arab nations had already begun to use oil as a political weapon. In October 1973, Israel had fought its fourth war with its Arab neighbors, and Arab governments decided to punish the United States and the Netherlands with an oil embargo because of their support for Israel.

The first to declare an embargo against the United States was Sheikh Zayed. Like the other Arab leaders, Zayed was bitterly opposed to the U.S. backing of Israel. Zayed was more than a prominent supporter of the OPEC price increases and the oil embargo. He was one of its biggest beneficiaries. In 1970, Abu Dhabi's oil revenues were $800 million; by 1975 they had soared to $8 billion.

As Zayed prospered, so did his bank; his money poured into BCCI. What is more, Abedi assisted in the management of Zayed's wealth, investing it overseas. Other oil-rich Middle Easterners were also stockholders and important customers of BCCI. The shareholders' list read almost like a *Who's Who* of the Middle East, including members of the ruling families of Dubai, Sharjah, Bahrain, Saudi Arabia, and Iran. Nowhere was BCCI's role in catering to wealthy Middle Easterners more noticeable than in London.

"Swinging London" conjures up images from the 1960s: Twiggy modeling miniskirts, boutiques on Carnaby Street, Beatles imitators with mop-top haircuts. To thousands of wealthy Arabs, however, London's golden decade was not the sixties but the seventies. When oil prices soared, they turned the British capital into their second home, a haven from the summer heat of the Gulf and a place to shop, drink, and gamble. Arab visitors rented suites at the Ritz, the Savoy, and other posh hotels. Hospitals furnished like five-star hotels sprang up seemingly overnight, since London was a preferred place for medical treatment. Top department stores like Harrods flourished as Arab customers swept in and scooped up everything that caught their fancy. For them, money was no object.

One item on many shopping lists was British real estate, and the buyers included some of BCCI's leading shareholders. In 1975, Sheikh Zayed bought a £300,000 (about $600,000) mansion in The Boltons, an exclusive neighborhood in West London. That same year Kamal Adham, the Saudi Arabian spymaster, paid £400,000 for an apartment in Grosvenor Square across from the American Embassy.

The newly rich Arabs also needed a place to deposit their money, and that was where BCCI came in, establishing branches in every part of London frequented by its wealthy customers. The head office, at 100 Leadenhall Street, was in the heart of the City of London. An office on Oxford Street was convenient to Selfridges department store and the Dorchester Hotel. A branch on Piccadilly was across from the Ritz. These branches were nothing like the traditional British banking halls, which often looked as though they hadn't seen a designer since Victorian times. BCCI's offices were generally of sleek design, with marble floors, smoked glass windows, and expensive furniture. Everything exuded a spirit of enterprise, success, and modernity.

BCCI's officers were trained to provide the ultimate in service. Privileged clients would be picked up at Heathrow airport in a Rolls-Royce and provided with a car and driver during their visits. They would be entertained at elegant restaurants, nightclubs, and casinos. The "entertainment" might also include the provision of female companions.

Thanks in part to the Arabs' mania for London, BCCI's British network grew at a mind-boggling pace during the 1970s. At the end of 1973 — its first full year of operation — BCCI had 19 branches in five countries. Of those, 8 were in the UAE, 4 in the United Kingdom. Two years later, when BCCI had 64 branches in thirteen countries, the UAE and the UK remained in the lead, with 19 branches each.

BCCI posted its fastest growth in Britain in 1977. The number of UK branches rose from 29 to 45, and the British work force nearly doubled, to 900. By the end of that year, BCCI's global network had grown to 121 branches in thirty-seven countries.

When BCCI set up shop in Britain, London was already well established as the leading international banking center. Regulation was relatively lax as long as an institution maintained good relations with the Bank of England. In London, there were hundreds of other banks from all over the world to do business with. The city offered good communications, including the largest international airport in Europe. It was also the center of the burgeoning Eurodollar market — a vast pool of dollars deposited outside the United States that was especially fed by the massive surpluses of the OPEC nations.

But BCCI didn't resemble the other foreign banks in London. One obvious difference was its astonishing record of growth. Rival banks found it difficult to understand how BCCI could open dozens of branches and lend hundreds of millions of dollars in the space of a few years and still make a profit. "People can't understand how they make all this money," said an American banker. "They've got all these little branches all over the place — and that must be very costly."

When asked to account for the bank's growth record, BCCI officials would explain that it had much to do with the Middle Eastern connections, suggesting that many of the petrobillionaires on BCCI's shareholder list channeled deposits to BCCI. As for profitability, that was explained by BCCI's practice of concentrating on lucrative niches neglected by other banks, such as catering to the needs of wealthy Arabs. Another was the so-called ethnic market in Britain. Over the years, thousands of Indians, Pakistanis, and Arabs, as well as ethnic Indians from Africa, had settled in Britain. (Many ethnic Indians expelled from Uganda by Idi Amin wound up in Britain.) These immigrants needed banking services but were mostly ignored by mainstream British banks. This oversight offered a tremendous opportunity to a newcomer like BCCI, which was led and staffed largely by Asians. Outside London, there were large immigrant communities in Bradford, Edinburgh, Glasgow, Leeds, and Leicester; BCCI had branches in each city. Many of these immigrants were active in the import-export business, and BCCI used its connections — and its Third World branch network — to provide trade financing.

Outside Britain, BCCI profited from the oil boom by catering to the banking needs of migrant workers in the Persian Gulf countries. The thousands of Pakistanis who poured into the UAE to work on construction projects during the oil boom would send a large part of their earnings to relatives at home. BCCI's branches in the UAE were well positioned to handle this business. The bank employed people who spoke the same languages as the workers and could transmit funds to BCCI offices in Pakistan.

"I think a lot of commercial banks disdained this business," said an American banker with experience in the Middle East. "They didn't realize you could make money on retail business." In fact, it could be quite profitable, particularly if a bank was willing to take advantage of its customers, this banker explained. "First of all, you clip the customer on the exchange rate. Then you charge him a fee for issuing the checks. Then you get the float for about a month. If the bank is mailing the check, then the bank could perhaps not mail the check right away."

BCCI officials also claimed that the bank's success was based in part on its unique management philosophy, which they referred to as "the Concept." An important part of the Concept was egalitarianism.

While other banks were run as hierarchies, BCCI played down status and rank. There were generally no titles on business cards and there were few private offices. In addition, decisions were supposedly made by consensus. This corporate culture was said to foster a spirit of harmony, inspiring each employee to work harder so that all might prosper. The British Pakistani writer Tariq Ali once described the Concept as "a curious, semi-mystical management philosophy" in which "BCCI's chief executive is a committee which embodies the bank's 'joint personality' and 'unity of thought.' " Another part of BCCI's corporate culture was its Third World identity. At every opportunity, Abedi played up the bank as an institution owned and run by people from developing countries. BCCI donated money to Third World causes, including scholarships for students from developing countries.

No one outside BCCI was really in a position to challenge these explanations. Because the bank was a privately held institution (its shares could not be bought on any stock market), it was not obliged to provide detailed information to the public and it was not scrutinized by stock market analysts. Anyone who did try to figure out BCCI by studying its annual reports would be stymied by its complicated structure: a maze of subsidiaries and affiliates incorporated in several different countries. To make matters even more confusing, there were the two separate holding companies, one in Luxembourg and one in the Cayman Islands.

If outsiders were unable to figure out what made BCCI tick, there seemed to be little doubt that it was an enormously successful operation and one with an insatiable appetite for growth. With the zeal of an evangelist seeking souls, Abedi exhorted his employees to bring in deposits. At the bank's annual management conferences, said one former officer, "the whole theme was deposits, deposits, deposits — bring in dollar deposits." To collect these funds, Abedi created a vast international network.

Abedi was like a military strategist plotting the conquest of the world. He tended to concentrate his efforts on one region at a time while continuing to fill gaps in other parts of the world. The first two pieces of terrain he captured were the United Arab Emirates and the United Kingdom. As BCCI grew, he solidified its base in those countries while planting flags elsewhere, mainly in the Third World. These outposts took several different forms. Some were BCCI branches. Others were branches of banks controlled solely by BCCI or in partnership with other investors. Still others were merely representative offices, which were not permitted to collect deposits or make loans.

In the Middle East, BCCI established offices in just about every country where it was permitted to do so, including Bahrain, Lebanon, Turkey, and North Yemen. It also set up joint venture banks in partnership with other foreign banks or local investors. National Bank of Oman was one of the first and most important of these banks. Started in 1973 as a joint venture with Bank of America, it eventually became one of BCCI's biggest units, with fifty-five branches. In Kuwait, BCCI established a 49-percent-owned subsidiary called Kuwait International Finance Company. Its chairman was Faisal Saud al-Fulaij, the former chairman of Kuwait Airways. Fulaij also became an investor in a series of companies and banks associated with BCCI in the United States and other countries. Before the fall of the shah of Iran, BCCI owned 15 percent of Iran Arab Bank, based in Tehran.

One of the biggest operations in the region was in Egypt, where a BCCI subsidiary eventually established a network of more than twenty branches. At its height, BCCI's Egyptian unit reportedly collected more than $1.2 billion from 68,000 depositors. The Egyptian unit was just one of several on the African continent. The late 1970s and early 1980s saw a major push into Africa — both the Arab countries of North Africa and the black African nations south of the Sahara. During BCCI's first few years, Abedi swept through Africa with a vigor that would have impressed General Erwin Rommel. In 1978, *Euromoney*, a bankers' magazine in London, noted that BCCI was about to launch a joint venture in Swaziland and that it "already has six branches in Egypt, easily the most profitable of the African operations; it also has two branches in Kenya, and a single branch in each of the following: Ivory Coast, Sudan, Gabon, Morocco, Djibouti and Mauritius. That's not all; there are joint ventures in Ghana and Liberia. And in Sudan another BCCI branch is due to open this month; unusual, because every other bank in the Sudan has been nationalized."

Asia was where Abedi had begun his banking career in the 1940s, at Pakistan's Habib Bank. In 1978, BCCI opened its first Pakistani branch. It later added two more branches. BCCI's biggest Asian outpost was Hong Kong, the region's leading international banking center. In 1979, BCCI bought 51 percent of a local institution called Hong Kong Metropolitan Bank. BCCI later boosted its stake to nearly 100 percent and changed the name to Bank of Credit and Commerce (Hong Kong) Limited.

Although BCCI made much of its status as a Third World bank, it was well represented in the industrial countries. A Canadian subsidiary was launched in 1979, and it eventually established eight branches. In Japan, BCCI started with a representative office in Tokyo in 1978. Four years later, it established a branch in the capital. One of the most important BCCI operations in Europe was Banque de Commerce et de Placements S.A., a joint venture in Switzerland. It was formed in 1976 in partnership with other financial institutions, including one of the "big three" Swiss banks, Union Bank of Switzerland.

By the end of 1977 — after just five full years of operation — BCCI was well on its way to becoming a global financial institution, with 146 branches in thirty-two countries. Total assets were $1.6 billion. One year later, its total assets hit $2.2 billion, enabling it to tout itself as the fastest growing bank in Britain and one of the fastest growing in the world.

BCCI's astonishing growth evoked tremendous pride among employees, as well as devotion to the man who had made it possible, Agha Hasan Abedi.

Abedi saw himself as an intellectual and was well read in foreign affairs, contemporary politics, and philosophy. "He was a nut on philosophy, a great reader of Sartre," recalls one of his former senior officers. Whenever an important new book came out on one of his favorite subjects, he would be among the first to read it — and would even quote from it, the former colleague adds. Abedi was also drawn to the poetry of the Sufis, as Islamic mystics are known. He was fond of private evenings with a few male friends — known as *mujras* — filled with poetry reading, drinking, camaraderie, and performances by professional dancing girls. Drinking alcohol was, of course, un-Islamic, but it was widely tolerated when practiced by intellectuals in such bohemian settings.

In his private life, Abedi had suffered considerable pain. Around the time BCCI was founded, his first wife left him under difficult circumstances. The banker later married an attractive woman, Rabia, who was much younger than he; she had been a stewardess for Pakistan International Airlines. Because of the traumatic end of his first marriage, says a former associate of Abedi's, the banker forbade Rabia from socializing, and he himself became somewhat reclusive. They doted on their daughter, Maha, who, having been raised in England, was more Westernized than her parents. (For example, in 1985, when she was eleven, she subscribed to *Archie* comics and twelve related titles.)

One of Abedi's most striking attributes was his ability to inspire the people who worked for him. Masihur Rahman, who was with Abedi at United Bank before joining BCCI as chief financial officer, recalled an incident that predated BCCI. "I and six other top aides were all given a brown envelope containing a book. We were told to read the book and to meditate about it." It was *Jonathan Livingston Seagull,* an inspirational book that had been a best-seller. When Rahman read it, he recalled that Abedi said "that he would take us on magical voyages to places we had never seen, that he would show us things we had never seen."

Just weeks later, at the beginning of 1972, Abedi was under house arrest and United Bank had been nationalized by Zulfikar Ali Bhutto. Whereas others might have sunk into despair, Abedi, mindful of the new venture ahead, worked to reinforce his hold over former subordinates. At Abedi's request, Rahman, who had become an adviser to Bhutto, visited the banker. "He told me he could not sleep anymore, because people like me had walked out of his life," said Rahman. "It sounds funny now, but I was touched. He talked to me about my family, my cat, and my dog. And I asked him, 'How do you feel about all of this. They say you are a crook.' He said, 'People like you and I will always build.' "

Within BCCI, Abedi was regarded as someone with little interest in mundane details. Bank officers who went to him thinking he wanted a two-hour presentation would often be shocked when it turned into a two-minute exchange. In considering a country, Abedi "would ask who the prime minister was and how long he would last," recalls one of his senior staffers. "Always the big-picture man." There were, however, exceptions. Abedi could be very finicky about physical appearance: the design of branches, how his employees dressed and groomed themselves. Everything had to look just right. He had expensive tastes, recalls the former BCCI officer Alberto Calvo, with a liking for "Persian rugs, Italian shirts and ties."

To handle the practical side of the bank, Abedi had Swaleh Naqvi. "Arrogant, self-sacrificing, a tireless worker, the man of detail and the administrative manager of the bank" is how Calvo characterized Naqvi. Abedi's deputy was always more an assistant than a director. The quiet and relatively shy Naqvi "would try to keep up with Abedi," another former BCCI officer recalls, and Abedi would make encouraging remarks to try to boost Naqvi's confidence. But though he was well read and knowledgeable, Naqvi was not a flamboyant intellectual like his mentor. "Abedi without Naqvi would still be the boss," said Calvo. "Naqvi without Abedi is nothing."

Despite BCCI's egalitarian rhetoric and the talk of management by consensus, Abedi was the unquestioned ruler of BCCI. He had established the institution, raised the initial capital, and recruited its top officials. Some employees were so devoted to Abedi that it was almost as if he were the leader of a cult.

To outsiders, BCCI appeared to be a commercial bank. To insiders, however, it resembled a secret society, with special rituals, jargon, and lore. In many important ways, BCCI had less in common with Citibank or Barclays than it did with the Reverend Sun Myung Moon's Unification Church.

If Abedi was the high priest, the bankers he had brought with him from United Bank were his disciples. Although some of his recruits were from elite Pakistani families, many others were poor, and Abedi gave them a chance to live a life they could never have experienced without him. Men who had grown up in modest circumstances in one of the world's poorest countries were transformed into international financiers. They bought expensive homes in the better parts of London, worked in tastefully appointed offices, and traveled first class. Many BCCI managers flaunted their affluence by sporting gold chains and Rolex watches and by gambling in the casinos of London, Monte Carlo, and the Spanish resort of Marbella. Other international bankers were able to live like this, but there was an important difference. If a BCCI officer lost his job, there was little likelihood that he would be able to find an equivalent position at another major bank. Because BCCI had a somewhat dubious reputation, there was little demand for its alumni.

The money and perks were not the only explanation for the loyalty of Abedi's minions. Many employees also regarded him as a visionary who was able to turn his dreams into reality. He had created BCCI out of nothing and transformed it into a major force in international finance. Employees were awed by his carefully cultivated image as an international statesman. He circled the globe in the bank's corporate jet and met with world leaders. Photographs of Abedi with these luminaries were sprinkled through the pages of *BCC International,* the bank's employee magazine. If Abedi was powerful, so the thinking went, then BCCI was powerful and, by extension, so were the people who worked for it.

Every cult has a liturgy, and BCCI was no exception. The Founding President, as Abedi was sometimes called, delivered homilies to his flock in the form of memoranda, letters, speeches, and articles in the employee magazine. These were often written in a peculiar jargon — a "BCCI-speak" — that gave them a kind of spiritual cast. To the irreverent, it sounds like pseudophilosophical mumbo-jumbo. Many employees, however, were taken in entirely, perhaps because they *wanted* to believe. A good example of BCCI-speak is an article in the October 1988 issue of *BCC International,* "Hope Is the Horizon." Based on a speech by Abedi, the article concludes:

> Hope is our vehicle. Hope is the experience of my being of future
> relationships. Hope is within possibility. Hope is moving into
> Relationships. The territory of Hope is Totality. Who hopes?
> Towards what does he hope? Into Totality — hope takes us into
> possibility. Into infinite relationship — like water. Hope
> is the Horizon.

The annual conferences at which Abedi expounded on his philosophy were amazing spectacles that were held in such European capitals as Athens, Vienna, Geneva, Luxembourg, and London. Hundreds of employees were flown in to attend — so many that BCCI typically had to book rooms in several hotels. No expense was spared. The 1984 meeting in Vienna, for example, was held in the ornate Auersperg Palace.

At a typical conference, the attendees would be in their seats by nine o'clock in the morning, eagerly awaiting Abedi's arrival. But the Founding President was seldom on time — that was part of his mystique — and the employees might have to wait an hour or two. Abedi would then sweep into the room, stride up to the lectern, and speak to his flock for hours on end.

The Vienna conference lasted for three days, stretching late into the evening each day. Abedi spoke most of that time. Only a few other top officials of the bank, including Naqvi, were allowed to address the throng. Speaking without a prepared text, Abedi would say little about BCCI's business strategy and financial performance. Instead, he would expound on his "philosophy," talking for hours about subjects like love and hope.

Some employees regarded this all this as gobbledygook. "He was always preaching bullshit — this bank by the grace of God will be the largest bank in the world, and the cosmic orientation that will flow through the bank," said Alvaro Lozano, a veteran American banker who worked briefly for BCCI in Spain. But many other employees were deeply touched. At the annual conferences, some of Abedi's acolytes would rise to their feet — like born-again Christians at a revival meeting — burst into tears, and pledge their devotion to BCCI and Abedi. At one conference, an employee stood up and said, "When I was in Pakistan, I was living in nothingness. Now I'm something. Why? Because of BCCI." Top managers were sometimes overcome by emotion. On one occasion Naqvi turned to Abedi and said, "You have moved me so much." Naqvi then broke down and wept for twenty minutes.

Abedi did not create BCCI single-handedly, of course. A cornerstone of the bank's success was his relationship with Sheikh Zayed, the onetime Bedouin chieftain who was now one of the richest men in the world. Like many other newly rich Arabs, Zayed spent staggering sums of money after the oil shock. So much money was spent on construction projects that Abu Dhabi sometimes looked like one big construction site. Generous welfare benefits were given to citizens. Subsidies were provided to the rulers of the other emirates, which lacked Abu Dhabi's wealth.

Zayed also spent freely on himself. "Better to have the problem of spending than the problem of no money," he once said. He built a string of palaces in Abu Dhabi and scooped up foreign stocks, bonds, and real estate, including a 1,200-acre vineyard in the Champagne region of France, a peculiar choice for a man whose religion forbids the consumption of alcohol. He was also generous to his family — an onerous responsibility. In the late 1970s, it was reported that he had been married as many as fourteen times, although, of course, he presumably never had more than four wives at one time (the limit under Islamic law). He reportedly had twenty-two daughters and nineteen sons. When his son Mohammed was married in 1981, Zayed treated his countrymen to the most expensive wedding ceremony of all time, according to *The Guinness Book of World Records*. The event lasted seven days and cost $33 million — partly because a stadium for 20,000 people was built just for the occasion.

In spite of his profligate ways, Zayed had plenty of money left over to support BCCI's growth with large deposits. In 1978, a U.S. bank examiner found that BCCI's deposits came mainly from the UAE. Much of that money would have come from Zayed personally, his relatives, and government entities that he controlled.

Abedi well understood the importance of Zayed's backing, and he went to extraordinary lengths to cater to the sheikh and to other VIPs in the emirates. Zafar Iqbal, one of Abedi's chief lieutenants, was stationed in Abu Dhabi, and one of his principal duties was to keep Zayed happy. Bashir Tahir was responsible for attending to the needs of Sheikh Rashid bin Said al-Maktoum, who ruled Dubai — the second most important sheikhdom in the UAE — until his death in 1990. These BCCI officials were so effective that they became confidants of the rulers and their families. Tahir, said a former BCCI official, "was adopted almost as a son" by Sheikh Rashid.

Zafar Iqbal spent far more time at Sheikh Zayed's palaces than he did at the BCCI office. A typical day might be spent with Zayed's son Sheikh Khalifa, the crown prince. "Sheikh Khalifa would get up at about midday," said a former BCCI official. "By that time, hangers-on would be sitting in his office," including middlemen representing foreign companies that wanted to do business in Abu Dhabi. "They would see Zafar Iqbal. Khalifa would have his breakfast at one in the afternoon." A few hours later, he would take his siesta, and Iqbal would go to his BCCI office, perhaps to return a phone call from Abedi. "Then he would go back to Khalifa, who might have a *majlis** in the evening until about ten or ten-thirty. Iqbal would have dinner with him and he would go home."

Zayed would typically spend his time praying or listening to news, recalled Akbar Bilgrami, a former BCCI official who looked after some of Zayed's investments. "He had a court jester–type person who made him laugh and told him poetry. He was a simple man, simple but shrewd."

When Zayed and Rashid traveled abroad, a BCCI man nearly always went along to attend to personal financial chores and other details. Bilgrami has described a two-week visit to Spain when Zayed arrived with two planeloads of 150 hangers-on, including relatives and servants. "The sheikh is a sort of father figure," said the banker. "It is hard for him to say no to people, especially because he knows that everybody knows that he has the money." To ensure a handy supply of gifts, Zayed "would carry about a briefcase filled with expensive watches — Cartiers, Rolexes." During the Spanish trip, Bilgrami was responsible for paying all of the bills — which amounted to $20 million. Zayed, according to the banker, "only spent $400 on himself the entire trip for two dogs, whose price he negotiated down from

---

*In a *majlis*, citizens can air grievances and make requests to the ruling family.

$1,000." Bilgrami joined Zayed's entourage, lugging two large suitcases containing as much as $5 million in cash. "I was like a mobile bank."

BCCI also helped manage and invest Zayed's wealth. Abedi ordered BCCI officers to set up a number of front companies for the ruler. Like other Middle Eastern potentates, he wanted to conceal his wealth and accumulate a nest egg abroad in the event of political turbulence at home.

The first company, Associated Shipping Services Ltd., was established in 1975 as a personal service company. Run by BCCI in all respects, it arranged limousines, travel, and cash transactions for Zayed and his associates. A nephew of Abedi's, Qamar Rizvi, helped set up the company and served as one of its major shareholders.

Other companies soon followed. Through the Hilal Foundation (*hilal* is Arabic for "the crescent moon"), Progressive Investment Company of Liechtenstein, and Bruna S.A., Akbar Bilgrami bought and managed millions of dollars worth of property in Spain, including a string of villas in Marbella. These villas, which were acquired by Bruna S.A. from the Fiores family in 1977, took care of some of Zayed's vacation needs. For the health of his family, he wanted to invest in some good medical care, so BCCI arranged for the construction of London's Cromwell Hospital. In 1978, Zayed's personal office, with the help of BCCI, set up Resal Investment Grand Cayman Ltd. to hold Zayed's investments in the hospital. BCCI also helped Zayed acquire valuable property in London's tony Regent's Park area.

Ownership was always carefully hidden. The Resal company in the Cayman Islands was in turn owned by a Liechtenstein entity, the Resal Foundation. The foundation was controlled by Sheikh Zayed, his son Khalifa, three trusted acolytes, and a lawyer from Liechtenstein. Abedi also set up Transocean Shipping Ltd., a shipping concern, for Zayed. Although the company was incorporated in London, its two main shareholders — Caminos Transocéanicos Naviera S.A. and Destinos Transocéanicos Navigación — were shell companies based in Panama.

Thanks to BCCI's close relationship with Zayed, the bank's operations in the UAE were given privileged treatment. After the 1973 oil shock, foreign and domestic banks hoping to cash in on the petrodollar boom opened hundreds of branches in the UAE, making it one of the most overbanked countries in the world. By 1979, according to one estimate, the UAE had 430 bank branches, or one for every 2,000 citizens, the highest ratio in the world. In 1982, the UAE government ruled that foreign banks would be restricted to eight branches apiece. Abedi got around the limit through the simple stratagem of setting up a new, "local" bank, Bank of Credit and Commerce (Emirates). BCCE, established in January 1983, acquired BCCI's "excess" branches. This transparent attempt to evade the limit was attacked by some bankers as "immoral," but they could do nothing about it. After all, Sheikh Zayed and other UAE officials were major shareholders in both BCCI and BCCE.

Although BCCI seemed to be an unqualified success, there was trouble brewing — inside and outside. One internal problem was factionalism. The top managers were split between two camps: the technocrats and the Gulf faction. The technocrats — experienced, Westernized bankers — were led by Swaleh Naqvi, Abedi's deputy. The Gulf faction consisted of officials working in the UAE and other Arab countries where BCCI's shareholders lived. This group was led by Zafar Iqbal, BCCI's top official in Abu Dhabi. Each group claimed credit for BCCI's success. The technocrats felt the bank would never have grown so rapidly without their skill and experience. Members of the Gulf faction, said a former official, "claimed that they were the ones who made the bank because of their access to the Arabs."

There was also an ethnic and religious dimension to the factionalism. As a former official explained, "Abedi was an Indian immigrant to Pakistan, Urdu-speaking and of the Shi'ite religion." Many of the technocrats came from the same background. By contrast, the Gulf faction was dominated by men who had grown up in the Punjab region of Pakistan and belonged to the Sunni branch of Islam. (Abedi did not plan it; it just happened that way in BCCI's clannish atmosphere.) The tension was palpable at BCCI's annual management conferences. Each faction stayed in a different hotel and sat apart during the proceedings. "They would never socialize," a former BCCI official said. "They would not even acknowledge [each other]. They would not even shake hands."

Outside BCCI, bankers and bank regulators were beginning to ask tough questions about Abedi's institution. *Euromoney* noted in 1978 that BCCI "is the talking point at bankers' cocktail parties, the source of gossip at conferences, and the object of speculation in the first-class cabins of planes ferrying bankers out to the Gulf."

Questions about the bank's profitability persisted in spite of BCCI officials' talk about lucrative niches and their unique management style. A British banker with extensive experience in many of the Third World countries where BCCI was active said, "They seem to be able to get a return on assets far greater than all the other [foreign] banks [even though] they pay their staff more and they don't have a more efficient way of operating. It's clear they have some means of operating different than other banks." Said a former BCCI official: "One thing is for damn sure — this bank makes lots of money and nobody knows how."

BCCI's ownership was also a mystery. There seemed to be no question that the biggest shareholders were Sheikh Zayed, associates of his, and Bank of America. But where did the rest of the money come from? Part of the answer lay in a strange entity in the Cayman Islands called International Credit & Investment Co. Ltd. (ICIC). Speaking a few years after the founding of the bank, Abedi said that BCCI had "about thirty or so" shareholders, with only ICIC holding a larger share than Bank of America. Together, these two shareholders held close to three-quarters of the stock, Abedi said, meaning that ICIC held about half the bank's stock. "The remaining stock," Abedi said, "is owned by twenty-five to thirty investors," who were "individuals from the Middle East." The most prominent one was apparently Sheikh Zayed, who, according to one newspaper account from the 1970s, subscribed to 20 percent of the bank's capital at its formation. Many of the others were relatives or associates of Zayed's, who depended on the sheikh for funds.

Abedi's vague statements about BCCI's ownership aroused suspicions that some of the rich Arab stockholders were simply nominees, especially because the use of fronts and nominees is widespread in the Middle East. Members of the ruling elites do not want others to know how much wealth they have accumulated.

Questions were also raised about BCCI's manner of doing business. The bank's extremely rapid growth began to cause concern in the financial community and among bank regulators.

A bank is not like a retailer. If a supermarket's sales rise, it is a good sign. If a bank grows very fast, that means it is lending more and more money each year, and every loan is a potential time bomb: Will the loan be repaid on time or will the borrower default? In BCCI's case, concerns about the quality of its loan portfolio were especially valid, since the bank's roots were in countries where modern concepts of banking and finance were alien.

In the more traditional parts of the Middle East, such as Abu Dhabi, the very notion of banking is inimical to many Muslims. Fundamentalists generally cite the famous prohibitions against *riba*, as usury and interest are termed in Arabic, in the Muslim holy book, the Qu'ran. Other passages in the Qu'ran seem to support the payment of interest, but they have done little to restrain a strong Muslim tradition against such payment. This has caused great difficulties for Western banking in traditional Muslim countries, as the collection of interest may not be enforceable in court.

Pakistan had a longer banking tradition than many Arab countries, but modern financial concepts had not really taken hold. Far more important was the borrower's status in the community and his personal relationship to the banker.

One Pakistani business group with close ties to Abedi was the Gulf Group, controlled by the Gokal family. The Gokals were international shipping magnates, and they became important customers of United Bank. When Abedi established BCCI, he brought in the Gokals as clients. BCCI lent increasingly large sums to the Gokals during the 1970s, even though the shipping industry is notoriously cyclical. The carrier trade to developing nations and the tanker business both went into a nosedive in the latter part of the decade, causing big problems for the Gokals. Instead of cutting his losses and turning off the spigot, Abedi continued lending to his friends. In so doing, he tied BCCI's fate ever more closely to that of the Gokals.

Abedi had no intention of curbing BCCI's lending or cutting back on the growth of its branch network. In Britain, where BCCI had forty-five offices, Abedi wanted hundreds. In January 1978, the *Sunday Times* of London reported that "BCCI will open five more branches by the end of next month and has plans for another 150 in the next two or three years." The Bank of England was not at all comfortable with these plans and made it clear to Abedi that if he wanted to open more branches, they would have to be in some other country. The British central bank ordered BCCI to freeze its UK branch network at forty-five.

Another setback came in October 1979, when Britain's Banking Act took effect. Under that law, every bank doing business in Britain was either given "recognised bank" status or classified as a "licenced deposit-taker." BCCI was relegated to the second-class status of a licensed deposit-taker — forbidden to call itself simply a bank — in spite of its large presence. (Britain's banking legislation was later changed, with all banks given equal status.) Abedi complained bitterly to the Bank of England, and his minions blamed it on "racism" in the City of London. If BCCI was being treated as a second-class citizen, it was because the financial establishment could not tolerate a successful Third World bank. As Abedi said in 1978, "It is not only the Bank of England that is against us, but the Club."

Bank regulators and jealous competitors, however, weren't the only ones who had concerns about BCCI. So did one of BCCI's largest shareholders, Bank of America. When the California bank agreed to become a founding shareholder in BCCI, it was a major coup for Abedi. Its participation gave Abedi's venture a measure of credibility and respectability. Over the years, however, Bank of America officials became nervous about BCCI's extraordinary growth and its questionable banking practices.

B of A auditors found that there was a high degree of concentration of lending. In the United States, nationally chartered banks were forbidden to lend more than 10 percent of capital and reserves to a single borrower. BCCI's loans to the Gokals' Gulf Group far exceeded that figure. Other concerns included large loans to insiders (directors, officers, and shareholders), inadequate loan-loss provisions, and lax internal controls. According to one (perhaps apocryphal) story, B of A auditors were once sent to check on a BCCI branch in the UAE. When they arrived, they discovered that the branch did not exist.

Bank of America gradually began to distance itself from BCCI. In 1976, it asked Abedi to remove its logo from BCCI's letterhead. That same year, it refused to contribute new capital to finance BCCI's expansion because it was alarmed by the rapid growth of BCCI's assets. In August 1977, *Euromoney* reported that Bank of America was thinking of selling its BCCI stock. "Subsequently," the magazine later said, "a representative from BCCI, Dildar Rizvi, visited *Euromoney*'s London headquarters to complain about what he termed the inaccuracy of the report. Rizvi claimed that Bank of America planned to retain its shareholding in the bank, and that it was very happy to do so. Bank of America confirmed that statement. Some months later, however, Bank of America issued a press notice, following a number of stories in the financial press, which said that it intended to divest itself of its interest in BCCI by 1980."

Bank of America's press release, issued in January 1978, stated that it would be selling its BCCI stock to another major shareholder "over the next 2 1/2 years" because "BCCI is now a fully fledged global bank" and because B of A "is currently increasing its direct presence in the Middle East." The buyer, according to Abedi's deputy Swaleh Naqvi, was the ICIC Staff Benefit Fund. B of A completed the divestiture in July 1980.

Few people in the financial community believed the official explanation of the pullout. The general assumption was that BCCI was a dubious outfit — a "cowboy" operation, as some British bankers put it — and Bank of America was fearful of being tainted. But the California bank did not sever all its ties with BCCI. It remained a joint venture partner with BCCI in National Bank of Oman and served as one of BCCI's main correspondent banks in the United States.

The setbacks with the Bank of England and Bank of America did nothing to dampen Abedi's obsession with growth. One former official said of BCCI's top officers, "Their objective — and they said so openly — was to become the largest bank in the world by the year 2000."

No banker with Abedi's ambitions could ignore the United States, the world's biggest economy and the seat of vast political power. It was also the country of the dollar, and BCCI's balance sheet was expressed in dollars. The United States was also alluring for cultural and emotional reasons. BCCI was a bank with a strong immigrant culture. America, of course, is the land of immigrants.

Abedi not only wanted to expand into the United States, he even dreamed of transforming BCCI into an American bank one day. Sani Ahmed, a BCCI officer who served as head of the bank's Washington, D.C., representative office, said, "Mr. Abedi told me four times, 'Our aims in the United States are very ambitious.' He wanted at least five hundred branches. We thought we would shift our headquarters there."

Abedi made the first important steps toward fulfilling this dream by arranging for a group of BCCI clients to buy stock in one of the most important banking institutions in the U.S. capital. In doing so, he touched off one of the biggest, most acrimonious, and most protracted takeover battles in American corporate history, attracting worldwide attention to BCCI. When it was over, Abedi emerged with far greater financial and political clout than ever before.

It all began in the fall of 1977, when Abedi met a banker from Georgia who happened to be the best friend of the president of the United States. His name was T. Bertram ("Bert") Lance.

3

COMING TO AMERICA

IT'S HARD TO IMAGINE a more unlikely pair than Agha Hasan Abedi and Bert Lance. While Abedi appeared refined and cultivated, Lance was almost the stereotype of the southern "good ol' boy." There was also a striking physical contrast. Abedi had an average build, but the Georgia banker was a bear of a man, weighing 240 pounds and standing six feet four inches tall. However, Lance and Abedi also had much in common. They both had a knack for making political connections and they both played fast and loose with banking regulations. These two characteristics were related: both men used their banks to acquire political clout.

Lance was born on June 3, 1931, in the rural community of Young Harris, Georgia. In 1950, he dropped out of college to marry his childhood sweetheart, LaBelle David, then worked as a teller at Calhoun First National Bank, which had been founded by LaBelle's grandfather. Seven years later, Lance and a group of investors bought control of the bank, and he ultimately became its chairman. One of the most popular men in town, Lance was utterly unlike the image of the conservative banker. Friends and neighbors found him an easy touch, and he lent liberally to himself and his relatives as well.

In 1966, Lance made the most important political connection of his life when he met a dynamic young Georgia politician, James Earl Carter, Jr., known to everyone as Jimmy. At the time, Carter was a state senator running for the governorship. Lance became an important campaign supporter and contributor. They eventually became best friends; Carter has likened Lance to a brother. Although Carter lost in 1966, he won four years later, thanks, in part, to Lance's help.

After he took office, he appointed Lance to the post of highway commissioner.

Lance enjoyed his stint in state government and made an unsuccessful bid for the Democratic nomination for governor in 1974 as Carter's chosen successor. It was later discovered that Lance's campaign committees wrote hundreds of bad checks against accounts at Calhoun First National and that the bank cleared them.

Although Lance failed to gain higher political office, his career as a banker flourished when he was recruited by Financial General Bankshares (FGB), a bank holding company based in Washington, D.C. FGB was an unusual institution. Although the McFadden Act forbade American banks to engage in interstate banking, FGB had been granted a special exemption and owned banks in several states. In most cases, it held a majority of the stock, with local investors owning the rest.

In January 1975, Lance became president of National Bank of Georgia (NBG), FGB's subsidiary in Atlanta. Five months later, he and a group of investors bought control of the bank from FGB and he was named chairman. As head of NBG, Lance became friendly with one of the most important financiers in the South, Jackson T. Stephens, the president and a controlling shareholder of Stephens Inc. of Little Rock, Arkansas, one of the largest brokerage firms in the country.

Lance and Stephens met in 1975. It was around that time that Stephens Inc. managed a public offering of NBG stock. "Their common interests, one acquaintance said, were Jimmy Carter — a Naval Academy classmate of Stephens's — banking, money, religion — both Southern Baptists — and Democratic politics," a reporter noted later. (Stephens would say that although he had met Carter at the Naval Academy, they did not become well acquainted until later in life.) In the 1976 presidential race, Stephens and Lance both assisted Jimmy Carter.

Not only was Lance a contributor to Carter in 1976, his bank was the biggest single lender to the Carter family's peanut warehouse business; the debt to NBG reached as high as $4.7 million. It was later alleged that these loans amounted to de facto financing of the presidential campaign — which would have been illegal. (After an investigation, Carter was cleared of wrongdoing.) Lance also let the Carter campaign use NBG's corporate plane without disclosing it as a contribution; the campaign was fined for this violation.

·　·　·

After Carter was elected president, he brought Lance to Washington as director of the Office of Management and Budget, one of the most important posts in the federal government. Lance's dubious financial practices did not cause a problem when he was up for Senate confirmation, for federal officials had withheld important information about his activities from Senate investigators. A handful of journalists — notably the *New York Times* columnist William Safire — began to dig into Lance's background and uncovered a number of apparent irregularities. It seemed that Lance had financed his purchase of NBG stock with loans from two big New York banks — Manufacturers Hanover Trust Company and Chemical Bank — and had then arranged for NBG to open correspondent banking accounts with them. In one column, Safire suggested that Lance received a $3.4 million loan from the First National Bank of Chicago not because of his creditworthiness but because of his closeness to Carter. This loan, according to Safire, enabled First Chicago's chairman, A. Robert Abboud, "to gain life-and-death financial control over the man closest to the President." (Abboud denied favoritism.)

In July 1977, the Senate Governmental Affairs Committee, chaired by Abraham Ribicoff, a Connecticut Democrat, looked into Lance's conduct and cleared him of wrongdoing. But Ribicoff acted too soon. More allegations of misconduct emerged almost daily, engulfing the Carter administration in its first major scandal, Lancegate. On August 18, the Office of the Comptroller of the Currency — the main regulator of nationally chartered banks — issued a report criticizing Lance's banking practices. Since the report did not accuse Lance of breaking the law, Carter treated it as an exoneration of his friend; at a press conference with Lance, the president made a remark that later came back to haunt him: "Bert, I'm proud of you." Nonetheless, Ribicoff announced that his committee would be holding new hearings on Lance.

In the meantime, there was growing pressure on Carter to fire his friend. On September 5, Labor Day, Carter met with Ribicoff and Charles Percy of Illinois, the ranking Republican on the committee, and the senators asked the president to dismiss his budget director. Lance turned for help to Clark Clifford, one of the most respected — and politically well-connected — lawyers in Washington. Clifford persuaded the committee to postpone Lance's testimony to give the banker more time to prepare.

The nationally televised hearings began with a parade of witnesses who recounted Lance's dubious financial practices. Lance defended himself on September 15 in a two-hour statement in which he lashed out at the committee for treating him unfairly. It was an impressive performance, winning him applause at the end. Hedrick Smith of the *New York Times* observed: "For the moment, he managed not only to push Senator Percy into regretful apologies about news leaks and misinterpretations, but also to win predictions from some members of the Senate committee that there would be 'a backlash of sympathy.' " Despite the rave reviews, Carter was unable to resist the pressure to fire Lance and on September 21 accepted his resignation with "regret and sorrow."

The resignation was by no means the end of Lance's woes. He was the target of investigations by bank regulators and federal prosecutors, which led to an indictment in May 1979 on charges of violating federal banking laws. Clark Clifford's protégé, Robert A. Altman, assisted Lance's defense team. A year later, the trial ended in a hung jury.*

On top of his legal troubles, Lance was in desperate financial straits. Around the time of his resignation, he was more than $5 million in debt, and the value of his biggest asset — his stock in National Bank of Georgia — had plummeted. His only hope was to sell the stock at well above the market price.

Hope soon arrived in the person of Agha Hasan Abedi.

Abedi was eager to expand in the United States. Although he could open BCCI branches, he realized that the quickest route to growth would be through an acquisition. But there were several obstacles. One was the McFadden Act banning interstate banking. BCCI was affected because Bank of America owned a large chunk of its stock. Thus, if BCCI wanted to buy a bank in any state other than California (B of A's home), regulators would think B of A was trying to circumvent the law. Even though B of A was planning to dispose of its stock, Abedi

---

*A few years after that, the incorrigible Lance was in trouble again. In August 1985, the Office of the Comptroller of the Currency (OCC) charged him with a series of offenses. The agency alleged that he had engaged in check kiting, had received proceeds of nominee loans from Calhoun First National Bank, and had obtained a payment from the bank's credit life insurance company that was owed to the bank.

The Lancegate affair finally concluded in February 1986. In a settlement with the OCC, Lance agreed to pay a $50,000 civil fine to the U.S. Treasury. He was also barred from serving as an employee, officer, or director of — or otherwise participating in the affairs of — any federally insured bank without the written permission of the appropriate banking agencies.

The story ended on a farcical note. Lance, according to the columnist Jack Anderson, paid the $50,000 fine with a rubber check. The hapless banker eventually made good.

would likely encounter opposition from regulators who were nervous about BCCI's rapid growth and its dubious banking practices.

One way around these obstacles would be for a BCCI client to take over an American bank. The first such attempt was made by a member of the Gokal family that controlled the Gulf Group, the shipping empire that Abedi had supported for years. In 1975, Abbas Gokal made an offer for Chelsea National Bank, a small institution in Manhattan, and the owners agreed to sell it to him. Before the deal could go through, the New York State Banking Department had to give its approval.

When the New York regulators checked into Gokal, they were far from impressed. John Heimann, then New York State banking superintendent, later said, "His uncertified financial statement showed total assets of $4.5 million, of which $3 million was in the form of a loan from his sister. His reported annual income for the prior year was, as I recall, approximately $34,000." The regulators also found that Gokal had no banking experience — but very close ties to BCCI. When Gokal negotiated with Chelsea's owners, he was advised and represented by BCCI. In a statement filed with the regulators in 1976, Gokal said he had been advised by Abdus Sami, a senior BCCI executive. In October, Gokal told the regulators that BCCI would help him run the New York bank. One regulator's notes of that meeting state: "Sami is to spin off management from Bank of Credit and Commerce to manage Chelsea (new information)."

This prompted the regulators to take a close look at BCCI, and they did not like what they saw. Heimann found that the BCCI group was structured in such a way that no single central bank or regulatory authority had primary responsibility for overseeing it. As Heimann and his staff dug further, they became increasingly alarmed. When they asked BCCI for details about large, unsecured loans to certain Arab customers, for example, the response typically was dismissive: "It's private." Because of their wariness about BCCI's role, the regulators told Gokal's lawyer that his answers were unsatisfactory. Chelsea National was sold to someone else.

Around the time that Gokal was trying to buy Chelsea National, BCCI officials were looking at another New York bank, Bank of Commerce, which was controlled by FGB, the same company that spun off NBG to Bert Lance. Abdus Sami also worked on this deal. Abedi and Sami met with FGB's controlling shareholder, the retired army general George Olmsted, and William Schuiling, FGB's chairman and CEO. Schuiling later said he had not been very impressed with

Abedi. The BCCI chief "was not the type of banker that I would care to be associated with. I doubted his judgment, and I went in to see General Olmsted and told him, maybe he can work with the Bank of America, but as far as I am concerned I do not wish to be associated with Mr. Abedi." One of Schuiling's former colleagues says that the American banker was much more blunt in private. (The former colleague says Schuiling pronounced the name "Ah-*bee*-dee" rather than "*Ah*-buh-dee," the correct pronunciation.) "I threw Ah-*bee*-dee out of my office when he tried to buy Bank of Commerce back in the seventies," Schuiling growled. He then muttered, "Bunch of unsavory people."

In late 1977, after meeting Bert Lance, Abedi finally succeeded in putting together a U.S. takeover.

The matchmaker was R. Eugene Holley, the former majority (Democratic) leader of the Georgia senate and a friend of Lance's. Holley was more than a local politician; he was involved in a Middle Eastern oil venture. In 1975, the evangelist Oral Roberts had introduced Holley to Roy J. Carver, the multimillionaire chairman of Bandag Inc., a big tire retreading company. Holley and Carver soon became involved in a project to develop an offshore oil concession granted by the government of Qatar.

Shortly before Lance's resignation, Holley visited London in an effort to obtain financing to develop the oil concession. One of the banks he called on was BCCI. Holley was not afraid to drop names, so he mentioned to a BCCI banker that Bert Lance happened to be his good friend. In case the banker didn't appreciate the significance of this, Holley told him that Lance was a close friend of President Jimmy Carter's. "On hearing of his presidential contact, the BCCI banker takes him straight to Mr. Abedi," according to a former BCCI official.

Abedi quickly agreed to help the stranger who said he was a friend of a friend of the president's and arranged for Holley to see executives of Attock Oil, a company in London associated with BCCI.* In the

---

*In spite of BCCI's assistance, Holley and Carver ran into trouble in Qatar when the government refused to renew their oil concession. In March 1978, the two men visited Qatar, and Carver complained to the U.S. ambassador that they were losing the concession even though he had paid a $1.5 million bribe to a Qatari official. The ambassador reported the conversation to the Justice Department. In April 1979, Carver earned the distinction of being the first person charged with violating the Foreign Corrupt Practices Act, which makes it illegal for Americans to bribe foreign officials. Carver agreed not to contest the charges and was enjoined from bribing foreign officials in the future. (Carver died in June 1981.)

course of the meeting, said the BCCI source, Holley mentioned "that his banker friend [Lance] will be leaving the government and want[s] to sell his bank and may also be in the market for a loan for a couple of million dollars." Abedi was interested.

Lance and Abedi met for the first time in early October, according to Lance, at the Waldorf-Astoria Hotel in New York. (Abedi has said that the first meeting was actually in London.) They met again on October 15 at a hotel in Washington, D.C. The two bankers had a strong mutual attraction. Lance wanted to get out of his financial mess by selling his National Bank of Georgia stock and refinancing his debts. Abedi wanted to expand into the United States. Perhaps even more important to Abedi was the chance to use Lance as a bridge to the American political world. Shortly after the meeting in Washington, Abedi hired Lance as a business consultant, to spot investment opportunities for BCCI.

At the time, there were about fifteen thousand banks in the United States, some of which were undoubtedly attractive prospects. Lance, however, recommended an ailing bank that was the target of a great deal of regulatory scrutiny, National Bank of Georgia. NBG's woes did not seem to bother Abedi, and he was soon involved in serious discussions with Lance and his investment banker friend, Jackson Stephens.

Despite Abedi's enthusiasm, there was little chance that a takeover by BCCI would be approved by U.S. bank regulators, but Abedi quickly found a solution. He arranged for NBG to be purchased by Ghaith Rashad Pharaon, a Saudi Arabian tycoon and BCCI client who was reputed to be one of the richest men in the world.

When Pharaon appeared on the American scene in the 1970s, the only other well-known Saudi businessman was Adnan Khashoggi, the flamboyant arms dealer who had been implicated in the Lockheed bribery scandal a few years earlier and would figure in the Iran-contra affair of the 1980s. In his well-tailored suits and Vandyke beard, Pharaon appeared to be much less vulgar than Khashoggi. Pharaon's aides pointed out discreetly that their boss had a Ph.D. from the Harvard Business School — a not very subtle reminder that Khashoggi was a college dropout.

Pharaon's Harvard degree was actually an M.B.A., but few people bothered to check. Former associates explain that Pharaon favored the title "doctor" because it was used by men like Henry Kissinger and Armand Hammer, although they, of course, had earned their degrees. (Pharaon's lawyer says that the term was intended simply as an honorific.) The Saudi businessman also liked to show off his art collection. Once, when a visitor to his office in Paris admired a full-length portrait, Pharaon gestured at it with his cigar and said, "It's Philip of Spain. It's by Titian, by the way." Later, the visitor learned that the picture had not been painted by the seventeenth-century Venetian master at all but by some anonymous copyist. One clue that should have alerted the visitor was Pharaon's failure to install a burglar alarm to protect the allegedly priceless artwork.

An additional deception was Pharaon's attempt to portray himself as an entrepreneur whose success was based on training and skill. In fact, Pharaon owed a great deal to friends in high places. His father — like Khashoggi's — had been a personal physician and top adviser to the late King Faisal. Pharaon's flagship company, Saudi Research & Development Corporation (REDEC), had been launched in 1966 in partnership with two of King Faisal's sons, Prince Abdullah and Prince Mohammed. (Pharaon later bought them out.) Over the years, Pharaon made a fortune by acting as a middleman on behalf of foreign companies doing business in Saudi Arabia.

There is some dispute about when Abedi and Pharaon met. Pharaon has claimed that it was in the late 1970s in Cairo. Other sources, however, say the relationship began much earlier, before BCCI was founded. A former BCCI officer says the introduction was made by Pakistan's Saigol family, which controlled the bank Abedi ran before founding BCCI. The Saigols had struck up a partnership with Pharaon "in a construction and trading company," said one source, and Abedi cemented the relationship by lending money to a hotel project in Jiddah, Saudi Arabia.

Pharaon eventually emerged as one of Abedi's closest associates, serving as a bridge to other important Saudis, including his partner in the Jiddah hotel project, Kamal Adham, a brother-in-law of King Faisal's as well as the head of Saudi Arabia's intelligence agency. Several of these Saudi contacts became BCCI shareholders, enhancing the credibility of the bank. Pharaon invested in it (for a time he was one of the biggest single shareholders), as did Adham and Adham's nephew Prince Turki bin Faisal al-Saud. Considered the brightest of King Faisal's seven sons, Prince Turki became deputy director general of intelligence in 1973, at the age of twenty-six. He succeeded Adham as the country's intelligence chief in September 1977.

Of all Abedi's clients, Pharaon seemed to be the one most suitable for the National Bank of Georgia deal since he had already passed muster twice with U.S. bank regulators when he invested in banks in Houston and Detroit. Toward the end of 1977, Pharaon agreed to buy Lance's 60 percent stake in NBG for $2.4 million, which worked out to $20 a share. A few weeks earlier, the stock had been trading for about $10 a share. (Pharaon later acquired all of NBG.)

The deal was a tremendous boon to Lance, of course, who had been teetering on the brink of bankruptcy. Lance and Pharaon portrayed the deal as a routine investment, but skepticism abounded. Of the thousands of banks in the United States, it seemed odd that Pharaon happened to choose one that was owned by a close friend, political supporter, and lender to President Carter — and that he would pay top dollar for it. Charges arose that "the Arabs" were trying to buy influence with powerful Americans. The controversy surrounding the NBG deal, however, would pale by comparison with what was in the works: a bid for one of the biggest banking companies in the nation's capital, Financial General Bankshares.

If Lance could engineer a takeover of FGB with Abedi's help, he could return to Washington in style, installing himself as chairman or president, and thus recover from the humiliation of Lancegate. Not the least of FGB's attractions was the company's headquarters at 17th Street and Pennsylvania Avenue, with an impressive view of the White House.

FGB traced its roots to the Morris Plan, a pioneering consumer-lending business. Arthur Morris, its founder, began his banking career around the turn of the century by making small installment loans to working people — a practice virtually unknown at the time. In 1910, he established the first Morris Plan bank: Fidelity Loan & Trust Company of Norfolk, Virginia. Within ten years, Morris Plan banks were operating in many states. In the 1940s and 1950s, the company became a financial conglomerate, with interests in such areas as insurance and mortgage banking. It was also exempt from the federal ban on interstate banking, as noted earlier. In 1977, FGB controlled banks in Maryland, New York, Tennessee, Virginia, and the District of Columbia.

General George Olmsted controlled FGB through a company called International Bank and various other entities. The Federal Reserve Board said this setup was illegal. International Bank, according to the Fed, was a bank holding company. It therefore could not simultaneously own FGB and certain other businesses not related to banking, such as an insurance company. So the Fed ordered International Bank and its officers and directors to dispose of large chunks of FGB stock. One potential buyer was Bert Lance, who was quite familiar with FGB since it had hired him to run its Georgia bank in 1975 and had then sold a controlling interest in it to an investment group led by Lance. In the fall of 1976, Olmsted offered to sell his FGB stock to Lance, but the Georgian turned him down, presumably because this would have prevented him from serving in the Carter administration.

The following April, Olmsted sold about 22 percent of FGB's voting stock to a group of some twenty investors led by J. William Middendorf II, a former investment banker who had served as the secretary of the navy under Presidents Nixon and Ford. Middendorf also received proxies for FGB stock from Olmsted and from another leading stockholder, the Washington real estate magnate Eugene B. Casey.

Lance's friend Jackson Stephens, the investment banker, was one of the biggest investors in the Middendorf group. Other major investors included Armand Hammer, the chairman of Occidental Petroleum; Jorge Pereira, a banker; the Washington lawyer Eugene J. Metzger; Thomas Wyman, a New York investor; and North Carolina National Bank. Smaller investors included Joseph Farland, a former U.S. ambassador to Pakistan and Iran; John Safer, a real estate developer from Alexandria, Virginia; the New York lawyer Jeremiah Milbank of Milbank, Tweed, Hadley & McCloy; Peter M. Flanigan, a former Nixon White House aide and a managing director of Dillon, Read, a New York investment banking firm; the Washington lawyer R. Robert Linowes; and William H. G. Fitzgerald, the chairman of North American Housing Corporation.

Middendorf became chairman and president of the company in June 1977 and almost immediately began to encounter opposition from other investors. The dissidents included Jackson Stephens, who, it was later alleged, wanted FGB to use a company he controlled, Systematics Inc., for its data processing business. (Stephens has denied that this was his intention.) Several shareholders argued that Middendorf should be replaced as CEO by a professional banker. One disgruntled investor, Eugene Metzger, suggested a scheme to wrest control of FGB from Middendorf, take the company private, and sell it to a foreign bank at a big profit. He outlined this plan in mid-October 1977 in a letter to an officer of North Carolina National Bank, a member of the Middendorf group, suggesting that Stephens could carry out the scheme with the help of a foreign bank or a Japanese client.

That same month, Metzger allegedly recruited Lance and Stephens, and the three men began collecting stock in FGB. If the scheme succeeded, it was later alleged, Lance would be given a senior position in FGB. On November 9, Lance, Stephens, and a Stephens Inc. employee named Curt Bradbury met with BCCI's Abdus Sami in Little Rock to discuss the National Bank of Georgia deal. Stephens and Bradbury allegedly recommended that BCCI purchase FGB stock or recommend the stock to its clients, but the BCCI officer said that he had no interest in FGB.

A few weeks later, the picture changed dramatically. On November 25, the Fed ordered Olmsted's International Bank and its affiliates to cut their ties with FGB by selling all of their FGB stock by the end of the year. A huge volume of stock would now be on the market. The next day, Lance and Stephens met with Abedi at the Omni Hotel in Atlanta and found a receptive audience. Abedi, after all, was already familiar with FGB, having attempted to buy its Bank of Commerce subsidiary in New York. He was aware of the company's unusual franchise — the right to own banks in different states. For someone as politically attuned as Abedi, the fact that it was headquartered in Washington, D.C., was plainly a major attraction.

When Abedi expressed some interest, Stephens offered to sell a block of shares equivalent to 4.9 percent of FGB. He also recommended that Abedi pursue the matter with Eugene Metzger. At the end of November, Abedi met with Metzger at a Washington hotel and authorized him to buy 115,000 shares of FGB that were being offered by one of Olmsted's companies. The next day, Abedi asked about other large blocks of FGB stock. He said that he had a client interested in acquiring FGB, adding that he did not want BCCI's involvement in the transaction to be revealed.

Over the next several weeks, Lance, Stephens, and Metzger collected millions of dollars' worth of FGB stock on the open market and through private purchases from large investors.* The shares would later appear in the names of four Arab clients of BCCI's:

- Kamal Adham, the former Saudi intelligence chief;
- Faisal Saud al-Fulaij, the former chairman of Kuwait Airways;

---

*Stephens now seeks to play down his role in the whole affair, insisting in an interview that he merely bought stock in FGB in response to buy orders from Metzger over a period of a few weeks around the end of 1977. Metzger was acting as an agent for others, Stephens says, but he insists he didn't know the identity of Metzger's clients. He does, however, remember meeting with Sami and Abedi and recalls their interest in U.S. banks and some discussion of the acquisition of NBG.

- Sheikh Sultan bin Zayed al-Nahyan, a son of Abu Dhabi's Sheikh Zayed;
- Abdullah Darwaish, a financial adviser to Zayed, acting on behalf of Zayed's son Mohammed.

By about the end of January 1978, BCCI's Arab clients held roughly 20 percent of FGB's stock. On top of that, Lance and his associates controlled about 8 percent. Since each of the four Arab investors held slightly less than 5 percent of FGB's outstanding stock, they kept their investment secret. Under U.S. securities law, any investor who buys 5 percent of the stock of a publicly held company is required to disclose the investment by filing a Schedule 13(d) with the SEC. This did not necessarily mean that Abedi's clients were acting within the law, however. If the investors were acting as a *group,* they were still obliged to file disclosure statements.

Lance and his associates now decided that it was time to confront the company's top management. Armand Hammer, the head of Occidental Petroleum as well as an FGB board member and major shareholder, arranged for Lance to have lunch with FGB's top executives on February 7. "Hammer apparently planned to play peacemaker, but the seventy-seven-year-old industrialist's private jet was grounded by bad weather and the meeting had to go on without him," the *Washington Post* later reported. Hammer, interestingly, had at least one connection to the BCCI network: Pharaon was a big shareholder in Occidental. Lance arrived at the Washington office of Occidental International Corporation, the site Hammer had picked for the meeting, and was joined by Middendorf, FGB's president, and B. Francis Saul II, who had replaced Middendorf as chairman in January after buying a large block of FGB stock. He was a prominent Washington real estate developer and financier.

What Lance said at the meeting has been hotly disputed. Middendorf and Saul later said in sworn statements that Lance told them he represented Abedi and BCCI and that BCCI "always wanted control." Lance also appeared to make a pitch for the chairmanship or presidency of FGB. He said that after the company was taken over, "he would play a significant role in running FG," in Saul's words. Lance also recommended that Saul and Middendorf meet with Abedi.

The next day, FGB issued a press release stating that it "has reason to believe that possibly in excess of 15% of its outstanding common stock has been purchased recently in a series of transactions." The statement added that FGB "has been informed that the purchases have been made by a foreign bank which may be seeking to obtain control of the Company." The *Washington Post* carried a story the following day headlined "Mideast Bank Buys Block of Financial General Stock," but the paper was unable to find out the name of the bank. Lance then telephoned Saul to say that there had been a misunderstanding. The buyers, Lance said, were not members of a group under the direction of BCCI but were acting as individuals.

BCCI and Lance were linked to the deal publicly a few days later, causing a flurry of press coverage. When reporters called BCCI for comment, bank spokesmen issued blanket denials, which were later found to be false. On February 13, for example, the *New York Times* reported that BCCI officials "flatly denied making any purchases of or having any involvement in efforts to acquire Financial General stock." Further, a BCCI official, Dildar Rizvi, "said that he had spoken today with Mr. Abedi, who also denied any connection with efforts to purchase Financial General stock."

In an effort to thwart what they viewed as a hostile takeover attempt, FGB lawyers met with officials of the SEC and the Federal Reserve. FGB also retained a New York law firm widely regarded as one of the leaders in mergers and acquisitions work, Skadden, Arps, Slate, Meagher & Flom.

On February 17, FGB sued Abedi, Lance, Stephens, Metzger, the Middle Eastern investors, BCCI, and two companies controlled by Stephens: Stephens Inc. and Systematics Inc. The complaint alleged that the "Lance group" began acquiring FGB stock in October 1977 in what amounted to an illegal tender offer. According to the complaint, the investors had been acting as a group, which meant that they had violated securities laws when they failed to file 13(d) disclosure statements. One month later, the SEC also sued the "Lance group," alleging violations of securities laws. The defendants were BCCI, Abedi, Lance, Stephens, Metzger, and the four investors in whose names the stock had been acquired: Kamal Adham, Sheikh Sultan, Abdullah Darwaish, and Faisal Saud al-Fulaij.*

To handle their defense, Lance, Abedi, and the Arab investors turned to the man who had assisted Lance with the Lancegate scandal the previous year, Clark Clifford.

. . .

---

*The SEC also named Middendorf as a defendant, alleging that he had violated certain disclosure rules.

Clark McAdams Clifford has been a Washington fixture since the 1940s, an adviser to every Democratic president since 1945, when he became a junior naval assistant in Truman's White House. Truman soon named him special counsel, a post he held until 1950, when he left the White House staff to form a law firm in Washington. At the time, the Truman administration was mired in scandals involving friends of the president who were accused of cashing in on their White House connections. They were nicknamed "5 percenters" because of the kickbacks they allegedly took for securing government contracts.

Elegant and patrician, Clark Clifford has always striven to differentiate himself from the common Washington influence peddler. "There is one point I wish to make clear," he once said. "This firm has no influence of any kind in Washington. If you want to employ someone who has influence, you will have to go somewhere else. . . . What we do have is a record of working with the various departments and agencies of the government, and we have their respect and confidence, and that we consider to be a valuable asset." Nevertheless, there is no denying that connections were a cornerstone of Clifford's career, as he himself acknowledged privately.

In April 1951, David Lilienthal, Clifford's friend and a senior Truman administration official, wrote in his diary about a lunch with Clifford. Lilienthal noted that his friend's law practice was flourishing — Clifford "earned probably as much as any professional man in the country" — but that he feared his practice would suffer if Truman were not reelected in 1952. "He was uneasy about what will happen after Truman is out, if he is; wonders if he will keep any of his clients. . . ." (Lilienthal added that this was "nonsense" because of Clifford's abilities.)

Clifford not only survived the Democrats' loss of the White House but prospered, forging new relationships over the next three decades. In the 1950s, a rising young senator named John F. Kennedy retained Clifford as his personal lawyer. After Kennedy became president, he appointed Clifford chairman of the Foreign Intelligence Advisory Board. Lyndon Johnson tapped him to serve as secretary of defense during the last year of his administration. Jimmy Carter used him as a presidential envoy to Greece, Turkey, and India.

Clifford's connections also enabled him to attract such corporate clients as General Electric, W. R. Grace Shipping, Phillips Petroleum (on whose board Clifford served), McDonnell Douglas, and Knight-Ridder (where he was also a board member).

One politician who envied Clifford was George Smathers, a Democratic senator from Florida. In *The Superlawyers,* a 1972 book on Washington law firms, Joseph C. Goulden wrote:

> Smathers said publicly that he intended to leave the Senate after his second term expired, in 1968. "I'm going to be a Clark Clifford," he said in 1966. "That's the life for me." And after only a few months of private practice he told a Miami reporter: "I've found the pastures outside are a lot greener than I had presumed. A fellow with my background can make more money in thirty days out here than he can in fifteen years as a senator."

Also important to Clifford's success were his persuasive style and commanding presence. With his distinguished profile and mellifluous voice, Clifford was everyone's picture of the elder statesman. He bears a striking resemblance to the late actor Ralph Bellamy, who portrayed Franklin Roosevelt in *Sunrise at Campobello.*

When Lance retained Clifford in connection with the Lancegate affair, he was assisted by his partner Robert Altman. Although Altman was just thirty years old and had become a partner only the year before, he had impressed Clifford with his energy and quick mind.

Lance's impressive performance at the previous Senate hearings owed much to Clifford's and Altman's assistance. The banker's opening remarks, for example, had been drafted with his lawyers' help. As Lance spoke, Clifford — like a ventriloquist — silently mouthed the words of the statement. Clifford seemed to awe some of the senators with his magisterial style. At one point, for example, Lance was subjected to harsh questioning about a complicated series of transactions. It was alleged that he had used the same collateral to obtain loans from two different banks. Clifford took the floor and said calmly that Lance had decided that "the simplest thing to do was to pay off the note, and he paid it off."

Clifford's powerful presence was evident at another point in the hearings. Years later, Phil Gailey of the *St. Petersburg Times* recalled the scene:

> Senators were whispering among themselves. Reporters and spectators were adding to the noise level. The lack of decorum annoyed Clark Clifford, the stately Washington lawyer representing then-President Jimmy Carter's beleaguered budget director.
>
> Clifford, with chiseled face and silver mane, did not ask the chairman to restore order. He simply raised a finger into the air. The room fell silent.
>
> Such was the prestige and the presence of Clifford — super lawyer,

adviser to presidents, political wise man and ultimate Washington insider.

In the FGB case, Clifford again asked Altman to serve as his right-hand man. They, in turn, were assisted by experienced takeover specialists from the New York firm of Wachtell, Lipton, Rosen & Katz, the archrival of Skadden, Arps, which represented FGB. The two firms so dominated takeover law that they were viewed as the Coke and Pepsi of the field.

Clifford's team quickly negotiated a settlement of the SEC's lawsuit — so quickly, in fact, that the defendants signed the consent agreement on March 18, the day after the suit was filed. It was an extremely favorable deal for Abedi and his associates. Without admitting or denying guilt, the Middle Eastern investors promised not to violate securities laws in the future. They also agreed to establish a special $1 million fund to compensate former FGB stockholders who had sold their stock in the open market at less than $15 a share. (If the sellers had known that rich Arabs were scooping up the stock, it was reasoned, they would have demanded higher prices.)

The most extraordinary aspect of the settlement was the provision that the investors make a tender offer to all FGB stockholders at $15 per share (subject to approval from the Fed to form a bank holding company). The SEC's apparent reasoning was that this would give the shareholders a chance to sell their stock at a high price. In effect, it meant that Abedi and his associates were actually being rewarded for having purchased the stock covertly.

The consent agreement was not the end of the story. It merely raised the curtain on one of the longest and most controversial takeover dramas in U.S. corporate history.

Many observers suspected that Abedi's Arab clients were trying to buy political influence in the United States. Bert Lance, said a *New York Times* editorial, "enjoys easy access to the White House, which may explain why wealthy Arabs have hired him to invest their oil fortunes in the United States." William Safire made much of Kamal Adham's status as Saudi Arabia's former intelligence chief. Thanks to Lance, he wrote, "the top Saudi spy will now be able to examine the intimate financial vulnerabilities of some of our nation's lawmakers and military leaders."

FGB's lawyers kept the pot boiling by pressing ahead with their suit against Abedi and his associates. Two of the Arab investors — Fulaij and Adham — retaliated in June by filing a countersuit against FGB's chairman and president, Saul and Middendorf, ten other board members, and FGB itself. The suit accused the directors of violating federal securities laws and making false statements to shareholders in order to maintain control of the company and to block the Middle Eastern investors from buying additional FGB stock.

FGB's lawyers, in turn, used the discovery process aggressively, demanding documents from the defendants and taking depositions from Abedi and his associates. They soon hit pay dirt. A particularly damaging disclosure concerned Lance's financial dealings with BCCI. The SEC had alleged in its complaint that Lance had "obtained substantial personal loans that were arranged by BCCI." BCCI's Dildar Rizvi told the *Washington Post* that Lance "was paid nothing by the bank"; Allaudin Shaik, another BCCI official, said that Lance had "received absolutely no loans from BCCI or loans arranged by BCCI."

These statements were false. FGB's lawyers discovered that BCCI had arranged for Lance's biggest debt — $3.6 million owed to First National Bank of Chicago — to be repaid on January 4, 1978. Abedi himself, in fact, later admitted that BCCI had lent Lance about $3.5 million. At a court hearing in March, Edward McAmis of Skadden, Arps alleged that BCCI had paid off the loan without even asking Lance to sign a note. Robert Altman reacted by accusing McAmis of deliberately misconstruing the loan as part of a campaign to smear Lance. Altman said formal loan documents were being drawn up but had not been completed because of the lawsuit and other complications. In fact, BCCI never gave a satisfactory explanation of the loan. When the *Wall Street Journal* published a story on BCCI in February 1980, it tried to determine what had happened to Lance's debt to BCCI. The bank said that the loan was no longer on its books — but declined to say how or by whom it had been repaid.

FGB's lawyers also uncovered many indications that the Arabs had acted not on their own behalf but possibly as front men for BCCI. They found, for example, that Fulaij had paid for his FGB stock by borrowing $3.55 million from the BCCI affiliate he headed, Kuwait International Finance Company.

As part of the takeover fight, Abedi was extensively deposed by Skadden, Arps's lawyers at Browns Hotel in London on March 8, 1978. Although he tried to distance himself from the transaction, Abedi gave several hints that he had played a key role in the run at

FGB. Abedi said that after a meeting with Eugene Metzger and BCCI's Abdus Sami, he "approved that they should start buying some shares." He later amended his story, saying, "I didn't approve. I had the instructions from an individual client who was interested in making an investment and who made his own decision." All he really meant, he explained, was that he was present when Metzger was asked to start making purchases.

Skadden, Arps also amassed a great deal of negative information on BCCI from the files of Bank of America. Douglas M. Kraus, a lawyer at Skadden, Arps, demanded that B of A turn over documents relating to BCCI. At a meeting with a B of A officer in London, he was shown several documents and asked that they be copied. The banker took the documents out of the room and said he would return shortly. But when he came back, he said that the bank's lawyers had advised him not to provide copies.

Kraus eventually obtained the documents, which revealed that B of A had serious concerns about the way BCCI did business. One document said that B of A thought BCCI's loan-loss reserves should be increased from $3 million to $17 million. Another damaging disclosure was that BCCI had loaned more than $80 million to "insiders" — companies and individuals connected to the bank.

Even more controversial than BCCI's business practices were the backgrounds of some of the Arab investors, who were alleged to be involved in corruption, repression, and terrorism.

Kamal Adham was not only the former Saudi intelligence chief and an adviser to the royal family, he had parlayed his connections into a lucrative career as a middleman for foreign companies doing business in the kingdom. Much of his work consisted of collecting "commissions" from arms manufacturers and other foreign companies. His net worth was about a quarter of a billion dollars, according to his lawyers.

One of Adham's clients was the Boeing Company. In a 1975 deal, he helped it sell $137 million worth of aircraft to Egypt — a country in which he had considerable influence, thanks in large part to his role in channeling Saudi money to the Sadat regime. Details emerged after the SEC and the Federal Trade Commission filed suit against Boeing. When the cases were settled in 1978, Boeing admitted paying $8.7 million to corporations in Liechtenstein; company spokesmen said they believed that the ultimate recipients were individuals who had arranged or provided financing for the sale. Although the names of those people were withheld by the government, the *Wall Street Journal* filled in the blanks by interviewing government sources. In June 1978, the *Journal* reported that Boeing had been assisted by Adham and Mahdi al-Tajir, a diplomat from the UAE, and Sheikh Zayed.*

Adham and Zayed were not the only figures in the FGB deal who were linked to questionable payments by Boeing. So was Faisal Saud al-Fulaij, another big buyer of FGB stock. From 1964 to 1977, he served as the chairman of Kuwait Airways, the state airline. The Federal Trade Commission identified him as the recipient of at least $300,000 in bribes from Boeing. The commission's draft complaint said, "The payment, at the direction of a Boeing Co. officer, was made through a fictitious Swiss consulting firm." Fulaij denied the allegation.

Some of the BCCI clients were also linked to human rights abuses. Adham was the head of Saudi intelligence at a time when the regime was ruthlessly suppressing opposition. Political opponents were rounded up and jailed; some of them, according to human rights groups, were tortured and executed. Some of the military officers who were arrested in the wake of a 1969 coup plot were tortured by the secret police; a few of them died in prison. In its human rights report for 1977 — when Adham was still the head of Saudi intelligence — Amnesty International said that it knew of two hundred political prisoners by name. Sheikh Zayed's human rights record was better, but his country was still an absolute dictatorship. A State Department human rights report states succinctly: "The UAE has no formal democratic institutions, and citizens do not have the right to change their government." The report notes that "political parties are prohibited."

Terrorism was another controversial issue. Both Saudi Arabia and the United Arab Emirates have provided important political and financial backing to the Palestine Liberation Organization, which the U.S. government classifies as a terrorist group.

Finally, there was the Arab oil embargo of the United States for its

---

*Al-Tajir had encouraged Zayed to lend Egypt up to $90 million to finance the aircraft purchases, U.S. officials said, while Adham had used his influence with the Egyptian government to ensure that Boeing would be the supplier. Asked to comment on the deal in 1991, a lawyer for Adham, Plato Cacheris, confirmed to a *Wall Street Journal* reporter that Adham had urged the Egyptians to use Boeing. He added that Adham was proud of the deal, because the Egyptians would otherwise have bought Soviet airliners.

support of Israel in the 1973 Yom Kippur War. Memories of long lines at the gasoline pumps were still fresh.

Despite all the controversy, the BCCI clients pressed ahead with their campaign, and the takeover battle dragged on into 1979. In January, FGB won an important victory when Maryland's attorney general issued a legal opinion that FGB's Maryland bank could not be acquired in a hostile takeover. On the basis of that opinion, the Federal Reserve ruled that the Arab investors could not take over FGB. The investors responded by asking a federal court to declare the Maryland law unconstitutional.

The investors then tried to mount a proxy fight. They chose three individuals who would seek election to FGB's board: Stuart Symington, a former Democratic senator from Missouri; Elwood R. Quesada, a real estate developer in Washington; and Donald D. Notman, the former chairman of National Bank of Washington. All three were close associates of Clifford's. Clifford served on the board of Notman's bank, and Symington and Clifford had been intimates since the 1940s. When Symington ran for president in 1960, Clifford was his campaign manager.

When Clifford first contacted Symington about FGB in August 1978, the retired senator was in Canada, fishing for salmon with the comedian Bob Hope. Symington later said that Clifford asked him to serve as "a trustee of some Arabian investors who were anxious to obtain control of Financial General." Telephone voices on Bob Hope's boat reverberated all over the craft, so Symington kept the conversation short, saying he would discuss it back in Washington. Upon his return, Symington talked it over with Clifford, who introduced him to Kamal Adham. Symington said he was impressed by the Arab sheikh. He also said he checked the proposal out with leading people in the banking business, who all told him they thought it was "a very good idea possibly to get petrodollars back into the United States." Symington agreed to become chairman of a Netherlands Antilles company called Credit and Commerce American Holdings N.V. (CCAH), a dummy company set up by the investors to carry out the acquisition.

Financial General's annual meeting was held on April 30, 1980, in an atmosphere of great anticipation. More than two and a half years had elapsed since Lance and his associates had started collecting FGB stock, and the battle might soon be over. The Arab investors had been soliciting proxies from other FGB shareholders. If they collected enough, they could take control of the board of directors. When the votes were counted, FGB's management claimed victory, but the tally was very close. Altman said that settlement talks would continue in an effort to end the fight.

FGB's board of directors finally capitulated, and the two sides signed a letter of understanding on May 21. After some additional haggling over price, a formal acquisition agreement was signed on July 25. Three representatives of the Arab investors — Clifford, Symington, and Quesada — were then elected to the board.

In spite of the agreement, the deal still had to be approved by the Federal Reserve Board, which has jurisdiction over bank holding companies. If the Fed gave its nod, FGB would be taken over by dummy companies set up for that purpose, the main one being CCAH.*

CCAH's shareholders included three of the original four BCCI clients who had bought stock in late 1977 and early 1978: Kamal Adham, Faisal Saud al-Fulaij, and Abdullah Darwaish.† There were also eleven other Middle Eastern investors:

- The Abu Dhabi Investment Authority, an investment vehicle controlled by Sheikh Zayed;
- Stock Holding Company, owned by the family of Sheikh Rashid bin Said al-Maktoum, the ruler of Dubai;
- Abdul-Raouf Khalil, a Saudi Arabian businessman close to Adham;
- Crescent Holding Company, owned by Sheikh Mohammed bin Rashid al-Maktoum, a son of Dubai's Sheikh Rashid;
- Mashriq Holding Company, a vehicle of Sheikh Hamad bin Mohammed al-Sharqi, the ruler of Fujeirah (part of the UAE);
- Sheikh Humaid bin Rashid al-Naomi, the crown prince and deputy ruler of Ajman, UAE;
- Ali Mohammed Shorafa, a top adviser to Sheikh Zayed;
- Mohammed Hussain Qabazard, an aide to Zayed;
- Gulf Investment Real Estate Company;
- Real Estate Investment Company; and

---

*CCAH was the parent of Credit and Commerce American Investments B.V. (CCAI), a Dutch company. CCAI, in turn, would own all the stock of a U.S. dummy company, which, in turn, would own FGB. The layering of companies in these jurisdictions is a common technique used to avoid taxes, known as a "Dutch sandwich."

†Shiekh Sultan, another son of Sheikh Zayed's and one of the four original investors, sold all of his FGB stock to Adham in the fall of 1978.

- Sayed Jawhary (sometimes spelled El-Gohary), a friend and business manager of Adham's.

The proposed takeover presented unusual problems to the regulators. When a large bank holding company is acquired, the buyer is usually an existing bank. In this case, FGB was to be bought by dummy companies owned by individual investors, none of whom was a banker. A further complication was that all the investors were residents of foreign countries. Could U.S. regulators effectively monitor the new owners?

Perhaps even more important, bank regulators had serious concerns about BCCI, and they did not want it to be involved in the ownership or management of FGB. Questions were raised by the Federal Reserve Board, the Federal Reserve Bank of Richmond, the Virginia commissioner of financial institutions, and the Office of the Comptroller of the Currency (OCC), the main regulator of nationally chartered banks. The investors would have to convince the Fed that FGB would be run by Americans who had solid banking credentials — and that BCCI wouldn't be involved.

To allay the regulators' fears, lawyers for the Arab investors devised a formula to insulate the company from the foreign investors. If the takeover went through, FGB would be controlled by a board of directors consisting of distinguished U.S. citizens, including former Senator Symington. To ensure the board's autonomy, Symington would have the right to vote the majority of the Arabs' stock for five years. In the words of one observer, "The lawyers proposed that there be a buffer in the form of a blue-ribbon board of directors, and the shareholders would basically agree to take a walk."

As far as BCCI was concerned, the application stated that "BCCI owns no shares of [FGB], CCAH or CCAI, either directly or indirectly, nor will it if the application is approved. Neither is [it] a lender, nor will it be, with respect to the acquisition by any of the investors of either [FGB], CCAI or CCAH shares." The investors would finance the takeover with their personal funds and by borrowing from financial institutions not affiliated with BCCI. Some of the money would be lent by a bank in Paris, Banque Arabe et Internationale d'Investissement. BCCI would have no involvement in the management of FGB, although it could act as an investment adviser to the Middle Eastern owners.

Some regulators continued to have doubts, including Virginia's state bank regulator and the OCC. In March 1981, the OCC sent a letter to the Fed expressing concerns about enhanced ties between FGB and BCCI because no individual regulatory body had a worldwide view of BCCI's operations. BCCI, the letter stated, "is not subject to regulation and supervision on a consolidated basis by a single bank supervisory authority."

The Fed also received letters from a wide range of people opposed to the takeover, including board members of FGB's banks, stockholders, customers, and ordinary citizens. Some raised valid issues, but there also seemed to be elements of xenophobia. One FGB stockholder wrote that "any group of Middle Eastern investors associated with Burt [*sic*] Lance" would be

> grossly unsound in terms of potential management. How aliens could effectively meet the high banking standards prevailing in the United States, when they come from economies which operate out-side the market system and which have no commercial banking industry of the type that flourishes here in our free enterprise society is a complete mystery to me.

An elderly couple in Winchester, Virginia, said that they were con-tented customers of the Shenandoah Valley National Bank (an FGB subsidiary) and were happy with it the way it was, adding, "In the event it loses control to Bert Lance & the Arabs, we will sever all connections with it." A woman on the board of another FGB bank expressed concern about the second-class status of women in Arab countries:

> Without casting aspersions on any party because of ethnic origin, I must point out as regards to women the basic cultural difference in the Arab world, from which the would-be acquirers come, and modern American society.
> These businessmen are products of a culture which looks on women solely as chattel and procreators and does not even allow women to eat with men nor walk by their side.

Because of the doubts and criticism, the Fed decided to hold a private hearing on the application. Only then would it decide whether BCCI's clients could take over FGB.

At 9:39 A.M. on April 23, 1981, more than two dozen people gathered in Room B-1215 of the Federal Reserve's Main Board Building, a grand, white marble edifice at 20th Street and Constitution Avenue in

Washington, D.C. It is now called the Eccles Building, after the Fed's former chairman Marriner S. Eccles. There were federal and state bank regulators, four of the Arab investors, one FGB official, and a host of lawyers, including Clark Clifford and Robert Altman. The meeting was chaired by Robert E. Mannion, a deputy general counsel of the Fed. Two of the Arab investors had been featured in the press for more than three years, Kamal Adham of Saudi Arabia and Faisal Saud al-Fulaij of Kuwait. The other two investors were much more obscure: Abdul-Raouf Khalil and Sayed Jawhary. Both were close associates of Adham's.

After Mannion and Clifford introduced the participants, Sidney Bailey, Virginia's commissioner of financial institutions, took the floor. A feisty chain smoker who has devoted his life to banking regulation, Bailey had an important interest in the matter, since FGB did more business in Virginia than in any other state, and he was strongly opposed to the takeover. He was skeptical that it was simply a routine investment. What was the motive, he asked, "giving rise to this protracted, expensive campaign to buy Financial General?" There was little doubt, he said, "that some incentive other than orthodox investment motives must have prompted this effort." In Bailey's view, there was a strong possibility that the takeover bid was prompted by political motives.

It was now Clark Clifford's turn to speak, and he was clearly in his element. For years he had used his considerable charm and skills of persuasion in settings just like this. The eminent lawyer spoke eloquently of the need for the United States to attract investment from the Middle East. There was, he said, "a growing feeling among many thoughtful and experienced Americans that it is in the interest of our country . . . to bring back to the United States as many of the dollars as we can that through the years we send over to the OPEC countries." He also spoke of his high regard for the Arab investors. Describing Adham as "a prominent businessman in Saudi Arabia," Clifford lavished praise on him: "I have come to have the deepest respect for his character, for his reputation, for his honor, and for his integrity. I'm proud to be an associate of his."

Clifford recounted what he described as a recent conversation with B. F. Saul, FGB's chairman. "He had occasion to go to London, maybe more than once," Clifford said. "He had occasion to go to the Middle East, the Persian Gulf countries. I remember later on his talking with me, and he said, 'I have looked into the reputation, particularly of the leader of the group, of His Excellency Sheikh Kamal Adham.' And he said, 'It's difficult to recall a time when I have heard such universal commendation for an international businessman. I hear it in London. I've heard the most commendatory comments. I've heard about him in countries of the Persian Gulf. I have not heard one whisper of criticism against this man.' And he said, 'I feel perfectly comfortable about this group, headed by this man, coming in and taking over our banks.' "*

In his statement and in response to questions from the regulators, Clifford described how Adham and his associates happened to buy their FGB stock; it contrasted sharply with the version in the SEC complaint. Adham, according to Clifford, got the idea not from BCCI but from a friend named Hassan Yassin, who worked at the Saudi Arabian Embassy in Washington. Adham then asked BCCI to evaluate the stock for him. In other words, it was pure coincidence that Abedi was being told about the same stock at the same time by Bert Lance and Jackson Stephens.

Clifford also did his best to play down Lance's role — a wise move, since the regulators regarded Lance as a kind of Typhoid Mary of the banking industry. Clifford provided an extraordinarily terse account of Lance's involvement in the deal: "At one time he did own a few shares of stock. He sold the stock. Retired from participation in it." (This statement is reminiscent of Clifford's remark in 1977 at the Senate hearing on Lance when he said his client had merely borrowed money and then paid it back.)

Clifford said that if the takeover was approved, the Arabs would be passive investors and the company would be run by "a top, very well regarded commercial banker," someone with twenty-five or thirty years' experience.

Each of the four Arab investors then took the floor to introduce himself and recount how he became involved with FGB. Adham talked about his business activities but did not discuss his long service as Saudi Arabia's intelligence chief. He echoed Clifford's statement that he had learned about the company from a Saudi friend. "Mr. Yassin

---

*Saul disputed Clifford's account several years later: "I never did go to the Middle East to meet him. I think I met Kamal Adham in Washington once. I don't think I ever met him in London. I met him for twenty minutes. I did not try to make a judgment whether they should own a bank. That was something for the Federal Reserve to do. All I was concerned about was whether this was in the best interest of the shareholders, and I thought it was. I didn't know these people."

advised me that the stock had become available for purchase in Financial General and that this company might provide an attractive investment opportunity," he said. "I asked BCCI to evaluate this property for me and advise me as to its suitability as an investment."

After a midday break, the meeting reconvened at 1:38, and the regulators questioned the investors and their lawyers about various aspects of their testimony, including how they happened to invest in the company and their relations to BCCI.

Adham stated firmly that he was not a front man for BCCI. "I think that from the line of questions, it appears that there is doubt that there is somebody or BCCI is behind all of this deal," he said. "I would like to assure you that each one on his own rights will not accept in any way to be a cover for somebody else." He added, "We don't need anybody to use us, to be a cover for them. We are doing it for ourselves."

The Fed's Mannion noted that the two dummy companies established to carry out the acquisition had names that were similar to that of BCCI: Credit and Commerce American Holdings and Credit and Commerce American Investments. Clifford brushed this aside as meaningless, saying, "I think generally the term 'credit' and the term 'commerce' are terms that are used extensively in the Persian Gulf in financial affairs. . . . I know of no additional reasoning behind it." (Clifford was mistaken. The only major bank in the region with those words in its name was BCCI.) Altman said that "there is no connection between those entities and BCCI in terms of ownership or other relationship." At one point in the proceedings Clifford said, "There is no function of any kind on the part of BCCI. I know of no present relationship. I know of no planned future relationship that exists."

The atmosphere of the meeting was cordial, and most of the regulators were deferential to Clifford and his clients. Throughout, Clifford referred to Adham as "His Excellency," a term that isn't always applied to Saudi sheikhs. In Saudi Arabia, "sheikh" is not a title of nobility but simply an honorific for a respected person — roughly equivalent to calling a distinguished Spaniard "don." Taking their cue from Clifford, however, the regulators began to refer to Adham as "His Excellency."

No one challenged Clifford's portrayal of Adham as simply a businessman, even though he had been identified repeatedly in the press as his country's intelligence chief. He had held that post until 1977 but continued serving as a royal adviser. There was no discussion of the Boeing bribery case — which involved Adham and Fulaij — even though the Fed's correspondence with the SEC makes it clear that the bank regulators knew about it.*

One regulator who asked tough questions was Virginia's Sidney Bailey, but he was an exception. Asked about the experience years later, Bailey said, "I felt like a voice in the wilderness. The Fed paid little attention to what I had to say." He said he felt like a "mouse in a room full of dancing elephants."

Throughout the approval process, the Fed ignored numerous clues that the investors may have been fronting for BCCI. On May 17, 1978, the London *Financial Times* published an article on BCCI based on an interview with Abedi, stating in part: "He is not yet sure who will make the offer [for FGB], but whoever makes it and if it succeeds, BCCI will probably manage Financial General."

Moreover, Clifford and Altman's assertion that the Arabs' purchase of FGB stock was a routine investment not connected with BCCI had been sharply contradicted three years earlier. In FGB's lawsuit against Lance and the Arab investors, among others, U.S. District Judge Oliver Gasch held that the Arab investors had acted as a group to take over FGB in violation of securities law. Gasch wrote in his opinion that Abedi had essentially put together the deal, assembled the investment group, and instructed Lance and others to buy stock for them. Further disputing Clifford's statement, Gasch held that it was Abedi — not Hassan Yassin — who had recommended the stock to Adham.

Another important sign of BCCI's involvement was that several members of the investment group had close ties to BCCI. Adham, Fulaij, and Sheikh Zayed were BCCI shareholders, and Fulaij was chairman of BCCI's Kuwaiti affiliate, Kuwait International Finance Company (KIFCO). Perhaps most important, Fulaij, as noted earlier, had financed his initial investment in FGB by borrowing $3.55 million from KIFCO. Adham had also borrowed from the bank, and other members of the group may have done so as well. When FGB's management was fighting the takeover, one of its lawyers said in an affidavit

---

*On July 5, 1980, the Fed asked the SEC for information about the Boeing case. Theodore Levine, an SEC lawyer, confirmed in a letter that the names of two of the investors had come up in the Boeing investigation.

that he had seen a Bank of America document revealing that BCCI had made loans to two of the initial four Middle Eastern investors.

The Federal Reserve brushed aside all these connections. One Fed document suggests profound ignorance — or willful blindness. A letter from a Fed official to Congressman Benjamin Rosenthal, a New York Democrat who raised questions about the takeover, contains this statement: "Staff has no knowledge of loans from or other involvement in the affairs of BCCI on the part of Applicants' principals [the Arab investors]." Another extraordinary statement appears in an internal Fed memorandum dated August 7, 1981. It says, in part: "There is no evidence in the record that BCCI ever owned or controlled shares of FG, or that the investors acted through BCCI to control FG." Not only was there no doubt that the investors had acted through BCCI to buy the stock, the Fed had it backward: the real issue was whether BCCI had acted through the investors to gain control of FGB.

On August 25, 1981, four months after the hearing, the Federal Reserve Board announced that it had approved the takeover of Financial General Bankshares.

There was a final regulatory hurdle before the takeover could proceed. The New York State Banking Board had to approve the deal because FGB controlled two small banks chartered by the state. This was not a major barrier, since the banks could always switch to a national charter, but the Arab investors nonetheless sought approval.

There was considerable opposition to the deal in New York, partly because some members of the state's large Jewish community were suspicious of the Arab investors. One opponent was Manfred Ohrenstein, the minority (Democratic) leader of the New York state senate. In March 1981, he sent a letter to Muriel Siebert, the state banking superintendent, in which he suggested that the Arab investors were trying to increase their political influence. "Financial General Bankshares," he wrote, "could be one of the most valuable bank holding companies in the United States to a foreign investor who desired maximum influence on American banking and political institutions" because the company controlled banks "in the Washington, D.C., metropolitan area."

One month later, Ohrenstein wrote to the Fed's chairman, Paul Volcker, raising the issue of terrorism. He asked whether any of the investors "or the organizations for which they act as representatives [are] affiliated in any way with any international terrorist organizations" or whether they provide "any financial assistance" to any terrorist organization. In a written response, Robert Altman gave a simple reply to both questions: "No."*

Clifford had gone to the state capital of Albany on May 12, 1981, to meet with Ohrenstein. The legislator said that Clifford tried to reassure him by describing the takeover as "a passive investment on the part of these people." Ohrenstein was unmoved. Two weeks later, he wrote to Clifford and accused him of providing inaccurate information about the Arab governments' policies toward foreign investment. Contrary to Clifford's assertions, Americans did not have the same rights and privileges in terms of investments as the Middle Eastern investors who were bidding for FGB. Ohrenstein listed restrictions on foreign investment in Kuwait, the UAE, and Saudi Arabia. He added that "the rulers of the governments imposing those restrictions are the same persons who are investing in Financial General Bankshares, high-ranking officials from the United Arab Emirates — Abu Dhabi, Dubai, Fujaira [sic] and Ajman — and Kuwait and Saudi Arabia."

On September 21, the New York State Banking Board conducted its own hearing on the takeover at the World Trade Center in Manhattan. Unlike the Fed meeting the previous April, this one was open to the public, and anyone was allowed to express an opinion. The atmosphere was much less polite as a series of speakers asked the kind of tough questions that had been skirted at the Fed meeting. A number of people said they feared that FGB would become a tool of Arab foreign policy. One suggested that Clifford may have violated federal law by failing to register with the Justice Department as a foreign agent. Another went so far as to describe him as a "front man" for the Arab investors. Clifford dismissed much of the criticism as the product of prejudice against the Arabs. "That's what it came down to as I listened to it," he said.

In November, the New York State Banking Board voted against the takeover. The following March, another vote was taken; this time the takeover was approved by a vote of 9–2 (one more vote than was needed). One reason for the reversal was that the Arab investors agreed that FGB would divest its New York City subsidiary, Bank of Commerce. The bank it owned in upstate New York would be allowed to expand into New York City.

---

*In 1989, Altman was asked to reconcile his answer with Saudi and UAE support for the PLO. He expressed offense at the question but refused to answer it.

Immediately after New York State gave the green light, the investors made a tender offer for all FGB shares. On April 19, 1982, the investors announced that the tender offer had been successful: they had acquired 96 percent of the company's outstanding common stock, paying just over $200 million for the shares. (During the next several years, the investment group was reshuffled from time to time, with some additional BCCI clients coming in. One man who invested in the mid-1980s was Khalid Bin Mahfouz, whose family controls National Commercial Bank, the largest bank in Saudi Arabia, and acts as banker to the ruling family.)

The takeover was followed by a shake-up of FGB's top management. Clifford had promised the Fed that the investors would recruit a seasoned banker to serve as president and CEO, and he fulfilled this part of the agreement by recruiting Robert G. Stevens, the former chairman and CEO of BancOhio Corporation, a large bank holding company in Columbus. (Stevens held that post until June 1989, when he was replaced by the longtime FGB executive Jack Beddow.)

To a great extent, Stevens was the CEO in name only, with Clifford and Altman dominating the company. The board included Clifford and four other directors close to him: Altman, Symington (as vice chairman), the retired army general James M. Gavin, and Elwood R. Quesada. The distinguished American elected chairman of the board was none other than Clark McAdams Clifford. What is more, Altman became president of a holding company that ranked above FGB on the organization chart.* Thus, of the four top positions, only one was held by a banker. The board also designated Clifford's law firm as the company's general counsel, a move that later raised conflict-of-interest questions. Even more questionably, the firm continued to do legal work for BCCI.

In August 1982, a new name for the company was unveiled: First American Bankshares, Inc. The change had been in the works before the takeover, but it was nevertheless an extraordinary move in view of the company's new foreign ownership. A more appropriate name would have been First Arabian Bankshares.

Just as First American's new management was settling in, the Federal Reserve learned that Abdullah Darwaish, one of the leading share-

---

*FGB Holding Company, the direct parent of FGB. In August 1982, it was renamed First American Corporation.

holders and Sheikh Zayed's financial adviser, had been accused of defrauding the sheikh out of nearly $100 million. Still more disturbing was that the accusation was made months before the takeover went through, yet, apparently, no one had bothered to tell the regulators about it.

Sometime around the end of 1981 or beginning of 1982, Darwaish was placed under house arrest and dismissed from his posts as chairman of Zayed's Department of Personal Affairs and chairman of the Abu Dhabi Investment Company. His chief deputy, Riaz Saleem Aslam, was jailed in late 1981. In March 1982 — the month before the takeover was consummated — Sheikh Zayed brought two lawsuits in U.S. courts against Darwaish, Aslam, and other defendants, charging that they had been involved in an elaborate scheme to defraud him of $96 million through investments in copper, gold, and U.S. government bonds.* Somehow the U.S. regulators managed to remain ignorant of the case, and Darwaish's name continued to appear prominently in documents related to the takeover. The formal tender offer document for FGB, filed with the SEC on March 3, 1982, listed Darwaish as one of the three controlling shareholders in the takeover group (along with Adham and Fulaij) and identified him with the titles he held before his arrest.

Fed officials said that they learned of the Darwaish case when the *Washington Post* published a story on the U.S. litigation on August 10, 1982. "Documents filed in that case," wrote Jerry Knight, "indicate Darwaish's troubles in Abu Dhabi were known weeks and perhaps months before he and his partners bought control of Financial General but were never disclosed to bank officials, stockholders, or regulatory agencies." He went on to say that the SEC and the Fed were never informed, according to sources at those agencies.

The same day this story appeared, Michael Bradfield, the Fed's general counsel, wrote to Clifford to ask for more information. In a reply dated August 16, Clifford stressed that Darwaish owned no shares in the company but was merely representing Zayed's son Mohammed, adding that Mohammed would be handling his own investments in the future. Clifford denied that any information had been withheld from regulatory agencies. He branded the *Post*'s story "inac-

---

*In March 1989, the New York Court of Appeals ruled unanimously that Zayed couldn't press his claim because he had refused to be deposed in the case. Darwaish was released from house arrest after a short time but was apparently forbidden to leave the UAE. Aslam remained in custody until October 1990.

curate, misleading, unwarranted, and irresponsible" and said that he had informed Benjamin Bradlee, the executive editor, of "the gross inaccuracies in the article." If the Fed had done some checking, it would have found that the *Post*'s story was entirely accurate. Despite Clifford's supposed complaint to the newspaper, the *Post* published no correction, letter to the editor, or follow-up article.

The Darwaish affair raised an obvious question: Had the regulators been misled about anything else? It appears that the Fed was disinclined to ask. The affair was apparently treated as nothing more than an unpleasant incident rather than a warning sign.

4

THE UNDERGROUND EMPIRE

THE TAKEOVER OF First American Bankshares was a remarkable achievement for Abedi. A group of BCCI clients — including several of the bank's most important stockholders — now controlled a major banking company in the American capital. Abedi had also forged close ties with Clark Clifford, one of the most powerful figures in Washington and a potential bridge to America's political establishment. This was bound to enhance Abedi's standing in the eyes of Sheikh Zayed, his chief patron. In 1980, the same year that First American agreed to be acquired, Zayed named Abedi to a new investment committee responsible for managing billions of dollars of Abu Dhabi's funds. He was the only non-Arab on the committee — indeed, the only member from outside the UAE.

With Zayed's backing, BCCI continued to expand its international network in industrial countries and throughout the Third World. By the end of 1983, eleven years after the bank was founded, Abedi had achieved his dream of a global bank. The international network consisted of 360 offices in sixty-eight countries. Of these, 91 were in Europe, 52 in the Americas, 47 in the Far East, South Asia, and Southeast Asia, 90 in the Middle East, and 80 in Africa. The annual report for that year stated proudly: "The Group's network now covers most of the principal financial trade and money centres of the world."

In Africa, BCCI's network extended from Cameroon in the west to Kenya in the east, from Djibouti in the north to Swaziland in the south. The Indian Ocean tourist mecca of Seychelles had a BCCI branch, as did the impoverished nation of the Sudan. By the end of 1987, BCCI had operations in twenty African countries. The biggest was in Nigeria, where BCCI had dozens of branches. BCCI was unquestionably the most important foreign bank in Africa.

In some countries, BCCI was regarded as a local bank, since it had taken over domestic institutions, as it did in Hong Kong. In 1983, BCCI bought a Colombian bank as well as a 26-branch Spanish bank, Banco de Descuento S.A., which was renamed Bank of Credit and Commerce S.A. Española. A former official of the Spanish unit says that important clients were treated to the ultimate in service. One client, he says, was a wealthy Arab who liked to gamble at the casino in Marbella. If the customer ran out of cash, a BCCI officer would open the branch at midnight to obtain currency.

BCCI did not buy any banks in the United States — its clients took care of that — but it did open branches and representative offices across the country. The bank made its American debut in 1978 with a representative office on Park Avenue in Manhattan. Since such offices were limited in what they could do, Abedi sought permission to open "agencies" in the United States. (Under U.S. law, foreign bank agencies have fewer privileges than full-fledged branches.) The first BCCI agency was opened in San Francisco in 1981. It was followed by six more agencies.* BCCI's Miami office was the headquarters for Latin America and the Caribbean.

By the end of 1988, BCCI's network included 417 offices in seventy-three countries. The annual report noted that the bank now served 1.3 million customers through 14,000 staff members of ninety nationalities. Total assets had soared to $20.6 billion — a hundredfold increase in fifteen years. Although these numbers were impressive, they actually understated the size and scope of BCCI's empire. Not mentioned in the annual reports were several other institutions with very close ties to BCCI — a kind of underground empire.

When Abedi's Arab clients sought approval to buy First American Bankshares, they told the Fed that BCCI would have no role in financing the takeover. Some of the money to buy the stock was borrowed from Banque Arabe et Internationale d'Investissement (BAII).

What was BAII? More important, was the Fed correct in regarding it as unaffiliated with BCCI? BAII was founded in Paris in 1973 as a

---

*BCCI's other U.S. agencies were opened in Miami (1982), Los Angeles (1983), Palm Beach (1983), Tampa (1984), New York (1984), and Boca Raton (1986). The agencies were supplemented by representative offices in Chicago (1984), Houston (1984), Washington (1984), and Beverly Hills (1985).

consortium bank — that is, an institution owned by several other banks. Like BCCI, BAII was owned by a Luxembourg holding company but had its headquarters elsewhere. In BAII's case, it was in Paris's glorious Place Vendôme, a stone's throw from J. P. Morgan & Company's grand French headquarters. Another similarity with BCCI was its parentage. Bank of America was a founding shareholder in BCCI and the only major U.S. bank to hold stock in BAII.

Perhaps the most important connection, though, was through a man named Yves Lamarche, BAII's longtime chief executive. Lamarche had been a senior official of Bank of America and had encouraged it to invest in Abedi's bank. He then joined BCCI's board of directors, remaining on the board after moving to BAII. Lamarche was more important in BCCI than his position on the board would imply. During its early years, BCCI had only a few directors. At one point its Luxembourg holding company had just three directors: Abedi, a Swiss politician named Franz Muheim, and Lamarche, who also became "a close friend and confidant of Mr. Abedi," according to a former BCCI executive.

On an operational level, there were a number of ties between the two banks. On many occasions, BAII popped up in BCCI-related deals. The financing of the First American takeover in 1982 was one example. Three years later, Ghaith Pharaon borrowed from BAII in order to buy a small California bank. It was later discovered that the real lender was BCCI, with BAII acting as a front.

While BCCI and BAII were very close, other entities had even closer ties to Abedi's bank, including financial institutions, industrial and service companies, and nonprofit organizations. Some of them were so closely associated with the bank that even low-level staff members regarded them as de facto affiliates of BCCI.

Each of these "satellites" had most — sometimes all — of the following characteristics:

- BCCI was involved in founding or acquiring it.
- Its shareholders were Arab investors with close ties to BCCI.
- Its shareholders were passive investors.
- BCCI provided financial support to the entity and/or its shareholders.
- Its officers had close ties to BCCI.
- Its logo resembled that of BCCI.
- It did a great deal of business with BCCI and with other BCCI satellites.

Attock Oil, in London, was a drilling, refining, marketing, and oil-trading company that was particularly active in Pakistan. In 1977, it was taken over by a group of BCCI-related investors, including men who later invested in U.S. banks with BCCI's help: Ghaith Pharaon, Kamal Adham, and Faisal Saud al-Fulaij. All three men wound up on Attock's board, with Pharaon as chairman. Another board member, Hasan Mahmood Kazmi, served as general manager of one of BCCI's most important units, International Credit and Investment Company (Overseas) Ltd., in the Cayman Islands.

Though Pharaon was chairman of Attock, he was seldom seen by its employees. "In terms of the day-to-day running of the business," says a former employee, "he was not involved or informed." Most decisions were made by Pakistanis recruited from BCCI, including an executive named M. A. Baqi. Baqi also had a family connection to BCCI: his brother-in-law was Agha Hasan Abedi.

Cromwell Hospital, in the Earl's Court section of London, was built at Sheikh Zayed's request and owned by dummy companies that Zayed controlled. Abedi handled all the details, recruiting doctors from Pakistan (including his personal physician) and Britain. While construction was in progress, Abedi provided the doctors with offices at the bank's headquarters as well as BCCI cars and drivers. "They spent two years in 100 Leadenhall Street," says a BCCI official.

International Travel Corporation (ITC), a London travel agency with offices in Pakistan, had its headquarters in BCCI's main office. Outlets of the travel agency shared space with other BCCI offices in London. Employees of BCCI and some of the satellites used ITC; in fact, some were required to use ITC even though they could have gotten cheaper tickets elsewhere.

South Publications, a company financed by BCCI, owned a monthly magazine called *South* and a quasi-academic journal called the *Third World Quarterly*. The man in charge, Altaf Gauhar, also ran a charitable organization sponsored by BCCI, the Third World Foundation. As we shall see, the foundation and the publications served as promotional tools for the bank.

Capcom Financial Services Ltd., a commodity futures and investment management firm in London, was founded in 1984. Its stockholders included several BCCI shareholders, and it was run by Syed Ziauddin Ali Akbar, who had headed BCCI's treasury department in London and brought several BCCI people with him to the firm. There is also a family tie: Swaleh Naqvi, Abedi's right-hand man, was married to Akbar's sister.

While most of the BCCI satellites were in London, some of the most important ones were in the United States.

When Pharaon and Lance held a press conference in December 1977 to answer questions about the National Bank of Georgia takeover, an Atlanta reporter asked Lance about a promise he had made to keep NBG in Georgian hands. Glancing at Pharaon, the banker said, "We want to make a Georgian out of him." Although the remark was obviously made in jest, things almost turned out that way. After the takeover, Pharaon developed close ties to the Peach State, using it as the base for his U.S. operations, which included investments in several parts of the country. His U.S. holding company, Interedec Inc., was in Savannah. He also purchased Richmond Hill, a spectacular estate near Savannah that had once been owned by Henry Ford, and he spent a fortune restoring it. "He loved this old plantation and the style he'd seen in *Gone With the Wind*," says a former associate.

Pharaon was well on his way to becoming a Georgian — at least an honorary one. In fact, although his business interests were scattered around the world, he spent several months each year in Georgia. However, there was one company he seldom visited: National Bank of Georgia. After acquiring the bank in 1978, Pharaon became an absentee landlord, turning over its management to a group of professional bankers, many of whom had close ties to BCCI.

When Pharaon bought the bank, the president and CEO was an experienced banker named Robert P. Guyton. In late 1979, Guyton was forced out and replaced by a former Bank of America executive, Roy P. M. Carlson, who also became chairman. (He gave up the title of president in 1986.) Carlson's ties to Abedi stretched back several years, as noted in Chapter 1. Before Abedi launched BCCI in 1972, he had outlined his plans to Carlson, then head of B of A's Mideast-Africa region. After B of A agreed to invest in the new bank, Carlson became responsible for monitoring the investment and often traveled with Abedi in the Middle East. Before Pharaon hired Carlson for the NBG job, Carlson met with Abedi in London. Carlson had a further link to BCCI. From 1975 to 1979, he was the managing director of Melli Industrial Group in Iran, a company controlled by Mohammed Rahim Motaghi Irvani, a prominent businessman with close ties to BCCI. (Carlson declined to comment on his ties to BCCI.)

NBG's staff also included three Pakistani bankers who had worked at BCCI. The most senior was Tariq Jamil, the assistant to the chairman. (He later returned to BCCI as regional general manager for the

Far East.) Some say that he was the de facto chief executive of the Georgia bank.

In 1982, NBG's logo was changed to resemble BCCI's. Around the same time, Jamil took part in a scheme for the joint marketing of NBG's and BCCI's services to potential clients. The Atlanta bank opened a branch in the Cayman Islands and also became involved with BCCI in Latin American business.

Several years after the NBG takeover, Pharaon bought another American bank with BCCI's assistance. This timing was odd because the transaction occurred when he was suffering from severe financial setbacks.

After the oil shocks of 1973 and 1979, Saudi Arabia's most prominent businessmen were avidly courted by foreign bankers. One big borrower was Pharaon's flagship company, Saudi Research & Development Corporation (REDEC). The boom times began to end in the early and mid-1980s, however, when an oil glut caused prices to fall. Saudi tycoons who had boasted of their "entrepreneurial" abilities a few years earlier began to suffer huge losses. In December 1985, REDEC declared a moratorium on the repayment of principal on its debt. The following year, after it stopped paying interest, creditor banks agreed to reschedule $353 million of the company's debt.

The crisis was a humbling experience for Pharaon. For years he had flitted around the world in private jets; at one point he owned three Falcons and two Boeing jetliners. He sold all of his jets and started using a far less impressive Cessna Citation II. For a globe-trotting tycoon like Pharaon, it was like checking out of the Plaza Hotel and moving into Motel 6.

In October 1985 — just two months before REDEC declared a moratorium on principal payments — Pharaon paid $23 million for Independence Bank, a small ($220 million in assets) institution in Los Angeles; its headquarters was in the San Fernando Valley community of Encino. The timing of the investment was not the only peculiar feature. The deal had much in common with Pharaon's purchase of NBG several years earlier. BCCI officers picked out Independence Bank and negotiated with the sellers. The purchase was largely financed by Banque Arabe et Internationale d'Investissement, which had also helped fund the First American takeover. In fact, of course, the money actually came from BCCI.

After buying Independence Bank, Pharaon became — as with

NBG — an absentee landlord. A Pakistani banker, Kemal Shoaib, was installed as chairman. He had been a top official of BCCI, supervising all its activities in North America from its London headquarters.

Soon there was another strange transaction — the sale of National Bank of Georgia by Pharaon. The buyer? First American Bankshares.

First American signed an option to buy NBG in November 1986, but the takeover could not go through until the Georgia legislature modified the state's banking legislation. In recent years, federal laws banning interstate banking have been eased considerably, but the states have a great deal of say on takeovers by out-of-state banks. Georgia permitted such acquisitions, but only if the buyer was from the southeastern United States. Washington, D.C. — the home of First American — was not considered part of that region.

In an effort to change the Georgia law, Pharaon mounted an aggressive lobbying campaign. Inducements of various kinds were allegedly provided to certain legislators, including campaign contributions, travel expenses, and lavish entertainment. At a cost of several thousand dollars, NBG took a group of state lawmakers on a junket to Florida on January 16–19, 1987. On February 12, the legislation permitting the takeover passed the Georgia senate by a unanimous vote, 52–0. On March 4, the House passed the bill, 155–4. The takeover was consummated later that year. Charles Jones, Pharaon's politically connected lawyer, was paid "in the vicinity of $1 million" for successfully lobbying the legislature, NBG's Roy Carlson later said.

Although Altman has described the purchase of NBG as an "arm's-length transaction," there are grounds for skepticism. At the time, Clifford indicated that Pharaon's ties to the owners of First American may have had something to do with the transaction. "Our investors encouraged us to consider the purchase," he said. "They had known of the ownership being in the hands of Pharaon. They encouraged us to do it." Pharaon himself acknowledged the importance of his ties to the owners of First American. "These are people we have been associated with for a long time," he said, referring to Adham and Fulaij. "We've had many contacts with them, so we know them. They said we should speak to [First American's] management in Washington, which we did, and that's how the deal came through."

To support the notion of an "arm's-length" deal, Altman said that

Pharaon engaged in serious negotiations with another potential buyer, NCNB Corp.,* before accepting First American's offer. One problem with that explanation is that NCNB felt the Georgia bank was worth less than $200 million, yet First American paid considerably more. In fact, embarrassment about the high price might help to explain why First American officials not only failed to announce the purchase price but provided conflicting information about how much it was.

At the time, the *Washington Post* reported that First American had paid about $200 million, citing sources close to the deal. Given the *Post*'s location, it is likely that this information came from First American. The *Atlanta Business Chronicle,* however, gave a much higher estimate: between $220 million and $240 million. When Altman was asked about the price in 1989, he said First American paid $227 million. In a 1988 deposition, however, he had quoted the price as $255 million. (Altman later said the deposition transcript may have contained a typographical error.) A Federal Reserve document issued in July 1992 states that First American paid about $220 million.

Although he disposed of NBG, Pharaon invested millions of dollars in other U.S. financial institutions. In 1986, he had bought American Southern Companies, an insurance group in Atlanta. Three years later, he set up DLF Finance Inc., a company in New York that traded in the bank debt of developing nations. He also bought a big chunk of one of the largest savings and loan associations in the country.

The 1980s was a boom time for the savings and loan business, thanks to the deregulation of the industry by federal and state authorities. S&Ls that had once been restricted to providing home mortgages and personal loans were now permitted most kinds of lending. Since deposits were insured by the federal government, even the most badly run S&Ls had no trouble collecting money — as long as they paid higher-than-average interest rates. And they were not restricted to raising funds locally; they collected money nationwide by using Wall Street firms as deposit brokers. In order to earn the high returns necessary to pay the high interest to depositors, S&L managers financed risky real estate projects and bought billions of dollars in junk bonds. Deregulation also lowered barriers to entrepreneurs who wanted to enter the

---

*NCNB Corp. was the parent company of North Carolina National Bank and several other banks. In 1991, it merged with a bank holding company called C&S/Sovran to form NationsBank.

industry. In some states, regulators made it so easy to buy or start an S&L that people with no banking experience entered the business. Some of them even had criminal records. It was, in short, a recipe for disaster. Since the late 1980s, taxpayers have been forced to spend hundreds of billions of dollars to rescue depositors in failed savings and loan associations.

One of the most notorious S&Ls was CenTrust Savings Bank of Miami. It had been a relatively obscure institution called Dade Savings and Loan until 1983, when a wheeler-dealer named David L. Paul took it over. He changed the name, installed himself as chairman, and embarked on a campaign to transform it into the largest S&L in the country. CenTrust did grow quickly — it eventually became the biggest S&L in the Southeast — but its portfolio was filled with junk bonds purchased from Drexel Burnham Lambert. Paul also drained money out of CenTrust by awarding himself a huge salary and lavish perks and using depositors' money to build an art collection — including a Rubens that he kept at home.

Federal and state regulators were suspicious of Paul's activities but were slow to crack down. One possible explanation is that Paul had impressive connections, thanks to his extraordinary generosity to political candidates. A political action committee set up by CenTrust gave $140,000 to federal and state politicians between 1987 and 1989. The company gave $131,000 more to other political action committees. One beneficiary — the Democratic Senate Campaign Committee — received $30,000. Paul also served as co-chairman of the committee with Senator John F. Kerry of Massachusetts. Kerry was one of several politicians who flew on CenTrust's corporate jet.

In Florida, one big recipient of Paul's campaign money was Comptroller Gerald Lewis, the state's chief bank regulator. In a 1991 profile of Paul, Peter Becker provided details of the banker's support for Lewis:

> Florida is the only state with a popularly elected bank comptroller, and David Paul was an active political supporter of Lewis. In June 1986 Paul hosted a fund-raising barbeque at his home. . . . The next day six of Paul's companies gave a total of $17,000 to Lewis's reelection campaign. Three weeks later Paul took Lewis on a fund-raising tour of New York, and in the next five weeks Lewis reported campaign contributions of $28,500 from New York financial companies or individuals.*

---

*Lewis later distanced himself from Paul and cracked down on CenTrust.

CenTrust's rise to prominence occurred as BCCI was emerging as an important bank in Florida. At the same time, David Paul became a close friend and business associate of Ghaith Pharaon's. The Saudi tycoon traveled with Paul on CenTrust's plane and even vacationed with him. From 1984 to 1988, according to his records, Paul and Pharaon were in frequent — sometimes daily — contact. They also became involved in important business deals. In 1987, Paul, Pharaon, and the Swiss investor Carlo Gritti spent millions in a secret attempt to buy control of Hercules Inc., an arms manufacturer in Wilmington, Delaware.*

That same year, Pharaon bought about one fourth of CenTrust's stock, becoming the largest shareholder. His investment came at a time when CenTrust was in very poor financial shape, and regulators were pressuring Paul to strengthen the balance sheet by issuing new stock or bonds. He responded by issuing $150 million in CenTrust junk bonds through Drexel Burnham Lambert's Michael Milken, which helped to allay the regulators' concerns. What the regulators did not know was that the offering only *appeared* to be successful, thanks to a sham transaction Pharaon arranged with his friends at Abedi's bank. BCCI bought $25 million in CenTrust bonds in May 1988, but they were only *parked* at BCCI. Two months later, BCCI sold the bonds to a CenTrust subsidiary. Because of this ruse, the regulators refrained from shutting down CenTrust.

CenTrust, Independence Bank, and National Bank of Georgia can all be regarded as BCCI satellites, although CenTrust was not as closely linked to BCCI as the others. In the case of NBG, even Clifford and Altman have acknowledged that its ties with BCCI were extraordinarily close. Altman has said that after First American acquired the Georgia bank, he found that senior managers had ties to BCCI, that the bank's logo resembled BCCI's, and that BCCI brochures were sometimes distributed to NBG customers. He and Clifford insisted, however, that First American was in a totally different category. Although it was owned by BCCI clients, they said, it was a wholly autonomous institution.

In fact, First American was the biggest BCCI satellite of all.

·   ·   ·

---

*The trio fell out after the October 1987 stock market crash left them carrying huge losses on their Hercules stock. In 1992, the investment in Hercules was the subject of litigation between Pharaon and Gritti in state court in Manhattan.

Clifford had grand ambitions for First American. He told the board of directors in 1984 that he wanted it to be one of the twenty biggest banks in the country within ten years, and he moved quickly toward that goal. The company shifted the headquarters of its New York subsidiary from Albany to New York City and renamed it First American Bank of New York (FABNY). An impressive office was opened on Park Avenue. In 1984, FABNY purchased 33 branches of the Bankers Trust Company in the Albany area, along with about $450 million in assets. And a few years later, as noted above, National Bank of Georgia was acquired from Pharaon; it was then renamed First American Bank of Georgia.

But most of the growth came in the Washington area, fueled by a booming real estate market. By the end of 1989, First American Bankshares had $11.5 billion in assets, making it the largest bank holding company with headquarters in the Washington area — about 50 percent bigger than its closest rival, Riggs National Corporation. Nationally, it was the fifty-second-largest banking company. As the company grew, memories of the bitter takeover battle faded, as did the once-provocative questions about the backgrounds and motives of the Arab shareholders and their ties to BCCI. Most customers probably assumed it was an American-owned company, thanks in part to the First American name.

In fact, the management used every opportunity to exploit the patriotic connotations of the name in its advertising and promotion. First American's logo, for example, incorporates the Stars and Stripes. In one commercial, an announcer touted First American's "All-American CD" and "All-American Money Market Account" while a fife-and-drum corps played in the background. The most powerful series of television commercials began with shots of photographs from family albums. As one portrait dissolved into the next, a narrator told his family's version of the American immigrant saga. The final image was a group shot of the immigrant's descendants. The speaker then identified his family. In some cases, they were typical American families. In others, they were the families of well-known Washingtonians, such as the columnist Robert Novak and the restaurateur Duke Zeibert. The commercials — a skillful blend of patriotism, nostalgia, and family values — ended with a voiceover: "Nearly every family can trace its heritage to one bold first American. We salute the spirit of the first Americans who made this country their own. We're First American — the bank for all Americans."

Officials of First American did more than simply wrap the company in Old Glory; they went to extraordinary lengths to conceal the identities of the company's shareholders. A handful of names had come out during the takeover battle — those of Adham and a few others — but most of the investors had never been identified publicly, and First American wanted to keep it that way. The efforts at concealment began even before the takeover was approved. At the Fed hearing in April 1981, for example, Altman noted, "We had requested that the names of the minority investors be maintained confidential." In November 1982, the Fed received a letter from Baldwin Tuttle, a lawyer for First American, asking it to keep the names of the investors secret. Tuttle wrote a similar letter to the Fed in July 1983.

Further evidence of First American's sensitivity about its ownership was displayed when it was defending itself from a lawsuit in 1988. The Middle Eastern investors, in taking over the company in 1982, did not acquire 100 percent ownership of all its banking subsidiaries. In 1987, First American Bankshares decided to buy out the minority shareholders in First American of Maryland and First American of Virginia at $42 a share. Several of the Maryland bank's investors complained that the price was too low and took advantage of a state appraisal system to win a higher price. In Virginia, which had no such system, the dissenting shareholders went to court. In September 1988, a federal jury in Alexandria awarded the investors $60 a share. (The verdict was sustained on appeal, then reversed by the Supreme Court.)

During the discovery phase of the case, the lawyers for the plaintiffs met stiff resistance when they tried to determine who owned the company. When the question was put to Altman during a deposition, he steadfastly refused to provide any names. The attorneys persisted, and Altman's lawyer snapped that the identity of the owners was "none of your business." When specific names were put to Altman, however, he did confirm their status as shareholders. In a pretrial motion, First American went so far as to ask the judge to forbid the plaintiffs' lawyers from mentioning in court the names or nationalities of the shareholders — or even that the company was foreign-owned. The defense lawyers argued that it was irrelevant to the case, largely because Clifford and Altman ran the company; the owners played no role, they said, in setting the price to be paid to minority shareholders. They also claimed that the disclosure that First American was owned by Arabs could stir up prejudice in some of the jurors.

First American's touchiness was understandable. The questions that had been raised during the takeover battle may have been largely forgotten, but they had never been satisfactorily answered. Why were these Arab VIPs so eager to own a banking company in Washington, D.C.? And were they really the owners — or merely front men for BCCI?

The Federal Reserve had approved the takeover of First American based on assurances by Clark Clifford and the Arab investors that First American would be autonomous of BCCI. After the takeover, an all-American board of directors led by Clifford was installed to act as a buffer between the BCCI clients and First American. Clifford, in turn, recruited several friends to serve on the board with him, notably his law partner and protégé Robert Altman.

There was one obvious flaw in this setup. At the same time that Clifford was supposed to guard First American from BCCI's influence, his law firm was receiving millions of dollars in fees from BCCI. If he did anything to displease Abedi, the fees could be cut off.

After the takeover went through, there were other indications of a close relationship between First American and BCCI. First American's Arab shareholders were more than simply passive; they were all but invisible. A former top official of First American said in 1990 that he knew of only two investors who ever visited the company's headquarters in Washington, Kamal Adham and the Saudi banker Khalid Bin Mahfouz. He met with Adham for no more than five minutes and was asked nothing about First American's performance. Adham, in this man's opinion, did not act like a major shareholder, let alone the biggest single investor. When Bin Mahfouz visited, it was to take a tour of First American's computer facilities. The former official referred to the two investors as "the so-called shareholders."

Further evidence of the investors' passivity emerged in the course of the lawsuit filed by former minority shareholders of the Virginia bank. The lawyers for First American said that its Middle Eastern stockholders had been told absolutely nothing about the buyout of the minority shareholders — a $30 million transaction. When Altman was deposed, he was questioned at length about how he communicated with the company's owners. He made it sound very haphazard. "Sometimes some of the investors call me or at times I will contact one of them," he said. "At times I will contact all of them." When asked if there is "some system of regular reporting to which you adhere," Altman said, "No." One surprising assertion by Altman was that First American's board of directors never had to ask advance approval from the share-holders for anything it did.

BCCI, by contrast, was very much in evidence. Clifford and Altman were in constant communication with Abedi and other top officials. Clifford, for example, made an average of two trips a year to London to meet with BCCI officials. Altman went even more often, sometimes monthly. The ostensible reason was that BCCI acted as a "communications link" between Clifford and the shareholders as well as being their investment adviser.

First American and BCCI also did a great deal of business with each other. Forty-seven BCCI branches, subsidiaries, and affiliates maintained accounts at First American Bank of New York. Since FABNY was a relatively small and obscure institution, it was an unusual choice — unless, of course, BCCI viewed it as an affiliate.

The first president of FABNY, a former Bank of America executive named Bruno Richter, was hired in 1983 after three meetings with Abedi. It was only after the last meeting that he was introduced to Clifford and Altman, who then offered him the job. Not long after Richter took over, he hired two BCCI executives as senior officials of FABNY at Abedi's recommendation. Aijaz Afridi left his job as a general manager of BCCI's Swiss subsidiary to become an executive vice president. (He later returned to the BCCI group to run its Spanish subsidiary.) Khusro Elley, who ran BCCI's representative office in New York, became FABNY's executive vice president and chief financial officer, making him one of the bank's top three officials.

While employed by First American, neither Elley nor Afridi completely severed his ties to BCCI. Both men used BCCI mortgages to finance houses in suburban Scarsdale, New York. Afridi received his mortgage in December 1983, just months before he joined First American. The terms were extremely generous. There was no down payment, and the interest rate was 5 percent on the first $100,000, 7 percent on the next $50,000, and one percentage point over Citibank's base lending rate on the remainder. When asked about the mortgages in 1989, Altman said he did not know whether BCCI required employees to repay concessionary loans when they left the bank. He suggested that Afridi may have been permitted to keep the mortgage because BCCI wanted to avoid expensive paperwork.

BCCI did have a policy on concessionary loans: departing employees were required to refinance such loans. For example, one employee who resigned in 1989 received a letter from the personnel department stating that he must repay all concessionary loans he received from the bank. The letter contains this statement of the bank's policy: "As you are aware, it is a condition of a staff concessionary loan, that these facilities be repaid immediately on leaving the employ of the Bank." Even if Altman's theory was right, it did not explain the concessionary mortgage to Khusro Elley. He received the cheap loan in July 1984, *when he was a First American employee.*

During Afridi's and Elley's tenure at First American, many former BCCI colleagues continued to regard the men as part of the BCCI family. As a BCCI official put it, Afridi and Elley did not really quit BCCI to work for an unrelated bank; they were *transferred* to First American by Abedi. This sense of kinship was reinforced at BCCI's annual management conferences. As noted earlier, hundreds of employees from around the world were flown in to attend these events. The guests also included members of BCCI's extended family: representatives of Attock Oil, Capcom Financial Services, Cromwell Hospital, National Bank of Georgia — and First American Bankshares.

When BCCI's Arab clients invested in National Bank of Georgia and First American, many observers suspected that they had political motives. As the *Washington Post* said in an editorial: "Mr. Lance's wealthy new friends from the Middle East may well be under the impression that they are buying, along with the stock, a degree of access to political power in this country."

Abedi and his clients insisted that there was no hidden political agenda; the Arab investors were merely recycling some of their petrodollars to the U.S. economy. That view was echoed in congressional testimony by such respected figures as Henry Wallich, a member of the Federal Reserve Board, and Joseph Sisco, a veteran State Department official.

Anyone who believed that it was nothing more than a business transaction did not know Abedi, for he was obsessed with power. He was a collector of people, and he used his connections to build BCCI's global network. The network — which now included the largest banking company in Washington, D.C. — became an instrument for acquiring still more power.

5

FRIENDS IN
HIGH PLACES

THROUGHOUT his career, Agha Hasan Abedi cultivated prominent
people, using the skills he had learned growing up in a family of
courtiers in India. His techniques varied, depending on the object of
his desire. Some people could be won over through contributions to a
pet charity. For others, a briefcase full of banknotes was more effective. In between, there was a range of inducements: flattery, travel
expenses, favorable press coverage, legal fees, jobs, consultancies, business deals, political favors, loans on highly favorable terms, or
"loans" that were not intended to be repaid.

Abedi made his first important contacts in India and Pakistan, then
extended his reach into the Arab world. Eventually he could boast of
connections with government leaders and international statesmen the
world over. In Third World countries, his contacts included high-level
government officials in the Middle East, black Africa, and Latin America. In Europe, current and former heads of government were close to
BCCI. In the United States, BCCI insiders had ties to prominent figures
in both the Democratic and Republican parties, including at least three
presidents: Richard Nixon, Jimmy Carter, and George Bush.

Friends of Abedi's helped him expand the BCCI network. Like the
medieval alchemists — who claimed to convert base metals into
gold — Abedi transformed the financial and political power of his
backers and allies into an international financial empire. The network,
in turn, was used to acquire still more political influence, which could
protect the interests of the bank and advance the political agendas of
Abedi's backers.

. . .

Abedi honed his approach in Pakistan during his days at United Bank, when he courted Arab VIPs. One way he earned goodwill was by procuring sexual companions for them. When Sheikh Zayed visited Pakistan, Abedi would provide young Pakistani girls to members of the ruler's entourage. A Pakistani woman named Begum Asghari Rahim was in charge of the prostitution operation, according to former associates of Abedi's.

Rahim recruited these "dancing girls," as they are called in Pakistan, by going to poor villages and making payments to their families. The girls were typically between sixteen and twenty years old, but some were even younger; a few had not reached puberty. Rahim would purchase fine clothes and jewelry for them and teach them how to behave as sexual companions for Arab sheikhs.

Abedi procured boys as well as girls. One prominent member of a UAE ruling family is widely reputed to be a homosexual with a penchant for underage males. "So BCCI brought boys from Peshawar," says a former bank official. "That's the rumor in BCCI." Pathan boys from the area around Peshawar — a city near the Afghan border in Pakistan's Northwest Frontier Province — are considered particularly desirable by pedophiles, explained a former BCCI banker as his wife quoted a homosexual love poem that compares a Pathan boy's bottom to a peach. Abedi's involvement was so widely known that some Pakistanis used to refer to him as "the great pimp."

Despite his success in the Gulf, Abedi suffered setbacks in Pakistan. In 1971, as noted earlier, President Bhutto* nationalized the banking industry and arrested Abedi. Many Pakistanis who were harmed by Bhutto's policies joined the political opposition. Abedi, however, never liked to make enemies of the powerful, so he sought a rapprochement with Bhutto. During the general election of March 1977, Abedi channeled 20 million to 30 million rupees (between $2 million and $3 million) to Bhutto's Pakistan People's Party, according to a government white paper issued after Bhutto's fall from power. The document included an affidavit signed by Afzal Said Khan, a secretary of Bhutto's, alleging that Abedi made frequent trips to Pakistan, "loaded with bagfuls of money"; the cash was for "election purposes." The white paper charged that the money came from "a foreign head of state" — believed to be a reference to Sheikh Zayed. If that is true, the financing enhanced the political clout of both Abedi and Zayed.

---

*After a new constitution was enacted, Bhutto became prime minister in 1973.

Four months after the election, however, Bhutto was overthrown in a military coup led by General Mohammed Zia-ul-Haq, the army's chief of staff. Always adaptable, Abedi began to court General Zia and members of his regime, with impressive results. Abedi's first major accomplishment was to persuade the dictator to permit a group of investors connected with BCCI to take control of Attock Oil, Pakistan's leading oil company. Attock had begun developing petroleum in Pakistan during its colonial days under Britain. Many Pakistanis had felt that Bhutto should nationalize the firm's Pakistani operations because of its strategic importance. Nevertheless, Bhutto had not only left Attock in the private sector, he had permitted a BCCI affiliate called Kuwait International Finance Company (KIFCO) to acquire 16 percent of the company. The deal was done in March 1977, the same month Bhutto won reelection with — alleged — financial support from Abedi. Three months after the July coup, the Zia regime allowed KIFCO to acquire 51 percent of Attock.*

Zia's dictatorship was extremely repressive. Zia jailed Bhutto and put him on trial for what were widely regarded as trumped-up murder charges. In March 1978, he was convicted and sentenced to death, provoking worldwide protests and appeals from foreign leaders to spare his life. Zia ignored these pleas, and Bhutto was hanged in April 1979.

The execution helped to turn Zia into something of an international pariah. Another black mark — particularly in Washington — was Pakistan's nuclear program, which American officials believed was aimed at developing a nuclear bomb. The same month Bhutto was executed, the U.S. government suspended economic and military aid to Pakistan.

The loss of U.S. aid was a serious blow since the country was suffering from a foreign exchange crisis, putting the very survival of Zia's regime into question. At this point, BCCI stepped in with a $100 million loan to the government's Rice Export Corporation. BCCI also secretly lent Pakistan's central bank $25 million to inflate its foreign currency reserves, according to BCCI's Nazir Chinoy. This markedly increased Pakistan's access to credits from the World Bank and the International Monetary Fund, Chinoy said. BCCI's assistance helped

---

*At the time, BCCI owned 49 percent of KIFCO. Other shareholders were BCCI clients who later bought into U.S. banks: Ghaith Pharaon, who bought National Bank of Georgia, and two of the lead investors in First American, Kamal Adham and Faisal Saud al-Fulaij.

Zia contain the financial crisis and cling to power. "Abedi," in the words of one expert on Pakistan, "saved Zia's financial neck."

BCCI's bailout was just one of countless ways in which Abedi ingratiated himself with the Zia regime. Abedi was unstinting in his generosity to Pakistani officials, showering gifts and favors on even middle-level bureaucrats. BCCI sometimes arranged for free medical treatment at London's Cromwell Hospital, one of the BCCI satellites mentioned earlier. A former BCCI officer jokes that Cromwell treated "just about every Pakistani bureaucrat who had a heart attack."

Many Pakistani officials visited London at the bank's expense. Upon arriving, they might be met by a chauffeur who would take them into town in a limousine. Cash for "expenses" might also be provided. The Pakistanis — like government officials and BCCI customers from other countries — could also take advantage of the kind of "lavish entertainment" Abedi provided when he ran United Bank. In those days, the job of finding prostitutes was, in effect, "contracted out." After BCCI was established, it was handled by bank employees. "It's a separate part of the bank," said one source. "It's become institutionalized within the bank." The operation was run out of an office in London known as the Special Handling Unit. If a BCCI customer wanted a woman during a visit, he could simply call a certain telephone number and say something like: "I'm a special client of the bank. I'd like a car and I want some other services, too."

Abedi also provided jobs to an extraordinary number of Pakistani officials. Some became employees or consultants to BCCI; others joined organizations connected with the bank. One example is Saghir Anwar, a top intelligence official who had terrorized the Bhutto family. Bhutto's daughter Benazir wrote in her memoirs of the traumatic morning of September 3, 1977, when soldiers led by Anwar burst into her parents' home, brandished weapons, and terrified the family. After rushing to her parents' bedroom, she saw what she described as

a fat thug of a man lolling on one of Mummy's delicate blue and white brocade Louis XV chairs. "Who is he?" I whisper to my father. "Saghir Anwar, Director of the Federal Investigative Agency," he tells me. "Do you have an arrest warrant?" my father asks the FIA Director. "No," he replies awkwardly, looking down at the carpet. "Then under what charge are you taking me from my home?" my father asks. "I am following orders to take you to military headquarters," Anwar says. "Whose orders?" my father asks. "General Zia's," the man replies.

Anwar later left government service to become head of London's International Travel Corporation, the BCCI satellite.

An even more prominent example is Ghulam Ishaq Khan. During Zia's years in power, he was the dictator's principal adviser. He held several senior posts, including finance minister, chairman of the Senate, and secretary-general of the cabinet. He was, according to the *Far Eastern Economic Review*, "one of the few who knew of the decision to hang Bhutto long before the execution." In the early days of the regime, Ishaq Khan, as finance minister, was involved in approving the 1977 takeover of Attock Oil by BCCI-related investors. In 1981, Abedi set up a nonprofit organization in Pakistan called the BCC Foundation, and installed Ishaq Khan as chairman. After Zia's death in 1988, he became acting president of Pakistan and then president.* He remained chairman of the BCC Foundation.

Many other Pakistanis were scooped up by BCCI after leaving the government, including central bank officials, military men, and ambassadors. Examples include Rashid Ahmed, the governor of the State Bank of Pakistan; Naziruddin Ahmed, the executive director of the State Bank of Pakistan; Ali Pirbhai and Mushtaq Yousufi, the ex-chairmen of the Pakistan Banking Council; Dr. Mahbubul Haq, the finance minister; General Rahimuddin Khan (retired), the chief of the military staff and a relative of Zia's; Akram Shaikh, the chief of the intelligence bureau; I. H. Usmani, the chief of the Pakistan Atomic Energy Commission; Yunus Khan, the ambassador to China; H. U. Beg, the senior civil servant in the finance ministry; Majid Mufti, a secretary in various ministries; and the ambassadors Iftikhar Ali and Sultan Mohammed Khan.

BCCI's relationship with the Zia regime was so close that it is almost surprising that the dictator himself didn't get a job with the bank. However, the general's son, Ijaz Zia-ul-Haq, was hired in 1978 by BCCI's most important Western banking partner, Bank of America. He later became a vice president and regional manager of B of A, based in Bahrain.

Within a few years of Zia's coup, Abedi achieved such a high status that when he traveled to Pakistan he was treated almost as a visiting head of state. A limousine would pick him up at the airport and whisk him to the presidential palace. The banker and the dictator became

---

*Under the current constitution, the president is the head of state. The government is led by the prime minister.

close on a personal level. According to a former BCCI official, "Zia and Abedi were the closest of personal friends — if Zia ever had a friend. He was a very religious and introverted man." Zia consulted so frequently with Abedi that the banker was widely viewed as one of his principal advisers. "The relationship was so close," says the former official, "that everyone amongst the elite knew that if they wanted a change in an economic policy or a different job within the government, the way to do it was to go to Mr. Abedi in London."

In the United States, Jimmy Carter benefited from the largesse of BCCI and Pharaon. When Abedi met Carter's friend Bert Lance, the Georgia banker was close to bankruptcy, as we have seen, and Abedi came to the rescue by hiring him as a consultant and arranging for Pharaon to buy his National Bank of Georgia stock. Not surprisingly, Lance and his new friends claimed that they were involved in routine business dealings with absolutely no political strings attached. At a press conference in December 1977, Pharaon denied that he was trying to get close to the president by helping one of his best friends: "I would not be where I am today if I had to do things like that."

Under Lance, NBG had been the biggest single lender to Carter's family peanut warehouse business, and it remained a big creditor after Pharaon took over in early 1978. Spokesmen for Carter have insisted that all borrowing was done at market rates of interest. In the early 1980s, Abedi used his friendship with Lance as a bridge to Carter.

When Carter left the White House, he refused to cash in on his status as a former president by joining corporate boards, in contrast to his predecessor Gerald Ford. Carter has also been compared favorably to Ronald Reagan, who accepted $2 million in speaking fees from Japanese companies during a brief trip to Tokyo in 1989. Nevertheless, it was possible to approach Carter in a different manner: by donating money to his favorite causes.

Carter and Abedi are believed to have met for the first time after Carter's presidency ended in January 1981. Bert Lance, not surprisingly, made the introduction, but there is some discrepancy about the date.* He said he introduced Abedi to Carter for several reasons. One was that the banker's daughter, Maha, wanted her picture taken with

---

*Lance says the meeting occurred in August 1982. However, Lord Callaghan, the former British prime minister, has said that he met Abedi through Carter the previous year.

Carter and his wife, Rosalynn. In addition, Carter was raising money for his presidential library in Atlanta, and Abedi was a potential donor. Finally, said Lance, Carter was involved in humanitarian programs in Africa and other parts of the developing world. "Mr. Abedi," said Lance, "had banking institutions there and could be helpful."

Lance flew to Albany, Georgia, with Abedi, his wife, Rabia, and their daughter and drove to Carter's home in Plains. "There was an immediate relationship that developed between the two of them," said Lance. "You could sense it as they talked to each other there in the living room of the Carter residence. That was where that relationship began." They all drove to the airport together, and Abedi showed the former president BCCI's corporate jet.

Shortly after that meeting, Abedi contributed $500,000 to the Carter Presidential Center, as the library is called. The donation, said Lance, was in the form of a cashier's check, placed in "a plain white, unmarked envelope addressed to the Carter Center in care of Jimmy Carter in Plains." Later, BCCI gave another $300,000 to the center. Other donations were made by parties related to the bank. The Saudi arms dealer Adnan Khashoggi, a BCCI client, financed a fund-raising event for the library. Clark Clifford is listed in a Carter Center brochure as a donor in the $5,000–$9,999 category. When the center was dedicated in 1986, Abedi was a guest of honor.

BCCI played a much bigger role in Global 2000, a nonprofit organization established at the Carter Center in 1986 to carry out health and agricultural projects in the Third World. Over the years, BCCI became the largest single donor, giving $8 million. In addition, the Abu Dhabi Investment Authority, which is controlled by Sheikh Zayed, has given at least $2.5 million to Global 2000. Abedi also played a role in running the organization. Carter served as chairman of Global 2000; Abedi was one of two "co-chairmen," with a Japanese businessman named Ryoichi Sasakawa.* The organization's British office was at BCCI's London headquarters. Finally, some of Global 2000's projects were done with Abedi's BCC Foundation in Pakistan.

Abedi and his bank were not only financial pillars of Carter's charitable ventures; Carter and the banker became close, traveling around the globe in BCCI's Boeing 707. (The luxurious plane boasted a pan-

---

*Sasakawa has been a prominent supporter of extreme right-wing elements in Japan since the 1930s. (He once described himself as the country's "wealthiest fascist.") After World War II, he was imprisoned by the Americans as a "class A war criminal."

eled library, a master bedroom with a bathroom, and a sumptuous living room with sofas, armchairs, and a large world map with red lights indicating each of BCCI's hundreds of offices.) Abedi and Carter made a five-country African tour in 1986, visited Pakistan that same year, and returned there in 1987, when they were entertained by General Zia.

In the spring of 1987, Abedi took Carter and his wife on a world tour, with stops in London, Hong Kong, Tibet, Peking, and Moscow. It was "almost a social trip," with big dinners scheduled at every stop, said Bill Kovach, a former editor of the *Atlanta Constitution,* who went on part of the trip. He later told a reporter that Carter and Abedi were not only friends but that the former president talked about the Pakistani banker "almost like a religious figure." Abedi and Carter were treated as equals by all the government officials they met, according to Kovach. He said that Abedi was excluded from meetings only when Carter raised issues that the State Department had asked him to discuss with Asian leaders.

Abedi's investment in Jimmy Carter paid big dividends. Inside BCCI, it boosted the banker's image, contributing to the personality cult. The staff magazine, *BCC International,* was filled with photographs of Abedi hobnobbing with Carter and other dignitaries. Outside the bank, it helped to burnish BCCI's image through a process that could be called "innocence by association."

One person in Carter's circle who met Abedi was Andrew Young. (Young says he doesn't recall who made the introduction, although he said it may have been Ghaith Pharaon.) His résumé would have been extraordinarily attractive to a man like Abedi. An ordained minister, Young had been a top aide to Martin Luther King, Jr., and a prominent civil rights leader in his own right. Later, as a congressman from Georgia, he was Carter's strongest black supporter during the 1976 presidential campaign. Young became Carter's ambassador to the United Nations, where he forged close ties to Third World leaders, but he was forced to resign in 1979 for having unauthorized meetings with members of the Palestine Liberation Organization. As a result, he is widely viewed in the Arab world as a victim of America's pro-Israel lobby.

From 1981 to 1989, Young was mayor of Atlanta, and he spent much of his time traveling abroad to attract foreign investment to the city. At the same time, he headed a consulting firm called Andrew Young Associates. One of his clients was BCCI. "Young," according to a former official, "used to come to London a lot to meet with Abedi and talk about Third World politics." In 1986, he accompanied Abedi and Carter on their swing through Africa.

The relationship was highly profitable to Young. He not only received a $50,000 annual retainer from BCCI, he accepted travel expenses from the bank and from parties connected to it. When he visited Saudi Arabia and the UAE in 1983, part of his expenses were paid by the UAE government. In addition, NBG paid part of his hotel bill in Dubai. In the late 1980s, says a former BCCI official, "he came to France as a guest of BCCI."

NBG gave Young's consulting firm a line of credit, which was transferred to BCCI's Panama branch in 1985. Five years later, when Young was making an unsuccessful bid for the governorship of Georgia, the loan balance of $150,000 was forgiven by BCCI.

Several BCCI insiders made high-level connections in the United States. Ghaith Pharaon's mansion near Savannah was the site of glittering parties that attracted such political figures as Andrew Young and Alexander Haig, President Reagan's first secretary of state. In 1983, Pharaon brought Jimmy Carter and his wife to Savannah to attend a fund-raising event for the symphony, historical society, and ballet. When the event failed to raise sufficient funds, Pharaon wrote a check to make up the difference.

NBG officials were also active politically. Tariq Jamil — the former BCCI official involved in running NBG — got to know several Georgia politicians. NBG's chairman, Roy Carlson, became active in Republican politics. Although he identifies himself as a Democrat in his *Who's Who in America* entry, he backed Ronald Reagan's bid for the White House. Carlson was the only Georgia resident on the 1980 National Steering Committee of Democrats for Reagan.

Pharaon's friend and business associate David Paul, the head of CenTrust Savings Bank, was involved with Pharaon in a donation to the Carter Center. Pharaon was approached for a contribution because "he was flashing a lot of money around," explained James Brasher, a fund-raiser for the center. In the spring of 1987, the Saudi was invited to lunch at the center and he brought Paul with him. Pharaon impressed Carter's aides as "bright, articulate," and "extremely well educated," Brasher said. Pharaon described how his father had once saved the life of the king of Saudi Arabia. After the lunch, CenTrust contributed $100,000 to the Carter Center with instructions to "credit it to Ghaith Pharaon." Pharaon is believed to have reimbursed Cen-Trust for the donation.

Abedi's relationship with Carter helped him make connections outside the United States. Carter introduced Abedi to Lord (James) Callaghan, Britain's prime minister from 1976 to 1979. Abedi channeled money into one of his pet causes, the Cambridge University Commonwealth Trust, of which Callaghan was a trustee. In addition, BCCI hired him as an adviser and paid some of his foreign travel expenses. Masihur Rahman, BCCI's chief financial officer, has recalled that Callaghan "would take us to lunch to meet members of Parliament."

BCCI did not limit itself to Callaghan's Labour party. Two Conservative members of Parliament became paid advisers to the bank, Sir Julian Ridsdale and Julian Amery. (Ridsdale's home in London happens to be next door to a house owned by Zayed.) A former Tory MP, Sir Frederic Bennett, served as an honorary director of BCCI's Hong Kong subsidiary until 1986 for $10,000 a year.

BCCI even managed to get close to the Conservative prime minister, Margaret Thatcher (now Lady Thatcher), through one of its clients, Nazmu Virani. One of the thousands of ethnic Asians who had settled in Britain after they were expelled from Uganda by Idi Amin, Virani eventually created a major property and leisure group called Control Securities. He was reputedly one of the richest people in Britain and was honored by his community in 1990 as Asian of the Year.

Virani's Horatio Alger story appealed to Thatcher, for it seemed proof of what was possible in the capitalistic system. "Mrs. Thatcher," said a former BCCI official, "had a weak spot for this Virani." The admiration was reciprocated, and Virani became a big supporter of the Conservative party, meeting frequently with Thatcher and the party secretary, Norman Tebbitt. Through Virani, several BCCI people met Thatcher. She may not have realized that Virani was not quite the self-made man he appeared to be. His company's growth was based in large part on millions of pounds of BCCI loans. This, of course, raises an obvious question: To what extent were BCCI's loans to Virani aimed at buying political access and influence?

Another man in Thatcher's circle who benefited from BCCI's generosity was Brian Griffiths (now Lord Griffiths), a professor at London's City University and a senior adviser to the prime minister. After Griffiths set up a think tank in 1985, BCCI provided some of the funding.

.   .   .

The world of think tanks and foundations was intriguing to Abedi. Like many American tycoons, he understood that they can be effective tools for acquiring influence. The Rockefellers, for example, have financed a series of public policy groups, including the Council on Foreign Relations and the Trilateral Commission. Similarly, Abedi set up his own organization, the Third World Foundation, which became a sophisticated instrument for winning friends and influencing people.

The brains behind it was a veteran Pakistani bureaucrat named Altaf Gauhar, who had a highly unorthodox background for the head of a supposedly philanthropic entity. Gauhar served as information secretary for President Mohammad Ayub Khan, Pakistan's dictator from 1958 to 1969. The bible of the regime, Ayub Khan's *Friends, Not Masters: A Political Autobiography*, is believed to have been ghost-written by Gauhar. He was also involved in nationalizing various newspapers as part of the regime's efforts to stamp out freedom of the press, earning him the nickname Goebbels.

When Zulfikar Ali Bhutto came to power in the early 1970s, Gauhar was jailed. A few years later, he moved to England and was introduced to Abedi, and the two men became close. In March 1978 they launched the Third World Foundation; the three trustees were Abedi, Gauhar, and Abedi's deputy, Swaleh Naqvi. When the foundation applied for registration as a charity in Britain, its stated goal was "to relieve poverty and sickness and advance education among inhabitants of the Third World Countries." Despite these lofty words, it appears that the main beneficiaries were Abedi, BCCI, and members of the Gauhar family. Gauhar and two of his children wound up on the payroll of the foundation or related entities.

BCCI's support made it easy for Abedi to rub shoulders with people of international stature. At one foundation event — a gala dinner party in London — the guests included Lord Callaghan, Jamaica's Prime Minister Michael Manley, and Sir S. S. ("Sonny") Ramphal, the secretary-general of the Commonwealth. Callaghan became a trustee of the foundation.

Gauhar realized that the easiest way to attract attention to the foundation was through a prize — a kind of BCCI version of the Nobel Prize. For maximum impact, the amount would be high; Abedi agreed on $100,000, making it one of the largest prizes in the world at that time. In 1979, BCCI endowed the prize with $10 million. Ramphal was a member of the selection committee.

Prizewinners included Willy Brandt, the former West German chancellor, former president Julius Nyerere of Tanzania, the International

Rice Research Institute of Manila, and Nelson and Winnie Mandela. Another recipient was Bob Geldof, the Irish rock musician who raised money for the relief of world hunger. Kurt Waldheim, the secretary-general of the United Nations from 1972 to 1981, was the guest of honor at the 1981 presentation. A photograph shows him chatting with Abedi.

Waldheim's successor, Javier Pérez de Cuéllar, reportedly used BCCI's jet over a period of five years. A U.N. spokesman denied the report but acknowledged that Pérez de Cuéllar had taken two trips on planes owned by Pharaon. There were other BCCI ties to the United Nations. When the Third World Prize was presented to Brandt, the foundation was allowed to use the U.N.'s Trusteeship Council Chamber for the ceremony.

Through a curious coincidence, the prize was often presented by leaders of countries where BCCI did significant business — or was seeking permission to expand. Colombia's President Belasario Betancur was the presenter in 1984 at a BCCI-sponsored conference in Colombia. In connection with the conference, Gauhar produced an impressive-looking book on regional cooperation in Latin America. The year before, Betancur's government had permitted BCCI to acquire a Colombian bank.

Abedi waged a long campaign for permission to open a branch in India, the country of his birth. But the Indian authorities resisted, partly because they were suspicious of a bank run by men from Pakistan — a country that has long been at odds with India. Abedi even made a personal appeal to Prime Minister Indira Gandhi, according to a source, who says that "she flatly refused him. She made a number of remarks to him about what they [BCCI] were doing in Pakistan. She had some kind of a dossier on him. And she said — basically — given what you are doing in Pakistan, we don't think [a BCCI branch] would be in India's national interest." In 1983, however, the government relented, permitting BCCI to open a branch in Bombay. The year before, the Third World Prize had been presented by Indira Gandhi; a close relative of hers was on the committee that chose Tanzania's Nyerere as the winner.

As Abedi built his political power base and his network, he did not ignore the news media. He understood that journalists were a potential threat to BCCI and he went to great lengths to influence their coverage of the bank.

One way BCCI fended off criticism was by blaming it on prejudice.

Back in 1981, for example, during an interview for an article on foreign banks in London, a BCCI spokesman was asked why his bank had a dubious image. He adopted a somewhat conspiratorial tone and said he would explain, but only if he would not be quoted by name. He then confided that BCCI's poor image was based on jealousy of BCCI's success and racism in the City of London. This tactic could be quite effective with Third World audiences. In Muslim countries, in particular, BCCI officials blamed the bank's outsider status on anti-Muslim prejudice in the West — particularly on the part of "the Zionist lobby." For the most part, though, the Third World media were not a problem, since freedom of expression is severely limited in most developing countries.

In the industrial countries, a favorite BCCI technique was to lie. That was what some BCCI officials did in early 1978, when it was revealed that clients of the bank, assisted by Bert Lance, had bought stock in First American.

In Britain, the bank took advantage of libel laws that are extraordinarily favorable to plaintiffs. One target was the *New Statesman,* a left-leaning British weekly, which published a series on BCCI in late 1981. It was written by Tariq Ali, a prominent left-wing British intellectual of Pakistani origin. This was the first major exposé of BCCI, and it was filled with serious allegations. Ali wrote that a BCCI manager who had stolen depositors' funds to maintain his gambling habit was given £300,000 in severance pay. He also questioned the bank's accounting practices, raising doubts about the reliability of its financial statements. More disturbing were charges that Abedi and his bank were heavily involved in corruption and influence peddling, using their power to "buy governments." BCCI's "dramatic rise may be due as much to the political wheeler-dealing of its founder, Agha Hasan Abedi, as to any intrinsic commercial skills," Ali contended. One shocking story concerned a former BCCI banker named Masood Asghar, who worked in the Cayman Islands before resigning in 1978. After threatening to sue the bank and write a book disclosing its misconduct, Ali wrote, Asghar was beaten and raped by a group of Pakistani soldiers.

BCCI sued the *New Statesman* for libel. After some legal fencing, the publication — already tottering financially — settled out of court, paying the bank "substantial damages" and printing a retraction and a groveling apology. The settlement hastened the end of the *New Statesman* as an independent publication; it was forced to merge with *New*

Society a few years later. BCCI, with its apology and retraction in hand, continued to practice business as usual.

The Asghar incident is not the only report linking BCCI to violence against a critic. A journalist who was attacked after probing into BCCI was the late Anthony Mascarenhas of the *Sunday Times* of London. According to a friend of his, Mascarenhas began looking into BCCI in the early 1980s and "said that the bank was totally bent [and that] they were laundering money." The journalist said he had been warned to stay away from the subject, but he persisted anyway. One night in London, he was attacked by thugs and injured so severely that he had to be hospitalized. "He suffered a broken jaw and a burst eardrum," said his friend. "He was knifed several times." Mascarenhas was certain that BCCI was behind the attack. While he was in the hospital, his file on BCCI disappeared from the newspaper's office.

There were, of course, limits to Abedi's ability to intimidate and influence the press, so the banker decided to play a more direct role in the media business. The man behind this venture was Gauhar, the former Pakistani bureaucrat who ran the Third World Foundation.

In the late 1970s, Gauhar approached the *Guardian,* one of Britain's leading newspapers, offering to prepare a special supplement on the Third World, to run in the paper on a regular basis. The *Guardian* agreed, and Gauhar became the co-editor of a monthly supplement called the *Guardian Third World Review,* which began appearing in 1978. On at least one occasion, Gauhar used this forum on behalf of the Zia regime. When the death sentence imposed on Bhutto provoked an international uproar, Gauhar published an article attacking him in the *Guardian* in early 1979. Not long after that, Bhutto was hanged.

Gauhar soon tapped into BCCI to start a series of publications. "Gauhar had the ideas and Abedi wrote the checks," says a former associate of Gauhar's. The *Third World Quarterly* was the house organ of the Third World Foundation. Gauhar modeled it after *Foreign Affairs,* the official organ of the Council on Foreign Relations, the prestigious public policy group in New York. In 1980, Gauhar launched *South,* a monthly news magazine on developing countries. *South* was conceived as a Third World version of the news magazines published in industrial countries. "Mr. Abedi always felt that the Third World should have its own magazine to compete with the *Economist, Newsweek,* and *Time,*" says a former BCCI official.

South acquired a loyal following but it never succeeded commercially. In fact, a former associate of Gauhar's estimates that the venture cost BCCI more than $50 million between 1978 and 1990, when it collapsed. It was, however, quite profitable for the Gauhar family. Impressive titles and salaries were awarded to Altaf Gauhar, his son Humayun, and his daughter Raana. BCCI used the publications to make connections.

South was not a pure propaganda vehicle for BCCI; the relationship was more complex. The staff included some respected journalists, and the magazine sometimes published stories that seem contrary to BCCI's interests. But the hidden hand of BCCI was always in the background. Government leaders who could help the bank were frequently the subjects of flattering profiles. The magazine seldom published negative stories about countries where BCCI had important interests.

South's first editor was the late Denzil Peiris, a highly regarded journalist recruited from the *Far Eastern Economic Review.* "He became increasingly frustrated," says a former colleague from the *Review,* Lawrence Lifschultz. "There was one incident in particular. The prepublication issue [distributed in mid-1980] contained an article attacking military dictators." It was by a Pakistani exile named Khalid Hasan who was then working for *South.* Although the article did not mention the general by name, Lifschultz notes that "it appeared just as Zia had embarked on public hangings of alleged criminals who had been convicted by summary martial law tribunals" and that it was illustrated with a cartoon depicting men hanging from the bemedaled chest of a military officer. "Denzil told me that Abedi saw it and had the entire issue of *South* destroyed," he continues. "Denzil was extremely embarrassed." After that incident, Hasan was forced out of the magazine.

Over the years, *South*'s coverage of the Zia regime was generally quite positive. Such subjects as human rights abuses, corruption, and government officials' ties to heroin traffickers were seldom mentioned. The magazine did publish an editorial criticizing Zia in February 1987 (nearly a decade after he seized power), but that was an exception. More typical is a "South Survey" on Pakistan in February 1988. The tone is captured by the lead sentence: "Today, 10 years after General Mohammad Zia ul Haq came to power, life in Pakistan has undeniably improved." The survey contained advertisements from several state-owned companies, including Pakistan International Airlines, United Bank, and Habib Bank. This attitude changed abruptly in the October 1988 issue when the publisher, Humayun Gauhar, wrote that Zia "consistently thwarted the democratic process with lies and deception to perpetuate his rule." By that time, of course, Zia was dead.

Sometimes BCCI's influence was easy to detect. An interview with Clark Clifford in November 1983 contained no reference to his role as a lawyer for the bank. In 1988, after BCCI was charged with criminal offenses in the United States, *South* did not find the story newsworthy — although it was covered by just about every major news organization in the world.

Several sources say that Gauhar helped BCCI expand its network by putting *South* at the service of the bank. A Pakistani journalist explained how the process worked. "Before Abedi moves anywhere he sends in Gauhar. Before they move into any country Gauhar interviews the president. The president becomes a cover story. This has repeatedly happened. Then following that the bank moves in through the contacts that Gauhar has established." One Third World official who was courted with Gauhar's help was Robert Mugabe, the first leader of independent Zimbabwe.

When Zimbabwe became independent in April 1980, it was one of the most economically advanced countries in black Africa, making it enormously attractive to foreign banks. "Everybody was trying to get in," recalled an official at a major U.S. bank. As things turned out, Mugabe permitted only one new bank to enter Zimbabwe. In November of that year, it was announced that the government had signed an agreement with BCCI to establish a joint venture bank, owned in part by the government: Bank of Credit and Commerce (Zimbabwe).

How is it possible that BCCI was the only foreign bank permitted in this market? Part of the answer, according to BCCI sources, is that Abedi had been cultivating Mugabe long before independence. What is more, Abedi hedged his bets by making connections with Mugabe's principal rivals. That way, BCCI would have a leg up on competing banks no matter who wound up as leader of the country. Some of the politicians may have received cash from the bank. Abdur Sakhia, a former BCCI executive, remembered driving one of his colleagues to a hotel in London where several Zimbabwean politicians were staying during independence negotiations. Sakhia's colleague "went with a briefcase and he came back without a briefcase, and I asked him, 'What happened to your briefcase?' And he smiled at me and he said, 'This was for those people.' I said, 'What did you carry — gold bars?' He said, 'No, some cash.' " After Mugabe was elected, said another source, a BCCI officer named Iqbal Rizvi flew to Zimbabwe and visited the new leader, who told him, "'Of course, the bank is yours.'"

After the election, BCCI continued to nurture the relationship. Mugabe was the subject of favorable articles in *South* that year. The prepublication issue distributed in mid-1980 had Mugabe's picture on the cover and a flattering article inside. The magazine's first issue, published in October, contained an interview with Mugabe. Around the same time, *South* discussed the possibility of publishing a newspaper for Mugabe's political party. *South* later ran a flattering profile of Zimbabwe's finance minister, Bernard Chidzero, a respected figure who has been a candidate for U.N. secretary-general. He became a member of the advisory board of the *Third World Quarterly*.

Abedi also drew on General Zia's help, arranging for the dictator to provide military assistance to the Mugabe regime, according to a former BCCI official. During a visit to Zimbabwe after the election, Iqbal Rizvi asked Mugabe what the bank could do for him. Mugabe said he wanted to fire the white Rhodesians who were running the country's armed forces and replace them with blacks, but there was a dearth of qualified blacks to take over the air force. BCCI immediately arranged for General Zia to send the number-two man in the Pakistani Air Force, Daud Pota, to help set up a black-led air force.

This instance is just one of many occasions when Zia used his clout to help BCCI. One BCCI banker has pointed out that most major international banks could rely on the assistance of their home governments in their efforts to expand abroad. BCCI, however, was literally a bank without a country. Its three most important bases were in Luxembourg, the Cayman Islands, and Britain, but it was not really a local bank in any of these countries. Pakistan often filled the role of a home country when Abedi needed political backing to enter new markets. Zia was particularly helpful in China.

When China began opening its economy to foreign businesses in the 1970s, international banks clamored for permission to establish offices there. Bankers naturally assumed that China would give preference to the top international banks from countries with which it had the strongest trading links — Japan, Britain, Hong Kong, the United States, and so on. In 1985, the Chinese government announced that certain foreign banks would be permitted to open offices in Shenzhen, a special economic zone bordering Hong Kong, and the first institution so privileged was the Hongkong and Shanghai Banking Corporation, a choice that surprised no one. Bankers were stunned, however, to learn that the second bank allowed in was BCCI.

What its rivals did not know was that Abedi had invested a tremendous amount of effort in cultivating the Chinese, drawing on the resources of BCCI and its most powerful allies. Abedi had taken advantage of Pakistan's special relationship with China by asking Zia to lobby government officials on BCCI's behalf. Abedi was also assisted by Pakistan's former ambassador to Peking, Sultan Mohammad Khan, a paid adviser to BCCI. Altaf Gauhar did his part as well. In 1983, the Third World Foundation invited China's Prime Minister Zhao Ziyang to present the Third World Prize. The ceremony was cosponsored by the Chinese Academy of Social Sciences. Two years later, *South* published an extremely optimistic "survey" on China, headlined "New Directions for Progress." Like the Pakistan survey, it was filled with advertisements from government-owned entities. There was even talk of launching a Chinese-language edition of *South*.

Abedi and Jimmy Carter arrived in China on June 18, 1987, two days before the start of a Third World Advertising Congress in Peking, organized by *South* magazine in partnership with a government agency called the China National Advertising Association for Foreign Economic Relations and Trade. It was a grandiose event, attended by 1,000 foreigners and 530 Chinese delegates and lasting nearly two weeks. Gauhar's son Humayun invited several members of his family, according to one attendee. "All his relatives were there."

"The main thing everyone was shocked about was that they secured the Great Hall of the People," says a source familiar with the event. "It would be like the U.S. Capitol being handed over for an advertising conference." He adds that "there were lavish receptions, lavish fashion shows. Of course, it was just one of the ways BCCI roped in Chinese bureaucrats as part of their entry into China."

It was later estimated that *South* magazine lost $2 million on the conference.

Political friends around the world helped Abedi expand the BCCI network. When, for example, BCCI wanted to buy an ailing bank that had been taken over by the Spanish government, it was represented by a former finance minister, Juan Antonio García Díez, in its negotiations. After the takeover was completed in 1983, García Díez wound up on the board of the Spanish bank.

Andrew Young earned his BCCI consulting fees by introducing Abedi to business and government officials in more than a dozen developing countries, including Nicaragua, Guatemala, Zambia, and Tanzania. Such connections not only enabled BCCI to expand its network but helped it to gather deposits from Third World central banks.

BCCI's highly placed "door openers" were not always successful. One embarrassing setback occurred in Singapore, one of the world's leading international banking centers. Over the years, BCCI applied repeatedly for permission to open a branch in Singapore. Abedi flew there in August 1979 and made a personal pitch for a license, but the man who spearheaded the effort was BCCI's board member J. D. van Oenen, someone the Singaporeans would not have wanted to offend. When he worked in Singapore for Bank of America, van Oenen had helped to launch the country as a banking center. But even he was rebuffed. Abedi then enlisted the help of one of his most prominent political allies, Lord Callaghan. In 1985, he flew to Singapore and lobbied Prime Minister Lee Kuan Yew. Lee turned him down.

Years later, officials of the Monetary Authority of Singapore said that they conducted a thorough investigation of BCCI in the early 1980s and concluded that it was a poorly regulated institution. They were also disturbed by such factors as BCCI's changes of outside auditors and its ties to Bert Lance. Tiny Singapore did something that the United States, Great Britain, France, Japan, and other major countries had failed to do. It said no to BCCI.

BCCI officials all over the world knew they would be judged not only as bankers but on the basis of their ability to get close to powerful people. One man who excelled at this was Abdur Sakhia, the manager of BCCI's Miami branch, then its senior official in the United States, based in New York. Florida was a very important market to BCCI, with four branches and the regional headquarters for Latin America and the Caribbean. When the headquarters opened in 1981, Sakhia threw a lavish party in the penthouse of Miami's Interterra Building. Lots of celebrities attended, including Andrew Young, John E. ("Jeb") Bush, a son of George Bush's, and Bob Graham, the Democratic governor and now senator. As he left the party, Graham said, "These banks are making a statement about South Florida. They are attracted here because of our growth, our ebullience, our confidence in the future."

The presence of Graham and the other political figures is not at all surprising in light of what is now known about Sakhia's penchant for collecting prominent people. Aziz Rehman, a Pakistani immigrant who was a chauffeur in the Miami office from 1982 to February 1984, has testified that Sakhia spent much of his time glad-handing government officials and other VIPs. In his less than perfect English, Rehman said, "When I saw Mr. Sakhia with manager of BCCI, he was more involved to get influence or get involved with this senator or politicians instead of banking."

Outside Miami, one of BCCI's biggest U.S. offices was in Washington, D.C., which was odd because the city is not an international banking center. Only a few foreign banks have opened representative offices in Washington, and they are typically staffed by a handful of people — one or two bankers and a few clerical employees. BCCI's representative office was unique. It occupied a large suite at the corner of 16th and K streets in Northwest Washington, which had been leased with the assistance of Clark Clifford's law firm. The office manager, Cathy Pyle, had spent several years as an employee of the law firm. About two dozen people worked there, including bankers, consultants, secretaries, and chauffeurs. The office even boasted four limousines: three Mercedes-Benzes and a Cadillac. In its five-year existence, the office spent more than $20 million. Many of the employees had nothing to do with conventional banking activities. Some of them attended to the needs of visiting dignitaries, especially those from the UAE and Saudi Arabia. One man who headed the office, Sani Ahmed, had run BCCI's protocol office in Pakistan; in that post, he attended to the personal needs of visiting sheikhs.

Drag Avramovic, a respected Yugoslav economist, put out a monthly newsletter for the Washington office on development issues while working on a scheme of Abedi's to launch a Third World bank in Washington. Abedi managed to attract several political backers for the project, but it never really had a chance. There was already such an entity in Washington, the International Bank for Reconstruction and Development, better known as the World Bank.

BCCI, incidentally, had a startling number of connections to the World Bank. Many of them were indirect, but together they show the extent of BCCI's reach. The British financier I. P. M. ("Peter") Cargill, who had been a senior official of the World Bank, served for a time on BCCI's main board of directors. Moeen Qureshi, a Pakistani bureaucrat who was effectively the second most important official at the

World Bank from 1988 to 1991, had close ties to BCCI. In the late 1980s, Abedi considered putting him in charge of First American Bankshares. In 1991, his brother applied for a banking license with BCCI in Pakistan.* Shahid Husain, the head of the World Bank's Latin American operation, also had close connections with Abedi and his crowd and discussed going to work for BCCI with bank officials. Avramovic, who worked on the Third World bank scheme, had served as an economist at the World Bank before joining BCCI in Washington. He customarily lunched at the World Bank even when he worked for BCCI. A. W. ("Tom") Clausen, the president of the World Bank from 1981 to 1987, had been the president of Bank of America, one of BCCI's first and largest shareholders. Clausen later returned to B of A for a second term as president.

The heavily staffed Washington office suggests that whoever ran it must have been Abedi's chief envoy to the U.S. political establishment. That was not the case. Abedi's number-one representative in Washington was Clark Clifford, superlawyer, *éminence grise* of the Democratic party, and preeminent power broker.

One obvious sign of Clifford's stature is that he played several important roles during Jimmy Carter's presidency. While advising Carter and acting as a presidential envoy, Clifford represented Bert Lance, the target of a criminal investigation by Carter's own Justice Department. Although Clifford might claim that there was nothing improper about it, more cynical observers might say it exemplifies much of what is wrong with Washington: he was part of the city's "permanent government" of fixers and lobbyists who wield power behind the scenes while elected officials come and go.

But Clifford's power was beginning to ebb as the years passed. When Abedi retained the lawyer in 1978, he was seventy-one years old and many of his contemporaries had retired or died. But he was not ready to retire, to sit around and "wait to die," as he put it. The BCCI connection was a major boost for Clifford, enabling him to, in effect, relaunch his career. His law firm went on to earn millions of dollars in legal fees from BCCI, its Arab clients, and First American Bankshares. In 1988, it was estimated that nearly a third of Clifford & Warnke's twenty lawyers did some work for First American. Perhaps more

---

*In an interview in 1991, Qureshi sought to play down his links with BCCI and First American, but did not deny them.

important, Clifford and Robert Altman ran First American, a major force in the financial community.

One source of power is money, and Clifford and Altman earned considerable goodwill by contributing to political campaigns. In addition, Clifford enjoyed a close friendship with Pamela Harriman, who also has contributed heavily to moderate Democrats. Along with her late husband, the party elder statesman Averell Harriman, she had formed a powerful political action committee, Democrats for the Eighties. Clifford has called it "one of the Democratic Party's most successful efforts." Through this association, Clifford also drew close to the Harriman family trust and Brown Brothers, Harriman & Company, an investment banking firm on Wall Street. Clifford and a Brown Brothers partner, William Rich III, are partners with Mrs. Harriman in Middleburg, an investment trust that manages Harriman money. Rich served on the board of First American Bank of New York.

Before the takeover of First American, Altman was little known outside Washington's legal circles. He was Clifford's acolyte, to be sure, but had little stature of his own. After the takeover, his status increased dramatically, since he was now involved in running First American. One sign of Altman's growing prominence was a lengthy — and highly flattering — profile of him in the *Washington Post* in October 1984. *American Lawyer* ran a feature on up-and-coming young lawyers in March 1986; Altman was one of the examples. Clifford was quoted as saying, "Twenty years from now I expect him not only to be the leader of this firm but to be the leader of the bar in Washington."

While Clifford concentrated on cultivating Democrats, Altman developed friendships with members of both parties. His social success owed much to his wife, the actress Lynda Carter. She was known for her starring role in the 1970s television show *Wonder Woman*, based on the comic book character. She later became a spokeswoman for Maybelline cosmetics, whose parent company was a client of Altman's. A company official introduced them, and they were married in January 1984. The ceremony, held in the posh Pacific Palisades section of Los Angeles, was a glittering affair. Clifford was the best man and the guests included Washington power brokers as well as such Hollywood celebrities as Loni Anderson, Ed McMahon, and Valerie Harper. Abedi attended the wedding, and he gave the bride an unforgettable present, a Jaguar XYS sports car. "He said I could have any one I wanted," she later recalled. "Well, I picked a black Jag, but he would have given me a Mercedes, a Ferrari, anything." In Hollywood, Lynda

Carter had never been more than a grade B television actress. In Washington, a city full of drab bureaucrats, she represented style and glamour, and the Altmans became prominent socialites. Their mansion in suburban Potomac, Maryland — purchased for $2.6 million in 1987 — was the site of many opulent parties attended by the cream of official Washington.

Lynda Carter has been nothing less than a magnet for several senior Republicans. Senator Orrin Hatch of Utah displays a picture of himself with the actress in his office and frequently refers to her husband as "my good friend." The Altmans' social circle also includes a large number of people close to George Bush.

Abedi's political friends not only enabled him to expand the BCCI network, they were useful in defending the bank from external threats. When, for example, BCCI was accused of criminal offenses in the United States in the late 1980s, such allies as Jimmy Carter and Lord Callaghan came to the bank's defense.

BCCI's connections were also useful as tools for advancing the foreign policy agendas of Abedi's patrons in the Middle East and other parts of the world. Pakistan's General Zia used Abedi to cement his relationships with rich Arab oil states and the United States — which together channeled billions of dollars in aid to Islamabad. For the Americans, BCCI became an important contact point between the United States government and Third World leaders. With his courtier origins, Abedi relished this role. A family friend told one investigator of the bank that Abedi "wanted to be bigger than the bank, he wanted to control countries and heads of state, obliging them with jobs for relations, balance of payments help, gifts."

Abedi's willingness to act as a foreign policy instrument was apparent early on. In 1977, as we have seen, he allegedly channeled millions of dollars to the political party of Pakistan's Bhutto; the money is believed to have come from Sheikh Zayed. Zayed and the rulers of neighboring Saudi Arabia viewed Pakistan as an important ally and worked hard to develop close ties with Bhutto and his successor, General Zia. Pakistan is near the Persian Gulf, is sympathetic to the conservative Arab countries, and is politically aligned with the West. What is more, Pakistanis are for the most part Sunni Muslims, the dominant branch of Islam in Saudi Arabia.

Thousands of Pakistanis, of course, worked in the thinly populated sheikhdoms of the Gulf as laborers and clerks. They also provided military muscle. General Zia became virtually a mercenary for wealthy Arab countries, providing troops in exchange for oil money. Zia, noted the *Far Eastern Economic Review,* "courted . . . petrodollars by declaring he and his soldiers would defend the Saudi royal family with their lives and sent a large number of soldiers to serve in Saudi Arabia." For several years, two regiments of Pakistani troops have been billeted in Saudi Arabia. Abedi is believed to have played a role in fostering military ties between Pakistan and the Arab states. "We had twenty thousand troops in Saudi Arabia in the late seventies," says a Pakistani journalist. "That deal is supposed to have been brokered by BCCI."

One threat to the conservative Arab monarchies is terrorism. It is not only Israelis and Westerners who are vulnerable to attacks from Palestinian terrorist groups, it is also officials of the conservative oil-producing states of the Gulf. In 1975, for example, the infamous Venezuelan terrorist "Carlos," with other members of the Popular Front for the Liberation of Palestine, kidnapped eleven oil ministers in Vienna, including Saudi Arabia's Ahmed Zaki Yamani and six other Arab ministers.

Since then, there have been few such attacks — partly because terrorist groups have extorted millions of dollars from Arab officials in a Mafia-style protection racket. One of those who agreed to pay up was Sheikh Zayed, and he used BCCI to deliver the funds. In 1984, Zayed paid $17 million to Abu Nidal, the notorious Palestinian terrorist whose nom de guerre means "father of destruction" in Arabic. Some of the money was deposited in BCCI bank accounts in London controlled by the Abu Nidal organization.

Abedi was ideally placed to help Zayed and the rulers of Saudi Arabia acquire political influence in the United States. BCCI and its satellites were, after all, owned by some of the most prominent people in the Arab world, and the bank had connections with powerful people in the United States.

Saudi Arabia's efforts to acquire American support date from World War II, when the United States was beginning to displace Great Britain as the dominant Western power in the region.

Colonel William Eddy, who took over as America's permanent representative in Saudi Arabia in late 1944, had the wind in his sails. The son of a Presbyterian missionary, he had grown up in Lebanon and traveled widely in the Middle East. He had the experience and Arabic language skills to capitalize on America's growing influence in the region.

When Washington upgraded its outpost in Jiddah, Eddy won the job of minister. The young colonel rode roughshod over his sniffy British rivals when it came to securing influence in Saudi Arabia. One advantage he enjoyed was that Washington could afford to provide substantial financial support to the Saudis. In 1943, President Franklin D. Roosevelt had authorized Lend-Lease aid to the Saudis, declaring that "the defense of Saudi Arabia is vital to the defense of the United States." Over the next two years, the Saudis received $99 million through the program.

In January 1945, Eddy took on the most important assignment of his diplomatic career. On orders from Washington, he secretly arranged for President Roosevelt to meet with King Abdel-Aziz Ibn Saud of Saudi Arabia, the founder of the desert kingdom. It was a milestone for both countries, the start of a relationship that would lead to the world's most powerful democracy allying itself closely with an absolute and intolerant theocracy.

After meeting in Yalta with Churchill and Stalin, Roosevelt sailed to Egypt for five hours of talks with the Saudi monarch. The U.S. Navy cruiser *Quincy* moored on the Great Bitter Lake off the Suez Canal. For Abdel-Aziz, this would be his first meeting with an "infidel" leader. The USS *Murphy* ferried the king to his rendezvous; there was some difficulty because he wanted to take a hundred live sheep aboard the vessel — they were essential to maintaining a correct and religious diet. The king insisted on sleeping on deck, ignoring the luxurious cabin that had been prepared for him.

The meeting centered on the issues that are basic to the bilateral relationship to this day: oil, defense, money, and Arab-Jewish disagreements. Roosevelt and Abdel-Aziz affirmed America's dominant role in developing Saudi Arabia's oil reserves and in providing for its defense. The U.S. Navy had already become one of Saudi Arabia's best customers for oil in these closing months of World War II. America had also made a commitment to match Britain's financial aid, and soon surpassed it. As the Americans distributed largesse, the British were desperately trying to persuade Abdel-Aziz to rein in his spending habits. Such a stingy approach from the imperialist British — who were already blamed by Abdel-Aziz and other Arabs for Jewish immigration into Palestine — hastened the decline in Britain's influence.

Not that Roosevelt and Abdel-Aziz found it easy to agree about Palestine and the aspirations of the Jews and Arabs who lived in that

British-administered territory. Roosevelt, eager to please the king, assured him that there would be no change in U.S. policy on the issue of Palestine without first having full consultations with both the Arab and Jewish sides. The president also promised to undertake no action that might be hostile to the Arab people. Abdel-Aziz strongly argued for giving the Jews "and their descendants the choicest lands and homes of the Germans who oppressed them." Roosevelt answered that the Jews had a dread of remaining in Germany as well as a "sentimental desire" to settle in Palestine.

Roosevelt was apparently impressed by the Saudi king. On his return to Washington, he told Congress, "Of the problems of Arabia, I learned more about the whole problem, the Muslim problem, the Jewish problem, by talking with King Ibn Saud* for five minutes than I could have learned in the exchange of two or three dozen letters."

The Arabs placed great faith in the promises the U.S. president made concerning Palestine. But his words were to have little effect. In April — within weeks of his meeting with Abdel-Aziz and days after setting out his pledges in a letter to the king — Roosevelt was dead. His successor, Harry Truman, decided not to hold to the understandings reached at the Great Bitter Lake. He told his advisers: "I'm sorry gentlemen, but I have to answer to hundreds of thousands who are anxious for the success of Zionism; I do not have hundreds of thousands of Arabs among my constituents." Truman recognized the new state of Israel in 1948, a move that had been urged on him by key advisers, who stressed the importance of the Jewish vote in the tough presidential election of that year.

Three decades later, Abdel-Aziz's son Fahd — as crown prince of Saudi Arabia — received quite different treatment from another American president, Jimmy Carter. Visiting Washington in May 1977, Fahd was received with great fanfare as a leader of a major American ally. One sure sign of the kingdom's new status was an administration proposal to sell F-15 Eagles to Saudi Arabia. Manufactured by McDonnell Douglas, they were the world's most advanced fighter planes. One year later, the Senate approved the sale, 54–44.

In 1981, the Saudis achieved another important victory. The Reagan administration proposed selling AWACS (airborne warning and control systems) — advanced radar planes — to the kingdom. This was a technology that had not been supplied to Israel and that threatened to

---

*In the West, the Saudi king was often called Ibn Saud.

alter the balance of power in the Middle East. On October 28, 1981, the Senate approved the AWACS deal, 52–48.

Before the Senate vote, Prince Bandar bin Sultan, a son of Saudi Arabia's defense minister and a future ambassador to Washington, had made much of the historic ties between Washington and Riyadh. As he drummed up support in Washington for the AWACS sale, he carried around a photograph of his grandfather, King Abdel-Aziz, meeting with President Roosevelt in 1945. This, Bandar would say, was evidence of the importance, history, and continuity of the U.S.-Saudi relationship.

Despite his efforts to invoke the past, a great deal had changed since 1945. Washington no longer viewed Saudi Arabia as a quaint backwater but as the world's leading oil exporter and an important ally in the Middle East. The al-Saud family shared Washington's desire to curb the growth of Soviet power and Arab radicalism in the region. Perhaps just as important was that the Saudis had learned how to manipulate the American political process to advance their own interests and to counteract the influence of the pro-Israel lobby.

Before the Senate's vote on the AWACS deal, the Saudis carried out a massive lobbying campaign, coordinated by Prince Bandar. His command post was a set of rooms on the sixth floor of Washington's Fairfax Hotel (now the Ritz-Carlton). As part of the the campaign, U.S. corporations that did business in Saudi Arabia were urged to use their political clout in Congress on behalf of the deal. The evening it was approved by the Senate, the Saudis, their lobbyists, and their political allies celebrated with a banquet at the Tunisian ambassador's house. The dinner was attended by congressmen, State Department officials, Arab ambassadors, and many others who had lobbied hard for the sale.

One man who should have been honored at the banquet was Agha Hasan Abedi. Since the founding of BCCI, he had been a potent weapon in the Arab arsenal, putting his contacts and the BCCI network at the service of his Middle Eastern patrons. For years, the Saudis had spent an enormous amount of effort and money to acquire influence in the United States, using such inducements as gifts, business contracts, and — allegedly — political contributions. The campaign was orchestrated and executed by an army of Saudi officials, lobbyists, and surrogates, an extraordinary number of whom had ties to BCCI and Abedi.

·   ·   ·

Adnan Khashoggi, the Saudi arms dealer, was one important surrogate. His father was a physician and adviser to King Faisal, and his own business career was based on his connections with other members of the royal family, including Prince Sultan, the defense minister. Foreign arms manufacturers paid Khashoggi millions of dollars in commissions on the understanding that he would channel some of the money to friends in the regime.

Khashoggi targeted Richard Nixon as a potentially valuable contact in the late 1960s. The two men first met in 1967 at the Ritz Hotel in Paris. At the time, Nixon was widely regarded as a political hasbeen, but Khashoggi cultivated him, taking steps to ensure that he would be received as a VIP during a visit to the Middle East; Khashoggi even offered to finance the trip. He soon became close to Nixon and to Nixon's best friend, Bebe Rebozo. Arab newspapers reported that Khashoggi also gave $1 million to Nixon's campaign coffers, but no proof was ever found. When questioned by the Watergate prosecutors, Khashoggi admitted having contributed $50,000 to the production of a phonograph record of Nixon's speeches. As president, Nixon involved Khashoggi in Middle East diplomacy, asking him to convey secret messages to King Faisal after the Yom Kippur War in 1973.

Khashoggi was connected to the BCCI network in several different ways. He was a friend of Kamal Adham's as well as other members of the royal family who owned stock in Abedi's bank. When he was implicated in the Lockheed bribery scandal of the mid-1970s, he hired several U.S. lawyers to represent him. One of those was Clark Clifford, according to press reports at the time. (Clifford has denied it.) Years later, Khashoggi played an important role in the Iran-contra affair, and he used BCCI's facilities.

The political clout of Saudi Arabia, the UAE, and other oil-producing states increased enormously after they learned to use oil as a political weapon. It was BCCI's patron — Sheikh Zayed — who was, as noted earlier, the first Arab leader to declare an embargo against the United States in 1973. Later that year, OPEC pushed oil prices to dizzying heights, and Arab leaders used their new wealth to buy influence in the West.

During Nixon's presidency, Arab leaders showered valuable gifts on top U.S. officials and their families. Prince Sultan gave a diamond bracelet to Nixon's wife and brooches to his daughters. King Faisal gave Vice President Spiro T. Agnew a diamond-studded, gold-sheathed dagger; his wife received diamond and pearl jewelry from Crown Prince Jabir al-Ahmad al-Sabah of Kuwait. The emir of Kuwait gave ruby and diamond jewelry to Adele Rogers, the wife of the secretary of state. Under U.S. law, the recipients were allowed to keep only presents worth $50 or less, but many of them pocketed the gifts. They turned them in only after the *Washington Post* ran an exposé in 1974 on how Secretary of State William P. Rogers had failed to hand over valuable gifts.

The presents were mere baubles compared with the rewards that awaited many Nixonites when they left government service. A long list of officials in the Nixon and Ford administrations wound up doing business in the Middle East. Ford's treasury secretary, William Simon, went on to manage a huge pool of money for the Saudi investor Suleiman Olayan. Gerald Parsky, who worked under Simon as an assistant secretary, pushed for policies to encourage Arabs to invest in the United States. He then joined the Gibson, Dunn & Crutcher law firm, which represented Sheikh Zayed's interests in Washington. George Shultz and Caspar Weinberger, who held several senior posts in the Nixon administration, both joined Bechtel, a giant construction firm that did billions of dollars' worth of work in Saudi Arabia. Shultz was president; Weinberger served as "special counsel." When the Saudis were lobbying for approval of the AWACS deal in 1981, Weinberger was secretary of defense. Shultz — still at Bechtel — wrote a letter urging approval to every member of the Senate. The following year, he became secretary of state.

Kamal Adham has had important connections in the U.S. government since at least the early 1960s, when he founded Saudi Arabia's intelligence agency with assistance from the CIA. In the 1970s, Adham and several other Arab investors with ties to BCCI hooked up with John B. Connally, the former governor of Texas and treasury secretary in the Nixon administration. At the time, Connally was widely regarded as a leading contender for the Republican nomination for president. Unlike the other candidates, he was sympathetic to the Arab point of view in the Arab-Israeli conflict. He was just the kind of politician who would have appealed to Abedi's backers.

Connally appears at least three times in deals by BCCI insiders. In 1975, First Arabian Corporation, an investment firm partly owned by Adham and Pharaon, took over Detroit's Bank of the Commonwealth. (Pharaon later sold out.) Many law firms could have assisted the investors, but they happened to choose Connally's firm in Houston,

Vinson & Elkins. Later, Connally's law partner Frank Van Court became Pharaon's chief representative in the United States. In September 1977, Connally bought Main Bank, a small ($66 million in deposits) institution in Houston, with Fredrick Erck, a Texas banker, and two BCCI associates, Pharaon and Khalid Bin Mahfouz, the Saudi banker. (In the mid-1980s, Bin Mahfouz became a BCCI board member as well as a major investor in both BCCI and First American.)

The third deal that has come to light concerns the silver market. When the Texas tycoons Herbert and Bunker Hunt tried to corner the world silver market in the late 1970s, they were acting with other investors, including — it is alleged — Bin Mahfouz, Pharaon, and leading members of the Saudi ruling family. Connally is said to have introduced the Hunts to Bin Mahfouz and Pharaon. One of the banks involved in financing the Hunts was closely associated with BCCI, Banque Arabe et Internationale d'Investissement. This escapade almost broke the Hunt family and badly dented the fortunes of the Saudis involved.

At the time of the Main Bank sale, there were charges that "the Arabs" were trying to buy influence with Connally, an allegation he hotly denied. "So what's the big deal? We bought a bank," Connally would say. "The big deal," noted his biographer James Reston, Jr., "was the appearance it created for a potential candidate for the U.S. presidency, when the United States was attempting to make itself more independent of foreign oil, when the special relationship with Israel was a cornerstone of American foreign policy, and when an Arab oil embargo hung as a persistent threat to American society, which now drew 55 percent of its petroleum from abroad." The Texan now had "a direct, personal, financial stake in a cozy relationship with the Arab world," Reston pointed out. Connally, of course, never made it to the White House, and the BCCI crowd soon began to target Jimmy Carter.

Arab governments began trying to acquire influence with Carter even before he won the Democratic nomination for president in 1976. One of his closest aides, the pollster Patrick Caddell, was simultaneously advising Carter and Saudi Arabia's embassy in Washington. For $80,000 a year, Caddell would presumably help the Saudis manipulate the U.S. political establishment — which would soon be headed by Carter.

After Carter became president, Abedi, of course, rescued Bert Lance by arranging for Pharaon to buy Lance's stock in National Bank of

Georgia — an indulgent lender to Carter's family business. Finally, as we shall see, Kamal Adham provided valuable support to Carter in the Camp David peace process. BCCI's involvement with Carter intensified after he left the White House. As noted earlier, the Carter Center and Global 2000 received millions of dollars from BCCI and related sources. Another major donor was King Fahd of Saudi Arabia, a relative of such BCCI shareholders as Kamal Adham and Prince Turki. Prince Bandar, a nephew of the king's and the country's ambassador to Washington, attended the dedication of the Carter Center.

As president, Carter was generally supportive of Israel, although he did take certain positions that antagonized the pro-Israel lobby, such as the sale of F-15 fighters to Saudi Arabia in 1978. Another setback for Israel occurred in April of that year, when the Palestine Liberation Organization was allowed to open an office in Washington, D.C.

Carter doesn't seem to be the sort of man who would become a mouthpiece for foreign governments, but even the most honorable person will listen sympathetically to the opinions of close friends. After leaving office, he seemed to move closer to the point of view of Abedi and his Arab patrons. Carter not only lobbied for the 1981 AWACS deal, he pushed for another arms sale proposed by the Reagan administration in 1986 — without having been asked to do so by the White House. In 1983, he spoke movingly about the plight of Palestinians in the Israeli-occupied West Bank but said nothing about human rights abuses by Arab regimes. And in 1989, he sharply criticized Salman Rushdie for offending Muslims in his novel *The Satanic Verses*. Although Carter disapproved of the "death sentence" imposed on Rushdie by Iran's Ayatollah Khomeini, he called the book "a direct insult" to "millions of Muslims."

Was First American Bankshares part of the foreign policy apparatus of Abedi's backers? Clifford always maintained that the takeover of First American was a straightforward business deal. In fact, there is considerable evidence that Abedi's patrons regarded First American — and Clifford — as political tools. One indication is that several people involved in the takeover had ties to the Arab lobby in the United States. Adham, the lead investor, was associated with two of Saudi Arabia's principal lobbyists in Washington.

At the Federal Reserve's April 1981 hearing on the takeover, Adham said he had learned about the availability of First American's stock from Hassan Yassin, whom he described as a friend at the Saudi embassy. This version seemed unlikely, since Abedi was recommending the stock to BCCI clients at the same time. Yet it is possible. In January 1978 — at the same time the BCCI clients were scooping up the stock — a member of the Saudi royal family, Prince Nawaf bin Abdul Aziz al-Saud, also bought 15,000 shares. His contract to buy the shares was delivered through Yassin. And who was Yassin? He happened to be one of Saudi Arabia's chief lobbyists in Washington. He was a registered foreign agent for the kingdom until December 1976, when he joined the embassy as director of the Saudi Arabian Information Office.

The kingdom's chief lobbyist in the United States was Frederick G. Dutton, a Washington lawyer. In 1974, when he was angling to get the Saudi contract, he made it clear in a letter to the Saudi government that he wanted to report to Adham. He stipulated that he would "be guided by and report to Sheikh Adham and shall not be assigned to work regularly under a ministry or bureaucracy, nor under other Americans." Before the Saudis awarded him the contract, Dutton went to Saudi Arabia and met with both Adham and Prince Turki, Adham's nephew and deputy in Saudi intelligence as well as a BCCI stockholder. Interestingly, Dutton was connected with another important character in the First American deal: in 1966–67, he was a partner in Clark Clifford's law firm.

An even stronger indication that the First American takeover had something to do with Arab foreign policy comes from Bert Lance, who was, of course, Abedi's key adviser in the deal. In early 1978, Lance met with Abedi and Sheikh Zayed in Pakistan. (During this trip, Lance spoke to Zayed through an interpreter.) Zayed talked about "his concerns of the treatment that he was receiving from the U.S. government," Lance later recalled. He added that Zayed felt "that he was being treated in a manner that really wasn't befitting the strategic importance or the fiscal importance of the UAE." The purchase of one of the most important banking companies in Washington could certainly help Zayed acquire the respect he craved.

While Zayed's remarks merely imply that there were political motives, a former Abu Dhabi official with intimate knowledge of the deal has been much more explicit, stating that obtaining political influence was *the principal goal of the takeover*. He said in a written account that he and other people involved in the deal "talked about the fact that having a Washington presence would mean that senators, congressmen, and other government servants would bank there and would require a range of financial service." The statement continued: "Knowing the BCCI style of personalized service" that had been "very successful in other parts of the world at the higher government levels, it naturally followed that over time, that we would gain influence."

BCCI and its backers understood the power of the pro-Israel lobby in Washington. "We were aware that the various anti-Arab lobbying groups exercised their influence through money," the former Abu Dhabi official said. "What better way would there be than if our bank became the creditor, lender, provider of funds to key U.S. government personnel over time? We knew the prices of houses in Georgetown and the mortgages." He continued: "Because of our ownership in and relationship at the top across the board, we were quite comfortable, especially because we have power brokers like Clifford in place; any influence that the ruler [Sheikh Zayed] needed to exercise in Washington could be done through BCCI's control of Financial General," which would soon become First American.

Did the Arab investors indeed use First American and Clifford to acquire influence in the United States?

Although Clifford bristles at terms like lobbyist, power broker, and influence peddler, he has acted as a mouthpiece for foreign governments for decades. When he left the Truman White House in 1950, Clifford announced, "I have not and will not register as a lobbyist, for that is not the kind of work we do. We run a law office here." In January 1951, however, he registered with the Justice Department as a foreign agent for Indonesia's Sukarno regime.

Clifford has long portrayed himself as a staunch friend of Israel — particularly since BCCI and its murky background have been in the news. He was, after all, one of the aides who advised Truman to recognize the Jewish state. When Clifford was asked in 1991 to name the "most rewarding experience" of his career, he said, "Helping play a role in the creation of the state of Israel. The behind-the-scenes maneuvering building up to that event was extraordinary." What he failed to mention is that his advice to Truman, according to Secretary of State George C. Marshall, was based not on sympathy for the Zionist cause but on electoral arithmetic: support for Israel could help Truman win Jewish votes in the 1948 election. (Clifford has asserted that his position was based on "the national interest.")

He has, in fact, proved highly adaptable over the years, arguing the brief presented to him by whatever client happens to be paying the bills at the moment. In 1971, Israel's great friend started representing the radical Arab state of Algeria. He failed to register as a foreign agent for Algeria until 1975, however, and then only after the Justice Department wrote to him about the oversight.

At the same time that Clifford was serving foreign interests, he was carrying out foreign policy errands for the United States. When Carter was in the White House, Clifford acted as a roving ambassador to the eastern Mediterranean. "On one occasion, [Carter] sent me to Greece," he later said. "On one occasion he sent me to Cyprus when there was a flareup." At that time, Clifford was representing Arab clients with major interests in the region. In January 1980, Carter sent Clifford to India to reassure Premier Indira Gandhi that increased U.S. aid to Pakistan (in response to the Soviet invasion of Afghanistan) would not undermine her country's security. He then returned to Washington to continue representing Abedi, one of the top advisers to Pakistan's President Zia.

After becoming chairman of First American Bankshares in 1982, Clifford placed other well-connected men on the board, including his old friends Stuart Symington, James M. Gavin, and Elwood R. Quesada. (Symington died in 1988, Gavin in 1990.) Symington had spent twenty-four years in the Senate, chairing the Armed Services Committee and serving on the Foreign Relations Committee. Gavin, a retired army general, had been one of the most respected American military leaders in World War II. During the 1960s, he served as Kennedy's ambassador to France and then as chairman of Arthur D. Little, the consulting firm. Quesada, another former general, had been a military aide to Eisenhower during World War II, then served in Eisenhower's administration and as a Lockheed executive before becoming prominent in Washington real estate. In 1988, Charles McC. Mathias, a former Republican senator from Maryland, joined the board. He had been a member of the Senate committee that investigated Bert Lance in 1977.

A closer look at the backgrounds of First American's board members reveals that several of them have been extremely helpful to the Arab lobby; a few were heavily involved in pro-Arab political activities.

Symington had chaired the Middle East Subcommittee of the Senate Foreign Relations Committee and was generally supportive of Israel. However, as a member of the Subcommittee on Multinational Corporations in 1976, he had helped to scuttle an investigation of Arab investments in the United States. When he voted against demanding records from American banks, the probe came to a halt. The inquiry had been launched partly because of the controversy that surrounded the investments in American banks by three men associated with BCCI: Ghaith Pharaon, Khalid Bin Mahfouz, and Adnan Khashoggi. Symington retired from the Senate shortly after that vote. In 1978, he began assisting Clifford in the First American takeover.

Mathias had taken flak from supporters of Israel for voting in favor of two important arms sales to Saudi Arabia: the Carter administration's F-15 deal in 1978 and Reagan's AWACS deal in 1981. He had also published an article in *Foreign Affairs* in the spring of 1981 that criticized the pro-Israel lobby, "Ethnic Groups and Foreign Policy."

First American's flagship bank in Washington, D.C. — First American Bank N.A. — had several board members with interesting connections.

- Charles J. DiBona was the president of the American Petroleum Institute, the lobbying arm of the major American oil companies. Many of these firms have been prominent advocates of Arab interests in the United States.
- Richard Lesher, the president of the U.S. Chamber of Commerce, had written to every member of the Senate on the day of the AWACS vote, urging them to support the deal.
- Lucius D. Battle was the president of the Middle East Institute, a public policy organization in Washington. Steven Emerson, author of a book on Saudi lobbying activities, has described the institute as a "public relations outlet" for Arab interests. Battle was also associated with the American Arab Affairs Council, another pro-Arab group.
- Robert Keith Gray, a Washington lobbyist and public relations man with the firm of Hill and Knowlton,* has had a number of Arab clients over the years, including the Arab League, Adnan Khashoggi, and Prince Talal bin Abdel-Aziz ibn Saud, an important member of the Saudi royal family. In 1990, the firm received millions of dollars in fees from the government of Kuwait to drum up support in the United States for military action against Iraq.

---

*Gray headed the Washington office of Hill and Knowlton, a major public relations firm, until 1981, when he started his own firm, Gray & Co. He returned to Hill and Knowlton five years later.

Hill and Knowlton has also done public relations and lobbying for both BCCI and First American.

Clifford's chairmanship of First American meant that he was now presiding over one of the largest lending institutions in the Washington area, and many of its customers were politicians. This was not a totally new experience for him. Long before the takeover, he had joined the board of National Bank of Washington (NBW), as did his friend Elwood Quesada. In 1972, a lobbyist named Robert Winter-Berger noted in his book, *The Washington Pay-off,* that NBW "does a great deal of business with congressmen." (NBW collapsed in 1990.)

A big proportion of First American's lending was to real estate developers, and this, too, was familiar to Clifford. In the 1970s, his law firm became involved in one of the biggest real estate projects in the Washington area: Avenel, a development of expensive houses — and mansions — in Montgomery County, Maryland. Some of the most prominent people in Washington either live or have bought houses there, including Richard Allen, Reagan's first national security adviser; Senator John Glenn, an Ohio Democrat; and Michael Armacost, who served as undersecretary of state in the Reagan administration (and is a brother of Sam Armacost, a former president of Bank of America). Other buyers included Brian Jensen, a senior official at the World Bank who went to work for BCCI's Washington office, and Gil Simonetti, a partner in Price Waterhouse, BCCI's accounting firm.

The Avenel project is intriguing for several reasons. For one thing, the source of the money used to pay for the land is a mystery; the bulk of it — $12.5 million — was transferred to the United States from a secret bank account in Basel, Switzerland. For another, the man who developed Avenel, Tony Natelli, had a very interesting background. In the 1960s, he headed the Milan office of Peat Marwick Mitchell, a leading accounting firm. One man who claimed to use that firm was Michele Sindona, a Sicilian financier with ties to the Mafia who later became involved in one of the biggest banking scandals in history.* Natelli was never accused of wrongdoing in the Sindona affair, but he was found guilty of violating U.S. law for his role in another famous

---

*In 1974, Sindona's Milanese bank, Banca Privata Italiana, and his New York Bank, Franklin National, collapsed as the result of fraud. Franklin had been the twentieth-largest bank in the country, and its collapse was the largest bank failure in U.S. history. Sindona was eventually convicted of fraud and other charges in both the United States and Italy. He died in 1986. Natelli has denied any business dealings with Sindona.

financial scandal, the collapse of National Student Marketing Corporation (NSMC). Using a variety of gimmicks, NSMC grossly inflated its profits, and when the company's true condition was revealed, the stock price plummeted and investors lost an estimated $200 million. Natelli was found guilty in 1974 of approving the filing of a false proxy statement with the Securities and Exchange Commission; he was fined and sentenced to sixty days in prison. (He was pardoned in December 1980 by President Carter.)

The Avenel project was the subject of an FBI investigation in 1986 because of questions about the way some of the land was acquired from a local utility company, the Washington Suburban Sanitary Commission (WSSC). One large parcel, which was used to develop a golf course, was sold by the WSSC for just ten dollars, according to the deed of sale. The justification for it was that the WSSC retained the right to build a facility on the golf course, but it has never been built. The FBI investigation was ended with no charges filed.

Clifford and his law firm were involved with Avenel in several different ways. The firm apparently represented the seller of the property, Sheffield Enterprises, Inc., a Liberian-registered company. It also acted as trustee for the money shipped in from the secret Swiss bank account. Legal experts say that this was apparently a conflict of interest for the firm. In addition, First American was a major lender to the developers of Avenel and to many of the people who bought houses there.

Under Clifford, First American also lent substantial sums to insiders, including some of the prominent people who served on the boards of its subsidiary banks. One such borrower was Robert Gray, who dabbled in real estate with some of the money he earned in his lobbying business. He owed the bank $2.5 million at the end of 1989, according to a list of insider loans. (Gray declines to comment.)

Another man who lobbied for Arab interests was also a big borrower, Michael Deaver. He was a senior official in the Reagan White House from 1981 until 1985, when he set up a lobbying firm. First American granted him a $1 million loan secured by his house. In an effort to attract business, Deaver shamelessly flaunted his friendship with Reagan and achieved considerable success. One lucrative client was Saudi Arabia. (Deaver was later convicted of lying to a federal grand jury and a congressional committee about his lobbying activities.) When asked about the loan, Deaver said it was unrelated to his business.

Robert Novak, a nationally syndicated columnist known for his harsh criticism of Israel, obtained a loan denominated in British pounds from First American. He says there was nothing untoward about this deal, and there is no evidence to the contrary. But he also appeared in a First American television commercial. (He gave the $10,000 fee to charity.)

One of First American's most intriguing transactions was a loan to a leading candidate for president of the United States.

In 1984, the main contenders for the Democratic nomination were Walter Mondale, a former vice president, and Senator Gary Hart of Colorado. The Hart campaign received about $700,000 in loans from First American — by no means a routine transaction. First American was the biggest single source of credit for the campaign.

Hart's campaign manager, Oliver Henkel, has said he doubted that Abedi brokered the First American loans. But a former BCCI official thinks this is exactly what happened. In early 1984, says this source, Abedi and Swaleh Naqvi were at the Helmsley Palace Hotel in New York, preparing to meet with BCCI officials from the Americas. The meeting was suddenly postponed, however, because "Abedi and Naqvi have gone to D.C. to meet with Gary Hart." Hart, this source continues, "was introduced to Abedi by Clark Clifford. Mr. Abedi liked him and financed his campaign."* Hart insists that he has no recollection of meeting Abedi. However, his memory does not seem to be totally reliable. For example, he says he recalls that National Bank of Washington rather than First American was the biggest lender to his campaign.

In the 1988 campaign, one Democrat was far more sympathetic to the Arab point of view than any other major presidential candidate in history: Jesse Jackson. During a visit to the Middle East in 1979, he embraced Yassir Arafat, the leader of the PLO, and called for the United States to recognize the organization. Jackson further alienated Jewish voters when he made anti-Semitic remarks five years later and would not repudiate the black Muslim leader Louis Farrakhan, an anti-Semitic demagogue.

Jackson was able to count on backing from Arab governments as well as many Arab Americans. In 1979, the government of Libya gave

---

*The Mondale campaign later made an issue out of Hart's acceptance of loans from First American because of its Arab ownership, and Hart repaid the loans.

$10,000 to Jackson's organization PUSH for Excellence (PUSH-Excel). The following year, the Arab League contributed to PUSH-Excel as well as to a group of Jackson's called the PUSH Foundation, according to Clovis Maksoud, the PLO's envoy to the United Nations. The Saudi Arabian government seemed to have a special regard for Jackson. In 1979, he attended a dinner in Washington in honor of Ahmed Zaki Yamani, the kingdom's oil minister. Representing the Carter administration was Patrick Caddell, who had been on the Saudi embassy's payroll three years earlier. In a speech after the meal, Yamani singled out three American politicians for praise: Charles Percy, the Republican senator from Illinois who would later help steer the AWACS deal through the Senate; John Connally, Pharaon's business partner; and Jesse Jackson. The host of the dinner was Kamal Adham's friend Hassan Yassin, the Saudi lobbyist who had been involved in the First American takeover.

When Jackson was running for president in 1988, he got a boost from Saudi Arabia's lobbyist Fred Dutton. In June, Dutton published an op-ed piece in the *Los Angeles Times* touting Jackson as a vice-presidential candidate. (The *Times* identified Dutton as a Democratic party activist, failing to mention that he was also a registered foreign agent for Saudi Arabia.)

One of Jackson's handicaps was that he was viewed as too radical by many members of the Democratic establishment. In March 1988, a few of his advisers got together to remedy that by staging a political breakfast in Washington at which Jackson could meet with party elders. One guest was Frank Mankiewicz, who happened to be the number-two man in the Washington office of Hill and Knowlton, under First American's board member Robert Gray. The breakfast was organized by a former BCCI consultant, Bert Lance, and the star attraction was none other than Clark Clifford. Afterward, Clifford praised Jackson and said that if he were elected, he would bring to Washington "the best brains the party and the country have to offer." Jackson, according to a campaign aide, "frequently told reporters that Clark Clifford was among his 'top policy advisers.' "

It may not be a coincidence that all of these people had ties to the BCCI network.

Abedi knew Jackson well. "Jackson and his son were regular visitors to BCCI-London," says a former bank official. Lance recalls that he introduced them in 1985, when Jackson was passing through London after meeting with Pope John Paul II. Jackson and his son had dinner with Abedi, Naqvi, Lance, and Lance's son at the home of Sonny Ramphal, the secretary-general of the Commonwealth. Not long after that, says Lance, Altaf Gauhar "talked to Jesse about doing some writing" for *South* magazine.

That same year, BCCI gave Jackson about $11,000 in travel expenses, according to Nazir Chinoy, a former bank official. He added that Jackson implied that he could help BCCI procure deposits from African central banks. (Jackson has acknowledged accepting the travel money but denied having any business relationship with BCCI or Abedi.)

During the 1988 campaign, senior BCCI officials were enthusiastic supporters of Jackson, according to former employees of the bank.

Associates of Abedi also had connections to the man who won the election: George Bush. BCCI and its allies had extensive ties to administration officials and relatives of the president's. Robert Altman, for example, hobnobbed with several cabinet members, while BCCI's Miami branch manager, Abdur Sakhia, socialized with Jeb Bush. The president himself had ties to BCCI associates. For example, when he ran the CIA in the 1970s, he worked closely with Saudi intelligence, then headed by Kamal Adham.

The CIA, in fact, was quite familiar with Adham and the entire Abedi network, and it suspected that BCCI was more of a political organization than a commercial enterprise. A classified memo on BCCI in the mid-1980s noted that its "principal shareholders are among the power elite of the Middle East, including the rulers of Dubai and the United Arab Emirates, and several influential Saudi Arabians." It also said that money wasn't the major motive for BCCI's backers. "They are less interested in profitability," the agency wrote, "than in promoting the Muslim cause."

The CIA was in a good position to analyze Abedi's bank. It was a customer of BCCI's and used the bank in a multitude of ways. In fact, the bank's relationship with the CIA was so close that BCCI became involved with the U.S. government in a series of covert operations.

6

COVERT OPERATIONS

THE SAUDI SPYMASTER Kamal Adham likes to work several sides of a deal. In 1965, Northrop, the arms manufacturer, received a letter from one of its agents, Kermit Roosevelt, stating that Adham appeared to be representing three foreign aerospace contractors simultaneously — and was trying to sign up Northrop as well. Adham, Roosevelt wrote, "already has a piece of the Lightning deal, the Mirage deal, and the Lockheed deal and is trying to complete the square by an arrangement with Northrop." In other words, Adham stood to receive a commission from just about every major military aircraft purchase that Saudi Arabia was making. Despite these apparent conflicts of interest, Roosevelt advised Northrop to hire Adham. "Without him," he wrote, "we are going to be weakly represented."

The CIA felt the same way about Adham, one of its closest friends anywhere outside the United States, for he became one of its principal liaisons for the Middle East in the mid-1960s. Even though he was the head of Saudi intelligence, he could also assist the CIA in furthering U.S. interests. There would be no conflict because there were enough similarities in policy aims. Besides, who else could the agency work with? In a theocratic and absolutist society struggling to come to terms with the modern world, Adham was one of a handful of Saudis at the center of power who had the background to cope with international issues of intelligence, foreign policy, and defense. A courtly figure, Adham is cosmopolitan — particularly by the standards of his country.

He was born in Turkey in 1929 to a Turkish mother and a father of Albanian extraction and taken a year later to Jiddah, the Saudi city with the strongest foreign influence. Every year in the month of *hajj* ("pilgrimage") in the Islamic calendar, Muslims from all over the world pass through Jiddah on their way to Mecca. In contrast, the central Najd region, where the capital of Riyadh is situated and the Saudi ruling family makes its home, is a more closed and austere society. Adham set out on an international course at a young age. He was educated at Cairo's Victoria College, which is modeled on Britain's elitist public schools, and he learned several languages. In addition to Arabic and English, he speaks some Turkish, French, and Italian.

Adham's entrée to the ruling al-Saud family was provided by a half-sister, Iffat, the favorite wife of King Faisal, the country's ruler from 1964 until his assassination in 1975. During this period, Adham was one of the most powerful men in Saudi Arabia. He has been described as Faisal's "closest confidant and adviser" and his "right-hand man." In 1963, with Faisal's backing, Adham became the first head of Saudi Arabia's intelligence service, a post he held until September 1977 (shortly before he began buying stock in First American). Until 1979, Adham remained, in his own words, the "king's adviser for security matters," and he continued as an adviser to the government.

At home, the Saudi regime faced many threats during Adham's early years in intelligence, from dissident members of the ruling family, foreigners who lived in the kingdom, Nasscrites, religious zealots, and rebellious members of the armed forces. In 1969, for example, there were at least two attempts at a coup. Externally, the ruling family was preoccupied with the threat of radicalism and subversion from its more populous southwestern neighbor, Yemen, which was then beset by factional fighting that periodically erupted into civil war. While the Saudis supported the traditional royalists, Egypt — at that time the fount of Arab nationalism under Gamal Abdel Nasser — backed those advocating a socialist republic. In a series of meetings with the Egyptians, Adham helped to calm the situation and prevent a more direct Saudi-Egyptian confrontation in Yemen. During these years, the early and middle 1960s, Adham became friendly with Anwar Sadat, the Egyptian vice president and future president. They became so close that Adham was known as Saudi Arabia's "Mr. Egypt." One way that he cultivated Sadat was by showering hundreds of millions of dollars in Saudi funds on him and his country.

Throughout his period as intelligence chief, Adham maintained close ties with the spy agencies of Britain, France, and the United

States. The British, for example, advised the Saudis on internal security during the early 1960s. A former British intelligence officer who lived in Jiddah and spoke frequently with Adham about the fighting in Yemen remembers him as an intelligent and genial man who liked to eye the girls lounging around the swimming pool.

The British, though, played second fiddle to America in Saudi Arabia, as they had since World War II. Saudi-British relations were marred by periodic disputes over the border between Saudi Arabia and Abu Dhabi, a British protectorate. Nevertheless, Adham was well connected in Britain. One of his friends was Julian Amery, a Conservative member of Parliament who served for a time as minister of air. Amery, as noted earlier, later supplemented his salary by acting as a paid adviser to BCCI.

Adham was always closer to the CIA than to the British intelligence services. In fact, the U.S. agency had not only helped him set up Saudi Arabia's internal security service in the early 1960s; some sources believe the CIA may have trained him at its headquarters in Langley, Virginia. Adham, for his part, was willing to help CIA alumni. When Raymond H. Close, the agency's station chief in Saudi Arabia for seven years, retired in December 1977, Adham arranged for him to be sponsored by a company called National Chemical Industries, which was run by a nephew of the Saudi's. (All foreign businessmen living in Saudi Arabia require a local partner or sponsor.)*

At the Saudi court, Adham was the leading advocate of a more engaged and pro-Western foreign policy. (Another adviser who held this view was Ghaith Pharaon's father, Dr. Rashad Pharaon.) And by the early 1970s Adham was not only Saudi Arabia's most important link to Egypt, he was also King Faisal's premier backchannel to the United States. Those two links would be invaluable to Western policymakers, who were desperate to draw Egypt, the most populous Arab nation, away from Soviet influence. Within weeks of Nasser's death in 1970, King Faisal sent Adham to Cairo to suggest to Sadat that he cut back his ties to the Soviets in exchange for increased aid.

By July 1972, Sadat had decided to signal to the United States that he was prepared to adopt a more pro-Western stance; Adham was the channel he used to communicate with Henry Kissinger, President

---

*In an interesting historical note, Close was a nephew of William Eddy, who had arranged President Roosevelt's historic meeting with King Abdel-Aziz and acted as interpreter.

Nixon's national security adviser. On July 13, a message was sent through Adham: if the United States had something to propose, Egypt would send an emissary to Washington. Days later, Sadat delivered "a bombshell," as Kissinger later termed it, giving fifteen thousand Soviet military advisers one week to leave the country; further, all Soviet military bases built since 1967 would become Egyptian property.

At about this time, Adham's path crossed that of Abedi. The Pakistani banker was regularly visiting Saudi Arabia, desperate to get a license there for BCCI, which was still being planned. Abedi's United Bank had a share in one of these coveted licenses, which eluded even such international financial behemoths as Chase Manhattan and Barclays Bank. But the Saudis just didn't want any more foreign banks; the existing ten or so were enough.

Abedi didn't give up; he set about building his influence and contacts in his time-honored way of socializing with the rich and powerful. Through the Jiddah representative of a Lebanese bank in Saudi Arabia, Abedi met Adham, according to a close associate of both men who was living in Jiddah at the time. Adham, so the story goes, was friendly with the glamorous secretary at the Lebanese bank. Sensing a job prospect with Abedi and seeking to impress him, the Lebanese banker introduced the two men. Adham himself says that he met Abedi through one of his own Pakistani secretaries.

Meanwhile, Adham continued to prove his value to the United States. In May 1973, he delivered a message to Frank Jungers, the chief executive of Aramco, the consortium of U.S. oil companies in Saudi Arabia.* Adham warned that Sadat might well wage war against Israel and that there could be an oil embargo.

Adham's role in encouraging favorable attitudes toward the West — and nudging Egypt into the American sphere of influence — made him a valued American asset. His importance became abundantly clear during the presidency of Jimmy Carter.

When Carter was urging Egypt to make peace with Israel, Adham's close ties to the Sadat family were of vital importance. Adham had not only been a conduit for Saudi aid to Cairo, he was a business associate of Sadat's wife, Jehan, and other members of the family.

Carter's foreign policy achieved a dramatic boost when, in November 1977, Sadat made a grand gesture toward an accommodation with

---

*Aramco was later acquired by the Saudi government and renamed Saudi Aramco.

Israel by flying to Jerusalem and declaring his commitment to negotiate peace. This in turn led to the signing of the historic Camp David Accords in September 1978 by Sadat and Menachem Begin, the Israeli prime minister. The following March, a formal peace treaty was concluded at the White House.

Adham had tried hard to persuade the Saudi ruling family to participate in the peace talks. The State Department tried to persuade Crown Prince Fahd that Saudi Arabia should be part of the peace process; the kingdom was already an important patron of Sadat's, supplying as much as $3 billion in aid to Egypt in 1977. Although Adham strongly supported the Americans, Fahd was guarded; the risks appeared too great.

So America was frustrated, and those who had sided with the U.S. cause in the debates in Saudi Arabia and the Persian Gulf sheikhdoms suffered. On January 19, 1979, King Khaled announced that Adham had been dismissed from his post as a royal adviser. He was being punished for criticizing Saudi Arabia's opposition to the peace initiative.

Such a public rebuke is rare in Saudi Arabia. But King Khaled and Crown Prince Fahd, his brother and successor, seemed ready to slight their adviser to help calm public anger at the Camp David settlement. To many Arabs, the Egyptians had abandoned their cause, relinquishing the strongest card that the Arab nations have to play: the formal recognition of Israel. With the exception of a few nations, such as Morocco and the Sudan, the Arab countries severed their diplomatic ties with Cairo.*

Even though Adham had been publicly humiliated, he remained influential in Saudi Arabia's ruling circles. In Washington, his stature rose dramatically. In 1981, the U.S. government permitted a group of BCCI clients led by Adham to acquire First American Bankshares, one of the most important banking institutions in Washington.

Was this a payment for Adham's help on Camp David — and the other assistance provided to Washington over the years — or was there no connection? The timing suggests a quid pro quo. The First American takeover battle occurred just as Adham was involved in Camp David. Another coincidence concerns one of the parties involved in the

---

*Egypt's estrangement from most other Arab countries lasted for several years. In December 1983, Jordan restored full diplomatic relations with Cairo. Many other Arab countries eventually followed suit.

acquisition. After the Camp David Accords were signed, the United States agreed to provide additional arms to Egypt, and it awarded an exclusive contract to ship the weapons to a little-known company called Tersam. The columnist Jack Anderson revealed that Tersam's silent partner and financial backer was Ali Mohammed Shorafa, a member of the group permitted to buy First American and one of Sheikh Zayed's top advisers.

The takeover, of course, enhanced Adham's status in Saudi Arabia, since he could use First American to promote the kingdom's interests in Washington. Abedi was happy to put his network at the disposal of his friends and patrons in the Middle East and Pakistan, including government officials and intelligence officers. He also helped the Americans: BCCI became an important tool of U.S. intelligence.

Abedi, with his taste for intrigue, found the world of espionage alluring. Intelligence agencies, for their part, are always on the lookout for "assets" — individuals and institutions in a position to gather secrets, transmit money, and exert influence behind the scenes. BCCI was a particularly attractive mechanism. Its network included offices throughout the Third World; in many developing countries, it was one of a handful of foreign banks — sometimes the only one. Wherever BCCI operated, Abedi and his minions tried to make connections with the local power elite, and they soon developed an intimate relationship with the CIA.

The precise origin of the CIA's relationship with Abedi is difficult to establish, but it may well have gone back to the bank's earliest days, perhaps to before BCCI's founding in 1972. When Abedi was placed under house arrest by Bhutto the year before, it was because he was suspected of helping the previous military regime. But Bhutto's hostility was also based on his suspicion that Abedi had ties to American intelligence. On several occasions, Bhutto said publicly that Abedi was in league with the CIA. Similar rumors swirled around the late Hussein Gokal — whose sons Mustapha, Abbas, and Murtaza ran the Gulf Group after he died around 1970. The Gulf Group was the biggest borrower from BCCI. The three brothers seemed to have impressive connections in the U.S. government; their companies were heavily involved in shipping goods to Third World countries supplied by American aid programs.

After Abedi launched BCCI, several people with intelligence backgrounds appeared on the bank's list of shareholders. Kamal Adham, of course, was the most notable example. Close associates of his in Saudi intelligence were also shareholders. Prince Turki bin Faisal al-Saud served as Adham's deputy from 1973 to 1977, when he succeeded Adham. As the head of Saudi intelligence, he has been the CIA's principal liaison in the kingdom. Abdul-Raouf Khalil, who has an engineering and communications background, was a senior aide to Adham and remained in the Saudi agency after Adham's departure. Khalil continues to serve in the Saudi government, according to his American lawyer. Like Adham, Khalil also held stock in First American.

Two top officials of Pakistani intelligence agencies worked for BCCI satellites. Akram Shaikh, the former director of the intelligence bureau, worked for Attock Oil in Pakistan until 1989, when he returned to the intelligence bureau. Saghir Anwar, the former head of the Federal Investigative Agency, worked for International Travel Corporation in London. A BCCI banker named Amjad Awan is the only son of Ayub Awan, a top-ranking police and intelligence official until his retirement in the late 1960s; he also served as interior secretary, director of the intelligence bureau, and director of Inter-Services Intelligence (ISI), Pakistan's military intelligence agency.

However BCCI began its association with the CIA, it was heir to a long tradition of shady banks with close ties to U.S. intelligence agencies. Several people connected with these institutions also play a part in the BCCI story.

Deak & Company, a money-changing and private banking group, was founded by Nicholas Deak, who had served in the Office of Strategic Services (OSS), the CIA's World War II precursor. Deak assisted the CIA on several occasions. In 1953, for example, he provided untraceable cash for a covert operation in Iran: the overthrow of Prime Minister Mohammad Mosaddeq, which enabled the shah to return to power.

Nugan Hand, an international banking group founded in 1973 that was active in Asia and the Middle East, was involved in money laundering and arms deals as well as covert operations. Nugan was connected to an extraordinary number of former U.S. military and intelligence officials, including William Colby, the CIA's director from September 1973 to January 1976. Colby was a lawyer for the bank.

During the 1960s and 1970s, several shady banks in the Caribbean were associated with the CIA, notably Castle Bank & Trust Company and an affiliate called Mercantile Bank and Trust Ltd. Both institutions were run by an OSS veteran named Paul Helliwell and were used by the CIA for covert operations. Helliwell had been the OSS's head of special intelligence in China during the war. Later he worked closely with the CIA, helping to establish several "proprietaries," companies that appeared to be normal private enterprises but were secretly owned by the CIA. He was involved in founding Civil Air Transport, Sea Supply, and Air America.

Helliwell was an old colleague of George Olmsted, the head of the OSS's China section during the war. Olmsted, of course, controlled Financial General Bankshares until 1977, when it was taken over by the Middendorf group, which, in turn, agreed to sell it to BCCI clients.* Before that deal, Olmsted's International Bank had bought two thirds of Mercantile after it was declared sound by auditors from Price Waterhouse. Olmsted claimed that he had been snookered. He maintained that $21 million of the $25 million of Mercantile's assets that Price Waterhouse had listed didn't exist. The money had been siphoned off to unidentified borrowers and would never be repaid. The Bahamian government shut the bank down in 1977 at a cost of $9 million to International Bank. Olmsted threatened to sue the auditors. A spokesman for Price Waterhouse maintains that the accounts were "true and fair" under Bahamian accounting principles, which are similar to British standards.

Three years after the collapse of Mercantile, Nugan Hand went bankrupt as the result of massive fraud. Interestingly, Nugan Hand also used Price Waterhouse as its auditor — as did BCCI. In yet another coincidence, Nugan Hand and BCCI used the same law firm in the Cayman Islands: Bruce Campbell & Company. The firm acted as the registered agent for Nugan Hand. In 1976, it set up BCCI's most secretive unit: International Credit & Investment Company Ltd. (ICIC). Bruce Campbell, which shared the same office building as ICIC, also organized and managed several other corporate entities related to BCCI.

ICIC and its sister companies later became a critical link in many of BCCI's more outlandish schemes, an off-the-books dummy company that was used in connection with a vast array of frauds. ICIC became

---

*There is another intriguing link to the BCCI network. Helliwell used Castle and Mercantile in connection with tax-avoidance schemes for a number of famous and infamous people, including American mobsters, prominent Asian politicians, and members of the Pritzker family of Chicago, which controls the Hyatt hotel chain. The Pritzkers later went into business with BCCI's Ghaith Pharaon, who developed Hyatt hotels in Saudi Arabia and Latin America.

indispensable by providing a façade of respectability to the financial affairs of Adham and several other BCCI insiders, many of whom, like Adham, had ties to the CIA.

General Olmsted was just one of several people at First American with intriguing intelligence connections. The investment group that acquired First American in 1977 was led by J. William Middendorf II, a financier with intimate ties to the national security establishment. Until a few months before the takeover, he had been secretary of the navy. In 1980, after Ronald Reagan was elected president, Middendorf served on his CIA transition team. In early 1981, a businessman who wanted to build a pipeline in Central Africa held discussions with both Middendorf and William Casey, the incoming CIA director. Middendorf, according to the columnist Jack Anderson, "reportedly said he liked the idea, but couldn't get involved because he anticipated getting a post in the Reagan administration." He was soon named ambassador to the Organization of American States. In that post he would have worked with the CIA, which was involved in several important covert operations in Latin America.

One member of Middendorf's investment group was Joseph Farland, who had been U.S. ambassador to Pakistan. In that post, he came into contact with several Pakistani officials who later worked for BCCI. Farland then served as ambassador to Iran, where BCCI had impressive political connections. A brother of the shah's, Prince Mahmood Reza Pahlavi, was a BCCI shareholder.

Farland's immediate successor in Tehran was Richard Helms, a man with an extraordinary number of connections to the BCCI network. Helms served as the CIA director from June 1966 until February 1973, a period when America's relations with Adham and the Saudis were becoming extremely close. Helms's tenure caused him considerable difficulties. In 1977 he was prosecuted for lying to the Senate Foreign Relations Committee four years earlier about the CIA's attempts to undermine Chile's President Salvador Allende Gossens. Helms retained Edward Bennett Williams and Clark Clifford to represent him. Williams, the legendary criminal defense lawyer from the Washington firm of Williams & Connolly, was at that time a member of the Foreign Intelligence Advisory Board, on which his friend Clifford had also served. Helms knew Clifford well, having run the CIA when Clifford was secretary of defense in the Johnson administration.

Helms's friends rallied around in his defense: former senator Stuart Symington, who had served on the Foreign Relations Committee, was called to testify before the grand jury; he showed his testimony to Williams before he testified. A close friend of Clifford's and a future board member of First American, Symington was intent on helping Helms. "If they prosecute Dick, the whole temple will come down," he warned an attorney in Williams's firm. Reading Symington's testimony, Williams was thrilled, deeming it so muddled that it would confuse the prosecutor.

With the help of his well-connected lawyers, Helms was able to work out a favorable settlement with the Justice Department. He pleaded *nolo contendere* — no contest — to misleading Congress (as opposed to perjury). The judge imposed a $2,000 fine and a suspended two-year jail sentence.

Helms had been forced out of the CIA in 1973, during Nixon's ill-fated second term. In a face-saving gesture, the president offered him an ambassadorship. Helms picked Iran and served there until 1977, when he left the government. In time-honored Washington fashion, he was quick to cash in on his connections by setting up a consulting firm. With a remarkable lack of subtlety, he called it Safeer — which means "ambassador" in Farsi, the language of Iran.*

One of Helms's associates was Mohammed Rahim Motaghi Irvani, an Iranian businessman who was a partner, through his Alvand Investments Company, with BCCI in Iran-Arab Bank, Abedi's joint venture in Tehran. Irvani also controlled the Melli Industrial Group, which was run by Roy Carlson, the former Bank of America official who had been involved in establishing BCCI. Both Carlson and Irvani were founding directors with Helms in the Safeer consulting firm, which was based in Atlanta.† Irvani held 80 percent of the equity, registered in the name of Northwest Investment Corporation, with Helms holding the balance of the shares, according to correspondence in 1977 relating to the establishment of the company. Its initial clients included Bechtel, Hughes Aircraft, Martin Marietta, McDonnell Douglas, Mitsui, and Itek, according to company records. When the shah was ousted in 1979, Carlson and Irvani both moved to Atlanta, and Carlson was named chairman of a BCCI satellite, National Bank of Geor-

---

*While Helms was the ambassador to Iran, his brother Pearsall ran a consulting company in Switzerland involved in U.S.-Iran trade.

†Helms and Carlson were also partners in another venture, the Brockton Leather Company of Boston.

gia. Helms took over all of Safeer's equity that year, at which time Carlson resigned from the board.*

Before Irvani moved to Atlanta, he was a director and shareholder in one of the dummy companies set up to acquire First American. Abedi asked him to become involved in the takeover fight, according to his son Bahman; Irvani dropped out before the acquisition was consummated. Helms provided advice to Irvani on his role in the dummy company in a telex dated October 20, 1978, setting out the legal language that Irvani should use to protect himself when he gave his power of attorney to "any partner of Clifford, Glass, McIlwain & Finney [as Clark Clifford's firm was then called] . . . with respect to the transaction involving Financial General Bankshares of Washington D.C." Helms has described reports of his involvement with Irvani's role in the takeover, including the telex, as absolute nonsense.

Regardless of what Helms says, no one can deny that virtually every major character in the takeover was connected in one way or another to U.S. intelligence: Olmsted, who controlled the company for years; Middendorf, who headed the group that acquired it from him; Abedi, who arranged for clients of BCCI to buy the company from Middendorf's group; Irvani, the chairman of one of the dummy companies set up to carry out the acquisition; Helms, who advised Irvani; Adham, the lead investor in Abedi's group; Clifford, who steered the deal through the regulatory maze and then became the chairman of the company; and Symington, who assisted Clifford and then became the vice chairman.

After the BCCI group gained control of First American, two men with links to U.S. intelligence joined the board of its Washington, D.C., bank. The lobbyist Robert Gray of Hill and Knowlton often boasted of his close relationship with the CIA's William Casey; Gray used to say that before taking on a foreign client, he would clear it with Casey. Karl G. Harr, Jr., a lobbyist for the aerospace industry, had been on the staff of the National Security Council in the late 1950s. He had served on the Operations Coordinating Board, which was involved in overseeing the CIA's covert operations.

Can this all be a coincidence? Or is it possible that First American was affiliated with U.S. intelligence all along and that it was simply passed from one group of CIA associates to another, and then another? No proof has emerged that this is what happened, but it is certainly not

---

*Carlson has declined requests for interviews and in 1992 refused to testify before Congress, citing his constitutional rights against self-incrimination.

a farfetched theory, especially when one takes other "coincidences" into account.

For example, a former BCCI official, Akbar Bilgrami, has testified that when he worked for the bank, he found indications that it may have secretly controlled First American. When asked what he learned, Bilgrami said he was told by Issan Kabbani that BCCI and First American were part of "the same group." Kabbani happened to be a Saudi official who went into business with Raymond Close, the former CIA station chief in Saudi Arabia, around the time the takeover battle began. Close, of course, was also a business associate of Kamal Adham's.

Another set of relationships is equally intriguing. In the early 1980s, Hassan Yassin, the Saudi lobbyist who, according to Adham, recommended that he invest in First American, served on the boards of two financial institutions: Hong Kong Deposit and Guaranty Company Limited and Tetra Finance (H.K.) Limited. Both of these companies were licensed by the Hong Kong government as "deposit-taking companies," which meant that they could engage in banking but were forbidden to take small deposits from retail customers. Both companies collapsed in 1983, and depositors suffered large losses.

Yassin was not the only person with ties to BCCI on the board of those companies. Serving with him was Ghanem Faris al-Mazrui, the head of Sheikh Zayed's Department of Personal Affairs as well as Zayed's representative on the board of BCCI. A third board member was John M. Shaheen, an Arab-American businessman.

Shaheen was very well connected in U.S. intelligence circles. He was a veteran of the OSS and one of the closest friends of the head of the CIA, William Casey. A few years after the collapse of the Hong Kong deposit-taking companies, Shaheen and two of his business associates — Roy Furmark and Cyrus Hashemi — played important roles in the Iran-contra affair, as did Casey and BCCI.

The BCCI network's ties to the CIA extended to the very top of the agency, for Adham worked with a series of CIA directors, including George Bush.

When Bush became director in January 1976, the CIA's image had never been worse. During the previous few years, journalists and congressional investigators had uncovered shocking and illegal conduct. American intelligence officers had secretly funded nonprofit organizations in the United States and publishing businesses abroad. They had spied on U.S. citizens and had even tried to assassinate foreign leaders. There were several schemes to kill Fidel Castro, one of which involved an alliance between the CIA and American mobsters.

Bush saw it as his mission to restore the CIA's image and improve relations with Congress. In his one year as director, he appeared more than fifty times on Capitol Hill. In the years since, it has become clear that he never really carried out a house-cleaning. Some of his appointees later acquired notoriety; Theodore Shackley, whom Bush appointed associate deputy director for operations, later became embroiled in the Iran-contra affair and other dubious covert operations. Bush also "ignored repeated signals that rogue, off-the-books operations by former agents were out of control, leading to Agency acquiescence in illegal activities," according to an article by Scott Armstrong and Jeff Nason, two experts on national security issues. It was during Bush's tenure that Edwin Wilson, a former CIA operative, began selling his services to the Libyans, using his access to the agency to advantage. Bush also helped to strengthen ties between the CIA and Saudi intelligence.

When, in June 1976, a terrorist bomb killed the U.S. ambassador to Lebanon, Francis E. McCloy, Bush successfully pushed the case within the administration for evacuating American citizens from that country, a move that could hardly be criticized. But he also instituted a more questionable policy. In an effort to obtain better information on terrorism, the CIA strengthened its relationships with so-called friendly Arab intelligence agencies. One of the most important of these was Saudi Arabia's intelligence service, run by Kamal Adham, Prince Turki, and Abdul-Raouf Khalil, all of whom were BCCI insiders.

Did the Arab spies get something in return? The CIA, according to intelligence experts, tacitly agreed to look the other way when friendly agencies conducted operations in the United States. The fruits of this policy quickly became apparent. A few years later, Adham and Khalil became involved in the First American takeover battle — with no hindrance from their friends at the CIA. Later, as we shall see, Adham, Khalil, and other BCCI insiders would forge connections with other sensitive industries, including telecommunications and cable television.

The threat of terrorism was not the only issue that helped to strengthen ties between America's military-intelligence establishment and the conservative autocracies of the Middle East. Even more important was a series of upheavals in 1979.

·　　·　　·

Shah Mohammad Reza Pahlavi of Iran was regarded as one of the West's most important allies in the Middle East. With his large military forces — equipped with billions of dollars' worth of American arms — the shah could act as America's "policeman" in the Persian Gulf. To ensure continued U.S. support, the shah, like the ruling family of Saudi Arabia, went to great lengths to cultivate influential Americans.

One strong backer of the shah was William P. Rogers, Nixon's first secretary of state, who favored increased U.S. arms sales to Iran. Some of those deals were financed with taxpayer-subsidized loans from the U.S. Export-Import Bank, which was headed by William Casey, a Nixon appointee. When Rogers and Casey returned to their New York law firm, Rogers & Wells, the shah awarded business to the firm and placed Rogers on the board of his Pahlavi (New York) Foundation. (Casey, of course, went on to become Reagan's CIA director.)

Although the U.S. government loved the shah, millions of Iranians were outraged at the corruption of his regime and the repression by his Savak (secret police), enabling the Ayatollah Khomeini to force him from power early in 1979. The Iranian revolution provoked fears that similar rebellions would erupt in the conservative Arab monarchies. Most of the sheikhs governed restive Shia populations who had often suffered discrimination at the hands of their Sunni rulers. Broadcasts from Iran urged Arab Shi'ites to rise up against their decadent rulers.

In November 1979, armed fundamentalists in Saudi Arabia seized the Grand Mosque in Mecca, the holiest Muslim shrine. Loudspeakers were set up, and the rebels began broadcasting attacks on the regime. The leader of the siege said he would rid the country of "corrupt princes." A Western journalist living in Saudi Arabia at the time recalled that "corruption in the royal family was one of the main things the rebels talked about," adding that "all of Mecca could hear what they were saying." After weeks of fighting left hundreds dead, the rebels were captured and as many as sixty-three of them were executed.* In December there was yet another upheaval, the Soviet invasion of Afghanistan, which posed a threat to the pro-West regimes in the region.

The traumas of 1979 led to a dramatic increase in military and intelligence cooperation among the United States, Saudi Arabia, and

---

*The mosque rebellion also caused more immediate problems for some of BCCI's close allies in Saudi Arabia. Pharaon later complained that his bank creditors flew away "like a flock of pigeons" in response to the uprising. He received some recompense, however: one of his companies was awarded the contract to clear up the damage done to the Grand Mosque.

Pakistan, resulting in multibillion-dollar arms deals, secret schemes to arm Iran and Iraq, and a massive covert operation to aid the Afghan guerrillas. BCCI, with its close ties to Washington, Riyadh, and Islamabad, was deeply involved.

After the fall of the shah and the invasion of Afghanistan, Saudi Arabia and its neighbors sought foreign friends with greater urgency than ever before. The al-Sauds and their counterparts in the UAE, Kuwait, Bahrain, and other rich Gulf states used every means at their disposal to ensure political and military support from the West, including access to sophisticated weapons. The principal source of such aid, of course, was the United States.

Pakistan, which shares a long border with Afghanistan, sought financial aid from the Arab countries to cope with the new Soviet threat. General Zia immediately flew to Saudi Arabia to request aid. He also turned to the United States.

Washington had suspended aid to Islamabad in early 1979 partly because of the nuclear weapons program. After the Soviet invasion of Afghanistan, Carter turned the spigot back on. The Reagan administration was much more generous, seeing a chance to fight the Soviet "evil empire" by aiding Pakistan as well as the mujaheddin rebels in Afghanistan. Much of the aid to the Afghans was channeled through the Zia regime. In addition, Pakistan itself became a favored recipient of U.S. assistance in the 1980s (surpassed only by Israel and Egypt). Between 1981 and 1986, the United States gave $3.2 billion to Pakistan.

Abedi would often boast to General Zia of his role, and that of his bank, in ensuring this continued flow of funds, according to a former associate. "Many times when the aid package was approved in the Congress, Abedi would take credit with General Zia," said this source, who added that the BCCI chief helped the Pakistani foreign minister arrange meetings with U.S. officials.

Together with the Pakistani government, the CIA embarked on a campaign to aid the Afghan rebels. It was in this operation that BCCI clearly emerged as a U.S. intelligence asset.

The CIA's support of the Afghan resistance received far less attention than a similar operation in Central America — where the United States backed the contra rebels against Nicaragua's leftist government — in large part because there was little congressional or public opposition. The Afghan rebels, however, received far more money than the contras — more than $2 billion. This operation has been described as America's biggest covert action program since World War II.

The war in Afghanistan led to an extraordinary ten-year partnership between the Pakistani military, its intelligence agency (the ISI), the Saudi intelligence agency, and the CIA. Zia built the ISI into his chosen covert operations unit. Working with the ISI, Prince Turki bin Faisal, the Saudi intelligence chief (and a BCCI shareholder), distributed more than $1 billion in cash to Afghan guerrillas during the late 1980s.

Abedi and several of his close associates were conduits for information and intelligence. In addition, BCCI handled transfers of funds through its Pakistani branches and acted as a collection agency for war matériel and even for the mujaheddins' pack animals, according to internal documents. BCCI was also extremely useful when the CIA, the National Security Council (NSC), or other agencies wanted to supply arms discreetly to allies like the mujaheddin.

The Afghan operation was so extensive that the CIA station in Islamabad "was one of the biggest in the world," according to Bob Woodward of the *Washington Post;* he added that the CIA's William Casey "had the closest relationship with Zia of any member of the Reagan Administration." Casey also became close to one of Zia's top advisers, Agha Hasan Abedi.

Abedi helped arrange Casey's sojourns in Islamabad and met with the CIA director during visits to Washington, according to former BCCI officials and sources in Washington. Typically, Abedi would stay at a luxury hotel and Casey would go to his suite. The two men, who met intermittently over a three-year period, would spend hours talking about the war in Afghanistan, the Iran-contra arms trades, Pakistani politics, and the situation in the Persian Gulf.*

Casey was quick to realize that Abedi and his network could be useful to U.S. intelligence around the world, whereas men like Adham and Prince Turki were primarily of value in the Middle East. "What

---

*The CIA has said it has no record of contact between Casey and Abedi and has denied that the two men ever met. Although that might sound like a sweeping denial, in the looking-glass world of espionage it could mean something else. Staff members of Senator Kerry's have pointed out that Casey's meetings with Abedi could have occurred "outside [the CIA's] record keeping and operations." They note that the CIA's legal department always maintained that it had no record of Casey's involvement in the Iran-contra affair even though the director was a major figure in the scandal. In Iran-contra, the agency explained, he was acting not as the CIA's director but as an adviser to President Reagan. Thus, Casey's relationship with Abedi may well have been handled in such a way that it was "undocumented, fully deniable, and effectively irretrievable."

Abedi had in his hand [was] magic — something Kamal Adham or even Prince Turki didn't have," said a former BCCI official. "Abedi had branches and banks in at least fifty Third World countries. The BCCI people in all these countries were on a first-name basis with the prime ministers, the presidents, the finance ministers, the elite in these countries — and their wives and mistresses." Casey could ask Abedi whether a country's leader had "a girlfriend or a foreign currency account," the BCCI official continued. "Abedi could say: 'We'll tell you how much he's salted abroad and how much money he gives to his girlfriend.' "

The BCCI network was also valuable as a mechanism for exerting influence abroad, thanks to the political connections Abedi and his minions had made over the years. The bank's network could also serve as a discreet channel for financial operations, including bribes, money laundering, and the financing of arms deals. As Abedi's relationship with Casey blossomed, BCCI became increasingly important to the CIA. The agency opened several accounts at BCCI as well as at its satellite in the capital, First American; the CIA used more than forty accounts at First American for routine business.

Throughout his tenure at the CIA, Casey bristled at Congress's attempts to impose controls on covert operations. The arena of greatest contention was Central America. To the frustration of Casey and other Reagan administration officials, Congress would approve aid to the contras for a brief period, then deny it, then approve it again. In an effort to circumvent Congress, Casey — together with NSC officials — cooked up a secret plan that Oliver North, a Marine colonel and NSC aide, later called "a neat idea." BCCI was intimately involved.

The administration's covert sales of arms to Iran created a political uproar when they became public in 1986. Why had the United States been supplying arms to its sworn enemy? And what were senior presidential advisers like Robert ("Bud") McFarlane doing, making a secret trip to Tehran with a Bible and a cake as gifts for the reigning mullahs?

The tale that unfolded in 1987, in the hearings held by the congressional Iran-Contra Committee, was worthy of the raciest fiction. Leading officials in the Reagan administration — with the help of the CIA — had secretly arranged sales of weapons to Iran. Some of the profits from the arms sales were illegally diverted to the contras. Casey, the Israeli government, and some of the firebrands in the NSC succeeded in getting approval from President Reagan for these secret arms shipments.

By 1985, Iran was struggling to maintain its war against Iraq. After five years of fighting, hundreds of thousands of Iranian soldiers had been killed or maimed by Iraq's better-equipped army. The United States and several other Western countries refused to supply matériel to Iran, and it was plagued by a lack of spare parts, rockets, missiles, and ammunition.

The U.S. government hoped to capitalize on this weakness and build new bridges to Iran. The Reagan administration wanted the Iranians to use their influence with terrorist groups to secure the release of American hostages in Lebanon. Middlemen were required to carry out the transactions, particularly to give the administration and the CIA some cover and the prospect — especially for the president — of "plausible deniability." But the middlemen had to work many different sides of the fractured politics of the Middle East.

Adnan Khashoggi, the flamboyant Saudi arms merchant, had connections in Saudi Arabia and other Arab countries but could also deal with Iranians and even the Israelis. He also got along well with Manucher Ghorbanifar, the Iranian arms dealer at the heart of the scheme. Both men smelled multibillion-dollar contracts just around the corner once Iran's trade with the United States got going again.

Khashoggi used BCCI to deposit money into North's Enterprise, as the covert slush fund was labeled by Arthur Liman, a lawyer for the Iran-Contra Committee. Money from the Enterprise was then funneled to the contras to circumvent the congressional ban on aid. Ghorbanifar also used BCCI to deposit millions of dollars. The arms transactions were profitable for the middlemen — and BCCI. As the planning of the shipments gathered pace, Khashoggi drew a chart for his colleagues showing how his company, Triad International Marketing, would buy $10 million worth of arms for Iran and extract $11 million in return. This transaction, he told them, would happen four times, creating a tidy profit of as much as $4 million, with BCCI receiving a share.

It is unclear exactly how many arms deals Khashoggi carried out with the help of BCCI. Some may have taken place outside the confines of Iran-contra. But the Saudi middleman was a critical link in at least four of the six Iran-contra transactions between August 1985 and October 1986. These deals were certainly very profitable for Khashoggi, Ghorbanifar, and BCCI. Khashoggi and Ghorbanifar sold

TOW missiles costing $3,500 for $10,000, and Khashoggi, in at least one case, made a profit of $2 million on the $10 million financing that he arranged for just two months.

Nazir Chinoy, a senior BCCI official in Paris, has said that he discussed the sale of U.S. arms to Iran through Israel with Khashoggi. Chinoy testified to the Senate in 1992 that he met Khashoggi in either late 1985 or 1986 to arrange these transactions. But it was the bank's Monte Carlo office, and perhaps later its Los Angeles office as well, that apparently provided the bulk of the financing for Khashoggi's shipments.

BCCI's manager in Monte Carlo, Muneer Kiran, a Frenchman of Lebanese origin, called Chinoy in 1986 and set up a meeting in Paris, saying it would involve a wealthy and well-connected Saudi businessman, Adnan Khashoggi. "Khashoggi was quite candid, open about it," Chinoy said. At this meeting, held at BCCI's posh office on the Champs-Élysées, Khashoggi asked for a $5 million loan that would be used "to supply arms to Iran, American arms through Israel, and sold to Iran." Advising Chinoy that discretion was needed, Khashoggi also indicated that he was working with "friends in the States, in Israel, and Iran" and that those friends included people in the U.S. government. Chinoy was leery, but Kiran had worked closely with Khashoggi, secretly doing about eight or nine transactions involving $15 million or $16 million that funded arms deals for Iran. And Kiran was prepared to lend a further $10 million. Chinoy said he was nervous about such business and tried to stop Kiran — who ranked below him in the bank's hierarchy — from doing business with the Saudi. But Khashoggi had Kiran at his beck and call, having given him "a bribe of $100,000," according to Chinoy. Also, it seems that Chinoy got no help from his superiors in London to restrain Kiran. (Kiran could not be reached for comment.)

Ghorbanifar, who helped to arrange the Iran-contra deals, maintained deposits of between $2 million and $2.5 million at BCCI's Monte Carlo branch, Kiran told Chinoy. When Chinoy said that Kiran should tell Ghorbanifar to take his accounts elsewhere, Kiran refused, saying that the Iranian arms merchant was in good standing with French officials, who credited him with helping to liberate French hostages in Lebanon. Thus, Kiran argued, Ghorbanifar's accounts would only help boost BCCI's status with French officialdom.

Further confirming BCCI's pivotal role in the arms sales, Albert Hakim, who acted as Oliver North's banker, testified before the Iran-

Contra Committee that Khashoggi transferred a total of $20 million from BCCI in 1986 to fund the operation. Intriguingly, Hakim also referred to other arms-trafficking deals totaling millions of dollars more that involved a party he simply called "IC" of Grand Cayman. These deals, congressional investigators speculate, could well have involved ICIC, BCCI's Grand Cayman affiliate. Hakim was also a customer of another BCCI-related institution: First American.

Beyond the Iran-contra arms trades, BCCI was an important part of Iran's efforts to obtain weaponry and matériel. BCCI had a natural sympathy for the Iranian cause, for Abedi's clique was mostly made up of Shia Muslims; most Iranians are also Shi'ites.

BCCI was prepared to do business with the Iranian banks, most of which were shunned by the major Western institutions after the Iranian revolution. BCCI was also willing to falsify documents and letters of credit to disguise arms sales to Iran to get around the U.S. and other Western embargoes. Through most of the Iran-Iraq war, BCCI's head office in London ran large accounts for Iran's Bank Melli which were used to pay for weapons, military supplies, pharmaceuticals, and other needs. Bank Melli periodically replenished the accounts with payments that were sometimes as large as $100 million, according to Arif Durrani, a Pakistani arms dealer who used BCCI to finance the export of weapons to Iran.

Another supplier financed by BCCI was Ben Banerjee, a British arms merchant of Indian origin. According to BCCI documents, in November 1985 the bank's Park Lane branch in London financed more than $11 million of goods sold by Banerjee and his company, B.R.&W. Industries Ltd., of Olney in Buckinghamshire. The buyer was Iran's Sepah Pasdaran, or revolutionary guards. Most of the goods were labeled *lift trucks,* but they were actually 1,250 TOW antitank missiles costing $7,500 each, manufactured in the United States in 1980 and 1981. The documents had to be falsified because of the arms embargo.

BCCI also financed the sale of $1.86 million worth of Polish rockets, launchers, missiles, and rifles that traveled with the TOW missiles to Tehran via Dubai in the UAE. The Iranians were so eager for these supplies that they refueled the airplane for free for the return journey and agreed to pay within forty-eight hours of delivery. Bank Melli's London branch transmitted the promise to refuel the aircraft.

Countries such as Poland, India, Brazil, Argentina, North Korea, and South Africa were among the most important arms suppliers to Iran, according to people knowledgeable about the trade. And many suppliers from these nations were paid through BCCI, according to Durrani, with the bank generally disguising the nature of the goods in an attempt to evade the arms embargoes. "You could get [BCCI officers] to word things any way that you wanted," said Durrani.

BCCI's biggest borrower — the Gokal family's Gulf Group — helped Iran in several ways. Mustapha Gokal, who now runs a financial company in Tehran, was a financial adviser to the Ayatollah Khomeini, according to a former BCCI official. The Gokals' companies were among the most important shippers and suppliers to Iran during its war with Iraq, supplying mostly nonmilitary goods, including foodstuffs and pharmaceuticals, but also war matériel and military clothing. A former manager of the Gokals' Karachi office said, "We did *everything* for Iran. *Everything.*"

Some arms merchants who used BCCI ran afoul of the law for selling to Iran. From a federal prison in Bridgeport, Connecticut, Durrani said that he used the bank to help finance his shipments of Hawk missiles and other hardware to Tehran. BCCI records show that its Los Angeles branch started financing his company in about 1984, although these documents, understandably, make no mention of Iran because of the U.S. embargo. When Durrani was arrested in 1986, BCCI's U.S. offices claimed ignorance. The bank's lawyer maintained in an internal memo that Durrani's company "deals in spare aviation parts sold to Argentina, Egypt, Pakistan etc." The hapless arms dealer — whose sister-in-law is related to some of Abedi's clique — was sentenced to ten years; he was scheduled to be released in the fall of 1992.

While in prison, Durrani struggled hard to link his own arms sales to the Iran-contra deals of the Reagan administration. He argued that he was only one part of a much wider campaign by the administration and the CIA to guarantee a stalemate in the Iran-Iraq war. Durrani now claims, for example, that his money helped bankroll a $10 million arms shipment arranged by Khashoggi through BCCI's Los Angeles office. The Los Angeles branch officer, Yacoub Wadawalla, said in 1991 that Durrani was indeed a valued client but declined to confirm his claim about the $10 million.

It is increasingly evident that there was significant arms trafficking to Tehran from the United States outside the Iran-contra transactions, such as that carried on by Durrani. For the moment, however, it remains unclear how much of this was sponsored by the U.S. government.

BCCI had no qualms about helping both sides in the Iran-Iraq war. The Iraqi dictator, Saddam Hussein, spent billions of dollars on arms during the 1980s. BCCI was involved in several deals, although the sums it lent were small in comparison with its substantial financing of trade with Iran. Records from BCCI's accountants at Price Waterhouse show that the bank was owed about $13 million by the Iraqi government in 1988 and 1989. Most of this money financed public works projects, including a major dam project, according to Durrani. Some of the loan proceeds, according to U.S. investigators, were used for a missile project.

Through its branch in Amman, Jordan, and its Swiss subsidiary, BCCI also financed merchants who supplied Iraq with arms and matériel. One of these, according to government investigators, was Wafai Dajani, a BCCI customer in Amman. That branch happened to be run by Fakhri Bilbeisi, whose brother Munther was also an arms dealer financed by BCCI. Before getting into that business, Dajani spent more than ten years in Saudi Arabia working for Ghaith Pharaon. Dajani has denied to U.S. investigators that he played an important role in supplying matériel to Iraq.

Iraq's favorite financier in the West was Italy's largest bank, the government-owned Banca Nazionale del Lavoro (BNL). During the late 1980s, BNL's Atlanta branch arranged for more than $4 billion in loans to Iraq, a staggering sum. As much as $1 billion of that money was used to finance a network of dummy companies that secretly acquired much of Iraq's military high technology.

When BNL's lending to Iraq was exposed by U.S. law enforcement authorities in 1989, bank officials in Rome claimed that the Atlanta branch manager, Christopher Drogoul, had orchestrated the entire lending spree without the approval of his superiors. In fact, however, further evidence has suggested that BNL executives were involved in the scheme and that officials of the Reagan and Bush administrations may have been aware of what was going on.

BCCI was involved in the BNL affair in a number of ways. Through its offices in the Cayman Islands, Luxembourg, and Switzerland, BCCI channeled kickbacks into bank accounts held for the Iraqi leadership. The money came from a 15 percent commission on BNL-sponsored loans transmitted through an account at a bank in Paris, Union de

Banques Arabes et Françaises. BCCI and BNL also did a substantial amount of foreign exchange and short-term deposit business, some of it through BNL's Atlanta branch. The Federal Reserve found that BCCI was one of many banks that lent money to BNL/Atlanta to fund it overnight; BCCI even took funds from its overseas branches so that it could increase its overnight lending to BNL. Investigators have thus speculated that there was "some larger arrangement between BNL and BCCI executives under which BCCI agreed to place funds in the U.S. for the specific purpose of lending them short-term to BNL." BCCI's Italian affiliate, Italfinance, also used BNL's treasury services for its own business.

BCCI was not alone in helping both sides in the Iran-Iraq war — so did the Reagan and Bush administrations. Most of the American aid to Iraq was in the form of government-guaranteed loans from such sources as the U.S. Export-Import Bank and the Department of Agriculture. A large portion of BNL's loans to Iraq was guaranteed by the Agriculture Department's Commodity Credit Corporation, which is supposed to finance exports of American agricultural goods. Nevertheless, some investigators suspect that money was diverted to the purchase of arms. (Of course, the whole concept of nonmilitary aid to such a militaristic state as Iraq is absurd, since it ignores the fact that money is fungible: every dollar provided to Iraq to import American food freed up one dollar to purchase arms.)

When BNL's lending to Iraq was exposed in 1989, it was a major political scandal in Italy, with front-page newspaper stories for months on end, parliamentary inquiries, and so on. The cost to the Italian taxpayer has been enormous. In its 1989 fiscal year, BNL reported a loss of $400 million, largely because of the Iraqi lending debacle.

In the United States, however, relatively little attention was paid to the affair for years, and the Bush administration certainly did not publicize it. After all, American taxpayers were stuck, since the government had guaranteed many of BNL's loans to Baghdad. Over the years, the Commodity Credit Corporation had guaranteed as much as $1.9 billion of the loans; when the FBI raided BNL's Atlanta branch in August 1989, about $750 million of these debts were still outstanding. More important, the weapons purchased by Saddam Hussein with BNL funds were used in the Gulf War of 1991 against American troops and their allies from Britain, France, Saudi Arabia, and other countries. It was not until February 1991 that the Justice Department secured the indictment of BNL's Christopher Drogoul and other defendants — one and a half years after the FBI began investigating the case. Through an odd coincidence, the indictment was announced just a few days after the Gulf War ended.

Congressman Henry Gonzalez of Texas, the chairman of the House Banking Committee, has been probing the BNL affair for years. He has alleged that officials of the Reagan and Bush administrations allowed Iraq to tap into U.S. government programs to finance its war machine. Gonzalez has singled out two Bush administration officials for supporting Iraq: Lawrence S. Eagleburger, the deputy secretary of state (and, since August 1992, the acting secretary), and Brent Scowcroft, the national security adviser. Before joining the Bush administration, both men had been employed by Kissinger Associates (Eagleburger as president), the consulting firm run by the former secretary of state. One client was BNL, and Scowcroft had been involved in advising the bank. Kissinger had other ties to people and organizations who were close to BCCI.

Kissinger's most notable foreign policy achievement during his years in the Nixon and Ford administrations was the U.S. rapprochement with China after decades of mutual hostility. To pave the way for normalization of relations, Kissinger traveled secretly to Peking in 1971. He received valuable assistance from the government of Pakistan, which has long enjoyed a special relationship with China. Before the trip, Kissinger sent diplomatic feelers to Peking through the Pakistani government. Once he was in China, Pakistani officials helped him fool journalists into thinking he was actually in Pakistan, recovering at a government guest house from a sudden illness.

Two of the Pakistanis involved were M. M. Ahmed, a senior foreign policy adviser to President Yahya Khan, and Sultan Mohammed Khan, the foreign secretary. Both men worked for BCCI in the 1980s as "consultants" to Abedi in the Washington, D.C., representative office. Kissinger also had dealings with Kamal Adham when, in the early 1970s, Egypt's Sadat used him as a "back channel" to send messages to Kissinger.

After Jimmy Carter became president in 1977, Kissinger launched his lucrative new career in the private sector as a consultant to multinational companies and banks. His clients have included American Express, Coca-Cola, Anheuser-Busch, H. J. Heinz, Volvo, ARCO, Hunt Oil, Chase Manhattan Bank, American International Group, and Freeport McMoran. In exchange for their fees, some clients have been able to gain access to some of the same foreign officials Kissinger dealt with in government service.

Kissinger hired other former government officials to work for his firm, including, as noted earlier, Brent Scowcroft and Lawrence Eagleburger. Scowcroft took time off to serve on a commission appointed by President Reagan and chaired by former Senator John Tower of Texas to investigate the Iran-contra affair. Much to the relief of George Bush, Reagan's vice president and heir apparent, the Tower Commission cleared him of misconduct.* When he became president in 1989, he nominated Tower to be secretary of defense (Tower failed to win Senate confirmation) and appointed Scowcroft national security adviser.

Another member of Kissinger Associates is Alan Stoga, an international economist who used to work for A. Robert Abboud, a banker with several links to the BCCI network. Abboud was the chairman of First National Bank of Chicago from 1975 to 1980, a period when the Chicago bank became the biggest single lender to Bert Lance, as noted in Chapter 3. BCCI arranged for that loan to be repaid in early 1978. Abboud then served as president of Occidental Petroleum, in which Ghaith Pharaon was an important stockholder. Its chairman, Armand Hammer, was a major investor in Financial General Bankshares. Hammer arranged the meeting in February 1978 at which Lance informed FGB's chairman and president that clients of BCCI controlled a large block of the company's stock. Later, Hammer tried to persuade FGB to agree to the takeover.

In 1988, a group of investors led by Abboud took over an ailing bank holding company in Houston called First City Bancorp of Texas; Abboud became chairman, a post he held until he was ousted in March 1991. While in charge, he provided financing to a Swiss company run by the Gokal family. Later, when BCCI ran into financial trouble and began to pare its international network, Abboud discussed buying some of its foreign offices, according to a former associate. Abboud says he doesn't recall the Gokal loan and denies discussing the purchase of BCCI's offices.

One country where the interests of Kissinger, Abboud, and BCCI intersected was Iraq. First City Bancorp was a lender to Iraq; more important, Abboud chaired an organization called the U.S.-Iraq Business Forum, which promoted business dealings between the two coun-

---

*Bush has maintained that he was "excluded from key meetings" at which the Iranian operation was discussed. In fact, he attended several such meetings.

tries. Stoga, of Kissinger Associates, took part in some of its activities. In June 1989, for example, he went to Baghdad as part of a Business Forum delegation and advised Saddam Hussein on international borrowing.

Kissinger's firm not only received consulting fees from BNL, Kissinger served as a member of the bank's international advisory board. He has striven mightily to distance himself from the BNL-Iraq scandal by pointing out that he left the board in February 1991, around the time of the indictment. Of course, this was long after the scandal exploded. And Kissinger did not totally sever his ties to the Italian bank. In June 1991, he gave a speech to the advisory board.

BCCI did not limit itself to procuring conventional weapons for its friends. There is mounting evidence that it was part of a scheme to obtain nuclear arms.

America's monopoly on nuclear weapons lasted only a few years after World War II. Other countries became nuclear powers, including the Soviet Union, Britain, France, and India. Pakistan's leaders were alarmed that this potent weapon was in the hands of India, their archenemy, and they decided that Pakistan needed nuclear weapons too. Another incentive was that the Muslim world lacked nuclear arms, although Israel had them. Thus, if Pakistan succeeded in developing a nuclear weapon, it would be the world's first "Islamic bomb."

Pakistan's nuclear project began in the early 1970s, when Zulfikar Ali Bhutto was in power. When his successor, General Zia, refused to halt the program, the United States, cut off economic and military aid in April 1979. But after the Soviet invasion of Afghanistan eight months later, such petty concerns were brushed aside by big-power politics.

BCCI soon became an instrument of the Zia regime, and there is evidence that the bank became involved in the Islamic bomb project. In the early 1980s, the late Anthony Mascarenhas, a journalist for the *Sunday Times* of London, began to investigate BCCI, as noted in Chapter 5. In the midst of his research, he was attacked by thugs and severely beaten. He told a friend that he had found evidence that BCCI was involved in procuring nuclear technology for Pakistan through a Liechtenstein shell company and that Libya was somehow involved.

The struggle to procure nuclear technology was something of a national obsession for Pakistan, involving many of its best-known politicians, some of whom were closely associated with BCCI. In 1984, Dr. Abdul Qader Khan, the man in charge of Pakistan's nuclear enrichment program, attributed its recent progress to "the personal interest and efforts" of President Zia, Finance Minister Ghulam Ishaq Khan, and their friends. Ishaq Khan, who has been president of Pakistan since 1988, spent years as the chairman of Abedi's BCC Foundation.

There is more recent and tangible evidence of BCCI's ties to this program. In July 1991, a retired Pakistani brigadier general, Inam ul-Haq, was arrested in Frankfurt, Germany, and the U.S. Justice Department sought his extradition for his alleged part in a scheme to smuggle metals out of North America for Pakistan's nuclear program. Investigators had also linked his procurement activities to BCCI's operation in Canada. Police there had discovered documents allegedly showing that ul-Haq had directed Arshad Pervez, a Canadian businessman of Pakistani origin, to acquire metals essential to producing nuclear weapons. Pervez was convicted in federal court in Philadelphia in 1987 on charges that he filed false documents as part of an attempt to export high-strength metal, so-called maraging 350 steel, used to manufacture weapons-grade uranium. (His conviction was overturned on appeal. In 1990, however, Pervez pleaded guilty in exchange for a reduction in his sentence to the time he had already served.)

BCCI allegedly helped to bankroll that purchase. Its senior officer in Canada, Omar Khan, said his bank was to have acted as the agent for the transaction because the Pakistani bank designated to handle the financing did not have a Canadian office.

Soon after news of ul-Haq's arrest leaked out in August 1991, a spokesman for Pakistan's foreign office denied that the retired general had any connection with the government, asserting that he was a private businessman. Ul-Haq's lawyer in Lahore said his client had gone to Germany for a routine business meeting and denied that he had anything to do with BCCI. In July 1992, however, ul-Haq was convicted in federal court in Philadelphia of conspiring to export maraging steel and beryllium. His lawyer filed an appeal in August.

Pakistan itself has denied being behind the scheme to buy the restricted materials and has often denied trying to build nuclear weapons. These denials are difficult to accept, however, since General Zia openly admitted his country's nuclear program. In an interview with *Time* magazine in March 1987, he said, "Pakistan has the capability of building the bomb. You can write today that Pakistan can build a bomb whenever it wishes."

.　　.　　.

From the days of the Arab oil embargo, the Saudis and other Gulf Arabs have railed at the Western media's coverage of the Middle East, and who can blame them? Western news organizations have often stereotyped Arabs, portraying them in editorial cartoons as camel-jockeys in headdresses malevolently withholding gasoline supplies from the West. But the Arab world has likewise stereotyped the media organizations of the West, convinced that the television and newspaper newsrooms in Washington and New York are in the grip of Zionists. As a result, Arab governments have often tried to use their political and financial clout to influence coverage of the Middle East.

Well-connected public relations men were hired, costly advertising supplements were placed in news magazines, reporters and editors were wooed with gifts and junkets, and occasionally outright intimidation was employed. In one notorious incident, Saudi Arabia threatened Western governments with retaliation if TV stations dared to broadcast *Death of a Princess,* a 1980 "docudrama" that depicted the treatment of a Saudi woman caught cheating on her husband. (She was publicly shot and her lover was beheaded in a car park in Riyadh.)

Outright infiltration of the Western media has long been suspected — and occasionally proved. Britain's *TV-AM,* the equivalent of America's *Today* show, was produced by a company chaired by Jonathan Aitken, a Conservative member of Parliament. In a parliamentary disclosure statement, Aitken said he was a director of a company that "receives payments from contracts with Saudi Arabian royal family interests and government agencies." One of King Fahd's sons, Prince Mohammed, became a secret investor in *TV-AM* in the early 1980s, according to a report in London's *Independent* newspaper.

In the United States, a group of BCCI insiders managed to develop very close ties to the men in charge of one of the country's most important media conglomerates: Tele-Communications Inc. (TCI). Although it is not a household name like CBS or Time Warner, it is a vast and powerful enterprise. TCI holds stakes in four of the largest cable channels in the country. It serves one of every five American households wired for cable TV. It also owns one of the country's largest chains of movie theaters. Through this long-secret relationship, the Saudis have even brought themselves close to — perhaps directly into — an ownership position in Ted Turner's Cable News Network (CNN). At the center of this scheme was a group of Saudi intelligence operatives with intimate ties to both BCCI and the CIA.

TCI was founded and remains headed by the visionary Bob Magness, a stubby, rough-cut Oklahoman who likes to chomp cigars. Beginning in 1956 with a grubstake raised from selling cattle, Magness formed a small cable television company in Texas. Twelve years later, he founded TCI. It eventually became the giant of the industry. With its affiliated companies, Liberty Media Corporation and West Marc Communications (also controlled by Magness and his close colleagues), TCI operates cable television systems in forty-eight states and has huge investments in microwave routes for transmitting pictures and information round the country. It produces revenues of about $4 billion a year, generating a cash flow of $1.7 billion. It was estimated in early 1992 that TCI would fetch as much as $15 billion in a takeover.

Magness's protégé Larry Romrell is a senior vice president of both TCI and West Marc, which manages the microwave routes that carry signals for cable television. Romrell, who was brought up in a church orphanage, sees Magness as the father he never had, by some accounts. He has spent his whole career working for Magness at TCI and its related companies.

Among Romrell's varied assignments on his way to his current post was a stint in Saudi Arabia in the 1970s. There Romrell met an American defense specialist named Kerry Fox, who was representing Martin Marietta and Rockwell International. There is some speculation that Fox was a CIA asset. "Kerry Fox either is agency or is connected to the agency," said a former senior Treasury official who dealt extensively with Saudi Arabia during his time in that department. (Fox declined requests for interviews.)

One of the Saudis with whom Fox became acquainted was Abdul-Raouf Khalil, who worked closely with Kamal Adham. Khalil's background in electronics and communications put him on the same technological wavelength as Fox. Khalil was the owner of Saudi Security & Technical Services Company, a firm founded in 1978 that advertises itself as an insurance company but is believed to provide electronic and computer equipment to the government of Saudi Arabia for its intelligence operations. (In 1991, when U.S. prosecutors needed to reach Khalil, they found they could most easily contact him through the offices of the CIA station chief in Saudi Arabia.)

In the summer of 1981, some years after Fox and Khalil became acquainted, Khalil traveled to the cool mountains of Colorado. Fox himself enjoyed going there in the summer, and this year his friend

Romrell from TCI was also vacationing in the mountains. The three men met, became friendly, and began doing real estate deals together. Khalil decided to back three investments: in Rockwall, Texas; Vail, Colorado; and New Smyrna Beach, Florida. Romrell and Fox managed the properties on Khalil's behalf and could use them. They later sold the house in Vail at a profit to Dr. Charles Howard of Houston North West Medical Center, a longtime associate of Khalil's. Fox also held a power of attorney for Khalil to acquire property for him in Florida.

By doing business with Khalil, Magness and Romrell came into BCCI's orbit. In the 1980s, the two men — apparently acting as nominees for Khalil — borrowed millions of dollars through three accounts at BCCI's Cayman Islands bank to finance real estate investments in Colorado and to cover interest costs associated with the borrowings, according to a report compiled by British investigating lawyers.

Khalil, meanwhile, was setting up another venture in London: Capcom Financial Services, a BCCI affiliate that would trade in commodity futures and options. Capcom was launched in 1984, and two years later BCCI's former treasury department chief, Syed Ziauddin Ali Akbar, became the head of the firm. Tens of millions of dollars would ultimately disappear from Capcom. Some of the evidence suggests that that money was used by BCCI insiders and Saudi intelligence operatives to penetrate American communications companies.

In February 1984, Romrell wrote to Akbar expressing his willingness to get involved in the new commodity trading firm. "Magness and I have discussed your proposal to invest in a U.S. brokerage firm in Chicago or New York," he wrote, "and to participate in the ownership and operation to the mutual benefit of BCCI and ourselves." Thus did Magness and Romrell became stockholders in Capcom, which was connected to BCCI in a multitude of ways.

Capcom got most of its business from BCCI, trading futures, options, and foreign exchange with the bank. The head of the firm, Akbar, was not only a BCCI alumnus, he was related by marriage to Swaleh Naqvi. Capcom's three biggest shareholders owned stock in BCCI and First American: Kamal Adham, Sayed Jawhary (Adham's business manager), and, of course, Khalil. Capcom's records later showed that Adham owned 17 percent of Capcom, Jawhary 15 percent, and Khalil 30 percent, making him the biggest shareholder. Another shareholder was an American named Robert E. Powell, a longtime associate of Adham's who ran an aircraft supply business in Southeast Asia during the Vietnam War. Powell now spends much of his time in Oman running Global Chemical Systems, a business that was set up in Saudi Arabia by Adham.

Romrell purchased his Capcom shares mostly with money borrowed from BCCI; a note to Romrell's file in November 1984 indicates that BCCI lent him $75,000 to buy the stock. Magness and Romrell later acquired stakes of 4 and 16 percent, respectively, in Capcom's commodities brokerage subsidiary in Chicago, according to company documents.

The cable television tycoons were not only important stockholders in Capcom, they held senior positions in the company. Romrell became Capcom's chairman; Magness sat on the board of directors. Even more important, the two TCI executives also looked to BCCI for capital.

Romrell wrote to Akbar in November 1984 saying that Magness had asked him "to determine whether there would be any interest on the part of BCCI" in providing loans to TCI and an affiliate. TCI, he explained, was "looking for around $200 million" and the affiliate "approximately $50 million to construct a new microwave route." He added, "There may be an opportunity to put this deal together with BCCI if you are interested."

BCCI may have already been a significant shareholder in TCI, according to government investigators. Akbar seems to have been, and he may have been fronting for BCCI or its Saudi backers. When Western Tele-Communications (WTCI), the microwave subsidiary, began trading independently on U.S. markets, Romrell discussed a $100,000 credit line from BCCI to purchase shares in Akbar's behalf — and an additional $100,000 credit line to purchase shares for himself. The stock offering was a tremendous success, with the price of the stock surging after the offering to the public — and with Romrell and Akbar apparently sharing in the riches. Romrell has denied that the investments went ahead.

These alleged stock purchases were apparently being made from London, raising questions about whether the purchasers fully reported the trading they had carried out; company directors are required to report insider transactions to the SEC, and failure to do so is a serious violation of U.S. securities law. Romrell even sent Akbar information intended for distribution to TCI's shareholders, suggesting that Akbar or Capcom owned shares in the parent company.

The TCI executives discussed a bewildering range of prospective investments with BCCI, including a proposal for a $90 million investment in Houston North West Medical Center, with BCCI providing half the funds, Magness and Romrell a quarter, and the center's doctors the remaining quarter. Other proposed investments included a $220,000 joint purchase of Stouffers Inn in Denver.

Their friends and associates also benefited. Romrell arranged for a friend to borrow $525,000 from Capcom to invest in a land deal in Phoenix, according to investigators. There was also contact with other entities connected to BCCI; in April 1988 Romrell made plans with Akbar to visit Independence Bank in Los Angeles, a BCCI satellite owned by Ghaith Pharaon.

There was also a clear understanding that the American executives would function as nominees for Khalil, Adham, Jawhary, and Akbar. In a 1987 letter, Romrell wrote: "As far as I personally am concerned . . . I have acted as nominee for one or more of the original shareholders" — meaning the Saudi investors. What earthly reason would Capcom or BCCI have to call on a couple of cable television executives to function as "nominees" for them? Romrell answered the question himself. At the time Capcom was active on the Chicago commodity market, and the Chicago Board of Trade was beginning to look askance at the company's offshore shareholders. Romrell wrote a letter explaining that he and Magness were all too happy to help Capcom "meet the needs of the Chicago Board of Trade." He added that "it was understood by the reorganized shareholders that they were nominees for the original shareholders."

As nominees for BCCI and its backers, Magness and Romrell received substantial financial benefits from the bank — the ones that BCCI commonly offered its nominees: no-risk loans secured by stock purchased in their names or so-called subordinated loans of stock. If the value of the stock fell, there would be no risk to Magness and Romrell. But if it rose, they would benefit. In addition, their loans were self-liquidating and would be paid off with funds paid into their loan accounts from profits on their own "managed investment" accounts, maintained by Capcom's Akbar. Although it was circuitously transported through shell companies in Panama and other far-flung money-laundering centers, this money, it would later turn out, came straight out of Capcom's coffers. BCCI was effectively giving Magness and Romrell the stock they held in Capcom.

One strange Capcom venture was the Capital Fund, an open-end investment fund established in the Cayman Islands in late 1985. Its stated purpose was to buy stocks, bonds, metals, options, and commodities. Though it was dressed up to look like a third-party investment fund, it was actually a vehicle controlled by Akbar. The shareholders in the $10 million fund included five members of the Adham family, four members of the Jawhary family, and entities controlled by Akbar. Together, the Akbar and Adham groups owned 90 percent of the fund's capital, but it was controlled primarily by Akbar — joined by Romrell's pal Kerry Fox, as fund manager. Through "matched" and "back to back" transactions and "artificial profits," an estimated $3.3 million was skimmed into the fund from at least seventeen accounts, according to an investigator.

At the time, Fox was president of American Telecommunications Corporation (ATC), a firm in Texas which counted Akbar as one of its directors. ATC went on to buy stock in U.S. Telephone, a provider of long-distance telephone lines on the West Coast. Fox tapped into his friends at Capcom and BCCI to fund a series of acquisitions, including the U.S. Telephone deal. In the fiscal year ending June 30, 1989, ATC's net sales totaled $12.5 million, up from $5.5 million the previous year.

But ATC was suffering from serious cash flow problems, and Fox turned to his friends for help. Writing to Akbar in May 1988, he asked for "another emergency loan" of $250,000 for ATC, saying that he had "nowhere else to turn" and that he faced "a near-term but critical cash flow problem." As for the longer term, Fox said he could probably use financing of between $2 million and $3 million from Akbar. Through two shell companies, Akbar even bought stock in ATC; investigators have seen indications that Kamal Adham, through Fox, also participated in grabbing a piece of the U.S. telecommunications industry.

In 1988, Khalil suddenly pulled out of Capcom, selling his entire stake to Akbar for £4 million (about $6.5 million) plus forgiveness of a substantial debt. Khalil's timing was impeccable; the U.S. government was investigating BCCI and Capcom at that time — raising the possibility that Khalil was tipped off by some American friends, perhaps his contacts in the CIA. As one investigator put it, "They knew the game was over, so they're cleaning up Khalil's act."*

By that time, TCI and its affiliates already dominated the U.S. cable industry. They owned large stakes in several of the leading cable channels, including the Discovery Channel and the Black Entertainment

---

*In a lengthy statement, Khalil maintains that he was duped by Akbar and BCCI and that they frequently used his name without his knowledge.

Network, not to mention the franchise to provide programming to millions of Americans. TCI would go on to acquire United Artists, making it a leading exhibitor of movies in the United States.

TCI's sales had grown at an average of almost 40 percent a year, to total more than $3 billion in 1989, up from only $181 million in 1981. The TCI stock price catapulted from $1.53 a share in 1981 to $17.88 in 1989, offering investors great returns on their money and boosting the fortunes of Magness and Romrell.

In late 1988, when BCCI and Capcom were charged with criminal offenses, Magness and Romrell resigned from Capcom, but they continued their contact with BCCI. They met with BCCI's executives in December 1990 to try to resolve the extensive real estate borrowings in which they were involved. But as of the summer of 1991, nothing had happened as a result of this meeting, and BCCI still had as much as $4 million in delinquent loans and overdue interest to these accounts.

Magness told Senate investigators that he lost every penny of the $90,000 he said he invested in Capcom and maintained that he was offered no inducements by the company and transacted no business with it. "I was just plain defrauded," he wrote in May 1992. Romrell told investigators that he was humiliated by his association with Capcom and BCCI. TCI, for its part, denied that it was connected with BCCI or Capcom.

The links that Capcom and BCCI forged with two of the country's most powerful cable television executives — and with Fox, a veteran of the defense industry — certainly look like more than just mutual interest in good business opportunities. Khalil and Adham — associates of both Saudi intelligence and the CIA — and Akbar and their allies at BCCI, certainly seemed to go out of their way to ingratiate themselves with Magness and Romrell, providing the two executives with juicy financial opportunities. Two of the most important men in Saudi Arabia deliberately sought and built a long-term relationship with TCI and its affiliates, a venture that clearly was becoming a major force in programming and channeling information into American living rooms.

Just as Khalil, Adham, and BCCI provided vital capital to the men in charge of TCI at a critical time in its development, TCI engineered the rescue of Ted Turner's cable television business. In the mid-1980s, Turner was desperately short of capital and on the verge of bankruptcy. In 1987, TCI's president, a Magness protégé named John

Malone, orchestrated a $560 million rescue of Turner's company. TCI wound up as the owner of 25 percent of Turner Broadcasting System and its main cable subsidiaries — including, of course, CNN, which would soon become one of the most influential news outlets in the world.

Were BCCI and its friends in Saudi intelligence behind the bailout of Turner Broadcasting? If so, were they seeking to influence public opinion in the United States and the other countries where CNN operates? It is also worth asking whether the CIA was aware of what was going on. It is hard to imagine that America's leading intelligence agency would be oblivious of an investment in such a sensitive industry by foreign intelligence operatives. It is more likely that the CIA simply looked the other way because of its own cozy relationship with Adham and company. After all, the CIA had done nothing to hinder the takeover of First American.

Although Turner declines to comment, there is no denying that the men in charge of TCI, the rescuer of his company, had intimate links with BCCI. There were other intriguing relationships as well. Turner, whose business is based in Atlanta, is very close to one of BCCI's most important American allies, Jimmy Carter. In 1986, Abedi, Carter, and Turner all attended the conference in Peking held by BCCI's *South* magazine, according to a BCCI official.

CNN also had a questionable relationship with Robert Gray, the lobbyist who served on the board of First American's Washington bank and who was close to the CIA. In the mid-1980s, Gray's firm arranged for CNN to broadcast programs on behalf of foreign clients, and the network did not (as the law requires) warn its viewers that this was anything other than the product of independent journalists. In March 1985, for example, CNN broadcast an "exclusive interview" with King Hassan II of Morocco which was essentially a video press release: the Moroccan government was a client of Gray's and the interviewer worked for him, not CNN. After the *Washington Post* reported the incident, a CNN official denied knowing that the material had originated with Gray's firm.

But this was not an isolated incident, according to Susan Trento, the author of a book on Gray. CNN also had a secret arrangement to run programs on behalf of another foreign client of Gray's, the Japan Center for Information and Cultural Affairs (JCIC), a government agency. The JCIC paid fees to both CNN and Gray's firm. "According to Gray and Company executives," writes Trento, "CNN was broadcasting pure propaganda, produced and paid for by a foreign country, to unsuspecting Americans and reporting it to no one."

The full story of BCCI's relationship with the intelligence agencies of the Middle East and the West will probably never be known. But there is little doubt that the CIA was intimately involved with BCCI, that it knew about the bank's illegal activities for years, and that it did little to stop them.

One man who became aware of the BCCI-CIA relationship was Norman Bailey, a senior member of President Reagan's NSC staff. Bailey has recalled that "very early on in 1981, after I joined the staff at the National Security Council, I began to see the name of BCCI on a number of different documents." It became clear to him that the bank was involved in a wide range of illegal activities, including "terrorist activities, gun running, guerrilla movements, technology-transfer violations, embargo-and-boycott violations, things of that kind." The CIA, according to Bailey, "used the BCCI for certain of its payments, and obviously doing that would make them less than totally favorable to blowing the BCCI cover."

The CIA may have had another reason for turning a blind eye to the activities of its Saudi friends. William Casey and other Reagan administration officials frequently asked the Saudi government to provide financial assistance for covert operations in Afghanistan and other parts of the world. It was a convenient arrangement for both sides. When the Saudis provided the funding, the administration was able to bypass Congress. The Saudis benefited by earning goodwill from the American officials who provided them with arms and military protection.

But where did the Saudis get all this money? Until the early 1980s, Saudi Arabia was flush with cash, but then oil prices dropped sharply, causing the kingdom's revenues to plummet. New sources of money had to be found. It was precisely at this time that millions of dollars were drained out of BCCI through accounts at Capcom that had been opened in the names of Kamal Adham and Abdul-Raouf Khalil, both of whom were associated with Saudi intelligence and the CIA. Over the years, even more money would disappear from the coffers of BCCI and other financial institutions connected to the Saudis. A number of investigators strongly suspect that some of the stolen money was used to fund covert operations sponsored by the U.S. government.

This theory is certainly consistent with what we know about Casey.

When Oliver North appeared before the Iran-Contra Committee, he testified that Casey used to say he wanted to find a way to finance covert operations without having to turn to Congress. Casey wanted to create a "self-financing" entity that would be "independent of appropriated monies." It would be an "off-the-shelf, self-sustaining, stand-alone entity that could perform certain activities on behalf of the United States," said North. "Some of those [operations] were to be conducted jointly by other friendly intelligence services, but they needed money."

7

THE DIRTY MONEY
MACHINE

AGHA HASAN ABEDI SPOKE OFTEN about moral and spiritual values, sounding more like a religious leader than a banker. In interviews, speeches, and articles in BCCI's staff magazine, he would expound on subjects like love, hope, and tolerance. BCCI was not simply a profitmaking enterprise, according to Abedi; it had a higher calling. "We serve a purpose for society and humanity at large, absolutely without any consideration or bias toward caste, creed, color, religion, or race," he once said. "This is the distinction between us and other business institutions." On another occasion he said, "Purity and chastity is the key to our management at BCCI." Masihur Rahman, BCCI's longtime chief financial officer, recalls that Abedi would frequently caution his lieutenants always to bear in mind "the moral balance sheet" as well as "the material balance sheet."

BCCI's "moral dimension," according to Abedi, was closely related to its identity as a Third World bank. He and other officials portrayed BCCI as an institution dedicated to the best interests of people in the world's poorest nations. This rhetoric struck a chord with many people in developing countries. Huge portions of the Middle East, Africa, and Asia had been colonies until recently, and there was widespread resentment of "First World" institutions. Most foreign banks that did business in Africa and the Middle East were run by white men — many of them from the former colonial powers of Britain and France. These banks were widely regarded as exploitative, neoimperialistic institutions that sucked the wealth out of former colonies. BCCI, by contrast, was run by dark-skinned people who had lived under colonialism and who could be expected to have some sympathy for the problems of developing countries. If anyone doubted BCCI's commitment to morality and Third World development, Abedi could point to the millions of dollars the bank gave to such causes as the Third World Foundation, the BCC Foundation in Pakistan, and Jimmy Carter's Global 2000. BCCI wasn't merely a commercial bank, it was a philanthropy!

The beautiful rhetoric masked an ugly reality. BCCI did indeed operate on a different moral plane from other banks — a much lower one. Abedi was willing to do virtually anything to accumulate power and wealth. Perhaps the most extreme example of his hypocrisy concerns the bank's conduct in developing countries. Far from helping these nations, BCCI exacerbated some of their most serious problems, including poverty, repression, crime, and corruption.

Until the Pakistani civil war of 1971, the country was divided into two pieces — West Pakistan and East Pakistan — separated by a thousand miles of Indian territory. During the civil war, East Pakistan broke away and became the new nation of Bangladesh. Ever since, Bangladesh has suffered from grinding poverty. On just about every indicator of underdevelopment, it ranks near the bottom, including per capita income (about $150 per year) and infant mortality (13 of every 100 babies die before their first birthday).

One reason for Bangladesh's poverty is overpopulation; it is one of the most densely populated countries in the world. Natural disasters have played a part: floods killed about a half-million people in 1975 and 130,000 in 1991. The country has also suffered from terrible misrule. The longest-serving autocrat was Lieutenant General Hussain Mohammed Ershad, who came to power in a 1982 military coup and ruled until a popular uprising forced him to resign in December 1990. (An elected government took office early the following year.)

Ershad's reign was characterized by political repression and appalling corruption. While people starved, Ershad enjoyed a life of luxury. According to one report, when Bangladeshi police raided his home, "they found among other items $500,000 in cash hidden in trunks, 40 bottles of Chanel cologne for men, 134 neckties, 62 bottles of Scotch whisky, golf clubs, a big-screen television and a silver tea set studded with emeralds." The new civilian government believed that Ershad and his associates accumulated several hundred million dollars by demanding kickbacks from businessmen and by diverting funds from foreign aid programs.

In the plundering of his country, Ershad received a great deal of assistance from BCCI, according to Bangladeshi authorities. BCCI, they say, helped him stash huge sums of money in foreign dummy companies and secret bank accounts. "This bank, this BCCI, was a smuggler's paradise," said Attorney General Aminul Haq. "They were the bankers of all the smugglers and the corrupt people here. . . . Of course they helped ruin us."

General Ershad has been labeled a strongman, autocrat, and despot, but a more fitting term is "kleptocrat." Under Ershad, Bangladesh was a kleptocracy — a regime whose principal purpose was to enrich the ruler.

Kleptocracy has flourished in the Third World during the last few decades, partly because of huge new flows of funds. The 1973 oil shock created overnight millionaires and billionaires in such countries as Saudi Arabia, Iran, Kuwait, and the UAE. In each of these states, a large portion of the revenue was skimmed off by members of the ruling families. In addition, politically connected middlemen fattened their bank accounts by taking "commissions" from foreign companies. These practices were not confined to the Middle East; graft was rampant in oil-producing states elsewhere in the world, including Mexico, Indonesia, Nigeria, and Venezuela.

The Third World lending boom that followed the oil shock created more opportunities for corruption. Between 1972 and 1982, the foreign debts of developing countries soared from $300 billion to $750 billion. Much of the money was used for grandiose projects whose main purpose was to enable government officials to enrich themselves through kickbacks.

The drug trade has also stimulated corruption in parts of Asia and Latin America, with traffickers buying immunity with bribes. In one of the most brazen examples, military men backed by Bolivia's cocaine kingpins actually seized control of the government in 1980 in what became known as the "cocaine coup."

Corruption has been a major scourge in the Third World, contributing to political upheavals, economic dislocation, and crime. For BCCI, it was a business opportunity, since kleptocrats were a huge potential source of deposits. BCCI was not the only international bank that collected money from corrupt politicians, to be sure. But it stands out because of the number of kleptocrats on its client list, including Ferdinand Marcos of the Philippines, Saddam Hussein of Iraq, Manuel Antonio Noriega of Panama, Samuel Doe of Liberia, and a vast number of Persian Gulf oil sheikhs. BCCI also stands out because of the intimate relationships it enjoyed with many of these officials. In some cases, BCCI helped officials enrich themselves in the first place by paying bribes and participating in frauds. In so doing, it became a chief accomplice in the looting of the Third World.

Abedi began collecting money from a Third World despot long before BCCI was even founded. In the 1960s, he persuaded Sheikh Zayed to deposit some of his wealth in United Bank, the Pakistani bank Abedi headed. When BCCI was founded in 1972, Zayed became the bank's most important backer and its biggest depositor. Abedi also helped to manage the ruler's wealth.

Several Arab middlemen who profited from their political connections had close ties to BCCI, as we have seen, including Kamal Adham, Ghaith Pharaon, and Adnan Khashoggi. In non-Arab Iran, where the shah accumulated a huge fortune after the oil shock, a brother of the ruler held stock in BCCI.

The fall of the Iranian monarch in 1979 turned out to be a boon for BCCI. It led to the so-called second oil shock — a new surge in petroleum prices — which added to the wealth of Sheikh Zayed and other BCCI customers. They would deposit much of this money in BCCI. It also touched off a flight of capital from the Middle East, with some of the money flowing to BCCI branches outside the region. When war broke out between Iran and Iraq in 1980, BCCI cashed in by financing arms deals for both sides, as we have seen. BCCI also collected loot from Iraq's ruler, Saddam Hussein.

Not long after the Iran-Iraq war ended in 1988, Saddam turned against a "brother" Arab state that had been one of his biggest financial backers: in August 1990, thousands of Iraqi troops poured into Kuwait. During the occupation, they carted off a staggering amount of booty, including furniture, hospital equipment, and valuable artworks. They were not warriors but plunderers. The Kuwaiti authorities suspected that much of this wealth went to the family of Saddam Hussein.

In early 1991, Saddam's forces were expelled from Kuwait by foreign military forces led by the United States. Kuwait hired Kroll Associates, a private investigative firm in New York, to hunt for the concealed foreign assets of the Iraqi regime and Saddam's family. Kroll's operatives soon found evidence that Saddam had hidden huge sums of money abroad, both to enrich himself and to enable his country to evade international sanctions. The investigators believed that Saddam's family had accumulated between $10 billion and $15 billion in liquid assets abroad. Much of it was held in accounts at more than forty foreign banks, according to the investigation, and some of the biggest deposits were in BCCI. Jules Kroll, the head of the firm, called BCCI "one of the more prominent banks in handling Iraqi money."

While Saddam Hussein was battling Iran, another despot close to BCCI was consolidating his grip on power in Pakistan. General Mohammed Zia-ul-Haq, who seized power in 1977, was an austere and remote figure, a person who commanded respect and fear but not affection. In official photographs, he looked something like a British military commander of World War I vintage, with a center part in his slicked-down hair and a clipped regimental mustache. Religion had as much to do with Zia's style as his military background. He was a devout Muslim with puritanical instincts, and he tried to impose conservative Islamic norms on his countrymen.

Zia's image contrasted sharply with the corruption that flourished in his regime. During the 1980s, large numbers of government officials and military men became millionaires by stealing American aid dollars and taking bribes from drug traffickers. Pakistan's Inter-Services Intelligence agency (ISI), which acted as a conduit for American aid to the Afghan rebels, was riddled with corruption. For example, a former BCCI official with high-level connections to the Pakistani government recalls that some of the American aid money was used to pay for heavy-duty trucks to transport weapons to the mujaheddin. "Half the trucks never got there," says this source. "A hell of a lot went to Iran for cash."

The war in Afghanistan coincided with an upsurge in drug trafficking in Pakistan. Parts of Pakistan, Afghanistan, and Iran comprise the so-called Golden Crescent, the world's second-ranking opium-producing region (after Southeast Asia's Golden Triangle). Before 1979, Pakistan was not a major exporter of drugs. After the Iranian revolution that year, the Khomeini regime cracked down on the opium trade, and Iran was quickly overtaken in importance by the other Golden Crescent countries. In 1984, it was estimated that 80 percent of all the heroin consumed in Britain and 30 percent of American imports came from Pakistan. In 1988, the State Department estimated that Pakistan produced up to 9 percent of the world's opium, adding that it was also the main transit country for opium from Afghanistan, the world's second-largest producer (after Burma). The amounts of money involved were staggering. In the late 1980s, Pakistan's drug revenues were estimated at between $8 billion and $10 billion, equivalent to one quarter of the country's gross domestic product.

The drug trade was closely connected with the Afghan war. Some of the rebel groups supported themselves by selling opium, and a number of Pakistani officials who worked with them provided protection to drug traffickers in exchange for payoffs. BCCI, with its intimate links to Pakistani officialdom, was ideally placed to handle their loot. Referring to stolen aid dollars, a former BCCI official says, "A lot of this money was being funneled by these generals into BCCI." Abedi's bank also laundered money from the drug trade. One of the most popular laundering centers was the UAE, where BCCI was the dominant foreign bank.

One high-ranking official involved with the Afghan resistance and — allegedly — the drug trade was Lieutenant General Fazle Haq (sometimes spelled Huq), who served as military governor of the Northwest Frontier Province, which borders Afghanistan. According to Alfred McCoy, an authority on the heroin trade, mujaheddin rebels "brought the opium across the border [and then] sold it to Pakistani heroin refiners who operated under the protection of General Fazle Huq." Many Pakistanis referred to Haq as "our own Noriega," according to Lawrence Lifschultz, a former correspondent in Pakistan for the *Far Eastern Economic Review* who has done extensive research on the Golden Crescent drug trade. The general, of course, denied any wrongdoing, but he also boasted that he was so close to President Zia that he "could get away with blue murder."

Fazle Haq was also close to Abedi. Both were key advisers to Zia, notes a former BCCI official, and the three men met frequently. "When Abedi would have dinner with Zia," says this source, "Fazle Haq was [often] there."

After Zia's death in 1988, Benazir Bhutto — the daughter of the man Zia had overthrown and executed — became prime minister in a free election. Unlike Zia, she took a tough line against drug traffickers. "When Zia went down," says Lifschultz, "many of the top people in the 'heroin circle' went down." In 1989, for example, Pakistani authorities arrested an air force officer with ties to General Zia on charges of smuggling heroin. He was suspected of laundering drug money with the help of a BCCI officer in Dubai, the second most important sheikdom in the UAE.

Benazir Bhutto was forced out of office in August 1990 by President

Ghulam Ishaq Khan, a high-ranking official in the Zia regime and an associate of Abedi's. (As noted above, Ishaq Khan had been chairman of Abedi's BCC Foundation.) In Bhutto's place, the president installed Nawaz Sharif, who also had ties to BCCI. In the 1970s, Sharif's family had launched a steel plant in the UAE with substantial financial backing from BCCI, according to a former associate. "BCCI," said Benazir Bhutto, "has connections to all the Zia cronies who ousted my government."

Haq, the reputed Noriega of Pakistan, was never prosecuted on drug charges. He was, however, arrested for the 1988 murder of a prominent Shi'ite cleric named Arif Husseini but was later released. In October 1991, Haq was assassinated in what was thought to be revenge for Husseini's death. He was hailed by Prime Minister Sharif as "a great soldier and a competent administrator who played a commendable role in national progress." With the death of Fazle Haq, the prime minister said, "the nation has lost a true patriot."

Nigeria, where BCCI had one of its largest operations, is by far the biggest country in black Africa, with about 100 million people. It is also endowed with vast petroleum reserves, making it one of the world's leading oil exporters. One other fact should be added to the list: corruption pervades Nigerian society. In a discussion of bribery, a senior government official once said, "The evil exists in every facet of society. You bribe to get your child into school; you pay to secure a job and also continue to pay in some cases to retain it; you pay 10 percent of any contract obtained; you dash [bribe] the tax officer to avoid paying taxes; you pay a hospital doctor or nurse to get proper attention; you pay the policeman to evade arrest. This catalogue of shame can continue without end."

The scale of the corruption grew enormously after the oil shocks of the 1970s. Officials not only took kickbacks from foreign oil companies, they sometimes stole the oil itself. Nigerian crude would be loaded onto tankers with no bill of lading issued, making it possible to sell the cargo abroad and pocket the entire proceeds. According to one estimate, 20 percent of the country's oil revenues from 1979 to 1983 were diverted through smuggling and fraud. (Some of the oil was smuggled to South Africa, in spite of Nigeria's role as a prominent critic of apartheid.) In 1983 alone, according to the former oil minister Tam David-West, $1 billion worth of petroleum was stolen.

This oil wealth enabled Nigeria to borrow heavily from foreign banks and from such "official" sources as export credit agencies. Between 1979 and 1983, its foreign debt soared from about $2 billion to more than $14 billion. Much of this money was squandered on white elephant projects and stolen by corrupt officials and their cronies. Nigeria, in short, seemed to be a country made for BCCI.

BCCI arrived in 1979 with a 40 percent–owned subsidiary called Bank of Credit and Commerce International (Nigeria) Limited. (Foreigners were forbidden to own more than 40 percent of a Nigerian bank.) The rest of the stock was held by local investors, including Ibrahim Dasuki, a wealthy businessman from the state of Sokoto who was also chairman of the bank. He was very close to General Ibrahim Babangida, who seized power in August 1985 in a coup d'état and then became president. Dasuki was frequently described as the president's "political godfather." His son Sambo served for a time as General Babangida's aide-de-camp.

One important indication of Dasuki's stature with the regime is an incident that occurred in 1988. On November 1 of that year, the sultan of Sokoto — the spiritual leader of Nigeria's large Muslim community — died. Two days later, it was announced that Muhammadu Maccido, his son, would succeed him. Although the choice was widely supported within the Muslim community, the government reversed the decision and named Dasuki as the new sultan. The decision touched off two days of riots in Sokoto, in which at least ten people died. Protesters also set fire to a building owned by Dasuki which happened to house a BCCI branch.

Most foreign banks found the Nigerian market disappointing because they had problems getting permission to convert profits from naira — the local currency — to hard currency and remit the money to their head offices. "You can make a lot of money," said a European banker, "but if you cannot get it out there is no point." Another problem affecting several foreign banks concerned technical service agreements (TSAs). When a TSA had been signed, the Nigerian subsidiary was supposed to be able to remit hard currency to the parent bank to pay for various services — auditing, computer work, and so on. If the Nigerian authorities blocked TSA payments — which was often the case — foreign banks could lose a great deal of money. Because of these and other problems, a number of international banks pulled out of Nigeria while others reduced their stakes in local banks.

At the same time, however, BCCI was expanding. "They were opening branches everyplace," said a French banker. By the end of 1987, BCCI had thirty-three branches in Nigeria, more than in any other country except Britain and Oman (where it operated a joint venture bank called the National Bank of Oman). Its total assets had reached $584 million.

Officials at other international banks could not explain why BCCI was just about the only foreign bank flourishing in Nigeria, but they did have some theories. It was widely suspected that BCCI's political connections helped it to obtain permission to move money out of the country. The main secret of BCCI's success was exposed in 1991: for years, the bank made huge profits illegally by converting naira to dollars and channeling the money abroad. Between 1985 and 1987, the illegal profits totaled between $150 million and $200 million. The fraud was believed to have started as early as 1982.

While BCCI — as an institution — was defrauding Nigeria, several employees ran their own free-lance scams, taking kickbacks from borrowers or engaging in black market currency dealings. "I had people working for me — Pakistani employees — who were rich," recalls a former executive of BCCI who was based in Europe. "They had made personal wealth in Nigeria." In fact, while officials at other foreign banks regarded Nigeria as a hardship post, many BCCI officials pleaded for a chance to work there. Abedi was not at all disturbed that his employees were lining their pockets this way, according to another BCCI veteran. When Abedi was told that an employee was taking kickbacks, "he would say, 'If you can't make money for yourself, how can you make money for the bank?' It was encouraged by senior management."

Attock Oil, a BCCI satellite in London, enjoyed such cozy relations with the Nigerian National Petroleum Corporation (NNPC) that it made profits there when it was losing money everywhere else in the world according to a former employee. The reason was that NNPC officials awarded sweetheart contracts to Attock, this source explained in 1990. There was one particular deal, he said, in which Attock purchased Arab light crude from Saudi Arabia and provided it to the NNPC's Kaduna refinery to be turned into lubricant. (Nigerian crude was not suitable for lubricant.) In return, Attock received Nigerian crude from the state oil company. One reason the deal was peculiar, said this source, was that there was no reason for Attock to serve as a middleman. "Why doesn't NNPC go direct to the Saudis and buy the Arab light?" he asked. Even more suspicious, he said, is that the deal was structured in such a way that Attock was virtually guaranteed a profit: "You'd have to be totally inept not to make money."

After the oil glut of the early 1980s, Nigeria's financial condition deteriorated rapidly. The country was eventually forced to reschedule its debts and turn to the International Monetary Fund (IMF) for assistance. The IMF insisted on various financial reforms, but Nigeria resisted. Partly to circumvent the IMF, Nigeria turned to countertrade: swapping oil for merchandise or loans.

One major barter agreement involved BCCI and Attock Oil. It was signed on November 29, 1985 — just three months after President Babangida seized power — by Tam David-West, then Nigeria's oil minister; Allauddin Shaik, the general manager of BCCI's central marketing division; and M. A. Baqi, the managing director of Attock Oil. It was a $1.25 billion loan, with principal and interest payments to be made in oil. As much as $250 million of the loan was used. Unlike most major financings, the terms and conditions were never announced. The deal was not even disclosed to Nigeria's other foreign creditors, many of whom had trouble collecting interest on their old loans. Nigeria's use of barter was widely attacked by economists for being wasteful and fostering corruption, but that didn't seem to faze the country's leaders. On the contrary, the opportunities for graft may have been a major attraction.

No one knows how much money was stolen by Nigerian officials and their associates in the 1970s and 1980s, but the amount is undoubtedly in the billions, much of which was smuggled out of the country and deposited in foreign bank accounts. The corruption led to an orgy of spending, as Nigerians scooped up Rolls-Royces, private jets, and country mansions in England. A real estate agent in London said that in the early 1980s his agency was "selling anything up to twenty properties a week to Nigerians." One Nigerian official reportedly approached an insurance company to cover the contents of his English vacation home. The company said it would be happy to oblige — although it would have to exclude the solid gold bathtub he had bought for $5 million. It was suggested that he leave the bathtub in a bank. If the bathtub was stored in a London bank, there's a good chance it was BCCI, since Abedi's institution was a favorite depository for the Nigerian elite.

A former Senate investigator, Jack Blum, discovered this fact in 1988, when BCCI was the target of a U.S. government investigation. When the probe was reported publicly, Blum received a telephone call from a Nigerian diplomat in Washington who wanted to know if the investigation was serious. When Blum asked why he was concerned, the diplomat explained that President Babangida had an account at BCCI.

BCCI's secret loan to Nigeria was just one of several examples of its dubious deals with Third World governments. Another intriguing loan was made to Suriname, a small country in South America known as Dutch Guiana until its independence in 1975. At the time of the loan, Suriname was ruled by a dictator named Desi Bouterse, whose human rights abuses and corruption had turned the country into an international pariah. Under Bouterse, Suriname also became a haven for Latin American cocaine smugglers.

BCCI was happy to do business with Bouterse, agreeing to a secret $200 million loan in March 1986. The loan agreement suggests that it was hardly a conventional deal. The money was to be lent by Camari Corporation, a dummy company in the Netherlands Antilles, with the proceeds to be deposited "in cash" in account 01007647 at BCCI's Miami branch. According to the agreement, the money was to be "used exclusively for social, economic and educational purposes." Some U.S. law enforcement authorities, however, suspected that the loan was actually a scheme to launder drug money through BCCI. When asked about the deal in 1991, Suriname's central bank governor, Henk Goedschalk, acknowledged signing the agreement but said the deal had not gone forward.

Stranger than BCCI's occasional loans to developing countries are the *deposits* the bank received from Third World central banks and governments. Central banks in particular usually deposit their countries' foreign exchange reserves in international banks with the highest credit ratings. BCCI was just the sort of bank a prudent depositor should have avoided. Not only was it weakly regulated, its main holding company was incorporated in Luxembourg, a country without a central bank. This meant that BCCI had no "lender of last resort" to help it out in the event of liquidity problems (temporary shortages of cash). Since BCCI was privately held, it was not scrutinized by stock market analysts. Finally, credit rating agencies like Moody's and Standard & Poor's did not analyze the bank's creditworthiness. Nevertheless, BCCI attracted deposits from governments or government agencies in Barbados, Belize, Cameroon, Guatemala, Jamaica, Nigeria, Paraguay, Peru, St. Kitts and Nevis (a small Caribbean country), Trinidad, Venezuela, and Zimbabwe, according to internal records. The records of BCCI's Paris branch for 1984 show substantial deposits from the central banks of Mauritania, Togo, and Tunisia. Even after BCCI ran into deep trouble with U.S. law enforcement in the late 1980s, many developing countries continued to do business with it.

Some of the government deposits were linked to lending by BCCI. Political connections also seem to have played a role. In Jordan, the brother-in-law of its army commander went to work for BCCI. Soon afterward, the bank reportedly took over the Jordanian army's deposits and banking business.

BCCI also paid bribes to get deposits and evade regulations. Abdur Sakhia, a veteran BCCI official, described an incident at the 1985 annual meeting of the World Bank and the International Monetary Fund in Seoul, Korea. "I saw one of the BCCI officers with a lot of cash, handing [it] out to the staff of the Central Bank of Nigeria. This is what I saw personally being given to them." U.S. law enforcement authorities say they have evidence that BCCI paid bribes to central bankers or finance ministry officials in about a dozen developing countries, including Argentina, Nigeria, Peru, Senegal, and the Sudan.

It is not only corrupt officials in the Third World who move their money to foreign financial havens; so do ordinary people. Much of the money borrowed by Third World countries during the 1970s and 1980s flowed right back out again in the form of capital flight. People who feared political and economic instability accumulated dollars and other hard currencies in foreign financial havens. The flight of capital contributed to the financial woes of debtor nations: hard currency that could have been used for economic development or to service foreign debts was instead stashed abroad in private bank accounts, real estate, and other investments. Capital flight was one of the principal causes of the Third World debt crisis, which exploded in 1982 when such major borrowers as Argentina, Brazil, and Mexico defaulted on their debts.

Because of the harmful effects of capital flight, most Third World countries imposed foreign exchange controls, which restricted the ability of residents to move money abroad. This did not prevent international banks from accepting such deposits, however. In fact, major international banks that had been at the forefront of the Third World lending boom — such as Citibank, Bank of America, and Chase Manhattan in the United States as well as major European banks — also collected huge amounts of flight capital. To deal with rich foreign customers, the banks set up special "international private banking" departments in such financial centers as London, New York, Geneva, and Hong Kong.

BCCI received a huge volume of petrodollar deposits after the 1973 oil shock, yet it was not a major lender to developing countries. Abedi even boasted that BCCI made few loans to foreign governments (so-called sovereign creditors). In a January 1983 interview with *Institutional Investor,* a financial magazine in New York, he said that "as a matter of policy from the beginning, we have not gone for sovereign risks." This, of course, was an extraordinary statement in view of BCCI's self-appointed role as a pillar of the Third World, yet Abedi gave no indication that he saw the contradiction.

Although BCCI avoided lending to developing countries, it contributed to the debt crisis by sucking billions of dollars of flight capital out of Third World countries. Flight capital, in fact, was a cornerstone of BCCI's business, helping to explain its phenomenal growth rate.

BCCI's network was ideally placed to collect deposits from capital exporters, with offices in dozens of developing countries as well as virtually every major flight capital haven, including London, Luxembourg, Geneva, Zurich, Miami, Panama, and Hong Kong. BCCI's brochures and advertisements were sprinkled with code words like "confidentiality" and "privacy." Potential customers were reminded of the bank secrecy laws in countries like Luxembourg and Switzerland. The bank also took advantage of the Third World origins of its staff. In many African countries, for example, ethnic Indians are active in retailing and import-export businesses. They tended to feel more comfortable dealing with BCCI officers of similar background than with European or American bankers.

BCCI's "personal service" also helped. Rich customers from Third World countries were courted with the same techniques Abedi used to make political connections — including gifts, limousines, and lavish entertainment. A former BCCI official recalls that one of his colleagues spent months courting a member of Saudi Arabia's al-Ibrahim family, who are related by marriage to the ruling al-Saud family. The banker's superiors told him to stick with the prospect, so he did nothing but socialize with the businessman for months. "Come six months," the source recalls, "this man says, 'I've brought in one of the biggest deposits — a half-billion dollars.' "

BCCI enjoyed yet another advantage over most competitors: Abedi and many of the people who worked for him had no qualms about colluding with customers in illegal schemes to move capital abroad. In at least a half-dozen developing countries, BCCI was formally charged with violating foreign exchange controls: Mauritius (in 1983), the Sudan (1985), India (1986), Kenya (1987), Colombia (1989), and Brazil (1989). It was found guilty in India, Mauritius, and Colombia. (There were also incidents of similar alleged foreign exchange abuses by BCCI officers in Jamaica, Sierra Leone, and Liberia, according to the former chief financial officer, Masihur Rahman.)

In Kenya, BCCI was charged with violating currency controls by permitting a coffee exporter to accumulate abroad $34 million worth of foreign exchange. The money should have been repatriated to Kenya. The bank's foreign exchange license was suspended and three BCCI officers were arrested: the general manager in Kenya, the credit manager, and the manager of the main Nairobi branch. BCCI eventually reached a settlement with the Kenyan government in which it agreed to turn over the $34 million to the government, and the charges were dropped in February 1988.

In the Indian case, employees of BCCI's Bombay branch were suspected of selling traveler's checks to people who were not going abroad. After an investigation, five BCCI employees were arrested and then released on bail. After further investigations, four of the employees were arrested again in January 1987 and released two weeks later by an order of the High Court of Bombay. Later that year, the bank was found guilty of violating India's Foreign Exchange Regulations Act and fined. The conviction was appealed, but the bank eventually dropped the appeal. BCCI's manager in India, Krishen Murari, disappeared. He later surfaced in Britain.

Members of the Indian elite were among those suspected of using BCCI's facilities to move money out of the country. In late 1987, the Indian government retained the Fairfax Group, an investigative firm in Falls Church, Virginia, a suburb of Washington,* to look into possible violations of the country's currency controls and bribery statutes. "We were essentially hired to handle the foreign part of six or seven investigations already under way in the [Indian] finance ministry," recalls Mike Hershman, the president of the Fairfax Group. "It was thirty days to forty-five days into our investigation that the links to BCCI became apparent." By tracing money that had been transferred abroad in violation of foreign exchange controls, investigators discovered a

---

*The Fairfax Group was later retained by the Bangladesh government to investigate General Ershad, the deposed dictator.

slew of offshore companies. "Many of them," Hershman said, "were set up by BCCI." These offshore companies and accounts were being used by several leading Indian businessmen and aides to former prime minister Rajiv Gandhi, who had together transferred "tens of millions of dollars" into overseas companies, according to Hershman.

These cases were exceptional. In many countries, BCCI was able to use its influence to avoid legal troubles. After all, the bank was bribing central bank officials, who were responsible for enforcing exchange controls. In several countries, the bank had cozy relationships with higher-ranking officials: heads of government and heads of state.

BCCI's role as a dirty money machine came naturally. The corporate amorality is one explanation. In addition, the bank was perfectly placed to service its unsavory clientele, thanks to its international network. Also important was Abedi's obsession with growth. For Abedi to achieve his goal of building the world's largest bank, he would need tens of billions of dollars in fresh deposits, and he cared nothing about their origin. Indeed, BCCI's most unscrupulous bankers were often the best marketers, since they did not hesitate to handle dirty money.

One man who joined BCCI in the mid-1980s after a long career at a major American bank says that Abedi and other top officials "put tremendous pressure on people to bring in deposits — at any cost." Many employees succumbed to the pressure, says this source, because they feared they would otherwise lose their jobs and would be unable to find comparable work at other banks. "It was a twenty-four-hour-a-day pressure," he says, accompanied by "threats, especially to these poor Pakistani bastards: 'If you don't bring in this money we'll put you on a plane.' The guy is living in a million-dollar house [in the United States] and the alternative is to go back to where they have no running water. After leaving BCCI no one will touch you with a ten-foot pole — especially those Pakistanis who had no professionalism. Their whole life was BCCI."

BCCI's involvement with dirty money was by no means limited to the Third World. Abedi's boast that BCCI did not discriminate on the basis of race, religion, or color was correct: he was happy to collect money from criminals of any background. Nazir Chinoy, a senior BCCI official who was convicted of laundering drug money, put it simply in 1991: "One never gave much thought to the law. One only thought about getting the deposits." The bank was so effective in this policy that it attracted tens of millions — perhaps hundreds of millions — of dollars in criminal money, including funds from drug traffickers, smugglers, and financial fraudsters. In some cases, BCCI officers became so intimately involved with such customers that they were full accomplices in the crimes.

Of the hundreds of international banks that have set up shop in London, one of the most peculiar was Arab Overseas Bank and Trust Company. For one thing, the name was misleading, since it was not really a Middle Eastern institution; it was licensed in the Caribbean country of Anguilla. For another, it was run not by Arabs but by an American named Wallace C. Kemper, Jr., who had been born and raised in Louisiana. Most important, it was not really a bank.

Arab Overseas was a shell bank, a totally unregulated institution consisting of little more than a receptionist and a box of stationery. During the 1980s, the Anguillan government made a fortune selling bank licenses to foreigners with little regard for how the licenses would be used. Kemper ran two Anguillan banks, Arab Overseas and an equally phony institution called European Overseas Bank. Both "banks" maintained illegal representative offices in London in a small building at 28 Black Prince Road, a back street off the Albert Embankment. Kemper attracted deposits by promising total confidentiality to customers. "No passports or references are required when you open your account," said one of his brochures. "You do not give your name. You need not give your address." What the brochure did not say was that Kemper had no intention of allowing his anonymous depositors to ever withdraw their money — at least, if he could get away with it. For Kemper, the bank charters were a license to steal.

Another scam was the so-called advance fee fraud. Kemper told would-be borrowers that he could arrange loans for them as long as they gave him large fees in advance. The fees were paid, but the loans did not materialize. The total take was in the millions of dollars.

The Anguillan government stripped Kemper's banks of their licenses in 1987, but the American continued to operate his illegal representative office in London for several more months until the British police caught up with him. In March 1988, a court in London sentenced Kemper to three years in prison for fraud and six months for possession of two forged passports. Around the same time, accomplices of Kemper's who had swindled several Americans pleaded guilty to fraud charges in the United States. The British police found that Kemper had maintained an account at a Croydon, England, branch of an authentic

Arab bank: Bank of Credit and Commerce International. When the police asked for Kemper's bank records, BCCI refused to cooperate on the ground of banking confidentiality.

In other advance fee cases, BCCI officials actually vouched for the con men, making them accomplices in the frauds. One case involved Morris J. Miller, a Florida man with several convictions on his record. Immediately after his release from prison, prosecutors said, he set himself up as a loan broker and collected fees and expenses across the country. (Miller was convicted by a federal jury in Washington in December 1988, but the conviction was reversed on a technicality; the appeals court held that a defense witness was improperly prevented from testifying.) Several of the people who dealt with Miller say they were told that they could obtain financing from a bank licensed in Montserrat, which was actually just a shell bank. The men who controlled the Montserrat "bank" reassured would-be borrowers by saying that they worked closely with a major international bank, BCCI. The victims were told that they could check out the Montserrat bank by contacting BCCI officers in New York or London.

A Florida businessman who owned a small computer company says he was told by a BCCI officer in New York that BCCI was working with the Montserrat bank and would be funding the deal. This man wound up paying about $7,000 to Miller and more than $32,000 to one of the men connected with the Montserrat shell bank. "Two members of my family lost their homes because they had to take out second mortgages," he says. The advance fee fraudsters, says this man, "ruined my business and ruined my personal life."

Financial fraudsters seem to favor sunny climates. Fort Lauderdale — Morris Miller's stomping ground — is infested with such crooks. Another popular spot is Orange County, California, south of Los Angeles. It has been the base for dozens of crooked investment firms, known as boiler rooms, including First American Currency (FAC), an outfit in Laguna Hills. The First American name had nothing to do with the Washington, D.C., banking company associated with BCCI. The firm was connected to Abedi's bank in another way: the men who ran the California boiler room hid some of their loot in BCCI.

Investors who fell for the pitch of FAC's smooth-talking salesmen were told they would be getting commodity futures contracts for precious metals. But FAC was not licensed to trade in commodity futures. What is worse, FAC's operators pocketed the bulk of the money. After nearly two years in business, FAC was raided in December 1985 by federal law enforcement authorities and forced into receivership. More than a thousand customers lost an estimated $16 million, according to investigators. About $3 million was traced to an account at BCCI in Panama.

The money lost by FAC's customers was pocket change compared with the losses in boiler room scams run by other BCCI clients. In these cases, the products were not precious metals but penny stocks, so named because they often sell for less than a dollar per share. Some penny stocks are legitimate, but many are grossly overpriced or worthless. In fact, some of the companies that issue the stock are just empty shells, set up by accomplices of the boiler room operators. During the 1980s, penny stock bandits collected huge sums of money in the United States and other countries; in 1989, U.S. state securities regulators estimated that American investors lost at least $2 billion each year.

Several of the most notorious penny stock crooks laundered their loot through BCCI. The bank's ties with some of them were so close that BCCI's officers must have known that the funds came from criminal activity. The most prominent swindler was Thomas F. ("Tommy") Quinn, the mastermind of what may have been the biggest boiler room fraud in history.

Tommy Quinn grew up in Brooklyn and attended college and law school there at St. John's University. After working as a criminal lawyer (some of his clients were mobsters), he became a criminal himself, specializing in stock market scams. As president of a small New York brokerage firm, Quinn was involved in a scheme to promote shares in a company whose assets, according to the Securities and Exchange Commission, were "almost completely illusory." In 1966, the SEC barred him for life from the securities industry because of "flagrant fraudulent practices." Quinn landed in even deeper trouble in 1970, when he was sentenced to six months in prison and disbarred from the practice of law. He settled another fraud accusation by the SEC in 1986 by agreeing to a permanent injunction not to violate securities laws.

That same year, Quinn left the United States and established a new base on the French Riviera. Operating out of a $6.5 million villa in Mougins, a town near Cannes, he set up a network of boiler rooms in Europe and the Middle East, with offices or sales representatives in such countries as France, Switzerland, Germany, Spain, Sweden, Cyprus, Gibraltar, Abu Dhabi, and Saudi Arabia. Salesmen used hard-sell tactics to promote penny stocks to gullible investors. Prospects were sent copies of newsletters with impressive names, such as *The Swiss Analyst* and *Strategy Market Letter.*

Complaints from investors touched off inquiries in Europe and the United States, and in 1988, French, German, and Swiss police arrested more than twenty members of the Quinn organization. French police picked up Tommy Quinn in July at his villa and charged him with fraud, illegal canvassing, and violating securities laws. In Switzerland, he was accused of fraud and forgery.* When investigators and prosecutors from several countries compared notes shortly after Quinn's arrest, they estimated that his victims had lost more than $500 million, making "Euroscam" — as the fraud was nicknamed — one of the biggest stock swindles in history. Some observers believe the total take was as much as $1 billion.

A large portion of Quinn's loot was channeled through BCCI, according to the authorities. "This bank," said a Swiss investigating magistrate, Laurent Kasper-Ansermet, "intervenes many times in my case." He added that accounts were maintained at BCCI by Quinn, by entities belonging to him, and by his lieutenant Kurt Meier. Tens of millions of dollars were deposited in BCCI accounts in France, the Channel Islands, Gibraltar, Luxembourg, the UAE, and the United Kingdom. Kasper-Ansermet said there were rumors that "there was someone inside the bank" helping Quinn's organization.

Long before Tommy Quinn moved to France, other boiler room operators from North America had begun fleecing investors in Europe. In the mid-1980s, there were at least twenty boiler rooms in Amsterdam. The Dutch city had several attractions: a central location, a good telephone system, and — perhaps most important — virtually no regulation of brokerage firms. Until 1986, securities firms did not even need to be licensed. One final asset was that the Netherlands had no extradition treaty with Canada, the native country of most of the boiler room bandits.

The biggest and most notorious outfit was First Commerce Securi-

---

*Quinn was eventually convicted in France of swindling ninety-three people, selling stock without authorization, and using false passports. In July 1991, he was sentenced to four years in prison.

ties, which set up shop in 1983. When the Dutch authorities cracked down on the boiler rooms in 1986, First Commerce was raided twice and then forced into bankruptcy in January 1987, causing its customers to suffer huge losses. A Dutch prosecutor, Jan Koers, says the victims lost a minimum of $100 million, and perhaps three or four times that figure. Jan van Apeldoorn, a lawyer in Amsterdam appointed as the bankruptcy trustee for First Commerce, says the figure may indeed have been as high as $400 million.

Dutch police say that the man behind First Commerce was Irving Kott, a stock promoter from Montreal with a shady past. In 1976, he had pleaded guilty to stock fraud in Ontario and was fined C$500,000, reportedly the largest such fine in Canadian history at that time. Although Kott always claimed he had nothing to do with First Commerce, police have no doubt that he is the prime culprit. Several close associates of Kott's — including his son Michael — worked at First Commerce. Kott himself spent months every year in Amsterdam and, according to several witnesses, he was the man who called the shots. A Bahamian accountant who was listed as the owner of First Commerce's parent company told police in a signed statement that he was a nominee for Irving Kott. Finally, his attorneys arranged a settlement in which Kott would pay partial restitution to victims of the fraud. (The amount of the settlement is quite small — the equivalent of about $4 million — because the prosecutors had little leverage over Kott. As long as he avoided coming to the Netherlands, he could not be prosecuted on criminal charges.)

Kott's principal front man was Altaf Nazerali, who served as chairman of First Commerce, its parent company in Luxembourg (Alya Holdings), and a Luxembourg affiliate called Asset International Management (AIM). One of Nazerali's duties was handling money sent in by investors. These funds were deposited in a variety of banks in Europe and Latin America, including a subsidiary of Algemene Bank Nederland, a Swiss unit of Banque Nationale de Paris, and Geneva's Trade Development Bank.* But the Kott organization appears to have had a particularly close relationship with BCCI.

When the First Commerce fraud was at its height, millions of dollars arrived in Amsterdam in the form of personal checks and wire transfers. Much of the money was then forwarded to BCCI. A former

---

*Trade Development Bank was controlled by Edmond Safra, a New York banker of Lebanese origin. In 1983, he sold it to American Express.

associate of Nazerali's remembers seeing him bundle up hundreds of checks in Amsterdam and fly the package to Luxembourg. The checks were then deposited at the Luxembourg office of Banque de Commerce et de Placements, BCCI's Swiss bank. From Luxembourg, the money was transferred to accounts in other countries, including Switzerland and Panama.

Nazerali's principal contact at BCCI was a senior official in Luxembourg, Kazem Naqvi, who was believed to be related to Nazerali or his wife. A former BCCI official says Kazem Naqvi was also related to the number-two man of the entire BCCI group, Swaleh Naqvi. (BCCI was asked about the family connection in early 1989; a spokesman declined to comment.) When First Commerce transferred money to BCCI, the payments were generally sent to the attention of Kazem Naqvi. The banker also visited AIM's Luxembourg office frequently, according to a former associate of Nazerali's. "Naqvi came to see Nazerali almost every day," he said. On at least one occasion, Naqvi met with Irving Kott in Luxembourg. In late 1986, Naqvi moved to Zurich and became a managing director of BCCI's Swiss bank. Even after the move, he continued to deal with Nazerali.

Naqvi's prominent role was noted by van Apeldoorn, the First Commerce bankruptcy trustee. "Monies usually were paid to the attention of one person who was probably in control of that account and that was — I think in all cases I have seen — Mr. Naqvi," said the Dutch lawyer.

The First Commerce organization had other ties to BCCI. A BCCI officer in Luxembourg, Joseph El Gamal, quit the bank and joined First Commerce's sister company in Luxembourg, Pétrusse Securities International (the new name of AIM). Three top officials of First Commerce came from one of BCCI's most important satellites, the Gulf Group, run by Pakistan's Gokal family.

From 1982 to 1984, Nazerali had been vice president of Transgulf Investment and Finance, a unit of the Gokals' Gulf International Holdings S.A. of Luxembourg, according to a résumé dated March 3, 1985.

Sinan A. Raouff, a board member of Alya Holdings and a "supervisory director" of First Commerce, was employed by a series of Gokal companies beginning in 1976: Mercantile and Marine (Texas) Inc. in Houston (in 1976), Gulf East Pte. Ltd. in Tokyo (1976–78), and Marcotrade S.A. in Geneva (1978–82). He went to work for Transgulf Finance Company S.A. in Geneva in 1982 — the same year Nazerali joined Transgulf, remaining until at least September 24, 1984, the date of the résumé from which this information comes.

Walter J. Bonn, a Dutchman who served as managing director of First Commerce, had worked for Stokvis International, a trading company owned by the Gokals in the Netherlands.

Some of the Gokal alumni may have been involved in the arms trade before joining the First Commerce group. Nazerali, according to a former associate, used to boast that he and the other Gokal alumni were involved in arms deals when they worked for the Gulf Group. On one occasion, Nazerali said he had sold arms to Africa.

Raouff had impressive Middle Eastern connections. His résumé states that he was employed by the Iraqi foreign ministry from 1959 to 1968, dividing his time between Baghdad and Iraq's embassies in Prague, Bonn, and Tokyo. Years later, BCCI, as we have seen, financed arms deals with both Iraq and its enemy, Iran.

The arms business was a field in which a BCCI client named Munther Bilbeisi was active. That wasn't all he did, though. He was involved in such a vast array of crooked deals that he was virtually a one-man crime wave. And he did it with the financial support and collusion of BCCI, making the bank a full partner in his criminal enterprises.

Munther Bilbeisi, a portly and flamboyant Jordanian merchant, was a man of the world and a bon viveur. One day he might be sipping coffee in a fashionable Geneva restaurant. The next day he could be found in a nightclub in the Middle East, leering at an Arabian belly dancer. His million-dollar-plus home was in "the Sanctuary," a development of luxury condominiums in Boca Raton, Florida, a posh suburb of Miami. The apartment was just minutes from a BCCI branch, which may not have been a coincidence. Bilbeisi once boasted that he gave so much business to BCCI that it set up the Boca Raton branch to serve him.

If anyone asked Bilbeisi what he did, he described himself as a coffee merchant. That was technically accurate, but it was only a fraction of his business activities, as a Florida lawyer eventually discovered after years of probing.

Bilbeisi's company, Coffee Inc., purchased coffee beans in Central America for resale in other parts of the world, including such Middle Eastern countries as Jordan. The banks that provided him with trade financing insisted that he insure these shipments, so he called on

Lloyd's of London, the international insurance market. A syndicate of Lloyd's underwriters provided coverage for coffee beans in transit and in warehouses and also insured some of Bilbeisi's personal property. In February 1987, Bilbeisi submitted insurance claims to Lloyd's, saying that some of the beans his company had received from Guatemala were not the grade he had paid for: someone had switched them for inferior beans.

Lloyd's was reluctant to honor these claims because of a bad experience with Bilbeisi. The previous year, he had tried to make a substantial insurance claim for the theft of an expensive Chinese vase — Sung dynasty, he said — and several Oriental rugs, which he said were worth hundreds of thousands of dollars. To check out that claim, Lloyd's retained a lawyer in Miami Beach named James F. Dougherty II; it could not have found a more aggressive advocate.

An alumnus of Notre Dame and a U.S. Marine Corps veteran of Vietnam, Dougherty is a cantankerous bulldog of a man with a mercurial temper and a crazed but infectious laugh. He is a tenacious investigator and a fearsome courtroom warrior. Dougherty unearthed records showing that Bilbeisi had bought the rugs two years earlier for just $11,439. The lawyer found other evidence undermining Bilbeisi's account of the supposed theft. The insurance claim was quickly rejected.

When Bilbeisi submitted his coffee claim in 1987, Lloyd's turned to Dougherty once again. This time, he conducted a thorough investigation that turned up evidence of wide-ranging criminality. The decisive breakthrough occurred when Dougherty located and deposed Tony Aramburo, who had worked for Bilbeisi in New Orleans. In his depositions of November 16–19, 1989, in Miami, Aramburo revealed Bilbeisi's coffee-smuggling scheme in full. "He broke the case," Dougherty said. Confirmation of Aramburo's allegations came from three disgruntled former employees of Bilbeisi's who knew many of the secrets of the Jordanian wheeler-dealer — Steve Calderon, Joseph Villalba, and José Antonio Otano — whom Bilbeisi had nicknamed "the boys."

Bilbeisi, it turned out, hadn't been shipping coffee to the Middle East at all. Instead, he had been involved in a multimillion-dollar smuggling scheme aimed at evading U.S. controls on coffee imports. (The United States, like most other countries, adhered to the international coffee agreement until 1986.) The coffee wasn't sold in Jordan but to roasters and brokers in New York City. Bilbeisi would bring in so-called non-quota coffee, which was cheap, then resell it at higher quota prices. Bilbeisi's "boys" and other sources explained to Dougherty how the coffee had been rebagged to disguise its true origin and allow it to get into the United States. The "boys" said that Bilbeisi himself had instructed them and others to prepare false cargo manifests.

There was also evidence of payoffs to government officials. According to the testimony of Carlos Dubon, a former associate of Anastasio Somoza Debayle, the late Nicaraguan dictator, Central American customs officials were bribed at Bilbeisi's direction to ensure that the smuggling continued.

As Dougherty continued the investigation, he found that Bilbeisi was not just an insurance fraudster and a coffee smuggler but a veteran arms trafficker. He had apparently sold machine guns to El Salvador back in 1969, at the time of its so-called soccer war with Honduras. In 1974, Bilbeisi's sale of Centurion tanks, Hawker Hunter jet fighters, and missiles to South Africa had been described on the front pages of a leading British newspaper. Britain's Foreign Office intervened and stopped the sale of the jets.

In 1980, Bilbeisi — then living in Warwick Gardens, in the Earl's Court section of London — had approached T. Weller Smith Aircraft in Atlanta, hoping to buy spare parts for F-14 fighter planes on behalf of a foreign country. The company refused to sell the parts to Bilbeisi, pointing out that only the United States and Iran operated these aircraft. The American embargo on arms supplies to Iran would make any sale without government authorization illegal. Bilbeisi had also helped the army of his native Jordan with sales of its military equipment. By the early 1980s, according to his own testimony, he had been "awarded the sale of all the surplus military equipment by the Jordanian armed forces." In his role as an agent, he had also negotiated or sold jet fighters from Yugoslavia to Honduras.

There were even indications, according to Dougherty, that Bilbeisi was involved in sales of material that might be used in the production of nuclear weapons. These consisted of a series of faxed messages, the Lloyd's lawyer said, one of which mentioned 2,000 pounds of enriched uranium that seemed destined for South Africa.

It was only after years in the arms trade that Bilbeisi branched out into coffee. In the early 1980s, he once explained to BCCI's Miami office, he decided to go into the coffee business with Mauricio Salavarría, described as a "longtime friend and former business partner from El Salvador." The two businesses went hand-in-hand, with

Bilbeisi dabbling in arms deals with some of the same Central American countries that supplied him with coffee.

In 1987 and 1988, Bilbeisi tried to sell ten Northrop F-5 jet fighters and eighteen Sikorsky helicopter gunships from Jordan to Guatemala, according to Dougherty. Although the fighter deal did not go through, Bilbeisi did succeed in arranging the sale of three helicopters. To help with this and other military sales, his company, Mura International, retained as consultants James Vaught, a retired four-star U.S. Army general, and Mauricio Coronado, Guatemala's former consul-general in Miami. By the fall of 1988, the helicopter sales were well under way. One of the three aircraft was *Royal Jordanian Air Force 719*, King Hussein's personal helicopter.

This deal was extremely profitable. Bilbeisi is believed to have paid $2.1 million for the helicopters but was able to sell them to the Guatemalans for $5.1 million. He tried to get financing for the deal from BCCI, but it is unclear exactly where the money eventually came from. Some investigators suspect it may have been routed through BCCI units in Jordan and Switzerland. The transaction also included some unusual payments to Guatemalan officials that amounted to payoffs, according to Lloyd's and to an internal investigation by BCCI. A list provided to Bilbeisi on October 17, 1988, includes a payment of $270,000 to Milton Cerezo, a half brother of Guatemala's president, Vinicio Cerezo, and planned payments of "$150,000 to the two generals." The $270,000 payment was made into an account at Bank Leumi le Israel, on Lincoln Road in Miami Beach. Milton Cerezo admitted receiving the money but insisted it was part of a legitimate business transaction.

Dougherty has alleged that it was these payments in Guatemala that hampered his attempts to investigate Bilbeisi's insurance claims there. He also said that "Bilbeisi tried to bribe our attorneys in Guatemala through one of the people named in the 1988 payoff list."

Bilbeisi even offered to supply arms to the Nicaraguan contras, according to an affidavit by Adolfo Calero, a contra leader. He said that Bilbeisi had offered to sell him and his associates machine guns, rockets, and other small arms. Dougherty and other investigators suspected that Bilbeisi might well have been involved in covert arms sales sponsored by the U.S. government. In his extensive investigation, Dougherty found a Salvadorean passport with Bilbeisi's picture but in the name of Munthur Araujo. The passport bears a visa for easy access to the United States granted by the American embassy in Switzerland shortly after the passport was issued. How, Dougherty asked, could Bilbeisi so quickly acquire such a visa for an apparently forged passport without some official U.S. government connivance?

Dougherty found that the Jordanian merchant would never have been able to carry out many of his schemes without the financial backing and cooperation of BCCI. "Without BCCI," Dougherty said, "Bilbeisi would have had a really difficult time organizing and financing his deals. With BCCI, they were a snap."

Bilbeisi's relationship with BCCI — which may have come about through his brother Fakhri, who ran the Amman, Jordan, branch — blossomed after he went into the coffee business. In a 1983 letter introducing himself to BCCI's Miami branch manager, the Jordanian boasted, "My contracts in military and defense equipment with Qatar, East, West, Central and Southern Africa, Central America, South America, Caribbean and other countries proved very successful." He said he had diversified into commodities, supplying the Jordanian government with twenty thousand tons of sugar, and also had become "the main supplier of cement clinker to the Kuwait Cement Co." Before long, Bilbeisi was providing BCCI with some of its biggest business in Florida. Between 1983 and 1987, BCCI's Florida offices lent more than $100 million to the merchant to finance the coffee shipments he said he was making from Central America to the Jordanian port of Aqaba. Bilbeisi also used BCCI's Amman branch to borrow money and service his schemes.

His relationship with BCCI was apparently so close that when he had a run-in with "the boys" — Calderon, Villalba, and Otano — he invoked his ties with BCCI to intimidate them. "The boys" had become testy when Bilbeisi fell behind on their payments. When they complained, the Jordanian suddenly produced a copy of Otano's bank statement from BCCI in London and showed it to Calderon, telling him that Otano "had better be careful with his money" and boasting of his close links with the bank.

BCCI's officers connived in Bilbeisi's smuggling activities. For years, they ignored the requirements — attached to the short-term loans — that the coffee be sent on to the Middle East. The bank also issued a huge number of cashier's checks to allow Bilbeisi to pay Central American coffee suppliers without leaving a record of their names. On one occasion, as many as thirty-one cashier's checks totaling $765,000 were issued by BCCI's Miami office, according to Dougherty and his associate Richard Lehrmann, a bright young New York lawyer. BCCI also helped transfer millions of Bilbeisi's dollars to offshore accounts in the Bahamas and Panama.

The bank helped Bilbeisi conceal the allegedly false insurance claims to Lloyd's. When Dougherty demanded records from BCCI, it provided copies of cashier's checks Bilbeisi had used to pay for his shipments but refused to turn over copies of the endorsed sides of the checks. BCCI also produced undated documents to support Bilbeisi's allegation that his coffee had been switched for inferior beans. Dougherty and his assistants also found that records had been deliberately destroyed and that BCCI was extremely reluctant to cooperate or provide any documentation about Bilbeisi's trading. Even when Lloyd's obtained court discovery orders, BCCI would produce only incomplete records.

Dougherty's widening investigation turned up other intriguing leads. Bilbeisi had been doing business with Gerardo Harris, an associate of the Panamanian strongman Manuel Antonio Noriega. For example, two letters from Bilbeisi to Saad Shafi of BCCI instructed the bank to pay Harris more than $550,000. Bilbeisi also had dealings with Amjad Awan, a BCCI officer who acted as Noriega's personal banker.

Lloyd's of London seized on the complicity of the bank and named BCCI as a co-conspirator with Bilbeisi in a suit it brought under the federal Racketeer Influenced and Corrupt Organizations Act (RICO) in May 1991. Lloyd's alleged that the coffee scheme required the participation of "a banking institution willing to underwrite the venture in exchange for a share in the profits." All of the smuggled coffee was financed by companies wholly owned by Bilbeisi using BCCI letters of credit, according to Lloyd's.

The RICO statute was designed to combat organized crime. In the summer of 1991, Dougherty discovered how apt Lloyd's use of the statute had been. Bilbeisi, it emerged, had links to alleged Mafia leaders in New Jersey. One of his associates was Thomas ("Corky") Vastola, a reputed member of the DeCavalcante crime family. Corky Vastola is identified in FBI documents as a member of La Cosa Nostra, "with cross-family ties between the Genovese and Lucchese LCN families." He has "widespread influence in the entertainment industry, especially in New York City, Atlantic City, Las Vegas and Chicago." One FBI document said that Vastola "handles arrangements regarding the booking of nightclub acts in Atlantic City and New York City." According to the FBI, as far back as 1982 Bilbeisi and Vastola considered making an offer for a huge parking lot in Atlantic City.*

Dougherty found so much evidence of criminality by Bilbeisi and BCCI that he felt obligated to inform high-ranking federal law enforcement authorities. On August 5, 1989, the lawyer met with William Rosenblatt, an assistant commissioner of the U.S. Customs Service, and described in detail what he had learned about BCCI and one of its biggest customers. In the presence of his own investigators, Dougherty says, he was told that the U.S. Treasury Department and the Customs Service "had no interest in pursuing the case." Even though he provided the agency with substantial information on the alleged smuggling, he says angrily, "U.S. Customs never followed up on any of the information we provided."

Years later, the federal authorities finally took action. In 1991, Bilbeisi and an associate were indicted for tax fraud. By that time, he had returned to Jordan to help manage his family's company, which imports products from Japanese companies. Bilbeisi seemed nonchalant about the indictment. "What can they do to me?" he asked as he sat back at his luxurious villa in Amman, sipping tea. "Coffee smuggler?" he said. "Let them say coffee smuggler, people will laugh. Evading taxes? I never evaded taxes." And there seemed to be little chance that Bilbeisi would ever return to the United States. "I'm not going to Miami. . . . If they want to investigate me they can come to Jordan." Why did he leave Miami? Why, he said, he "couldn't stand the crime."

---

*The owner of the lot was MMRT Associates, a partnership that included Kenneth Shapiro, a man identified by federal authorities as a nominee for Nicodemo ("Little Nicky") Scarfo, a reputed Mob boss in Philadelphia. On December 21, 1982, Bilbeisi sent a telex to the partnership in which he said, "We contemplate an offer in the area of $18 million," and identified "our bankers" as BCCI in Amman, Jordan, Arab Bank Ltd., a major Jordanian bank, and France's Banque Paribas. The deal didn't pan out, but Bilbeisi and Vastola stayed in touch. The visitors' log for March 4, 1986, shows that Vastola visited Bilbeisi's condominium in Boca Raton.

8

FALSE PROFITS

YEAR AFTER YEAR, like some latter-day prophet, Agha Hasan Abedi would trumpet BCCI's rising profits in his speeches and his annual business reviews. For BCCI was a huge success story, a rapidly growing and highly profitable Third World enterprise that had succeeded in breaking into the privileged confines of high finance. From cramped offices in Abu Dhabi in 1972, BCCI had grown into a worldwide institution boasting plush offices in hundreds of locations.

Abedi's gushing comments on the group's 1980 results are typical: an 84 percent increase in operating profits had him purring about the bank's "increasing return" on its "earlier investments" and how this justified BCCI's "policy for establishing a global network within a reasonably short passage of time." In that year, the shareholders, according to this review, enjoyed a 23 percent return on their investment in BCCI, compared with an already healthy 16 percent in 1979. Abedi's deputy, Swaleh Naqvi, echoed his mentor's message. "Let me mention to you one word — profit," he said in a speech in London in 1988. BCCI was, Naqvi contended, a solid and successful institution, as was apparent in its financial statements. "The balance sheet," he said, "is the proof of the reality of our vision."

Yet these proud words and healthy appearances masked an altogether different reality. From the very beginning, BCCI violated almost every principle of sound banking, with the result that it soon had a huge volume of shaky loans to a handful of cronies on its books. The most notable example was the Gulf Group, the collection of shipping and commodities companies controlled by Pakistan's Gokal family. Abedi had lent hundreds of millions of dollars to the Gokals, enabling them to turn the Gulf Group into an international business empire. In so doing, he ignored the famous banking dictum that warns, "If you owe the bank a million dollars, the bank owns you. But if you owe the bank a hundred million dollars, you own the bank." The Gokals, of course, did not literally "own" BCCI, but their debts were so large that the bank's fate was inextricably tied to that of the Gulf Group.

Conventional rules of banking meant little to Abedi, partly because he saw himself as a visionary, someone who had invented a new style of banking that transcended the traditional ways. His hubris really knew no bounds. He once boasted to the bank's employees that he understood management far better than Peter Drucker, the highly acclaimed management guru, whom he dismissed as an "apprentice."

For all his avant-garde rhetoric, BCCI's banking practices were really a throwback — an extension of what Abedi had learned when he began his banking career in India and Pakistan. He came from a culture in which personal connections were far more important than the fussy statistical guidelines of accountants, financial controllers, and bank regulators. His approach was also influenced by his craving for political influence. The Gokals, for example, were more than simply businessmen; they could help Abedi make valuable political connections in both the Third World and the West.

Abedi soon learned that the rules really did apply to him. No one can engage in reckless lending for very long without incurring big losses. In an attempt to evade the consequences of his folly, he engaged in a massive fraud, culminating in the biggest bank robbery in history.

Abedi believed in lending money to friends, particularly friends who impressed him as powerful and influential. That, after all, is how banking has often been conducted in Pakistan and many other developing countries. Traditional money changers and corner-shop financial companies had mostly filled the role of bankers until the second half of the twentieth century. It was only in 1941 that Habib Bank — the first sizable bank in the subcontinent to be owned and run by Muslims — was established in Bombay at the urging of Mohammed Ali Jinnah, a champion of the Muslim cause who became the father of Pakistan.

When the Indian subcontinent was partitioned in 1947, Habib Bank moved its headquarters to Pakistan, becoming its biggest bank. There was a woeful shortage of financial skills in the new nation. Masihur Rahman, BCCI's chief financial officer, has recalled that "banking was very poor in Pakistan in '47." It was a world in which accounting skills — and, thus, reliable financial statements — were hard to come by. Bank lending was typically an incestuous process involving friends and influence, where the very owners of a bank might be among its biggest borrowers. Banking supervision was at best rudimentary, and bankers found it easy to undermine the regulatory process by providing jobs and payoffs to supervisors. The regulators did nothing to curb Abedi's lending to the Gokals.

During the 1960s and 1970s, the Gokal brothers — Mustapha, Abbas, and Murtaza — expanded into the international shipping business with loans from United Bank. When Abedi founded BCCI in 1972, some of the seed capital may have come from — or via — the Gokals, according to former associates of Abedi's. In addition, Abedi seemed to follow in the Gokals' footsteps in the way he structured BCCI. The brothers had chosen London, Geneva, and Toronto as the headquarters for their major companies. Abedi used a similar setup, with bases in London, Luxembourg, and the Cayman Islands.

Shipping was a thriving business in the early 1970s, boosted by growing world trade, and the Gokals were trying to ride it for all they could. They were well positioned to scoop up business with newly independent, developing countries in Asia and Africa, where their Muslim and Third World background was a major asset. Abedi was happy to finance their ambitions.

From the very beginning, the Gokals were major customers of BCCI. Masihur Rahman said that BCCI "earned a lot of money from them in the early days." The Gokals placed deposits with the bank's London and Luxembourg offices and started borrowing money from BCCI almost immediately. "They grew and grew," said Rahman, "and the bank benefited from their relationship because they generally became major players in the world trading market, in shipping; [they] became holders of very large vessels." In 1975 alone, loans from BCCI made it possible for them to buy seventeen vessels.

When Abedi wanted a favor, the Gokals would reciprocate. In 1975, for example, he needed an ally to acquire New York's Chelsea National Bank. Abbas Gokal, as we have seen, told the New York bank regulators that he would be buying the bank; BCCI would simply help him run it. (The skeptical regulators vetoed the deal.)

Abedi was extremely impressed by the Gokals. They were cosmopolitan men, thoroughly experienced in Western ways, who carried themselves with style. Abbas Gokal was something of a dandy. He sported a goatee and usually had a square silk handkerchief poking out of the breast pocket of his double-breasted suit from London's Savile Row. The Gokals' offices were elegantly appointed. In Geneva, for example, their base was a plush building on the Cours de Rive with expensive Italian marble even on the back stairs.

The Gokals had superb connections in both the Third World and the West. Because of their upbringing in Iraq, they were fluent in Arabic and quite familiar with the Arab world, which was starting to gush with oil money. They also built connections to Washington, where they became important shippers of goods for U.S. aid programs.

BCCI's loans to the Gokals were made in an extremely relaxed and cozy manner. If they wanted a loan, they wouldn't approach a credit officer, they would go to Abedi directly. He would then instruct Swaleh Naqvi to lend the funds, paying little attention to such formalities as loan documentation, statistical reviews of creditworthiness, or the volume of loans BCCI had already provided to them.

This casual approach inevitably led to a great concentration of risk. BCCI treated other favored borrowers similarly, but the Gokals were the most extreme example. The danger of these practices became apparent in the late 1970s, when the international shipping market contracted sharply. BCCI soon found itself propping up the Gokals with little concern for their real financial health.

Abedi engaged in another reckless practice: making large loans to "insiders" — a term that refers to the shareholders, directors, and officers of a bank. When the First American takeover battle began in 1978, lawyers for the company discovered that a number of BCCI shareholders were also borrowers. The Gokals, of course, may also have been insiders since, as noted above, they were suspected of providing some of BCCI's start-up capital.

Sheikh Zayed, the most important shareholder, was either unaware of these risky practices or did nothing to stop them. The other major founding shareholder, Bank of America, soon discovered that something was amiss. In late 1977, B of A cut its stake in BCCI from 30 to 24 percent and pulled out entirely by 1980. It was so eager to withdraw that it even lent money to a BCCI-linked unit in the Cayman Islands, ICIC Overseas Ltd., so that it could pay for the shares on behalf of BCCI.

Bank regulators were largely oblivious of BCCI's practices. Abedi had organized BCCI in such a way that no single regulatory authority had a worldwide view of its activities. During its early years, the only major regulatory setback occurred in 1978, when, as we have seen, the Bank of England froze the bank's British branch network at forty-five because it was concerned about BCCI's rapid growth.

The first regulator to take a serious look at BCCI was a U.S. bank examiner, and what he found was highly disturbing.

Robert Bench, a ruddy-cheeked career bank supervisor, was the associate deputy controller for international banking at the Office of the Comptroller of the Currency (OCC), the federal regulatory agency with primary responsibility for nationally chartered banks. In early 1978, Bench decided to commission a study of BCCI. He now says that he can't remember what prompted him to order the study, but it's likely that the National Bank of Georgia (NBG) deal had something to do with it; Ghaith Pharaon, the acquirer of NBG, was a big shareholder in BCCI. In addition, there was already speculation that Arab banking interests might want to buy into First American. In fact, it was at that time that BCCI clients were buying up a large block of stock in that company.

The man assigned to the job was Joseph E. Vaez, a diminutive Hispanic who had spent eight years as a bank examiner. Vaez was an excellent choice, for he was a careful and thorough examiner who took great pride in his work. It also helped that he was based in London, BCCI's corporate headquarters. His main job was to keep track of the London operations of American banks, including Bank of America.

Vaez's first step was to quiz B of A officials in London. For several weeks, Vaez waded through B of A's credit reviews of the mysterious young banking institution run by ambitious Pakistanis. The latest balance sheet data at that time dealt with BCCI's condition as of the end of September 1977.

In February 1978, Vaez produced his report for Robert Bench. It proved to be an extraordinarily prescient document, exposing dangerous practices at BCCI that would lead to huge losses years later. Vaez noted that BCCI had an "extremely complex conglomerate structure," making it very difficult to understand how the pieces fit together. He sought to depict the bank's structure with a graphic containing more than twenty different companies and the names of several Arab sheikhs.

It was impossible, he said, to determine how much money had been borrowed by BCCI or companies associated with it, including Cayman Islands entities grouped under the name ICIC, themselves major BCCI shareholders. When B of A's auditors looked over BCCI, they had not been able to examine the books of ICIC or other Cayman units. With a financial institution, it is critical to look at all its units simultaneously because money can be moved very quickly from one to another.

Although it was difficult to gain a complete understanding, Vaez found plenty of signs of dangerous practices. One warning was BCCI's phenomenal growth rate. Rapid growth in loans can indicate that a bank is not paying adequate attention to risks or that it is shoveling out too much money to a small number of borrowers, producing a threatening concentration of risk. From early 1976 to September 1977, BCCI's loans had more than doubled — from $511 million to $1.08 billion. That alone set off alarm bells for Vaez.

And how was this lending being financed? Most foreign banks in London funded a large part of their U.S. dollar lending by tapping into the so-called interbank market where banks deposit money with one another — but not BCCI. "BCCI's name in the interbank market is virtually unknown," said Vaez. Most of the bank's $2 billion in deposits came from "wealthy Arabian sources," he noted, and were "mainly generated in the United Arab Emirates." Vaez also found that BCCI's lending procedures seemed to be highly questionable. His report referred to BCCI's "highly personal relationships with major clients," delays in reporting loans to its own board, and weak credit analysis and loan documentation.

Sizable loans to insiders were another red flag. Some of BCCI's biggest borrowers were members of the ruling families of the UAE, many of whom were also BCCI shareholders. The emirate of Sharjah had borrowed more than $75 million. There was a total of $203 million of real estate loans in the UAE, about half of which were guaranteed by the ruling families. Such guarantees, of course, might well end up at the door of Sheikh Zayed, the richest UAE ruler and a benefactor of most of the rulers of the other sheikhdoms. One of the most disturbing findings was that BCCI seemed to have no policies aimed at preventing an excessive concentration of lending. There was, in Vaez's words, "no internal maximum lending limit" at BCCI. In Western banks, a standard rule of thumb is that a bank should lend no more than 10 percent of its capital to a single borrower. At the time of the report, BCCI's total capital was $63 million, which meant it should have lent no more than about $6 million to any one customer. However, its loans to the Gokals' Gulf Group totaled a staggering $185 million — equivalent to *three times* the bank's capital and *thirty times* the accepted ratio.

These ratios were not some academic issue; they meant that BCCI's very survival was at stake. If the Gokals failed to repay just a third of their loans, BCCI's entire capital would be wiped out and the bank would be out of business.

And BCCI's loan portfolio was anything but solid. Between June 1976 and September 1977, questionable loans had soared from $27 million to $226 million. By far, the biggest problem area was the Gulf Group: fully $122.5 million of the bank's $185 million of loans to this group were categorized as substandard.

Vaez's report may have played some role in the OCC's attitude toward the First American takeover. On a number of occasions, the agency told the Federal Reserve that BCCI was poorly regulated and thus should have no role in the ownership or management of First American. But there is no sign that the OCC alerted foreign bank regulators about Vaez's findings. BCCI's reckless banking practices not only continued, Abedi and Naqvi embarked on a bold scheme of deception to mislead regulators and auditors about the true condition of the bank.

A central part of the scheme apparently began in 1977, after the Bank of England imposed new rules aimed at curbing concentrations of lending. The new regulations created a terrible dilemma for Abedi and Naqvi. If BCCI cut back its lending to the Gokals, the Gulf Group could well collapse, pulling down BCCI with it. It was possible, of course, that Sheikh Zayed might agree to pump in fresh capital to rescue BCCI, but this was by no means certain. There was, however, another solution: a cover-up. BCCI could conceal the bad loans from regulators and auditors.

Abedi transferred a large portion of the Gokal loans — as well as other dubious credits — to the Cayman Islands, where banking supervision was virtually nonexistent. In a masterpiece of understatement, Masihur Rahman later said, "There was obviously more flexibility in record-keeping in Grand Cayman." So many bad loans were transferred there that BCCI officers used to refer to it as "the dustbin." As Shahid Suleri, a BCCI branch manager, later told a reporter, "All of us had, in BCCI that is, had our, you know, Cayman horror stories. What amazed us to begin with was that [it] appeared to be the place where every problem loan was transferred to, was dumped." And no one, he added, knew what happened to those loans once they were transferred to the Caymans.

At the center of this growing fraud was a loose collection of dummy companies in the Caymans, many of which were collectively known as the ICIC Group and constituted a bank within the bank. The ICIC Group worked closely with BCCI's Caymans branch, itself the least regulated part of the far-flung group. The initials stood for International Credit & Investment Company and had originally been used by Abedi between 1972 and 1976 to refer to a charitable trust and other entities he had set up in that period to hold a large proportion of BCCI's stock — up to half the bank's shares in its early days. The ICIC Group included a host of other entities, among them subsidiaries, a charitable foundation, and the BCCI staff benefit fund.

In April 1976, Abedi had formally incorporated two holding companies in the Cayman Islands: ICIC Holdings Limited and ICIC Overseas Limited. To serve as nominee shareholders of ICIC, Abedi recruited a handful of trusted lieutenants, men who were also of Muslim Indian origin from Uttar Pradesh and who had worked with him since the 1950s. The ICIC entities were clearly part of the BCCI group, yet their accounts weren't consolidated with the parent bank's. What this meant was that the auditors were never able to gain a complete picture of the group. In addition, the Caymans branch was the head office for BCCI's Bank of Credit and Commerce International (Overseas) Ltd. holding company, which was separate from BCCI's Luxembourg holding company and, until 1986, audited by a different firm.

Abedi and Naqvi were personally in charge of this scheme: audits from the Grand Cayman branch went directly to them. Naqvi's assistant Hashim Shaikh took direct responsibility for managing the Gokal accounts. Price Waterhouse, which audited ICIC, accepted the story that there were several accounts they weren't allowed to examine because they belonged to secretive Arab sheikhs and were "confidential."

To manage the deception, Abedi and Naqvi established a so-called special duties department. Based at BCCI's Leadenhall Street headquarters (about two hundred yards from the Bank of England) and including a few other bankers in nearby Cunard House, the department employed around a dozen people. Most of them were based in London, but — according to an auditor's report — a few were in other

BCCI offices, including A. Abbas, the manager of BCCI's Bahrain branch, and the general manager of the Grand Cayman branch, Syed Ziauddin Ali Akbar until 1986 and thereafter S. M. Akbar.

If anyone outside the bank found out what was going on, it could spell disaster for BCCI, so Abedi took various steps to ensure secrecy. One precaution was to physically separate special duties employees from other BCCI staffers. Some of them worked in a small office on an upper floor of the head office, where they would have relatively little contact with others. Another precaution was to use people in whom Abedi had total confidence. All of the department's employees were of Pakistani origin, most of them Shi'ites whose families came from around Lucknow, and all were very loyal to Abedi and Naqvi.

Hasan Mahmood Kazmi, a central figure in the scheme, was a prime example. He was devoted to Abedi, having worked for him since the 1950s. The ties between their families went further back, to the court of the rajahs of Mahmudabad near Lucknow and its ruling clique of Shia Muslims. Kazmi's forebears had worked as servants for the rajah and his family, ranking below such courtier families as the Abedis.

Money was also a factor in the loyalty of certain members of the special duties department. Abedi had brought most of them to England, paying them much higher salaries than they could have earned in Pakistan. In addition, BCCI granted nearly all of them sizable loans that they knew they probably wouldn't have to repay if they left the bank. If any of these trusted clerks did choose to leave, he might also receive a handsome farewell check. Jamshid Khan, who handled the accounts of Kamal Adham and his associate Sayed Jawhary, received $300,000 upon leaving the bank, according to an auditor's report. Another employee, Hashem Sheikh, walked away in 1988 with a $1.7 million payment from Naqvi, the same report says. These were staggering sums for people who were essentially doing clerical work — but it was clerical work of a very confidential nature.

In carrying out this scheme, it wasn't enough simply to move questionable loans to the Cayman Islands. BCCI officials also used a series of dummy companies to shift loans from one place to another in a massive and complicated shell game. Almost as soon as the Gokal accounts were moved to the Caymans, Naqvi and Hashem Sheikh began to manipulate them, moving money around to make it appear as though regular interest payments were being made. The Gokals helped with this manipulation, which involved the manufacture of false documents, the deliberately exaggerated use of accounts, and the secret transmission of funds. Money would be whisked around the BCCI empire, through the London, Grand Cayman, and Madrid branches and through BCCI's affiliated banks in Switzerland and Oman. The Gokals even provided the special duties department with stationery for their companies, including account opening forms and letters with payment instructions, to speed up the document fabrication necessary to spirit funds around the globe to conceal their growing debts. It would soon be hard for investigators, even for the perpetrators of the fraud, to sort out the reality from the fiction, the false profits from the real losses. (The Gokals, through their lawyer, deny any wrongdoing.)

The deception showed results very quickly. Vaez's report stated that BCCI's loans to the Gokals stood at $122.5 million in September 1977, as we have seen. Accountants from Price Waterhouse, however, estimated that they owed just $80 million at the end of 1977. It is almost inconceivable that the Gokals repaid more than $40 million in just three months. Their primary business, international shipping, was headed into a prolonged dive. In addition, the supposed shrinking of these debts occurred at the same time the brothers were trying to expand their way out of the shipping recession by using borrowed funds to buy cargo ships and companies. A commodity trader who dealt with the Gokals in Geneva recalls that there were frequent rumors that the brothers were in terrible financial trouble.

The answer, of course, is that the Gokals' debts did not diminish. They had simply been transferred off the BCCI balance sheet to shell companies controlled by BCCI in the Caymans. What is more, BCCI continued shoveling money to the Gokals during the remainder of the 1970s and throughout the 1980s. "Their loans just jumped and jumped and jumped," said Masihur Rahman, "till it was about $600 million to a single party."

Like lies, frauds tend to multiply: the commission of one fraud usually requires at least two others to cover it up. The account manipulations perpetrated by Abedi, Naqvi, and their special duties department were no exception. To disguise the scale of their debts to BCCI, the Gokals borrowed through more than sixty companies, including entities with such names as Marcotrade and Harpon Trading as well as myriad companies with Gulf in their titles. Just managing this scheme would eventually involve no less than 750 accounts at BCCI through which a staggering total of $15 billion was routed in the 1970s and 1980s.

Other bad loans were also moved to the Cayman Islands, causing the balance sheet of BCCI's Grand Cayman branch and the ICIC companies to grow rapidly over the next few years. By the mid-1980s, the total assets in the Caymans were as high as $2.5 billion — about 15 percent of the BCCI group's assets.

BCCI's "bank within a bank" in the Cayman Islands was involved in yet another sensitive operation: making loans to many of BCCI's own stockholders. At any bank, lending to insiders can be risky, but at BCCI, it was part of an audacious fraud: the manufacturing of fake equity capital.

Equity capital is the foundation of a corporation and the most essential buffer for a bank. When a company is established, investors contribute money and receive shares of stock in return. If the company becomes profitable, some of the profits may be retained by the company to strengthen the capital base. If the firm loses money, the equity serves as a kind of shock absorber. Losses come out of equity capital, but if there is sufficient equity, the bank has time to regroup, improve its strategy, and return to profitability.

In BCCI's case, a strong base of equity capital was particularly important. It was, after all, a somewhat mysterious bank with holding companies incorporated in two weakly regulated financial centers: Luxembourg and the Cayman Islands. Luxembourg had no central bank, which meant that there was no institution to provide BCCI with temporary loans if it ran into liquidity problems.

If potential depositors expressed concerns about BCCI, bank officials would say that there was no need to worry. BCCI was owned by fabulously wealthy oil sheikhs who had injected millions of dollars into the bank over the years, and they would certainly be willing to help it out if it ran into trouble — if only to safeguard their investments. "When we wanted to deal with many official bodies, large corporations, various agencies," explained Abdur Sakhia, who was BCCI's senior man in the United States, "they would always ask us, who is the lender of last resort? And we would say, 'the richest man in the world,' because we were owned partially by the ruler of Abu Dhabi." BCCI's bankers would also point to their balance sheet, which Sakhia and others would boast was "one of the best . . . in terms of ranking, in terms of financial ratios, in terms of liquidity."

So where did BCCI's equity capital really come from? When Abedi founded the bank in 1972, he certainly did raise some of the start-up capital from Bank of America and Sheikh Zayed. But he was always vague about the rest of the money.

When, in 1978, Abedi was a defendant in a lawsuit by First American, he had said in a deposition that a large portion of BCCI's stock — as much as 50 percent — was held by ICIC. He said that the balance of the stock was split about equally between Bank of America and twenty-five to thirty Middle Eastern investors. But what exactly was ICIC? Even Abedi seemed unsure. He described it as "an institution which is in the process of evolution." It would become a staff benefit fund and a charitable foundation. For the time being, though, Abedi told his mystified audience, ICIC's owners were "nominee shareholders of the foundation" who "have no beneficial ownership as such."

Later, the explanations and the details kept changing. In July 1978, *Euromoney* published a lengthy article on BCCI and obtained shareholder information from the bank. A chart identified ICIC as owning 41 percent of the bank, Bank of America, 24 percent, and "Middle East interests," 35 percent. This group was further identified (with no percentages listed) as comprising members of the "ruling families" of Bahrain, Sharjah, Abu Dhabi, Dubai, Saudi Arabia, and Iran as well as "Middle Eastern businessmen."

In 1983, the bank released a list of its shareholders in connection with an offering of floating-rate notes in the international capital market. The list contained some of the richest Arab sheikhs in the Persian Gulf: Sheikh Zayed's eldest son, Khalifa, owned 13.05 percent of the bank's stock and ranked as the second-largest shareholder; Zayed's Abu Dhabi Investment Authority held 10 percent of the stock; the Saudi officials Kamal Adham and Abdul-Raouf Khalil were the fourth- and fifth-biggest individual shareholders, with respective holdings of 3.87 and 3.44 percent. Powerful members of Saudi Arabia's ruling family were also named: Prince Turki bin Nasser bin Abdul Aziz al-Saud owned 1.21 percent of the bank's shares, and the interior minister, Prince Naif bin Abdul Aziz al-Saud, held 0.16 percent.

But there were some curious changes in the bank's various shareholder lists. Swaleh Naqvi was on the 1983 list as the owner of 0.03 percent of BCCI's stock. On another list released five years later, his name was missing. Ghaith Pharaon was cited as the biggest single shareholder in 1983, but his stake later dropped and then disappeared altogether in 1986, while that of his brother Wabel rose sharply.

The reality was that many of the wealthy Arab sheikhs on these lists had not risked their personal funds at all; they had borrowed from

BCCI itself to finance the stock purchases with the understanding that they would not have to repay the loans. What this means, of course, is that the very foundation of BCCI was to a great extent artificial. Much of the bank's equity capital was simply made up of loans that might never be repaid. It was a bank built on sand.

At the very founding of the bank, Abedi had used nominees equipped with borrowed money to provide capital. According to some of Abedi's associates, the visionary banker lent more than $2 million to a group of his friends in his last months at United Bank. These credits were then written off as bad debts, and the money was used to capitalize BCCI.

Certainly, it was only by using such front men over the years that Abedi was able to boost BCCI's share capital from just $2.5 million in 1972 to $845 million in 1990. To compensate the nominees for the use of their names, Abedi and Naqvi agreed to buy back shares at particular prices. They also promised that the nominees would earn specific rates of return on their share investments. To achieve these returns, Naqvi and his associates manipulated the price of the bank's privately held stock. Much of the stock manipulation was done through ICIC. As early as the late 1970s, ICIC was buying and selling BCCI stock to manufacture profits, boost the share price, and maintain confidence in the bank.

With the exception of Bank of America's stake, it is possible that *all* of BCCI's original capital was financed by bank loans. Congressional investigators have concluded that while Sheikh Zayed and his acolytes had supported BCCI with deposits from the beginning, they themselves may not have put much capital into the bank. "Abu Dhabi appears not to have capitalized BCCI, but instead to have insisted on guaranteed rates of return for the use of its money," a congressional report on BCCI said in the fall of 1992.

To disguise the funding of its nominees, Abedi and Naqvi used the ICIC group to move money in and out of the bank. By March 31, 1991, out of the $485 million of loans ICIC had made, as much as $160 million had been lent to BCCI shareholders to finance purchases of shares in the bank and its related companies. Effectively, ICIC was enmeshed in the most incestuous trading and funding of shares in BCCI, which was simultaneously its subsidiary and its parent.

Fees were paid to nominees willing to lend their names to such irregular share transactions. Faisal Saud al-Fulaij, a Kuwaiti investor who frequently acted as a nominee for BCCI, received $100,000 a year and a $606,000 payment on August 23, 1990, according to British investigators. Mohammed Hammoud, another important nominee, received as much as $1 million a year in the late 1980s, according to the investigators. Naqvi and his team often guaranteed returns, too, in lieu of payments. In December 1979, for example, ICIC Overseas guaranteed a return of 1.75 percent over the prevailing interbank deposit rate to Sayed Jawhary in exchange for a $2 million investment in BCCI shares.

The use of such nominees to hold the company's shares was so extensive that by the end of 1989 as much as 45 percent of BCCI's entire share capital was in the hands of front men, with a further 11 percent owned by ICIC entities. Through such devices, Abedi could increase the bank's capital at will. A former senior BCCI officer recalls meeting with Abedi at the bank's headquarters in London to discuss BCCI's need for additional capital. "Why don't we increase the capital?" Abedi said. "Why don't we increase it to $800 million?" And, miraculously, the capital soon grew to $800 million from its previous level of $600 million. "I don't know where the money came from," the senior BCCI officer says. Subsequently, the two men again discussed the bank's capital. "Why don't we make it $1 billion?" Abedi said. Again, the capital soon jumped to $1 billion. The banker recalls wondering at the time, "Is this guy printing his own money?"

Some of the more devious accounting tricks were performed under the supervision of Kazmi, whose title was general manager of ICIC. He would write to some of BCCI's coterie of sheikhs, assuring them that they had no liability for the many transactions that were being carried out in their names. "Your Highness. . . . You wouldn't be liable for the repayment of the [loan] under any circumstances," Kazmi assured the ruler of the emirate of Ajman, Sheikh Humaid bin Rashid Al Naomi, in 1983. It was just as well. Unlike Sheikh Zayed, Sheikh Humaid had no huge oil wealth to call on to honor his loans. Kazmi also wrote similar letters to Kamal Adham. This practice of essentially renting the sheikhs' names with their consent — used from the very outset at BCCI — became increasingly common as the bank sought to hide its growing losses and increase its "capital."

Judging by their correspondence with ICIC, at least some of these nominees knew precisely what their role was. Wabel Pharaon, Faisal al-Fulaij, and others wrote to ICIC, setting out their roles as nominees. "I ratify and confirm all your actions by way of acquisition, purchase and sale of the said shares [in BCCI] in my name as your nominee," Wabel Pharaon wrote to ICIC on December 4, 1984.

Many, if not most, of BCCI's loans to its own shareholders to finance share purchases or other secret BCCI ventures weren't repaid. Moreover, the recipients of the funds generally didn't pay much interest at all, if any. BCCI itself had to cover up these holes; otherwise it would have become plain that the bank was using nominees and was involved in a huge deception. This amounted to a massive fraud on BCCI's depositors, duping them into believing that the bank was backed by wealthy oil sheikhs and was thus a safe place for them to leave their savings. Many of these depositors were poorer people from developing nations who had to struggle hard to gather their meager deposits in BCCI. The bank went even further: it began to steal its depositors' money.

Abedi, Naqvi, and members of the special duties department took to collecting customers' deposits without even recording these liabilities on the bank's books and using the money to make interest payments on its loans to the nominees.

Just as BCCI had transferred many of its big and suspect loans to the Cayman Islands, so it began to transfer lots of its big-dollar deposits there. A large portion of this money had been collected in developing countries, much of it from Islamic banks. Like a centrifuge spinning out of control, the frauds in and around the bank were spreading exponentially.

To bolster its supply of "unrecorded deposits," Naqvi and his special duties team began to use ICIC to misappropriate money from BCCI. These funds were then directed into the accounts of the Gokals' Gulf Group and other delinquent accounts to allow them to seem solvent and to conceal the extent of their borrowings from BCCI. By booking excessive interest payments and other charges against the Gokal loans, BCCI also was able to provide itself with apparent profits.

Once this mechanism for routing money illicitly was set up, it was also easy to loot the bank directly, by siphoning out depositors' money. As the looting gathered pace, straight transfers were made to less regulated companies like ICIC, Capcom, and other BCCI satellites as well as to senior BCCI officials. For example, on March 26, 1985, ICIC approved an interest-free loan to Swaleh Naqvi of £325,000 (about $600,000). Abedi clearly intended that the loan would not be collected, according to a BCCI file memo relating to a conversation between ICIC's clerk Kazmi and Abedi in January 1988: Abedi asked Kazmi "to write off the loan" and instructed him to pay Naqvi £3,000 a month. Much bigger sums were also involved. Imran Imam of the special duties department instructed ICIC to draw down a loan of $50.6 million in the name of Ghaith Pharaon, then to pay this money to National Commercial Bank's Jiddah office.

This was the ultimate abuse of the trust placed in a bank by its depositors. Abedi and his associates had cynically turned a Third World institution into a mechanism for robbing depositors from developing countries. And the beneficiaries were rich sheikhs from the Persian Gulf, BCCI's associates around the world, and the bank's own management.

By stealing depositors' money, BCCI had become a Ponzi scheme. This type of fraud is named for the Italian-American swindler Charles Ponzi (1883–1949), who attracted deposits in the 1920s by offering returns that were well above the market's expectations. To make these high interest payments, the con man dips into the deposits entrusted to him. This, in turn, produces a growing hole in the accounts. But, by appealing to the greed and credulity of depositors, the operator of the scheme is — for a time, at least — able to continue attracting deposits. Ponzi, through his Securities Exchange Company in Boston, collected more than $15 million in less than a year by offering to double depositors' money in six months. Ponzi's scheme ran at breakneck pace. Meanwhile, its perpetrator moved from a shabby garret to a twenty-acre estate with a fabulous mansion and a heated swimming pool within just a few months.

BCCI's Ponzi scheme developed more gradually, but it was much larger and more difficult to detect because of the multiple jurisdictions in which the bank did business and the secretive maze of companies and front men. In essence, however, it was the same scam that Ponzi had perpetrated. BCCI was plundering its deposits because it needed an ever-greater supply of funds to keep paying high returns to its nominees and investors and to cover the growing holes in its balance sheet. Money also went into the pockets of BCCI officials.

In this heady atmosphere, where "capital" and "profits" could be conjured out of the air, Abedi and his staff joined in the looting. And they used depositors' funds to take huge risks in the foreign exchange, commodity futures, and options markets.

As the fraud grew, so did the need to move large sums of money out of the sight of regulators. Just about the only places to do that were the futures and options markets, which happen to be the riskiest markets in the world. But these markets could also offer Abedi and Naqvi the chance to hit the jackpot and make enough money to cover the gaps in BCCI's balance sheet.

Several BCCI associates had already been burned in the commodity markets. Sheikh Zayed, for example, had fallen out in 1980 with Abdullah Darwaish, who ran his private office and had been his ambassador to Pakistan, as noted in Chapter 3. Darwaish and Riaz Aslam, a Pakistani and one of the sheikh's financial advisers, invested in the metals markets, incurring losses of about $100 million. The resulting squabble dragged through the U.S. courts for years before Zayed dropped the suits. Darwaish was briefly detained, but Aslam was not released until 1990.

But nothing would match the wild gambling spree by BCCI's treasury department in the early and middle 1980s. At every major bank, the treasury department plays an important role. If the bank needs additional deposits to fund its loans, the treasury department raises the money in the interbank market or issues certificates of deposit to investors. If the bank has surplus cash, the treasury department places it in the interbank market or invests it in short-term instruments such as U.S. Treasury bills and certificates of deposit. The treasury department is also responsible for dealing in foreign exchange and other financial markets. At conservative banks, the treasury department tries to raise money cheaply and avoid losses. More aggressive institutions treat the treasury department as a profit center, hoping its traders can make a few million dollars by maneuvering more skillfully than other players in the market. BCCI's treasury department took risks far beyond those of even the most aggressive banks. The treasury department, quite literally, bet the bank in its efforts to control and maintain the sprawling frauds at BCCI.

The chief trader at BCCI responsible for this gambling spree was Syed Ziauddin Ali Akbar, who became head of the treasury department in 1982. He was a smooth and debonair banker in his thirties with intimate ties to BCCI's top management. Akbar wore two hats at BCCI: while running the treasury department in London, he managed the Grand Cayman branch. This combination may sound absurd, but it made sense in the context of BCCI. For one thing, all the important decisions about the bank's Caymans entities were made in London.

For another, the treasury department for the entire BCCI group was part of its Caymans holding company (rather than its Luxembourg holding company). The Grand Cayman branch was also where BCCI maintained the accounts of some of its most important customers and shareholders, including Kamal Adham, Abdul-Raouf Khalil, Ghaith Pharaon, and the Gokals. It thus fell to Akbar to manage these monies under Naqvi's supervision.

After taking over the treasury, Akbar claimed to be making big profits on the bets he took in the financial markets. Not that it was easy to verify these claims; with characteristic sloppiness, BCCI consolidated its treasury results with those of the Grand Cayman branch, rather than providing a separate and detailed account of the bank's trading activity.

Top officials of BCCI were impressed by Akbar's apparent profits, and he was given all the bank's surplus funds for his trading and investment schemes. This wasn't, of course, the bank's own money; these were deposits purloined from BCCI's customers. Akbar took wild risks with these funds, carrying out many of these trades in the names of some of BCCI's rich clients, in many cases with their permission, according to the auditors. It is hardly surprising that these rich clients — many of whom were Arab sheikhs — would agree to Akbar's free use of their names. He wasn't using their money, after all, but was merely renting their names.

Two of these sheikhs, Adham and Khalil, appear to have benefited enormously from Akbar's shenanigans, receiving large transfers of money to their accounts at Capcom from BCCI's treasury department. Akbar also would use the names of some of Khalil's companies, including Razat Associates Inc. and Maram Trading Company, according to Price Waterhouse. This was apparently done with Khalil's knowledge and permission, and — according to some accounts — Akbar was often doing Khalil's bidding in these transactions. (Khalil denies any wrongdoing.)

Akbar was an old friend of Khalil's and Adham's. He had known them since the mid-1970s, when he worked at National Bank of Oman, the joint venture bank owned by BCCI and Bank of America. Akbar and Khalil were also engaged in several U.S. real estate ventures together, as we saw in Chapter 6.

The Gokals also became involved in BCCI's plunge into speculative markets. As part of their diversification, the brothers acquired a commodity trading outfit in Geneva called Tradigrain, which they later conveniently sold to Ghaith Pharaon. Gil Miller, a veteran of the Chicago futures business, traded frequently with the Gokals. He remembered the sangfroid with which Abbas Gokal would receive news of massive losses. Most other people, Miller said, would have been screaming or crying at such setbacks. Abbas "loved the game, he loved currencies," Miller recalled in the summer of 1991. Like many players in the dangerous commodity markets, Abbas was "addicted to it."

Like Abbas Gokal, Akbar took enormous risks in highly speculative markets — such as that for options on U.S. Treasury securities. Options are notoriously volatile investments that can bring wonderful windfalls or wounding losses. By investing in options to buy U.S. Treasury bonds at a particular yield on a particular future day, an investor is betting on the likely course of U.S. interest rates. Akbar, under Naqvi's supervision, was "taking positions on silver, and on twenty-year bonds, suggesting that twenty-year bonds would [yield] 7 percent or 8 percent, which anybody who understands treasury" would think was absurd, Masihur Rahman, the bank's finance director, has said.

BCCI took on huge risks in these markets, totaling an astounding $11 billion, according to Rahman. This, he added, was eleven times the maximum exposure that the bank's treasury committee had set for investments in the commodity and options markets. But Akbar, using the bank's Caymans units, had apparently been able to ignore this limit without the knowledge of some of his superiors. Naqvi knew the details of Akbar's strategy, according to Rahman. The huge exposure of $11 billion of options contracts was possible only because of the practice in the commodity and option markets of requiring investors to put up only 10 percent of the total amount they were investing.

Inevitably, Akbar began to incur huge losses. Dating all BCCI's losses in the commodity futures and options markets precisely is difficult particularly because of the complex deceptions that Akbar used to cover them up. Other people, including BCCI's auditors and regulators at the Bank of England, have stated that the losses began perhaps as far back as 1977, years before Akbar became involved. Others maintain that the "options losses" were just a convenient cover for all the bank's many different losses and for the looting of its treasury.

Senior BCCI officers and those who have struggled to understand the bank generally agree that the most spectacular losses apparently occurred between 1983 and 1985, when Akbar took big bets in the U.S. Treasury bond options market. This insane trading, which had many professionals in the market wide-eyed, went on for years without a peep from the auditors or the bank regulators. Under the cover of a huge volume of transactions, Naqvi, Akbar, and others made large transfers, robbing the bank of hundreds of millions of dollars in the process.

Pierre Jaans, the chain-smoking chief of Luxembourg's bank regulatory agency, the Institut Monétaire Luxembourgeois (IML) and a veteran of the Bundesbank, Germany's central bank, had met with senior BCCI officers every few months since the bank was incorporated in Luxembourg in 1972. The government had been eager to boost the tiny country as a banking center, and Jaans was impressed and encouraged by Abedi's arrival with rich Arab backers. BCCI swiftly became one of the biggest banks in Luxembourg, although it was something of an anomaly in the grand duchy's growth as a financial center. This goal had been achieved mostly by attracting subsidiaries of big international banks that wanted to take advantage of tax breaks for issuing and listing international bonds.

In late 1985, Jaans and his colleagues at the IML became concerned about gossip regarding BCCI's unbridled trading activity. This timid and understaffed agency, which had been blithely unaware of BCCI's outrageous practices for years, now asked the bank's auditors at Price Waterhouse to review its treasury activities.

The auditors discovered evidence that the bank had suffered big losses on its futures and options trading and that it had not recorded them properly. Naively, perhaps, Price Waterhouse assumed that the losses were the result of incompetence. Several years later, it reported to the Bank of England that it had gradually become convinced that Akbar had fraudulently inflated the treasury division's income: he often wrote options contracts toward the end of the month and, by accounting incorrectly for the fee income accrued, generated false profits for the treasury division. The options contracts incurred huge and growing losses. But they were not charged to BCCI. Instead, they were booked against clients' accounts or covered up with bogus loans or unrecorded deposits.

BCCI's commodity trades were in any case a zero-sum game. For every loser, there's a winner on the other side. And to understand these huge losses properly, investigators would also have to learn who was on the other side of these trades. If BCCI was the loser, who was the winner? In the London markets there were direct counterparties, but in the more regulated U.S. markets the counterparty is always the exchange itself. Even in the United States, though, counterparties can effectively be created by arranging so-called mirror trades, whereby another trader or firm agrees to perform a simultaneous trade with the exchange, thus becoming the other side of the transaction.

Many of the big commodity trading companies certainly benefited greatly from Akbar's apparent foolhardiness, and none more so than Capcom, the BCCI satellite in London. The other main brokers used by BCCI were Refco, Rudolf Wolff, and Bear Stearns. (Rudolf Wolff even had a separate office to deal with BCCI and, according to the auditors, allowed the bank an overdraft of $40 million on December 31, 1984, which the auditors suspect was used to help hide the bank's losses.) Until BCCI stopped its trading in options and futures, the bank was Capcom's main source of business, generating revenues of some $16.7 million in 1985. But once the scale of the bank's losses became apparent in October 1985, it stopped trading in these markets.

When it withdrew, BCCI was left in a terrible quandary. If it closed out its options contracts, it would have to report losses of hundreds of millions of dollars. It delayed announcing its 1985 results, but news of the problems leaked out. A story in the European edition of the *Wall Street Journal* in late May 1986 quoted BCCI sources as saying that the bank had lost as much as $150 million on its trading in U.S. Treasury bond options. In response, BCCI issued a statement on June 2 confirming the *Journal*'s story.

The bank's official version of the losses was that a total of $285 million had been lost, of which $150 million was charged in 1985, $75 million in 1984, and $60 million in 1986. The reality was much worse than even these horrific figures. Not only had BCCI's stated equity been wiped out, the bank's liabilities vastly exceeded its assets. For years, though, the auditors apparently didn't properly understand, or disclose, the scale of the fraud that produced the losses.

Abedi and Naqvi, however, knew what had happened. When Akbar left the bank in 1986, he gave Naqvi a detailed summary. This document — which the auditors said they didn't see for several more years — shows accumulated losses of $849 million for the years 1982–86 and states that Akbar inflated profits by $108 million in 1982, $136 million in 1983, and $234 million in 1984.

To help cover up the losses, Akbar had used $400 million of deposits that weren't even recorded in BCCI's books, $250 million of money managed by ICIC, bogus loans, deposits from the bank's Abu Dhabi subsidiary, and funds from other sources, auditors said in 1991. More than $60 million of the unrecorded deposits belonged to the government of Cameroon, in West Africa. But the biggest chunk — $246 million — came from Feisal Islamic Bank, an institution in Cairo that is controlled by the Saudi ruling family. The special duties department seemed to prefer to use Islamic bank deposits because they didn't accrue interest and didn't have to be accounted for in an orthodox way. Arjmand Naqvi, the account officer for Feisal Islamic Bank, was an important member of the special duties department.

Capcom was probably the most important vehicle for looting money from BCCI between 1984 and 1986, company documents show. For example, in four separate transactions, a total of $221 million was transferred to Capcom from BCCI. Much if not all of this money went to accounts in the names of Adham and Khalil.

The huge transfers out of BCCI to Capcom were made up of a number of different payments, according to work carried out by auditors and investigators in 1991 and 1992. A profit schedule found in Akbar's desk in London showed a Capcom account — called ARKY — making $53 million out of its transactions with BCCI. Some U.S. investigators believe this account was controlled by Khalil. According to one investigator's notes, "These profits were made from October 1984 to September 1985, the period in which BCCI lost $430 million at Capcom. This is the clearest evidence that the shareholders of Capcom and/or Akbar stole funds from BCCI through artificial market transactions." The picture is really not that clear, however, since Akbar may have used the names of Adham and Khalil without their knowledge.

On June 25, 1985, BCCI's treasury division transferred $68 million to a Capcom subsidiary "for an unknown purpose," Price Waterhouse said in 1991. Payments totaling $50 million were made to Capcom in March 1986 out of BCCI's treasury "for which no liability for payment was recorded," the auditors said. These payments were made on Naqvi's instructions. It is unclear exactly where this money went after it reached the Capcom accounts apparently controlled by Adham, Khalil, and Akbar. Many Capcom documents were deliberately destroyed in late June 1991 by a company official.

Some U.S. investigators are intrigued by Adham's and Khalil's intelligence connections. Both men, of course, were veterans of Saudi intelligence and were closely associated with U.S. intelligence operatives. This relationship has fueled speculation that some of the money may have been used to finance covert operations by the Saudis and the CIA.

·   ·   ·

BCCI's reckless lending and trading — and the looting of deposits to cover up the losses — left the bank little more than an empty shell. Abedi, Naqvi, and their associates could not possibly let the truth come out. If they did, the whole edifice would come crashing down, and many of the thieves would be rounded up and thrown in jail. And so they began to steal even more money, to hide BCCI's losses and lack of capital.

The Ponzi scheme became even bigger and more complicated in the mid-1980s. Huge sums were taken from depositors and routed through various accounts to make it appear that loans were being serviced in a timely fashion. In 1986 alone, the special duties department routed an extraordinary $1.6 billion through a maze of accounts. Many transactions through BCCI's Swiss unit, Banque de Commerce et de Placements, even carried the advice "Pay without mentioning our name."

As the deception grew, the special duties department created more and more fictitious loans so that the bank could show apparent profits. When, for example, sheikhs who had bought BCCI shares on guaranteed terms demanded their money back, the returned funds would often be booked as fictitious loans.

The auditors and regulators now say they had little idea at the time of what was going on. For example, they say they were unaware of BCCI's cozy relationship with Capcom. But one incident should have been enough to alert even the most obtuse person that something was very rotten at both BCCI and Capcom.

When Akbar left BCCI in 1986, he became head of Capcom. Who owned Capcom? Its controlling shareholders included major BCCI stockholders like Adham and Khalil, the same people who had been "victimized" by Akbar's reckless trading. Why would they willingly hire Akbar? Moreover, wasn't it also strange that BCCI continued to deal with Capcom after Akbar took over, even though he had presided over the options-trading debacle? Akbar had not even been fired from BCCI, according to former bank officials. He left of his own accord and was even allowed to keep his company car and other benefits.

The treasury fiasco removed one barrier to trying to get a handle on BCCI's affairs; henceforth the banking group would have only one auditor. Ernst & Young (then called Ernst & Whinney), which had previously audited BCCI's Luxembourg units, insisted that it be given the whole BCCI group to audit or it would resign. Abedi balked, and the big accounting firm did resign, leaving the whole audit to Price Waterhouse.

Outsiders, though, still couldn't learn much from BCCI's annual reports. All anyone reading the reports from the mid-1980s would know was that BCCI had lost a total of about $285 million in the U.S. Treasury options market and that new capital had been supplied by an anonymous shareholder — widely believed to be Sheikh Zayed. That was a reasonable assumption. Abedi had, in fact, flown to Abu Dhabi in a desperate attempt to obtain money from Zayed. "At that time, we were literally stripped of capital," says Rahman. Soon afterward, $150 million of new capital was injected into the bank. BCCI and its auditors called this "a shareholder subvention."

Many years later it was discovered that the money wasn't from Zayed or from one of the other sheikhs in BCCI's shareholder group. It was not even new capital. The money actually came from the staff benefit fund, which was part of the ICIC group. Without consulting anyone, Abedi had plundered his staff's pensions to keep the bank alive.

The $150 million wasn't nearly sufficient, so Abedi looked for capital from new sources. He soon found some willing investors, the Bin Mahfouz family of Saudi Arabia, bankers and friends of the ruling family's. Significantly, the Saudis — whose very own Adham and Khalil are suspected of benefiting so greatly from the fraud at BCCI — were stepping in to rescue Abedi's ailing empire.

Salim Bin Mahfouz, the patriarch of the family, was a canny banker whose family came from the Hadrahmut, the southwestern corner of the Arabian Peninsula. He and his sons own a majority of National Commercial Bank (NCB), Saudi Arabia's largest bank, which they run as a family company. Khalid, the most ambitious and cosmopolitan of Salim's sons, had long cherished the ambition of adding a sizable international arm to the bank. But banking is a sensitive issue in Saudi Arabia, a theocratic state that pays particular heed to the words of the Qu'ran and its admonitions against charging interest. The Saudi government had limited the Bin Mahfouz's international ambitions to such a degree that they barely had a foreign presence. This left their bank ill prepared for the internationalization of financial markets and the opening up of the Saudi economy, both of which gathered force in the 1970s.

BCCI looked like a perfect match for the Bin Mahfouz: it had a network of offices spanning the globe, mostly Muslim management, and a need for capital. The details of the arrangements between BCCI and the Bin Mahfouz are obscure, but in 1986 the family reached an agreement with Abedi to buy into the bank and into First American, with an option and understanding that the investment would be increased.

The agreement, which gave the Bin Mahfouz family the right to increase its stake to 30 percent, also involved the Saudi family's issuing capital notes of about $300 million or $400 million, which were redeemable into capital after a certain number of years, according to Rahman. The Bin Mahfouz also obtained an agreement from Abedi that was characteristic of many of his understandings with his shareholders: he would buy them out at no loss whenever they wished. As an added sweetener for the Bin Mahfouz family, Abedi deposited $250 million in NCB, according to Rahman and others, raising questions about how genuine the Bin Mahfouz investment in BCCI really was. (The Bin Mahfouz have maintained that they made a genuine investment and then later sold it.)

The investment achieved Abedi's desire. It brought in much-needed cash and gave the prestigious Saudi family an initial stake of at least 10 percent of the bank. The money was immediately put to work to shore up some of BCCI's more bizarre accounting. A September 24, 1986, memo from Imran Imam of the special duties department to Sharaful Hasan, the manager of BCCI's Cayman Islands operation, said that $256.6 million would be credited to the bank's accounts, divided between the Cayman accounts of Faisal Saud al-Fulaij and the ruler of Ajman, both of them important nominees whose accounts were routinely manipulated by Imam and his colleagues. An accompanying memo, "Appropriation of $US 256.6 million received from NCB," breaks down the amounts of money owed to these two accounts, implying that money had already been temporarily moved to cover the interest owing on the accounts.

The Bin Mahfouz family even became involved in running BCCI when Khalid Bin Mahfouz joined the board of directors in 1986. But he soon became nervous about his new partners and within just a few months wanted to cut back the investment and end his association with Abedi. But Abedi and Naqvi needed help to find the money to buy out the Bin Mahfouz stake. Abedi turned to Zayed, whose Abu Dhabi Investment Authority seems, according to the bank's accountants, to have provided an off-the-books loan to finance the secret buyback of shares. In addition, the special duties department quietly created fictitious loans of $213 million in the Bin Mahfouz family's name to finance the repurchase of the shares.

With the temporary help of the Bin Mahfouz investment, Abedi and Naqvi survived the increasing strains of backing the Gokals' crumbling empire, of huge treasury losses, and of handing out favors to some of BCCI's backers in the Persian Gulf. But they had incurred massive costs: the bank's books were now a catalogue of manufactured loans, false profits, hidden loans, and stolen deposits. They had also plundered the staff pension fund, stealing the future livelihood of their own employees. And they had had to offer lucrative enticements to draw in a big new backer.

Keeping the bank going without fraud being detected would remain a major challenge. It would require a continued huge influx of deposits. And BCCI's need to use these deposits as it chose meant that the bank would increasingly turn to depositors more concerned about secrecy than security. Among those who fit the bill were the drug barons of Latin America, men who had accumulated billions of dollars as North Americans and Western Europeans acquired a taste for their costly merchandise: cocaine.

9

EL DORADO

ONE DAY IN SEPTEMBER 1983, a young American businessman named Steven Michael Kalish had dinner with two Panamanians during a business trip to Panama City. César Rodríguez and Enrique Pretelt had impressive political connections, and they arranged for Kalish to dine the next day at the home of the most powerful man in the country, General Manuel Antonio Noriega, the head of the National Guard. They suggested that he bring a gift, a normal gesture for a dinner guest. When Kalish arrived at Noriega's house, he brought his host an aluminum Halliburton briefcase, the type used by many photographers. The case was not the present, however, but merely the wrapping. Inside was $300,000 in cash.

Noriega appreciated the gesture, and he reciprocated by providing valuable assistance to Kalish's business, which happened to be drug smuggling. With Noriega's protection, Kalish transported huge quantities of Colombian cocaine and marijuana through Panama to the United States. In addition, Rodríguez helped Kalish launder his drug money. Kalish would load millions of American dollars onto private planes, fly the money to Panama, and turn it over to Rodríguez, who would launder it through his two favorite banks, the government's Banco Nacional de Panamá and a foreign institution called Bank of Credit and Commerce International.

Rodríguez wasn't the only member of this group who used BCCI. Accounts were opened by Kalish and Pretelt as well as Noriega himself, who channeled tens of millions of dollars through BCCI, much of it representing payoffs from drug traffickers like Kalish.

The laundering of drug money was not a sideline for BCCI in

Panama, it was one of the bank's principal businesses. In fact, money laundering was a lucrative business for BCCI all over the world.

To international bankers, one of the most mystifying things about BCCI was its ability to thrive in markets where other foreign banks found it difficult or impossible to turn a profit. Nigeria, as we have seen, was one such market. Others were Hong Kong and the UAE.

In 1983–84, the Hong Kong economy was in turmoil. Britain was negotiating the colony's future with the Chinese government and many Hong Kong Chinese began to panic. New investment dried up as businessmen exported capital to other countries. Most foreign banks reacted to these economic woes by retrenching, yet BCCI's Hong Kong unit expanded to the point where only three of the colony's 161 foreign banks had networks as big or bigger. Around the same time, the UAE was battered by plunging oil prices. Once again, BCCI seemed to weather the storm much better than other foreign banks. This phenomenon is captured in the headline of a 1986 article on BCCI's local affiliate, Bank of Credit and Commerce (Emirates): "BCCE — A Growing Bank in a Shrinking Market."

When BCCI officials were asked to explain such anomalies, they would make bland remarks about the bank's "efficient" manner of operating or its ability to exploit lucrative "niches." A BCCI official in Hong Kong, for example, said the bank made money in trade financing and foreign exchange dealings. The problem with that explanation is that *all* the leading banks in Hong Kong were active in those businesses.

The banker could have mentioned another niche: money laundering. The UAE and Hong Kong were major centers for heroin money. Banks in the UAE catered to traffickers from the Golden Crescent countries of Afghanistan, Pakistan, and Iran. Hong Kong banks received huge sums from traffickers in the world's leading opium-producing region, the Golden Triangle, which comprises parts of Burma, Thailand, and Laos.

One customer was General Khun Sa, a warlord in Burma who was reputed to control up to 80 percent of the region's opium trade. (In 1990, he was indicted in the United States on federal drug charges but remains a fugitive.) In mid-1991, it was estimated that he had deposited at least $300 million in BCCI. The accounts, according to an associate of his, were fed from Taiwan and Hong Kong.

BCCI officers in the United States also dealt with heroin traffickers. One client of BCCI's Miami branch was a Nigerian drug dealer named

Olutende ("Steve") Fafowora. In late 1987, a federal jury in Washington, D.C., convicted him of racketeering and conspiracy to distribute heroin. (In March 1989, the conviction was sustained on appeal.) Fafowora deposited money in BCCI in the name of a company he controlled, Afro Caribbean Connections. The prosecution called it "a sham corporation through which Fafowora invested his drug proceeds." Records seized from BCCI "were totally consistent with money laundering" because all of the deposits were in cash and cashier's checks.

The trafficker's brother, Oladapo Fafowora, happens to be a prominent figure in Nigeria. In the early 1980s, he was its deputy permanent representative to the United Nations and later became head of the Manufacturers Association of Nigeria. He should not, of course, be blamed for the sins of his brother. But it is worth noting that the two brothers were the sole owners of the company used to launder heroin money through BCCI.

Heroin has been overtaken in importance in recent years by another illegal drug, cocaine. Sales of the white powder generate tens of billions of dollars in revenues each year, and the prospect of getting a chunk of that money encouraged BCCI to embark on a major expansion into Latin America.

Latin America was the last part of the Third World penetrated by BCCI when, in 1979, it set up shop in Panama, a major offshore financial center.* Until 1983, BCCI's only other sites in the area were representative offices in Venezuela and Colombia. Meanwhile, other major banks were opening offices all over the region and lending huge sums of money to Latin American governments. The lending spree ended abruptly when the Third World debt crisis exploded in 1982 — at which point BCCI began its expansion. The timing is easy to explain. BCCI wasn't interested in making loans in Latin America, it wanted to collect money, including flight capital, deposits from central banks, loot from corrupt politicians, and cash from cocaine dealers. To Abedi, Latin America represented a wealth of potential deposits — an El Dorado to enrich his bank.

---

*BCCI was active in the Caribbean, however. The Cayman Islands was the site of one of BCCI's main holding companies as well as various dummy companies used in connection with frauds, as we have seen. During the 1980s, the Caribbean presence grew to include branches in Jamaica (1981), the Bahamas (1983), Barbados (1983), Curaçao (1983), and Trinidad & Tobago (1986).

The man behind BCCI's Latin American expansion was Kemal Shoaib, one of Abedi's chief lieutenants. (His family, like Abedi's, were Shi'ites from Mahmudabad, India.) His professional credentials were more impressive than those of most other BCCI executives; he had a master's degree in engineering from the Massachusetts Institute of Technology and had served as president of Pakistan's Muslim Commercial Bank. His father, Mohamed, was also prominent in the financial world, having been Pakistan's finance minister and a senior aide to Robert S. McNamara when he was president of the World Bank. Shoaib was assisted by Akbar Bilgrami, a young BCCI officer who was married to a Colombian and had a good command of Spanish. In the 1970s, Bilgrami had helped to acquire Spanish real estate for Sheikh Zayed. In 1983, Bilgrami was involved in BCCI's purchase of a Spanish bank.

One potential problem for BCCI was its reputation as a weakly regulated institution. Shoaib's solution was to hire a man with a solid reputation to deal with bank regulators: in 1980, he recruited Alberto Calvo, an Argentine economist who had spent several years as a senior official of the Inter-American Development Bank. "Calvo," says a former BCCI official, "gave [BCCI] tremendous legitimacy and credibility." When central bankers expressed concerns about BCCI, says this source, Calvo reassured them by saying that its dubious image was based on nothing more than rumors and speculation. In spite of these soothing words, BCCI broke the law in its first major move into Latin America.

In 1983, BCCI acquired 49 percent of Banco Mercantíl, a twenty-four-branch Colombian bank later renamed Banco de Crédito y Comercio de Colombia. BCCI didn't buy all the stock because foreigners were forbidden to hold a majority interest in local banks, but it got around that restriction through the use of front men. One of the board members was Rodrigo Llorente, who was one of the most prominent politicians in the country. He was a leader of the Conservative party, a former finance minister, and a former president of the central bank. "There was a [secret] voting trust to show all the power was in the hands of BCCI," says a former BCCI official. There was also "a buy-back agreement saying they can buy the shares back at any time for one dollar."* He adds that "the regulators are always taken in by

---

*The law was later changed, and in 1985 BCCI "bought" the stock from the nominees, increasing its stake to 99 percent.

the big name that's making the investment, without verifying the source of the funds."

BCCI planted three more flags in the region in 1984, opening a representative office in São Paulo, Brazil, a finance company in Uruguay, and a branch in Paraguay. In 1985, BCCI bought a 30 percent stake in a Buenos Aires bank (increased to 99 percent two years later).

In 1987, BCCI established a 50-percent-owned Brazilian subsidiary, with the remaining stock supposedly owned by local investors. In fact, BCCI used the same strategy it had employed in Colombia: the other investors were merely front men.

For creating this network, Alberto Calvo expected to be rewarded with the job of regional general manager for Latin America and the Caribbean. Instead, the job was given to S. M. Shafi, a Pakistani banker who had served as head of a BCCI joint venture in the Middle East, National Bank of Oman. Calvo resigned in early 1988 and went to work for BCCI's ally Ghaith Pharaon.* Shafi's qualifications for the post were singularly unimpressive. He spoke no Spanish and, according to a former BCCI official, had probably never visited Latin America. He even had a weak grasp of the region's geography. Shortly after his arrival at BCCI's Latin American headquarters in Miami, a colleague mentioned that he had just returned from a trip to Paraguay. Shafi remarked that the man must be tired after flying all the way from Africa.

Despite the limitations of Shafi and some of his associates, they were extremely adept at making political connections in Latin America. One man who assisted was Andrew Young, who, as noted earlier, was a paid consultant to BCCI. An internal memo states that Young provided "patronage and help" for the bank's "endeavors in Central America." In a few years, BCCI forged relationships with some of the most powerful people in the region, including Alan García Pérez, who served as president of Peru from 1985 to 1990.

When García was elected president, he was one of the youngest heads of state in the world — just thirty-five years old. Thanks to his youth and good looks, he was often compared to John F. Kennedy; like Kennedy, he projected a progressive image and seemed to embody a

---

*A few years earlier, Kamal Shoaib had become chairman of Independence Bank in California, a BCCI satellite owned by Pharaon.

new style of politics. Nevertheless, García has been linked to a number of murky financial transactions, some of which also involved BCCI. One was a secret arms agreement with France which he is suspected of having negotiated before he even took office.

One of García's favorite haunts was Paris, where he had been a university student, and he took a brief vacation there before assuming office in July 1985. On his return, García allegedly secretly canceled an arms deal Peru had made with the French in 1982, substituting a new agreement. Some of his political opponents have alleged that he negotiated the new deal during his trip. Under the old agreement, Peru was to have purchased twenty-six Mirage 2000 jet fighters from a consortium of French arms companies — Avions Marcel Dassault, Snecma, and Thomson-CSF. These planes could be signed over only if the French government agreed. Under the new contract, Peru would buy only twelve planes; the remainder would be sold to another country. This was potentially a very profitable deal, for the value of the planes had soared since the original contract was signed. Peru had agreed to pay between $12 million and $14 million per plane. It could now sell them for as much as $30 million apiece.

The surplus planes were sold to Morocco by two Arab arms dealers, Abdul Rahman el Assir (a former brother-in-law of the Saudi tycoon Adnan Khashoggi) and his partner Hazem Eissa, according to a consultant close to the transaction. The two arms dealers, the consultant says, banked the profits with BCCI.

García's progressive image was based in part on his willingness to challenge the international banks. When García took office, Peru owed $14 billion to foreign creditors, most of it to commercial banks. In a move that rocked the world financial community, the Peruvian leader insisted that his country would limit payments on its debts to an amount equal to 10 percent of export earnings — far less than it was obliged to pay. The banks responded by cutting off new credit, and García feared that they would also try to seize Peruvian assets, including funds that the central bank had deposited abroad. BCCI stepped in with a solution. In 1986, the Peruvians agreed to place central bank funds in BCCI.

On the surface, this appears to have been a bold act of Third World solidarity — perfectly in line with Abedi's rhetoric. In fact, this could easily have made things worse for Peru, since BCCI was systematically stealing the depositors' money as part of its schemes to cover up its disastrous financial condition. BCCI could well collapse, causing big losses to the Peruvian central bank. Some of the Peruvian officials who agreed to park the money in BCCI may have also had dishonest motives: BCCI allegedly paid $3 million in bribes to two Peruvian central bankers to garner the deposits. It was later alleged that García also accumulated millions of dollars through graft and used BCCI as a conduit for the funds. He denies the allegations.

While Alan García represented a new style of Latin American politician — in form, at least, if not necessarily in substance — the old guard was personified by Paraguay's Alfredo Stroessner. An aging army general, he was the epitome of the Latin American *caudillo* and had ruled his country with an iron hand since 1954, when he seized power in a coup d'état. Stroessner, whose father was Bavarian, had a soft spot in his heart for escaped Nazi war criminals. He had harbored other fugitives as well, including two deposed Latin American dictators, Juan Domingo Perón of Argentina and Anastasio Somoza Debayle of Nicaragua. (Before taking refuge there, Somoza had called Paraguay "the last place on earth for the worst people in the world.")

Smuggling was a pillar of the economy. Cigarettes, liquor, and cars imported to Paraguay found their way to neighboring Brazil. Another popular racket was the laundering of stolen cars: thousands of automobiles stolen in Brazil were taken to Paraguay and "legalized" after the payment of a small registration fee. The Stroessner regime was also linked to the drug trade. During the 1980s, U.S. authorities complained that Paraguay was importing large amounts of chemicals used to convert coca paste into cocaine, but Stroessner ignored requests to destroy the chemicals.

This corrupt and impoverished backwater was not the sort of place likely to appeal to most foreign banks, but BCCI, of course, was not like other banks. Paraguay was one of the first Latin American countries where BCCI set up a branch.

Ghaith Pharaon was also drawn to Paraguay, perhaps because it was the kind of country where foreign tycoons could easily secure an audience with the head of state. When he flew to Paraguay in late 1987, his trip was announced in advance in the local press, which described him as "one of the richest men in the world." The articles were based on press releases from Stroessner's office. Pharaon dazzled the general with grandiose plans to make major investments in the country, including a bizarre scheme to build a $300 million Disneyland-style theme park in President Stroessner City, right near the point where Paraguay, Argentina, and Brazil meet. The old *caudillo* was overthrown in 1989 and the theme park was never built.

Pharaon made more progress in Argentina, however, where he built a Hyatt Hotel in Buenos Aires, bought a jojoba plantation, and, by 1988, was apparently so taken by the country that he applied for Argentine citizenship. There was at least one false statement in his application: he claimed to be a major shareholder in BCCI, even though he had sold his stock in 1986. (Pharaon blames an employee for the mistake.) He managed to develop ties to some of the most powerful people in the country. One entrée, of course, was Alberto Calvo, whom he had hired from BCCI. He also did business with Javier Gonzalez Fraga, a top economic adviser to President Carlos Saul Menem. The president later named Gonzalez Fraga head of the Argentine central bank. Before assuming that post, Gonzalez Fraga had been involved in arranging a complicated debt-equity swap with BCCI which enabled Pharaon to build the Hyatt Hotel. The deal later touched off a criminal investigation in the United States. (Gonzalez Fraga has said there was nothing untoward about his dealings with Pharaon. "I am not now, nor have I ever been, 'Pharaon's man,' " he told an Argentine newspaper.)

The Saudi's most important link was with the family of President Menem's wife, Zulema Yoma. In cultivating the Yomas, Pharaon took advantage of an ethnic connection, for the Yoma family originated in Syria, as did Pharaon's. Members of the family were guests of Pharaon's at parties he held at such tony spots as the jockey club in Buenos Aires.

During the same period that BCCI and Pharaon were becoming active in Argentina, the country was emerging as an important transshipment center for South American cocaine destined for Europe. Traffickers in Spain would then distribute the drugs all over the continent. Pharaon was not implicated in the trafficking, but the names of some of his Argentine friends came up in a drug investigation by the Spanish police that began in late 1990. In July 1992, Amira Yoma, Menem's sister-in-law and former appointments secretary, was charged in Argentina with money laundering. She had allegedly carried suitcases of drug money from the United States to Argentina.

The most important center for the cocaine trade was, of course, Colombia, and that is where BCCI showed its most impressive growth in the region. After acquiring its Colombian bank in 1983, BCCI added seven new branches over the next four years while its total assets grew to $213 million. An item in a 1988 issue of the staff publication, *BCC International*, boasts:

> From small and difficult beginnings in 1983 something of value has been built in Colombia. The bank has experienced a growth unsurpassed in recent Colombian banking history. We are not here only to take, but also to give and to be responsible members of the society in which we move. Our present and future are linked to the evolution of the city and the country. When Colombia and Bogota prosper, we prosper, if they do not, we do not.

BCCI's "prosperity" in Colombia was closely tied to the drug trade. Indeed, that was one of the main reasons that BCCI bought the bank. "We knew that the money that we would be getting in Colombia would be drug money," BCCI's Abdur Sakhia later said. Two of the Colombian unit's branches were in Medellín, the home of the country's most important cocaine kingpins, and BCCI officials aggressively solicited deposits from them. In the words of one U.S. investigator, BCCI "absolutely and specifically sought out narco money." He added that the bank offered counseling to those people and told them how to invest and cover the money. One client was José Gonzalo Rodríguez Gacha, a cartel leader who stashed millions of dollars in BCCI. An Interpol report states that seven BCCI employees — one Colombian and six Pakistanis — gave "instructions as to the administration of his bank accounts in Luxembourg."

BCCI was playing a very dangerous game. U.S. law enforcement authorities had begun to crack down on money laundering, and there was a constant risk that they would discover what the bank was doing. In fact, not long after the Latin American expansion began, a former employee of the bank approached U.S. law enforcement officials with potentially explosive information about BCCI.

Aziz Rehman, as noted earlier, was a Pakistani immigrant living in Florida who had been hired by the Miami branch of BCCI in 1982 as a chauffeur and clerk. He was in a position to observe a great deal, and what he saw was highly disturbing, including signs that the bank was engaged in wide-scale money laundering. When BCCI fired Rehman in February 1984, he contacted the FBI and offered information about the bank. The bureau referred him to the Internal Revenue Service. In a series of meetings with IRS agents, Rehman told a fascinating tale, which he repeated years later in a deposition to a U.S. Senate investigator.

The manager, Abdur Sakhia, Rehman said, spent much of his time hobnobbing with politicians, as noted in Chapter 5. Rehman added that the office handled huge amounts of cash, even though it was not licensed to do retail banking. Starting in 1983, one of Rehman's duties was to transport bags of cash to other banks in Miami — as much as $700,000 at a time. When BCCI opened a branch in Jamaica that year, large amounts of currency started arriving from that country.* The cash would be brought in by companies like Wells Fargo and Brinks, and Rehman would take it to other banks in Miami — "sometimes twice a week, sometimes every second day or third day. In three months I deposit[ed] about $3 million," he said.

BCCI customers often made large cash deposits in the Miami branch — and he was sure that the bank did not fill out currency transaction reports (CTRs), as federal law required. (A law aimed at curbing money laundering requires banks to fill out CTRs for cash transactions of $10,000 or more.) Some BCCI officials, according to Rehman, took deposits to their homes, "because they want to fly it to some different places." He went on: "They fly it to basically Panama and Grand Cayman" by private plane. The bankers would do this, he said, when they received large amounts of cash and did not want to deposit it in the United States, since CTR forms would have had to be filled out. It appeared to be a very profitable business, according to Rehman. He said that when the bank took in cash, there was a lag in the payment of interest to the depositor.

Rehman also described what appeared to be a classic money-laundering technique: a customer would borrow money in the United States secured by a deposit in the Bahamas. He added that BCCI officers in Miami accepted deposits for its Nassau, Bahamas, branch when no such branch existed. "They would take the money from here and issue a receipt for Nassau, Bahamas, that you deposited the money, not in Miami, but in Nassau." To buttress his story, Rehman gave the IRS agents a pile of documents, including a thick computer printout of transactions for 1982–84.

The Miami office employed a large number of Pakistanis to do jobs that Americans could easily have done, Rehman said. His theory was that BCCI felt it could trust the Pakistanis with the sensitive cash transactions.

---

*Jamaica is a major exporter of marijuana.

Rehman asserted that BCCI fired him because he had complained about moving large amounts of cash; he was concerned about his personal safety. When the bank refused to give him a favorable reference, he was unable to find another job for a year and was forced into personal bankruptcy. He also claimed to have received threatening telephone calls.

The IRS agents took Rehman very seriously. They held a series of meetings with him over a period of several months and also gathered information about BCCI from other sources. In order to go further, however, they felt they would have to conduct an undercover investigation of BCCI, which required approval from their superiors in the agency. But permission was never granted — in spite of repeated requests — and BCCI continued to launder drug money with impunity in the United States and other parts of the world for several more years.*

The IRS's failure to pursue Rehman's allegations is particularly striking because BCCI's name popped up repeatedly during the next few years in drug investigations by the Drug Enforcement Administration (DEA) and other federal agencies.

From 1984 to 1987, the DEA conducted Operation Pisces, a probe of Colombian drug traffickers. Undercover agents dealt with Anibal Zapata, an accountant for the Medellín cartel leader Pablo Escobar Gavíria. Zapata gave millions of dollars to the agents and told them where to deposit the money; it turned out that one of his preferred banks was BCCI. The agents, in the words of one report, "made 80 wire transfers to named and numbered accounts provided by Zapata at BCCI . . . in Panama. The total involved was more than $26 million."

In a 1985 investigation, the head of an Iranian heroin ring introduced an undercover DEA agent to a BCCI officer, who explained the best ways to hide drug money. The Iranian was then investigated by the IRS, but BCCI was not.

In 1987, a Federal Reserve examination of BCCI's Miami branch

---

*Shortly after Rehman approached the IRS, the agency conducted a sting operation that resulted in the indictment of Shahid Riky, an employee of BCCI's Chicago office. The probe was apparently unrelated to Rehman's allegations. Between April 1985 and August 1986, according to the indictment, Riky and three other men laundered more than $1.5 million for an undercover agent. Riky was charged with conspiracy, mail fraud, wire fraud, and failure to file CTRs and was arrested on September 4, 1986. The charges were dropped in 1987 because of a legal technicality, according to a source close to the investigation.

turned up evidence of potential money laundering. The Fed made a criminal referral to the Treasury and Justice departments, but there was apparently no follow-up. That same year, the Nigerian heroin trafficker Olutende Fafowora was convicted on federal drug charges in Washington, D.C., as noted above. A source close to the case says that BCCI should have known that Fafowora was depositing dirty money.

It appears that no one at the federal law enforcement agencies asked why so many traffickers used BCCI. As a result, it was never targeted for investigation. The U.S. crackdown on money laundering did, however, have an effect on the dirty money business. Several launderers shifted their activities to other countries — where BCCI was ready and willing to serve them. One such country was Canada, where banks were not obliged to report large cash transactions.

Between 1985 and 1987, a Canadian lawyer named Patrick Anthony Good allegedly laundered about C$7.5 million in cash through BCCI's Vancouver branch. About C$3 million was converted to U.S. dollars, with the rest transferred overseas. To make the transfers, the lawyer allegedly brought cash into the branch — as much as C$396,000 at one time — purchased bank drafts, then sent them to Luxembourg. When Good first went to BCCI, he was asked about the source of the money, says a Canadian police official familiar with the case. "He said he was a lawyer [and that they shouldn't] ask him any questions. They never questioned him any further and they left it at that." He became such a familiar face at the bank that he was soon accorded privileged treatment — even though he had never opened an account there. The Canadian police official says that bank employees would typically find him a seat in a vacant office, pour him a glass of liqueur, and run the money through a counting machine. Good was later charged with possession of money that he knew to be the proceeds of crime, and he was to be tried with another man in September 1992. (The third defendant was a fugitive.) Just before the trial was to begin, the prosecutors stopped the proceedings because they were denied the right to obtain evidence from Luxembourg that they felt was crucial to proving the case, and the defendants went free.

Panama became another growth center for money laundering, and BCCI achieved some notable successes there. It not only attracted deposits from a host of drug traffickers, it persuaded the country's dictator to become a customer. The man most responsible for BCCI's impressive performance was Amjad Awan.

·   ·   ·

In many ways, Awan was a typical senior manager of BCCI. Born in 1947 in Kashmir, he grew up in an elite Pakistani family. His father, Ayub Awan, was one of the country's highest-ranking police and intelligence officials. In his late twenties, Awan graduated from Punjab University with a degree in economics and went to work for an investment bank in Pakistan. He later joined United Bank, which was then headed by Abedi. Awan moved to Britain in 1971 and continued working for United Bank for five more years. He then joined International Resources and Finance Bank, a subsidiary of Bank of Montreal, as vice president of marketing, and he worked in Montreal, London, and Dubai. It was during this period that Awan became a British citizen. Along the way, he married the daughter of Asghar Khan, one of the most prominent politicians in Pakistan.* On December 7, 1978, Awan was hired by BCCI as marketing manager in its flagship branch in the City of London.

Around this time, BCCI was seeking permission for a branch in Panama. One of the people involved was Awan's boss, Allaudin Shaik, who managed the Leadenhall Street office. Courting foreign VIPs was something of a specialty for Shaik; he was one of those who provided "lavish entertainment" to influential people.

At the time, Panama's president was Arístides Royo Sánchez, but he was little more than a figurehead. The real ruler was Omar Torrijos Herrera, who had come to power in a coup in 1968. Although he was a dictator, he enjoyed considerable popular support, for he had a strong populist streak and considerable charm. But there was a less attractive side to the general. His main power base was his position as commander of the National Guard, and he bought the guardsmen's loyalty by allowing them to enrich themselves through smuggling, drug dealing, and other rackets. Torrijos's right-hand man and intelligence chief, Colonel Manuel Antonio Noriega, was involved in a wide range of criminality. As far back as the early 1970s, U.S. law enforcement agencies found indications that he was heavily involved in the drug business.

One of the Panamanians cultivated by BCCI officials was Guillermo Vega, the country's ambassador to London. Vega's diplomatic qualifications were slight, but he was very close to Noriega. Shaik and

---

*After serving as commander in chief of the Pakistani air force, Asghar Khan became a leading opponent of Premier Zulfikar Ali Bhutto as the head of a coalition called the Pakistan National Alliance. After the death of General Zia in 1988, Asghar Khan was an unsuccessful candidate for prime minister.

Awan met with the ambassador as well as Panamanian officials who visited London, including President Royo, General Torrijos, and Colonel Noriega. Awan was once asked to take President Royo around London. Awan later recalled his first meeting with Noriega: "He was visiting London, and we met at a dinner arranged by the ambassador." Allaudin Shaik was also at the dinner, and he used the occasion to ask for Noriega's help in obtaining a branch license. Not long afterward, the Panamanian authorities granted BCCI's application, and the branch was established in 1979 on Vía España in Panama City.

The following year, Awan was given the opportunity to head a BCCI office in one of three countries: Britain, Zambia, or Panama. He chose Panama and in early 1981 became BCCI's country manager.

One of the first things Awan did in Panama was to renew his acquaintance with Noriega, who was head of G-2, the intelligence branch of the National Guard. "I was looking for government accounts," Awan later said. "The bank's object was to obtain deposits from whatever sources we could, and certainly, that was one of the sources I was looking at." Noriega, he explained, "was the only person that I knew in the armed forces, in the first place. In the second place, I knew that intelligence services normally do have funds available to place with banks. I had some knowledge of that fact."

When Torrijos died in a plane crash in July 1981, Noriega emerged as the country's new strong man. The title of president was held by civilian politicians, but Noriega was generally regarded as the power behind the throne. He was now an even more attractive prospect to BCCI, and Awan pressed ahead with his courtship. "I met with him several times socially and visited his office," he said, "and asked him to give some of the Defense Forces accounts to us."

Awan's persistence paid off in January 1982 — about a year after his arrival in Panama. At a meeting in Noriega's office, the dictator agreed to open a G-2 account at BCCI and was told that he would have signatory authority as the head of G-2. "He was the head of intelligence at the time and told me that this was a secret account, a secret service account," Awan said. The account, Awan later said, "was to be maintained in Panama with full confidentiality, which is one of the services the bank offered. So, we opened what we called a manager's ledger account, which is more or less the same as a numbered account." The banker added, "I was to handle the account, personally."

Over the next few years, Noriega channeled tens of millions of dollars into BCCI. The highest bank balance, said Awan, was "in the region of $20 million — $20 million, maybe $25 million." Most of the deposits were in cash, according to the banker, including the first one of "several hundred thousand dollars." On January 21, 1982, a few days after the account was opened, Noriega deposited $45,000 in cash. Awan later recalled, "I believe it was in bundles of hundred-dollar bills." Awan has described how he collected the money. "I would receive a call from General Noriega advising me that a deposit was going to be made and somebody would then bring in the funds to the bank," he said. "On occasion I used to go down to his office and pick up the funds from him."

Noriega's wife, Felicidad, also put money in the account. These deposits were usually in cash and were as high as a half-million dollars at a time. "She would normally call me and I would pick the cash up from her," said Awan, adding that the money "would be in a bag or a briefcase or a suitcase."

Noriega had told Awan that the account was for the military intelligence service, and some official expenses were charged to it, such as overseas trips during which Noriega met with foreign officials. But the dictator and his relatives also withdrew large sums for personal expenses. For example, BCCI issued VISA Gold Cards to Noriega, his wife, and his three daughters. The family used the credit cards on shopping sprees, and BCCI would debit the bank account to pay the Gold Card invoices.

In 1983, Noriega transferred his account from Panama City to London because he felt there would be more security there. "The general," said Awan, "had expressed a desire that he wanted complete confidentiality regarding this account, and I think I suggested to him that it might be a better idea that we transfer it to London, where it would be far more confidential than it would be in Panama City." Members of Noriega's family also opened accounts at BCCI in London. Cash deposits were still made in Panama, however. Upon receiving the funds, Awan would notify his colleagues in London to credit Noriega's account.

Over time, the banker and the dictator became close on a personal level. "It was a banker-customer relationship," Awan said. "But apart from that, I think it was a friendly relationship." The banker was a guest in Noriega's home and the two men sometimes socialized together. As the friendship grew, so did Noriega's political power. In 1983, he became head of the National Guard. When a presidential election was held in May 1984, the National Guard resorted to vote fraud to ensure the victory of the general's candidate, Nicolás Ardito Barletta.

Awan helped out during the campaign. On a regular basis, Noriega instructed him to disburse money to certain candidates. A politician would appear at the BCCI office bearing a note from Noriega indicating that he was entitled to a certain amount of money and Awan would hand over the cash. (A former colleague of his adds that "Awan would walk around with sackfuls of money. He used to tell me that Noriega would call him up [at] two o'clock in the morning and tell him to pay off this one or that one. He would put the money in the boot of his car.")

After Barletta took office, he proved to be too independent for Noriega's taste and was forced out of office when he agreed to investigate the murder of Noriega's critic Hugo Spadafora.*

Noriega's large deposits in BCCI could not possibly have come from his official salary. What was the source? Some of the money came from the U.S. government. For decades, Noriega was on Washington's payroll as an informant, and the size of the payments increased in proportion to his political power. In January 1991, the U.S. government admitted that the CIA had paid Noriega $322,000 in cash and gifts over the years, but it is widely suspected that he received additional money through other channels. The CIA deposited Noriega's "paychecks" into his BCCI account after first channeling the money through dummy companies. One former BCCI officer says he was told by a colleague who worked in Panama that Noriega used BCCI at the suggestion of the CIA.

Another source of money was the drug trade. U.S. authorities, as noted above, suspected Noriega of being involved with drug traffickers as far back as the early 1970s. In 1982, investigators for a Senate committee reported that it was "common knowledge" that the National Guard — led by Noriega — "has ties to and income from various traffickers in drugs, arms, and other contraband." The investigators went on to say that the National Guard "provides warehousing for narcotics on their way north, assures the release, for bribes received, of drug traffickers arrested, guarantees the nonarrest of offenders wanted elsewhere who have paid a kind of 'safe conduct' fee,

---

*After Spadafora denounced Noriega, he was abducted by military men and killed. His headless corpse was discovered in September 1985.

supervises the air transport of gold, arms, spies bound to and from North America, Cuba, and Central America." Between 1982 and 1984, according to a federal prosecutor, Noriega received $10 million in bribes from Colombia's Medellín cartel in exchange for protecting shipments of fifteen to twenty tons of cocaine destined for the U.S. market. This was just one of several alleged payoffs.

Some of Noriega's cronies who were involved in the drug trade were also BCCI customers, including Enrique ("Kiki") Pretelt and César Rodríguez. Both men were Noriega's partners in a variety of businesses, including drug trafficking. Like Noriega, they dealt with Amjad Awan. Pretelt, who owned a chain of jewelry stores in Panama, was the first to become a client, according to Awan. Pretelt, in turn, introduced Awan to Rodríguez. In 1983, as we have seen, Pretelt and Rodríguez brought Steven Michael Kalish to Noriega.

Kalish had started in the drug business in the 1960s when, as a high school student in a suburb of Houston, he peddled marijuana. He dropped out of high school in the early 1970s and became a marijuana importer. After a conviction in Texas, Kalish fled to Florida, adopted an assumed name, and teamed up with Leigh Bruce Ritch, a young Tampa native. Together, they set up a smuggling organization and distribution network. It was a sophisticated operation, replete with computers, money-counting machines, and private planes — including a Learjet. From their base in Tampa, Kalish and Ritch smuggled in huge quantities of drugs from Colombia. Between 1981 and 1985, they imported 500,000 pounds of marijuana and 3,000 pounds of cocaine. Ritch has said that the marijuana alone was worth hundreds of millions of dollars.

By 1983, Kalish "had a Ferrari, a BMW, a Chevy Blazer and more money than he could handle," in the words of John Dinges, a biographer of Noriega's. Kalish and his partners collected so much cash that handling it became a logistical nightmare. "The currency filled entire rooms," Kalish later said. "Although we were sending out millions of dollars to our Colombian suppliers, at one point we had in excess of $35 million in Tampa. We used money-counting machines, but had to stop any counting because we could not keep up with the volume."

One of Kalish's friends said he knew someone in Panama — a man named César — who might be able to handle the mountains of cash. And so, in September 1983, Kalish flew there and contacted the man, who turned out to be César Rodríguez. The following day, as noted earlier, Kalish delivered $300,000 to Noriega. Ritch described the payment as a "security fee," which made it possible to smuggle drugs through Panama with impunity. The payment was just the first of several bribes. Over the next several months, said Kalish, "I spent millions of dollars in Panama to bring myself closer to Noriega."

The dictator was allowed to use the Learjet owned by the Kalish-Ritch organization. Noriega, said Kalish, used it "quite extensively on flights to Washington, D.C., to New York City, to Las Vegas, numerous flights." Kalish has said that Noriega eventually "became a full-scale co-conspirator in my drug operations." Rodríguez took responsibility for money laundering, channeling millions of dollars from the Kalish-Ritch organization into bank accounts in Panama — much of it in BCCI accounts, where it was handled by Amjad Awan.

Awan may have been skillful as a marketer and a money launderer, but he had some shortcomings when it came to conventional banking. In 1984, he cleared $3.7 million in checks that turned out to be forged. He was blamed for the loss, and his superiors decided to transfer him to a job outside Panama. But Noriega did not want his personal banker to leave. In fact, he was so upset that he made a personal appeal to Abedi to cancel the transfer. Awan later recalled that Abedi "told him no, I had to move, but I would be available to him whenever he needed me."

Awan moved to the United States in mid-1984 to work in BCCI's Washington, D.C., representative office. He would come into contact with government officials from the United States as well as other countries, which prompted some colleagues to nickname him "the ambassador."

Even though he had left Panama, Awan's relationship with Noriega remained close. Noriega provided several hundred thousand dollars in loans to the banker, making it possible for him to purchase some expensive real estate in the Washington area. (Awan has said that he repaid the loans.) He bought a house at 4201 Cathedral Avenue, a tony address in the northwest quadrant of the capital, which takes its name from the imposing National Cathedral. The banker later acquired a house in suburban Bethesda, Maryland, and a condominium.

Awan continued to serve as Noriega's personal banker, transferring money from one account to another, paying bills for travel expenses, and handling other chores for the dictator. On a typical visit to New York, Noriega would stay at the Helmsley Palace Hotel. (As a welcoming gesture, BCCI sometimes sent flowers or fruit baskets to the room.) He would instruct the hotel to send the bill to BCCI's New York office. It would pay the bill and then send a memo to Awan asking for reimbursement. Awan would send a check to BCCI/New York, debiting one of Noriega's bank accounts. Since BCCI did not have a branch in the capital, Awan sometimes channeled money through an account maintained by the representative office. The account was at a local bank that had a very cozy relationship with BCCI–First American.

Over the years, dozens of checks representing transfers of Noriega's money were cleared by First American. Records show that at least $500,000 was transferred from Noriega's BCCI accounts into a BCCI account at First American. Additional amounts totaling more than $250,000 were wired simply to "BCCI Washington." In some cases, Noriega himself signed letters ordering transfers of funds to First American. BCCI's employees made no effort to conceal that they were channeling Noriega's money through the U.S. bank: his name was actually written on the memo line of several checks. On February 13, 1987, for example, Awan and another BCCI officer signed a $1,814.26 check payable to BCCI's New York representative office. In the lower left-hand corner of the check is the word FOR, followed by a line on which is written "M. Noriega."

Awan also went to Panama every few months to discuss Noriega's finances in person. Noriega met with his banker during trips to the United States: Awan would fly to New York to see him and stay at the Helmsley Palace. The banker even organized a trip to Las Vegas for Noriega and his cronies and flew in to join them.

In August 1987, Awan was transferred from Washington to Miami to become a marketing officer for Latin America and the Caribbean. He sold his home in Maryland and paid about $700,000 for a house in Coral Gables. The house was just one of many symbols of his success. Awan wore expensive suits and adopted the ostentatious manner of some of his drug-dealing customers. A former BCCI official describes him as "a flamboyant, showy, obnoxious bastard."

Awan also started doing business with a professional money launderer from Tampa — a man who claimed to have access to vast sums of cash from some of the biggest drug traffickers in Colombia. He liked to boast that his "clients" were tycoons on the scale of Chrysler's chairman, Lee Iacocca — except that "one sells cars and one sells coke." Awan soon began socializing with him, just as he had with Noriega. It was a client Awan should have avoided, for his relationship with this particular customer would prove disastrous for him and BCCI.

10

TROUBLE IN TAMPA

ROBERT MUSELLA, a financial consultant in Tampa, had all the trappings of a successful entrepreneur: a beachfront condominium, limousines, yachts, and private airplanes. His clients were drug traffickers, and he made a fortune from laundering their money. In early 1987, Musella decided to open an account at an international bank so he could serve his customers more effectively. One day, when he was caught in a traffic jam in downtown Tampa, he glanced around and, he later recalled, "I just happened to see the sign" on BCCI's local branch. It was at 100 West Kennedy Boulevard, in the Riverside Plaza Building. A few days later, Musella walked in and explained "that I was a businessman based in the Tampa area with a large number of Colombian clients for whom I transferred funds." He opened an account at the branch and returned four months later to open another account — at BCCI's branch in Panama.

In his initial contacts with BCCI, Musella did not say that he was handling dirty money, but he dropped plenty of hints, and the bankers indicated that they understood his desire for secrecy. In one conversation, Musella recalled, "I was the recipient of what appeared to me to be a rather well-polished pitch by the officer that he could assist and the bank could assist in the secret transfers of funds." He was also advised to use cash-intensive businesses to hide the source of his money. One BCCI staff member in Tampa told him, "It's the dumb people that get caught."

Musella soon began depositing checks in BCCI's Panama branch which represented the proceeds of cocaine sales. One of the checks contained a mistake: he had written $110,000 in numerals and $110,300 in words. In late November 1987, a BCCI officer in Panama named Syed Aftab Hussain telephoned him about the discrepancy. In the course of the conversation, Hussain suggested that they get together to discuss Musella's business and the kind of services BCCI could provide.

In early December, they met in Miami. Hussain said that if Musella was interested in hiding money, he was going about it the wrong way: checks could be traced back to him. Hussain told him that BCCI could suggest much more effective ways of concealing the source of the money. For example, Musella could purchase a certificate of deposit from BCCI in Luxembourg and then use it as collateral for a loan in Panama. At another meeting about a week later, Musella stated bluntly that he was handling drug money. "There are things best left unsaid, as you told me once," he said, "and I will discuss this only with you and never again. . . . Obviously this money comes from some of the largest drug dealers in South America."

Eager to assist Musella, Hussain introduced the money launderer to some of his BCCI colleagues, including Amjad Awan. Over the next several months, Hussain, Awan, and other BCCI officials helped him launder $14 million through bank accounts in the United States, Latin America, and Europe.

The bankers' trust in Musella was misplaced. For one thing, he had lied about his name. It was actually Robert Mazur. More important, he was not a professional money launderer but an undercover agent from the U.S. Customs Service. Mazur's dealings with BCCI were part of an elaborate sting operation aimed at catching drug traffickers and the crooked bankers who were their accomplices. As the bankers schemed with Mazur, a tape recorder concealed in his briefcase captured their incriminating words.

The reaction of Hussain and his colleagues is not surprising. They were under great pressure from their superiors to bring in fresh deposits so that the bank's huge losses could be concealed. At a marketing meeting in New York, for example, bank officers were told that "deposit marketing is the lifeblood of the BCC organization."

In addition to the financial strains, BCCI was suffering from factionalism, as the so-called technocrats led by Swaleh Naqvi clashed with the "Gulf group," the BCCI officers in the Persian Gulf led by Zafar Iqbal. This dispute was contained for years by the force of Abedi's personality, and no one knew what would happen if Abedi were no longer on the scene. They found out when the BCCI founder was felled by a serious illness.

. . . .

On February 9, 1988, Abedi suffered a massive heart attack and a stroke at his home near London. He was rushed to Cromwell Hospital, the BCCI satellite funded by Sheikh Zayed. Abedi's heart was so severely damaged that doctors recommended immediate heart transplant surgery. When Jimmy Carter learned of the banker's condition, he contacted a renowned heart surgeon, Dr. Norman Shumway of Stanford University, and asked him to assist Abedi's doctors. Shumway agreed to fly to London. Another noted specialist brought in was Dr. Charles Rackley, the chief of cardiology at Georgetown University Hospital in Washington, D.C.

Despite a successful transplant, Abedi remained in very poor health, and he later suffered more heart attacks. When the severity of Abedi's condition became apparent, Naqvi was named acting chief executive of BCCI. For years he had served as Abedi's right-hand man. He was also the chief orchestrator of the Ponzi scheme as well as the account manipulations and creative accounting aimed at concealing the true condition of the bank. Although he appeared to be the natural choice, his ascension provoked open warfare between the technocrat and Gulf factions. When Abedi was in charge, members of the Gulf faction "would never take orders from Naqvi," says a former BCCI official, because "he had no relationship to any of the Arabs." When Naqvi took over, the Gulf faction refused to obey him, resulting in the paralysis of BCCI's senior management. In their rebellion, the members of the Gulf faction were emboldened by their intimate ties to Sheikh Zayed and other Arab shareholders.

For the most part, the dissension was concealed from the public. On a few occasions, however, rumblings of discontent surfaced in the press. In June 1988, *Forbes* magazine said there was a clash among shareholders over who would run the bank and that a compromise candidate had been suggested: Bert Lance! Although Lance denied the report, his name appeared two months later in *The Times* of London. A columnist reported a rumor that Lance was "on the brink of becoming a senior executive at the Leadenhall Street office of the Bank of Credit and Commerce International" and "is expected to assume some of the responsibilities currently being handled by BCCI's chief executive, Swaleh Naqvi." This rumor may have been a trial balloon floated by Lance's allies at BCCI. Nevertheless, it is virtually inconceivable that regulators would have permitted the discredited Georgia banker to take a senior post in the bank. Lance says the rumors were "totally groundless."

Abedi's illness also raised questions about the ownership of the bank. Large blocks of BCCI stock were held by two Cayman Island entities that had been controlled by Abedi: the ICIC Foundation and the ICIC Staff Benefit Fund. His illness touched off a power struggle over who would run them now, according to a former BCCI official. "When Abedi was incapacitated — seemingly permanently — there was a jockeying for influence," this source recalled in early 1989. It seemed most likely that control of the Cayman entities' BCCI stock would be given to Naqvi, but other candidates were also mentioned, including Ghaith Pharaon and Robert Altman.

In an effort to maintain his grip on the institution, Naqvi met with Zafar Iqbal to try to come to terms with the Gulf faction. Eventually, a kind of modus vivendi was worked out in which Iqbal would deal directly with Naqvi and would not have to take orders from any of his subordinates. It was only a truce, and many people within the bank felt that Naqvi would eventually be toppled by the Gulf faction or by a representative of Sheikh Zayed's. As a former BCCI official put it, "People said it was a question of time that either Zafar Iqbal will become president or Sheikh Zayed will take charge."

Under Naqvi, BCCI's rampant criminal activity continued just as before, with vast sums drained from the bank through fraudulent loans and other schemes. Another form of crime also continued: the laundering of dirty money, including cash from drug traffickers.

Illegal drugs have long been regarded as one of the most serious problems in American society, and presidents from Richard Nixon to George Bush have responded by launching highly publicized campaigns against drugs. Nixon, whose election in 1968 owed much to law-and-order campaign rhetoric, declared "war on drugs" shortly after taking office. Ronald Reagan called for "a national crusade against drugs, a sustained, relentless effort to rid America of this scourge by mobilizing every segment of our society against drug abuse." The results have been disappointing, partly because the same presidents supported foreign leaders who were in bed with traffickers, including Pakistan's Zia and Panama's Noriega.

One federal law enforcement official who had no qualms about offending foreign leaders was William von Raab, who became U.S. Customs commissioner in October 1981. Von Raab, a New York lawyer, was utterly unlike the colorless and ultra-cautious bureaucrats and political hacks who run so many federal agencies. Pugnacious and outspoken, he was always ready with a sound bite for reporters on the drug beat. He was also popular with many conservative Republicans, notably Senator Jesse Helms, the fire-breathing right-winger from North Carolina. But his zealotry alienated many administration officials — as well as officials of drug-producing countries.

One of the most famous incidents of von Raab's career occurred after Enrique ("Kiki") Camarena Salazar, an agent of the Drug Enforcement Administration (DEA), was kidnapped in Guadalajara, Mexico, in 1984. (He was eventually found dead.) DEA officials who investigated the disappearance complained that they were getting little cooperation from the Mexican authorities, and they suspected that corruption was involved. The DEA administrator, Francis ("Bud") Mullen, asked von Raab to have Customs agents question people crossing the border. He replied, "I'll do better than that. I'll question *everybody*." The result was a virtual paralysis of travel and trade — and a major diplomatic row — between the two countries. But von Raab seemed to produce results. Mullen told him, "Willy, you can't believe it. The Mexicans are starting to respond to us."

Reflecting the style of their boss, Customs agents became increasingly aggressive in the drug war. In addition to targeting smugglers — a traditional task of Customs — agents began to investigate money launderers. In July 1986, the Tampa office of the Customs Service launched an undercover operation aimed at catching launderers, Operation C-Chase.*

Customs agents would pose as professional money launderers and — if all went well — drug traffickers would take the bait. Although the concept itself was straightforward, the scheme was fraught with potential pitfalls. The agents would have to put on a convincing show, yet they could not engage in entrapment. (The case would fall apart if a court ruled that government agents went too far by inducing the defendants to commit crimes they weren't predisposed to commit.) There were also considerable personal dangers. Like a professional actor, the lead agent would have to create a new identity for himself. If he were spotted as a phony, he might be killed. The risk of detection was heightened because the agent would be carrying a concealed tape recorder much of the time.

The Tampa office of the Customs Service assembled a team of agents

---

*The name was derived from Caliber Chase, an apartment complex where one of the undercover apartments was located, according to Robert Mazur.

to carry out the sting. They would later be assisted by agents from the Internal Revenue Service (IRS) and, to a lesser degree, the FBI and the DEA. When the laundering spread to Europe, the Customs agencies of Britain and France would also join the investigation.

Robert Mazur, the star of this dangerous drama, was a veteran federal agent who had taken part in several undercover operations over the years. He grew up on Staten Island, New York, where his schoolboy sport was wrestling. After earning a degree in business administration, he joined the IRS in 1972 as a special agent in the Criminal Investigation Division. He was based in Manhattan and began doing undercover work early in his career. In 1983, he transferred to Customs, working out of New York and then Tampa. With his black hair and dark complexion, he easily passed for an Italian American, which helps explain the pseudonym Musella.

Mazur set himself up as the head of a firm called Financial Consulting Inc. and assumed a lifestyle commensurate with the successful image he wanted to project. Through an informant, he made his first important contact: a Colombian money changer named Gonzalo Mora, Jr., who handled cash for cocaine dealers. Mazur convinced Mora that he was in a position to collect and launder the money discreetly, thanks to his connections with businesses that handled large amounts of currency, including airlines and jewelry stores. He claimed to have ties to a brokerage firm with a seat on the New York Stock Exchange, and he sometimes hinted of connections to New York mafiosi.

As Mora grew to trust Mazur, he arranged for the undercover agent to pick up hundreds of thousands of dollars in cash from drug sales all over the United States. Later, Mazur and his colleagues would handle millions. They would deposit the funds in cooperating American banks and issue checks to Mora. The checks would then be cashed by money changers in Latin America, with the funds turned over to Colombian drug dealers. The laundering operation grew even bigger in early 1987, when Mazur attracted other clients, including Roberto Alcaino, a Chilean who ran a jewelry store in Los Angeles. "The Jeweler," as he was called, handled millions of dollars for Colombian traffickers.

At a certain point, Mora suggested that his friend set up an account with an international bank so that he could do business in Panama. So, as we have seen, Mazur started dealing with BCCI. He and his colleagues would deposit Mora's cash in U.S. bank accounts, wire the money to BCCI/Panama, and then issue checks to Mora.

Mazur's first important contact at the bank was Syed Aftab Hussain, the BCCI officer in Panama who met with him in December 1987. The following month, Hussain introduced the agent to two of his colleagues in Miami, Amjad Awan and Akbar Bilgrami. Years before, Bilgrami had managed some of Sheikh Zayed's investments, as we have seen. He also helped establish BCCI's Latin American network.

In his first meeting with Awan, Mazur made it clear that he was handling drug money. "The people with whom I'm dealing," he said, "are the most powerful and largest drug dealers in Colombia." Awan didn't balk. He sold the agent a $1.1 million certificate of deposit, which would be used to secure a loan from BCCI/Panama.

Panama's growing notoriety as a money-laundering center soon prompted BCCI officers to suggest that Mazur start washing his funds in other financial centers. In a June 1988 conversation, Awan boasted to Mazur that he could launder as much as $10 million per month in U.S. currency if it were delivered to London. Mazur took the advice and started channeling money through London, Paris, Geneva, Luxembourg, Uruguay, and the Bahamas. In the Bahamas, he dealt with BCCI's country manager, Saad Shafi, whose father, S. M. Shafi, was the bank's Latin American chief.

As the operation spread, Mazur was introduced to one BCCI officer after another. In nearly every case, he repeated that he was handling dirty money and the bankers were happy to assist. In Paris, Mazur was lavishly entertained by BCCI. The bankers transferred much of the drug money through institutions with close ties to BCCI, including BCP, its Swiss bank, and Capcom Financial Services, the commodity futures firm in London run by Syed Ziauddin Ali Akbar. Money was also wired through an American bank with very close ties to BCCI — First American.*

Of the $14 million in drug money laundered by BCCI, nearly half was transmitted through First American. Starting on January 26, 1988, there were seven transfers of funds through First American Bank of New York, totaling $6,870,510.

Thanks to his dealings with Mazur and Noriega, Awan was becoming one of the most successful marketers in BCCI's history, a man who had been able to attract millions of dollars in deposits. He was also in grave

---

*No evidence has emerged that First American's employees knew it was drug money.

danger — not only because of C-Chase, but because law enforcement authorities were closing in on many of his clients. Customers from his Panama days were being indicted, arrested — and worse.

Steven Michael Kalish had been arrested in Tampa in July 1984, and his partner, Leigh Bruce Ritch, was picked up in 1986. That June, both men were indicted on federal drug charges in Tampa. Ritch was convicted the following year and sentenced to thirty years in prison with no possibility of parole. Kalish's lawyer made a deal with the Justice Department: in exchange for a reduced sentence, Kalish pleaded guilty and agreed to tell the prosecutors everything he knew about Noriega. César Rodríguez's fate was far worse. In March 1986, his corpse was found in a village near Medellín, Colombia. His arms were tied behind his back, his tongue was cut out, and he had been shot through the head.

Noriega himself — the man who had protected Kalish, Ritch, Rodríguez, and other traffickers — was increasingly in danger. After supporting him for years, the U.S. government began to turn against the dictator. Noriega had long been a valuable asset to Washington, but he was no longer reliable. In various disputes in the region, he seemed to be playing both sides — helping the Americans but also cozying up to left-wing elements. His involvement in the drug trade was also worrisome. The United States had ignored this for many years, but Noriega had become too brazen by taking huge payoffs from the Medellín cartel.

As part of a campaign to undermine the Panamanian strong man, officials in President Reagan's National Security Council (NSC) leaked negative information about him to the press. Based in part on these leaks, the investigative journalist Seymour Hersh published a lengthy exposé in the *New York Times*. The first article, headlined "Panama Strongman Said to Trade in Drugs, Arms and Illicit Money," appeared on June 11, 1986 — the same day Noriega traveled to Washington for an official visit. Awan was with him when the story appeared. The banker later recalled that "we were traveling together from New York to Andrews Air Force Base [near Washington]. He had a copy of the newspaper with him. He was agitated and upset." But the embarrassing article did not deter Noriega from making his rounds. He called on several American officials, including Oliver North of the NSC and William Casey of the CIA.

In February 1988, federal grand juries in Miami and Tampa indicted Noriega. He was charged with drug trafficking, laundering drug money, and providing assistance to traffickers in exchange for millions of dollars in bribes. Leon Kellner, then the U.S. attorney in Miami, said that Noriega had "utilized his position to sell the country of Panama to drug traffickers." The names of BCCI customers were sprinkled throughout the Tampa indictment, which was based heavily on testimony by Steven Kalish. It charged Noriega with taking $4 million in payoffs from Kalish and Ritch to protect their drug operation. Indicted with Noriega was Kiki Pretelt, who had helped introduce Kalish to Noriega. (Pretelt eventually pleaded guilty and agreed to testify against the dictator.) Several months later, a prosecutor revealed that Awan was an unindicted co-conspirator because of his role in handling drug money from traffickers connected to Noriega.

At BCCI, Noriega's status as a customer was widely known. Although Awan had assured his client of confidentiality, few precautions had been taken. Noriega's name appeared in hundreds of internal BCCI documents — including bank statements, checks, telexes, and memoranda. Documents mentioning his name were seen by employees in London, Washington, New York, and other cities.

It appears that neither Awan nor any of his superiors took steps to distance BCCI from Noriega after the indictments. On the contrary, the bank came to his aid. Days after the indictments were announced, Noriega told Awan he wanted to close the accounts in London that had been opened for him and his family and transfer the money to safer havens. Awan discussed the matter with Swaleh Naqvi.

At the time of the indictments, Noriega had $8 million on deposit in personal and corporate accounts at BCCI and $15 million in a Panamanian Defense Forces account. All of that money was in London, and he feared that U.S. authorities would be able to seize it. At Noriega's instructions, BCCI transferred the $23 million to a BCCI account in Luxembourg. The money was later shifted to other European banks in order to obscure the trail. One of those institutions was Union Bank of Switzerland, a part owner of BCCI's Swiss bank, BCP. For additional security, the deposits were held in the name of the government-owned Banco Nacional de Panamá.

Shortly before the Noriega indictments were announced, the Senate Permanent Subcommittee on Investigations conducted hearings on Noriega, and one of the witnesses was Steven Michael Kalish. He appeared on January 28 and talked at length about his relationship with Noriega but also made some references to BCCI. At one point he referred to an aircraft deal with the general which involved the withdrawal of $500,000 from a Kalish account at BCCI. His partner, Leigh Bruce Ritch, appeared before another congressional committee eleven days later, the Subcommittee on Terrorism, Narcotics, and International Operations of the Senate Foreign Relations Committee, chaired by John F. Kerry of Massachusetts.

At the time of the hearing, Kerry was not regarded as a political powerhouse. He was relatively young (forty-four) and a newcomer to the Senate, having been elected in 1984. His credentials were impressive. Kerry was a graduate of Yale with a law degree from Boston College and was a highly decorated Vietnam veteran. After his discharge from the navy, he became a prominent antiwar activist as national coordinator of Vietnam Veterans Against the War. Before his election to the Senate, he served as a prosecutor and as lieutenant governor of Massachusetts. In Washington, however, Kerry was overshadowed by the state's far more famous senior senator, Edward M. Kennedy, who had served since 1963. Adding to the identity problem was that Kerry was sometimes confused with another Democratic senator, Bob Kerrey of Nebraska.

But Kerry was by no means a lightweight. It would just take time for him to find the right issue to make his reputation. BCCI turned out to be that issue.

Ritch told the Kerry Committee that he had dealt with the Banco Nacional de Panamá and BCCI and that he had been referred to those banks by Noriega's friend César Rodríguez. Kerry then asked him, "Was this [BCCI] a bank favored by General Noriega?" Ritch replied, "Having been recommended by César Rodríguez, I would say yes, sir." BCCI's name came up the following day in testimony by José Blandón, a former Panamanian diplomat who had turned against Noriega. He told the Kerry Committee that BCCI "was used by César Rodríguez and is used by Pretelt for money laundering." He added, "It is a bank where normally Noriega carries out his international operations, so it is a very — it's a bank that would be very interesting to study." A committee staff member, Jack Blum, later recalled that Blandón "put a chart up that showed what he called Noriega's criminal empire and at the center of the chart he had BCCI."

Blandón's remark — that BCCI would be an interesting bank to study — was taken to heart by the committee. In the following weeks, the staff launched an intensive investigation of Noriega and his dealings with BCCI. The committee's point man was Jack Blum, a forty-six-year-old lawyer who had spent most of his professional life on

Capitol Hill chasing all manner of villains — from bribe-paying multinationals to Latin American drug pushers. With a roly-poly figure and rumpled suits, Blum does not fit the stereotype of the sleuth, but he proved to be more of a threat to BCCI than any other investigator the bank had encountered.

Blum was born in 1941 in the Bronx and raised in Elizabeth, New Jersey. His father was a doctor and his mother, a teacher. He attended high school at an orthodox yeshiva in Manhattan and then enrolled in Bard College. There, according to a profile of Blum,

> he came under the powerful influence of two refugees from Nazi Germany, philosophy professor Heinrich Bluecher and his wife, Hannah Arendt, whose "Origins of Totalitarianism" was already a classic and who was then at work on "Eichmann in Jerusalem."
>
> "I spent time in their apartment in New York, where W. H. Auden and Mary McCarthy were regular visitors," he recalls. "I remember they were so worried about Auden, because he lived this derelict life, so the two women [Arendt and McCarthy] went to the Lower East Side and cleaned his apartment."

After graduation, Blum obtained his law degree from Columbia in 1965 and then went to Washington. After a stint at the Federal Communications Commission, he became a congressional staff member. Corporate skulduggery was one of his principal areas of interest. As a member of the late Senator Frank Church's staff, Blum investigated ITT's activities in Chile and the bribery of foreign officials by Lockheed and other multinational corporations. He also probed Investors Overseas Services, the mutual fund group that was taken over and looted by Robert Vesco. Blum went into private practice in 1976, returning to Capitol Hill in 1987 to work for Senator Kerry as special counsel to the subcommittee on terrorism and drugs.

Initially, Blum investigated allegations that the contra rebels in Nicaragua, backed by the United States, were involved in drug trafficking. He soon began to take a broader look, collecting evidence that government officials in several countries in the region were involved in the drug trade, most notably Noriega.

BCCI was not an unfamiliar name to Jack Blum. He had heard of the bank a few years earlier, when he was in private practice. A client was planning to do business with Attock Oil, a BCCI satellite, and the bank's name came up at a meeting with officials of Mellon Bank in Pittsburgh. "We sat down with Mellon Bank and said that the party on the other side of the transaction was affiliated with BCCI," Blum recalls. "And the entire senior international staff at Mellon just about threw up on the table. They would not accept under any circumstances letters of credit from BCCI. I later found out that almost none of the serious banks I talked to were interested in doing business with them — and they wouldn't say why."

After several witnesses close to Noriega fingered BCCI as his favorite bank, Blum decided to take a look at the institution and started making calls to some of his contacts. One friend told him that a mutual acquaintance of theirs had worked for BCCI; when Blum called him, the banker agreed to meet. Over the course of a day and a half, the banker told Blum an amazing tale. BCCI appeared to be the ultimate "hot money" bank, in Blum's words, an institution dedicated to collecting and laundering every conceivable type of dirty money, including loot from corrupt politicians and cash from cocaine dealers. This confidential source "laid out all the problems that were going on. He told me about Awan. He told me about Awan's relationship with Noriega. He told me about the bank in Colombia and [its] dealings with the [cocaine] cartel. He told me about Pharaon being a front — a dummy shareholder. And he told me about BCCI's [relationship with] First American."

On March 22, Blum circulated a memo to all the members of the Foreign Relations Committee, asking for the authority to subpoena BCCI records and to compel testimony from two BCCI officials. A few days later, the committee voted to issue the subpoenas. When Justice Department officials learned about the Kerry Committee's probe, they feared that it could compromise Operation C-Chase and asked the committee to delay its investigation. "We were in a very difficult position," Blum recalls, "not wanting to screw up a major undercover operation." Justice later gave a green light and the subpoenas were issued at the end of July.

BCCI was "commanded" to produce a vast number of documents, including all records relating to Noriega and companies controlled by him. The bank was also told to produce two witnesses: S. M. Shafi, the head of the Latin America region, and Khalid A. Awan. The latter name was garbled because Blum did not know the banker's first name; he picked an Awan out of a Florida telephone book who turned out to be the wrong person.

When BCCI officials learned that the bank was the target of a Senate investigation, they turned to the Washington lawyers who had played an important role in the bank's affairs for more than a decade, Clark

Clifford and Robert Altman. The first thing Clifford did, Blum recalls, was to call Senator Claiborne Pell, the chairman of the Foreign Relations Committee. Pell, a patrician Yankee from Rhode Island, is a gentleman from the old school — not the sort of person likely to resist a reasonable request from a distinguished attorney like Clifford. It didn't hurt, of course, that the two men had been friends for years.

Clifford "requested an extension," Blum recalls, "and got that extension put in the middle of the August recess." He also tried to limit the scope of the inquiry to Noriega, according to Blum. Clifford "wanted very much to prevent a wide-ranging discussion of what was afoot." In addition, Clifford and Altman tried to discourage the committee from talking to Amjad Awan; "they said Awan's life was at risk," according to Blum. Clifford also met with Senator Kerry and used the occasion to vouch for BCCI. "He saw Kerry and said what a terrible thing this was — that he'd known the BCCI people for a long time and that they were people of repute."

A far different picture was emerging from Blum's investigation. The lawyer continued to receive disturbing information about BCCI. Among his sources were current and former employees — including two of the principal targets of Operation C-Chase.

Shortly after the Senate's subpoenas were issued, Blum received an anonymous call from a woman with a British accent suggesting that he talk to "Ali Akbar" — a reference to Syed Ziauddin Ali Akbar, the head of Capcom. "So I picked up the phone and called him," Blum recalls. "And Akbar says, 'You want to talk to me about BCCI? I've got a lot to say. Fax me a letter.'" Blum responded immediately, inviting Akbar to discuss "certain international banking issues."

Akbar had explosive information about BCCI. When he ran the bank's treasury department — and later, as the head of Capcom — he was involved in the fraudulent trades in the futures and options markets through which a huge volume of depositors' money was siphoned out of BCCI. What would he say?

A few days after the phone conversation, says Blum, "Akbar turns up in my office." He was "exceedingly dapper, incredibly well tailored. Very well spoken. Very gentlemanly. I took him to be surprisingly young for being the self-described head of a commodity trading company with offices in London and Chicago. We talked about BCCI, we talked about its capitalization, and I said I knew that there were some strange things in the books. And he said, 'Ah, you mean the capital problem.'"

Akbar also told Blum that the U.S. Marshals Service had served the Senate subpoena on the wrong Mr. Awan. What is more, recalls Blum, he said that "lawyers for BCCI are trying to tell [Awan] to leave the country so he won't have to be served with a subpoena." Akbar added that he was a friend of Awan's and might be able to arrange for Blum to meet him. He would be going to Miami soon and would talk to the banker.

About a week later, Akbar agreed to meet with Blum and another committee staff member at the Intercontinental Hotel in New York. "It was one of the most oppressively hot summer days in my memory," says Blum, "and this man comes breezing into the lobby for lunch — absolutely crisp. He came in and sat down and said, 'I've got wonderful news. I've met with Awan and he wants to cooperate.' " In the course of the lunch, Akbar also talked about BCCI's problems in India and Kenya, where the bank had been accused of violating foreign exchange controls. He teased Blum with indications of the mess inside the bank and its involvement in questionable activities but did not reveal the rampant fraud.

Blum was nonetheless surprised by Akbar's willingness to go that far — and to fly to the United States at his own expense. Years later, he learned of a possible explanation. Akbar allegedly told senior BCCI officials that he was thinking of cooperating with Blum and used this threat to extract hush money from the bank. If this allegation is correct, silence was golden: Akbar got a $30 million payoff, according to BCCI's auditors at Price Waterhouse. Akbar, says Blum, had computer disks that "would have laid out in detail the fraud at the heart of the bank."*

Akbar did help Blum get in touch with Awan, who agreed to come up to Washington to see him. They went to the lawyer's home in Maryland and discussed BCCI for about eight hours. Like Akbar, Awan strove to appear helpful by providing tantalizing bits of information about BCCI, but he revealed only a fraction of what he knew.

At the same time that Akbar and Awan were providing information to the Senate, they were becoming ensnared in the Customs Service's sting operation. Both men were completely duped by Robert Mazur's

---

*Some BCCI officers disagree with this version of events; one says he believes that the payment to Akbar was really to help boost the capital of Capcom or to transfer more money to the company as a way of taking it out of BCCI. Akbar has denied that he was bribed.

façade. The Customs agent had an extraordinary gift for winning the confidence of the people he was investigating. At one point during C-Chase, the money launderer Roberto ("the Jeweler") Alcaino was arrested for smuggling cocaine, thanks to a tip from Mazur. Alcaino, in the words of one journalist,

> turned to the friend he most trusted to help his wife hide an emergency cache of funds. He turned to the man he knew as Robert Musella, a.k.a. Robert Mazur.
>
> "When you become very close to a person," Alcaino testified after pleading guilty, "you consider them a friend, so you talk about your wants and needs and the things that you have done and what you are planning to do. That's why I'm here today."

Awan was a man who — to paraphrase Will Rogers — never met a money launderer he didn't like. He developed such a close relationship with Mazur that he would gossip about BCCI, outline his plans for the future, and even discuss his relationship with Noriega. In these conversations, Awan revealed one of the darkest secrets of BCCI — its covert ties to U.S. financial institutions.

Early in their relationship, Awan boasted to Mazur that the BCCI group could well be much bigger than it appeared. In January 1988, he casually mentioned that First American was "unofficially owned by us" but did not go into detail. Two months later, he indicated that BCCI had been close to both First American and National Bank of Georgia. The following September, Awan went into greater detail about BCCI's ties to First American and the men who ran it, Clark Clifford and Robert Altman.

Friday, September 9, 1988, was a hot and humid day in Miami as Awan arrived at the Grand Bay Hotel in Coconut Grove to meet with Mazur. Awan took a seat and waited for his friend, who appeared shortly after five P.M. Mazur ordered a Scotch and water, and the two men settled down for a chat. The conversation began on a light note as they talked about Awan's grueling travel schedule. When Mazur said, "You must be a stranger at home," Awan joked that "even the dogs don't recognize me," and both men laughed.

The conversation soon took a more serious turn. They talked briefly about Mazur's dealings with BCCI, and Awan told his friend about the Kerry Committee probe. The committee had served a subpoena on the bank, demanding information on its activities in Panama. The principal target, of course, was Noriega. As he put it later in the conversation, "I'm the only guy who knows Noriega's activities, his accounts, his, uh, what he has, what he doesn't have." The investigation posed a serious dilemma, he explained. If he failed to cooperate, the Senate could make life difficult for him. If he did cooperate and Noriega learned about it, his life could be in danger: "If I say anything about Noriega and it's reported by the press, I'm dead. He's gonna kill me."

As Awan unburdened himself, Mazur's concealed tape recorder captured one startling statement after another. He suggested that BCCI, Clifford, and Altman were trying to impede the committee's investigation by moving him out of the country — a remark that jibed with what his friend Akbar had told Blum. On September 3, six days before this conversation, Altman "suggested to the bank that I should be immediately transferred from the U.S. to Paris," Awan said. BCCI took the advice, "so they duly transferred me to Paris." (Altman has denied giving such advice.)

Awan told Mazur he didn't agree with the transfer. "As long as I am an employee of the bank, I can be anywhere, I can, I can be in Timbuktu, if they throw a subpoena on me, they can demand that the bank produce [me]. And if they don't, they can do what they did to [Bank of] Nova Scotia. They can fine them $100,000 a day or whatever."* Ultimately, Awan said, he agreed to be questioned, although he insisted that it be done secretly so that Noriega would not find out. Awan said he told the committee, "I want to make a deal with you, that whatever I say should be in executive session, and not in open session." He also retained his own lawyer because, he said, he did not trust Clifford and Altman.

Awan then dropped another bombshell: he explained why he did not trust the two lawyers. He said that Clifford and Altman ran a bank in Washington called First American, that he suspected that it was secretly owned by BCCI, and that the lawyers could be "screwing" BCCI as part of a scheme to take over First American.

AWAN: It might be farfetched, it might sound stupid, but my assessment is that we own a bank in Washington. I may have mentioned it to you before.
MAZUR: That you what?
AWAN: We own a bank, uh, based in Washington, it's called the First American Bank. The holding company is in Washington, and

---

*In 1983, a U.S. court imposed a fine on Bank of Nova Scotia, one of Canada's largest banks, for contempt when it refused to turn over records from its Bahamian branch. When the judge increased the fine to $25,000 per day, the bank capitulated.

there are five banks actually. First American of New York, First American of Washington, D.C., First American of Virginia, Maryland, Tennessee, and Georgia. There's six banks. . . . BCCI was acting as adviser to [the shareholders], but the truth of the matter is that the bank belongs to BCCI. Those guys are just nominee shareholders.

MAZUR: Uh-hum.

AWAN: Clark Clifford and his, uh, law partner Robert Altman are the chairman and capital holders. I personally feel it would suit them if BCCI withdrew.

MAZUR: Ah hah.

AWAN: And they just take over that entire part of the bank. I wouldn't be, I mean because Altman is a young man. He's very ambitious. He has political aspirations. And being a bank president is, you know, is, it's not just being another Washington lawyer. . . . I wouldn't be at all surprised if, you know, if they're totally screwing BCCI to take over this bank.

The same day Awan had that conversation with Mazur, Robert Altman went to Capitol Hill to meet with the Kerry Committee's staff regarding the documents it had subpoenaed. Altman said that BCCI did not have any documents in the United States relating to Panamanian bank accounts. But Blum did not believe him — his own sources at BCCI had told him such records did exist.

On September 14, Altman began delivering BCCI documents to the Kerry Committee, and these records gave a highly misleading impression of the bank's relationship with Noriega. The papers suggested that the bank had done little more than handle routine transactions for Noriega and that the relationship had ended when he was indicted in February. Thousands of pages of documents that would have given a true picture of the relationship were withheld, including records that would have shown that the bank had moved some of Noriega's money to Luxembourg after the indictment.

Blum also received disturbing reports that the bank was systematically destroying records. His BCCI sources, Blum later said, began calling him to say "that Mr. Naqvi had flown over from London and the documents had been shipped up from Miami and were being shredded in the Washington office, that there was a team of people at work shredding documents that were due us under the subpoena." When Blum contacted Altman about this, Blum said, he "assured me

nothing like that could be going on." Nevertheless, Blum's informa-
tion was correct. In a conversation with Mazur that same month,
Awan said that the bank was destroying records that the Senate
wanted. (Years later, Abdur Sakhia, BCCI's top official in the United
States, testified that papers related to Noriega were sent from Miami to
London after the bank received the Senate's subpoena.)

At the same time BCCI was withholding and destroying documents,
its attorneys were continuing to vouch for the bank. On September 26,
Clifford met with Senator Kerry to discuss the production of BCCI
documents. At that meeting, Kerry later recalled, Clifford told him,
"This is a good bank." *

As Awan worried about how he would respond to the Kerry Committee, he decided to leave BCCI and resigned in mid-September. His plan
was to join his friend Syed Ziauddin Ali Akbar of Capcom Financial
Services. Awan and Bilgrami would set up a Capcom affiliate in Miami
and bring some BCCI customers with them — including Noriega. In
August, the banker had traveled to Panama to meet with Noriega and
discuss the movement of his funds. "He wanted me to send the money
back to Panama in the first place," Awan later said, "and then possibly
get it out of there, as well as into another place in Europe." Awan later
transferred some of Noriega's money from European banks to Capcom.

Awan also planned to channel some of Mazur's drug money to
Capcom. Shortly after Awan resigned from BCCI, Mazur went to
London and met with Akbar. Again, the agent made it clear that he
was handling drug money. In a conversation on September 21, Mazur
said that his clients "are extremely professional. If they were in a room
with Lee Iacocca, you would think that they were on the board of
Chrysler. The only difference is that Lee Iacocca sells cars in the U.S.

---

*Clifford's own integrity was being called into question at precisely this time. Former
minority shareholders of First American Bank of Virginia had sued First American Bankshares, Clifford, and other defendants for allegedly misleading them when the parent
company bought them out. When the trial was held in U.S. district court in Alexandria,
Virginia, in September 1988, the jury heard evidence that an "independent" appraisal of
the value of the bank stock was anything but independent. First American told a Wall Street
firm it was willing to pay $42 per share, and then asked the firm to appraise the stock. The
firm was also told that if First American decided to go ahead with the buy-out, the
brokerage firm would be hired to handle the tender offer. Not surprisingly, the brokerage
firm said the stock was worth $42 per share. The jury ruled for the plaintiffs, and an appeals
court sustained the verdict. The U.S. Supreme Court reversed the verdict on technical
grounds.

and these guys sell cocaine in the U.S." After that meeting, Mazur wired drug money from BCCI to Capcom.

Ultimately, Awan decided to cooperate with the Kerry Committee. But he did not inform BCCI and he did hire his own lawyer. On the morning of Friday, September 30, he arrived in Room S-116 of the U.S. Capitol. The only people in the room besides Awan and his attorney were congressional staff members and a court reporter. Awan spent the next two and a half hours answering questions from Jack Blum about BCCI and Noriega. He revealed that Noriega had deposited millions of dollars in BCCI — mostly in cash — and that the bank had been intimately involved in managing the dictator's personal finances.

Although Awan seemed to be forthcoming, his testimony was riddled with lies. He said, for example, that Noriega's BCCI accounts had been closed in early 1988, around the time of the indictments. He was asked about drug money several times, and he said he never knowingly accepted deposits of drug money or laundered drug money. This was, of course, also a lie. In the C-Chase operation alone, $32.7 million in drug money had been laundered — $14.3 million of it through BCCI.

C-Chase was turning out to be a huge success, exceeding everyone's expectations. The original goal was to catch drug traffickers, but the Customs agents had done that and more: they had also snared a major international bank.

And what a bank it was! Mazur had picked out BCCI by chance, yet it turned out to be Noriega's bank and it seemed to have a countless number of sleazy officers on its staff — men like Awan, who had no compunctions about handling the dirtiest money. Its connections to the United States were also intriguing — the links to Clark Clifford, First American, and National Bank of Georgia. Mazur was convinced that he and his colleagues would continue to hit pay dirt as the investigation progressed, that they might even be able to implicate officials at the very top of BCCI. In September, Nazir Chinoy, a senior BCCI official in Paris, told Mazur he might be able to arrange for him to meet with higher-ranking executives — perhaps even the head of the bank, Swaleh Naqvi.

But Mazur's superiors decided to halt the investigation in October. Justice Department officials have portrayed the decision as a purely technical matter. They felt the Customs agents had gone about as far as they could, and they feared that prolonging the operation would increase the risk of exposure. There may have been other factors, however, including politics. Everyone knew that a presidential election was scheduled for November 8, and a high-profile drug arrest could help the Republican nominee, Vice President Bush. It would certainly boost the stock of the Customs commissioner, William von Raab, who wanted to be appointed to the new post of drug czar.

At the U.S. Attorney's office in Tampa, the prosecutor in charge of the case was Mark V. Jackowski, who had been working with the C-Chase agents for months. He happened to be one of the few federal prosecutors in the country who had ever heard of BCCI: he had prosecuted two of Awan's old clients, Steven Michael Kalish and his partner, Leigh Bruce Ritch. Jackowski had also assisted other members of the office in preparing the Tampa indictment of Noriega, which was based largely on testimony by Kalish. Jackowski's desire to nail the Panamanian was obvious to anyone visiting his office. Displayed prominently on the wall was a picture of Noriega in the form of a dartboard.

On October 4, a federal grand jury in Tampa indicted ten current and former BCCI employees and four corporate entities related to BCCI.* The bankers were:

- Syed Ziauddin Ali Akbar, the head of Capcom and the former head of BCCI's treasury department;
- Iqbal Ashraf, the manager of the Los Angeles branch and the former manager of the Tampa branch.†
- Amjad Awan, a marketing officer for the Latin American region, in Miami, until mid-September 1988;
- Asif Baakza, the director of the corporate unit for BCCI in London;
- Akbar Bilgrami, the head of marketing for the Latin American region, in Miami, until mid-September;
- Nazir Chinoy, the regional general manager in Paris for Europe and French-speaking Africa;
- Sibte Hassan, an assistant to Chinoy;
- Ian Howard, the country manager for France;
- Syed Aftab Hussain, an officer in BCCI's Panama City branch; and
- Saad Shafi, the country manager for the Bahamas.

---

*Several suspects with no ties to BCCI were also charged as a result of the C-Chase probe, including drug traffickers and cash couriers.

†All charges against Ashraf were later dismissed.

The four corporate entities were Capcom Financial Services Ltd. and the three main units of the BCCI group: BCCI Holdings (Luxembourg) S.A., the main holding company of the group; BCCI S.A. (also in Luxembourg), the flagship bank of the group; and BCCI (Overseas) Ltd., the group's holding company in the Cayman Islands.

All of the BCCI defendants were accused of conspiracy to possess with intent to aid and abet others with the distribution of cocaine; conspiracy to defraud the Internal Revenue Service; and conspiracy to launder the proceeds of cocaine sales. All of the BCCI defendants except Ashraf and BCCI S.A. were also accused of knowingly laundering about $14 million of cocaine revenues.

The indictment was sealed so that the defendants would not disappear; it would be made public only after the arrests. But Customs faced a daunting problem. Many of the defendants — including most of the bankers — lived outside the United States. Before Customs agents could spring the trap, they would have to lure their prey to American soil. It was time for "Bob Musella" to get married.

During the two years that he posed as a professional money launderer, Robert Mazur was an extraordinarily good actor. He had to be — his life depended on it. The men he was investigating not only trusted him, some of them also became good friends. Mazur visited their homes, spent hours drinking and gossiping, and partied at discos. All of this was necessary to maintain his cover, but there were limits on how far he could go. Some of the people he was investigating tried to fix him up with prostitutes. Partly to avoid such entanglements, Mazur was teamed with a female undercover agent named Kathy Ertz (known to the traffickers as Kathy Erickson), who posed as his fiancée.

The phony romance between Bob and Kathy became the foundation of a scheme by Customs to lure the suspects to U.S. territory. Mazur's new friends were sent formal invitations to attend the wedding of "Robert L. Musella and Kathleen Corinne Erickson." The blessed event would be held on Sunday, October 9, at the Innisbrook Resort and Country Club in Tarpon Springs, Florida, just outside Tampa. A great deal of preparation went into the event — just as for a real wedding. Customs agents rented a room at the country club and had a sign set up to indicate where the "Musella-Erickson Wedding" would be held.

Amjad Awan and Akbar Bilgrami flew in from Miami; others came from as far away as Panama, France, and Colombia. One of the guests — the launderer Gonzalo Mora, Jr. — sent $20,000 worth of

Colombian red roses. Some of the bankers Mazur had dealt with in Europe could not come to Tampa, so alternate arrangements were made: British and French Customs agents were asked to make those arrests.

By pure coincidence, BCCI was holding an important event that very weekend: a conference in London involving about a hundred BCCI officers from around the world. The theme could not have been more appropriate: "The Moral Dimension of BCCI." A report on the conference in the bank's employee magazine said: "The spirit of BCC is permeated by a moral dimension and this eases the burden of management. The challenge of BCC will be met with happiness and will be achieved in happiness. The times that we live through demand that BCC leadership ignites in every member of our family the highest quality of vision and the highest moral quality. Courage and purity will prevail."

Saturday was to be "Bob Musella's" last night as a bachelor, so a stag party was organized at a restaurant on the top of a building in downtown Tampa. That evening, Awan and other out-of-town guests were taken there by limousine. It was supposed to be a raunchy affair, complete with strippers, and some of the guests were eagerly looking forward to the action. On the way to the party, Mora turned to an agent and said in Spanish, "I really need a good fuck tonight!" The agent replied, "Gonzalo, don't worry, I can assure you you're really going to get fucked tonight!"

As each guest stepped out of a parking garage elevator, a pair of handcuffs was slapped on his wrists and he was greeted warmly: "Welcome to Tampa. You're under arrest." The men were so startled that it took a while for them to realize what was happening. One banker even thought that the handcuffs were part of the fun — the prelude to some kind of kinky sexual game! The cold reality soon became apparent as the visitors were hustled back into their limousines, driven to the Tampa Federal Building, and booked.*Five of the men arrested that night in Tampa were BCCI bankers: Awan, Bilgrami, Hassan, Howard, and Hussain.

As Customs commissioner, William von Raab attracted criticism from many quarters, but no one could deny that he was a master of public relations. The Operation C-Chase indictment was announced with

---

*During the next few days, two BCCI bankers were arrested in London, Asif Baakza and Nazir Chinoy, as was Capcom's S. Z. A. Akbar.

considerable fanfare. On the morning of Tuesday, October 11, about fifty journalists and photographers gathered at the Sheraton Grand Hotel in Tampa. The turnout was large because the press officers from Customs had alerted the media the day before that the press conference concerned one of the most important drug money cases in history. An information kit was distributed, including a press release, a copy of the indictment, and background on the investigation. There were even photocopies of the Musella-Erickson wedding invitation.

Von Raab and U.S. Attorney Robert W. Genzman were flanked by representatives of the other federal agencies involved in the case: the IRS, FBI, and DEA. There were also senior officials of European law enforcement agencies: Brian Unwin, the chairman of British Customs, and Jean Weber, the director general of French Customs. Von Raab declared that Operation C-Chase was "the most important money-laundering case in U.S. Customs history," and he branded BCCI a corporate criminal — "an institution that was prostituting itself to money laundering."

In spite of the publicity blitz, von Raab and the prosecutors withheld one of the most important bits of information from the press. They never mentioned that Noriega's personal banker was now in custody. At Jack Blum's urging, Kerry held a press conference the next day in which he disclosed Awan's ties to the Panamanian and released a copy of Awan's deposition. Kerry also told reporters that his committee had information suggesting that BCCI was implicated in a vast array of misdeeds. He said that the bank had been involved in arms transactions in the Middle East and huge deals with Colombian drug dealers.

The failure of the Justice Department and the Customs Service to disclose Awan's ties to Noriega was obviously deliberate. Von Raab has asserted that he did not want to distract attention from the work of the Customs agents, but it is much more likely that he and the prosecutors wanted to avoid embarrassing George Bush less than a month before the presidential election. Bush's candidacy could only be harmed by a reminder that the Reagan administration's attempts to dislodge Noriega had failed and that the dictator was continuing to thumb his nose at the United States.

This curious omission was not the government's first questionable action in the C-Chase case. Earlier, as we have seen, the investigation was brought to an end over the objections of Robert Mazur. There would be many more dubious decisions in the months to follow, which would ultimately lead to charges of a cover-up.

11

CONTAINMENT

OPERATION C-CHASE thrust BCCI into the spotlight for the first time since the takeover battle for First American. The bank would be scrutinized as never before.

Federal agents obtained search warrants and seized thousands of documents from BCCI branches in the United States. "We have literally a truckload of documents," said Steve Cook, a Customs agent who had coordinated the C-Chase probe. "We have so many documents that we had to subcontract out the copying to a private firm." British Customs agents seized records from the bank's headquarters in London. At the same time, federal and state bank regulators conducted detailed inspections of BCCI's American branches. They also began to query First American about its ties to BCCI. Jack Blum continued to gather information on BCCI — with the help of several "deep throats," including current and former employees of the bank.

BCCI was also being examined by the news media. The day the indictment was announced, Operation C-Chase was one of the lead items on the network news. As newscasters talked about millions of dollars in drug money, viewers watched BCCI officers with manacles on their wrists being hustled into police vans. During the next few days, the case was front-page news around the world. The London *Financial Times*'s story was headlined "Luxembourg-based bank indicted on drug money charge." Paris's *Le Monde* carried a front-page story, *"L'argent de la drogue 'blanchi' par une banque internationale"* (Drug money "laundered" by an international bank). Press interest intensified when Senator Kerry revealed that BCCI was the favorite bank of Manuel Noriega.

A much bigger potential threat to BCCI than the news media was federal law enforcement agencies. "I would predict," said the Customs chief William von Raab, "that this case is going to go on for a year or more, just a constant turning over of more rocks, following down more leads." It seemed inevitable that federal agents and prosecutors would uncover the full extent of BCCI's criminality, including its covert ties to First American and the multibillion-dollar Ponzi scheme at the heart of the bank. BCCI reacted by launching a massive counter-offensive. The bank and its allies called in the political chits they had accumulated over the years and spent millions of dollars on lawyers, lobbyists, and public relations experts. The goal was containment.

When the indictment was announced on October 11, 1988, the switchboard at BCCI's London headquarters was flooded with calls from journalists wanting the bank's reaction. The person in charge of dealing with reporters was John Hillbery, a polished Englishman who had long acted as BCCI's chief spokesman. He had often been forced to deal with provocative questions, and he developed a standard patter. There was nothing strange or sinister about BCCI, Hillbery would assure journalists in soothing tones. The bank had grown rapidly because of its Middle Eastern connections. It made its money by concentrating on certain niches, such as trade financing. If other banks looked down their noses at BCCI, that was because of their jealousy at its success — coupled with ethnic prejudice. Hillbery's response to the crisis in Tampa could be of vital importance to BCCI. Banks depend on confidence, and any erosion of confidence can provoke a run on deposits.

Hillbery quickly issued a statement. "The bank," he declared, "is wholly unaware of any violation that allegedly has been committed. It would seem, however, that the concerted action by authorities in three countries is part of an international investigation which involves many individuals and institutions. BCC finds itself involved in a malicious campaign against itself which will have to be unravelled in the courts. The bank wishes to state categorically that at no time whatsoever has it been involved in drug-traffic-related money laundering."

The comment about a "malicious campaign" was absurd on its face. If there was such a campaign, how could Hillbery have learned about it so quickly? Of course, there was no such campaign; bank regulators and law enforcement authorities had been largely oblivious of BCCI's criminality for years. It was by happenstance that U.S. Customs had started looking into the bank.

Two days later, BCCI issued a statement aimed at reassuring depositors. It referred to the "unfailing support" of shareholders and to the bank's financial health — "$1.6 billion in capital funds" and 1987 profits (before taxes and provisions) of $185 million. At the time, of course, no one outside BCCI knew that its annual reports were works of fiction. The statement also sought to distance BCCI from the individual bankers who had been indicted. None of the individuals was a senior executive, BCCI said. "The only relatively senior person among the defendants is based in Paris supervising French-speaking Africa" — Nazir Chinoy. What is more, it was bank policy "that all governing rules, regulations, and laws must be strictly observed by the staff in the conduct of bank business." The clear implication was that if the individual defendants were involved in money laundering, they were rogue employees acting purely on their own.

Whatever skills Hillbery possessed, they were unequal to the job of dealing with a public relations disaster of this magnitude. BCCI was soon getting advice from hordes of professionals, notably Clark Clifford and Robert Altman.

Clifford and Altman were not the attorneys of record in the Tampa case, but they assembled the defense team, coordinated its work, and briefed BCCI officials on the case. The same day Hillbery put out his reassuring statement, Altman and two criminal defense lawyers met with BCCI executives in London. Altman returned to London four more times before the end of the year, with Clifford accompanying him on the last visit. During the first half of 1989, Altman made six more trips to Europe to meet with BCCI officials, three of them with Clifford.

The indictment occurred at the same time that BCCI was riven by the power struggle touched off by Abedi's illness, with members of Zafar Iqbal's Gulf faction vying for power with the technocrats, who were led by Swaleh Naqvi. One result was that Altman's influence increased enormously. Some executives said — only partly in jest — that Altman was the de facto head of the bank. If true, it would mean that Altman, a Jewish lawyer from Washington, D.C., was calling the shots at two of the biggest Arab-owned banks in the world, BCCI and First American.

It was not simply a lawyer-client relationship. In the BCCI drama,

Clifford and Altman played so many roles that they were like vaude-ville actors, frantically rushing on and off the stage for quick costume changes. They were — simultaneously — lawyers for BCCI, lawyers for First American, top executives of First American, and paymasters for the Tampa defense lawyers. And these were just the roles that were known at the time. Later, as we shall see, it emerged that they had borrowed from BCCI to buy stock in First American.

An obvious pitfall in their playing so many roles is the possibility of conflicts of interest. One clear example concerns BCCI's relationship with First American. Could First American really be regarded as wholly independent of BCCI's influence when the men who ran it were receiving substantial legal fees from BCCI? A test of First American's autonomy occurred in 1988, when BCCI was investigated by the Kerry Committee and the Customs Service. Investigators found that Amjad Awan had channeled millions of dollars of Noriega's money through a BCCI account at First American. Even worse, defendants in Operation C-Chase had laundered nearly $7 million in drug money through First American. Clifford and Altman — wearing their First American hats — should have been outraged. If they had been running Citibank or Chase Manhattan, it's a good bet they would have told BCCI to take its business elsewhere. But when they put on their BCCI lawyer hats, the situation became awkward. How could they tell BCCI to get lost without undermining an important client? Whose interests would they put first, First American's or BCCI's?

There were other important interests at stake as well — their own. Before the indictment in Tampa, there had already been allegations that Altman was involved in wrongdoing. Awan, as noted earlier, had suggested in a conversation with Mazur that Altman was trying to interfere with the Kerry Committee's probe by advising BCCI to trans-fer him out of the country. (The lawyer denied the allegation.) In the same conversation, Awan said he suspected that BCCI secretly owned First American. If BCCI had acquired control of the banking company, did it do so with the knowledge — perhaps even the collusion — of Clifford and Altman?

The legal defense team put together by Clifford and Altman was headed by three Washington attorneys: Raymond Banoun of Arent, Fox, Kintner, Plotkin & Kahn; E. Lawrence Barcella, Jr., of Laxalt, Washington, Perito & Dubuc;* and Lawrence Wechsler of Janis,

---

*Laxalt, Washington went out of business in 1991.

Schuelke & Wechsler. (They were assisted by lawyers at other firms, notably Miami's Holland & Knight.) Wechsler was an old friend of Altman's; he was one of a number of pals who often went to Altman's mansion in Potomac, Maryland, to watch football games on Sundays.

Banoun, Barcella, and Wechsler had known one another since the 1970s, when they worked as prosecutors in the office of the U.S. Attorney for Washington, D.C. After going into private practice, all three men developed reputations as white-collar crime experts. Banoun, for example, served as chairman of the White Collar Crime Committee of the American Bar Association. Wechsler's firm represented the arms dealer Albert Hakim, a central figure in the Iran-contra scandal.

Barcella was perhaps the best known of the three, having handled two cases that attracted tremendous press coverage. As a federal prosecutor, he investigated the 1976 murder of Orlando Letelier, a former Chilean diplomat living in Washington. After Letelier became a prominent critic of the Pinochet dictatorship, he was killed in a car bombing. Barcella also prosecuted Edwin Wilson, a former CIA agent who had sold arms to Libya's Moammar Qaddafi. Barcella secured a conviction. Because of the Letelier and Wilson cases, Barcella developed excellent contacts in the press and a great deal of credibility. This would come in quite handy when he became one of the most forceful apologists for BCCI.

BCCI received advice on lobbying and public relations from several sources, including Kissinger Associates, the advisory firm owned by the former secretary of state, according to internal BCCI records. Henry Kissinger's ties to associates of Abedi's dated from at least the early 1970s, as noted in Chapter 6, and there were other connections over the years.

In 1985, Kissinger provided advice to Roy Carlson, the chairman of National Bank of Georgia, according to NBG records. (Carlson, of course, had helped to arrange Bank of America's investment in BCCI when he worked for the California bank.) Kissinger has said that this was a one-time briefing that included other bankers, and he denied that he was paid by NBG. Not long after that, Kissinger Associates hired a BCCI front man, Sergio Correa da Costa, who served as Brazil's ambassador to the United States until 1986. While he was a consultant to Kissinger's firm, he was also a nominee shareholder in BCCI's Brazilian subsidiary as well as its chairman. (A spokesman for Kissinger says that if Correa da Costa also worked with BCCI, that was his affair.)

Shortly after he started working for Kissinger's firm, Correa da Costa began trying to forge a relationship between BCCI and the consulting firm. He tried to arrange for Kissinger to meet Ghaith Pharaon, but Kissinger declined. One employee of the firm was more responsive: Alan Stoga, an international economist. In May 1987, Correa da Costa introduced Stoga to Abol Fazl Helmy, a BCCI officer in New York.

On October 6 of the following year (five days before the Tampa indictment became public), Helmy had lunch with Stoga. The following day, Stoga wrote to him, saying he had enjoyed the lunch "and, even more, your suggestion that BCCI might be interested in developing a relationship with Kissinger Associates." On October 12, Stoga called Helmy with advice from Kissinger on how to deal with the case, according to a memo sent by Helmy to Swaleh Naqvi that day. "Dr. Kissinger," wrote Helmy, "recommends that a public relations offensive be made by us and in that context has suggested using Burson-Marstellar, a highly reputable public relations firm."* Helmy remained in touch with Kissinger Associates for the next few months, keeping Naqvi apprised of his contacts. In a December 19 memo to the BCCI chief, Helmy noted that two of Kissinger's partners would be joining the incoming Bush administration, a reference to the national security adviser, Brent Scowcroft, and Deputy Secretary of State Lawrence Eagleburger.

When asked years later about the firm's dealings with BCCI, Stoga acknowledged that there were meetings until January 1989 but said that the firm was never hired by the bank. He denied advising BCCI about which PR firm to hire. Stoga did, however, recommend a lawyer. In February 1989, he suggested that BCCI retain William D. Rogers of Arnold & Porter. Rogers, a former undersecretary of state,† used to work in the Washington office of Kissinger Associates. BCCI took the advice. In 1989 and early 1990, Rogers and three of his partners assisted BCCI. To handle PR, the bank retained Hill and Knowlton.

John Hillbery, BCCI's chief spokesman, signed a contract with the London office of Hill and Knowlton three days after the indictment was made public. The bank agreed to pay £25,000 (about $44,000) per month plus expenses.

---

*The correct spelling is Burson-Marsteller.
†He should not be confused with William P. Rogers, a former secretary of state.

Hill and Knowlton had a close relationship with Clifford's law firm and First American. "We've worked with Clifford & Warnke on many things over the years," said an official of the PR firm. Robert Keith Gray, the head of its Washington office, was on the board of First American's Washington bank, as noted in Chapter 5.

Gray boasted high-level connections in the Republican party. He worked on Reagan's campaign in 1980 and then served as co-chairman of the inaugural committee. Gray did not neglect Reagan's successor. He was co-chairman of Bush's inaugural committee after the 1988 election. In late 1990, Hill and Knowlton acquired a lobbying outfit headed by Craig L. Fuller, who had been chief of staff for Bush when he was vice president. (Fuller left Hill and Knowlton in early 1992.) Gray was also connected to the intelligence world. He had been brought into the Reagan campaign by the campaign manager, William Casey, who soon became CIA director. Back in the 1970s, Gray served on the board of a company controlled by Edwin Wilson, the renegade CIA agent who was prosecuted by Larry Barcella.*

Hill and Knowlton also employs well-connected Democrats; ideological purity is much less important than access and influence. A top official in the Washington office is Frank Mankiewicz, a veteran party activist. In the 1968 presidential race, he was a senior aide to Robert F. Kennedy. Four years later, he served as press spokesman for the party's nominee, Senator George McGovern. During the 1988 campaign, Mankiewicz attended the breakfast for Jesse Jackson organized by Bert Lance. Clark Clifford, as noted in Chapter 5, was the star attraction. In defending the firm's willingness to represent BCCI, Mankiewicz told the *National Journal* in 1991 that the bank had "a pretty good reputation" in 1988. When he was reminded that at least three Hill and Knowlton employees refused to work on the account because of BCCI's sleazy reputation, Mankiewicz shrugged off the contradiction: "A lot of people don't work on a lot of our accounts."

One way in which Hill and Knowlton tried to help BCCI was by telling reporters that several other major banks had run afoul of U.S. laws — downplaying the fact that these cases nearly always involved the failure to file currency transaction reports, a far less serious of-

---

*Gray has asserted that he was only a casual acquaintance of Wilson's and that the arms dealer used his name without permission. In fact, Gray and Wilson had extensive business and personal ties.

fense. Hill and Knowlton also promoted the idea that BCCI was a solid and stable bank. A "backgrounder" dated October 26, 1988, said the bank "stresses conservatism, prudence and liquidity in its deposit taking and lending activities." That same day, Hill and Knowlton officials met with Swaleh Naqvi and agreed on a "plan of action." The plan makes it clear that image-building could be a costly exercise for BCCI. The "account team" included twenty-two Hill and Knowlton employees in ten countries. One item in the "plan of action" was to spend about $75,000 to produce "a video for staff of an interview with Mr. Naqvi" to be distributed around the bank's branches. "It could be used not only for staff but also in segments on 'real' TV stations."

The PR men also advised BCCI executives on which journalists they should see and which ones to avoid. When, for example, Jeff Gerth, a veteran investigative reporter for the *New York Times,* started looking into BCCI, Hill and Knowlton advised bank officials not to talk to him.

BCCI was not an easy client. For one thing, Naqvi was so mistrustful of Western journalists that he would not even talk to them on a background basis. Another problem was the bank's penchant for telling lies. (As noted earlier, BCCI officials told several whoppers to journalists when the First American stock purchases were exposed in 1978.) Cultural barriers were another obstacle. Some BCCI officials wanted to give reporters copies of speeches and other material written in the bank's peculiar argot — the pseudo-philosophical "BCCI-speak" that Abedi and some of his associates used. A Hill and Knowlton official says he "told Naqvi the material was worthless." But the biggest constraint on the PR men was that the bank was under indictment, which meant that the lawyers would be in charge. Anything more than routine information would have to be vetted by the legal team. On January 11, 1989, Naqvi sent a memo to Clement R. ("Kim") Gagné III, a lawyer in Larry Wechsler's firm, saying that all inquiries "that relate in any fashion to the legal investigations in and proceedings concerning the U.S. criminal case or related matters" should be referred to Gagné. From that point on, Gagné and the "two Larrys" — Wechsler and Barcella — became de facto PR men for BCCI.

Much of the information provided to reporters by Wechsler and Barcella later turned out to be false or misleading. Most of the time, this did not reflect on them; they were simply acting as conduits of information from the bank. Sometimes, though, they made dubious statements on their own authority.

Barcella, for example, was asked on March 26, 1990, about the bank's compliance with U.S. laws on cash transactions. He replied that "BCCI's policies and procedures were consistent with industry norms in the countries in which they were operating," including the United States. That remark conflicts with findings by American bank regulators. On September 30, 1988, the Federal Reserve and the New York State Banking Department conducted a joint examination of BCCI's New York agency. One part of their report dealt with the Bank Secrecy Act — the federal law that requires banks to fill out currency transaction reports (CTRs) for large cash transactions. It stated, in part, that "the agency was found to be *deficient in all respects* concerning compliance with the requirements of the Financial Recordkeeping and Reporting Regulations" (emphasis added).

What is even more curious is that Barcella's remark was contradicted by the findings of auditors and investigators who were assisting the defense team. On January 5, 1990, Whitney Adams, a law partner of Barcella's, sent a memo to a BCCI official discussing the results of a study by investigator Charles Morley. A paragraph headed "Bank Secrecy Act Compliance" states:

> Mr. Morley's memorandum describes in detail the areas of deficiency with respect to Bank Secrecy Act compliance. In general, the system is inadequate with respect to reporting currency transactions exceeding $10,000, identifying suspicious currency transactions, accounting for CTR exemptions, or reflecting regulatory changes in the BSA regulatory requirements which are expected to occur shortly.

At the bottom of the memo are the names of the eight people who were to receive copies of it, including E. Lawrence Barcella.

Some months after the March 1990 interview in which Barcella vociferously defended BCCI, he did some legal work for one of the bank's chief accusers, the former Panamanian diplomat José Blandón. As noted in Chapter 10, Blandón had told the Kerry Committee that BCCI was at the heart of Noriega's criminal empire.

One potentially explosive issue — BCCI's relationship to First American Bankshares — was handled personally by Robert Altman.

The Tampa indictment raised the specter that news organizations would start to ask embarrassing questions about BCCI's ties to First

American for the first time since it was acquired by BCCI's clients in 1982. The biggest source of concern to Clifford and Altman must have been the *Washington Post,* since most First American customers live in the Washington area. In addition, the *Post* is read by thousands of federal officials, some of whom could make life difficult for BCCI and its Washington lawyers.

The initial signs were encouraging. The *Post's* front-page story on the indictment contained no reference to First American. The paper corrected this oversight the next day with a brief article in the business section, noting that the shareholder groups overlapped and that Clifford and Altman were associated with both banks. But the bulk of the story was devoted to remarks by Altman playing down the relationship. He said the overlap was "not as great as you might think," that Abedi played no role in setting policy at First American, and that Abedi sometimes spoke to First American officials to check on the company's progress on behalf of its Arab owners.

The city's other daily newspaper, the *Washington Times,* ran a much more forceful story that day. Splashed across the top of page 1, it highlighted Clifford's role in dealing with the Kerry Committee's investigation. The article also contained an explosive allegation attributed to committee sources: First American could be secretly owned by BCCI. This story attracted little attention, however, perhaps because few journalists take the paper seriously. It is connected with the Unification Church of the Reverend Sun Myung Moon (the "Moonies") and often prints half-baked stories. A business writer at the *Post* published a column the following week which was apparently aimed at debunking the *Washington Times* article. The *Post's* Rudolph A. Pyatt, Jr., portrayed First American as a victim of guilt by association. First American, he wrote, "is being subjected to innuendo and wild speculation in the wake of the allegations against BCCI."

One weapon in BCCI's armory was the threat of libel suits. This is particularly effective in Britain, where the law heavily favors plaintiffs. Over the years, countless scoundrels have taken advantage of British libel law to prevent the press from exposing their wrongdoing. One notable example is the late Robert Maxwell. The lack of scrutiny by the press made it easier for him to commit massive frauds, including the looting of employee pension funds.

Like Maxwell, BCCI used Britain's libel laws to intimidate and punish nosy journalists. In the early 1980s, as we have seen, BCCI sued the *New Statesman* after it published a major exposé about the bank. The cost of litigation helped to drive the publication out of business.

The author of that article, Tariq Ali, tangled once again with BCCI after the C-Chase indictment. Ali was now the producer of *Bandung File,* a television program on Third World affairs on Britain's Channel 4. (It takes its name from a 1955 conference of nonaligned states held in Bandung, Indonesia.) Soon after the indictment, Ali began work on a television exposé.

When the bank got wind of the program, its lawyers complained to the British government that the show could be prejudicial to the BCCI defendants who were to be tried in England. On January 12, 1989, government lawyers told Channel 4 to cancel the program and threatened to seek a court injunction to prevent the broadcast. Channel 4 resisted, and the attorney general backed down. The program was shown on January 16.

Several months later, Ali was planning another broadcast on BCCI; this time the bank did not resort to the legal process. In late 1989, Ali said, he was approached by "a very distinguished Pakistani, a man of medicine," who claimed to be acting on BCCI's behalf. Ali said the man offered him £2 million (about $3.3 million) to fund a television drama series written by Ali. There was one important condition: the program on BCC would be canceled. Ali rejected the bribe and the program was broadcast as scheduled.

Although Ali could not prove that the man was working for BCCI, a former bank official says that many journalists were paid off by the bank. He says, for example, that a journalist in the United States who covered the Middle East was paid a monthly retainer by a BCCI front man. After the indictment, this journalist gave BCCI advice on how to influence other reporters. At the same time, the journalist was covering the story for his own publication.

In their attempts to manipulate public opinion, some BCCI officials exploited anti-Semitism by spreading the word that the bank's troubles in the United States were the fault of the "Zionist lobby." They would point out that some of the bank's antagonists had "Jewish-sounding" names, including Jack Blum and Mark Jackowski. While it is true that Blum is Jewish, Jackowski has a Polish-Catholic background. Whatever their ethnicity, there is no evidence that the probes were motivated by anything other than BCCI's own conduct.

Blum encountered this allegation repeatedly during a visit to Pakistan in June 1989. "The bank has laid upon everybody that this is a

Zionist plot," he said shortly after his return, "and this has been published in Pakistani newspapers." In an effort to disabuse Pakistanis of that notion, Blum said he "told people there were two thousand tapes where the various defendants explain to people how to launder drug money."

With BCCI's encouragement, the Zionist plot story was widely disseminated. When an English-language newspaper in Kuwait printed an article on this theme, bank officials gave reprints to many of their customers. "I saw a copy of it in a BCCI office in South America," says a former official. "Management had circulated it globally."

In June 1989, defense lawyers for BCCI were asked whether the bank actually believed it was the victim of the "Zionist lobby" and whether it had ever spread that story. In a written reply, Wechsler and Barcella said, "The management of BCCI has not and does not contend that any 'Zionist lobby' is behind investigations of the Bank by U.S. authorities. The Bank's position on the indictment is reflected in its press release of 13 October 1988, a copy of which is attached for your reference." This reply, of course, ignored the question about whether the bank had spread the story.

While BCCI's propagandists tried to limit the damage to the bank's image, the wheels of justice were turning in Tampa. The bankers who had been arrested in October asked to be released from jail on bond, but the prosecutor, Mark Jackowski, argued that there was a "flight risk." The judge released two defendants (Hassan and Ashraf) and agreed to a compromise for the other four (Awan, Bilgrami, Howard, and Hussain) — a kind of "house arrest." They would move into apartments in the Tampa area and wear electronic monitoring devices on their ankles. The apartments would be guarded by off-duty policemen. (Three defendants connected to BCCI had been taken into custody by British Customs: Akbar, Baakza, and Chinoy. The Bahamas branch manager, Saad Shafi, was never arrested.)

During the bond hearings, Jackowski dropped several bombshells. He claimed, for example, to have evidence that the bankers were acting not on their own behalf but on behalf of the bank. "As far as we are able to tell, Your Honor, none of these defendants received any personal remuneration in connection with any of their activities," he said. At one point during the investigation, Jackowski said, one of the bankers rejected a payoff from an undercover agent, saying, "No, no, no. I don't need a bribe. I get paid by the corporation." Ian Howard, said the prosecutor, "indicated that notwithstanding his personal distaste with respect to drugs, he continued to transact business with the undercover agents . . . because he had decided to subjugate his own personal interest to . . . that of his employer."

Although the bankers did not profit, Jackowski said, BCCI benefited in two ways. It received cheap deposits and it used deposits of drug money to artificially inflate ("window-dress," in banking jargon) its balance sheet. Some of the defendants, according to the prosecutor, indicated that high-level officials at BCCI knew what was going on. In one taped conversation, Awan, Hassan, and Bilgrami told an under-cover agent that there was an "inner circle" of senior officials who were aware of drug-money activities and, said Jackowski, "had given their approval to those activities." One of the defendants went so far as to say that he "had the support of the board."

Shortly after the bond hearings, BCCI's defense lawyers provided some clues about their strategy. One defense motion asked that the case be dismissed on the ground of "outrageous government con-duct" — similar to the defense of entrapment. The motion said that "the government agents sought out the defendants for the specific purpose of luring them into criminal activity."

While prosecutors and defense lawyers fired salvos of paper at one another, investigators continued to gather information on BCCI. Shortly after the indictment, British Customs agents arrived at BCCI's headquarters in London with a warrant to search for records relevant to C-Chase. In the course of the search, they stumbled upon a treasure trove of documents related to Noriega. BCCI's lawyers fought unsuc-cessfully to prevent British Customs from turning the records over to their American counterparts. The documents were sent to the United States in early 1989.

Brian Ross, an investigative reporter for NBC-TV, revealed the exis-tence of the documents in a broadcast on June 15, 1989. He reported that the records showed that BCCI had transferred more than $20 million of Noriega's money from London to Luxembourg in early 1988 — right after he was indicted. U.S. Customs tried to find out who had leaked the documents to NBC, says Jack Blum, adding that he was a suspect. In July, Customs officials contacted Blum and said they wanted to talk to him. When he explained that he and his wife were on their way to the airport to begin a month-long vacation in Europe, the officials dashed to the airport and held the plane while they questioned him about the leak. "I never saw those documents," he says. "I had left the Senate by then."

The NBC story was significant for two reasons. First, it suggested that BCCI was helping a criminal defendant put his money out of reach of U.S. law enforcement authorities. Second, it meant that the bank had withheld important documents concerning Noriega from the Senate.

When Senator Kerry learned of the NBC report, he was incensed. On July 7, he wrote to Clifford demanding "prompt production of the documents." (BCCI's lawyers have argued that the Senate subpoena did not cover records held outside the United States. The records were nonetheless turned over to Kerry.)

By this time, Jack Blum had returned to private practice. His contract had expired on March 31, and the probe was handed over to two young lawyers on Kerry's staff, David McKean and Jonathan Winer. Before leaving the Senate, Blum had shared some of his findings with prosecutors and federal agents in Florida. He had even persuaded two former BCCI officials to talk to federal authorities. One informant was Amer Lodhi, a lawyer who had worked for BCCI and Ghaith Pharaon.* Lodhi had detailed information on BCCI's misconduct — including its very close ties to U.S. financial institutions.

Blum heard about Lodhi in March 1989. "I was in the process of cleaning out my desk," he later recalled, when "I received a telephone call from a former client of mine who said, 'I was talking to this guy who was very highly placed at BCCI, and I brought your name up, and he said your investigation almost brought the house down there and that there was a full court press to make sure that it did not get anywhere.' And I said, 'Would this guy talk to me?'"

Through his former client, Blum got in touch with Lodhi and arranged to meet him later that month at the Embassy Suites hotel near the Miami airport. Blum notified Mark Jackowski in Tampa, and the prosecutor arranged for Customs and IRS agents to bug the room. "There were all sorts of funny scenes," Blum recalled. The agents "discovered that the Embassy Suites used cinder block between rooms, and you can't drill through cinder block to run a wire through the wall. So they had to figure out how to get the wire through the wall." For the next few days, Blum spent about ten hours questioning Lodhi about BCCI. Toward the end, he persuaded Lodhi to go to Tampa with him to meet with federal prosecutors.

---

*Blum says he has never disclosed the names of his informants. Lodhi was identified as an informant in the *New York Times* on September 15, 1991. The article was apparently based on a leak from a law enforcement source.

There was something of a Keystone Kops atmosphere to their reception, Blum recalled. "We get to Tampa, get taken to a hotel near the airport, and the Customs people find that the hotel is overbooked and we don't have a place to meet. So we now pile back into the car and three carloads of cops start tearing around Tampa looking for a place to meet. We pull up in front of the HoJo's [Howard Johnson's]. You've got to see the scene. One of them is on a portable telephone to his secretary [who was trying to find a hotel room]. Lodhi is getting increasingly irate." Eventually, Blum pointed out that hotels usually have conference rooms, and a small meeting room was booked at the Howard Johnson's.

Once again the questioning was taped without Lodhi's knowledge. For the next several hours, Lodhi was questioned by prosecutors and federal agents attached to C-Chase. He talked about BCCI's political connections and the bank's involvement with the drug trade. He said he suspected that BCCI's financial statements were phony, that the "capital" might even be nonexistent. He also had detailed information about BCCI's ties to First American and other financial institutions.

The previous year, Amjad Awan had told Robert Mazur that he suspected that BCCI secretly owned First American and National Bank of Georgia. Lodhi now repeated the allegation, adding that BCCI may also have controlled Independence Bank. Although he did not provide proof, Lodhi was certainly worth listening to, since he had worked closely with Ghaith Pharaon, the man who supposedly owned NBG and Independence.

Two weeks later, Blum persuaded another former BCCI official to come to Tampa — the same man who had talked to him about the bank when he began his probe in early 1988. This source repeated much of what Lodhi had said.

If Blum's informants were right, it meant that BCCI, which was effectively an international criminal organization, had acquired three American financial institutions, including the largest banking company in the nation's capital. The implications were shocking. Consider National Bank of Georgia, which had supposedly been acquired by Pharaon in early 1978. NBG was a major lender to the family business of Jimmy Carter. If Pharaon was a front man, it meant that BCCI, in effect, was owed large sums of money by the president of the United States. Even if Carter did not know of BCCI's role, this kind of financial relationship would be highly disturbing.

The allegations could also help to explain First American's 1987 purchase of NBG from Pharaon. Several observers felt that First American had paid too much, but the deal made perfect sense if BCCI secretly owned both institutions. At the time, BCCI was desperately in need of money, and the takeover would enable it to drain money from a relatively healthy subsidiary — First American. A parent-subsidiary relationship between BCCI and First American might also help to account for First American's sometimes dubious loans to American politicians — such as the $700,000 lent to Gary Hart during the 1984 presidential campaign. Who was the real lender, First American or BCCI?

What about CenTrust, the Miami savings and loan in which Pharaon was also a big shareholder? Was BCCI also the owner of this stock? If so, this would raise questions about campaign contributions by David Paul, the savings bank's chairman. Paul had been one of the biggest single donors and fund-raisers for the Democratic party. When he showered that money on politicians, was he acting on his own behalf or was he also buying influence for BCCI?

There were other serious questions. Were the Arab shareholders of First American — who included some of the most prominent people in the Middle East — participants in a fraudulent scheme to take over the U.S. banking company? Were Clifford and Altman accomplices? What about the police and the bank regulators? If BCCI had really assembled this "underground empire," how was it possible that the authorities knew nothing?

The prosecutors and federal agents in Tampa appeared to take the allegations of Blum's informants quite seriously. On May 2, the U.S. attorney in Tampa subpoenaed records relating to BCCI and First American. On June 12, a subpoena was served on the Federal Reserve Banks of Richmond, Atlanta, and San Francisco for documents relating to BCCI, First American, and NBG. A federal grand jury was empaneled in Tampa to investigate BCCI's ties with First American.

There were also signs that the U.S. Attorney's office was planning an aggressive prosecution of BCCI in the drug money case. In May, a federal grand jury in Tampa returned a superseding indictment that contained new charges as well as sweeping allegations about the bank's practice of collecting dirty money. The indictment included three new defendants: BCCI's Colombian bank and two officers of that bank, Haroon Qazi and Surjeet Singh. In addition, BCCI officers were accused of laundering drug money as far back as 1983 — three years before Operation C-Chase was launched. (This charge was based mainly on information from Steven Kalish.)

More important than these changes, however, was a passage in the indictment alleging for the first time that the laundering of drug money was corporate policy. BCCI and its Colombian subsidiary, the indictment said, implemented "a corporate strategy for increasing BCCI's deposits by encouraging placements of cash from whatever sources, specifically including 'flight capital,' 'black market capital,' and the proceeds of drug sales, in conscious disregard of the currency regulations, tax laws, and antidrug laws of the United States and of other nations."

BCCI's legal defense team would find it hard to fight these charges. Under U.S. law, a company can, in certain circumstances, be found guilty even if the prosecution does not prove that top managers knew what their underlings were doing. Even if BCCI were found innocent, it would be a Pyrrhic victory, since the verdict would come after months of damaging testimony about the bank. The negative publicity could provoke panic among depositors, prompting them to pull their money out of the bank. The best outcome from BCCI's point of view would be a plea bargain. As part of their efforts to obtain a settlement, BCCI's lawyers tried to demonstrate that the bank was reforming itself.

Accountants from Price Waterhouse (assisted by lawyers and private investigators) conducted a massive "special audit" of BCCI's U.S. operations, aimed at testing the bank's compliance with American laws related to money laundering. In the course of the audit, they uncovered a number of suspicious transactions by BCCI customers and turned the information over to the government.

Although it is questionable whether BCCI really cleaned up its act, there is no doubt that the lawyers and accountants "cleaned up." The professional fees for C-Chase and related matters were enormous. BCCI paid $18.7 million in fees, plus another $2.8 million in expenses, with much of the money going to lawyers for the individual defendants. Separately, Clifford & Warnke received substantial fees from BCCI, which was already a lucrative client. Between 1978 and 1990, BCCI paid about $6 million (plus expenses) to Clifford's firm. In addition, First American and related companies paid about $11 million to the firm over the years. Of course, First American, according to Clifford and Altman, had nothing to do with BCCI.

Publicly, BCCI consistently maintained that it was innocent of all charges. Privately, however, lawyers for the bank tried for months to work out a settlement. The first attempt was made just days after the indictment, according to a prosecutor. A lawyer from Holland & Knight said the bank was willing to plead guilty to one count, and the offer was quickly rejected. In late 1988 or early 1989, says this source, a similar offer was made by Wechsler and Barcella. In the latter part of 1989, the negotiations became more serious, and Altman briefed BCCI on the progress of the talks. He discussed the case with the board of directors on August 18 and, according to the minutes of the meeting, "touched on settlement strategy." Altman also dealt with this issue at a board meeting on November 27. On December 13, three BCCI lawyers — Barcella, Wechsler, and Peter E. George of Holland & Knight — met with federal prosecutors to discuss a possible settlement.

Barcella even tried to enlist the support of Jack Blum. At a breakfast meeting in early November, Blum recalled a few weeks later, Barcella said "they were ready to plead guilty and that the prosecution wouldn't get anything more out of a trial." He wanted Blum to "pass the word around" to the prosecutors. Barcella tried to convince Blum that BCCI was reforming itself in a serious way, saying, "I've been given carte blanche to clean up the bank." Blum responded that BCCI was much dirtier than Barcella realized, that the whole thing could be criminal. Blum said he "tried to get him to see that — with any luck — the charges [in Tampa] are just the beginning."

Barcella also contacted a lawyer who had represented Colombia's Banco Occidente in a similar case. The Colombian bank had also been indicted on drug money charges, but the Justice Department agreed to make a deal. When Barcella asked why Banco Occidente was treated more favorably, the lawyer replied, "The problem is that your client is BCCI."

When Mark Jackowski was asked in early November if a plea bargain was in the works, he stated firmly, "I'm preparing for trial." The Justice Department's apparently resolute attitude was reflected in a speech delivered in October by Attorney General Richard Thornburgh at a conference on money laundering held in Miami. Thornburgh declared that the battle against money laundering was a crucial part of the war on drugs.

The BCCI trial was scheduled to begin on Tuesday, January 16, 1990, at U.S. District Court in Tampa. The presiding judge was William

Terrell Hodges. Fifteen months had passed since the bankers had been arrested, and there was great anticipation. The trial was expected to be an exciting courtroom drama, pitting the prosecutors, Mark Jackowski and Michael Rubenstein, against an array of high-priced legal talent assembled by BCCI.

But there was no battle of the titans that day. The bank had copped a plea. If Judge Hodges accepted the agreement, BCCI would be spared the indignity of a messy trial. Under the terms of the deal, the government would drop all charges against BCCI's Luxembourg holding company and its Colombian bank. Bank of Credit and Commerce S.A., the flagship bank of the group, and Bank of Credit and Commerce (Overseas) Ltd., the Caymans holding company, would plead guilty to money-laundering conspiracy charges and thirty specific acts of violating federal laws against money laundering. (Separately, charges were dismissed against the Los Angeles branch manager, Iqbal Ashraf. The government never extradited the two employees added to the case in the superseding indictment, Haroon Qazi and Surjeet Singh of BCCI's Colombian bank.) BCCI would be on probation for five years and would be subject to increased regulation by the Federal Reserve. It would also be required to "forfeit" about $15 million.

The most extraordinary part of the plea bargain was that the U.S. attorney in Tampa would agree "not to charge" BCCI or any of its units "with committing any other federal criminal offenses under investigation or known to the government at the time of the execution of this agreement or relating in any manner to the charges that were the subject of the instant prosecution." In other words, the federal prosecutors in Tampa would not follow up the vast number of leads they had — including the allegation that BCCI illegally owned First American.

The proposed plea bargain was widely denounced. To some critics, it appeared that the government had things backward. If BCCI was a criminal organization, shouldn't prosecutors have done a deal with the individual bankers in exchange for their testimony against their superiors? The monetary penalty was considered meager in light of the bank's resources. "This agreement," said the *New York Times* in an editorial, "looks feeble alongside Mr. Bush's macho oratory about coordinated drug-smashing programs, the Panama invasion and interdiction along the Colombian coast."

Senator Kerry said he thought BCCI should have been kicked out of the country. "Any bank that is caught violating the law with respect to money laundering and drug profits ought to be shut down. Absolutely. Don't allow them to operate in the United States. Why should we?" On January 19, he and three other Democratic senators* sent a letter to Attorney General Thornburgh harshly criticizing the deal. "The Administration and the Congress have placed the highest priority on stopping the flow of illegal drugs into the United States," they wrote. "Money laundering enterprises of this type are essential to drug traffickers. We do not see how this agreement will serve to deter similar illegal conduct in the future. We do not understand why the plea agreement should preclude further review of allegations concerning the structure, operations, and practices of BCCI." Senators Kerry and Metzenbaum — along with four House Democrats† — wrote to Judge Hodges on February 1, asking him to reject the plea bargain and impose a harsher sentence.

The criticisms were to no avail. The judge approved the agreement.

Although the Justice Department had allowed BCCI to get off with what was widely regarded as a slap on the wrist, there were hopes that bank regulators would take a tougher line. One man in a position to do something was Gerald Lewis, the state bank regulator in Florida, where BCCI had its biggest presence in the United States. On February 13, a senior Justice Department official sent a very peculiar letter to Lewis. Charles S. Saphos, the chief of the narcotics and dangerous drugs section, asked Lewis to allow BCCI to continue doing business in Florida! "We are . . . requesting that BCCI be permitted to operate in your jurisdiction," Saphos wrote, "with the understanding that certain accounts may be maintained by the Bank at the request of the Department of Justice which otherwise would be closed to avoid legal and regulatory violations." When Lewis asked for an explanation, Saphos wrote back that he had been misunderstood. "The Department of Justice," wrote Saphos, "is *not* requesting that you permit BCCI to be licensed." Lewis wasn't sure what the department wanted, and he made his own decision. The following month, he refused to renew BCCI's license to operate in Florida.

When Saphos's strange letters were made public much later, the Justice Department claimed it was all a misunderstanding. In fact, identically worded letters were sent to state bank regulators in New

---

*Howard Metzenbaum of Ohio, Howell T. Heflin of Alabama, and Dennis DeConcini of Arizona.

†William Hughes of New Jersey, Mel Levine of California, Edward Feighan of Ohio, and Charles Rangel of New York.

York and California. Saphos apparently never cleared the letters with the U.S. Attorney's office in Tampa. The bank knew about the letters, however. Saphos wrote them after he was lobbied by BCCI's criminal defense lawyers, and he sent the lawyers copies of the letters.

Justice Department officials have strongly defended the plea bargain, arguing that it was not a sweetheart deal. If the case had gone to trial, they say, it is unlikely that the penalty would have been any more severe. Others are not so sure. Some observers say the government went easy on BCCI and suspect that one reason it did so was that it wanted the bank's cooperation in the prosecution of Noriega. The timing certainly fits this scenario. The United States invaded Panama in December 1989, and Noriega turned himself in to U.S. authorities on January 3 — thirteen days before the BCCI trial was to begin. Twenty-three American soldiers and several hundred Panamanians lost their lives in the invasion. The financial cost to American taxpayers was $164 million. Because of these costs, there was tremendous pressure on the Bush administration to secure Noriega's conviction. The Justice Department's obsession with winning a guilty verdict became apparent when the trial began in September 1991. Several notorious drug traffickers were given reduced sentences or other favors for assisting the prosecution. One of Noriega's lawyers, Frank Rubino, joked that the prosecutors had made so many deals that the trial "is going to relieve prison crowding." With the help of such witnesses, Noriega was convicted in April 1992.

BCCI — as the dictator's main banker — was in a unique position to help the prosecution. In fact, one provision of the plea bargain was that BCCI would assist the United States in its prosecution of other persons. One official involved in Operation C-Chase openly acknowledged a link to the Noriega case. The day the BCCI plea bargain was announced, Bonni Tischler, the head of the Customs office in Tampa, told a reporter that she approved of the deal because the bank had agreed to help in other drug cases, including the prosecution of Noriega.

What about BCCI's political connections? The Justice Department has denied that lobbying affected its handling of C-Chase — a contention supported by an investigation ordered by Congressman Charles E. Schumer of New York. But several observers suspect that influence peddling played a role.

William von Raab, who served as the Customs commissioner until July 1989, has testified that the government took a "constant pounding" from "influence peddlers who either had been flattered, bought, or were just plain on contract to BCCI." He singled out Clifford, Altman, and Hill and Knowlton's Frank Mankiewicz. * "Therewasn'ta single influence peddler who wasn't being used to work this case," von Raab said. "The result was that senior U.S. policy-level officials were constantly under the impression that BCCI was probably not that bad, because all these good guys that they play golf with all the time were representing them." Von Raab called the plea bargain "a real triumph of the Washington power broking establishment."

One of the leaders of this "power broking establishment" was, of course, Clark Clifford.

Clifford and Altman used to reassure BCCI executives that the drug money case could be taken care of, according to a former official of the bank. Some of the bankers took this to mean that their lawyers would pull strings in Washington. "It's a perception you're born with in the Third World," he says. "You think anyone is for sale."

Internal records make it clear that BCCI intended to use political influence to fight the indictment. On December 1, 1988, M. M. Ahmed, a former Pakistani diplomat employed in BCCI's Washington representative office, sent a memo to Naqvi outlining "the legal, regulatory, the public relations, and the political aspects of the Tampa indictments against the BCC and nine of its officials." Under the heading "Political aspect," Ahmad included these items:

- "Contact with Bush administration by friendly Arab countries and Pakistan."
- "Activization of other contacts with well-connected persons known to us in USA."

There is also no doubt that Clifford and other lawyers for BCCI tried to use political influence to squelch the Kerry Committee's investigation and to silence critics of the plea bargain.

In February 1989, Clifford and some of his law partners developed a sudden interest in Kerry's political career. Clifford, Altman, John R. Kovin, and J. Griffin Lesher each contributed $1,000 to the senator. (Kovin and Lesher both did legal work related to BCCI.) Clifford gave

---

*Mankiewicz took exception to von Raab's testimony, insisting that he had worked on behalf of First American, not BCCI. This, of course, is hair-splitting, since he reported to Altman, a lawyer for both banks. In addition, Mankiewicz's firm had previously done PR work for BCCI.

Kerry another $1,000 in June 1990.* When Clifford was later asked about his 1989 donation, he said, "There was nothing unusual about it. Every time Kerry has run I have contributed to him. I have a group of Democratic senators and congressmen and I contribute to them every time." In fact, federal records showed that he had never contributed to Kerry before. When confronted with this fact, Clifford said his remark about earlier contributions was simply a mistake.

Through a curious coincidence, Frank Mankiewicz also donated $1,000 to Senator Kerry in February 1989 — his only direct contribution to any federal candidate in the 1989–90 election cycle. In May 1990, Clifford gave $1,000 to Senator Claiborne Pell.† As chairman of the Foreign Relations Committee, Pell controlled the purse strings of Kerry's subcommittee.

Kerry has said that he did not solicit Clifford's contribution, and there is no indication that he was influenced: he continued to investigate BCCI. Some of his Senate colleagues, however, showed little inclination to probe the bank. Kerry said later that he tried to get support from Joseph Biden of Delaware, the chairman of the Judiciary Committee; Donald Riegle of Michigan, the chairman of the Banking Committee; and George Mitchell of Maine, the majority leader. "It was like pulling teeth," Kerry later said.

BCCI and its allies used other politically connected law firms in Washington besides Clifford & Warnke. Sheikh Zayed was represented by Patton, Boggs & Blow. One of its partners, Thomas Hale ("Tommy") Boggs, Jr., is one of the most powerful Democratic fixers in town. Another partner, Ronald H. Brown, is chairman of the Democratic National Committee.

The senior partner of Barcella's law firm was Paul Laxalt, who had been the governor of Nevada and then a U.S. senator. He was a close friend and major political backer of President Reagan and had chaired Reagan's campaign committees in 1976, 1980, and 1984.

John C. Culver, a former Democratic senator from Iowa, was a partner in Ray Banoun's law firm. In early 1989, Jack Blum recalls, he

---

*Earlier, Kerry had been involved in Democratic fund-raising activities with David Paul, the chairman of CenTrust, the savings and loan association connected to BCCI. Kerry has denied that he knew of CenTrust's links to BCCI at that time, and there is no indication that his ties to Paul affected his treatment of BCCI.

†BCCI-related money also flowed to the Republican party. In 1989, Hassan Parvez, the manager of BCCI's Miami branch and a stepson of Swaleh Naqvi's, gave two contributions totaling $1,750 to the National Republican Senatorial Campaign Committee. He was apparently invited to a June 1989 fund-raising dinner at which President Bush spoke.

received a telephone call from Culver asking for a draft copy of his report on BCCI. When Blum refused, Culver told him that Kerry had said it was all right. "I said, 'Excuse me, but when I'm told to give you a copy by Senator Kerry, I'll give you a copy.' That was the last I heard from him." Culver popped up once again when Kerry complained to Clifford the following July about BCCI's failure to turn over documents concerning Noriega (the ones discovered by British Customs). In response, Banoun and Culver visited Kerry. Culver had little to do with the BCCI case, but, as a liberal Democrat, he was the kind of person who might impress Kerry.

BCCI's political clout became apparent after the plea bargain, when the bank was defended by a powerful Republican senator, a former British prime minister, and a former president of the United States.

On February 22, 1990, Senator Orrin Hatch, a Utah Republican, gave a speech in the Senate chamber about BCCI. As an influential member of the Judiciary Committee (which oversees the Justice Department), he was likely to be taken seriously. Hatch strongly defended the plea bargain and attacked members of Congress who had criticized it. He even praised BCCI's management "for the responsible way the company has responded to the charges." He called BCCI's willingness to cooperate with the authorities "the kind of reaction one might hope to see from a responsible corporate citizen."

The effusive praise is not the only strange thing about the speech. It was filled with inaccurate and misleading statements. Hatch portrayed C-Chase as a case in which a handful of low-level employees had been engaged in money laundering without the knowledge of their superiors and "in violation of the bank's own written rules." This, of course, ignored the superseding indictment, which stated that the laundering of drug money was part of BCCI's "corporate strategy." The senator also lumped BCCI with institutions like Bank of America and First National Bank of Boston, even though they had not been accused of laundering drug money. (They had committed a much less serious offense: failing to file currency transaction reports.)

Hatch said the allegation that BCCI was "Noriega's bank" constituted "guilt by association," partly because other banks had deposits from the Panamanian dictator. This remark ignored BCCI's intimate relationship with Noriega, as reflected in Awan's testimony to the Kerry Committee. Hatch said that most of the money belonged to the Panamanian Defense Forces when, in fact, BCCI records showed that Noriega had personal control over the funds and treated the money as his own property. Hatch also ignored the BCCI documents discovered by British Customs, which revealed that BCCI had helped Noriega hide his money after he was indicted.

Toward the end of his speech, Hatch suggested that BCCI might have been the victim of ethnic prejudice. He said that "we must be aware that efforts to make an example of this foreign bank . . . could be seen by some as discriminatory. It will not be lost on the international community — including our friends in the Middle East — that BCCI's critics seem to be singling out this foreign bank for unusually harsh, punitive treatment."

Shortly afterward, Hatch was asked to explain what had prompted his speech. He said that he had been briefed by Justice Department officials and by four BCCI lawyers: Robert Altman, Larry Wechsler, Larry Barcella, and Ray Banoun. (In his speech, Hatch said that he had been briefed by the Justice Department but neglected to mention the defense lawyers.) He said, "It's no secret that some of these guys were concerned that their client was being seriously slandered and libeled and they were concerned that some of the people up here on the Hill would be misled."

Hatch's concern about people being misled is, of course, admirable. Unfortunately, the senator made several remarks suggesting that he had been misled more than anyone. "The bank had relatively little to do with Noriega," he said. "What the bank did do wrong was strictly wire transfers." That remark is flatly contradicted by Awan's testimony to the Kerry Committee, in which he said that most of Noriega's deposits were in the form of cash. Hatch also referred to the individual bankers in the Tampa case as "lower-tier" people. In fact, BCCI — which tried hard to promote this line — was forced to admit in a press release that Nazir Chinoy was a "relatively senior person."

Why was Senator Hatch so willing to believe the defense lawyers — obviously not the most objective sources of information? He said he was impressed that men of such caliber were making the case. Wechsler and Barcella, he noted, "are former prosecutors, and so I relied fairly heavily on them." Referring to Altman, the senator said, "I know him well."

Hatch's friendship with Altman wasn't the senator's only connection to BCCI. Many months later, as we shall see, journalists and government investigators would discover several other curious ties between the senator from Utah and the BCCI network.

.   .   .

Two political figures much more prominent than Hatch also defended BCCI in early 1990: former president Carter and former British prime minister Callaghan. Both men, as we have seen, were beneficiaries of BCCI's financial largesse.

Carter's initial reaction to the indictment was to play down his relationship with BCCI. Immediately after it was announced, he said that BCCI was "one of a large number of contributors to Global 2000. We have more than 200. I don't know how much money they've pledged to Global 2000." At best, this was disingenuous, since BCCI was by far the biggest donor. In the months that followed, Carter continued to associate with BCCI officials. In the summer of 1989 — after the superseding indictment had accused the bank of laundering money as a matter of corporate policy — Carter visited Nigeria with BCCI officials, including Swaleh Naqvi.

Of course, it could be argued that the former president wanted to avoid judging BCCI before the verdict, but he even spoke up for the bank after the guilty plea. In a February 1990 interview with the *Atlanta Constitution,* Carter said that Global 2000 would continue to accept donations from BCCI because, without that money, "we would have to cancel all of our projects in Africa and Asia." This is odd in view of his earlier remark that BCCI was just one of hundreds of donors. More important, he dismissed the drug money case as an "unfortunate incident" involving "a few unsavory characters."

On April 23, Callaghan defended BCCI's management on the floor of the House of Lords during a debate on money laundering. "I have no hesitation in saying that in my judgment they are certainly people of the highest integrity and probity," he declared. "The purpose and philosophy of the bank are honorable and those who are at the head of it are fit and proper people to control it."

In subsequent months, some of BCCI's attorneys tried to use their political influence to thwart congressional investigations, according to a confidential memorandum by Roma W. Theus II of Holland & Knight, the law firm in Miami that assisted BCCI in the Tampa case. The memo, dated September 24, 1990, was apparently based on information obtained from a "mole" inside the Senate. In one passage, Theus wrote that Altman and another BCCI lawyer, Raymond Banoun, were "opposing the subpoenas" issued by the Kerry Committee and that they were "doing everything within their power to call in 'political markers.' "

·　　·　　·

The Justice Department has argued that BCCI's plea agreement did not preclude it from continuing to investigate the bank, since it was binding only on the U.S. attorney in Tampa. Nevertheless, many important leads developed in Tampa were either ignored or not pursued aggressively. Shortly after the Tampa prosecutors met with Jack Blum's informants, they started a grand jury investigation of First American, but it was "temporarily suspended" in October 1989. When asked a few years later to explain this, Mark Jackowski compared the BCCI case to a meal. The money laundering charges in the C-Chase indictment were the "main course." First American and the other issues were the "dessert." He also belittled the importance of Blum's informants, referring to one of them as an "alleged witness," and said the information they provided "appeared to be primarily hearsay, gossip, rumor, and innuendo." He also asserted that Blum said he wanted to be paid for any future assistance — a charge that Blum denies.

After the plea bargain, Jackowski and his colleagues proceeded with the "main course" — the money laundering case against the individual BCCI bankers. Somehow, they never got to the "dessert."

On January 16, 1990, the trial of five BCCI bankers — Amjad Awan, Akbar Bilgrami, Sibte Hassan, Ian Howard, and Syed Aftab Hussain — began in Tampa. It quickly became clear that the biggest culprit was absent: BCCI. In his opening statement, Assistant U.S. Attorney Michael Rubenstein echoed one of the allegations in the superseding indictment — that the laundering of drug money reflected the bank's corporate policy: "The Bank of Credit and Commerce International had a clear, well-defined corporate policy that came down from the highest levels of the bank to take in as many deposits as you can, as fast as you can, and not to be too careful about where they came from." He went on to say that the bankers did not launder drug money for their personal gain but "to advance their careers at BCCI."

On July 29, the jury returned guilty verdicts against the five bankers. They were sentenced in December. Awan and Bilgrami got the stiffest penalty: twelve years in prison and a $100,000 fine. Hussain was sentenced to seven years and three months in prison, Howard to four years and nine months, and Hassan to three years and one month. Awan could have been sentenced to nineteen and a half years, but Judge Hodges said he was lenient because Awan did not profit personally from the laundering. Most of the sentences were later reduced, including Awan's. One way in which Awan earned goodwill was by testifying at Noriega's trial.

Two defendants connected with BCCI, Asif Baakza and Syed Ziaud-din Ali Akbar of Capcom, were tried in London for conspiring to launder drug money. Baakza was convicted in September 1990 and sentenced to two years in prison, but half the sentence was suspended. Akbar was found guilty in October; he was sentenced to eighteen months and fined the equivalent of about $100,000. Nazir Chinoy was extradited from Britain to the United States in April 1991. He pleaded guilty in December to three counts of laundering drug money and was sentenced in May 1992 to three years and ten months in prison.

The plea bargain in Tampa was a stunning victory for BCCI. Thanks to the effectiveness of its lawyers and lobbyists — and the weaknesses of the opposition — the bank avoided the trauma of a long trial. What is more, bank regulators allowed it to remain in business — except in Florida, where Gerald Lewis refused to renew its license.

Shortly afterward, Swaleh Naqvi sent a message to BCCI's employees in which he reveled in the victory, writing: "Our conscience is clean, our intention is clear. We shall through individual and joint effort achieve what we have set out to achieve. The divine forces lead to a common good, towards universal good, towards the good of all humanity." Naqvi also sent his thanks to Clark Clifford. "On behalf of BCC and on my own behalf kindly accept our gratitude for guiding us in the most traumatic experience," he wrote. "We were guided by your wisdom, experience, realisms and purity of your relationship with BCC. Mr. Clifford, sir, you are aware of the moral values on which BCC has been founded. We all thank God for his mercy and beneficence."

In Naqvi's Orwellian doublespeak, BCCI's "moral values" meant fraud on a massive scale. After the plea bargain, BCCI collected millions of dollars in fresh deposits from customers all over the world while its top managers stole the money through fraudulent loans and other scams. It was business as usual.

Federal prosecutors had stopped probing BCCI's ties to First American, and the two banks continued to do business with each other. Shortly after the plea bargain was approved, two First American officials even wrote to BCCI to say that the U.S. institution valued its relationship with BCCI. The letter, dated February 21, 1990, was signed by two executives of First American Bank of New York: Maurice Acoca, senior vice president and chief financial officer, and Mansoor Shafi, vice president. (The letter was prompted by an article in the *Financial Times,* which said the Federal Reserve wanted First American to stop dealing with BCCI.) It reads as follows:

We bring your attention to the fact that recently an article appeared in the Financial Times of February 13, 1990 ascribing certain comments to an unnamed senior First American officer. We have taken exception to the report where it states that, in the future, our two institutions shall not be dealing together.

To set the record straight, we wish to reiterate that First American values the relationship between our two institutions, and we are continually desirous of enhancing it. As you are aware, we are maintaining about forty accounts of the BCC Group's various locations. Additionally, sizable credit facilities are also available in all categories.

The cover-up of BCCI's criminality might have continued for years if it were not for a handful of people who felt a duty to expose it. One man who played a crucial role in this process was Jack Blum, who had spent months gathering evidence on BCCI — collecting documents, deposing witnesses, and meeting with informants. Blum had also turned over many of his findings to federal prosecutors and even persuaded some of his sources to meet with the prosecutors.

Instead of pursuing these leads, the Justice Department allowed the bank to avoid the indignity of a trial and even spared it from further investigation. The day after the plea bargain was announced, Blum exploded: "I'm pissed. Enraged. What happened in Tampa shows the power of BCCI to fix anything. What the government did in this settlement is a fucking outrage."

If the federal government was unwilling to investigate BCCI, Blum was asked, who would do it?

"The State of New York."

12

THE ENFORCERS

THE USS HARRY F. BAUER was among the first ships to sail into action in the days before the invasion of Okinawa in the spring of 1945, one of the hardest-fought battles of World War II. In the two and a half months of almost constant fighting, the American destroyer downed thirteen Japanese planes and protected U.S. forces from air, surface, submarine, and shore fire. The *Harry F. Bauer* continued to fight — and to assist other vessels — even after she was severely damaged, with an unexploded Japanese bomb lodged in her hull.

The presidential citation extolling the "extraordinary heroism in action" of the vessel and its company concluded: "A seaworthy, fighting ship, complemented by skilled and courageous officers and men, the *Harry F. Bauer* achieved a notable record of gallantry in combat, attesting to the teamwork of her entire company and enhancing the finest traditions of the U.S. Naval Service."

The executive officer of that ship was Robert M. Morgenthau, the twenty-six-year-old son of Franklin D. Roosevelt's treasury secretary, Henry Morgenthau, Jr., and the grandson of the U.S. ambassador to Istanbul who sought to expose and prevent Turkish pogroms against Armenians during World War I. Morgenthau's father almost certainly enjoyed the closest friendship with FDR of all his cabinet officers. That had allowed the treasury secretary considerable influence in foreign policy and other areas usually outside the responsibility of his office. All this changed at FDR's sudden death on April 12, 1945. Henry Morgenthau, Jr., not only lost his best friend, as he told the press, but he was also soon out of a job.

The new president, Harry Truman, wanted his own team, including a young naval officer, Clark Clifford, who in July 1945 went to work in the White House for James K. Vardaman, Jr., a naval aide to the president. Like both Vardaman and Truman, Clifford was a Missourian, although he had not known Truman before. Within months of his move to the capital, and after a few poker games with Truman, Clifford would succeed Vardaman and in time become an important adviser to the president. His career as a Washington insider was safely launched. Truman's favorite poker companion, according to Clifford, was Fred Vinson, Morgenthau's successor at Treasury. Clifford, in his memoirs, would judge "Henry Morganthau" (*sic*) one of the "holdovers from the Roosevelt administration" who had "a style that was incompatible with that of President Truman." It's certainly hard to imagine FDR and his cerebral friend Morgenthau settling down to play poker together on the presidential yacht *Williamsburg,* as Truman and his cronies liked to do. Although Clifford and Robert Morgenthau had both been wartime naval officers and would both become famous lawyers, their paths wouldn't even cross until almost half a century after World War II.

A kinsman of such prominent financier families as Lehman and Wertheim, Morgenthau is a member of the German-Jewish East Coast elite, the patricians of the American Jewish community. Among them are the "Our Crowd" families of Straus, Sulzberger, and Loeb, who have had a remarkable impact on American politics, business, and culture. Following his family's tradition of noblesse oblige, Robert Morgenthau dedicated his life to public service. And the courage and stubborn determination that he and his crew showed at Okinawa became the hallmarks of his long and distinguished career as a New York prosecutor.

As for many young people of his generation, for Morgenthau World War II and the Holocaust shaped the rest of his life. He had a lucky war, surviving twenty-four hours in the water after the sinking of his destroyer as well as months of fighting off Okinawa. Even in peacetime, Morgenthau seemed to lead a charmed life. After Yale Law School, he went to work for Robert Patterson, the former secretary of the army who headed the law firm of Patterson Belknap & Webb. One day in 1955, the two men were on their way to La Guardia Airport when Patterson suddenly remembered some vital documents and sent Morgenthau back to get them. It was the last time they saw each other. The plane crashed, killing Patterson.

Morgenthau was politically ambitious, and he helped with Herbert

Lehman's campaign for the Senate in 1949 against John Foster Dulles and with John F. Kennedy's campaign for the White House in 1960. The new president's brother and attorney general, Robert F. Kennedy, appointed Morgenthau U.S. attorney for the Southern District of New York, which comprises Manhattan, the Bronx, and Westchester County. Morgenthau held the post until 1970, two years after President Nixon began trying to replace him. He had fallen afoul of the White House, attempting to expose crimes committed by Americans who used secret Swiss bank accounts; some of the malefactors had contributed to President Nixon's campaign. But after four years in private practice, Morgenthau found his way back to public life. In 1974, he was elected to the first of five consecutive four-year terms as Manhattan district attorney.*

Since the days of Thomas E. Dewey, who was elected district attorney in 1937 in a wave of outrage against public corruption, the Manhattan D.A.'s office has had a reputation for not shirking cases, for having loyal and smart people who take pride in their jobs and are willing to work long hours for little pay. Dewey was succeeded by Frank S. Hogan — "Mr. D.A." — a legendary prosecutor who served for thirty-two years, until 1973.

In his long career as a public prosecutor and politician, Morgenthau has seen spectacular victories, controversies, and defeats, but he has always maintained a stubborn and unswerving desire to bring home his case no matter who is affected. He convicted the Democratic boss Carmine DeSapio, but he never succeeded in convicting the notorious New York lawyer Roy Cohn. Morgenthau's 1962 run for governor of New York was overwhelmed by Nelson Rockefeller, yet in his nearly two decades as the Manhattan district attorney he has become a legend, obtaining convictions against some of the nation's toughest criminals.

He "particularly enjoyed nailing big shots involved in white-collar crime," according to *Mostly Morgenthaus*, the family history written by his elder brother, Henry Morgenthau III, a journalist and television producer. It is the D.A.'s belief that, as he puts it, "crime in the streets" prospers because of "crime in the suites." The drug seller on a street corner is able to peddle cocaine because he is assisted by financiers prepared to launder money, businessmen who transport bales of nar-

---

*The official title is New York County district attorney; the Borough of Manhattan and the County of New York are coextensive.

cotics, accountants who connive in tax evasion, and bank regulators who look the other way as drug money passes through the payments system.

Robert Morgenthau ordinarily wouldn't have the authority to take on an international bank like BCCI. But if the right person showed him a way to get started, he would make the most of the opportunity.

When Jack Blum left the Kerry Committee at the end of March 1989, he had been probing BCCI for a year. He shared some of his findings with the federal prosecutors in Tampa, but he had serious doubts that they would follow up. While some at the working level in Customs and the IRS were enthusiastic, resources were scarce, and Blum suspected that senior officials were unwilling to go very far. He decided against trying other avenues in Washington, believing that was, as he put it, "way too treacherous" and ran the risk of being smothered by lawyers and lobbyists.

Blum knew that Morgenthau routinely worked on major fraud cases and had a reputation for incorruptibility. As he later explained, "This isn't a guy who is going to be shut down by two or three fixers sliding in and saying [their] client didn't do anything." With the encouragement of Senator Kerry, Blum decided to call on Morgenthau.

Blum was familiar with the Manhattan D.A.'s office; he had almost gone to work there after graduating from law school in 1965. "I was screened by all the underlings, and they were all ready to hire me," Blum recalled. "In the final interview, they dropped it on me: it would pay something like $4,800 a year and you were required to live in Manhattan. The interview took place on a winter day. My memory of this is that I go there and the heat is up full blast — and the pervasive smell is urine coming off the radiators. The combination of $4,800, you have to live in Manhattan, and the smell — I couldn't hack it."

Years later, while working for Senator Kerry, Blum met Morgenthau. When the Kerry Committee held hearings on drug trafficking in early 1988, Morgenthau was one of the witnesses. Morgenthau, in turn, had learned something about BCCI: some of the other witnesses had identified BCCI as Noriega's bank.

In April 1989, Blum flew to New York to meet with Robert Morgenthau.

The Manhattan district attorney's office is a couple of blocks from City Hall, at One Hogan Place (named after Morgenthau's noted predecessor). A heavy but impressive Art Deco complex, it was built during the Depression to house the New York County prison and courthouse. Above the entrance to the courthouse is the inscription: "Where law ends, there tyranny begins." Inside is a warren of offices, many of them in need of paint, where heavy old rotary telephones were the rule long after most of the city worked with sleek push-button models. Lawyers, cops, and suspects stride and shamble through the shabby corridors that echo with voices and slammed doors.

Behind a locked and guarded door are the offices of Morgenthau and his senior aides. The office of "the Boss," as he is called by his staff, is a long, rectangular, untidy room filled with memorabilia, such as a huge Pat Oliphant cartoon of Nixon desperately trying to stop Morgenthau — wearing a Sherlock Holmes deerstalker hat — from prying into the Swiss bank accounts of the president's backers.

Blum took a seat in Morgenthau's office that April day and began dramatically: "I want to tell you about the biggest bank fraud in the world."

BCCI, according to Blum, was deeply involved with dirty money, laundering funds for some of the world's most notorious drug barons. What is more, he suspected that it secretly owned several U.S. financial institutions, including First American Bankshares, the biggest banking company in Washington. He also suspected that BCCI was defrauding its depositors. Much of the bank's capital appeared to be phony, which would mean that it had collected billions of dollars in deposits under false pretenses. The whole thing, according to Blum, could be a massive Ponzi scheme.

He also mentioned the possibility of political corruption. In 1987, he said, First American bought National Bank of Georgia from Ghaith Pharaon after the Georgia legislature changed the state banking law to make the takeover possible. Blum had heard from BCCI insiders that some members of the legislature had been bribed to alter the law. When asked why federal authorities in Tampa couldn't handle the case, he said, "I don't think Tampa is equipped, and I don't think Tampa wants to hear about it."

When Blum was partway into his account, Morgenthau summoned one of his deputies, Michael Cherkasky, to sit in on the extraordinary tale. It appeared that the New York prosecutors were taking Blum seriously. (Blum didn't realize it at the time, but there was, in fact, a fair degree of skepticism at first. John W. Moscow, an assistant D.A., later told friends that Blum's story was so bizarre that prosecutors laughed about it for ten days.)

One potential problem for Morgenthau was jurisdiction. Whereas the U.S. Justice Department can handle cases anywhere in the country, he could only prosecute crimes committed in New York State. Blum pointed out that many of BCCI's alleged crimes had in fact occurred in Morgenthau's backyard. A large part of the drug money laundered by BCCI passed through New York, channeled through the dollar payments system operated by the Federal Reserve Bank of New York. In addition, First American Bankshares owned a bank based in Manhattan: First American Bank of New York. If BCCI had lied to the Federal Reserve Board about the ownership of the holding company, it had also lied to the New York State Banking Department about the ownership of FABNY.

Blum had turned up at an opportune time. In recent years, Morgenthau had been overshadowed by Manhattan's chief federal prosecutor, U.S. Attorney Rudolph Giuliani. Occupying the post Morgenthau had held years earlier, Giuliani had attracted enormous publicity by cracking down on insider trading on Wall Street. The press had begun to fuel a perception that Morgenthau's star was fading, that Giuliani was more effective at combating white-collar crime. Nobody knew then that few of Giuliani's indictments would stick: many defendants were found not guilty; others had their convictions overturned on appeal.

Morgenthau decided to conduct his own probe of BCCI, and he assigned one of his best prosecutors to the case: John Moscow. The son of a famous *New York Times* reporter, Moscow looks every inch a Victorian prizefighter, with a Roman nose and stocky build. His habit of rocking back and forth on the balls of his feet only serves to accentuate the image. A Harvard Law School graduate, he could probably earn far more in the private sector than the $90,000 salary he earns in the D.A.'s office, but money has been less attractive to him than the chance to prosecute challenging crimes. He had chased down con men who had forged bonds supposedly issued by the government of Indonesia. He had also worked on the John Grambling case of the mid-1980s, a complex fraud through which a young financier had bilked banks out of millions of dollars. Brian Rosner, who was the lead prosecutor on the Grambling case, describes Moscow as "a tough, hard-nosed prosecutor. He's one of the best trial attorneys down there. His success record [was sometimes] spotty — because he took on cases that nobody else even wanted to touch. He has a superb relationship with Morgenthau. They're on the same wavelength."

With his Big Apple lapel button and his quick one-liners, Moscow is a quintessential New Yorker. When he suspects that a defense lawyer is playing him for a fool, he's likely to say, "I may have been born at night, but it wasn't last night." Some of his more cryptic remarks later prompted Federal Reserve investigators to nickname him "the Riddler." Critics sometimes accuse Moscow of being a hothead, of pushing too hard, of bullying, but no one denies his energy and intelligence.

Morgenthau and Moscow, as it turned out, would be Jack Blum's last best hope of getting any justice in the BCCI case. Blum's fear that the federal government was either unable or unwilling to mount an aggressive probe turned out to be justified.

Even before the October 1988 indictment of BCCI, there were signs that the Justice Department wanted to limit the inquiry. The investigation was brought to a close that month over the objections of Robert Mazur. The Justice Department also played down the importance of the arrests by failing to reveal that Noriega's banker, Amjad Awan, was one of those in custody. There was also some peculiar behavior by two other federal agencies, the CIA and the Federal Reserve.

Around the time of the indictment, William von Raab, the Customs commissioner, contacted William Gates, the CIA's deputy director (and currently the director), and asked if the agency had any information about the bank. Gates quipped that BCCI was known as "the Bank of Crooks and Criminals" and gave the Customs chief a report the CIA had prepared. It was a skimpy document, von Raab later said, which was of little value to investigators. Gates never told von Raab that the CIA had prepared several other reports over the years, some of which mentioned the bank's close relationship with First American.

The Federal Reserve Board — the country's premier bank regulator — did not seem particularly eager to probe BCCI's relationship with First American. This indifference went back nearly a decade. When the Fed permitted a group of BCCI's clients to take over the company in the early 1980s, it brushed aside a vast number of clues that they were front men for BCCI, such as the large overlap between the shareholder groups of the two institutions. During the Customs drug money investigation, new information on BCCI's ties to First American emerged. On at least three occasions, Awan told Mazur that he thought BCCI secretly controlled First American. On December 27, 1988, David Burris, an IRS agent attached to C-Chase, spoke with William Ryback, the deputy director of banking supervision at the Fed. When Burris told the regulator about Awan's remarks, the reaction was surprisingly lukewarm. Unless the IRS agent could provide documentary evidence to support Awan's allegations, Ryback said, there was little the Fed could do.

Burris made another attempt the following February. Accompanied by his supervisor, Maurice Dettmer, he flew to Washington and met with Ryback. They briefed him on the evidence they had obtained and even offered to provide him with witnesses. Once again, the Fed official seemed to show little interest. (Ryback has asserted that no witnesses were mentioned.) Later that month, the Fed gave the BCCI–First American relationship a clean bill of health. The Federal Reserve Bank of Richmond said in a report that there were "no irregularities" in the relationship and that the original commitments about the ownership and control of First American had been complied with. The report made no mention of the information provided by the IRS. That same month, the Fed allowed First American to take over a Florida bank: Bank of Escambia in Pensacola. There were other strange incidents in 1989. Jack Blum, as we have seen, persuaded two former BCCI officials to meet with the federal prosecutors in Tampa in March. Both informants said they believed that BCCI controlled First American. The federal prosecutors issued a few subpoenas but did little else to investigate these allegations.

While the Justice Department and the Federal Reserve dawdled, the Manhattan district attorney's office mounted an aggressive investigation of BCCI. Morgenthau would eventually uncover new information on BCCI's relationship with First American. The New York prosecutor would also discover that BCCI was a corrupt financial empire of vast proportions.

John Moscow started out with valuable leads provided by Blum. He quickly developed his own informants, including former officials of BCCI and First American. The federal prosecutors, of course, were in a position to help, but they showed little inclination to do so. Justice Department officials have claimed that there were "procedural" problems that made it difficult for them to cooperate, but there was clearly more to it. In fact, it seemed that the federal prosecutors were going out of their way to hamper the probe. Telephone messages left by Morgenthau with his federal counterparts were ignored. On at least one occasion, Morgenthau said, he was even forced to send a fax to the U.S. attorney in Tampa "asking him to please answer his telephone." Moscow's reaction was much more blunt. When someone asked him about the federal prosecutors, he growled, "Cooperation with the Justice Department? Hand me the Vaseline."

One incident concerned the tapes that the Tampa prosecutors had made of Blum's informants. Blum says he never told Moscow about the tapes because he had promised that their existence would remain confidential, and he did not want to give anyone an excuse for accusing him of compromising the federal government's case against BCCI. Somehow, Moscow learned about the tapes and asked the U.S. attorney's office in Tampa for copies. For months, said Moscow, Tampa insisted that there were no such tapes, at one point sending back letters that, in one investigator's eyes, were "insulting to Morgenthau." Moscow persisted anyway. (He called Tampa's denial "the Easter Bunny story"; it amused him, but he didn't believe it.) Eventually, according to Moscow, Tampa "found" the tapes and claimed that they had been mislaid. (Officials in the U.S. Attorney's office in Tampa recall things quite differently. One prosecutor says the existence of the tapes was not revealed at the outset because of the need "to protect confidential relationships." He and his colleagues also insist that they gave considerable assistance to Morgenthau's office.)

Moscow managed to gather a great deal of information about BCCI, and he began to share many of his findings with the Fed, partly because he hoped that the bank regulators would help him. In August 1989, for example, Morgenthau's office provided information on First American to a Federal Reserve investigator: one of the D.A.'s informants had stated that BCCI owned or controlled First American. (In an internal memo, the Fed investigator wrote that "the allegation that BCCI owns First American is serious, and is an allegation that we have heard from other law enforcement agencies.") In spite of his progress, Moscow knew that he would have to get documentary evidence to back up his informants' allegations. Bank regulators in Europe were beginning to obtain just the kind of evidence he needed, but it would be months before he could get it.

Since the 1970s, there had been complaints that BCCI was poorly regulated. One reason was that each regulator had only a partial view of the group. There was a similar problem for the auditors. For most of BCCI's existence, the Luxembourg holding company and bank were audited by Ernst & Young (then called Ernst & Whinney). Another firm, Price Waterhouse, audited the Cayman Islands holding company.

Not until the late 1980s were steps taken to deal with this structure. In 1987, Ernst & Young resigned and Price Waterhouse became the sole auditor for the main components of the BCCI group. The following year, bank regulators formed a committee to coordinate supervision of the bank. Called the College of Supervisors, it included representatives of Luxembourg, Spain, Switzerland, and the United Kingdom.* It began meeting in May 1988. Despite these reforms, the auditors and the regulators remained oblivious of the extent of BCCI's criminality. Incredibly, no one detected the massive Ponzi scheme that siphoned billions of dollars out of the bank.

Eventually, several forces converged to prod the regulators to take a closer look at the bank: the Tampa indictment, concerns about BCCI's financial stability, and the Morgenthau investigation. In the fall of 1989, the Bank of England and the Institut Monétaire Luxembourgeois asked Price Waterhouse to conduct the first of a series of special audits of BCCI.

In the past, Price Waterhouse had shown a singular lack of aggressiveness in its audits of BCCI. When, for example, the auditors asked about major loans on BCCI's books, bank officers would often refuse to identify the borrowers, invoking "client confidentiality." By accepting such nonanswers, Price Waterhouse had no way of determining whether the loans were going to be repaid — or if they were fraudulent transactions aimed at stealing money from the bank. This time, however, the auditors took a much tougher approach. They insisted that major borrowers confirm in writing that they actually owed the money that the bank said they did. Around the end of 1989, Price Waterhouse began providing some of its findings to the College of Supervisors. Additional reports were submitted in early 1990. (In March, BCCI's Swaleh Naqvi made a great show of assisting in the inquiry by setting up a special task force. It was, of course, an absurdity — since Naqvi had been in charge of the looting of BCCI.)

The Price Waterhouse reports make horrifying reading. A report submitted in January portrayed BCCI's accounts as a shambles, saying that there were "no loan agreements" on many of its largest loans. In many cases, there were no official, third-party witnesses to sums totaling hundreds of millions of dollars. Furthermore, in many cases there weren't proper appraisals on which these loans should have been based. Subsequent reports went even further. They highlighted the frequent absence of critical information to back up huge loans, irregu-

---

*Hong Kong and the Cayman Islands joined in 1989, the UAE in 1990, and France in 1991. The Federal Reserve never joined the panel.

larities in loan approval procedures, unreliable management represen-
tations, and other dubious practices. Some of the questionable loans
were in the names of Kamal Adham and his associate Abdul-Raouf
Khalil. The Khalil loans hadn't been properly serviced for five years.

There were also indications that large sums of money had been
siphoned out of the bank. The early 1990 audits, for example, described irregular transactions that caused hundreds of millions of dollars simply to vanish.

Price Waterhouse also found that BCCI had made huge loans to
some of its own shareholders and that the borrowers used BCCI stock
as collateral. The report of April 3, 1990, showed that BCCI had
apparently lent its own shareholders $1.48 billion against security of
about 60 percent of the bank's shares. At the very least, this showed
that the bank was involved in the massive manipulation of its own
share price. But there was a much more frightening possibility: it could
mean that much of BCCI's equity capital was fictitious.

Ever since its founding, BCCI had reassured depositors by saying
that wealthy Arab sheikhs had injected millions of dollars in equity
capital into the bank. But if most of these shareholders had really
bought the shares with BCCI loans — and were not obliged to repay
the debts — it would mean that they were straw men. BCCI, in other
words, may have manufactured equity capital out of thin air and had
merely "borrowed" the names and reputations of wealthy Arabs to
bolster confidence in the bank.

The Price Waterhouse audits shed light on another important mystery: the true ownership of First American Bankshares.

When BCCI's clients sought permission to acquire First American,
they assured the Fed that they were investing their personal funds —
supplemented by money borrowed from banks not related to BCCI.
Price Waterhouse discovered that several stockholders had borrowed
heavily from BCCI, putting up their First American stock as collateral.
This alone violated the agreement with the Fed. Beyond that, several of
the investors failed to make interest payments, which enabled BCCI to
take possession of the shares.* It was later estimated that BCCI wound

---

*The March 18, 1990, Price Waterhouse report described a chaotic situation. BCCI's
"task force" found the arrangements under which shares in First American's holding
company were pledged to BCCI as "informal," with the bank holding share certificates and
signed blank transfer forms backed by powers of attorney. To complicate matters further,
there were several cross pledges under which one borrower's shares were pledged against
another's loans.

up with at least 60 percent of First American's stock. This was the "smoking gun" — the proof of what had been suspected for so many years: Arab investors who held a majority of First American's stock were merely front men. BCCI secretly owned First American.

Since late 1988, the Federal Reserve had done little to pursue the allegations about First American because, as Ryback maintained, there was no documentary evidence. Now the evidence had been found. In late 1989, when the Bank of England obtained information on the secret ownership of First American, it informed the Federal Reserve. The Fed's reaction was incredibly mild. Instead of mounting an aggressive investigation, the central bank did little more than write to a BCCI lawyer asking if the information was true! In a letter dated December 13, 1989, Ryback asked Altman if First American's stockholders had borrowed money from BCCI.

On February 5, Altman replied, "We don't have access here to such information." He also enclosed a letter from Swaleh Naqvi denying that BCCI had provided such financing; Naqvi wrote that "none of the shareholders involved in the acquisition had any personal loans from BCCI during the years 1981 and 1982." Naqvi held open the possibility that the shareholders may have borrowed from BCCI to finance other parts of their businesses and holdings. The same day Altman wrote to Ryback, the judge in Tampa approved BCCI's plea bargain.

The cover-up of First American's true ownership continued — as did the cover-up of the massive fraud against BCCI's depositors.

The fraudulent loans uncovered in Price Waterhouse's audits meant that BCCI had suffered enormous losses. Price Waterhouse could not possibly sign BCCI's 1989 annual report — at least not without a major qualification. A heavily qualified opinion would have been a red flag to depositors, touching off a run on deposits. But there was another alternative. If the shareholders could be persuaded to pump in new equity, BCCI might be able to survive. The only major shareholder in a position to do that was Sheikh Zayed.

Swaleh Naqvi had been running BCCI for two years — ever since Abedi's heart attack in early 1988. When it became clear that BCCI desperately needed capital, he went to Abu Dhabi and pleaded with the sheikh for help. Zayed, according to a former BCCI official, spurned the banker's appeal: "I can't put in any more money," he is said to have told Naqvi. "You've done enough damage." BCCI officials then enlisted Abedi's help. If anyone could convince the sheikh to rescue the bank, it would be Abedi.

While BCCI was living on borrowed time, its founder was living with a borrowed heart. In spite of his frail condition, he agreed to make a personal appeal to Sheikh Zayed. In early 1990, Abedi was flown to Abu Dhabi. He waited patiently while Zafar Iqbal — the leader of the bank's Gulf faction — tried to arrange an audience with the ruler. But Zayed did not want to see him, according to a BCCI insider. "After about ten days," says this source, "Zayed told Zafar Iqbal, 'Why don't you take Mr. Abedi out of here because I don't have the heart to break his heart.' "

But the bankers persisted, and Zayed eventually agreed to back a rescue plan at an estimated cost of $928 million. About half the money was used to cover losses, with the rest replenishing BCCI's equity. In exchange, Zayed and investors connected with him (his son Khalifa, the Abu Dhabi government, and the Abu Dhabi Investment Authority) acquired 77 percent of BCCI's stock. BCCI announced that some of the stock had been acquired from the Bin Mahfouz family, which owns National Commercial Bank, the biggest bank in Saudi Arabia. As part of the package, Naqvi was replaced as chief executive by Iqbal — the BCCI official closest to Zayed — representing the triumph of the Gulf faction over Naqvi and his technocrats. (Naqvi remained on the bank's payroll, however.)

Zayed's bailout meant that BCCI would be kept alive, but it still posed a dilemma for Price Waterhouse. What should the auditors do about the internal frauds they had discovered before the rescue operation?

When BCCI's 1989 annual report was issued on April 30, 1990, it was duly signed by Price Waterhouse; the firm stated that it gave a "true and fair" view of BCCI's financial condition. There was no hint of the widespread irregularities the auditors had uncovered. When asked about this much later by the *Wall Street Journal,* Price Waterhouse said that it gave a clean opinion because Abu Dhabi "was committed to maintaining the capital of the bank." What the firm was saying, in effect, was that if a rich shareholder says he will prop up a company, it doesn't much matter what the financial statements say.

Although BCCI would remain in business, it would be a smaller institution. It would close most of its U.S. offices and also trim its UK branch network. In June, BCCI said it would lay off 4,000 of its 14,000 employees; in Britain alone, 900 employees would lose their jobs. In addition, BCCI would shift its headquarters from London to Abu Dhabi. The move took place in September.

The restructuring of BCCI and the transfer of its headquarters occurred with the full blessing of the Bank of England and other regulators. It seemed to be a convenient solution to a messy problem. BCCI would simply fold up its tent and creep away in the night. Of course, this "solution" meant that BCCI's crimes would remain concealed from the public and that the culprits would not be punished, but those shortcomings didn't seem to bother the regulators at all.

Other people, however, saw this as an outrageous cover-up, notably Robert Morgenthau and his team of prosecutors and detectives. John Moscow pressed ahead with his investigation, and he mounted a concerted effort to obtain copies of the Price Waterhouse reports. At the same time, new information about BCCI — and First American — was emerging in the press.

In 1988, Larry Gurwin began working as a free-lance financial journalist in the Washington area. He had written about international banking for several years and was familiar with BCCI and its shady reputation. He also remembered the controversial takeover battle for First American. In September, he offered to write stories about BCCI for two publications: the *Economist* of London and *Regardie's*, a monthly business magazine in Washington. The story for the *Economist* would seek to determine if BCCI's dubious reputation was justified; the *Regardie's* article would focus on the ownership of First American and its ties to BCCI. He did not know that bank was under investigation at the time; no information had emerged publicly about the probes of BCCI by U.S. Customs and the Kerry Committee. After BCCI was indicted in October, both magazines suddenly became quite interested in BCCI and Gurwin got his assignments.

By early 1989, he had located a number of former BCCI employees who told him explicitly that the bank had secretly acquired control of First American and a host of other organizations, including National Bank of Georgia, Independence Bank in California, Capcom Financial Services, Attock Oil, International Travel Corporation, and South Publications. None of these sources was able to provide proof, but Gurwin was able to find a great deal of evidence that BCCI had suspiciously close ties to First American and these other entities. When asked about this, spokesmen for BCCI flatly denied anything other than "arm's-length" relationships.

The most vociferous denials came from Robert Altman during an interview in July 1989. It was hard to accept them at face value, though, because a number of his statements were misleading. For example, he gave a blow-by-blow account of the First American take-over battle without once mentioning the involvement of Bert Lance. When asked about Lance, Altman denied that the Georgia banker had recommended the stock to the Arab investors. Altman was also asked if he had ever attended BCCI's annual management conferences, and he said, "I went once." When Altman was told in a follow-up interview that witnesses placed him at more than one conference, he admitted that he had been to two or three. (The correct number is three.)

When it was clear that Gurwin intended to proceed with the article for *Regardie's,* Altman attempted to have the story killed by threatening libel action. In September 1989, Gurwin received a letter from John W. Vardaman, Jr., of Williams & Connolly, saying, in part, "Robert Altman . . . informs us that you have been inquiring into whether First American is somehow owned or controlled by a foreign bank holding company, the Bank of Credit and Commerce International (BCCI). As Mr. Altman has informed you, this allegation is absolutely false and would, if disseminated, cause serious injury to First American."

Other lawyers were enlisted in Altman's campaign to kill the story. Michael Barnes, a former Democratic congressman from Maryland, worked for Arent Fox, one of the Washington law firms that represented BCCI in the Tampa case. Although Barnes was not involved in the BCCI case, he was an acquaintance of Bill Regardie's, the publisher of the magazine. Barnes contacted the publisher. The BCCI lawyer Larry Barcella called the magazine's editor, Brian Kelly, and suggested that Gurwin was looking for facts to fit his own theories about BCCI and First American. The magazine's libel lawyer, Ed Weidenfeld, later said he had never seen such a concerted effort to suppress an article.

Regardie did not succumb to the pressure, however. The story was published in May 1990; it showed that there were extraordinarily close ties between BCCI and First American — far from the "arm's-length" relationship claimed by BCCI and Altman. There was no proof that BCCI secretly owned First American, but there was strong circumstantial evidence. The story also revealed that at least $500,000 of Noriega's money had been channeled through First American by BCCI officers.

A few days after the article appeared, BCCI and First American had to deal with another public relations nightmare: a page 1 exposé of BCCI in the *Wall Street Journal,* written by Peter Truell and John Fialka. They portrayed BCCI as a "rogue bank" that had broken numerous banking and money-laundering laws. The story revealed that CenTrust, the big Miami savings and loan association owned in part by Ghaith Pharaon, had attempted to fool regulators about its financial stability by parking millions of dollars in junk bonds at BCCI. It also mentioned the overlapping shareholding between BCCI and First American, noting that some believed there might be a degree of ownership and control.

BCCI and First American did their best to limit the damage from the two articles. In response to the *Regardie's* story, First American distributed an eight-page "Fact Sheet": it claimed that the article was "filled with innumerable errors and outright falsehoods." One person who passed out copies of the "Fact Sheet" was Frank Mankiewicz of Hill and Knowlton.

On May 8, lawyers for First American met with William Ryback and other regulators. Altman was accompanied by his law partner J. Griffin Lesher and Baldwin Tuttle of Milbank, Tweed, Hadley & McCloy. Altman attempted to discredit the *Regardie's* and *Journal* stories, but he did say he had heard that BCCI was owed between $400 million and $1 billion by First American's shareholders. He added that there were no loans to the Abu Dhabi shareholders. He had also been told, he said, that these credits were properly documented by Price Waterhouse.

Other measures were taken inside BCCI and First American to cope with the negative publicity. BCCI's top management circulated a memo to senior officials around the world rebutting the *Journal* story. At First American, employees who asked about the *Regardie's* article were given the "Fact Sheet." On May 24, both stories were discussed at a board meeting of First American. Clifford, according to minutes of that meeting, "discussed in detail the events leading up to the publication of the articles appearing in *Regardie's* magazine and the *Wall Street Journal* newspaper in May which pertained to an alleged questionable relationship between the Company and the Bank of Credit and Commerce International (BCCI). He noted that the Company and BCCI have both issued fact sheets for their own internal use discrediting the articles' unfounded disclosures and stating the correct facts."

Throughout 1990, BCCI officials struggled to maintain a façade of

innocence. The BCCI group was not, they contended, a criminal institution but a respectable bank. The money laundering that had been
exposed in Operation C-Chase was not a reflection of BCCI's corporate policy but the work of a few renegade employees. The bank's plea
bargain in Tampa was not really an acknowledgment of guilt; it was
aimed at avoiding a costly and protracted legal battle. The massive
losses revealed in the spring of 1989 were not the result of fraud but
the product of mismanagement. As for the First American connection,
BCCI and its American lawyers continued to insist that there was
nothing more than an arm's-length relationship. BCCI and its allies did
their best to discredit critics and skeptics. When, for example, the
Kerry Committee asked First American to comment on the article in
Regardie's, Mankiewicz sent a copy of the "Fact Sheet" to Senator
Kerry. Jack Blum was portrayed as a crank; he later heard that BCCI
spokesmen had told at least one prominent politician that he had been
fired from Kerry's staff.

The campaign of disinformation seems to have had some success,
particularly with regard to the First American connection. Price Waterhouse's findings about BCCI's ties to the bank were still secret. What is
more, Clark Clifford had given his word that the allegations were
false — and many people were inclined to trust him. One measure of
the success of the campaign is that few journalists followed up on the
Regardie's and *Wall Street Journal* stories. It would be many more
months before Clifford's statements were seriously challenged by others in the media.

Behind the façade, BCCI's financial empire was gradually crumbling.
Financial institutions close to BCCI — and BCCI itself — were in
serious trouble.

CenTrust Savings Bank was taken over by regulators in February
1990. It was eventually discovered that Pharaon, who supposedly
owned about a fourth of the S&L, had actually been a front man for
BCCI. The demise of CenTrust was blamed on bad real estate loans,
huge losses on its own junk bond portfolio, and the rampant over-
spending of corporate funds on personal luxuries for the chairman,
David Paul. At the time, it was estimated that the cost to taxpayers
would be more than $2 billion — much more than if the regulators had
acted sooner. But BCCI's bond-parking scheme had delayed the shutdown.

Another institution in the BCCI orbit was in severe trouble because of huge loan losses: Banque Arabe et Internationale d'Investissement. BAII, the consortium bank in Paris, had long had very close ties with BCCI, as noted in Chapter 4. Run by a board member of BCCI, Yves Lamarche, BAII had played a critical role in some of BCCI's dubious schemes, lending $50 million to help finance the takeover of First American and also providing funds to allow Pharaon to buy Independence Bank in Los Angeles. In both transactions, BAII had merely fronted for BCCI. In the summer of 1990, BAII was taken over by Banque Nationale de Paris at a cost of 600 million francs — more than $100 million.

BCCI's biggest satellite — First American Bankshares — was also in trouble. Since 1989, Clifford had been working on a scheme to sell the company. Goldman Sachs, a leading Wall Street investment banking firm, was asked to find potential buyers. One institution that expressed interest was NCNB Corporation (now called NationsBank), a large bank holding company based in North Carolina. In a letter dated May 10, 1990, Christopher Flowers of Goldman said that NCNB had submitted a preliminary offer of $1 billion. When word of its interest leaked out in June, Clifford told the *Washington Post* that "the bank isn't for sale." This remark was at best disingenuous, since Clifford was the prime mover behind attempts to sell the company.

In all probability, there was little likelihood of a quick and easy sale. The economy in and around Washington, D.C. — the core of First American's business — had turned sluggish. The real estate market, which had boomed through so much of the 1980s, was souring. Five of six other banks approached by Goldman showed little or no interest.*

On September 27, 1990, Clifford told First American's board that he and Altman would be visiting the bank's Arab investors in October

---

*This was one of several times that NCNB made a cameo appearance in the First American story. In 1977, it was a member of the Middendorf group that bought control of First American. Later that year, when Bert Lance's associate Eugene Metzger suggested selling the company to a foreign bank, he did so in a letter to an NCNB official.

A decade later, when First American bought National Bank of Georgia, Clifford and Altman said they did so after engaging in a bidding contest against NCNB. The presence of NCNB has helped them to argue that First American's purchase of the Georgia bank was an "arm's-length" transaction.

NCNB's "offer" for First American has also been useful to Clifford; he has cited it repeatedly as proof that the company was well managed during his tenure as chairman. Interestingly, investigators for Senator Kerry have found that Goldman Sachs approached NCNB at *Clifford's* suggestion and that NCNB never conducted a serious study of First American.

"to arrange for the possible injection of more capital." On November 6, Clifford and Altman informed the board that they had requested a $125 million bridge loan and a $30 million capital infusion from the shareholders. When the year was out, the company had lost $158.5 million. (In May 1990 — in response to the *Regardie's* article — First American had described itself as a highly profitable and well-capitalized institution.)

While attempting to stave off a financial crisis at First American, Clifford and Altman were themselves in jeopardy. The *Regardie's* exposé prompted the *Washington Post* to take a close look at First American. Assigned to the story was Jim McGee, an investigative reporter who had recently joined the paper from the *Miami Herald*. McGee worked slowly and methodically, collecting documents from the Federal Reserve and interviewing Clifford, Altman, and other sources at length. At a certain point, he learned that the Price Waterhouse audits had revealed that BCCI had lent more than $500 million to First American's stockholders and that the borrowers had used First American stock as collateral. When Altman was asked to comment, he responded in classic BCCI fashion by invoking "confidentiality." In a September 27, 1990, letter to the *Post,* he stated: "We are not kept informed by our shareholders of their personal financial dealings, and obviously could not, in any event, make any comments to the press about their private financial dealings."

The biggest threat to Clifford and Altman was not the press but the Morgenthau probe. Prosecutors have an array of tools not available to journalists, including the power to issue subpoenas and the ability to offer immunity to informants. Through the deft use of such tools, John Moscow was able to piece together a large part of the hidden history of BCCI.

Moscow and his colleagues interviewed dozens of people in the United States and abroad who had been associated with BCCI. When Bert Lance visited Long Island's Hofstra University for a conference on Jimmy Carter's presidency, investigators from the D.A.'s office showed up and served him with a subpoena to testify about BCCI. Some of the most valuable information came from former officials of the bank, including Amer Lodhi, one of Jack Blum's informants, and Abdur Sakhia, who had headed BCCI's Miami office and then became the bank's top official in the United States. One man with special insight into BCCI's misconduct was Masihur Rahman, the former chief financial officer.

Rahman, a soft-spoken accountant from East Pakistan (now Bangladesh), had worked with Abedi at United Bank and was one of his first recruits at BCCI. He has always maintained that he knew nothing about the frauds at the heart of the bank until he began investigating in 1989. Speaking about what he found, he later said, "These were items which horrified me and I wanted to resign forthwith, as soon as I finished my report." He quit the bank at the beginning of August 1990 and soon began cooperating with officials in Morgenthau's office and other law enforcement authorities.

One thing many of Moscow's sources agreed on was that it was common knowledge within BCCI that First American was part of the "group." If that was the case, how was it possible that BCCI's Washington lawyers were in the dark? Inevitably, Clifford and Altman would become targets of Moscow's probe, and they knew it.

In the summer of 1990, Moscow telephoned Altman to ask him about BCCI and First American. Altman had for months been telling reporters and regulators that his conscience was clear — and he would reiterate that months later when queried by congressional committees. But when the New York prosecutor called, Altman's reactions did not quite jibe with his public posture. Rather than simply answer Moscow's questions, Altman turned the matter over to his attorney, Robert B. Fiske, Jr., a top litigator with the blue-blood New York firm of Davis Polk & Wardwell. Fiske soon appeared in Moscow's office and said, "If you want to meet with my client, you will have to give him immunity." Pouncing on this virtual admission of guilt, Moscow took on a puzzled air and replied, "You have to tell me what I am giving him immunity for. What has he done that is wrong? What crime has he committed?" (Fiske has denied that he asked for immunity.)

In spite of the progress he was making, Moscow still didn't have the documentary evidence he needed, the Price Waterhouse audits. Yet, from the evidence given by former BCCI officers, he knew of phony loans, phony capital, the widespread use of nominees, and other alleged crimes. When he asked Price Waterhouse's New York office for a copy of the audits, it refused, explaining that its U.S. and British partnerships were separate and distinct: the Americans said they did not have the power to obtain audit papers from their British colleagues. This was oddly reminiscent of BCCI's behavior — using legal entities in different countries.

The Bank of England not only refused to give the auditors' reports to Moscow, it tried to prevent Price Waterhouse from cooperating. The British central bank would later maintain that Moscow had made his approach in the wrong way, contacting middle-level regulators rather than going to the top. "They didn't give much indication of what they were doing, and basically said, 'Hand over your papers,' " recalls a British regulator.

Moscow did manage to obtain a portion of one of the earliest Price Waterhouse reports from a confidential source. Eventually, the Bank of England came around after Morgenthau worked his charm on Eddie George, the deputy governor. The Manhattan D.A. reminisced about the time he had spent in England during World War II and chatted with George about mutual acquaintances. There was also some not-too-subtle pressure. Michael Cherkasky, a senior prosecutor who helped coordinate the investigation, later said, "Morgenthau told George, 'We are going to charge this bank. And when we charge them, you are going to be looked at publicly. We would like to be able to say that the Bank of England helped us.' "

In late 1990, the Fed finally began to take serious action on the First American issue. The past two years had witnessed the C-Chase indictment of BCCI, the allegations from the IRS about the BCCI–First American relationship, exposés in the press, and Morgenthau's relentless investigation. In addition, the *Washington Post*'s Jim McGee was preparing a follow-up to the *Regardie's* story, with additional evidence of close ties between BCCI and First American. If the Fed lagged behind the press once again, it would be a serious embarrassment.

In December, the Fed's William Ryback visited London, where he met with BCCI's CEO, Zafar Iqbal, and was allowed by the Bank of England to inspect the Price Waterhouse reports. Upon his return, he talked with Tom McQueeney, a senior bank regulator with the Federal Reserve Bank of New York. On December 18, McQueeney sent a memo to his boss, Robert O'Sullivan, summarizing the conversation. Ryback, wrote McQueeney, was "very impressed with Iqbal," who had offered to open BCCI's books to U.S. regulators and "is anxious to get these matters settled." But Ryback — whose credulity seemed to know few bounds — was finally convinced that action was necessary. He felt that BCCI "has been lying to us for years," McQueeney wrote, and "would like to have Clark Clifford and Robert Altman investigated for their role in withholding that vital information from us." Ryback certainly wasn't going out of his way to help Morgenthau's investigation, however. "Bill hasn't committed anything to writing on this," McQueeney wrote, "lest Mr. Moscow of the New York District Attorney's office subpoena such records."

But the Manhattan D.A.'s office was ahead of the Fed. In late 1990, Morgenthau informed Ernest Patrikis, general counsel of the New York Fed, that there was as much as $854 million in BCCI loans to First American shareholders, all of them backed by pledged stock.

On January 4, 1991, the Federal Reserve finally ordered an investigation into BCCI's control of First American. Later that month, the Fed made criminal referrals to the Justice Department about possible misrepresentations concerning the relationship between the two institutions. By acting when it did, the Fed managed to avoid being scooped by the press once again. On February 3, McGee published a lengthy article in the *Washington Post*. It confirmed the May 1990 *Regardie's* story and added new information about ties between BCCI and First American. It said, for example, that BCCI officials had been involved in the hiring of First American executives and that there had been joint marketing of BCCI and First American services.

Clifford and Altman continued to deny that First American was controlled by BCCI. "There has been no participation, directly or indirectly, by BCCI," said Clifford. Its only role, he said, was "a limited, arms-length relationship" that conformed with the assurances he had made to the Federal Reserve back in 1981. But Clifford's word didn't have the ring of authority it once did. Regulators and investigators now pressed on regardless of these pious assurances from the eighty-four-year-old Washington icon. On March 4, the Fed issued an order stating that BCCI had illegally acquired about 60 percent of First American, and it ordered BCCI to submit a written plan within sixty days for the divestiture of this stock. BCCI was also ordered to cease all banking operations in the United States.

Confronted with these orders, Clifford and Altman were forced to acknowledge the illegal ownership, but they insisted that they had been in the dark all along. "If the Federal Reserve had been deceived," said Clifford, "so had I."

The credibility of Clifford and his protégé took a serious beating in May, when the *Washington Post* revealed that they had made millions of dollars in quick profits on transactions in First American stock. They had bought the stock in 1986 and 1987 with a total of $18 million in loans from BCCI. In 1988, they sold 60 percent of their holdings. After deducting interest and expenses, Clifford made $6.5 million; Altman walked away with $3.3 million. BCCI had put the whole deal together, finding the stock for the two lawyers and then providing a buyer at the right price, the Lebanese merchant Mohammed Hammoud. Investigators believe that Hammoud was simply a straw man for BCCI in this transaction — that he borrowed the money to pay for the stock and then put up the shares as collateral. Masihur Rahman has described Hammoud as "one of our most flexible fronts."

The stock deal was unusual for several reasons. For one thing, it was arranged by BCCI in such a way that there was virtually no risk to Clifford and Altman. BCCI provided 100 percent financing, and the loans were secured entirely by the stock. Thus, if the stock went up in price, they could sell it, repay the loans, and pocket the difference. If the price of the stock dropped, they could simply walk away from the loans. The interest rate was also suspicious. BCCI lent the money at LIBOR (the London Interbank Offered Rate) — the rate of interest that banks in the Eurodollar market pay on *deposits,* not the rate they charge borrowers. The whole transaction smacked of a scheme by BCCI to pour money into the pockets of Clifford and Altman.

Moreover, Clifford and Altman had failed to disclose these loans to the Federal Reserve. In December 1989, Ryback had asked Altman whether any of First American's stockholders had financed their investments with loans from BCCI. When Altman replied, he said nothing about the loans that he and Clifford had received. When confronted with this discrepancy, Altman claimed that Ryback later told him the Fed was interested only in loans to the original investors and in loans still outstanding to current investors. Ryback has said that he doesn't recall altering his original request.*

---

*Once again, the Clifford-Altman public relations machine swung into action to try to salvage something from these stunning revelations. Frank Mankiewicz distributed a six-page memorandum claiming that "this wasn't a secretive ownership," that "the compensation of Mr. Clifford and Mr. Altman is modest" compared with the earnings of executives of other big banks, and that the directors and shareholders of First American had encouraged them to buy stock. The ownership also was reported to the regulators, Mankiewicz wrote. On May 10, 1991, the *Washington Post* published a letter from Clifford and Altman disputing points in articles about their shareholdings. They maintained, for instance, that "First American was not prohibited from having financial dealings with BCCI." That was true, but the two men had certainly given their assurance that BCCI wouldn't play a role in financing shareholders in First American, though Altman would maintain that that assurance related only to the time of the actual takeover in 1982.

While Clifford and Altman were fighting a rear-guard action in Washington, bank regulators in Europe were beginning to close in on BCCI.

After BCCI was bailed out by Sheikh Zayed in the spring of 1990, the bank's top managers tried to portray it as a new, reformed institution, and the regulators tended to go along with the charade. After all, wasn't it true that the bank was now run by a new man, Zafar Iqbal, rather than the discredited Swaleh Naqvi? Conveniently ignored was that Iqbal and his minions were as much a part of the old guard as Naqvi and his technocrats: the "new" BCCI was being run by veterans of the old BCCI. Incredibly, Abedi and Naqvi — the masterminds of BCCI's frauds — remained on BCCI's payroll until October 1990, with Naqvi serving as a "consultant" to the bank.

Iqbal, in fact, was himself suspected of wrongdoing. Price Waterhouse suspected him of withholding vital information about BCCI. As far back as April 1990 — and perhaps much earlier — Iqbal knew much, if not all, about the frauds at the core of BCCI, but he withheld this information from the auditors and regulators for months. There were other ominous signs. For example, BCCI refused to issue a financial statement covering the first half of 1990, provoking a clash with its regulators.

The move to Abu Dhabi made it easier for BCCI officials to conceal what they were doing. Documents containing evidence of fraud were systematically destroyed. Other records were packed in boxes and moved to Abu Dhabi — putting the evidence out of reach of UK bank regulators and law enforcement authorities. The man responsible for moving many of the incriminating documents was none other than Swaleh Naqvi, and he did so with the acquiescence of Sheikh Zayed.

Naqvi must have known that in London, at least, the game was up. Some of the bank's top lieutenants had quit, enabling investigators and journalists to learn more about BCCI's illegal ways. He and other top managers escaped just in time. Price Waterhouse has said that within days of Naqvi's departure, it came across the so-called Naqvi files, a secret set of accounts that revealed that he and his special duties department had manipulated the bank's accounts for years.

Price Waterhouse summarized the material in a thirty-page report that it presented on October 3, 1990, to BCCI's directors and the Bank of England. The report estimated that as much as $1.5 billion of new capital was required to cover potential losses on the accounts of some of BCCI's major customers, including Ghaith Pharaon and Kamal Adham.

Here, at last, was the definitive and damning evidence that proved BCCI's top managers had been involved in fraudulent dealings for years. The complex and tangled Naqvi files eventually revealed that he and his special duties team had created fictitious companies; manufactured loans — sometimes with the knowledge and acquiescence of the supposed borrowers, sometimes not; and had lent huge sums to BCCI's own shareholders, many of whom were just nominees.

There is considerable controversy surrounding these files and what access Price Waterhouse had to them before 1990. Some BCCI officers have said that the files weren't squirreled away in a secret office — as the auditors have asserted — but were kept in easily accessible cabinets at Leadenhall Street and in nearby Cunard House. In addition, Price Waterhouse, as the auditor for ICIC Overseas Ltd., certainly had the opportunity to find signs of the strange routing of funds and other shenanigans carried out by Naqvi and his associates.

Once it received Price Waterhouse's report, the Bank of England immediately insisted that both Naqvi and Abedi be removed from BCCI's payroll. The two men officially resigned the next day, October 4. Zafar Iqbal's title was changed from acting chief executive to chief executive.

In London, Price Waterhouse was finally handed the smoking gun behind the Naqvi files. In January 1991, about fourteen weeks after the auditors say they first found the files, Iqbal tipped off the auditors about $600 million of unrecorded deposits. This was firm evidence that the bank was involved in stealing: accepting deposits and not recording them in its books. It also indicated strongly to the accountants and regulators that the bank itself was a Ponzi scheme, misappropriating deposits to pay interest and expenses.

Amazingly, BCCI tottered on. For years, the bank had papered over its outlandish practices by wooing influential friends, by masking the true state of its finances, and by bringing in fresh cash from depositors around the world. To BCCI insiders, there appeared to be no reason why the bank couldn't remain in business even after these new disclosures.

The man in charge of the efforts to keep BCCI afloat was Ghanem Faris al-Mazrui, the head of Sheikh Zayed's Department of Personal Affairs since the early 1980s. Mazrui had served on BCCI's board of directors since 1981, representing Zayed and his eldest son, Crown Prince Khalifa. Mazrui and his team spent months working on a scheme to restructure the bank with advice from management consultants at Booz Allen & Hamilton. They began discussing — with the Bank of England and the Luxembourg supervisors — plans to split BCCI into three separately capitalized parts, based in London, Abu Dhabi, and Hong Kong, the so-called Oasis banks.

The management consultants began hiring staff to run the new organization. A former senior executive from Lloyds Bank International, Leonard Kingshott, was to head the Oasis banks, which were all expected to be fully operational by the end of 1991. Trying to maintain its composure, BCCI's board met in Luxembourg in early April, formally ratified Iqbal's appointment as chief executive, and approved BCCI's 1990 accounts.

In late May, Sheikh Zayed's government, as part of the restructuring, gave a comfort letter to the bank, saying he would pay up to $600 million to guarantee the unrecorded deposits at the bank. In addition, Abu Dhabi agreed with bank regulators — under the so-called financial support arrangements signed on May 22, 1991 — that it would take on $4 billion of shaky loans as part of the restructuring. The loans were transferred to new companies owned directly by Abu Dhabi, and in return, BCCI received $3.1 billion of promissory notes and guarantees of $750 million from Zayed's government. Mazrui also struggled to get BCCI's 1990 accounts approved by the bank's most important regulators: the Bank of England and the Institut Monétaire Luxembourgeois.

The strain took a toll on Mazrui. He became increasingly withdrawn and religious, retreating to the desert to pray and frequently breaking from work to go to prayers. He wore a long beard of the kind favored by devout Muslims. But he was optimistic that the ordeal would soon be over. The regulators' attitude seemed favorable.

At first, the regulators were inclined to go along with Mazrui's restructuring scheme, but the alarming new information they were receiving from the auditors created grave doubts about the viability of BCCI. On March 4, 1991, the Bank of England's head of banking supervision, Roger Barnes, wrote to Christopher Cowan, a partner in Price Waterhouse, requesting an intensive new study of BCCI. The investigation, to be carried out under Section 41 of Britain's 1987 Banking Act, would seek to ascertain if BCCI's accounting transactions had been false or deceitful.

The probe would, as with the previous audits, be shrouded in secrecy. But this time it would be kept secret even from top officials of BCCI. Price Waterhouse took the precaution of using code words: BCCI's holding company in Luxembourg was Sandstorm; Zafar Iqbal was Blackbird; Feisal Islamic Bank, an institution in Cairo from which BCCI had purloined deposits, was Tumbleweed. The names, apparently selected by a British lawyer from the firm of Allen & Overy, also leaned heavily on gardening terms: Fork was the name for ICIC Overseas Ltd.

The secret investigation revealed a catalogue of fraud, raising doubts about whether it would ever be possible to restructure the bank. In a letter dated June 22 summarizing its findings, Price Waterhouse said that accounting records had "been falsified . . . for a substantial number of years." The complicated manipulations involved the use of nominee and hold-harmless agreements with "a substantial number of prominent Middle Eastern individuals" and "the fraudulent use of funds placed under management by the ruler of Abu Dhabi and his family." In addition, Naqvi and his team had created "a significant number of companies" and operated accounts outside BCCI "to disguise the nature of transactions and route funds." BCCI's manipulators had also engineered "the creation of a further seventy or so companies to assist in the financing of the Gulf Group" operated by the Gokals. There were also "agreements and unrecorded borrowings through third party banks," such as Saudi Arabia's National Commercial Bank, and investment institutions, such as the Abu Dhabi Investment Authority. Price Waterhouse concluded that the falsification of the accounting records was so widespread that it might never be possible to reconstruct the financial history of BCCI.

Eddie George, the deputy governor of the Bank of England, took the report home with him on June 27. It gave him a restless night, for it showed that BCCI was riddled with fraud and that many of the people involved in the restructuring were suspected of wrongdoing. It seemed likely that some of these same people would be involved in running the "new" banks that would be established in the restructuring.

There was another major concern at the Bank of England: the Morgenthau investigation. The Bank of England had been cooperating with the Manhattan district attorney in recent months, so it had a fairly clear idea that a New York grand jury might indict BCCI. In the view of the British regulators, massive legal action against an already crippled bank would produce chaos, making it impossible to wind the bank down in an orderly fashion. The indictment of a functioning international bank could also cause upheavals in international financial markets. "It was clear," George later said, "that in light of the new information, the restructuring couldn't go ahead." BCCI would have to be seized.

Before that could happen, other regulatory authorities would have to be convinced. The day after reading the report, George called an emergency meeting of the College of Supervisors for July 2. It would be chaired by Brian Quinn, the Bank of England director charged with overseeing banking regulation. Abu Dhabi was deliberately excluded because the regulators did not want the sheikhdom to pull its own deposits from BCCI, damaging it further. The Federal Reserve, which did not usually attend, was invited to send representatives. This was because E. Gerald Corrigan, the president of the Federal Reserve Bank of New York, was concerned that the demise of a bank as large as BCCI could disrupt the dollar markets. The meeting was attended by William Taylor, the head of banking supervision at the Fed in Washington, and Ernest Patrikis, general counsel to the New York Fed.

Although Eddie George was firmly convinced that BCCI had to be shut down, some of the other regulators balked. Some suggested appealing to Abu Dhabi to wind down the bank. Resistance began to melt, however, when George's fellow regulators absorbed the contents of the Section 41 report. They began to see that BCCI was beyond salvation: it was riddled with fraud. By the end of the day, the regulators agreed on the need for swift and decisive action.

The next problem was timing. The European regulators wanted the seizure to occur on Friday, July 5, but the New York Fed objected because of its concern about the dollar markets. U.S. markets would be closed the day before for the Independence Day holiday, and trading would be thin on Friday because many people would give themselves a long weekend. To allay the Americans' concerns, the Europeans agreed to shut down BCCI late Friday — after the close of the West Coast markets. The eight-hour time difference between California and London would mean that BCCI would be closed early Saturday morning in Europe.

Sheikh Zayed's representative, Mazrui, would be informed on Friday morning in Luxembourg, at a meeting with the Luxembourg regulator Pierre Jaans and Brian Quinn of the Bank of England. Mazrui thought the purpose of the meeting was to discuss the restructuring of BCCI.

When Quinn arrived in Luxembourg on Thursday, he discovered that there was a problem with the timing of the closure. Luxembourg regulators told him that a local court order essential to the shutdown could be obtained only during business hours, meaning it would have to happen during the day on Friday. So, in a series of hasty transatlantic telephone calls, the regulators agreed that the seizure of the bank would occur at 1:00 P.M. London time — just before the New York financial markets opened.

On Thursday evening, the mood in Washington was festive, and there was a spectacular fireworks display to celebrate the holiday. The Federal Reserve held its annual party where employees could watch the show. William Taylor attended with his family. But they left early that evening: Taylor had to be at his desk before dawn to prepare for the shutdown of an international bank.

On Friday morning in Luxembourg, Ghanem Faris al-Mazrui headed to the Institut Monétaire Luxembourgeois (IML) to meet with Pierre Jaans and Brian Quinn. He must have felt relieved. It had taken him months to get BCCI's messy accounts for 1990 past the auditors. Finally, long after other banks had published their results for that year, Mazrui thought he could get the accounts approved by Jaans and Quinn. Later that day, BCCI's board of directors would approve the restructuring scheme. This, in turn, would mean that it could go ahead; some order would be restored. There would be relative peace and quiet and an end to Mazrui's constant shuttling between Abu Dhabi and London. Most important, Sheikh Zayed's name would be out of the newspapers, and the ruler wouldn't have to add much to the monies he had recently put into the bank.

Mazrui was carrying three binders detailing the latest draft restructuring plan, which would turn BCCI into Oasis Bank of Europe and Canada, Oasis Bank of the Middle East and Asia, and Oasis Bank of the Far East. Copies had been sent to the Bank of England and the IML on July 3, just two days before.

At 10:00 A.M., Mazrui stepped from his limousine and hurried into the concrete office block housing the IML. Wearing traditional Arab dress — white robes and kuffiya headdress — he was received by Jaans, the graying IML chairman. He walked into Jaans's office and exchanged pleasantries with him and Brian Quinn.

To Mazrui's dismay, the two regulators expressed skepticism about whether the restructuring plan was feasible. They also criticized

BCCI's audited accounts. Suddenly, they began explaining that they and the group of regulators they represented had decided three days earlier to close BCCI. Jaans and Quinn told a stunned Mazrui that they had decided that they couldn't approve the 1990 accounts. BCCI, they stressed, had no capital after recognition of its real losses. It was therefore insolvent and would have to be wound up. The news was devastating to Mazrui, and he would be held responsible back in Abu Dhabi. He had assured Zayed and his circle that the restructuring was on track.

In anguished tones, Mazrui asked Quinn and Jaans why they had decided to do this.

Because of the fraud at the heart of the bank, Quinn replied.

Mazrui was still puzzled. And his reply betrayed a chilling candor about what sort of bank BCCI really was. "But we've known about that for a long time," the Arab official said. "We thought you did too."

If Quinn and Jaans were taken aback, they didn't let on. Instead, they talked about the new information contained in the Price Waterhouse report submitted to them in the past two weeks. There was no alternative, they said.

By keeping Mazrui in the dark until the seizure was about to happen, the regulators had, of course, hoped to prevent Abu Dhabi from pulling deposits out of BCCI and thus harming other depositors. But Mazrui boldly maneuvered to minimize the prospective losses to Zayed. According to one account, he told the two regulators he had to telephone Abu Dhabi immediately to convey the regulators' decision. From a nearby office, he hastily called the sheikh's office in Abu Dhabi and told an associate to stop a planned transfer of $650 million from the National Bank of Abu Dhabi to London that was to have helped recapitalize BCCI. This money was to have been a central component in the restructuring.*

After the meeting, Jaans had to deal with some of the practical problems involved in closing down a global bank. For the seizure to be legal, a Luxembourg judge would have to sign an order to liquidate BCCI's Luxembourg holding company. After trying to catch up with telephone calls from his counterparts in London, Paris, and Madrid,

---

*Surprisingly, the regulators didn't seem to mind Mazrui's move. "Once the bank was closed, you would expect the government of Abu Dhabi to stop the transfer," a British regulator said. In any case, he added, when you're closing a multibillion-dollar institution, you can't worry about individual transfers.

Jaans rushed over to the courthouse to get the order. When he did, no judge could be found.

It was lunchtime and, by coincidence, July 5 was the day for the judges' picnic, so all of them had gone to a pleasant orchard outside town. Jaans was crestfallen. This was the most important day of the year for him — perhaps of his whole career — and things were already going wrong.

After a high-speed chase around town, a judge was finally found and brought back to the court. Jaans got the order for the liquidation, which was premised on the insolvency shown in BCCI's 1990 accounts. The court later disclosed that BCCI lost more than its entire capital and reserves in 1990. This alone gave the regulators legal justification for closing down the bank.

With the court order in hand, Jaans telephoned Quinn, who had remained at the IML, portable telephone in hand. They could proceed. Quinn immediately called London and the international swoop on BCCI's offices began.

13

THE SHUTDOWN

THE SHUTDOWN CAME with stunning, brutal swiftness. At 1:00 P.M. on Friday, July 5, 1991, bailiffs marched into each of BCCI's twenty-five offices in Britain. It was lunchtime, and most of the bank's clerks had left for a sandwich. Using their full legal authority, the bailiffs told the remaining employees to gather their personal effects and leave the premises. Moments later, notices were posted on the glass doors of every BCCI branch telling customers that the bank had been closed by order of the Bank of England.

There were similar scenes in France, Luxembourg, Spain, and Switzerland. In the Cayman Islands, where some of the most spectacular frauds had been committed, the governor of the British colony appointed a receiver for three BCCI units: its Caymans holding company, ICIC, and Credit and Finance Corporation. The governor also froze the assets of as many as eight companies believed to be linked to BCCI, most of which were in the ICIC group.

The Bank of England and other regulators contacted the banking authorities in as many as sixty other countries where BCCI operated, asking for their cooperation in closing the institution. Most regulators complied quickly. In some countries, BCCI accepted the inevitable and quietly closed on its own. On Saturday, July 6, BCCI's manager in Tokyo told the Japanese finance ministry that he would be shutting the office "temporarily." The governor of the Bank of Japan, Yasushi Mieno, announced soon afterward that his investigators had started looking into BCCI's branch, which held $391 million in deposits at the end of the first quarter of 1991. On July 22, a Tokyo court would order the winding up of the branch, the first liquidation of a foreign bank branch since World War II.

Seizing a bank is tricky at the best of times. If some depositors find out before the closure, they will rush to pull out their money. Unless there is a system of deposit insurance, all the other depositors will suffer unfairly, since there will be less cash to go around. The closure of a bank can disrupt the system of payments between banks. All of a sudden, a bank that is a party to many different transactions is removed, leaving gaps in thousands of payments.

At the New York Fed, dealers carefully monitored the dollar markets, mindful that their boss, E. Gerald Corrigan, was concerned about the potential harm the closure might cause to the New York money markets. BCCI's balance sheet was denominated in U.S. dollars, and its largest holdings were short-term dollar investments. As it happened, there was little noticeable effect because of the massive size of the markets and because few financial firms traded with BCCI.

The shutdown of BCCI touched off angry protests by depositors from Britain to Hong Kong, sometimes erupting into violence. The timing of the swoop — at midday on Friday — meant that the first big demonstrations in London didn't take place until Monday, when depositors and employees demonstrated outside BCCI's headquarters and the Bank of England. Protesters carrying picket signs chanted, "Give us back our money."

In Hong Kong, where BCCI had a large branch network, customers took to the streets on July 8 and 9 when the colony's financial secretary, Sir Piers Jacobs, said the government would liquidate BCCI. This would mean big losses for the bank's forty thousand depositors. Wielding batons, officers of the Royal Hong Kong Police battled demonstrators, who burned an effigy of the Hong Kong banking commissioner, David Carse. Rumors quickly spread that other institutions were in trouble, causing runs on two foreign banks.

What particularly infuriated the depositors in Hong Kong was that Carse had initially said in a widely distributed press statement that "the operations of BCC (Hong Kong) remain sound and viable." The offices opened for business as usual on Saturday, but Carse was forced to close them two days later, after he learned that Abu Dhabi wouldn't support the bank as he had hoped.

Some of the most pathetic scenes occurred in Bangladesh, a desperately poor country where BCCI's four branches had collected money from some forty thousand customers. Crowds thronged the commercial district of the capital, Dhaka, in the days after the seizure. One demonstrator was so distraught that he even talked of dousing himself with gasoline and setting himself on fire. Another shouted that the closing of the bank was "a conspiracy against poor countries."

The nineteen-year masquerade had ended. The bank could not make new loans or accept deposits. Most important, BCCI's criminal rampage was over.

The victims of that rampage included nearly one million depositors who had entrusted BCCI with more than $10 billion.* In Britain, about 120,000 residents had deposited £250 million ($400 million) at the bank. No one knew how much of that money would be recovered. Britain, unlike the United States, does not have a generous deposit insurance program backed by the government. The British depositors could only count on getting back 75 percent of the first £20,000 they held with the seized bank, even if the money was held in different accounts.

For the hundreds of small Asian businesses in Britain that relied on BCCI for credit and other banking services, the seizure was catastrophic. Many of them had been drawn to the upstart bank in the belief that it was run by Third World financiers who would be sensitive to their special needs. Now, they found out, their funds were frozen, and much of the money was likely lost. "We are the ones getting hurt," lamented Mohammed Choudary, whose textile business in the Yorkshire town of Bradford was brought to a halt when it lost all its trade financing, which had been provided by BCCI. "It does not seem fair." His factory, which had employed sixty people making bed linen, was reduced to only one seamstress because it lost access to bank credit.

The victims also included BCCI's employees. Most of them were not involved in any wrongdoing, yet they suffered in several different ways. Thousands had been laid off before the shutdown; those who remained would now lose their jobs. They would later learn that the pensions they had counted on would never come: Abedi had raided the staff benefit fund in the mid-1980s to cover trading losses. Many employees were also depositors. One of them, who had left the bank in January 1991 after more than ten years, had more than £200,000 on deposit. He stood to collect only £15,000 from deposit insurance, and that would likely take several months. "I'm buried," he confided on the day of the seizure.

---

*BCCI's deposits had plummeted from more than $20 billion after the controversies of the previous few years.

More surprising, about thirty of Britain's local authorities (munici-
palities) were big depositors, with £81 million in BCCI. Many of them
had taken to borrowing money in the market and then depositing the
funds at BCCI at a higher interest rate. The hardest hit was the Western
Isles Council — the local authority on Skye, a remote island off the
northwestern coast of Scotland — which had £23 million on deposit.
Why were the thrifty people of Skye — many of them from the clan
Macleod — investing their money with BCCI? "Over the years that
this authority has used BCCI," a local official would later explain to
government investigators, "it has consistently paid a higher rate of
interest." The reason BCCI paid a higher rate, of course, was that the
market viewed it as a risky bank, but this was apparently ignored.

In time it emerged that Donald Macleod, the Western Isles' director
of finance, and his colleagues had borrowed as much as £16.5 million
of the money they had on deposit at BCCI. The borrowings had been
made from a life assurance company, a state-owned company, and
from another nearby local authority. Scotland's controller of audit
would later issue a report that severely criticized Macleod, saying he
had gone beyond his authority by borrowing so heavily. He was suspended from his job after the seizure of BCCI. In December 1991, a
committee of inquiry in the Western Isles recommended the immediate
dismissal of both Donald Macleod and George Macleod, the chief
executive of the local authority.

Other local government depositors included the town of Bury, with
£6 million; Harlow, with £4 million; Rochester on Medway, with £4
million; and Westminster, with £3.58 million. Again, many of these
authorities had borrowed money to deposit in BCCI and take advantage of its higher interest rate.

The British deposit brokerage firm of R. P. Martin Bierbaum was
one of five or six such companies that were giving out the name of
BCCI as a potential deposit taker immediately before the seizure. A
government report estimated that R. P. Martin was connected with
£42 million of the total of £81 million deposited by local authorities.
An R. P. Martin spokesman told a government inquiry that it did not
provide investment advice and that "the proposition that local authorities rely on brokers for creditworthiness assessments is absurd."

A cross-party committee of British members of Parliament, the so-
called Treasury Select Committee, would in December 1991 criticize
the Bank of England and call for stricter rules governing the conduct of
money brokers and the advice they were obliged to give local authority

customers. The report also said that local authorities shouldn't borrow money merely to lend it to banks, as many had been doing in the case of BCCI.

The week after the closure, depositors began to form action groups, hoping to secure some compensation for their deposits. In Britain, a group of members of Parliament from the main parties tried to help these victims. Some depositors tried to find relief in the courts. In Manchester, the law firm of Alexander Tatham organized a pressure group, and there was talk of a series of lawsuits against BCCI's top officers, the bank's auditors, and others. Few of the suits materialized; a major hurdle was that in Britain, accountants don't have third-party liability (as they do in the United States). This means that accountants are responsible to their clients but not to anyone else who relies on the financial statements they have prepared.

In the United States, depositors brought actions against BCCI and other defendants blamed for the collapse. The first suit was filed in August in San Francisco by a customer named Shrichand Chawla; similar actions followed in San Diego and Los Angeles. These claims were soon consolidated into one suit by the class action lawyers Milberg Weiss Bershad Specthrie & Lerach of San Diego. The suit named dozens of individual and corporate defendants, including Price Waterhouse, Sheikh Zayed, Ghaith Pharaon, Clark Clifford, Robert Altman, First American board members, Bank of America, and even Hill and Knowlton, the public relations firm. The judge tried to throw the case out, but Milberg Weiss countered by petitioning for a new judge, claiming that the ruling judge was biased. As of the fall of 1992, the case was still in limbo.

The effects of the collapse were most severe in the developing countries where BCCI had a large presence. In Cameroon, as in many sub-Saharan African countries, the bank was a part of the establishment, having cozied up to political leaders and members of the business elite for years. BCCI's seizure paralyzed businesses and denied critical financing to the few active areas of the economy. Incredibly, the Cameroon government had deposited more than one third of its foreign exchange reserves in BCCI. Uncle Sam suffered too. The U.S. Agency for International Development had $10 million in BCCI's Cameroon bank.

Depositors in Cameroon were allowed to take out only 10 percent of their money. Richard Massot, a shipping executive, stood in line at a BCCI branch to withdraw the meager share of his company's deposit. "Our account is blocked, which means we can't pay people," he told a reporter. "Our customers' money is blocked, which means they can't pay us."

In many developing countries, depositors blamed Western regulators for the failure of BCCI and spoke warmly of the seized bank, even though they had lost so much. "BCCI was a Third World dream, and a lot of people had sentimental feelings for the bank," said Ghulam Mohiuddin, a young Bangladeshi who had graduated from MIT. He had used BCCI's facilities to pay for the Apple computers he imported to Bangladesh. Many people would take months to come to terms with the bank's manifest and rampant corruption. To this day, some believe it to be a fabrication of the Western press or financial system. Bankers in the United States and Europe, they argue, couldn't tolerate a successful bank managed by Third World people. Some people in Muslim countries blamed anti-Muslim and Zionist forces.

The sad reality was that a bank owned and run by Muslims from developing countries had systematically robbed their own people. Many of the victims were in Egypt, where BCCI had looted Feisal Islamic Bank, which had collected deposits from devout Muslims because it promised to invest their money in conformity with Islamic law, which forbids the payment of interest. Their religious scruples made it easier for BCCI to steal their money.

In the heart of the City of London stands an imposing white stone building, designed by the famous British architect Sir Edwin Lutyens, that houses the Bank of England. One of the world's oldest central banks — founded in 1694 — it is steeped in tradition. The guards in the entranceway wear powder pink tailcoats and top hats with buckled hatbands. Denizens of the City often refer to this venerable institution as "the Bank," implying that if it is not the only bank around, it is clearly the most important one. Another familiar nickname — the Old Lady of Threadneedle Street — derives from a 1797 caricature by James Gillray, a famous political satirist. It depicts a scoundrel assaulting the Bank of England, which is portrayed as an elderly woman clothed in a long dress made of pound notes. The drawing refers to the recent first issue of pound notes, an event not appreciated by much of the populace, who were more fond of traditional gold and silver coins.

Britain's central bankers have learned to live with paper money, but they still strive to project an aura of wisdom, strength, prudence, and inscrutability. They are, after all, charged with the vital task of ensuring the stability of the country's financial system and have long played a leading part in international financial relations. But for years they did little to protect the public from BCCI.

The regulators were on the defensive the very day of the shutdown. At 4:00 P.M., Robin Leigh-Pemberton, the governor of the Bank of England, discussed the seizure at a hastily arranged press conference. He said that the swoop on BCCI "followed the discovery of large-scale fraud going back several years." The culture of the bank was criminal, he said, adding that this fraud "had been perpetrated at the highest levels within" BCCI and was "on a worldwide scale." Reporters were quick to ask him why the Bank of England had not acted sooner; one journalist pointed out that Price Waterhouse had qualified the accounts of ICIC in 1989. Leigh-Pemberton responded that the Bank of England did not have solid evidence of fraud until 1991.

Authorities in Abu Dhabi insisted that the regulators shouldn't have seized the bank at all. On the day of the closure, the government of the UAE issued a statement criticizing the Bank of England for acting precipitately, given that a restructuring of the bank had been negotiated and was in progress. But some days later, when an American journalist visited the UAE's central bank governor, Abdel-Malik al-Hamr, he refused to answer so much as a single question about BCCI. The local BCCI affiliate, BCC (Emirates), continued to operate normally, with Abu Dhabi's oil wealth and the UAE's central bank standing behind it.

The timing of the shutdown allowed all the parties involved a breathing space over the weekend. Friday in the Islamic world is the Muslim holy day, *yaum al-jamaa* — literally, the day of gathering (at the mosque). Abu Dhabi is quiet, with most people away from their offices. Big crowds mill around the more popular mosques after noon prayers. The three-hour time difference with London also meant that the shutdown didn't occur until 4:00 P.M. Abu Dhabi time.

Four days later, Governor al-Hamr of the central bank headed a delegation of UAE officials that met with Bank of England officials in London. One member of the group was Ghanem Faris al-Mazrui, who, as Zayed's adviser, had spent months on the aborted restructuring scheme. The Arabs were furious. They wanted to know why BCCI's assets had been seized with no warning to Abu Dhabi. Worse, in their view, the Bank of England had allowed the emirate to put money into BCCI after the regulators had decided to close the bank.

The Bank of England tried to persuade the visitors that it was the

UAE's responsibility to cover any shortfall in the bank's books. For their part, the Abu Dhabi officials continued to criticize the Bank of England for the closure and held auditors responsible for failing to discover the bank's irregularities. On July 15, Robin Leigh-Pemberton and his director in charge of banking supervision, Brian Quinn, flew to the UAE for additional meetings. They sought to explain their reasons for moving against BCCI and also asked Abu Dhabi to help compensate depositors.

On July 18, the British Parliament erupted at prime minister's question time, a weekly session at which the leader of the government takes questions from all comers. Opposition Labour party members pointed out that former BCCI employees had written to the Treasury, the Bank of England, and to ministers in June 1990 to report widespread corruption and nepotism in the bank. The speaker of the House of Commons shouted himself almost hoarse calling for order as the parliamentary session degenerated into near-chaos several times. Labour's head, Neil Kinnock, said that Prime Minister John Major had been "utterly negligent" for failing to act sooner against BCCI. Major protested that he had learned of the scale of the fraud only on June 28. "If you are saying I am a liar, you had better say so bluntly," he rounded on Kinnock.

The following day, Sheikh Zayed published a full-page advertisement in Britain's major newspapers lambasting the Bank of England and criticizing Price Waterhouse as well. The same ad ran four days later in the *Wall Street Journal,* the *New York Times,* and the *Washington Post;* it was signed by the government of Abu Dhabi, the Abu Dhabi Investment Authority, and the Department of Personal Affairs of Sheikh Zayed.

Partly to try to defuse the issue, on Friday, July 19, Britain's chancellor of the exchequer, Norman Lamont, announced an independent public inquiry into the supervision of BCCI. The surprise statement severely undercut Leigh-Pemberton, who only a day before had said that such a formal probe would be inappropriate. On July 22, Prime Minister Major's government commissioned Lord Justice Bingham to head the public inquiry and to determine whether the action taken by the regulators was "appropriate and timely." Bingham had enjoyed a highly successful career as a barrister, and he had a reputation for intelligence, independence, and disciplined investigation; his 1977 inquiry into the major oil companies didn't shy away from tagging some of Britain's most powerful firms for evading government sanctions against trade with Rhodesia. But, typically for Britain, Bingham's inquiry would be conducted in secret and wouldn't have subpoena powers. If people didn't want to provide information, they wouldn't have to.

It soon became clear that the Manhattan district attorney, Robert Morgenthau, was driving the investigation of the BCCI affair. His prosecutors and investigators were familiar with complex business fraud because of New York's role as a world financial center and they had a two-year head start. Morgenthau's office knew where many of the bodies were buried, while others were only just beginning to realize that the burial ground existed. The New York D.A.'s investigation forced regulators in both Europe and the United States to take action against several BCCI allies. A prime target was Ghaith Pharaon.

Morgenthau's office had established that Pharaon was essentially a front man for BCCI when he invested in National Bank of Georgia, Independence Bank, and CenTrust. BCCI secretly lent him the money to make these investments, and Pharaon put up the stock as collateral. He even gave blank, signed stock transfer forms to BCCI, enabling it to take possession of NBG shares at any time. There was also evidence that BCCI officials had been involved in managing some of its secret U.S. subsidiaries. Kemal Shoaib, a senior official at the London headquarters, was allegedly responsible for monitoring NBG and Independence Bank. In 1985, Shoaib had "resigned" from BCCI to become chairman of Independence.

When Morgenthau's investigators turned this information over to the Federal Reserve in the spring of 1991, it moved swiftly. On May 6 — two months before the seizure — the Fed ordered BCCI to sell its stock in Independence Bank. On July 12, the Fed published an order seeking to bar four BCCI insiders from U.S. banking for life: Abedi, Naqvi, Pharaon, and Shoaib.

Just over two weeks later, Morgenthau dropped his own bombshell.

On the morning of Monday, July 29, his office at One Hogan Place in Lower Manhattan was filled with reporters and cameramen. The night before, the D.A.'s office had alerted the main television networks that there would be an important announcement so that camera equipment could be set up ahead of time. A plastic sheet was thrown over Morgenthau's desk to conceal his papers from any inquisitive eyes.

The D.A. arrived at eleven o'clock and sat down behind a spray of microphones. He was flanked by a protective group of young investigators buttoned into bulging suit jackets.

Morgenthau and his team were astonished at the size of the gathering. Even in high-profile cases, it was rare to see more than three or four television cameras at press conferences. On that day, there were about twenty-five. The *New York Times,* the D.A.'s local paper and a barometer of news interest, hadn't given much space to this case, so the investigators were even more shocked by the large and international crowd that packed the office. In addition to a full turnout by the big American networks, there were crews from European, Latin American, and Asian television stations.

The D.A. cleared his throat, winced, and began describing a startling array of alleged crimes as camera shutters clacked and videocassettes whirred. "A New York County grand jury," Morgenthau read from his text, "has returned a twelve-count indictment that charges that the Bank of Credit and Commerce International, BCCI, its related entities, and two of its founders engaged in a multibillion-dollar scheme to defraud its depositors." The perpetrators, he continued, had "falsified bank records to hide illegal money-laundering, and committed larcenies" totaling many millions of dollars, and had "paid off public officials." The wily prosecutor looked up from his notes. "This indictment," he said, "spells out the largest bank fraud in world financial history."

After more than two years of tortuous investigation, Morgenthau and his team felt they had finally unraveled some of the complex dealings of Agha Hasan Abedi and Swaleh Naqvi. The indictment charged BCCI, Abedi, and Naqvi with larceny, money-laundering, and fraud. From its very inception, said Morgenthau, BCCI had been a fraud, because it misled depositors about its ownership and financial condition. Since all of BCCI's deposits — which at one point totaled $20 billion — had been collected under false pretenses, the BCCI affair was a $20 billion fraud. An essential part of the scheme, Morgenthau went on, was the use of prominent Arab investors as front men. In exchange for payments from BCCI, they posed as shareholders. The D.A. called this technique "rent-a-sheikh." Four alleged front men were named in the indictment: Pharaon, Adham, Sayed Jawhary, and Faisal Saud al-Fulaij. All four were listed as stockholders; all but Pharaon were also on First American's list of shareholders.

BCCI had achieved its ends partly through bribery, Morgenthau charged, citing the $3 million in payoffs that the grand jury alleged

BCCI paid to two officials of Peru's central bank. In exchange, Morgenthau said, BCCI received central bank deposits. The D.A.'s office said it had information showing that Peru's former president, Alan García Pérez, knew about the bribes.* Toward the end of the press conference, Morgenthau made it clear that the indictment covered only a fraction of BCCI's criminality. It represented, he said, only about one quarter of the potential case against the bank, its operators, and its allies.

Later the same day, the Federal Reserve issued a 100-page order that fined BCCI $200 million for alleged breaches of U.S. banking laws. It also sought to ban several alleged front men for life from U.S. banking. The timing was not coincidental; it had been carefully coordinated with the D.A.'s office. The order was based primarily on investigative work performed by Morgenthau's team and by two lawyers from the Fed's enforcement division, Richard Small in Washington and Thomas Baxter in New York.

In exquisite detail, the Fed's order spelled out how Abedi and his associates had used front men to acquire a majority ownership of First American Bankshares secretly. The alleged front men included Adham, Jawhary, and Fulaij as well as Abdul-Raouf Khalil.

Adham was BCCI's most important front man after Pharaon. Both men, however, would occasionally put in some of their own money alongside their nominee holdings. The former Saudi intelligence chief was a nominee shareholder in BCCI, Attock Oil, and First American. In addition, he was a holder of Capcom's shares. His reputation for great wealth had helped to bolster confidence in BCCI. When, in 1981, Adham sought approval from the Federal Reserve to invest in First American, he claimed to have a net worth of nearly a quarter of a billion dollars.

Unlike most of the other sheikhly shareholders in First American, Adham really seems to have had occasional contact with Clifford and Altman. The lawyers maintained that he represented other shareholders and was a conduit for information. But some believe his more active role may actually indicate that he was an architect of the scheme

---

*Around the same time Morgenthau made his accusations against the central bankers, the Peruvian parliament was investigating allegations that García had enriched himself through corruption and had deposited millions of dollars in BCCI. Later in the year, García was charged with embezzlement, but Peru's supreme court ruled that he was immune from prosecution. García denied the charges. After President Alberto Fujimori assumed dictatorial powers in April 1992, García fled to Colombia, where he was granted political asylum.

to take over First American and perhaps of some of the other frauds at the bank. Adham was certainly a convenient and willing nominee for BCCI. Despite assurances to the U.S. regulators that he would invest his own funds in First American, he had actually bought the stock with money borrowed from BCCI, and the loans were never serviced. The Fed says that he was paid at least $2 million for his services as a front man.

The Saudi spymaster was also suspected of involvement in the looting of BCCI, partly because of his links to Capcom, which had played such a critical role in the fraud. In addition, his ties to the Saudi court may help to explain why BCCI got so many deposits from Feisal Islamic Bank. The Saudi ruling family controls Dar al-Mal al-Islami, the 50 percent owner of that bank.

In 1991, Adham was unwilling to acknowledge any wrongdoing. Speaking through his Washington lawyer, Plato Cacheris, he insisted several times that he had always acted properly. In early 1992, he managed to negotiate himself a safe passage to talk to investigators in London, where he began to bargain with his pursuers.

Khalil, long an aide to Adham and a top Saudi intelligence official, was listed as a shareholder in BCCI, First American, and Capcom. The listings were misleading, since he was mostly a secret nominee. In all likelihood, he was a nominee in BCCI brought in by Adham. Although perhaps not at the outset, Khalil became a nominee in First American, according to Fed investigators. Shares registered in his name were pledged against the BCCI loans that were used to purchase them. BCCI paid Khalil $15 million in February 1987 for the use of his name in investment transactions through the end of 1986 and for the profit on his shares, according to an agreement signed by him and BCCI.

Jawhary, an adviser to Adham, was listed in 1988 as the owner of 0.75 percent of BCCI's stock, but he was merely a nominee. Jawhary had also acted as a front man in the takeover of First American, borrowing from ICIC to pay for the shares, according to the Fed. He was paid $150,000 a year for acting as a nominee in the holding of both BCCI and First American shares. Again, the loans from BCCI and ICIC used to finance his share purchases were never serviced.

Fulaij, the chairman of Kuwait Airways until 1977, was listed as a shareholder of BCCI, its affiliate Kuwait International Finance Company (KIFCO), and two companies secretly controlled by BCCI: Attock Oil and First American. A former UAE official expressed surprise that the Western regulators took Fulaij seriously, remarking that he and others in Abu Dhabi knew the Kuwaiti didn't have the money needed to finance the kind of investments he supposedly made. Fulaij's entire shareholding in KIFCO was financed with loans from KIFCO.

Fulaij was also a nominee for BCCI in his shareholdings in First American. BCCI and ICIC altogether paid him about $100,000 a year for the use of his name. And in 1990 they gave him an additional $606,000 for such services.

After years of ignoring increasingly strong warnings about BCCI, the Fed had finally begun to act. Even now, the central bank's performance was not quite as impressive as it appeared. The Fed's orders generally tracked work that had already been completed by Morgenthau's team, and there was sometimes a curious lack of follow-up. In early 1992, Khalil's lawyer, James Linn, said that neither he nor his client had ever been served with the Fed's July 29, 1991, order. Only Morgenthau, Linn judged, was serious about following the case through.

When a bankrupt financial institution is taken over by regulators, it has to be liquidated. The liquidator sells off assets and uses the cash to pay off liabilities, which consist mainly of deposits. In BCCI's case, a court in Luxembourg (where the bank's holding company was incorporated) appointed as liquidator Brian Smouha, a partner in the London office of Touche Ross, one of the world's biggest accountancy partnerships. Smouha had performed this role after another spectacular bank failure: the 1982 collapse of Italy's Banco Ambrosiano. He was the liquidator of Ambrosiano's Luxembourg holding company.

In Britain, the liquidation didn't go as smoothly as the Bank of England had hoped. On July 30, a judge granted a four-month delay in the winding up of BCCI to allow time to consider a possible rescue plan by Sheikh Zayed. The concession to Abu Dhabi, which was still insisting that the bank could be saved, came after Zayed's government had pledged to pay £45 million in partial compensation to British depositors. The Bank of England had pressed the court to favor the immediate liquidation of the bank. Smouha, on the other hand, wanted to continue negotiating with Abu Dhabi. In his view, the best solution for the depositors was a quick and amicable settlement with Sheikh Zayed.

Similarly, in U.S. Bankruptcy Court in Manhattan, a judge issued an order in August blocking most U.S. legal action against the bank until November 1. Smouha's strategy was to subordinate any U.S. settlement to a worldwide liquidation agreement involving Abu Dhabi, Luxembourg, and London.

Many depositors hoped that the Bank of England would succeed in pressuring Sheikh Zayed to compensate all the bank's depositors fully. But Abu Dhabi was in no such mood, and it would take months of secret negotiations between the liquidators and Abu Dhabi officials before Zayed and his government made any offer to help.

The shutdown of BCCI was a serious blow to several companies and financial institutions close to the rogue bank. One of the biggest borrowers in Britain was Control Securities. This conglomerate was headed by Nazmu Virani, the Asian entrepreneur who had introduced BCCI officials to British politicians. After the bank was seized, it became clear that there was much more than an ordinary lender-borrower relationship. BCCI had channeled huge amounts of money to Control Securities and even held a large block of its stock. Control Securities was also a big depositor, and the firm announced in late July that it had made a £3.8 million provision against potential losses on those deposits. The business went into a tailspin, and Virani was soon under investigation by the Serious Fraud Office as part of its probe into BCCI. The London Stock Exchange suspended trading in the company's shares.

The biggest customer casualty was the Gokal family's Gulf Group. BCCI had propped up the Gokals with a huge volume of loans — many of them fraudulent — since the 1970s. When the bank collapsed, parts of the Gulf Group went into liquidation.

And then there were the companies and banks that BCCI secretly owned. The biggest by far was First American Bankshares, and confidence in the institution was severely shaken by the scandal.

Clark Clifford and Robert Altman had always portrayed First American as a success story. When, for example, the May 1990 *Regardie's* article suggested that its performance was mediocre compared with that of similar banks, its spokesmen issued an angry rebuttal. In reality, its profitability had been poor in the late 1980s, and there were more problems on the way because it had engaged in a reckless lending binge, providing far too much money to real estate developers in the Washington area. At First American Bank of Virginia, the largest unit in the group, 27.6 percent of total assets were in real estate lending. At the Maryland bank, the figure was more than 30 percent — higher than at several other local banks. American Security Bank of Washington had 24 percent of its assets in real estate loans, while the figure at Riggs National — the capital's largest bank — was just 11 percent. Moreover, First American's capital base was inadequate, in the regulators' view.

After proof emerged that BCCI owned First American, Clifford and Altman said that they — like the regulators — had been duped by BCCI. They also insisted that BCCI had no influence on how the company was managed. In fact, there appear to be several signs of negative influence.

First American had expanded aggressively in New York in the early 1980s because it was encouraged to do so by "the investors," according to a former top official of the company. The New York unit never earned more than $2.6 million in any one year, and those "earnings" were inflated by accounting gimmickry. (A large part of the New York bank's lease payments on its headquarters was charged to the parent company, which had the effect of understating the bank's expenses and thus overstating its profits.)

First American's takeover of NBG could be another example of pernicious influence by BCCI. Several observers believe that First American paid too much in what may have been a scheme to transfer money from First American to BCCI. Clifford and Altman have contended that this was an arm's-length transaction. At the time of the deal, however, Clifford stated that First American was encouraged by its Arab shareholders to buy NBG.

Among the most dubious deals were investments in certificates of deposit (CDs) issued by one of BCCI's most notorious units, ICIC, in the Cayman Islands. In 1986 and 1987, First American bought $74 million in CDs, even though ICIC was not a conventional bank but a secretive dummy company controlled by Abedi and Naqvi. Moreover, according to the Fed, First American received below-market rates of interest.

Altman continued to deny in the summer of 1991 that BCCI had influenced First American. Speaking through his lawyer, he said, "It is absolutely not true that First American was a source of funds for BCCI. All money from the Middle East flowed into First American. Both internal audits and exams by the regulators confirmed there was not a single instance of improper financial dealings with BCCI."

Even without these peculiar deals, the stench of the BCCI connection was highly damaging to First American. Some depositors began pulling their money out after *Regardie's* and the *Wall Street Journal* published their exposés in May 1990. The real hemorrhage began after the July 1991 shutdown of BCCI. On August 1, *American Banker,* a trade publication, reported that First American's banks in Washington, Virginia, Maryland, and Georgia were losing deposits to rival institutions. Company officials tried to minimize the problem, but it was actually quite grave. First American would not own up to it until well into 1992. In April of that year, it released its 1991 annual report, which showed that deposits had dropped by about $2 billion during the year. In an effort to maintain confidence, First American's Washington-area banks posted stickers on many of their automated teller machines reminding customers that their monies were protected by the Federal Deposit Insurance Corporation. The stickers started appearing before the shutdown. To counter negative publicity, all depositors were sent pamphlets in which First American sought to play down the BCCI connection.

The seizure of BCCI killed an effort by Charles McC. Mathias, a First American board member and a former U.S. senator from Maryland, to bolster confidence in First American by placing its stock in the hands of a trustee. The man Mathias had in mind was Paul Volcker, the chairman of the Federal Reserve Board from 1979 to 1987. He is an old friend of Mathias's, and the two men sit on the board of the German American Foundation. Volcker is one of the most respected figures in international finance, but he also bears some of the responsibility for the First American mess. It was during his tenure as chairman that the Fed allowed BCCI's clients to acquire First American. Volcker seems somewhat amnesiac about the takeover. Occasionally in 1991 he even referred to the seized bank as BBCI.

The Federal Reserve was certainly nervous about First American's financial condition. When the July 29 order was considered at a Fed board meeting, William Taylor, the director of banking supervision, noted that the company had suffered an outflow of deposits. The board agreed unanimously that Clifford and Altman had to go.

Neither Clifford nor Altman was named in the Morgenthau indictment or the Fed orders, but their claims to have known little about BCCI's activities were regarded as increasingly improbable. Unable to convince the regulators that they had merely been duped by Abedi and his cohorts, they resigned on August 13. Clifford was replaced as chairman by Nicholas deB. Katzenbach, who had been an attorney general in the Johnson administration and later general counsel to IBM. Clifford had pushed hard to ensure Katzenbach's appointment.

It is unclear why the Fed thought Clifford should have any say in the matter. At the time, he was under investigation for violating banking laws. The appointment of Katzenbach is surprising for another reason. Before taking over First American, he had served on the board of Miami's Southeast Banking Corporation, which was in disastrous financial shape. In September — within weeks of Katzenbach's arrival at First American — the Miami banking company collapsed. Nine months later, the bankruptcy trustee would sue Katzenbach and other former directors, accusing them of gross mismanagement and negligence. Katzenbach has denied any wrongdoing.*

At the time of his resignation, Clifford tried to promote the idea that First American's problems were a matter of image rather than substance. Announcing his departure, he told reporters he was concerned that "highly sensationalized publicity" might hurt the company. He stoutly defended his record at First American and said that during the past decade it had become "the largest and one of the most respected bank holding companies in Washington, D.C."

But Clifford and Altman would increasingly be forced to defend themselves in the press, in congressional hearings, and in interviews with prosecutors in New York and Washington as more information about their tenure at First American filtered out.

The seizure of BCCI focused enormous attention on the bank in the news media, with another wave of press coverage after the Morgenthau indictment and the Fed order of July 29. There were front-page stories in major newspapers, special television reports, and cover stories in *Time, Newsweek,* and the *Economist.* Months later, in a survey of American newspaper editors, BCCI was ranked as the second most important business story of 1991 — surpassed only by the recession. The *Wall Street Journal* disclosed the contents of one of Price Waterhouse's 1989 special audits in a page 1 feature published a week after the shutdown. The article discussed BCCI's huge loans to the Gokals and to such front men as Pharaon, Adham, and Khalil.

News of BCCI's links to terrorists also leaked out. Ghassan Ahmad Qasim, the manager of BCCI's branch on London's trendy Sloane Street, told reporters that the infamous terrorist Abu Nidal had used

---

*A Federal Reserve official says that Katzenbach was chosen by First American's board of directors. The Fed knew about the problems at Southeast but did not feel that they were adequate grounds to veto the appointment.

the bank extensively. The banker said that he had even accompanied Abu Nidal on shopping trips around London. One of the terrorist's operatives, Samir Najm al-Din, had put tens of millions of dollars in the bank in 1981. There were also disclosures about BCCI's involvement in covert operations, including its role in financing arms sales to Iran orchestrated by Oliver North and his associates. The most sensational article was a cover story in *Time* magazine alleging that there was a "black network" operating out of BCCI's Karachi office, fronting for an armed criminal gang of international mafiosi involved in extortion, bribery, kidnapping, and murder. Substantiating *Time*'s assertions proved difficult. Pakistan's finance minister, Sartaj Asis, denied them outright, saying to Britain's *Financial Times*, "I am not aware of any such activities."

The growing scandal prompted congressional investigations. Senator Kerry, who had been looking into BCCI since 1988, began a series of hearings on the bank. Testifying on August 1, Jack Blum and William von Raab blasted BCCI's lawyers and lobbyists for their role in the affair. A few days later, Masihur Rahman, BCCI's chief financial officer, told the Kerry Committee that a bank official had threatened to kill him if he revealed what he knew. Just before Rahman left BCCI on August 1, 1990, he quarreled with two of his colleagues, he told the Senate panel. One of them "became furious," Rahman recounted, saying, "If you open your mouth, or if you go to court, I've personally killed people in my life in Multan in Pakistan, and I'll use the same gun on you."

The banking committees of both the House and the Senate also announced hearings on BCCI. The House panel turned out to be quite aggressive, thanks to its chairman, Henry Gonzalez. Things were somewhat different on the Senate committee, which is better known for participating in financial scandals than for investigating them. Five members, including the chairman, Donald Riegle of Michigan, had been investigated for taking huge campaign contributions from Charles Keating, the savings and loan crook. Because of the Keating Five affair, one congressional staff member jokes that Senate Banking is "the best committee money can buy."

Some of the biggest apparent culprits in the BCCI affair seemed to be well beyond the reach of Western law enforcement agencies. In many cases they were living in luxury on the monies they had stolen. Pharaon, for example, flitted between Pakistan and Saudi Arabia, though he had to cancel a stay on his yacht in Cannes in August for fear of the French authorities.

In early September, Sheikh Zayed's government arrested more than thirty BCCI employees, including Swaleh Naqvi, the man who had orchestrated the multibillion-dollar Ponzi scheme. Ostensibly, the arrests showed that Abu Dhabi was eager to get to the bottom of the scandal, but there was widespread skepticism in the West. If Zayed wanted to uncover the truth, why were American and British investigators prevented from interrogating the detainees? This stubborn refusal to make witnesses available increased the suspicions in the West about the possible involvement of members of Zayed's circle.

In Pakistan, there was widespread skepticism of the BCCI seizure, which several commentators ascribed to Western jealousy of the bank's success and to anti-Muslim prejudice. The old canard about a "Zionist conspiracy" was repeated. There seemed to be little likelihood that Abedi, who was living in Karachi, would ever be turned over to law enforcement authorities in the West. Jam Sadiq Ali, the governor of Sind province, in which Karachi is located, said publicly that he would not allow the banker to be extradited. The governor's protective attitude was understandable. When he lived in exile in Britain, Abedi had given him money and a house in the Belsize Park section of London.

Abedi's wife, Rabia, conveyed her husband's reaction to his indictment by the New York County grand jury. He insisted he would be cleared. His nonchalance seems to have been warranted. When the Western bank regulators ordered the seizure of BCCI, Pakistan was one of the few countries not to comply, and on Monday, July 8, BCCI's three Pakistani branches opened as usual. A spokesman for the State Bank of Pakistan said, "BCCI hasn't violated any banking rules in Pakistan and there is no complaint against it." But depositors didn't believe him; crowds surged around BCCI's offices in Karachi, Rawalpindi, and Lahore, withdrawing their funds.

In September, Abedi's lawyers published an advertisement in the Pakistani press warning reporters to watch what they said about him. The ad, signed by Sher Sultan Pirzada, a former Pakistani attorney general, appeared on the front page of *Dawn,* an English-language daily. "Mr. Abedi's integrity is unassailable," it insisted. "The allegations and criminal charges are defamatory, baseless, unwarranted and unjustified."

14

CLIFFORD AND ALTMAN

HE HAS BEEN CALLED an elder statesman of the Democratic party, a superlawyer, even a Washington monument. Thus, it was only to be expected that, after more than four decades in public life, Clark McAdams Clifford would recount his life and career in a book.

Clifford's memoirs, co-authored by Richard Holbrooke, a former State Department official, is a weighty tome that deals principally with his life in public service, as reflected by its title, *Counsel to the President*. It was published with great fanfare in the spring of 1991, and extracts appeared in the prestigious *New Yorker* magazine. A book party was held at the home of Pamela Harriman, the widow of Governor Averell Harriman of New York, another adviser to presidents. In her own right, Pamela Harriman has been a major force in the Democratic party as both a campaign contributor and a spotter of political talent.

On the evening of May 22, hundreds of guests arrived at Harriman's elegant town house on N Street in the heart of Georgetown. Some of the most powerful people in Washington were there, including House Speaker Tom Foley and such fellow House Democrats as John Dingell of Michigan, Jack Brooks of Texas, Steny Hoyer of Maryland, and Patricia Schroeder of Colorado. Representing the Senate were Democrats Edward Kennedy of Massachusetts, Alan Cranston of California, Claiborne Pell of Rhode Island, Paul Simon of Illinois, Christopher Dodd of Connecticut, Howard Metzenbaum of Ohio, Sam Nunn of Georgia, and Frank Lautenberg of New Jersey. Media heavyweights at the party included William Safire of the *New York Times,* Al Hunt of the *Wall Street Journal,* Jack Nelson of the *Los Angeles Times,* Tim

Clark Clifford and Robert Altman swear to tell Congress the truth,
September 11, 1991

The mastermind:
Agha Hasan Abedi
in his prime

Below left: Sheikh Zayed
bin Sultan al-Nahyan,
Abu Dhabi's ruler and
Abedi's patron

Below right: Abedi's
loyal deputy: Swaleh
Naqvi, 1988

The Saudi spymaster Kamal Adham, a BCCI insider and the lead investor in Washington, D.C.'s First American Bankshares

The general and the tycoon: Alexander Haig meets BCCI's favorite front man, Ghaith Pharaon

Below: The president and the king: George Bush and Saudi Arabia's Fahd (*at right*), 1990

Right: BCCI beneficiaries Jimmy Carter and Bert Lance

Courtesy, Carter Presidential Center

Below left: Presidential first-born George W. Bush (*at right*) and Arkansas financier Jackson Stephens, the man who helped BCCI buy into Washington

Below right: CIA Director George Bush, 1976

Mike Stewart/Arkansas-Democrat Gazette

Arnaud de Borchgrave/Gamma Liaison

Superlawyer and Wonder Woman: Clark Clifford with Lynda Carter, Robert Altman's wife

Below left: Cable TV entrepreneur and BCCI associate Bob Magness
Below right: CIA chief William Casey

UPI/Bettmann

Above: U.S. Customs chief William von Raab, investigator Jack Blum, and Senator John Kerry
Below left: Under arrest: Amjad Awan (*at center right*) and his colleagues in Tampa, October 8, 1988
Below right: French authorities nab Syed Ziauddin Ali Akbar, September 5, 1991

Tampa Tribune/*Sipa-Press*

Reuter

Above left: BCCI's friend on the Hill: Utah's Republican senator Orrin Hatch
Above right: CenTrust's David Paul, the shady S&L operator, generous political donor, and BCCI partner

Ailing financier: Agha Hasan Abedi, Pakistan, 1991

Harry Ben

The Manhattan D.A. and his sleuths (*foreground, clockwise from left*):
John Moscow, Robert Morgenthau, and Michael Cherkasky

Russert of NBC News, and Katharine Graham, the chairman of the Washington Post Company.

Finally, there were Clifford's fellow Washington power brokers: Richard Moe, Frank Mankiewicz, Lloyd Cutler, Sol Linowitz, and James Symington. Mankiewicz's firm, Hill and Knowlton, had done public relations work for both BCCI and First American, as we have seen. James Symington, a former congressman, was the son of the late Senator Stuart Symington, an old friend of Clifford's who served on First American's board.

It should have been a glorious moment, a time to celebrate a lifetime of achievement. Instead, something of a pall hung over the proceedings, for Clifford's memoirs were coming out at the height of the investigations into BCCI and First American. In fact, the day after the party, officials of the Federal Reserve told the Senate Banking Committee that they had been deliberately misled for a decade about the ownership of First American.

Clifford was so anxious to avoid having his reputation tainted by the BCCI scandal that he tried not to mention the bank at all in his memoirs. When it became clear that the subject could not be omitted entirely, a long footnote was added shortly before the book went to press. "In 1991," he began, "an unfortunate controversy arose concerning the relationship between First American and an international bank, the Bank of Credit and Commerce International (BCCI)." Clifford went on to describe how First American was acquired and how he was asked to become chairman. "The investors and BCCI," he wrote, "never interfered with our operations." After BCCI came under scrutiny in 1988, investigators "began examining the possibility that certain secret financial dealings overseas resulted in an illegal transfer of control of certain shares of First American stock to BCCI." Clifford said that when he "was first informed that United States law might have been violated, I was both appalled and embarrassed. Never, in my nine years as the bank's chairman, had I received any instructions from any BCCI representative." He said that if "the Federal Reserve Board and other authorities had been deceived, so had I." He asserted that First American had been a well-run bank, and he concluded, "No event in my entire career caused me greater anger and outrage."

Throughout 1991, Clifford was on the defensive. He and Robert Altman, his partner and longtime protégé, were interrogated by journalists, prosecutors, and congressional committees. After years of being regarded as pillars of the establishment, they were now suspected of fronting for an international criminal enterprise. At one point Clifford felt obliged to say that "the furthest thing from my mind would be to permit myself or my partner to become involved in some criminal conspiracy."

The lawyers' claims that they were ignorant of BCCI's role were greeted with widespread skepticism — sometimes derision. The columnist Michael Kinsley compared Clifford to Captain Reynault, the French prefect in *Casablanca,* who was "shocked, shocked" to learn that gambling was going on at Rick's Café. (An employee of the café then handed Reynault his winnings.) Altman and his wife were even the subjects of a story in a sleazy tabloid called the *Globe.* WONDER WOMAN'S HUBBY PROBED IN DRUG SCANDAL, the headline screamed. The kicker read: "Shattered Lynda was queen of Washington, now nobody wants to know her."

The central question asked of Clifford and Altman was the one that had dogged Richard Nixon during Watergate: What did they know and when did they know it? What, specifically, did they know about BCCI's relationship with First American? When did they learn that BCCI owned the U.S. banking institution? The first time they had a chance to provide detailed answers in a public forum was at a hearing of the House Banking Committee.

On the morning of Wednesday, September 11, 1991, the Wright Patman Room of the Rayburn Office Building was filled with reporters, photographers, and spectators. It was appropriate that the hearing would be held in a room named for Patman. The late Texas congressman had been a feisty populist who was suspicious of the power of the big banks. As chairman of the Banking Committee, he was a driving force behind the Bank Secrecy Act, which requires banks to report large cash transactions. It was this law that helped spur investigations of money laundering, including Operation C-Chase, which led to the indictment of BCCI. When Patman held hearings in the 1960s, one of his star witnesses was Robert Morgenthau, then the U.S. Attorney in Manhattan, who had prosecuted financial criminals. That was a quarter of a century before Morgenthau — as Manhattan's D.A. — helped bring BCCI to justice. The current chairman of the committee, Henry Gonzalez, is a Texas populist in Patman's tradition. Regarded as fearless and scrupulously honest, he was willing to follow the BCCI trail wherever it led.

When Clifford and Altman arrived, they were a study in contrasts. Clifford was eighty-four years old, with wavy silver hair and a pale complexion. He walked slowly up the aisle and took his seat before the committee. His gray fedora was in his hand — a reminder that he was of another generation, another era. Altman, roughly half Clifford's age, had black hair and a dark complexion. Despite these differences, his mannerisms sometimes mirrored those of his mentor. Altman would press his fingertips together in what has been called "the Clifford steeple."

The two lawyers were accompanied by their wives. Margery Pepperell Kimball Clifford, known as Marny, was the picture of the upper-class matron in her black dress and pearls. Lynda Carter Altman wore a tight minidress and seemed to personify Hollywood glitz. The two women took their seats behind their husbands.

Gonzalez called the committee to order and made his opening statement. The purpose of the hearings, he said, was to determine how BCCI — which he said was "tantamount to a racketeering bank" — had "gained a foothold in the United States, and how regulators and bank officials failed to detect or understand, or report, the invasion." He then turned his fire on Clifford and Altman. Referring to the millions of dollars they had earned in legal fees and stock deals, he said, "If Mr. Clifford and Mr. Altman did not understand BCCI's role in the takeover of First American, they did have an appreciation of the value of BCCI's money." The chairman was particularly disturbed by the potential conflicts of interest arising from their roles as executives of First American and lawyers for the bank. "Bank officers," he said, "cannot serve one moment in the decision-making capacity in the bank and, in the next moment, don their legal caps to give sanction to these same decisions."

There was another apparent conflict of interest that Gonzalez could have cited. In connection with the banking committee's probe (and other investigations), Clifford and Altman were represented by Robert Bennett and Carl Rauh of Skadden, Arps, Slate, Meagher & Flom. Throughout the hearing, Bennett sat behind Clifford and often whispered advice into his ear. Skadden, as noted in Chapter 3, had represented First American (then called Financial General) during the takeover battle. Lawyers for the New York firm dug up considerable evidence that BCCI was a shady outfit and that Abedi's Arab clients were front men for BCCI. The opposing legal team was, of course, headed by Clifford and Altman. Now, two lawyers from Skadden were arguing that Clifford and Altman had no way of knowing that BCCI was a sleazy bank or that the Arabs were front men.*

The chairman's criticisms were mild compared with the opening statements of some of his colleagues. To be sure, some members leavened their criticism by paying homage to Clifford's accomplishments in government service. There was effusive praise from Joseph Kennedy of Massachusetts, whose uncle, the late president, had been a client of Clifford's. The young congressman described Clifford as "one of the greatest public servants in modern American history." The poignancy of the occasion was captured by Democrat Jim Bacchus of Florida, who said that Clifford was under investigation at a time of his life when he should be able to look back on his accomplishments. "I'm very saddened to see you here," the congressman said.

Most committee members, however, showed only slight deference to Clifford, portraying him as little more than a liar. Some of the harshest comments, not surprisingly, came from Republicans. Chalmers Wylie of Ohio, the ranking Republican on the committee, said that Clifford and Altman "almost certainly had to be aware that First American maintained an extensive relationship with BCCI." None was more aggressive than Wisconsin's Toby Roth. "Mr. Clifford and Mr. Altman, I've looked at the facts presented to this committee and studied your statements," he said. "And it pains me to say this, but others may believe your story, but I must say I don't believe a word of it." The two lawyers, he continued, "allowed a vast criminal enter-

---

*In 1978, Skadden had argued in a seventy-one-page legal brief filed in U.S. District Court in Washington, D.C., that BCCI had "closely controlled and directed" the acquisition of a big block of First American stock.

When Bennett was asked about this apparent conflict of interest in the fall of 1991, he said that he and his colleagues had "thoroughly examined" the matter and had "determined there were no conflicts." He pointed out that he hadn't joined Skadden until April 1990, long after the takeover battle. (Rauh joined at the same time.) Moreover, Clifford and Altman did not object. (Skadden's former client — First American — had to give its permission, but it, of course, was controlled by Clifford.)

Others were not so sure. Peter Brown, who was employed by Skadden as a paralegal during the takeover battle and spent some time on the case, expressed strong criticism. "The news that Skadden has switched sides," he said, "magnifies the incestuousness of this whole affair in Washington."

There were other possible conflicts concerning Skadden's Carl Rauh. He had represented Akbar Bilgrami, one of the BCCI officers convicted in the Tampa drug money case. (Clifford and Altman, of course, had recruited the lawyers for the individual defendants.) Bilgrami has said that he gave Rauh permission to work for Clifford and Altman.

prise to gain a foothold in the United States." Roth said the committee's investigation had shown that "you have been in bed with BCCI for at least ten years. You're telling us all you got was a back rub."

Democrat Charles Schumer of New York used milder language, but his message was much the same. Clifford and Altman, he said, "are asking us to believe that when their house was on fire, they didn't smell the smoke, feel the heat, or hear the alarms. They claim they were duped." The lawyers' defense of themselves, said Schumer, "assumes a high degree of naiveté and disinterest that is out of character with men of such business acumen. Their explanation strains credulity to the breaking point."

Soon it was time for Clifford and Altman to state their case. Congressional hearings were familiar to Clifford. He had often appeared before such committees to defend clients in trouble. Bert Lance — the client who had introduced him to Abedi — was one notable example. Clifford was such an effective advocate that senators and congressmen sometimes seemed in awe of him. This time, however, he had been cast in an unfamiliar role: as the target of an investigation.

Referring to himself and Altman, Clifford told the committee that "our consciences are clear. We have not been guilty of not only any legal infraction, we've not been guilty of any misconduct and not even conscious of being guilty of any impropriety on our part." Throughout his presentation he referred to his honor, integrity, and reputation. "What I tell you today," he said at one point, "will be the total and complete truth." In his sixty-three years as a lawyer, "there has never been a cloud placed against my name until now."

Rather than reading his prepared statement, Clifford decided to talk about his involvement with BCCI and First American in a narrative fashion. If anyone thought that his age had seriously diminished his mental faculties, this presentation proved otherwise. The octogenarian showed a mastery of detail that would have been impressive in a man half his age. Seldom referring to notes or documents, he spoke forcefully and eloquently. During the presentation, he touched all the right chords. He mentioned his role as an adviser to Presidents Truman, Kennedy, Johnson, and Carter — a reminder of his status as an elder statesman of the Democratic party. He also referred to his long legal career — something likely to evoke sympathy from a panel filled with lawyers — and to his desire to remain active and useful in his old age.

When he agreed to take over the chairmanship of First American, he did so not for the money but because he feared drifting away from life. "I've worked all my life. That's what my life has been, just work. And it's kept me alive and kept me able — I hope able — and kept me vigorous. I didn't want to retire. I didn't want to just sit on the porch and rock and wait to die." He later added wistfully, "I think it's been good for me until this last year. Maybe it's kept me alive for nine more years."

Most of Clifford's remarks, of course, were devoted to his relationships with BCCI and First American. He said that his law firm began representing BCCI and its Arab clients in early 1978, when they were accused of violating U.S. securities laws in their initial purchases of First American stock. Before accepting BCCI as a client, Clifford made sure it was reputable. One indication of its high standing was that Bank of America was a major shareholder. There were other signs as well, including a favorable article about BCCI published by the *Economist* in 1977. When the Arab investors sought regulatory approval to take over First American, Clifford investigated their backgrounds and found that "they were persons of reputation, wealth, and stature." He also provided a justification for his and Altman's investments in First American stock. The lawyers had received little compensation for running the company and felt that the stock deal was an appropriate reward.

As for BCCI's influence, Clifford said, "At no time did BCCI exert any control whatsoever over First American." He stated firmly, "You have my word for it — I give you my word under oath, at no time did we turn to them for a decision."

If it seemed hard to believe that Clifford and Altman had been deceived about BCCI's character and its ownership of First American, Clifford noted that many others had apparently been deceived as well, including the Bank of England, Lord Callaghan, Price Waterhouse, and Jimmy Carter. Clifford again touched on his reputation. He said he was "going to work as hard as I can in an effort to preserve my good name."

Altman's statement was shorter and less emotional. In a flat baritone, the lawyer insisted that "First American was not controlled by BCCI in the management decisions that were made." Abedi, he said, acted as "an investment adviser to the shareholders" and as "the communications link between us and the shareholders," but the bank did not control First American. "We are secure in the knowledge that whatever concealed interests BCCI may have had never translated into actual control over First American's operations."

Clifford's statement had been a tour de force, helping to explain why he had been such a formidable figure. During a break in the proceedings, Congressman Wylie said, "Mr. Clifford is most impressive. Mr. Clifford could sell hams in a synagogue." But when the questioning began, it quickly became clear that most members still doubted that Clifford and Altman had been ignorant of BCCI's true role.

Chairman Gonzalez made much of the fact that Clifford and Altman wore many hats — as directors, shareholders, lawyers, and bank executives. These multiple roles even put Altman into the position of writing a letter to himself. On one occasion, Robert A. Altman sent a letter on behalf of First American's parent company to all of the company's shareholders — including Robert A. Altman. Just about everyone in the room, including Altman, burst into laughter when Gonzalez said, "Now it seems to me that the only place I've seen where anybody can be in two places at the same time is in *Star Trek.*"

Wylie said that although Clifford's presentation was impressive, "it did not pass the so-called straight-face test." He questioned Altman about his handling of the Fed's investigation of BCCI's loans to First American shareholders. When William Ryback of the Fed wrote to Altman seeking information about those loans, the congressman asked, why did Altman fail to reveal that he and Clifford had financed their own investments in First American by borrowing from BCCI?

Altman replied that he spoke with Ryback after receiving the letter and was told that the Fed was interested only in loans from BCCI to the original investors in First American and loans to current investors that were still outstanding. Since Clifford and Altman were not among the original investors and had repaid their loans, there was no need to disclose them to the Fed. (Ryback has said he does not recall altering his request.)

The harshest remarks again came from Toby Roth, the Wisconsin Republican. Addressing Clifford, he said, "You reported regularly to BCCI on the operation of your bank. You yourself have mentioned you went to London twenty-six times, and Mr. Altman reported as well. You provided them with financial statements. You even cleared job candidates with BCCI. You went to BCCI conferences. You even accepted BCCI payments for your legal fees. . . . And it's interesting that they didn't come to you, but you went to them in London. So if you weren't reporting like good subordinates to the real owners, what did you think you were doing?" Roth concluded with a tirade against political insiders: "I think that the insiders in this country are milking — they know the system and they are milking the system, and the people are going to get as upset with our government and with what's going on in Washington as they did in the Soviet Union, they are going to come and clean up Washington one of these days."

Henry Gonzalez was not only concerned about the conduct of Clifford and Altman, he also wondered why First American's board of directors seemed oblivious of BCCI's true role. Clifford had packed the board with close friends, including Altman and three aging cronies: James Gavin, Elwood Quesada, and Stuart Symington. Two members of the geriatric trio died before the BCCI scandal exploded: Symington died in December 1988 at the age of eighty-seven, Gavin fourteen months later at eighty-two.

Clifford's dominant role was amply documented in the lawsuit filed in the late 1980s by former minority shareholders of First American Bank of Virginia. Directors of both the parent company and the Virginia bank testified that Clifford essentially ran the company as an autocracy — admitting, in effect, that the board members were little more than ciphers. One startling example of the lack of oversight emerged in early 1991, when the *Washington Post* revealed that Clifford and Altman had purchased stock in First American's ultimate holding company, CCAH (Credit and Commerce American Holdings), with loans from BCCI. Clifford and Altman said the deal had been approved by CCAH's board members. At the time, the board consisted of four people: Clifford, Altman, Symington, and Quesada. By 1991, Symington was conveniently dead and Quesada said he couldn't remember whether he had approved the deal.

The conduct of the board was the focus of a hearing by Gonzalez's committee on September 27, roughly two weeks after Clifford and Altman testified. Five directors of First American — three of whom were also officers — appeared as witnesses. Gonzalez made his skepticism clear in his opening statement: "Unfortunately, too many directors bring to the table only one thing — a huge rubber stamp with one word, 'Yes,' for all management decisions." The directors claimed to have known nothing about BCCI's secret ownership of the company. What is more, they said, they had not even known the names of the

Arab stockholders until quite recently. Vincent Scoffone, the senior vice president and treasurer, said under oath that he did not know the investors' names until early 1991. This remark seemed odd, since most of the Arabs' names had been published in May 1990 in the *Regardie's* article.

Clearly, a position on the board of First American or one of its subsidiary banks was not very demanding. It could be quite rewarding, however. In addition to receiving director's fees, several board members borrowed substantial sums of money. At the end of 1989, loans to directors of First American Bankshares and its subsidiaries exceeded $200 million. Three directors owed more than $30 million apiece. And some board members also got business from the bank. Robert Gray's firm, Hill and Knowlton, did public relations for First American. The law firm of former Senator Mathias — Jones, Day, Reavis & Pogue — also received fees from First American. Directors of First American told the committee there was nothing questionable about this because Mathias did not participate in the decision to use his firm.

At one point in the hearing, Mathias said he had asked Clifford about the stockholders after joining the board in the late 1980s. "He responded that they were the most wonderful people," Mathias recalled. That was presumably enough to satisfy his curiosity. At the time of the hearing, it appeared that the former senator still failed to grasp the nature of the BCCI–First American relationship. He testified that First American's stockholders had contributed more than $400 million in capital over the years — apparently unaware that much of the money had been stolen from BCCI's depositors.

The House Banking Committee was not the only congressional panel looking into Clifford and Altman's role at First American. On October 24, the lawyers appeared before the Senate's Kerry Committee, which had been probing BCCI for years. The atmosphere was more cordial, but the questioning was generally more incisive.

Senator Hank Brown of Colorado, the ranking Republican on the committee, is both a lawyer and a certified public accountant, and he questioned Clifford and Altman closely about their investment in First American's stock, which they had financed with nonrecourse loans from BCCI. Brown pointed out that it was a no-risk deal, that "if the value of the stock went up, you could enjoy the value of that stock. If the value of the stock went down, you would have no liability."

Kerry confronted Clifford and Altman with a series of documents that suggested BCCI had been heavily involved in the affairs of First American Bank of New York. When the bank was being launched in 1982, one man who helped get it off the ground was Khusro Elley, BCCI's senior officer in New York. Elley helped to lease space for FABNY's Park Avenue headquarters and assisted in a variety of other matters. On October 13, 1982, he wrote to Swaleh Naqvi, then BCCI's number-two man, referring to a recent meeting with Altman. Among the matters Elley said they had discussed were the leasing of FABNY's headquarters; the selection of board members; the recruitment of key staff; the selection of auditors, lawyers, and data processing equipment; employee compensation; the projection of the first year's operations; and coordination with the holding company and its shareholders. In 1983, Elley and another BCCI official, Abol Helmy, negotiated with Bankers Trust officials regarding FABNY's purchase of several Bankers Trust branches.

When asked for an explanation of Elley's involvement in the Bankers Trust deal, Altman said that Elley was acting at his direction, not BCCI's. As for Elley's involvement in other matters, Altman asserted that this did not violate understandings with the Fed — since BCCI did not make the final decisions.

Not long after the Bankers Trust transaction, Elley was hired by FABNY and soon became involved in a scheme for the joint marketing of BCCI, National Bank of Georgia, and First American, according to internal BCCI documents. The joint marketing was apparently made official in something called the Americas Coordinating Committee of the Bank of Credit and Commerce International. Clifford and Altman said this was done behind their backs.

When the congressional hearings concluded, there was still no proof that Clifford and Altman knew that BCCI had owned First American. Nonetheless, there was a multitude of clues — dating from the earliest days of the takeover battle — that could have alerted them to BCCI's true role.

- BCCI was obsessed with growth, and it established a presence in every major market where it was permitted to do so: in Britain, continental Europe, and throughout the Third World. Did it not seem odd to Clifford and Altman that BCCI would be content with nothing more than a few branches in the United States, the world's largest economy?
- The Arab investors were not only passive, they were all but

invisible, as noted in Chapter 4. Altman himself said that the Middle Eastern investors were told nothing about First American's buyout of the Virginia bank's minority stockholders, although it was a $30 million deal.

- After First American acquired National Bank of Georgia from Pharaon in 1987, it discovered pervasive BCCI influence there, according to Altman's testimony before the Kerry Committee. Did it not occur to Altman that this suggested that Pharaon was a front man for BCCI? If BCCI was willing to use one front man to control NBG, does it not follow that it would be capable of using other investors to pose as owners of First American?
- Clifford and Altman bought stock in First American with nonrecourse loans from BCCI, meaning that if they failed to service the loans, the stock would fall into BCCI's hands. Did it not occur to them that First American's Arab shareholders might have bought their stock in exactly the same way?

BCCI was not only forbidden to own stock in First American, it was also barred from exercising "controlling influence" over it. This meant, in essence, that First American had to be managed as a wholly autonomous institution. Nevertheless, journalists and congressional investigators turned up an extraordinary number of instances in which BCCI was involved in First American's affairs. Examples included the involvement of BCCI officials in the launching of FABNY, the purchase of the Bankers Trust branches, schemes for the joint marketing of services, and even the hiring of executives. Two senior officials were interviewed by Abedi before they were offered jobs: Robert G. Stevens, who served as president of First American Bankshares from 1982 to 1989, and Bruno Richter, the president of FABNY from 1983 to 1985. When confronted with each example, Clifford and Altman would typically reply in one of two ways: (1) it was done behind their backs or (2) it didn't matter, because BCCI didn't make the final decisions.

But there were also peculiar financial transactions of which the two lawyers were fully aware, deals that certainly undermined their claim of First American's autonomy. One strange deal was First American's 1987 purchase of NBG at what many observers regarded as an inflated price. Another was First American's investment in certificates of deposit issued by BCCI's ICIC dummy company. Finally, there were the investments by Clifford and Altman in First American's stock, a deal that could only make them feel beholden to BCCI.

. . .

In spite of this evidence, Clifford and Altman continued to insist that they did not know about the secret ownership and that they never permitted BCCI to influence First American. When that was not enough to silence the skeptics, they would swear that they were telling the truth. Clifford, in particular, repeatedly invoked his reputation. At the Kerry Committee hearings, he said, "Did [BCCI] corrupt First American? Not in any way. Do I ask you to take my word for that? I do. My word has been important here for a great many years in Washington."

But the credibility of Clifford and Altman was seriously damaged by a series of dubious statements to regulators, journalists, and congressional investigators. Clifford, for example, provided several conflicting accounts of who had asked him to run First American, which resulted in the following question from the Republican senator Jesse Helms. "Mr. Clifford," he asked, "I would like to clear up a question about who exactly asked you to take over the chairmanship of First American. In your testimony before the House Banking Committee and in press interviews, you stated that Mr. Abedi and Mr. Adham asked you to take the position. In your written responses to questions submitted by the House Banking Committee, you stated that you were asked by Mr. Adham. Finally, in your written statement before the House Banking Committee, you stated that the investors asked you to take the post. For the purposes of clarification, just who did ask you to take the post?"

Many other instances could be cited, but a few are sufficient to make the point.

- In August 1982, the Federal Reserve asked Clifford about a *Washington Post* article that said one of the investors in First American — Zayed's financial adviser Abdullah Darwaish — had been accused of defrauding the sheikh. Clifford, as noted in Chapter 3, told the Fed he had written to the *Post* to complain about "the gross inaccuracies in the article." When the Kerry Committee asked him for a copy of the letter, he replied in an affidavit: "I do not recall having written to the Editor of the *Washington Post* in response to that article."
- In a 1984 interview, Altman discussed how he and Clifford began representing BCCI and its Arab clients. The relationship, he said, did not come about through Bert Lance but stemmed from the law firm's "international practice." In 1991, however, he and

Clifford gave a different version: Lance had introduced them to BCCI.

- When First American was sued by former minority shareholders of its Virginia bank, the defense lawyers described the banking company as 100 percent foreign-owned; they based these statements, of course, on information from First American's management. Those statements were false because Clifford and Altman also held stock in the company.

- In a July 1989 interview, Altman said he had been to only one of BCCI's annual management conferences, when he had actually been to three.

- In May 1990, *Regardie's* magazine revealed that BCCI had channeled at least $500,000 in Noriega money through First American. When asked about this by the *Wall Street Journal,* Altman said that nothing in First American's files would have revealed that Noriega money had been channeled through the bank. In fact, First American cleared dozens of checks with Noriega's name clearly written on the memo line.

- In their prepared statement to the Kerry Committee, Clifford and Altman said, "There is no basis for any suggestion that First American may have been used by BCCI for money laundering." This, of course, is flatly contradicted by the fact that about $7 million in drug money was laundered through First American by BCCI officials in Operation C-Chase.

- Clifford and Altman have maintained in interviews and congressional testimony that BCCI became a client in February 1978. The law firm was hired because BCCI had just been sued by First American for its role in collecting stock in the banking company. Investigators have now found two documents that seem to contradict this version. One is an invoice from Clifford's law firm which covers work done in *January.* Another is a telex to Abedi from BCCI's Abdus Sami, stating that Clifford had been hired to assist BCCI in connection with the stock purchases. The telex is dated January 30, 1978 — more than two weeks before the lawsuit was filed.

One of the most sensitive issues for Clifford and Altman is that they were in constant communication with BCCI over the years and yet had little contact with the Arab investors who ostensibly owned the bank. Their response is that BCCI acted as an investment adviser and communications link to the Arabs. The problem with this answer is that they have provided several, often conflicting, descriptions of BCCI's role.

- In November 1978, Altman said in a letter to the Federal Reserve Bank of Richmond that BCCI had advised three of the initial investors in First American: Kamal Adham, Faisal Saud al-Fulaij, and Abdullah Darwaish. He said that people related to BCCI would probably advise the investors in the future.
- In April 1987, Altman was quoted as saying that BCCI advises the investors, presumably meaning *all* of the investors.
- In October 1988, Altman told the *Washington Post* that Abedi (not BCCI) advises the investors.
- In July 1989, Altman said that Abedi advised the initial four investors in First American until his illness. This is odd because Abedi became ill in early 1988, yet two of the initial investors (Sheikh Zayed's son Sheikh Sultan and Abdullah Darwaish) withdrew from the investment group several years before that. It is also worth noting that Altman did not tell the *Washington Post* that Abedi's advisory role ceased at the time of his illness.
- In March 1990, Altman said that Abedi had advised the investors at the time of the acquisition. Abedi continued as an adviser to some of the investors until his health problems. Altman added that BCCI was not now, as far as he knew, an adviser to the investors.
- In February 1991, Clifford was quoted in the *Washington Post* as saying that he had briefed BCCI's top executives about First American over the years because the shareholders had designated BCCI as their adviser.
- In a written statement to the House Banking Committee dated September 10, 1991, lawyers for Clifford and Altman said that Abedi had acted as an "investment adviser to the shareholders."
- In his September 1991 testimony to the House committee, Clifford referred to Abedi and BCCI as "investment advisers to these investors." He also indicated that Kamal Adham was involved in this process as well. "The shareholders," he said, "turned the responsibility of monitoring this investment over to Mr. Abedi and to Kamal Adham, and we understood that, so we reported to them rather than going around to report to fourteen other individual shareholders scattered all through the Persian Gulf."

- At the same hearing, Altman identified Abedi alone as the point of contact: "Mr. Abedi, we were told, had been selected by the shareholders. He was the investment adviser for these shareholders. He was the communications link between us and the shareholders."
- In their prepared statement to the Kerry Committee — and in their testimony — Abedi the adviser suddenly vanishes. "BCCI," says the statement, "performed the same communications function with respect to all the shareholders, including Sheikh Zaied [Zayed] and others." In oral testimony, Altman said, "It was understood by the regulatory authorities at the time, not that Mr. Abedi was the adviser to the shareholders, not that Mr. Abedi was the communications link, but that BCCI performed and would continue to perform those functions."

However it is expressed, this alleged "advisory" role is a critical part of Clifford and Altman's defense. The reason they met so often with BCCI officials and provided information about First American is that First American's shareholders wanted them to do so. In view of this, the Kerry Committee asked lawyers for Clifford and Altman to supply "all documents that reflect statements by the investors as [to] their desire that you keep BCCI informed of the financial progress of First American." There is apparently no such documentation. On October 11, 1991, the committee received this reply: "Messrs. Clifford and Altman were not instructed to do so in writing."

The very notion that Clifford and Altman had to use BCCI to communicate with First American's stockholders has been ridiculed by one former BCCI official, Abdur Sakhia. "They were not Bedouins in the desert who were being communicated [with]," Sakhia has said. "These were intelligent people who owned banks and businesses. The Abu Dhabi Investment Authority has several billion dollars' investment in this country, and if they can manage those businesses they did not need a channel via Mr. Abedi to First American. They could have done it directly."

During his tenure as a leader of Washington's legal community, Clark Clifford was the envy of many other attorneys. His firm was not very large — never more than about twenty lawyers — yet the client list included some of the most impressive names in corporate America. If larger firms can be compared to department stores, Clifford & Warnke was a boutique, with the patrician elegance of its founder. The decor resembled that of an old-fashioned men's club, with dark wood, hunting prints on the walls, and leather chairs. There was an air of permanence about the place; it seemed clear that the firm would outlive its founder for many years.

Clifford & Warnke did not survive. Like so many other individuals and institutions, it was engulfed in the BCCI scandal. In October 1991, a majority of the firm's seventeen lawyers were reported to be negotiating to join another Washington firm, Howrey & Simon. A partner there told a journalist that he was not concerned about the BCCI taint because none of Clifford & Warnke's banking lawyers would be joining his firm. By early December, only five lawyers remained: Clifford, Altman, and three others.

The disintegration of the law firm was just the latest in a series of blows to Clifford and his protégé. Their credibility had been battered in the press and in congressional hearings, and they had lost control of First American. Now the law practice that Clifford had established and nurtured was disappearing. But it was not the end of their traumas. For nearly two years, Robert Morgenthau's team of prosecutors and investigators had been gathering evidence on the two Washington lawyers who had played such an important role in the affairs of BCCI. Clifford and Altman might soon be fighting for their freedom.

15

THE WATCHDOGS

ON THURSDAY, SEPTEMBER 5, 1991, the U.S. Department of Justice announced the indictment of Swaleh Naqvi, five other former BCCI officials,* and a reputed Colombian drug baron, Gerardo ("Don Chepe") Moncada, on racketeering charges. The indictment, which had been returned on August 23, accused the defendants of channeling millions of dollars in drug money through BCCI. Assistant Attorney General Robert S. Mueller III said that at BCCI, racketeering was "a corporate strategy, a corporately countenanced operation."

The new indictment and Mueller's tough language made it appear that federal prosecutors were finally getting serious about BCCI. But there were a few peculiarities. For one thing, the indictment was based almost entirely on information developed in Operation C-Chase. Whereas Robert Morgenthau had broken important new ground in his indictment of the previous July, the Justice Department was serving up warmed-over information from an investigation that had ended nearly two years before.

Another peculiarity was the timing of the announcement. The new indictment was unveiled just minutes after Congressman Charles Schumer issued a report that sharply criticized the Justice Department and other federal law enforcement agencies for their handling of BCCI. The New York Democrat doubted that this was a coincidence. "I think they wanted to take the sting out of the report," Schumer told a

---

*Also named in this indictment were Syed Ziauddin Ali Akbar, Dildar Rizvi, and three former officials of BCCI's Panama operation: Bashir Shaikh, Wilfredo Glasse, and A. M. Bilgrami (not to be confused with Akbar A. Bilgrami, who had been convicted in the Operation C-Chase case). Another defendant was Capcom Financial Services Ltd.

reporter. "If they had done what we suggested in the report, they would have had these indictments years ago."

Justice's sensitivity about its image was understandable. After the seizure of BCCI, federal law enforcement agencies were subjected to withering criticism. BCCI had been used by such notorious criminals as Noriega, the Colombian cocaine baron José Gonzalo Rodríguez Gacha, and the penny stock fraudster Tommy Quinn — yet for years the cops had seemed as befuddled as Inspector Clouseau, the clumsy French detective in the *Pink Panther* movies.

The Schumer report showed that federal law enforcement agencies had received valuable information about BCCI long before Operation C-Chase. In 1983, the Customs Service was tipped off about Munther Bilbeisi, the Jordanian arms dealer and coffee smuggler who was later accused of trying to cheat a Lloyd's of London syndicate. The following year, the Internal Revenue Service was approached by Aziz Rehman, the former chauffeur at BCCI's Miami branch, and told of possible money laundering. Although IRS agents in Miami wanted to launch an undercover investigation of the bank, their superiors said no. In 1985, agents of the Drug Enforcement Administration and the IRS obtained strong evidence that BCCI was involved in laundering heroin money. That August, the head of an Iranian heroin ring introduced an undercover DEA agent (posing as a drug buyer) to a BCCI official. The agent taped a conversation in which the banker explained how to hide and launder drug money. (In the same conversation, there was an apparent reference to BCCI's secret takeover of Independence Bank.) This evidence was turned over to the IRS, which tried to collect back taxes from the Iranian, but the IRS did not open an investigation of BCCI.

No one put the pieces together. "Despite the fact that BCCI was cropping up repeatedly in a variety of places and in an array of questionable activities," said the Schumer report, "no one in the law enforcement community noticed the pattern." (After this report was issued, Schumer's staff did additional research and found that federal agencies had actually received hundreds of tips relating to BCCI over the years.) The report also criticized the government's decision to end Operation C-Chase in October 1988. Robert Mazur, the lead undercover agent, felt that if the probe had continued, he might have been able to meet representatives of Pablo Escobar, the cocaine kingpin. The Customs agent was even trying to set up a meeting with Naqvi, who was then the head of BCCI.

After the Tampa indictment, the government obtained new information about possible wrongdoing by BCCI, but there was little follow-up, partly because of a shortage of money and staff. Documents seized from BCCI filled dozens of boxes and contained a great deal of information and many further leads, according to the report. But much of this material was, according to one federal agent, "at best glanced at." Schumer's report put much of the blame on the Customs Service. Mazur was so disenchanted with the agency that he resigned in early 1991 and joined the DEA. He later compared the C-Chase team to "a reconnaissance squad that had been out in the middle of the desert and [was] encountering the enemy, and I sent word back to the fort that we needed some help. And [we] waited and fought and fought and fought but no help came."

The Justice Department also failed to devote adequate resources to the case. The Schumer report noted that Justice assigned only a handful of prosecutors to the case, compared with a veritable army on the other side. It noted that "over 50 lawyers from 20 different firms reportedly played a role in the case."

Schumer backed away from a full-scale condemnation of Justice. For example, his report rejected attacks on the plea bargain. "Recent criticisms that the plea agreement was unduly lenient would appear to be inaccurate," it said.*

One controversial clause of the agreement was that the U.S. attorney's office in Tampa would not charge BCCI "with committing any other federal criminal offenses under investigation or known to the government at the time of the execution of this agreement." Officials in the U.S. attorney's office have said repeatedly that this did not tie the hands of the government. During a hearing on the plea bargain on February 5, 1990, for example, Greg Kehoe, the first assistant U.S. attorney in Tampa, told Judge William Terrell Hodges that the agreement would not prevent other parts of the Justice Department from going after BCCI. The Schumer report accepts that argument: "The plea agreement plainly binds only the U.S. attorney's office for the

---

*One peculiar feature of the plea bargain that has generally been overlooked is that the defendant Capcom — which the government knew to be an affiliate of BCCI's — was not included in the deal, yet the prosecutors did not pursue that company. Capcom was apparently ignored by the Justice Department for a year and a half, when it was named as a defendant in a federal indictment announced on September 5, 1991. Justice Department officials maintain that British Customs had agreed to take responsibility for following up on Capcom.

Middle District of Florida, and that office only with respect to further prosecution of the convicted BCCI subsidiaries based on information known to the U.S. attorney's office at the time."

That may have been how the agreement was worded, but the Justice Department nonetheless failed to follow up other leads for several months. For example, Dexter Lehtinen, who served as acting U.S. attorney in Miami until January 1992, told the Kerry Committee that when he tried to pursue BCCI in 1990 in connection with other alleged crimes, his superiors in Washington told him that he could not do so — because of that clause in the plea bargain. Lehtinen wanted to prosecute both BCCI and Munther Bilbeisi for coffee smuggling and other offenses. In August 1991 — after the BCCI affair became an international scandal — Lehtinen was allowed to indict Bilbeisi along with his accountant. By that time, the statute of limitations for some of the most serious alleged offenses — including coffee smuggling — had passed, and Lehtinen was only able to charge the Jordanian (and his accountant) with tax fraud. By that time, of course, Bilbeisi was ensconced in Jordan, thumbing his nose at U.S. law enforcement.

The federal authorities' conduct was the target not only of criticism but of ridicule. One editorial cartoonist depicted the Justice Department as a band of policemen ready to charge into BCCI's headquarters with their guns drawn in order to arrest the criminals inside. But the building was gutted, the vault was empty, and all the culprits had fled.

One man who took much of the blame was Attorney General Richard Thornburgh, who ran the department until August 1991, when he resigned to run for the U.S. Senate in Pennsylvania in a special election occasioned by the death of the Republican John Heinz. James Carville, the campaign manager for the Democratic candidate, Harris Wofford, used the BCCI affair as a weapon against Thornburgh, and Wofford was elected. (Carville went on to manage the 1992 presidential campaign of Governor Bill Clinton of Arkansas.)

William P. Barr was named acting attorney general on Thornburgh's resignation, and soon after, President Bush appointed him to the post. On the eve of Barr's Senate confirmation hearing in November, a Justice Department spokesman said, "There've basically been three rules: aggressively pursue, spare no expense, and follow evidence wherever it leads." On November 12, Barr promised the Senate Judiciary Committee that he would do everything in his power to investigate BCCI and bring any miscreants to justice.

Just three days later, the Justice Department announced a new indictment, accusing BCCI, Abedi, Naqvi, and Pharaon of engaging in a racketeering conspiracy involving BCCI's illegal ownership of Independence Bank and 25 percent of CenTrust Savings Bank. The indictment also charged them with stock fraud because of the scheme to park CenTrust junk bonds at BCCI. That same day, the Senate Judiciary Committee voted unanimously to recommend Barr's confirmation; he was confirmed by the full Senate on November 20.

The November indictment certainly seemed to be a positive sign, but Justice was still playing catchup with Morgenthau. The federal prosecutors had yet to match the sweeping New York State indictment accusing BCCI of a multibillion-dollar fraud against its depositors. Moreover, there were indications that Justice was not nearly as aggressive as Barr had promised it would be. Important leads were still not followed, documents were not seized, potential witnesses were not interviewed. In late 1991, for example, a journalist telephoned several people who had been employed in BCCI's mysterious Washington representative office to find out what BCCI had been up to in the capital. Several of them were willing to talk to the reporter. When he asked if they had been approached by federal agents or prosecutors, they all said no. Around the same time, the reporter asked Pakistan's ambassador to Washington, Abida Hussain, about U.S. efforts to bring Abedi to justice. She insisted that no one from the federal government had mentioned to her any request for Abedi's extradition to the United States.*

Law enforcement authorities were not the only watchdogs criticized for their handling of BCCI. Bank regulators were also on the defensive. The BCCI affair was, after all, the biggest and most spectacular banking scandal of all time. BCCI insiders and their allies stole billions of dollars from depositors; secretly bought banks and companies in the United States, Britain, and other countries; laundered millions of dollars for drug traffickers and other criminals; and assisted in — or perpetrated — a vast array of other crimes. Throughout, bank regulators seemed to be largely oblivious.

It is particularly striking that this rampage occurred almost literally under the noses of two of the world's leading central banks. BCCI's

---

*In 1992, however, the Justice Department, working through the State Department, did apply for Abedi's extradition on behalf of the Manhattan district attorney's office and the U.S. attorney in Washington, D.C.

headquarters was just around the corner from the Bank of England. First American Bankshares' head office is a few blocks from the Federal Reserve.

The U.S. central bank allowed a group of BCCI's clients to buy First American in spite of a vast number of clues that they were front men for BCCI, as we have seen. In the fall of 1991, a congressional investigator discovered yet another clue that the Fed had overlooked. Kidder Peabody & Company, the Wall Street firm that assisted in the takeover, had registered with the Justice Department as a foreign agent. In a series of disclosure statements filed from 1978 to 1981, Kidder stated that its clients included BCCI, Abedi, and three dummy companies. There was no reference to the Arab investors who were supposedly buying the company!

After the takeover, the Fed and other U.S. regulators failed to detect — or ignored — several signs of the close ties between BCCI and First American. For example, the Fed was informed that Clifford and Altman had bought stock in First American, but years went by before regulators asked if the stock had been purchased with loans from BCCI. (Regulators were also oblivious of BCCI's quite open ties to NBG — including the fact that BCCI brochures were distributed to NBG customers.)

While the Fed was apparently in the dark, Robert Mazur of Customs stumbled on information about the true ownership of First American. When this information was passed on to the Fed in late 1988, there was hardly any follow-up. Similar information from other sources was brushed aside for two more years.

One of the strongest critics of the regulators was Henry Gonzalez of the House Banking Committee. He expressed astonishment that for so many years the Fed had been unaware that BCCI owned First American. The Federal Reserve, he said, "would have us believe that BCCI was a stealth banking operation, undetected on the regulators' radar screens." He then pointed out that criminals might well be the owners of other American banks without the regulators' knowledge. "If U.S. banks can so easily be invaded by foreign operators and if the takeovers can be kept secret so successfully, what protection exists in our banking system? What other foreign entities, or criminal elements, are secretly in control of U.S. banks at this very moment?"

On September 13 — a Friday, as it happened — the House Banking Committee questioned several Fed officials, including the general counsel, a nervous J. Virgil Mattingly, Jr., and the New York Fed's gravelly voiced president, E. Gerald Corrigan. The legislators wanted to know how BCCI might have used First American to influence important people in Washington. Mattingly responded that the Fed was investigating loans from First American to some former public officials in Washington. He noted that there was nothing necessarily wrong with such loans, since First American was, after all, a leading local bank. The Fed's counsel declined to provide any details of who, or what, the central bank was looking into.

Mattingly and his colleagues seemed confused and defensive when asked about their supervision of BCCI and the four U.S. financial institutions in which it had secretly acquired stock: First American, National Bank of Georgia, Independence Bank, and CenTrust. In an apparent attempt to shift some of the blame, the Fed officials alleged that the Bank of England had kept them in the dark about the huge loans that BCCI had made to finance the acquisition of First American. But Corrigan, toward the end of the September 13 hearing, slipped in the startling information that in the fall of 1989, a Bank of England official — the chairman of the College of Supervisors set up to monitor BCCI — told a Fed official that there were such loans and had even "asked if he could provide further information."

Unfortunately, no one on the committee seemed to recognize the importance of this disclosure. Corrigan was admitting that the Fed had been told in 1989 that BCCI had financed First American's shareholders on a large scale and that the Fed had effectively replied, "We don't want to know." It was a staggering admission of negligence. (It also completely undercut the Fed's earlier criticism of the Bank of England for not passing on such information.) It was not until December 1990 — after strong evidence was provided by Morgenthau and the College of Supervisors — that the Fed took serious steps to check out the allegations it had been hearing for two years.

In the wake of the Gonzalez hearing, the Federal Reserve — like the Justice Department — seemed eager to prove that it was now doing its job. On September 17, the Fed announced that it intended to fine Ghaith Pharaon $17 million for his role in the acquisition of Independence Bank. Acting on the Fed's behalf, the U.S. attorney in Manhattan obtained a court order freezing Pharaon's considerable U.S. assets.* On September 25, the Fed sought to impose a $20 million fine on Kemal Shoaib, the BCCI executive who had served as chairman of Independence until 1989. (Around this time, board members of the California bank filed a federal racketeering suit against Pharaon and Shoaib.)

At the time of the Fed's actions, Independence was in disastrous shape. It had already been weak when BCCI secretly acquired it in 1985; it was now virtually insolvent. By the end of September, its capital had dwindled to just $5.5 million, less than 1 percent of total assets. Some regulators wanted to use $35 million of BCCI's deposits in California to shore up the bank, but the scheme was vetoed by some of their colleagues. The bank was soon declared insolvent and taken over by the Federal Deposit Insurance Corporation in January 1992.

The Federal Reserve's aggressiveness in the summer and fall of 1991 could in no way make up for its incredible inaction in previous years. How could this possibly be explained? In defending their conduct, Fed officials have stressed repeatedly that BCCI was never licensed to collect retail deposits in the United States. Its state-licensed agencies in Florida, New York, and California were allowed to accept funds only from nonresidents, and those deposits were not covered by federal deposit insurance. That may have been the law, but it was flouted by BCCI — even after scrutiny of the bank was increased following the C-Chase indictment. From 1987 to 1990, BCCI conducted an illegal telemarketing program in the United States to collect deposits, and much of the money came from U.S. residents.

As far as First American was concerned, Fed officials denied that they had grounds for suspecting that the BCCI clients who took over the company were front men. Mattingly told Gonzalez's committee that "the Fed is not authorized to deny an application on suspicion or rumor, or even because it wants to. Under the law, we must have

---

*The prosecutor who filed the motion, Assistant U.S. Attorney Thomas Zaccaro, said that Pharaon had planned to sell his American Southern Insurance Company to Vista Resources for $35 million on September 18. The previous May, he had apparently sold his 80 percent stake in DLF Inc., which traded in the bank debt of Eastern European and Latin American companies.

In both deals, the buyers had interesting backgrounds. Vista Resources was controlled by the Georgia tycoon J. B. Fuqua. One of Pharaon's key lieutenants in the United States, Dooley Culbertson, used to work for Fuqua. (It is also worth noting that Fuqua was a prominent political supporter of BCCI's old friend Jimmy Carter.)

DLF was taken over by three former executives of Manufacturers Hanover Trust Company, which had been a major creditor of Pharaon's Saudi company, REDEC. One of the executives, Fulvio Dobrich, served as chairman of Independence Bank from 1989 until 1992.

evidence. The Fed had no grounds for denial and therefore gave its approval in August 1981."

The Fed tried hard to promote the idea that it did not have sufficient powers to police foreign banks in the United States. At the regulators' urging, Congress quickly enacted legislation giving it additional authority. The Fed can now review the establishment of any branch, agency, or commercial lending company by a foreign bank. It can also close foreign bank offices for a violation of the law or for unsound banking practices. Foreign banks are also required to report any loan secured by 25 percent or more of a U.S. bank's shares. But was the new legislation really needed? Sidney Bailey, the chief bank regulator in Virginia — and the only regulator who had opposed the takeover of First American — argued that the Fed already had the authority to block the acquisition in the early 1980s.

Rather than focusing on new laws, it would make sense for bank regulators in the United States and elsewhere to concentrate on changing their own practices and attitudes. Regulators in different countries took far too long to exchange information on BCCI. Many of the regulators also seem to have been terribly naive and gullible, incapable of imagining that a bank could be run by criminals.

The European regulators were just as blind as the Americans, in spite of having been warned of the dangers of allowing an international bank to fall between the regulatory cracks. Nearly a decade before BCCI was seized, the international financial world was shaken by a major banking scandal: the collapse of Italy's Banco Ambrosiano. In several ways it was a precursor of the BCCI affair. The chairman, Roberto Calvi, had committed massive frauds using banks he controlled through a Luxembourg holding company. When Ambrosiano crashed in 1982, it became clear that the Bank of Italy had little idea of what Calvi did outside Italy. The Institut Monétaire Luxembourgeois (IML) knew absolutely nothing because the Luxembourg holding company had not been licensed as a bank.

After that debacle, bank regulators took steps to coordinate the supervision of international banks. In spite of these reforms, BCCI remained a weakly regulated institution. No single regulator had a complete overview of its activities, and BCCI exploited these blind spots to the fullest. Abedi and his minions shifted loans and deposits from one corporate entity to another in a massive shell game.

Problems could have been averted if the regulators had exchanged information, but this was not done for years. One notable example concerns the report on BCCI prepared in 1978 by Joseph Vaez of the Office of the Comptroller of the Currency. Vaez, as we have seen, found that BCCI was in an extremely precarious financial condition, yet there is no indication that his report was passed on to the European regulators with primary responsibility for the bank. Of course, there is no reason that the Bank of England or the IML could not have uncovered this same information by conducting a similar inquiry. Had they done so, they could have forced BCCI to strengthen its balance sheet, sparing untold suffering to depositors in the 1990s.

It was not until 1988 that BCCI's regulators took serious steps to coordinate regulation by forming the College of Supervisors. But the Federal Reserve did not become a member, and it only began sending observers in 1991. While the Fed was absent, the other regulators discussed BCCI's huge loans to First American's stockholders — the "smoking gun" that later exposed many of these investors as front men.

After BCCI was shut down in July 1991, the Bank of England was sharply criticized by British politicians. At a hearing that month, Alan Beith, a Liberal Democrat member of Parliament, blasted Governor Robin Leigh-Pemberton. "Here was a bank," he said, "that had been convicted as a corporate body of money laundering. Here was a bank about which you knew, or had been told, that there were transactions which were false or deceitful, which you had been told about in April 1990 . . . yet a lot of people, some in public service, others in small businesses, continued to believe the bank enjoyed a clean bill of health from the Bank of England."

In the face of such attacks, Bank of England officials have insisted that it is not their job to detect crime. If people go out of their way to deceive the regulators, it is hard to find out the truth. "I really believe it is asking a lot of [auditors] or of supervisors necessarily to uncover deliberate and well-designed fraud," Leigh-Pemberton told the parliamentary panel. "The operation of a bank within a bank, the holding of files, which, as it were, were locked away and not shown to auditors in the normal audit seems to me to be a form of deception against which it is extremely difficult to guard and uncover."

In a similar vein, Pierre Jaans, the head of the IML, said that bank regulators should not be expected to play detective. "I was aware of rumors for years," he said, but "I was never able to find hard evidence." He added that if he had tried to withdraw BCCI's Luxembourg banking license, he probably would have lost in court.

When the Bank of England was accused of negligence, officials claimed that they did not have convincing evidence of fraud until early 1991. The Price Waterhouse reports from previous years, one central banker said, were mainly technical. "It was seen to be a bad bank but not a crooked bank," one official said. There are some at the Bank of England who now concede that they might have moved more swiftly to investigate BCCI. But, claims a senior official, this might have saved months, but certainly not years, in the time it took to unravel the fraud.

After BCCI was finally shut down, Leigh-Pemberton said the regulators acted because they had discovered that the bank had a "criminal culture." This, of course, ignores the substantial evidence of criminality that had emerged over the previous two and a half years as a result of the Tampa indictment. Leigh-Pemberton tried hard to downplay the importance of that case. In parliamentary testimony, he said, "There was no evidence that group level management was implicated or, except for two junior officers, [that] anyone in the UK management team was implicated." This statement is hard to accept. Shortly after the indictment, the prosecutor, Mark Jackowski, said in bond hearings that some of BCCI's bankers had told an undercover agent that their superiors were aware of the money laundering. In addition, the April 1989 superseding indictment stated explicitly that money laundering was part of BCCI's "corporate strategy." When BCCI pleaded guilty in January 1990, the Bank of England would have been fully justified in throwing it out of the country. An eloquent appeal to do so was made by an investigative reporter, Michael Gillard of the London *Observer,* five days after the plea bargain was announced.

> Under the Banking Act of 1987, the Bank of England can revoke or restrict a bank's authorization if it does not "conduct its business in a prudent manner." One of the key criteria is "whether the institution's business is carried on with integrity." The Bank's definition of integrity requires a bank to observe "high ethical standards in carrying on its business," declares its Statement of Principles regarding the powers to give or revoke authorization. "Criminal offences or other breaches of statute will obviously call into question the fulfilment of this criterion," the Bank warns.
>
> It is difficult to see how the required "high ethical standards" fit with BCCI pleading guilty to conspiring with its own officials and two representatives of Colombia's Medellín Cartel to commit tax fraud and launder the proceeds of cocaine sales or to launder some $14 million on behalf of the cartel.

The Bank of England did not revoke BCCI's license but allowed the bank to continue collecting deposits in Britain, even as evidence of

BCCI's "criminal culture" mounted. By the end of 1990 and the beginning of 1991, bank regulators had overwhelming evidence of BCCI's criminality. Even then, regulators in Britain and other countries dragged their feet about shutting down the bank.

The conduct of the bank regulators in the BCCI affair is not simply a matter of ineptitude. In some cases, BCCI had very cozy relationships with people responsible for supervising it. Some were lavishly entertained, others were given valuable gifts and expense-paid trips. Several bank regulators have been accused of taking bribes.

In the United States, BCCI had its biggest (overt) presence in Florida, which happens to be the only state where the chief bank regulator is elected to the post. Since the mid-1970s, that job has been held by Gerald Lewis, whose title is state comptroller. Lewis has acknowledged that BCCI offered him favors: the use of a car and driver and free lodging at a posh condominium in Miami. "I politely declined," he said. But he did fly on a corporate jet owned by CenTrust. Lewis's 1986 reelection campaign, according to a press report, "reimburse[d] CenTrust $1,506 for the airfare — exactly one day after receiving a $1,600 contribution from [Chairman David] Paul's bank subsidiary, CenTrust Finance Corp." As things turned out, Lewis proved to be one of the few regulators willing to take tough action against BCCI — even after he received a strange letter from a Justice Department official, Charles Saphos, asking him to allow BCCI to remain in business. In March 1990, Lewis refused to renew BCCI's license.

One curious transaction with a former state bank regulator occurred shortly after the First American takeover. The acquisition had to be approved by the New York State Banking Board, a panel that advises the state banking department on regulatory and legal matters. When the board took its first vote in November 1981, the takeover was rejected. In a vote four months later, the measure was approved. One of the votes switched was that of Muriel Siebert, the state banking superintendent. One condition attached to New York's approval was that First American would sell Bank of Commerce, a New York bank it controlled. The bank was disposed of with the assistance of none other than Muriel Siebert, who had just returned to the private sector. Siebert says she received a fee of "$50,000 or $100,000" for helping to find a buyer. She says this had nothing to do with her former role as a regulator.

On the federal level, several regulators wound up working for law firms with ties to First American. The Washington lawyer Baldwin

Tuttle worked in the Fed's general counsel's office until 1977, when he joined Kutak, Rock & Huie; he later joined Milbank, Tweed, Hadley & McCloy. Tuttle was an important member of the legal team led by Clifford that persuaded the Fed to permit BCCI's clients to take over First American. After the takeover was approved, he assisted Clifford and Altman in their representation of First American and BCCI. In his dealings with the Fed, Tuttle was, of course, negotiating with old colleagues, including one of his former bosses, the deputy general counsel Robert Mannion. It was Mannion who presided over the April 1981 hearing on the proposed takeover. In 1983, Mannion joined the Washington law firm of Arnold & Porter, which has done important work for First American and was also retained by BCCI after the Tampa indictment. Mannion has said he hasn't been directly involved in that work.

Perhaps the most intriguing job change was that of Robert Bench, a former associate deputy comptroller of the currency. It was at his request that Joseph Vaez prepared the report on BCCI in early 1978. This extraordinarily prescient document showed that BCCI had engaged in extremely reckless banking practices and could well be insolvent. In 1986, Bench was sent a copy of a CIA report on BCCI containing serious allegations of wrongdoing. (Bench, as we shall see, apparently suffered a bout of amnesia when asked about this report at a congressional hearing.) In 1988, Bench left the government to join Price Waterhouse. He consulted extensively for BCCI in 1988, 1989, and 1990. Curiously, Bench's arrival seems to have had little effect on Price Waterhouse's attitude toward BCCI.

The BCCI network even had a friend at the very top of the Federal Reserve. In January 1991, the Fed took its first serious disciplinary action against BCCI and First American: it issued cease and desist orders against both banks, requiring them to sever whatever connections they had with each other. Before the orders could be issued, they had to be voted on by the Federal Reserve Board. The only member "abstaining from this action," according to the minutes of the meeting, was the chairman, Alan Greenspan. He later explained that he had socialized "on several informal occasions" with Robert Altman.

Outside the United States, BCCI developed extremely close ties with a number of regulators, particularly in the Third World. In Pakistan alone, the bank hired a long list of bank regulators — either as employees or consultants. Examples included two former central bank governors, Rashid Ahmed and Iqbaluddin Ahmed. BCCI also recruited Naziruddin Ahmed, a former executive director of the State Bank of Pakistan, and two former chairmen of the Pakistan Banking Council, Ali Pirbhai and Mushtaq Yousufi.

BCCI also paid bribes to regulators, according to several sources. Alvin Rice, a former vice chairman of Bank of America who was involved in monitoring its investment in BCCI, has said that the bank thought nothing of making payoffs. As he put it, bank officials thought they could get around regulators by giving out "baksheesh." Robert Morgenthau found evidence of bribes to central bankers during the course of his investigation. In July 1991, as we have seen, he accused officials of Peru's central bank of taking $3 million in payoffs from BCCI. One year later, he would allege that BCCI made similar payments to central bankers or other financial officials in another eleven developing countries.

Akbar Bilgrami, one of the bankers convicted in Operation C-Chase, has described a payoff to an African central banker. In about 1980, said Bilgrami, Swaleh Naqvi asked him to take a senior official from Sudan's central bank on a shopping spree at Harrods in London. BCCI paid the bill — about £78,000 (well over $100,000). In return, the official was asked to place several million dollars of his country's foreign exchange reserves in BCCI.

BCCI's efforts to ingratiate itself with bank regulators were not confined to the Third World. In Britain, the bank is alleged to have lavished gifts on a Bank of England official. It was well known within BCCI that Abedi had given the official presents of Persian rugs, alleged Javangher Masud, who worked both for the Abu Dhabi Investment Authority and for one of the sheikhs who was a shareholder in BCCI. No proof has ever come out.

Robin Leigh-Pemberton, the governor since 1983, has not been accused of any wrongdoing, but he came to the Bank of England from an institution that had very close ties to BCCI, National Westminster, one of Britain's "big four" banks. NatWest acted as BCCI's clearing bank in London, which meant that it handled a huge volume of transactions for BCCI.

After the July 1991 shutdown, Abedi granted a few interviews to reporters. He was feeble and his mind was not very clear, but he recalled some of the friends who had helped him over the years. He spoke of politicians like Jimmy Carter and Lord Callaghan but also referred to British financial institutions: "They were all helpful, the

Bank of England, NatWest, they all helped, and if I go to them again they will again be helpful."

To a certain extent, criticism of the conduct of law enforcement agencies and central banks is misplaced. These agencies may be staffed by civil servants, but the people who run them are chosen by politicians. In the United States, that means the president. The Federal Reserve chairmen, attorneys general, and other top officials whose handling of BCCI has been criticized were all chosen by Carter, Reagan, or Bush. It thus seems reasonable to ask whether political influence helps to explain the conduct of the watchdogs. After all, BCCI was for years protected and defended by friends in high places.

The Reagan-Bush Justice Department certainly seems to have been vulnerable to lobbyists. Richard Thornburgh, the former attorney general, often talked tough about crime, but he seemed to have a blind spot when it came to white-collar crooks, including savings and loan bandits and money-laundering bankers. In March 1990 — two months after the Tampa plea bargain was announced — Thornburgh "withdrew the Justice Department's longstanding support for tough mandatory sentences for corporate criminals," the *Washington Post* reported. Thornburgh switched his position "following an intense lobbying campaign by defense contractors, oil companies and other Fortune 500 firms, according to administration officials and department correspondence."

In August 1991, Jack Blum appeared as a witness before the Kerry Committee and spoke of how BCCI had employed well-connected lawyers and lobbyists after the C-Chase indictment to squelch investigations of the bank. There was "an army of people working in Washington on all sides trying to say this bank was a wonderful bank, the people involved in it were honest, good, and true people, and that anybody who said they were the criminals that I was making them out to be had to be crazy."

Shortly after Blum made these remarks, another Washington insider enlisted in that army, a young lawyer who had been employed in a sensitive position in the White House. He would now be working for one of the prime culprits in the BCCI affair.

16

===

THE POLITICIANS

ED ROGERS WAS ON A PLANE to Jiddah, Saudi Arabia, savoring the comforts of life in the private sector. It was August 31, 1991, just over three weeks after the ambitious young lawyer had left the White House and his job as political director for President Bush's chief of staff, John Sununu. The thirty-three-year-old Rogers and his old friend and new law partner Haley Barbour — a former Reagan White House official — were planning to cash in their government experience. Their mission: to negotiate a fat contract to represent Kamal Adham, the BCCI front man. American and British prosecutors were building strong criminal cases against the Saudi sheikh, and he wanted to cut an advantageous deal.

Rogers would later explain to congressional investigators how he and Barbour marketed themselves to clients. Their particular expertise, he said, was "managing other people's affairs, managing other people's problems, managing other people's business." In Adham's case, there was "an organizational problem," because the Saudi businessman had "a large business concern that needed a lot of different kinds of representation." Rogers intimated that the organizational difficulty he was managing for Adham was "the sheikh's problems with the feds."

After Rogers and Barbour spent three days talking with Adham and his legal and financial advisers, they struck a deal. The sheikh would pay Rogers $600,000 to represent him for two years. Shortly after returning home, Rogers received a check for $136,000 as a down payment on his contract. Once he had the money, he registered with the Justice Department as a foreign agent, saying that his work on behalf of the sheikh might "border on the political."

In late September and October, Rogers returned to the Middle East for meetings with Adham and the sheikh's advisers. On the latter trip, Rogers twice ran into Assistant U.S. Attorney David Eisenberg, who had come to Jiddah from Washington to hear Adham's version of his dealings with BCCI. Both Rogers and the Justice Department maintain that these were but fleeting encounters.

While Rogers was in Jiddah in October, news of his work for Adham broke in the United States and in the international media. The sheikh's hiring of a political operative who had so recently left the Bush administration and who had virtually no legal experience provoked an uproar. Rogers's involvement underlined to the public how BCCI and its backers routinely tried to buy influence to get around obstacles. In the *New York Times,* William Safire lambasted Rogers as "a Sununu toady" who was helping "an oil-backed elite."

The Bush administration lost no time in criticizing Rogers's contract. On October 25, at a White House press conference, President Bush said that he didn't know what Ed Rogers "is selling." Not long after that, Rogers said that he had canceled the contract.

It is heartening that Bush would distance himself from the Adham-Rogers deal, but it is also somewhat inconsistent. BCCI and its allies had an extraordinary number of connections to associates of President Bush, including financial supporters, top administration officials, and members of his immediate family. There may even have been a connection to the president himself. During the same press conference, Bush said he didn't "know anything about the man," without making it clear whether he was referring to Rogers or Adham. Bush had sat in numerous meetings attended by Rogers, according to Rogers's own testimony to congressional investigators. As for Adham, Bush was head of the CIA when Adham ran Saudi intelligence, and the two agencies worked closely together.

Weeks after the press conference, Adham spoke about his relationship with Bush in an interview in Cairo with the Middle East News Network. "There was a period of overlap," he said, referring to their respective jobs. "But whatever the case, it isn't possible for a president to say that." Referring to the press conference, Adham added, "The next day, nobody mentioned the White House spokesman came out and said that the president knows Mr. Adham and he did not like what was written in the papers." (The White House denies that Bush knows Adham.)*

---

*Through his lawyer, Adham says Bush did not know him personally but that Bush most likely would have known of him.

Senator Kerry's staff conducted an investigation of Rogers's involvement with Adham but came to no firm conclusions about how he had ended up working for the sheikh. When Kerry's staff members asked Rogers who had steered him to Adham, he maintained that the suggestion came from Samir Darwisch, the general manager of Washington's Grand Hotel, in the summer of 1991, a version of events that the investigators eventually judged "shallow and unconvincing." During an apparent misunderstanding in one interview, Rogers seemed to imply that he had met with a representative of Adham's in March 1991, though he then quickly denied it. The investigators have speculated that Rogers may indeed have started to negotiate much earlier than he now admits, and might well have had such a meeting in March 1991 — five months before he left the White House. Rogers insists that he never heard of Adham when he worked at the White House, adding, "There's no evidence that I did anything wrong."

Certainly, Rogers admitted meeting an intriguing assortment of characters as he made his overtures to Adham. These included the Saudi arms dealer Adnan Khashoggi; Sam Bamieh, a big Bush campaign contributor with ties to Khashoggi and Adham; and Sandra Charles, a former aide to Frank Carlucci. (Carlucci served in the Reagan administration as deputy secretary of defense and national security adviser. Under Carter, he was deputy director of the CIA.) Rogers admitted discussing Adham with Charles and Bamieh but denied talking about him with Khashoggi.

The Rogers incident for the first time focused attention on the role of the White House in the BCCI affair, and especially on President Bush. BCCI's connections to associates of Bush fueled public suspicion that political influence may help to explain the administration's astonishingly slipshod handling of the entire scandal.

There were tantalizing signs that seemed to indicate that the president knew more about the bank than he was prepared to admit. Over the years, his own career had at times taken him very close to BCCI and its backers in Saudi Arabia.

During Bush's tenure as CIA director, the agency was allegedly involved in a very curious business deal with James R. Bath, a Texas businessman who is a friend and sometime financial backer of one of Bush's sons. Bath was also a business associate of Khalid Bin Mahfouz, an important BCCI insider.

For years, the CIA secretly owned several airline companies — "proprietaries" in agency jargon. The most famous of these was Air America, which ferried CIA agents around Southeast Asia during the Vietnam War. After the CIA scandals of the 1970s, the agency was obliged to dispose of much of its fleet, and in 1976 it sold several planes to Skyway, a firm managed by Bath, according to Bill White, a former business partner of his. Bath denies any CIA involvement in the deal. White, who has been in bitter litigation with Bath for years, also says that Skyway was owned by Saudi interests, including Bin Mahfouz. Later, as we shall see, Bath provided financing to George W. Bush, the future president's eldest son, when he went into the oil business.

Returning to the private sector in early 1977, Bush became chairman of the executive committee of the First International Bank of Houston. He traveled on the bank's behalf and sometimes marketed to international banks in London, including several Middle Eastern institutions. Some speculate that he met with BCCI officers at this time.

When Bush ran for president a decade later, several people connected with BCCI offered to help. One intriguing example is Mohammed Rahim Motaghi Irvani, an Iranian immigrant with multiple ties to BCCI, as noted in Chapter 6. In 1987, Irvani wrote to James A. Baker III, Bush's campaign manager, saying he would like to help in the race. The letter was forwarded to Baker by former CIA director Richard Helms, with a note describing Irvani as "a man of substance and decency."

One important Bush supporter was Jackson Stephens, the Arkansas investment banker. Stephens, of course, had played a crucial role in BCCI's penetration of the U.S. market by collecting First American stock for Abedi's supposed clients. Stephens's wife, Mary Anne (they have since been divorced), ran Bush's 1988 campaign in Arkansas. In that campaign, Stephens was a member of Team 100 — individuals who had given $100,000 to the party. In May 1991, his brokerage firm, Stephens Inc., kicked in $100,000 to a Bush dinner committee.

As regulators, journalists, and prosecutors probed the failed bank in the fall of 1991, they found that Stephens and some of his associates had retained their connections with the BCCI network long after the First American takeover. Stephens has tried hard to convey the idea that he played a peripheral role in the events leading up to the First American takeover battle and that, in any event, his involvement with BCCI ended a long time ago. In fact, close associates of Stephens's have been involved in the BCCI saga during the 1990s. After BCCI was seized, the banking authorities in Hong Kong tried to find a buyer for Bank of Credit and Commerce (Hong Kong) Ltd. Through the end of

1991, it seemed likely that Indonesia's Lippo Group would take over the bank, paying out as much as forty cents on the dollar. (The plan was scuttled in February 1992, when Hong Kong investigators discovered previously unrecorded claims of $145 million against the bank.) Lippo is run by Mochtar and James Riady, financiers and associates of the Indonesian president, Suharto. The Riadys are very close to Stephens: together they controlled Stephens's Worthen Bank of Little Rock, Arkansas; one of them even lived in Little Rock for a few years.

Also in Bush's Team 100 was the California real estate investor Sam Bamieh, who was, of course, one of the people with whom Ed Rogers discussed working for Adham. A Palestinian American, Bamieh has developed strong ties to the Republican party in recent years. Rogers explained to congressional investigators in 1992 that he met Bamieh in 1988 through their mutual friend the late Lee Atwater, who helped to mastermind Bush's victory in 1988 and then became chairman of the Republican National Committee.*

After Bush took office in January 1989, he recruited a number of people with ties to BCCI associates. Two of his most important foreign policy advisers were Brent Scowcroft, the national security adviser, and Lawrence S. Eagleburger, the deputy secretary of state (and, since August 1992, acting secretary of state). Both men, as we have seen, had come from Kissinger Associates, which also employed a BCCI front man as a consultant (the former Brazilian diplomat Sergio Correa da Costa) and which provided advice to BCCI after the Tampa indictment. While serving as head of the National Security Council, Scowcroft has done business in Pakistan, where the government is headed by a BCCI ally, Prime Minister Nawaz Sharif.

Scowcroft was also an important shareholder in the now-defunct National Bank of Washington (NBW), as were several other people with intriguing connections. A major shareholder in the bank was the Saudi investor Wafic Said, who is close to the kingdom's defense minister, Prince Sultan. A board member of Said's holding company and NBW was the banker Robert Abboud, who had ties to the Bin Mahfouz family. A large chunk of NBW stock was owned by partners in Paul Laxalt's law firm, which represented BCCI in the Tampa case. NBW's directors had included Thomas Hale ("Tommy") Boggs, Jr., whose law firm, Patton, Boggs & Blow, would later represent Sheikh Zayed and BCCI. (Back in the 1970s, Clifford had been on the board of NBW.)

---

*Bamieh also had ties to the Democrats. In the late 1970s he paid for a trip to the Middle East by Ruth Carter Stapleton, President Carter's sister.

Several Bush Cabinet members and White House aides socialized with Robert Altman and his wife. In the fall of 1990, the Altmans held a surprise birthday party at their Potomac, Maryland, home for Michael Boskin, chairman of the President's Council of Economic Advisers. Several of Boskin's friends lined up in the mansion's huge atrium wearing Groucho Marx masks to lampoon the economist's prominent nose, eyebrows, and spectacles. The guests included Secretary of Commerce Robert Mosbacher, White House Chief of Staff John Sununu, and Jack Kemp, the secretary of housing and urban development.*

Altman was particularly close to Mosbacher and Samuel Skinner, who served as transportation secretary and then as White House chief of staff. Lynda Carter, Altman's wife, socialized with their wives, Georgette Mosbacher and Honey Skinner. Mosbacher, an oil tycoon from Texas, had raised large amounts of money for Bush's 1988 presidential run before taking over the Commerce Department. In 1991, he left that post to become director of Bush's reelection campaign. When he served in the cabinet, he talked to Altman at least every couple of weeks, according to an aide; he once left Scowcroft on hold in the middle of a conversation as he chatted with Altman on another line.

One Bush administration official who pops up in the story is Nicholas Brady, the treasury secretary. A confidant of the president's, Brady has spent most of his career as an investment banker with Dillon, Read in New York. An important client in the 1970s was Sonatrach, Algeria's government-owned oil company. During the same period, Clark Clifford was a foreign agent for the Algerians, and one of his duties was assisting Sonatrach in its foreign borrowing.

Another Dillon, Read client at that time was General George Olmsted, who controlled First American. When the Federal Reserve forced Olmsted to dispose of his stock, he was advised by Brady's firm. In 1977, he sold a controlling stake in the company to the Middendorf group, which included Peter Flanigan, a managing director of Dillon, Read. In other words, Dillon, Read officials were on both sides of the transaction.†

---

*When the BCCI scandal blew up in 1991, Boskin tried to distance himself from Altman. He admitted, through a spokesman, that the two families had twice vacationed in Colorado, but said they "skied on different mountains."

†Dillon, Read also had a Saudi connection. In 1981, the firm was acquired by Bechtel, the San Francisco construction concern which then did a massive volume of business in Saudi Arabia. Around that time, two top officials at Bechtel joined the Reagan administration, Secretary of State George Shultz and Caspar Weinberger.

When Brady was named treasury secretary in 1988, he became the boss of William von Raab, the Customs commissioner whose agency was responsible for Operation C-Chase. In early 1989, von Raab was suddenly removed from the case (as was William Rosenblatt, the assistant commissioner for enforcement), ostensibly because he was suspected of leaking information to journalists. Von Raab says that this was the only time he was ever taken off a case during his eight years as head of Customs. He says he doesn't know if Brady personally made the decision to remove him, but he says it had the effect of undermining the investigation: "Effectively, the engine — the generator — from the commissioner's office with respect to the BCCI case was stopped. It's very important in a police organization when they see the head of the organization is no longer driving the case."

Was Brady lobbied by BCCI as part of its efforts to secure a plea bargain? Brady has denied meeting with Clifford. Von Raab has no knowledge of a Clifford-Brady meeting but he does think the BCCI's aggressive lobbying campaign had some effect on the department. "I believe," he says, "that the Treasury Department was influenced by lobbying."

In the White House press conference in October 1991, Bush implied that he knew very little about BCCI or its backers. If he had wanted to find out more, he could have asked his own children. His daughter Dorothy is said to be close to the Altmans. Furthermore, two of the president's sons were linked to BCCI in several different ways.

John E. ("Jeb") Bush socialized frequently with Abdur Sakhia, the manager of BCCI's Miami branch and later the bank's top official in the United States. Sakhia has said that his family and Bush's got together several times, maybe a dozen in all. (Bush plays down the relationship, but declines to discuss it in any detail.) Jeb Bush's real estate company, Bush Klein Realty, also manages Grove Island apartments, a complex of luxury condominiums where Sakhia lived and where BCCI financed several real estate deals. Bush was involved in real estate projects with a number of controversial businessmen in Florida, including Alberto Duque, a BCCI customer.*

George W. Bush has even closer ties to the BCCI network. He likes

---

*Duque, a Colombian coffee importer, made a big splash in Miami in the late 1970s by investing heavily in real estate and by cultivating prominent people. When his business empire collapsed in the early 1980s, it turned out that one of his creditors was BCCI.

to point out that he is a second-generation oilman. In 1953, his father cofounded Zapata Petroleum, which turned into a highly successful company. The way he tells the story, it sounds like a classic entrepreneurial venture. What he seldom mentions is that wealthy friends of the Bush family provided important financing.

Decades later, George W. Bush plunged into the oil business in Texas. He has not been nearly so successful, but there is an important similarity: rich and powerful friends have financed him. When he set up Arbusto Energy Inc. in the 1970s, some of the financing came from James R. Bath, the Texas businessman who, as we have seen, was allegedly involved with Khalid Bin Mahfouz in the purchase of airplanes from the CIA. Bath had other ties to BCCI insiders: he has invested money in the United States on behalf of Bin Mahfouz and he was a part-owner of Houston's Main Bank with Bin Mahfouz and Ghaith Pharaon. Arbusto fell on hard times in the mid-1980s, when it merged with another struggling oil concern to form Spectrum 7 Energy Corporation. But Spectrum 7 didn't prosper, either. In 1986, Harken Energy Corporation rode to the rescue, swapping some of its shares to acquire Spectrum 7. George W. Bush got roughly $600,000 worth of stock, joined the board of directors, and became a consultant to Harken for $120,000 a year.

Harken, a small and relatively obscure firm, was not particularly successful either. In 1987, it was rescued from financial trouble through a debt restructuring. A few years later, the company's fortunes changed dramatically. In January 1990, Harken Energy was awarded one of the most coveted oil deals in the world: a concession to drill for crude oil off the coast of Bahrain. The decision stunned many people in the industry. Harken was not only a small firm, it had never drilled outside the United States, nor had it drilled offshore. The only explanation that made sense to many oil executives was that the Bahrain government wanted to do a favor for the family of President Bush.

The deal was certainly profitable for George W. Bush. After the concession was awarded to Harken, its stock price rose sharply. In mid-1990, Bush sold two thirds of his Harken shares at a big profit. (He failed to disclose this sale for several months — a violation of SEC rules.) The *Wall Street Journal* reported in December 1991 that "his remaining stake could still be worth millions if Harken hits a gusher in Bahrain."

The Bahrain contract was signed on January 30, 1990, exactly two weeks after the BCCI plea bargain was announced. Although no proof has emerged that the Bahrain deal influenced the drug money case, it is worth noting that an extraordinary number of people connected to Harken or the oil deal have ties to BCCI.

- Harken's investment banker is the same firm that helped Abedi's front men scoop up stock in First American: Stephens Inc. It was Stephens Inc. that helped Harken cope with its debts in 1987, and it did so by arranging financing from Union Bank of Switzerland (UBS), BCCI's partner in its Swiss affiliate Banque de Commerce et de Placements. Former Stephens Inc. executives represented Harken in the Bahrain deal.
- Bahrain's prime minister, Sheikh Khalifa bin-Salman al-Khalifa, helped to ensure that Harken was awarded the offshore drilling contract. Sheikh Khalifa, a brother of Bahrain's ruler, was a BCCI stockholder, according to a 1990 shareholder list.
- Sheikh Abdullah Taha Bakhsh, a big shareholder in Harken, has made investments in Saudi Arabia with Ghaith Pharaon, BCCI's most important front man. The sheikh's principal banker is another BCCI insider, Bin Mahfouz. Bakhsh took over Union Bank of Switzerland's shares in Harken when UBS ran into regulatory snags. (Bakhsh's investments are managed by a board member of Harken, Talat Othman, who has visited the White House on three occasions to discuss Middle Eastern policy with President Bush.)
- One of Harken's consultants on the Bahrain deal, Michael Ameen, considers Kamal Adham a close friend and has a long-standing acquaintance with Pharaon.
- The U.S. ambassador to Bahrain at the time of the deal was Charles Hostler, an old associate of another BCCI front man, Mohammed Hammoud. Hostler, who was appointed ambassador after contributing $100,000 to Bush's 1988 election campaign, has said that he had no involvement with the Harken deal.

All these parties deny any attempt to influence the Bush administration by helping either Harken or George W. Bush. The White House and the president's son also deny any impropriety. Marlin Fitzwater, the White House spokesman, says, "There is no conflict of interest, or even the appearance of a conflict of interest, in these business arrangements."

Any organization hoping to wield power in official Washington would of course be happiest if it could gain the president's ear or influence those closest to him. But ties to the legislative branch can also be valuable. Conveniently, anyone who set out to influence Congress wouldn't have to make connections with hundreds — or even dozens — of members. It would be sufficient to forge ties with a few critical people in the Senate and the House. And BCCI and its allies were unquestionably interested in securing influence on Capitol Hill. Powerful congressmen could help the bank and its associates by intervening on their behalf to slow, contain, or perhaps even stop legal and enforcement action. Equally important, congressmen could also hurt them. BCCI was fully aware that congressional committees could hold embarrassing hearings on their operation. BCCI's Middle Eastern patrons were eager to ensure continued access to American arms and military support. Not surprisingly, then, the bank and its allies seem to have cultivated a number of congressmen, those with influence in the judiciary, commerce, defense, banking, and foreign affairs committees. These were all potential pressure points on the bank or its Arab backers.

Clifford and his partners helped to foster several of these relationships by giving money to political campaigns. In 1991, it was estimated that members of Clifford's firm had given almost $150,000 to Democratic campaign committees since 1985. Beneficiaries of Clifford's contributions have included several moderate Democrats who have been contenders (or potential contenders) for the presidency, including Congressman Richard A. Gephardt of Missouri and Senators Joseph R. Biden, Jr. (Delaware), Bill Bradley (New Jersey), Al Gore, Jr. (Tennessee), Charles Robb (Virginia), and John D. Rockefeller IV (West Virginia).

Altman has also been a generous donor. In 1991, it was reported that he had made about $23,872 in federal contributions since 1987. He gave $500 to two Democratic candidates during the 1988 presidential race, Governor Michael Dukakis of Massachusetts and Congressman Gephardt. Altman's wife contributed $4,000 to candidates for federal office in 1987–88, including $1,000 to the presidential campaign of the Republican senator Robert Dole of Kansas. She also gave to Congressman John Dingell of Michigan.

Dingell was one congressman whom BCCI might have feared. He chairs the powerful Energy and Commerce Committee and is widely regarded as the Grand Inquisitor of Capitol Hill because of that panel's aggressive investigations. He might well have used his authority to look into either BCCI or some of its affiliates, such as Capcom, the bank's futures and commodities affiliate. But Dingell has never drawn a bead on BCCI, perhaps because of his high regard for Altman. The Michigan congressman and the Washington lawyer have been close for years, as have their wives. Dingell, a keen hunter, taught Altman how to shoot. The congressman has also borrowed from First American. In 1988, he received a $90,000 mortgage for seventy-two acres of property and a hunting lodge in Virginia. (Dingell says that he and his wife have been customers for many years and that the loan was granted at market rates.) When Clifford came under attack in early 1991, the congressman's wife, Debbie, told a reporter, "I just don't think Clark Clifford could be involved with anything that isn't on the up-and-up."

Claiborne Pell, who chairs the Senate Foreign Relations Committee, could have played a leading role in investigations of the bank. But he has deferred to his junior, John Kerry. Pell has never been totally comfortable with Kerry's inquiry, perhaps because he is an old friend of Clifford's and has received campaign money from the venerable lawyer. In May 1991, when Kerry was busily probing BCCI, Pell attended the party held by Pamela Harriman to celebrate the publication of Clifford's memoirs.

Senator Sam Nunn of Georgia, the chairman of both the Armed Services Committee and the Permanent Subcommittee on Investigations, was another person who could certainly have hurt or helped the bank. In recent years, his investigations panel has conducted complex probes of organized crime and the abuse of bank secrecy by money launderers and other criminals. In fact, it was at a hearing of this committee in January 1988 that Leigh Bruce Ritch, the convicted drug trafficker, said he had used BCCI's facilities in Panama. There was apparently no follow-up. By contrast, testimony by Ritch's partner, Steven Michael Kalish, and other witnesses prompted the Kerry Committee's probe of Noriega and BCCI. One possible explanation for Nunn's failure to look into BCCI is that such a probe would draw attention to his own connections to the BCCI network.

Nunn is well acquainted with Charles Jones, a lawyer in Hinesville, Georgia, who represented Ghaith Pharaon for years. It was Jones who spearheaded the lobbying campaign that made it possible for First American to buy National Bank of Georgia. (Before the takeover could go through, the Georgia legislature had to modify state banking law.) The senator has acknowledged meeting with Pharaon on four occasions between 1984 and 1990; he says they discussed Middle Eastern affairs.

Bob Graham, a Florida Democrat who sits on the Senate Banking Committee, was also acquainted with BCCI. He attended the opening of BCCI's Latin American regional headquarters in Miami as governor of Florida. He also met with Abdur Sakhia, BCCI's former Miami branch manager. Like many other politicians, Graham flew on Cen-Trust's corporate jet.

The Senate Banking Committee could have been an ideal vehicle for probing BCCI, but the chairman, Donald Riegle, ignored repeated requests from Kerry in 1990 and early 1991 to do so. Finally, in May 1991, one of the subcommittees conducted a single hearing on BCCI. The timidity of this committee is not surprising in view of the ties of Riegle and four of the other members to Charles Keating, the head of Lincoln Savings and Loan who was later convicted of fraud. It would certainly have been awkward for Clifford and Altman to appear before the full committee with their lawyer, Robert Bennett, at their side, for it was Bennett who had headed the Senate Ethics Committee's investigation of "the Keating Five."

After the July shutdown, Riegle was no longer able to resist pressure for an inquiry, and he assigned two investigators to the task. One of them was Timothy McTaggart, a lawyer who had worked for San Francisco's Morrison & Foerster. McTaggart was certainly familiar with the bank. While employed at the San Francisco firm, he some-times assisted one of its most important clients, BCCI.

Other important congressional committees have done little or noth-ing to look into BCCI. Neither the Senate nor House Intelligence Committee has shown much interest in the scandal in spite of BCCI's ties to the CIA and the involvement of Saudi intelligence officials in the affair.

The Senate Judiciary Committee, which is responsible for overseeing the Justice Department, has not held a single hearing on the conduct of federal law enforcement agencies in the BCCI case. (In contrast, Congressman Schumer of New York, a member of the House Judiciary Committee, has issued two critical reports on the Justice Department.) The chairman of the Senate's panel, Joseph Biden of Delaware, has received campaign money from the chairmen of two U.S. financial institutions in which BCCI invested through front men: Clark Clif-ford of First American and David Paul of CenTrust. Paul and his associates gave Senator Biden $10,000 for his 1988 presidential cam-paign.

A senior Republican on Biden's committee, Orrin Hatch of Utah, went to great lengths to publicize CenTrust's ties to BCCI and Paul's extraordinary generosity to Democratic politicians. In August 1991, he issued a strongly worded report on the "interlocking relationship" between CenTrust and BCCI. One obvious motive, of course, was to embarrass the rival political party. But Hatch could well have had another goal: to deflect attention from his own intriguing ties to BCCI.

Senator Hatch seems to be the very picture of rectitude. He's a conservative politician from a conservative state and a bishop in the Mormon church. Throughout his political career, he has campaigned against immorality and advocated traditional family values. During the 1991 hearing by the Judiciary Committee on Clarence Thomas's nomination to the Supreme Court, Hatch seemed to be a kind of Cotton Mather figure, a Puritan who felt profound, visceral disgust at the subjects under discussion: pornographic films, sexual advances, and crude speech. It therefore seems strange that Hatch, of all people, would rush to the defense of BCCI, a bank that had pleaded guilty to money laundering. But that is what he did in his speech to the Senate on February 22, 1990.

Hatch said that he had been briefed about the plea bargain by Justice Department officials, adding in a subsequent interview that he had "chatted with people around [Attorney General Richard] Thornburgh." He also acknowledged having met with BCCI's defense lawyers — something he had failed to mention in the speech — and that Robert and Lynda Altman were close friends of his. But the senator's ties to the BCCI network were much closer than those remarks suggested.

It was only in November 1991, almost two years after the strange speech, that the true story of Hatch's relationship with BCCI began to emerge. Several of his connections were revealed in the *Wall Street Journal* and on the *NBC Nightly News*. Since then, further revelations have come from Hatch's office and people close to the senator.

As it turns out, Altman met with the senator several times before he gave the speech, according to a close associate of the senator's. There were so many meetings, says this source, that he "practically lived in Hatch's office." Moreover, Altman and other lawyers for BCCI did more than simply brief the senator, they essentially outlined the speech for him. Nearly all of its essential elements are contained in a January 9, 1990, letter from Altman to Hatch. In one passage, for example,

Altman stated, "It isn't alleged that the bank employees charged ever dealt with or accepted cash." He also implied that BCCI and its employees were largely blameless in the Tampa case, the victims of "unscrupulous customers."

When Hatch was later criticized for his speech, he claimed that he believed at the time that BCCI was a reputable bank. In fact, he had been warned months before that BCCI was anything but respectable, according to Michael Pillsbury, a former member of Hatch's staff. Pillsbury has told investigators that he gave a series of memos to Hatch in the late fall of 1989 in which he explicitly warned the senator about having dealings with BCCI. Nevertheless, said Pillsbury, Hatch persisted in dealing with Altman.

But does Pillsbury have clean hands? Although he says he warned Hatch to stay away from BCCI, it appears that Pillsbury himself was assisting the bank. Investigators for Senator Kerry have found considerable evidence that Pillsbury provided advice to BCCI's defense lawyers and its PR firm, Hill and Knowlton, in 1989 and 1990. According to notes taken by one of the defense lawyers, Pillsbury offered suggestions on how to deal with Kerry's investigation.

Even though Senator Hatch's speech, as noted in Chapter 11, was filled with inaccuracies, it was very helpful to BCCI. At the time, the bank was trying to persuade state bank supervisors in New York, California, and Florida not to pull its licenses, and its lawyers sent copies of the speech to the regulators.

One good turn deserves another, of course. Shortly after delivering the speech, Hatch asked BCCI to lend money to a friend of his. He called the chief executive, Swaleh Naqvi, to ask whether BCCI would finance Monzer Hourani in his Texas real estate business. When NBC News asked Hatch whether he had approached BCCI, he denied it. When it became clear that NBC knew about the call, he admitted that it had taken place, adding that Altman had given him Naqvi's name and telephone number.

For his part, Hourani said that he followed up by sending a detailed loan proposal to BCCI at Hatch's suggestion. In a three-page letter to Naqvi dated April 2, 1990, Hourani asked BCCI to finance four real estate projects in Chicago, Minneapolis, and Clear Lake, Texas. These, he wrote, included multifamily and office buildings. Hourani proposed that BCCI provide him with "equity for [these] projects in the form of letters of credit." The projects, he wrote, ranged in size from $10 million to $20 million, and he sought "approximately $10 million" of financing from Naqvi's bank.* It isn't clear what assistance, if any, BCCI gave Hourani. (Hourani has claimed that he never received any financing from BCCI.)

Hatch reacted quickly to the embarrassing disclosures. In interviews and a press release, he sought to portray the telephone call as entirely normal, just a piece of networking for a friend. "Hourani was having problems finding financing for his real estate developments," the senator said in late November 1991, "and I thought perhaps an Arab bank would consider helping him." He explained that his friendship with Hourani dated from the mid-1980s and was partly based on their shared devotion to the Mormon faith. Hourani, a Lebanese American, was a convert, Hatch explained. He denied in an interview in late 1991 that he had ever made other calls to Naqvi, an assertion contradicted by Pillsbury, who says the senator called Naqvi as many as nine times.

Hatch's relationship with Hourani was actually much closer than the senator implied. They were such good friends that Hourani once gave Hatch an abstract painting worth $1,000, according to a financial disclosure statement filed by the senator. In addition, Hatch's office had once intervened with regulators to help Hourani.

In 1986, Hatch wrote to the office of the director of the Federal Savings & Loan Insurance Corporation (FSLIC) on behalf of Hourani, who was then in trouble over borrowings from Houston's Mainland Savings, which had been taken over by the FSLIC. Hatch, who said he was writing "at the request of constituents," wrote that his staff had found possible grounds for "substantial legal process against Main-

---

*The same day Hourani wrote that letter, Naqvi's right-hand man, Dildar Rizvi, sent a note to Altman in which he mentioned Senator Hatch:

"Dear Bob,

"A friend of ours in London, Sir Julian Ridsdale, who is a Member of the British Parliament and belongs to the Conservative Party, shall be visiting Washington DC from April 17th to 21st 1990. He has known Mr. Abedi, Mr. Naqvi and other senior executives of BCCI for a number of years and has been very supportive to us during our recent ordeal in Tampa.

"I was wondering if you and Mr. Clifford would be able to spare a few minutes to meet him and exchange greetings. He has volunteered to speak to selected members of the Senate or Congress, including Senator Hatch and assure them of BCCI's seriousness to act as good corporate citizen. Since he has known the senior management personnel of BCCI for a number of years he may be able to convey this message forcefully. I leave it entirely to you to weigh and decide whether any advantage can be had from this approach.

"Yours sincerely,

"[signed] Dildar

"Encl. Resume of Sir Julian Ridsdale with Washington DC contact phone number."

land Savings/FSLIC by Hourani and his associates." The letter seemed to cajole the FSLIC, saying the difficulties it had with Hourani "may be capable of resolution." Yet the letter claimed "we certainly don't want to interfere in any way with your processes." The FSLIC's general counsel, Harry Quillian, replied to Hatch on September 19, 1986, countering that the FSLIC believed it might be Mainland that had claims against Hourani. Both sides — Hourani and the FSLIC — had made offers to settle the disputes, Quillian said, but the FSLIC recognized its obligations to maximize the amount of money it could recover. Hatch now claims that he never saw the letter to the FSLIC sent out over his signature. He maintains that it was signed with his "automatic pen" by a former staff member, but he says he takes full responsibility for the letter.

Hourani has even been involved in managing the senator's personal finances. Hatch, according to his financial disclosure statements, is the beneficiary of a trust administered by Hourani. One asset of the trust is a small apartment, worth about $20,000. It was registered in Hourani's name.

Hatch's relationship with the BCCI network goes far beyond his friendship with Altman and his efforts to get money for Hourani. There's also the matter of First American's loan to COP, the Chiefs of Police National Drug Task Force, a nonprofit group run by Randy Anderson, whose father is the columnist Jack Anderson. First American wrote off the loan rather than force Randy or his father to honor the guarantees they had signed. Randy Anderson said COP would eventually repay the money. Hatch was the chairman of COP.

Hatch also had some links to the netherworld of spies and arms dealers of which BCCI was such an important part. He acknowledges having met with Adnan Khashoggi, who — with the help of BCCI — was an important middleman in the Iran-contra arms transactions. For several years, Khashoggi had based much of his business empire in Salt Lake City. Hatch said that in meeting Khashoggi, he was simply extending the courtesies he would to any big investor in Utah. Hatch was also a booster of the Afghan rebels.

But Hatch's most intriguing connection to BCCI concerns a Middle Eastern businessman named Mohammed Mahmoud Hammoud. A fascinating and enigmatic character, he appears repeatedly in the sordid history of the bank. He was an important BCCI front man, with connections to an assortment of powerful people in Washington.

· · · ·

Hammoud, a Shi'ite Lebanese merchant, first appears in the story in the 1950s, when he became friendly with Charles Hostler. Three decades later, as we have seen, Hostler became a major campaign contributor to George Bush; he was also Bush's ambassador to Bahrain when the government awarded the oil concession to Harken.

When Hammoud and Hostler met, the American was a foreign service officer in Beirut and his Arabic tutor was Hammoud's wife. Hostler had come to the State Department from a background in intelligence with both the CIA and its predecessor, the Office of Strategic Services. In 1974–76, during Gerald Ford's presidency, Hostler was a senior official in the Department of Commerce. He then became active in the real estate business in San Diego. Hammoud used Hostler as a consultant on some of his real estate investments in the United States, which were financed by BCCI. Hostler, speaking through a spokesman from the U.S. embassy in Bahrain in December 1991, admitted to giving Hammoud some advice on real estate over the years but maintained they hadn't had "any direct business dealings."

Hammoud's association with BCCI may have begun in the early 1970s, when the bank was founded. He soon became a pliant front man for Abedi, serving as a nominee shareholder in both BCCI and First American. Hammoud played a role in the dubious investments by Clifford and Altman in First American stock. When BCCI arranged for the two lawyers to sell a large part of their holdings in 1988 at a big profit, Hammoud was supposedly the buyer. The Lebanese businessman paid $6,800 per share for stock that had sold for just $2,430 per share seven months earlier. In 1990, the stock changed hands for $2,774 per share. Investigators believe that Hammoud was nothing more than a front man for BCCI in this transaction.

Hatch apparently met Hammoud in the early or middle 1980s. When his relationship with the Lebanese was revealed in the press in late 1991, the senator said he had met with Hammoud on one or two occasions in Washington to discuss the hostage situation in Lebanon. Hammoud, the senator explained, had also visited him in Washington later, as part of a Lebanese delegation sponsored by the United States Information Agency. In the mid-1980s, when Hatch chaired the Senate Labor Committee, he went to Geneva for International Labour Organisation meetings. On one such trip he tried unsuccessfully to look up Hammoud at his house in Évian, France, just a few miles from Geneva.

Other people close to the senator also knew Hammoud, including

Hatch's friend Monzer Hourani and Michael Pillsbury. In fact, the Hammoud family was going to publish a monograph that Pillsbury planned to write on modern Lebanese politics. Investigators for Senator Kerry would later raise questions about the project, wondering whether it was a quid pro quo for Pillsbury's assistance to BCCI's lawyers and PR men after the crisis in Tampa. Pillsbury claims that there was nothing improper about it.

In spite of all these links between Hammoud and Hatch's circle, the senator has claimed that he had no idea that Hammoud was connected with either BCCI or First American. That is simply not true, according to Pillsbury. He maintains that Hatch not only knew of Hammoud's ties to BCCI but that Hammoud even lobbied the senator on the bank's behalf. In late 1989 and early 1990, he says, Hammoud met with Hatch and urged him to stand up and support the BCCI plea bargain. Pillsbury adds that Hammoud also met with other U.S. politicians at that time, including the late John Tower, a former Republican senator from Texas.*

It was just after these alleged meetings that several important events occurred. Hatch was lobbied by Altman and other BCCI lawyers; the BCCI plea bargain agreed to by Bush's Justice Department was announced; the government of Bahrain awarded its oil concession; Hatch delivered his speech defending the plea bargain; and Hatch called BCCI's Naqvi to solicit financing for Hourani.

Hatch continues to insist that he was in the dark about Hammoud's ties to BCCI throughout this period. He said he did not learn of the connection until May 1990, when the article in *Regardie's* identified Hammoud as a shareholder in BCCI and First American. A few days after the article came out, Hammoud died — or seems to have died.

The Lebanese businessman, who had gone to Geneva from Évian, reportedly collapsed and died in his doctor's office in early May. According to a medical report and a statement written by his wife, he died during an endoscopy, an examination that involves inserting a rubber tube down a patient's throat. The cause of death, according to the autopsy report, was the rupture of a main artery close to the heart. Insurers, however, wouldn't pay out on his life policies, according to a London lawyer acting for Hammoud's mother, because the body was ten centimeters (about four inches) shorter than at the time of Ham-

---

*Tower was close to President Bush, who, after the 1988 election, nominated him as secretary of defense, but the Texan failed to win Senate confirmation.

moud's last medical examination. This lawyer also expressed amazement that the family sent him a videotape of Hammoud's funeral. The obsequies had apparently taken place in Beirut and been attended by senior Syrian government officials.

One person who doubts that Hammoud really died is Nazir Chinoy, a BCCI official who was convicted in the Tampa case. Conversely, a federal investigator who is working on the BCCI case thinks the Lebanese really is dead, and he suspects foul play. Hammoud, says this source, knew too much about BCCI's machinations and he was too talkative for his own good.

A medical report on Hammoud's death prepared in October 1990 by a physician from Harley Street, the home of some of London's most prestigious doctors, was very critical of the treatment Hammoud was apparently given before his death and also of the autopsy report. The circumstances weren't right for an endoscopy, the report by Dr. D. Forecast said, as Hammoud had eaten a full breakfast and was due to catch an airplane within an hour of the procedure. It added that Hammoud was "a known hypertensive suffering from intermittent chest pain." Forecast also said that the autopsy report was "surprising and clearly inadequate." An emotional statement given by Hammoud's wife, Violette, to the Swiss authorities raises further questions about the medical treatment. The account insists that Hammoud didn't want an endoscopy but that the two doctors present insisted, even preventing Violette Hammoud from reaching her husband when he was choking on the tube.

After Hammoud's apparent death, Michael Pillsbury, it seems, tried to help the family liquidate Hammoud's First American stock. A message faxed to Altman in April 1991 from Pillsbury shows that the former Hatch staff member was right in the middle of negotiations with Kassem Hammoud, Mohammed Hammoud's son, about the proposed transfer of First American stock from the father's name to that of the son. The message to Altman, in which Pillsbury addressed him as "Bob" ended: "I will call again today about meeting Senator Hatch, or you may hear from [his] personal secretary Ruth Carroll." Pillsbury also forwarded to Altman an April 24 message that Kassem Hammoud had faxed to BCCI's chief executive, Zafar Iqbal. It sought — unsuccessfully, as it turned out — to establish title to Mohammed Hammoud's stock in First American and have it reregistered in the names of his heirs. Pillsbury now plays down his relationship with Altman, saying that he has met with him only twice in his life and that he was involved on only one occasion in the negotiations over the Hammoud stock in First American. That involvement, he says, resulted from his friendship with the Hammoud family.

If Hammoud really died, he certainly took a lot of secrets with him. It would be interesting to know about his role as a front man for BCCI, his purchase of First American stock from Clifford and Altman, and, of course, his friendships with powerful Americans like Hatch. When the Utah senator was asked in October 1992 about his ties to Hammoud and BCCI, he explained through a spokesman that he had asked the Senate Ethics Committee to look into the matter and did not want to discuss it for the time being. At Hatch's request, the committee is also investigating Michael Pillsbury.

Hammoud's relationships with American politicians are also being examined by some of the law enforcement officials who have been digging into BCCI's past. Several investigators believe that Hammoud was more than simply a front man for BCCI, that he was also a bag man for the bank — a purveyor of money and favors to powerful people. Intercepts of telephone conversations made by a U.S. intelligence agency indicate that Hammoud knew a tremendous amount about BCCI's clandestine activities. In a conversation just hours before his "death," Hammoud told a friend, "If anybody knew how dirty the Americans are in this BCCI business, they'd be surprised — they're dirtier than the Pakistanis."

BCCI's political power was impressive, but it was not, of course, unlimited. Some members of Congress have been willing to investigate the rogue bank, notably two Democratic party mavericks: Senator John Kerry and Congressman Henry Gonzalez. After the shutdown of the bank, they learned increasingly shocking information about BCCI — including details of its ties to the CIA.

One area that intrigued Kerry's staff was how much the CIA had known about the bank and whether it had circulated that information to other federal agencies. William von Raab, the Customs commissioner, contacted the CIA around the time of the Tampa indictment to find out what the agency knew about BCCI. Robert Gates, who was then the CIA's deputy director and is now the director, provided a report that von Raab has described as "well-written pabulum." He said he later discovered from British Customs agents that the CIA had used BCCI to make payments for clandestine operations in many parts of the world.

During the fall of 1991, investigators for Kerry discovered that over the years the agency had prepared hundreds of reports mentioning BCCI, some of which contained allegations of serious crimes. A few of these reports were distributed widely within the federal government, yet somehow the crucial information did not reach the people responsible for dealing with BCCI. Even when reports did reach appropriate officials, the information failed to make an impression.

One report, dated September 30, 1986, contained allegations of BCCI's involvement in drug trafficking and money laundering. It also stated that BCCI had secretly gained control of First American. The report was distributed to the State, Treasury, and Commerce departments and other agencies; but, according to Senator Kerry, it was not given to the one agency responsible for First American Bankshares: the Federal Reserve.

At Treasury, the report apparently went to Robert Bench, the associate deputy comptroller of the currency who went to work for Price Waterhouse in 1988. But Bench told the Kerry Committee that he had no specific recollection of the document. His response is puzzling because Douglas P. Mulholland, an assistant secretary of state who had been with the Treasury Department, said that Treasury documents confirm that Bench received the CIA report. While Mulholland didn't recall specifically to whom he gave it at Treasury, he said Bench was his regular contact at the Office of the Comptroller of the Currency (OCC). Mulholland added that a secondary record indicates that he showed the report to Donald Regan, then treasury secretary. (Regan said that he didn't recall seeing the report and suggested that it may have gone to James Baker, his successor, who at the time was traveling in Morocco. Regan told the reporter, "Call Morocco!")

In May 1989 — seven months after BCCI was indicted — the CIA issued a further substantial report in which it repeated the assertion that BCCI controlled First American. This document was also sent to the State, Commerce, and Treasury departments, but it was not given to the prosecutors in Tampa who were planning to put BCCI on trial. Treasury's failure to forward the report is particularly striking. Operation C-Chase had been run by the Customs Service, which is part of the Treasury Department. Another unit of Treasury is the OCC, the chief regulator of nationally chartered banks, including banks owned by First American Bankshares.

Chairman Gonzalez of the House Banking Committee uncovered connections between the BCCI affair and another multibillion-dollar scandal: the secret funding of Iraq by Italy's Banca Nazionale del Lavoro (BNL). There were disturbing parallels to the BCCI affair. The Federal Reserve, which was responsible for regulating BNL's Atlanta branch, had failed to detect the massive fraud. At a hearing on BCCI, Gonzalez said that "the existence of another foreign bank entity [BCCI] engaged in criminal activity comes as no great surprise," particularly because BNL "became Baghdad's banker in the U.S. before our regulatory cops at the Federal Reserve could locate Iraq on the map."

There were also signs of a cover-up of BNL's activities by the Reagan and Bush administrations. Why was no one indicted until February 1991, eighteen months after BNL's lending spree was discovered? There were suspicions that the White House was eager to sweep this messy scandal under the rug, since it threatened to highlight the government's role in supporting Saddam Hussein before the invasion of Kuwait. As early as 1983, President Reagan had instructed the CIA to provide intelligence to help Iraq in its war with Iran. Washington continued providing aid to Baghdad for the next seven years — up to the time of the invasion.

When the lead defendant, BNL's former Atlanta branch manager, Christopher Drogoul, pleaded guilty, he was not obliged to make a public accounting of what had occurred, and the judge suggested that this smacked of a cover-up. Marvin Shoob of the U.S. District Court in Atlanta said in the summer of 1992 that an independent counsel should be appointed to investigate the matter. The House Judiciary Committee also requested an independent counsel, but Attorney General William Barr refused, maintaining that the department's investigation had been adequate. In September, shortly before his sentencing, Drogoul hired a new defense lawyer and started to set out evidence that pointed to a much wider conspiracy than the government had alleged. Soon after that, the plea agreement was canceled.

Congressman Gonzalez held a hearing on BNL in September during which he quoted from a confidential CIA document that said the agency had long been aware that the bank's head office was involved in the Atlanta branch's loans. Gonzalez also released State Department cables showing that senior BNL officials had met with the U.S. ambassador to Italy in late 1989 and asked that the U.S. government use "damage control" to address the spreading BNL scandal. Gonzalez said the documents undercut the Bush administration's argument that Drogoul had acted without the knowledge of his superiors.

In the course of his BNL probe, Gonzalez had found evidence of close ties between BCCI and the Italian bank. Alfred Hartmann, a board member of BCCI who ran the bank's Swiss subsidiary — Banque de Commerce et de Placements (BCP) — also happened to be chairman of BNL's Swiss bank, Lavoro Bank A.G. Hartmann has asserted that there was no particular significance to these overlapping roles.

But there were many other strange coincidences. For example, Hartmann had been vice chairman of Bank of New York–Intermaritime, a bank in Geneva controlled by Bruce Rappaport, an oilman thought to have ties to U.S. and Israeli intelligence.* The Swiss banker was also associated with Charles Keating, the S&L bandit who had so many friends on the Senate Banking Committee. (Hartmann and Keating served on the board of a shadowy investment company in the Bahamas called Trendinvest Ltd.) As the investigations continued, it sometimes seemed as if half the characters in the BCCI and BNL affairs were either spies or politicians.

As the charges and countercharges about BCCI echoed through Washington, most of the people responsible for its crimes were beyond the reach of the law. Many of them were shielded by friends in high places.

After the collapse of the bank, two of the Gokal brothers, whose companies had received an enormous volume of fraudulent loans from BCCI over the years, left Western Europe. Abbas Gokal is believed to have moved to Pakistan; his brother is said to be in Iran.

Kemal Shoaib was also out of reach. He had helped to assemble BCCI's Latin American network, had been involved in overseeing its underground empire of U.S. financial institutions, and then served as chairman of one of those secret subsidiaries, Independence Bank. The Federal Reserve and U.S. prosecutors regarded Shoaib as one of the most important culprits in the BCCI affair, but that didn't seem to matter at all to the Pakistani government. After all, Prime Minister Nawaz Sharif had long been close to BCCI. The government even decided that Shoaib was fit to run a bank. In the fall of 1991, Pakistani authorities awarded ten new bank licenses and Shoaib was one of the

---

*Rappaport was also a major investor in Bank of New York, which happened to be one of BCCI's principal correspondent banks in the United States.

lucky recipients. Another recipient was Arshad Nawabi, who had been BCCI's top man in Dubai. He had financed a steel mill owned by Prime Minister Sharif's family, according to an accountant familiar with the transaction. (BCCI's customers should have been enraged, but there was no uproar in Pakistan, because the government bailed out local depositors. BCCI's depositors in most other countries, of course, were not so lucky.)

Banking licenses aside, the ethics of Sharif's government certainly seemed lacking in matters of high finance. In May 1992, the Securities and Exchange Commission brought its first-ever action against a foreign government when it charged Pakistan with offering unregistered bonds that appeared to be tailor-made for money laundering. Earlier in the year, Pakistan's government had run advertisements for the bonds in major American newspapers containing such promises as "No Questions Asked About Source of Funds!" and "No Identity to be Disclosed!"

The most important political allies of BCCI were not just in Pakistan, of course, but also in the UAE. The backing of Sheikh Zayed had been crucial to the success of BCCI, and in late 1991 and early 1992, investigators were increasingly focusing on his role.

Zayed's advisers and spokesmen have portrayed the sheikh as an innocent dupe of BCCI and as the biggest single victim of BCCI's crimes. Over the years, according to his advisers, the Abu Dhabi ruler pumped hundreds of millions of dollars into BCCI, and he is expected to pay out even more money as partial compensation to depositors. The compensation could exceed $2 billion.

Many observers readily accepted this characterization of the victimized and innocent sheikh. In a series of feature articles on the seized bank in November 1991, the *Financial Times* published estimates that BCCI had stolen more than $2 billion from Zayed, attributing the information to "sources close to the investigation of the scandal-ridden bank."

If Zayed were indeed innocent, it would stand to reason that he would do his utmost to bring the suspects to justice. Curiously, though, there seemed to be little sense of urgency in Abu Dhabi when BCCI was taken over by the regulators. It was not until September 1991 that Zayed's government arrested BCCI employees suspected of crimes. Among the suspects were Naqvi and Iqbal. The conditions were not particularly onerous: the detainees were lodged at the Abu Dhabi Officers' Club. Moreover, law enforcement officials in the

United States and Britain were forbidden to interrogate the BCCI officials in Zayed's custody.

One man who was angered by the lack of cooperation was Senator Kerry. Eventually he was able to extract some commitments from an Abu Dhabi official. At a hearing in May 1992, Ahmed Al-Sayegh, a financial adviser to the Abu Dhabi government, claimed that "the idea of cooperation has just taken off." He added that "from this point on, nothing will obstruct it." Months later, these appeared to be empty words. At the opening of a hearing on BCCI, Kerry said, "I regret to report that we are now at the end of July and we have been informed by both the Justice Department and the district attorney of New York that no such cooperation has taken place. Not a document and not a witness held in Abu Dhabi have been produced to U.S. law enforcement concerning BCCI."

Around the same time Kerry made this complaint, investigators were discovering that people close to Zayed had been withholding information about BCCI for years. Lord Justice Bingham, who began investigating BCCI at the request of the British government, found that Abu Dhabi officials had known about massive fraud at the bank long before the shutdown and yet had failed to turn this information over to Price Waterhouse and the Bank of England. A portion of Bingham's draft report, leaked to the press in July 1992, highlighted the importance of an April 1990 meeting involving Swaleh Naqvi and senior Abu Dhabi officials, including Crown Prince Khalifa, Zayed's eldest son. The report concluded that if that information had been communicated, the bank would probably have been closed much earlier.

The behavior of Zayed's government only fueled suspicions that the Abu Dhabi ruler wasn't really the biggest victim of the BCCI affair but one of the biggest villains.

Spokesmen for Sheikh Zayed have tried hard to play down his role in BCCI. James Lake of the public relations firm of Robinson, Lake, Lerer & Montgomery, which represents the sheikh's interests in Washington, D.C., even tries to avoid describing Zayed as a stockholder. Instead, the PR man uses the vague expression "the majority shareholders." This is a distinction without a difference, because "the majority shareholders" comprise Zayed, members of his immediate family, and the Abu Dhabi Investment Authority (ADIA), which is controlled by the sheikh.

Lake has also promoted the idea that Zayed and his entourage were "passive" investors in the bank. This is not simply misleading; it is false. Zayed, as we have seen, was by far the most important investor in BCCI and was represented on the board by one of his financial advisers, Ghanem al-Mazrui. More than a year before the bank was seized, Zayed acquired majority ownership and removed Naqvi as the CEO. Long before that happened, BCCI officials were so intimately involved in managing investments for the sheikh (and handling other chores) that they were de facto members of his court.

Beyond these connections, several people close to Zayed were involved in dubious financial dealings with BCCI. Price Waterhouse had found that Mazrui had benefited from riskless transactions in shares of BCCI arranged by Abedi and Naqvi. In 1985, Mazrui for no apparent reason received payments from ICIC, the notorious BCCI dummy company in the Cayman Islands. In addition, his signature appears on a confirmation for what was in reality a fictitious loan in the name of Zayed's eldest son, Khalifa. (Mazrui told Price Waterhouse in early 1991 that he didn't recall signing the confirmation and said his signature may have been forged.) Allegations of misconduct by Mazrui were contained in the first book on the BCCI scandal: *Bankrupt: The BCCI Fraud,* by the British journalists Nicholas Kochan and Bob Whittington. When the book was published in November 1991, Mazrui retained a libel lawyer and had it withdrawn from British bookstores. It was soon reissued with deletions and amendments to the contested passages.

BCCI also made loans to Zayed and several close associates, according to a summer 1991 copy of its loan portfolio. This document shows loans to Zayed, his relatives, his government, and courtiers totaling more than $1.5 billion. Zayed's lawyers at Washington's Patton, Boggs & Blow say such documents from BCCI are questionable and insist that the sheikh is a victim who has lost billions of dollars in the whole episode. There are some borrowings they don't dispute, however. For instance, BCCI made a $55 million loan on a thirty-nine-story office tower in New York. The firm that owns that building, 330 Madison Company, is 75 percent controlled by the ADIA.

Members of Zayed's family were also enriched by BCCI, benefiting from no-risk transactions in the bank's shares, according to Price Waterhouse. In addition, BCCI had structured transactions in its own shares that benefited ADIA.

Investigators also found that an extraordinary number of people close to Zayed had acted as front men by posing as shareholders in

BCCI and First American. Some of the nominees were Abu Dhabi government officials. Ali Mohammed Shorafa, who had been the director of presidential affairs in the UAE and one of Zayed's most senior advisers, was a nominee in First American. In 1985, BCCI paid him $300,000 for the use of his name and $100,000 a year for two more years. The ranks of the nominees also included members of the ruling families of neighboring emirates, who depend on handouts from Zayed. The rulers of Fujeirah and Ajman — Sheikh Hamad al-Sharqi and Sheikh Humaid al-Naomi — allowed their names to be used in the acquisition of First American. Sharqi was paid an annual fee of about $400,000 for his services by BCCI and another $500,000 a year as a profit on the other shares he held for BCCI's benefit. At one point, as much as 24 percent of First American's stock was held in Sharqi's name.

Had Zayed and his relatives also acted as front men?

When Abedi arranged for a group of clients to acquire stock in First American (then Financial General) in late 1977 and early 1978, the purchases were made in the names of four men: Kamal Adham of Saudi Arabia, Faisal Saud al-Fulaij of Kuwait, Zayed's son Sheikh Sultan, and Zayed's financial adviser Abdullah Darwaish. (Darwaish was holding the stock on behalf of Zayed's young son Mohammed.) Sheikh Sultan soon sold his stock to Adham. Other investors later joined the group, including Zayed's ADIA and his son Khalifa.

By mid-1991, U.S. and British investigators had confirmed that several of First American's stockholders were front men for BCCI, including Adham and Fulaij. But they were unable to prove that Zayed and his associates were also nominees. One reason their role in First American was obscure is that his government refused to provide critical documents and witnesses. Eventually, though, investigators began to obtain evidence from other sources.

One informant was Akbar Bilgrami, a BCCI official who had been convicted in the Tampa drug money case. In the late 1970s and early 1980s, he had been involved in Zayed's real estate investments in Spain. In the summer of 1992, he told members of Senator Kerry's staff of an incident in early 1978, when Abedi was scooping up stock in First American. Bilgrami, who was visiting Spain, was told that he would be receiving a set of documents by courier and that he should have them signed by Zayed's financial adviser Abdullah Darwaish. Bilgrami said that the documents indicated that Darwaish would be paying for the stock with a BCCI loan. The papers also included a blank power of attorney form for him to sign. The clear implication of Bilgrami's statement is that Darwaish was fronting for BCCI at the very beginning of the takeover attempt.

One man with far more extensive information on the takeover is Riaz Saleem Aslam, a Pakistani accountant who served as financial adviser and deputy to Darwaish, the chairman of Zayed's Department of Personal Affairs (DPA). In the early 1980s, Abu Dhabi authorities arrested both men on fraud charges, as noted in Chapter 3. Darwaish was soon released but was apparently forbidden to leave the country; Aslam was not freed until 1990. These may have been trumped-up charges. Some investigators now suspect that their real offense was knowing too much about the illegal takeover of First American and being able to incriminate Zayed. Abedi is believed to have encouraged Crown Prince Khalifa to order the arrests.

The detention of Aslam silenced him for more than a decade. After his release, he returned to his native Pakistan to spend time with his family, but he also went to Europe to meet with lawyers and advisers. Through intermediaries, he started to provide evidence to law enforcement authorities and bank regulators in the United States and Britain.

The Pakistani accountant wrote some of the statements recently, but he maintains that others were written while he was in detention and that they were smuggled out. He did this, he said, because he feared for his safety and wanted to make a record of Zayed's and Abedi's acts to protect himself from "unforeseen circumstances."* A statement from early 1983 bears the signature of M. A. K. Afridi, Aslam's lawyer at the time, and is marked as follows: "This note was handed over to my associate, Hussain Abdullah Samahoni of the law firm of A. R. Hilal and Associates on February 20 1983." According to Aslam's current lawyer, Afridi has sworn an affidavit in London that he made that notation in 1983. This document, which covers thirteen pages, describes the relationship between Zayed and BCCI. It also contains

---

*Aslam has stated that he was harshly treated while in custody. (The UAE's human rights record has been criticized by Amnesty International and other observers.) In making his allegations against Zayed, Aslam has exposed himself to considerable risk. Should he return to Abu Dhabi, he could be arrested; the statutory penalty for publicly defaming the ruler ranges from twenty years' imprisonment to death. He could also be forced to pay fines even if he does not return. When Aslam was released in 1990, the Abu Dhabi authorities made him sign a document agreeing to a claim of $110 million against himself and his family. This claim, according to the document, can be enforced at the sole discretion of Zayed. The claim was registered in Abu Dhabi, Pakistan, and Switzerland. The U.S. consul in Abu Dhabi refused to register it.

serious charges against several of the people involved in the takeover of First American.*

Aslam was a senior financial adviser in the DPA from 1975 to late 1981. During his tenure, he said in one of his statements, "I became aware of certain acts which upon recollection were unlawful — but have been hushed up and/or suppressed and/or ignored as they were for the benefit of the DPA and certain interested parties." The most important of these, he wrote, was the First American takeover, "which involved directly, the Ruler Sheikh Zayed and the [DPA's] chairman Abdullah Darwish carrying out actions upon the advice of Mr. A. H. Abedi" and other employees of BCCI.

In the events leading up to the takeover, "it is my specific knowledge as an employee of the DPA, that certain misstatements, forging of documents, fraudulent statements, fraudulent information, perjury under oath, suppression of material facts, misuse of privileged information for personal gain and conspiracy to effect all or some of the above took place and were perpetrated partly or wholly by Sheikh Zayed, Sheikh Sultan bin Zayed, Sheikh Mohammed bin Zayed (then a minor), Abdullah Darwish, Agha Hassan Abedi, S. H. Naqvi," and others. Aslam stated that his knowledge of these events was based on his direct participation in meetings as well as conversations with Darwaish and with BCCI employees.

Aslam strongly denied that he was guilty of defrauding the sheikh and said he was arrested because the authorities were fearful that he would reveal what he had learned while working for Zayed. They were particularly concerned that he would talk about the First American acquisition. (Aslam obtained his freedom only after signing a document in which he promised to remain silent about his work for the ruler.)

He described the takeover as a "collaboration between Mr. Abedi, acting in his usual role as primary banker and advisor to Sheikh Zayed and with his known ambitions (previously deterred) to own a bank in the U.S., and Sheikh Zayed personally and through his private department seeking a safe haven for his funds politically protected." It was also imperative that the takeover be completed without the disclosure of Zayed's name. In a statement written in 1991, Aslam said, "The

---

*These statements have not been released publicly, but the authors of this book have obtained copies along with supporting documents. In his statements, Aslam uses alternate spellings for the names of certain individuals.

record shows that from the first purchases of Financial General's stock in 1977 and 1978 until now there have been many violations of U.S. law and misrepresentations to U.S. authorities which masked the involvement of Sheikh Zayed until it became uncontainable recently."

On several occasions, according to Aslam, Darwaish said that Zayed gave Abedi full discretion in the takeover. "Mr. Abedi," he wrote, "never concealed his intent to control [First American] as the effective arm of BCCI, which he said would benefit the ruler both through ownership of BCCI and direct ownership of a Washington D.C. bank."

Zayed was himself involved in the initial purchases of shares, according to Aslam: "The shares which were ultimately represented as purchased by the two sons [of Zayed] through BCCI had been allocated to them as nominees for Sheikh Zayed, who purchased them with his own knowledge, his own funds, and designated his sons as nominees to keep secret his ownership."

Those holdings, Aslam said, were reallocated to Zayed's sons Sultan and Mohammed only after "the implications of adverse publicity and regulatory violations became evident." Furthermore, these original purchases were made with DPA funds, which came through BCCI. In order to disguise this switch in ownership, a BCCI officer "produced fictitious entries in the bank records at BCCI Emirates to show that Sultan and Mohammed paid funds from their personal accounts to mask the fact that they had actually been paid for by the DPA, which was undeniably Zayed's money by ownership and control and beneficial interest."

Dildar Rizvi, a former senior BCCI officer, is believed to have corroborated Aslam's statements in September 1992. In interviews in Pakistan with investigators from the Justice Department and from Morgenthau's office, he gave an account of the takeover that closely agreed with that of Aslam, according to people close to the investigation.

While investigators were trying to figure out who was behind the crime, BCCI's depositors were clamoring for their money, and they hoped to get it from Zayed. This was more than a little ironic; defrauded depositors were expecting to be paid by the ruler of an emirate that was harboring many of the people who had organized the heist, a ruler who may even have been a central figure in the fraud. The dimensions of the fraud had gradually become clear after months of work by the court-appointed liquidators from Touche Ross. In a report issued in December 1991, they estimated BCCI's total liabilities at $10.64 billion and its realizable assets at $1.16 billion. In other words, a staggering $9.48 billion had vanished through a combination of mismanagement and fraud. There was no longer any doubt that the BCCI affair was one of the biggest larcenies in history.

BCCI's depositors desperately sought to recover as much as they could from the ruins of the bank. Their best hope, of course, was that the liquidators would be able to extract significant amounts of money from Zayed and some of the bank's other backers and would also succeed in pursuing many of those who had been involved in looting BCCI.

The liquidation was extraordinarily complex and would therefore take months, if not years. For a start, BCCI owed money to 800,000 depositors with 1.2 million accounts in more than seventy countries, according to Sir Donald Nicholls, Britain's vice chancellor (one of the country's senior legal figures).

The Touche Ross report implied that depositors would be able to recover only about ten cents on the dollar, because BCCI's liabilities far exceeded assets. In fact, there would be even less money available, because the liquidators had been incurring huge expenses to wind up the bank. According to their report, they had already run up expenses of £113 million (about $200 million). They also estimated a further $239 million in expenses before the liquidation was complete, meaning that the liquidators would altogether spend some $440 million — almost 40 percent of the bank's estimated realizable assets.

Depositors were furious when they found out that the senior liquidator, Brian Smouha, had been flying on the Concorde. A huge number of Touche Ross employees in Abu Dhabi seemed to be living quite comfortably, according to several sources. They set up their own soccer team and had special shirts made up. Aggrieved depositors, some of whom had lost their life savings, were further embittered when they saw how quickly the expenses were mounting up. There were also doubts about Smouha's strategy. He wanted to recover money from Zayed through negotiation rather than through the courts, as some of the depositors advocated.

No settlement would be possible until Smouha resolved the criminal and civil cases that had been brought by U.S. authorities. BCCI had been indicted on federal charges as well as state charges in New York. It was accused of an array of offenses, including money laundering, larceny, tax evasion, and a bewildering variety of frauds. In addition, the Federal Reserve had accused BCCI of violating a long list of banking laws and regulations. Around the end of 1991, Smouha negotiated a guilty plea on behalf of BCCI to all charges brought by New York State, the federal government, and the Federal Reserve.

The U.S. District Courthouse in Washington, D.C., where parts of the Watergate and Iran-contra scandals had unfolded, now became the setting for an important episode in the BCCI saga. At a hearing on January 9, 1992, Smouha agreed to settle with Uncle Sam. Judge Joyce Hens Green would formally approve the controversial agreement on January 24. The deal entailed BCCI's liquidators giving up $550 million, all of BCCI's American assets. These assets consisted mostly of cash and liquid investments in New York. The funds would be split into two roughly equal parts. One portion would go to the worldwide victims' fund that would be used to pay BCCI depositors as part of a global settlement of the bank's obligations. The other part would be used to shore up First American and Independence Bank. (No money ultimately went to Independence, since it was soon taken over by the regulators.) The liquidators also agreed that $10 million of the forfeited money would be paid as a fine to the Manhattan district attorney's office. As part of the settlement, the Federal Reserve agreed to drop a $200 million fine that it had assessed BCCI in the summer of 1991.

Before the settlement, the liquidators had been negotiating with the authorities in Abu Dhabi, Luxembourg, and London in an attempt to sort out BCCI's tangled affairs. Luxembourg approved the deal the liquidators had made with Morgenthau's office, the Justice Department, and the Federal Reserve, but Abu Dhabi wasn't part of it.

The U.S. settlement was only a portion of the worldwide agreement that Smouha was trying to pull together. On January 15, the High Court in London issued its much-delayed order to liquidate BCCI's British operations. Similar orders followed in the Cayman Islands, Scotland, and the Isle of Man.

The formal winding up of BCCI meant that the compensation of depositors could begin properly in many countries. Until then, various ad hoc measures had allowed depositors in some countries to get back small percentages of their funds. In Britain, a payment of £45 million from Abu Dhabi had allowed depositors and staff to receive some monies; depositors had also been able to get an emergency payment of up to £3,000 from the Bank of England. In Canada, Arthur Andersen, the accounting firm that acted as liquidators of BCCI Canada, had in December allowed that its six thousand depositors would receive ten Canadian cents on the dollar as a first payout on their C$203 million in deposits. The Canadian Deposit Insurance Corporation had already paid out C$22.5 million.

There were attempts to stop BCCI's settlement with the U.S. government, especially by parties who had their own claims against the bank. For example, a syndicate of underwriters at Lloyd's of London, which had for years pursued claims against the Jordanian merchant Munther Bilbeisi and BCCI for an alleged coffee-smuggling scheme, contested the settlement in federal courts in both Washington and New York. But the suit was thrown out on January 23.

The next major piece of the proposed worldwide settlement fell into place in February, when Abu Dhabi indicated it would contribute $1.7 billion to the settlement of depositors' claims over a period of four years in three separate payments. The complex agreement proposed that if depositors' claims totaled more than $10 billion, the emirate would contribute more money to an eventual maximum of $2.2 billion. But if claims were significantly less than $10 billion, Abu Dhabi's contribution could drop to $1.2 billion. There were some caveats, however. The whole scheme required at least 70 percent of BCCI's depositors, by value of funds, to waive their rights to claim against Abu Dhabi.

To many depositors this contribution seemed meager, especially since Abu Dhabi had apparently been prepared to contribute more than $4 billion in capital and guarantees to the proposed restructuring of BCCI back in April 1991. Smouha and his colleagues, as part of the deal, also agreed to give up the bank's claims to more than $3 billion of promissory notes issued in early 1991 by Abu Dhabi as part of the aborted restructuring. Some depositors were also outraged that the liquidators had agreed that if more than $2.5 billion was realized from the liquidation of BCCI's assets, those excess monies would be divided equally between Abu Dhabi and the liquidators. The BCCI Depositors' Association was skeptical of the proposed agreement and said that the creditors needed more time to study it in detail. Mourad Fleming, a lawyer for the association, said that the creditors were being asked to give up "very considerable rights," including the right to sue Abu Dhabi.

Smouha was defensive about the agreement. "It's not a cover up or anything like that," he told the *Financial Times*. "This is meant to make peace with the United Arab Emirates." He argued that under the proposed agreement with Abu Dhabi, depositors could expect to get as much as 10 percent by the end of 1992 and as much as 30 to 40 percent eventually. Without Abu Dhabi, he said, there were only remote prospects of a worthwhile dividend and there might even be no payout until the year 2000.

The proposed settlement, however, needed the approval of courts in London, the Cayman Islands, and Luxembourg as well as the agreement of the depositors, and some of that proved hard to get. A committee of BCCI's biggest depositors was especially critical of the proposal, though the London and Caymans courts approved it. The Luxembourg court would finally ratify the settlement on October 22, 1992, after it had been approved by a sufficient majority of the bank's creditors.

The liquidators now began to go about the business of trying to collect more money from those who allegedly shared responsibility for the scandals at BCCI. On March 12, the liquidators' lawyers issued writs in England against Price Waterhouse and Ernst & Young, former auditors for the bank. The suits, which named thirty-six defendants, alleged breach of duty and of contract as well as negligence in audits of BCCI carried out in 1985 and 1986. Those audits covered the period when BCCI suffered huge losses in its treasury division, estimated at more than $600 million.

By the fall of 1992, however, the liquidators had done little to press their claims against Price Waterhouse. For years, the auditors had been satisfied with bland assurances and scanty documentation from BCCI. Why wasn't more being done to hold Price Waterhouse accountable?

In the months following the seizure, it often seemed that few investigators — apart from those at Morgenthau's office — were eager to get to the bottom of the affair and to bring the perpetrators to justice.

17

ROUNDING UP
THE SUSPECTS

HARRY W. ALBRIGHT, JR., was finally settling down to enjoy a bit of retirement, starting to mix in a few games of tennis with a little part-time legal work. A soft-spoken and gentlemanly family man, he was beginning to feel relaxed and healthy again. The last year had been traumatic. At the age of sixty-five, Albright had been struck by severe coronary problems that required open-heart surgery just as he was at the point of retiring as chairman of Dime Savings Bank, one of New York's biggest financial institutions.

One day in December 1991, Albright received a telephone call from his old friend Bob Morgenthau. The two men had been partners at Patterson Belknap in the 1950s. (Years later, Albright served as New York State's banking superintendent.) "Your Uncle needs you," Morgenthau said. Albright was puzzled. "That's your Uncle Sam," Morgenthau explained, saying that he wanted Albright to act as trustee for First American Bankshares of Washington, D.C. As the trustee, he would control and vote a majority of the bank holding company's shares. The shares had belonged to BCCI, but the Federal Reserve had ordered that a trustee be appointed to control the stock; and as part of the settlement of the government's case against BCCI, Morgenthau won the right of veto over the choice of the trustee.

Albright was surprised and flattered, but he didn't want to move to Washington, and he was concerned about the reaction of his wife and family to his taking on such a responsibility so soon after major surgery. But Morgenthau wouldn't take no for an answer, and he eventually persuaded his friend that there was a major public interest in ensuring that First American was managed properly and that majority control was in the hands of a person not connected to Washington's lobbyists and political fixers. After talking it over with his wife, Albright decided to accept Morgenthau's offer.

It was a measure of Morgenthau's success with the BCCI case, how he had become the driving force in exposing the affair, that he had succeeded in getting the power effectively to choose the trustee of First American. Here was a district attorney from Manhattan deciding who should control a major banking institution in Washington, D.C. There was a widespread feeling in the press and the public that only Morgenthau had the ability and the moral authority to deal with this mammoth financial and political scandal. Clearly, there had been a terrible breakdown of the supposed system of law and regulation in the capital if a widely respected district attorney felt he could trust only his own appointee when it came to ensuring that First American was run independently.

The Federal Reserve didn't seem to share Morgenthau's enthusiasm for Albright, presumably because he was not a Washington insider. Some on the staff are believed to have resisted his appointment, but Morgenthau prevailed with the help of a few allies at the Fed. In June 1992, Judge Joyce Hens Green approved the appointment of Albright.

Meanwhile, Morgenthau's probe into BCCI was becoming more focused on some of its Saudi Arabian backers. One important target was Khalid Bin Mahfouz, the Saudi banker, who had long been an associate of several people in Abedi's circle. In 1977, for example, he and Ghaith Pharaon were among the four investors who took over Houston's Main Bank. But it was a decade later that his relationship with BCCI became close, and it was this period that intrigued Morgenthau's investigators.

Khalid Bin Mahfouz certainly does not fit the stereotype of the conservative banker. He used to wear a ponytail, and he has a taste for fast cars. But there is no denying the importance of his status — and that of his family — in the affairs of Saudi Arabia. The Bin Mahfouz family owns a controlling stake in National Commercial Bank (NCB), the largest bank in the kingdom, with hundred of branches. It was founded by Khalid's father and run by his sons, with Khalid acting as the first among equals. One sign of the family's status is that the Bin Mahfouz act as bankers to King Fahd and other members of the ruling family.

When BCCI admitted in the spring of 1985 that it had suffered substantial losses in options trading, its image was seriously damaged. The following year, however, Abedi won plaudits when he announced that the Bin Mahfouz family had acquired a large block of BCCI stock. Pierre Jaans, the Luxembourg bank regulator, was certainly pleased. "It seemed most impressive," he later said, "the way Abedi was able to come up with capital when he needed it."

Khalid Bin Mahfouz and his three brothers paid nearly $1 billion for their stake in BCCI, and Khalid joined the board of directors. As of October 1988, BCCI listed the brothers as the owners of 20 percent of the bank's stock. (Internal BCCI records showed that they actually owned close to 30 percent.) Around the same time, the family bought a large stake in First American. Khalid, who would tell Western investigators that he ran NCB with "absolute authority," had been attracted to BCCI by its far-flung international network, which he saw as a good complement to his family's own banking operations in Saudi Arabia. He and his brothers also liked the Muslim character of the bank. Further, they had all the introductions they thought they needed to BCCI's management; Khalid's right-hand man, Haroon Kahlon, was a Pakistani bureaucrat who was well acquainted with several of BCCI's senior officers.

One of the main reasons the Bin Mahfouz investment helped BCCI's image was that National Commercial Bank was generally regarded as strong and profitable. The reality, though, was quite different. NCB had done quite well for a number of years, but it was now in financial straits. Oil prices were falling sharply, and this was, of course, disastrous for the Saudi economy. Many of NCB's borrowers stopped servicing their debts, and the bank would soon suffer large losses. But BCCI didn't know this at the time, just as the Bin Mahfouz family did not know that Abedi's bank was effectively a bankrupt institution. This was like two drowning men clinging to one another, each believing that the other is strong and buoyant.

It did not take long for Khalid Bin Mahfouz to realize that BCCI was far from healthy. In fact, he and NCB took part in some of the fraudulent activities that damaged BCCI, it was later alleged. Price Waterhouse said in its spring 1991 report to the Bank of England that the "collusion" of Bin Mahfouz and NCB "appears to have been a major factor in hiding the fraud at BCCI." The auditors focused on the family's purchase and subsequent sale of their stake in BCCI. They termed BCCI's purchase of the shares "unauthorized" and said that $190 million of the money used to buy the stock was of questionable origin, although they did not say exactly why. A report dealing with ICIC said that NCB received "undisclosed payments" in the settlement of the share purchase.

In addition, the auditors charged that NCB lent about $400 million to BCCI's customers on behalf of BCCI, taking cash collateral from Abedi's bank. But, Price Waterhouse said, NCB had represented to auditors that this cash collateral was made up of routine interbank deposits. These transactions allowed BCCI to pretend it had increased the strength of its balance sheet greatly and also helped to conceal fraud at BCCI, the auditors said.

BCCI's last chief executive, Zafar Iqbal, approved certain questionable transactions booked through the accounts of Crown Prince Khalifa of Abu Dhabi, according to evidence unearthed in early 1991 by Price Waterhouse. Iqbal apparently took instructions from Naqvi in structuring these transactions, which involved routing funds to repurchase BCCI shares held by Bin Mahfouz. These dealings were themselves illegal because they weren't reported to regulators. Price Waterhouse had also found an account at NCB's Bahrain bank that, it alleged, was used by BCCI "for the purposes of fraudulently routing funds."

Price Waterhouse, of course, had qualified its reports to the Bank of England, indicating that these findings were what the firm believed to be the case but stressing that it felt more research was necessary to reach definitive conclusions about the nature of the frauds.

When the auditors' statements first became public in the *Wall Street Journal* in February 1992, Lawrence G. Smith, an NCB official in New York, said, "We reject in the strongest terms any implication of collusion or fraud." He pointed out that many of BCCI's records were erroneous and suggested that Price Waterhouse's conclusions might well be based on such misleading records. Smith went on to say that the auditors' charges were "absolutely untrue" and complained that Price Waterhouse would make such "an extraordinarily serious charge" against a man of "honor, dignity, and prominence" like Khalid Bin Mahfouz. The account at NCB's Bahrain branch, Smith said, "was an account. Money came in, money went out. We didn't know what it was used for."

In spite of the vociferous denials, Morgenthau's investigators took the Price Waterhouse reports quite seriously, and they began to develop additional information on the conduct of Khalid Bin Mahfouz. Of particular interest was the secret deal the Saudi banker made with

Abedi when his family invested in BCCI. Abedi, as we have seen, had agreed that Bin Mahfouz could sell the stock back — at a profit — whenever he wanted to. What this means, of course, is that the investment did not really represent an infusion of capital. It was, in effect, a loan that could be called at any time.

Morgenthau's team found evidence of other irregularities connected to this investment. When the Bin Mahfouz family paid for the stock, $755 million of the funds were fraudulently recorded on BCCI's books as deposits. In addition, the investigators found that BCCI had lent Bin Mahfouz $270 million to help him come up with most of the remaining purchase money. When the Bin Mahfouz family disposed of their BCCI stock in 1987, all of it was bought by ICIC, Abedi's dummy company, and most of the money, the investigators believed, was stolen from BCCI depositors. In addition, Khalid Bin Mahfouz kept the sale secret from the regulators until 1989. (Even more oddly, BCCI had told the public that some of the stock Zayed bought in 1990 came from Bin Mahfouz.)

The failure to disclose the sale also meant that BCCI's depositors were led to believe that Saudi Arabia's top banking family stood behind BCCI. Two months after the Tampa indictment, BCCI released the names of its "shareholders"; the list named Khalid Bin Mahfouz and his three brothers as owning a total of 20 percent of BCCI's stock.

As the New York D.A. closed in on Khalid Bin Mahfouz in the spring and summer of 1992, there were increasing signs that NCB was in serious trouble. It had not released any financial statements since the end of 1989, and regulators wondered what horrors the family was hiding. In Saudi Arabia, there were rumors that members of King Fahd's family had borrowed huge sums from NCB — as much as $3 billion — and often had failed to make interest or principal payments.

Morgenthau's investigators decided that they understood enough about Bin Mahfouz's dealings with BCCI to move against the Saudi. The New York D.A. was the first prosecutor to take any action. Only his office had figured out how important the most powerful Saudi Arabian banking family was to keeping BCCI in business with its prestige and with underhanded financial transactions. The federal prosecutors were still wrestling with problems that Assistant District Attorney John Moscow and others on Morgenthau's staff had researched for as long as two years.

On July 2, 1992, Morgenthau announced that a New York County grand jury had indicted Khalid Bin Mahfouz and his aide Haroon

Kahlon for defrauding BCCI and its depositors of as much as $300 million. Depositors' funds had been used to buy the Bin Mahfouz shares, and he was aware of their provenance. The indictment also included several infractions of New York banking laws, many involving Bin Mahfouz's alleged practice of not informing regulators about large and questionable financial transactions with BCCI.

The indictment was a sign that the Saudi elite may have been intimately involved in BCCI's criminality. Until now, Abu Dhabi's Sheikh Zayed had attracted most of the attention when the media focused on the bank's Arab backers. Attention soon shifted to other prominent Saudis: Kamal Adham, who had for years helped with BCCI's corrupt schemes, and Abdul-Raouf Khalil, another Saudi intelligence officer with ties to the CIA. Both men, of course, had acted as front men for BCCI in its purchase of First American, although Khalil denies wrongdoing.

At a press conference to announce the indictment of Bin Mahfouz and Kahlon, Morgenthau refused to speculate on Bin Mahfouz's links to Adham, the Saudi royal family, or other members of the kingdom's elite. The D.A. stayed close to the text of his prepared statement. There was one flash of humor, albeit a somewhat pejorative one: "Is he [Bin Mahfouz] married?" one journalist asked. "How many times?" Morgenthau replied with a grin.

The Saudi establishment was stunned by the indictment; its intensive lobbying of the State Department had been to no avail. Morgenthau's office refused to kowtow to foreign policy considerations, in any case. King Fahd called Ambassador Charles W. Freeman, Jr., to voice his shock and sadness at the news. The king even asked if the U.S. government would make a public statement vouching for the safety and stability of the Saudi banking system. Ambassador Freeman had to demur politely and explain that the law — or at least a maverick prosecutor's office in New York — had to take its course.

One week after the New York indictment, the Federal Reserve charged that Bin Mahfouz had been scheming to obtain control of both BCCI and First American in 1986. For a variety of banking offenses, the Fed fined Bin Mahfouz $170 million and Kahlon $6 million. Also, the Fed alleged, though Bin Mahfouz's family bank lost money from its investments in BCCI, Bin Mahfouz personally made $120 million from the transactions.

The Fed had also come under tremendous pressure from the Saudi authorities, who had sought to settle the issue of Bin Mahfouz's involvement with BCCI quietly. The Saudi Arabian Monetary Agency (SAMA), the kingdom's central banking authority, wanted desperately to keep the name of King Fahd's banker out of the press. "They are concerned about what implications it will have for the Saudi banking system as a whole," a senior Bush administration official told a reporter shortly after the New York indictment.

Even after the announcement of the indictment, officials from SAMA and their lawyers from the New York firm of Davis, Polk & Wardwell were still closeted in talks with Fed officials in New York. If the Fed planned to keep the affair as quiet as possible, it failed. Leaks to the press forced the Fed to announce its action on July 8, almost a week after the indictment. The Fed's order had been signed on July 2, so why hadn't it been made public earlier? Some suspected the effects of pressure from the Saudis and the State Department. But a Fed spokesman denied any such thing, blaming the July 4 holiday and other factors for the time lag.

Khalid Bin Mahfouz and his family appeared to come under considerable financial pressure after the New York charges were announced. Some bankers in London and New York cut back on the amount of business they were prepared to do with NCB. On July 7, NCB sold a large quantity of silver. Dealers at the bank told traders that the sales were on behalf of clients and totaled less than 20 million ounces. Many observers believed those particular clients to be members of the Bin Mahfouz family, though at least one associate of the family denied this. The price of silver dropped dramatically as others sold with NCB. Traders estimated that about 40 million ounces were dumped on the market on July 7, as the price of silver plummeted 15.8 cents, to $3.90 an ounce. That was a huge amount of silver to hit the market in one day; altogether it equaled about 7.5 percent of the annual worldwide sales of the precious metal.

As this drama unfolded in the New York courts and the world's metals markets, Bin Mahfouz himself was in Jiddah, well beyond the reach of Morgenthau's office.

Other investigators, including Britain's Serious Fraud Office, were starting to play an active role in the BCCI case. Police in London made their first arrest in the BCCI scandal in early February 1992 when they detained Mohammed Abdul Baqi, the former managing director of BCCI-controlled Attock Oil Company, as he arrived at Heathrow Airport. Baqi allegedly had told Price Waterhouse that BCCI had lent more than $76 million to Attock when it had done no such thing. These bogus loans had been used to help dress up the bank's shaky accounts. The sixty-six-year-old executive was charged with conspiring with BCCI to deceive its auditors.

On March 20, 1992, the SFO had charged Imran Iman — the BCCI officer who handled the accounts of Pharaon and First American — with conspiring to falsify records and concealing $105 million of loan guarantees. This action, though, didn't endear the SFO to Morgenthau; Iman had crossed the Atlantic to testify about BCCI as a cooperating witness with the Manhattan D.A.'s office. That same month, the SFO arrested the British-Asian businessman Nazmu Virani and charged him with conspiracy to mislead BCCI's auditors and other offenses. In the fall of 1992, he was in custody awaiting trial.

The SFO also had begun investigating several people who had worked for Price Waterhouse. One target was Richard Fear, a former partner who had been involved in auditing BCCI. Fear left the firm in 1986 and moved to the Cayman Islands. Two years later, he received two payments — one for $80,000, the other for $20,000 — from Capcom, the infamous BCCI satellite in London. Capcom's records do not indicate what the payments were for; a company ledger listing the second one simply reads "Paid to Richard Fear." (On several occasions, Fear was asked — through his lawyer — to comment on the payments. He did not respond.)

A Price Waterhouse spokeswoman said that the firm had conducted its own investigation of the payments and determined that they were "unconnected with [Price Waterhouse's] audits of BCCI." However, law enforcement authorities apparently suspect that there may be some suspicious connections between Fear and BCCI. In June 1992, the Cayman Islands police raided the homes of both Fear and another former Price Waterhouse official, Richard Harris, according to two people familiar with the BCCI case. The police, who were working on behalf of the SFO, also raided the office of a Caymans law firm that had represented either Harris or Fear as well as Price Waterhouse's Caymans office.

The SFO, like Morgenthau, also focused considerable attention on Kamal Adham. The Saudi was just as interested in his potential prosecutors; he had for months arranged meetings with them ostensibly to protest his innocence but also to sound out the possibility of making a deal. Adham likes to travel in the West and enjoys his apartment in Belgravia, arguably London's poshest district. He didn't want to spend his days hiding out from the SFO and Morgenthau's investigators. He missed Paris, and, furthermore, he had property and investments in the United States and Britain that could be seized by prosecutors. He is also a kinsman of the Saudi ruling family — a brother-in-law of the late and respected King Faisal — so settling his case might remove some of the taint that the Saudis had suffered from the BCCI scandal.

The indictment of Khalid Bin Mahfouz and the SFO's new cooperation with Morgenthau had a galvanizing effect on Adham and his business manager, Sayed Jawhary. They realized they could be next.

In July, Morgenthau's office notified Adham's lawyer, Plato Cacheris, and Jawhary's lawyer, Sarah Moss, that it was preparing to indict their clients for a list of alleged infractions of state laws. After months of on-again, off-again negotiations, the defense lawyers informed Morgenthau's office that Adham and Jawhary were prepared to make a deal. If Morgenthau dropped some of the charges, Adham would pay a large fine and agree to assist the prosecutors. If the plea negotiations ended successfully, it would be a major breakthrough for Morgenthau. It would mean that Adham, who had played a central role in BCCI's illegal takeover of First American, would testify against others, including Clark Clifford and Robert Altman.

Morgenthau's investigation of BCCI had been widely praised, but there was also a degree of cynicism. Defense lawyers and reporters pointed out that the indictments had only included foreigners with strange names who were thousands of miles outside the jurisdiction of the New York courts. The D.A. had now been investigating BCCI for more than three years, and skeptics were beginning to wonder if he would ever bring charges against any Americans, let alone such a personage as Clifford.

Nevertheless, Morgenthau was preparing to do just that, and he was receiving valuable assistance from the federal authorities. The Justice Department and the Federal Reserve were also investigating Clifford and Altman, and they were exchanging information with the Manhattan D.A.'s office. Since the arrival of Attorney General William Barr a year earlier, cooperation between the Justice Department and the D.A.'s office had improved considerably.

In broad outline, the federal and state investigations were quite similar, but they dealt with the laws of two different jurisdictions. The Justice Department and the Fed were looking for evidence that Clifford and Altman violated U.S. laws and banking regulations in connection with the ownership and management of First American. Morgenthau had to prove violations of New York State laws, but he had more flexibility than this might suggest. For example, if one or more acts in an alleged conspiracy had occurred in New York, he could argue that state law had been violated.

By the summer of 1992, the federal and state investigators had found a great deal of information that seemed to undermine the assertions of Clifford and Altman that they had been dupes of BCCI. As early as 1983, for example, Altman attended two BCCI conferences at which one of the speakers, a National Bank of Georgia official named Bill Batastini, expressed his happiness at being part of the BCCI family. This was a clear indication that BCCI had secretly controlled at least one U.S. bank. Four years later, an official of First American Bank of New York (FABNY) sent a memo to Clifford and Altman regarding an employee who had recently been dismissed. Attached to the memo was a letter in which the former employee made it clear he regarded First American as a BCCI subsidiary. In one passage he wrote, "Either FAB must take over and become First American Bank and buy out BCCI shares, or let them have it."

Other information gathered by the investigators suggested that BCCI officials had an important say in the management of First American. In 1982, according to the Fed, Abedi and Naqvi chose a suite of offices at 350 Park Avenue as the headquarters for FABNY. When Clifford and Altman objected that the rent was too high, Abedi overruled them, according to the Fed. Conveniently, BCCI's New York office was just down the street, at 320 Park Avenue. BCCI also played a role in the hiring of First American executives; about nine prospective employees were interviewed by Abedi or other BCCI officials.

Beyond the evidence relating to the ownership and control of First American, the prosecutors and the Fed believed that Clifford and Altman had lied repeatedly to the authorities. One example concerns First American's controversial investment in certificates of deposit issued by ICIC, the BCCI dummy company. Altman, according to the Fed, had made the decision to buy the CDs, yet, when questioned by the Fed, he testified that he did not know who made the decision. Altman also allegedly lied about the lucrative investment in First American stock that he and Clifford had made. In testimony to the Fed, Altman said he did not know how the price was determined when he and Clifford sold most of the stock. According to Imran Iman, a

BCCI official who worked on the transaction, Altman himself had been involved in fixing the sale price.

Iman was just one of several witnesses to the alleged wrongdoing by Clifford and Altman, but Morgenthau was hoping to get still more. Adham and Jawhary could be of tremendous help, but their lawyers said the Saudis would not make a deal unless they were guaranteed full immunity from future prosecution in the United States. Morgenthau could give them immunity in New York, but the Justice Department would have to agree to immunity from federal charges.

While trying to work out a deal with the Saudis and the Justice Department, Morgenthau was racing the clock. Some of the charges he was contemplating had to do with First American's acquisition of National Bank of Georgia. The takeover had occurred in 1987, and there was a five-year statute of limitations. By late July, Morgenthau decided to seek an indictment from the grand jury.

On July 22, a Manhattan grand jury returned sealed indictments against Clifford, Altman, and other suspects. Within days, two of the most important witnesses against them made their deal. Adham and Jawhary stole into New York on Monday, July 27, to sign cooperation agreements with the Manhattan D.A.'s office and the Justice Department. Both men pleaded guilty to violating New York State banking law. A company controlled by Adham, Arabian Industrial & Commercial Company, pleaded guilty to charges of fraud. As part of the deal, Adham agreed to pay a fine of $105 million, about $90 million of which was divided roughly between the Federal Reserve and the liquidators of BCCI. Most of the rest of the money was split among various law enforcement agencies. The trustee for First American received as much as $2 million to help finance his operation; some of that money would be used to hire an investigator to look over First American to make sure that it was fit for sale and that there weren't any hidden horrors in its books.

On Tuesday, July 28, the news broke in the press that Morgenthau was planning to announce the indictment of Clifford and Altman the next day. The Justice Department, eager to avoid being scooped by the New York D.A., raced to finish its own indictment. One problem was that Justice was planning only to charge Altman. Clifford, it appeared, was going to be spared because of his advanced age and heart problems. (Some cynics wondered whether his political influence played a role.)

Ironically, Justice's plan to keep Clifford's name out of the indictment could actually hurt the lawyer, because it could mean that he would be facing Morgenthau's well-prepared prosecutors in a New York courtroom rather than Justice Department lawyers, who were relative newcomers to the case. If, however, he were charged in both places, he might be tried only in Washington because of New York's strict double jeopardy law.* Clifford's lawyers, according to one source, even urged the Justice Department to put him back in the indictment. (An attorney for Clifford says this is false.)

It was now the Justice Department's turn to race the clock. Morgenthau scheduled his press conference for Wednesday morning. For the federal charges to be announced at the same time, a bill of indictment would have to be presented to a federal grand jury in Washington early that morning. The prosecutors worked for hours on the document, finally completing it at 4:00 A.M. A few hours later, the grand jury voted to indict.

At 11:00 A.M. on Wednesday, July 29, Assistant Attorney General Robert S. Mueller III announced that a federal grand jury in Washington had returned a three-count indictment against Clark Clifford and Robert Altman. They were accused of conspiring to defraud the Federal Reserve Board by misleading it about BCCI's relationship with First American and obstructing the Fed's inquiries into BCCI. They were accused of seeking to "curry favor with BCCI" by arranging for First American to buy National Bank of Georgia and depositing $45 million in ICIC. The grand jury also alleged that Clifford and Altman had lied to the Fed about BCCI's loans to First American shareholders, including the loans that the Washington lawyers had themselves received. As Mueller provided details of the federal charges, Robert Morgenthau was holding his own press conference in New York, making even more sweeping allegations.

Morgenthau announced two indictments containing charges against a total of six defendants. One of the indictments accused Abedi, Naqvi, Pharaon, and Fulaij with participating in "enterprise corruption," New York State's version of RICO (the federal Racketeer Influenced and Corrupt Organizations Act). This indictment alleged that

---

*Although the U.S. Constitution forbids trying a person twice for the same crime, the Supreme Court has ruled that it is sometimes permissible for a person to be tried twice — once in federal court and once in state court — on similar charges. The theory is that each court system represents a different "sovereign." New York State, however, has a double jeopardy law that gives defendants more protection than the Supreme Court rulings.

BCCI had been a criminal enterprise since 1972 and that it had used an array of fraudulent schemes to achieve its ends, including the bribery of public officials. According to the indictment, the bank had paid millions of dollars in bribes to central bankers or other financial officials in a dozen developing countries: Argentina, Cameroon, Colombia, the Congo, the Ivory Coast, Morocco, Nigeria, Pakistan, Peru, Senegal, Tunisia, and Zambia.

The second New York indictment accused Abedi, Naqvi, Clifford, Altman, and Fulaij of participating in a scheme to defraud. Much of the indictment dealt with BCCI's illegal takeover of First American; the grand jury alleged that the defendants began conspiring to acquire the banking company in 1977. Clifford and Altman were also accused of conniving in transactions that weakened First American but benefited BCCI, such as the takeover of National Bank of Georgia. In exchange for their help to BCCI, Clifford and Altman received tens of millions of dollars in legal fees and profits from stock deals. The grand jury characterized these as bribes.

The charges carried maximum penalties of eight years in jail and $80 million in fines for Clifford and twenty years and $80 million for Altman. In practice, though, neither man would suffer such penalties even if convicted on all counts; sentences invariably run concurrently, meaning that neither man would have to serve more than four years, the maximum prison sentence for any of their alleged crimes.

Morgenthau told reporters that now perhaps half the BCCI story had been made public, but that much still remained to be investigated and revealed. The prosecutor sharply criticized Abu Dhabi, maintaining that the emirate hadn't given any cooperation to the New York investigators despite its promises: "We haven't gotten a single thing in the past year."

That same day, the Federal Reserve issued a long order detailing Clifford's and Altman's many alleged infractions of banking regulations. It said it was considering whether to ban the two men from U.S. banking for life, but it wouldn't impose a fine against them for fear of triggering the double jeopardy clause of the Fifth Amendment to the Constitution, which would bar criminal prosecution.

Clifford and Altman pleaded not guilty to all charges and vowed to fight to clear their names. Through their lawyers at Skadden, Arps, they released a brief statement claiming that the charges were "a cruel and unjust abuse of the prosecutorial function" and the product of a horse race between prosecutors and investigators at the Manhattan district attorney's office, the Justice Department, and the Federal Reserve. The three agencies were "seeking public acclaim for their role in fighting BCCI corruption and to deflect criticism for their past failings." Clifford and Altman said they had become "the most visible, convenient targets for government bodies that wish to demonstrate that BCCI wrongdoers will be brought to justice." In this rush to bring indictments, "political considerations and public posturing have overwhelmed the merits of this matter." The two men said they would hold a press conference at their lawyers' offices in Washington the following day "to comment in person on these charges."

Clark Clifford shuffled toward the podium in the crowded conference room. Journalists perched on cupboards because of the crush of people as the eighty-five-year-old lawyer blinked before the banks of lights and television cameras that faced him. He and Robert Altman were fifteen minutes late for their 10:00 A.M. press conference, ensuring that most of the stragglers had arrived at the Washington office of Skadden, Arps, Slate, Meagher & Flom, a stone's throw from the Treasury Department.

Wearing a gray pinstripe suit, white shirt, and striped tie, every curl of his snow-white hair in place, Clifford presented the immaculate figure of the elder statesman. "I wish to thank you for being present here this morning," he began in his clear, deep voice. "It demonstrates a wish on your part to have a fuller understanding of this case rather than just what one reads about the charges that have been brought." The system itself is biased, Clifford explained to his hushed audience. "I have felt that there is a gross unfairness in the manner in which the publicity about a criminal proceeding is brought," he continued. "The indictments are filed, the next day the papers are filled with the government's charges, and then, after a mere denial by the defendant, weeks, months, and sometimes even years go by before you ever get to hear about what the defense is in the case."

That, Clifford said, was why he and Altman had decided to call this press conference. "We wish as quickly as possible here to bring to your attention the other side of the case," he said as Altman and their lawyer, Carl Rauh, sat impassively behind him. Surprisingly, Robert Bennett, the lawyer who had taken the most visible role in defending Clifford and Altman, had decided to remain on vacation in Montana.

Clifford insisted that he and Altman weren't at all overwhelmed by the "nature of the publicity this morning and the amount of attention given to it." The plain fact, Clifford said, was that "neither the district attorney in New York nor the Justice Department in Washington has any direct, credible evidence of our participation in any wrongdoing." The prosecutors, Clifford said, had found neither witnesses nor documents to support their case, despite "the fact that for over a year the most massive investigation has gone on that many have ever seen." The investigators, he said, raising his voice for emphasis, have found "not one scintilla of direct evidence of proof, either oral or in writing." The prosecution has two approaches, he said: either that he and Altman were willing partners in a criminal endeavor with BCCI or that First American's management was indeed controlled by BCCI and that the two lawyers were aware of that fact.

In time-honored fashion, Clifford told the story of his involvement with BCCI: how he had met Abedi and represented the banker's Arab clients, "men with excellent reputations, men of fabulous wealth" from the Middle East. Abedi appeared respectable, able, and softspoken, Clifford said, and "seemed to be what he pretended to be." Clifford helped Abedi's associates take over First American and, in 1982, decided to accept the "challenge" of becoming chairman of the board despite his seventy-five years. During his tenure, Clifford said, he had received only an annual compensation of $50,000. The bank didn't even assign a car to him for five years, Clifford explained, and then only "because people began to lose faith in my driving ability."

First American had done well under his management, Clifford averred, growing by billions of dollars in assets. It had done so well that — after consulting with the holding company board — he and Altman had bought some of the company's stock. They sold it two years later, at a fair profit. "You've seen a great many numbers, greatly inflated numbers," Clifford told his audience; all he had really ended up with was "a profit of something like $2.6 million." These profits, he argued, were only fair rewards for a job well done. He quoted senior Federal Reserve officials, including the former head of banking supervision, William Taylor, to show that they hadn't found any evidence of BCCI's influence on First American, as prosecutors now alleged.

Clifford said he would have given almost anything to have been warned of BCCI's criminality and to have avoided unwittingly becoming involved with it. But now he vowed that he would clear his name, despite his advanced years. "I have not even begun to fight," he declared defiantly as he brought his fluent presentation to a close. As he moved back to sit down beside Rauh, the glow disappeared from Clifford's face. He was once more a tired old man.

Altman quickly followed his mentor to the podium. "Deals," he charged, "have been made with true scoundrels" by prosecutors trying to gain information. All the direct evidence, however, Altman claimed, "establishes our innocence." The government had to twist events, he maintained, to obtain even the circumstantial evidence it planned to use against the two lawyers. The case, he argued, "should disturb decent Americans" as "anyone, and particularly prominent, well-known people, had become fair game" for prosecutors. "We shall fight to the end to clear our good names," Altman concluded, echoing Clifford's sentiments, if not his exact words.

Neither man offered any reply to the questions shouted at them by some of the assembled journalists. "Did you tell the Federal Reserve about your borrowings from BCCI?" yelled one persistent reporter.

Rauh quickly stood up. These investigations, he said, had been "a brutal ordeal" for Clifford and Altman, yet they had always sought to cooperate with the government. This was especially courageous of Clifford, Rauh said, because of his age and his "very poor health." Rauh said that Clifford suffered from "severe coronary disease" and has "90 percent blockage in three coronary arteries and a 70 percent blockage in a fourth." Because of his age and infirmity, Clifford "very much wants the opportunity to be vindicated before he dies" and "hopes to have an immediate and speedy trial here in Washington."

More shouted questions greeted these remarks, but Rauh simply said, "We will have no questions and no questions will be answered." The hungry media would have to make do with prepared statements from Clifford, Altman, and sundry lawyers, officials, and First American bankers who seemed to support their arguments. A joint statement from Clifford and Altman claimed that the Justice Department's case was "contrived" and that Morgenthau's office had "adopted an old trick — throw everything against the wall in the hope that something sticks."

Although Clifford and Altman insisted that the case against them was based on flimsy evidence, the reality was that investigators for the Manhattan district attorney, the Justice Department, and the Federal Reserve had obtained a great deal of damaging information about the two lawyers. Some of it was laid out in the indictments and in the Federal Reserve order of July 29, 1992. But there was also other information that had not been released publicly, including statements from dozens of witnesses who were familiar with the relationship between BCCI and First American.

One such witness was Riaz Saleem Aslam, the former financial adviser to Sheikh Zayed with direct personal knowledge of the takeover. Aslam, as we have seen, accused Zayed and assorted BCCI officials of wrongdoing in the takeover. He also alleged that Clifford and Altman were accomplices and that their complicity dated back to late 1977, just weeks after the takeover attempt began.

Aslam believed that the Washington lawyers had urged Zayed to keep him in prison because they were fearful of what he could say about their conduct. He noted that they had been BCCI's principal U.S. lawyers until October 1990 (when Zayed replaced them with Patton, Boggs & Blow). During that period, according to Aslam's attorney, BCCI's lawyers wrote "memos to Zayed's Department of Personal Affairs to press for his continued incarceration." The same month the Clifford firm was dropped, Aslam was freed.

Zayed played an integral role in the founding of BCCI, according to a statement Aslam claimed to have written in 1983. When the institution was established, "Zayed was probably the largest single shareholder and also provided a large subordinated loan to augment the small capital of the bank." Much of BCCI's capital, however, was "internally created" by coopting bank loans and deposits and with fraudulent accounting entries. The sheikh supported BCCI "by placing long-term deposits with it" that were "far in excess of what a normal investor would have considered prudent."

The sheikh was intimately involved in Abedi's attempt to acquire Financial General (as First American was then called), according to Aslam. It was understood at the outset that Abedi would control the banking company. One of Zayed's motives, Aslam said, was to increase his political power in the United States. "Mr. Abedi never concealed his intent to control FGB as the effective arm of BCCI," he wrote, "which [Abedi] said would benefit the Ruler both through ownership of BCCI and direct ownership of a Washington D.C. bank, especially if this could result in a mutually profitable relation with a close confidant of the President of the United States" — a reference to Bert Lance.

Abedi and his associates lied to regulators about the identity of the investors, and Zayed went along with the deception, according to Aslam. The initial stock purchases in late 1977 and early 1978 had ostensibly been made by Kamal Adham, Faisal Saud al-Fulaij, and two of Zayed's sons, Sheikh Sultan and Sheikh Mohammed. (Mohammed, a minor, supposedly acted through Aslam's boss, Abdullah Darwaish, the chairman of the ruler's Department of Personal Affairs.) In reality, Aslam said, the stock was accumulated by Abedi and placed in the names of the four investors. The real owners were Zayed and BCCI.

Zayed's pivotal role in the affair became apparent to Aslam after a meeting in Pakistan in early 1978, during Lance's visit. It was attended by Zayed, Abedi, Lance, and advisers to the ruler, including Majid Ali and Darwaish. According to Aslam, the meeting "was called by Abedi to allow Sheikh Zayed to formally inform Darwish that certain shares had been bought in FGL and that Darwish was to liaise with BCCI in all matters relating thereunto."*

The collection of the stock had been handled clumsily. "Lance had clearly inspired Abedi to act impulsively," Aslam stated, "without proper allowance" for U.S. securities laws. This was a reference to the requirement that anyone who buys 5 percent of a public company's stock should file a disclosure statement with the Securities and Exchange Commission; Abedi quickly exceeded that limit and failed to make any filings.

Realizing his legally perilous position, Abedi retained Clifford's law firm. According to Aslam, this was done in December 1977 — not, as Clifford has maintained, the following February, when the investment group was sued by the banking company.† By late January 1978, BCCI controlled about 17 percent of the stock, more than three times the disclosure threshold. It became imperative to disguise BCCI's control of the stock — and its violation of securities law — by parceling out the shares to four nominees.

Evidence of BCCI's efforts to round up front men is contained in documents unearthed by U.S. government investigators. For example,

---

*In his statements, Aslam spells the name of Zayed's adviser as "Darwish" and the name of Abedi's deputy as "Naqui." First American is generally referred to by its old name, Financial General Bankshares, which is sometimes abbreviated as FGB or FGL. (The "L" is for Limited, probably because Limited is used in corporate names in Aslam's native Pakistan.)

†Aslam's recollection jibes with new findings by Senator Kerry's investigators. They discovered an invoice sent to Abedi by Clifford's firm which covers work done in January 1978. Moreover, the Abdus Sami telex mentioned in this chapter states that Sami had retained Clifford in connection with the takeover. Financial General's lawsuit was filed on February 17, more than two weeks after the telex was sent.

on January 30, 1978, BCCI's Abdus Sami sent a telex to Abedi in which he urgently requested "two other names immediately" in addition to the two he already had, Adham and Fulaij. Abedi quickly came up with Zayed's sons Sultan and Mohammed. In a written statement dated 1991, Aslam said, "The shares which were ultimately represented as purchased by the two sons through BCCI had been allocated to them as nominees for Sheikh Zayed, who purchased them with his own knowledge, his own funds, and designated his sons as nominees to keep secret his ownership."

Clifford and Altman were accomplices in BCCI's scheme to conceal the true ownership of the stock, according to Aslam. In his words, they helped Abedi "rectify the mistakes and guide the acquisition in conformance to U.S. regulation." With their guidance, "a reorganized, although false, edifice of ownership of shares in FGB was created." In statements to the SEC and Financial General, noted Aslam, the owners were "referred to as the 'Arab investors.' " Disclosure statements filed with the SEC stated that Mohammed and Sultan acquired close to 5 percent of Financial General on January 26, 1978. This, of course, was four days before Sami asked Abedi to supply two more names. Either Sami's telex is wrong or the SEC filings are false.

After Financial General sued the four Arab "stockholders" (along with Abedi and his associates), Darwaish had to go to Washington to be deposed by lawyers for the banking company. He was extremely anxious about the deposition, according to Aslam, and talked nervously about "the big guns" he would have to face. Clifford and Altman did more than simply prepare him for the deposition, according to Aslam; they coached him on what to say.

In his 1983 statement, Aslam described one alleged coaching session which, he said, took place in London in an apartment near Hyde Park. "I recollect a meeting in the summer of 1978 held at Darwish's (rented) penthouse at the Quadrangle Apartments in London. The following were present — A. H. Abedi, S. H. Naqui, Clark Clifford, R. Altman, B. T. Lance, Abdullah Darwish, and R. Aslam." The purpose of the meeting "was to discuss strategy and bring Darwish up to date," Aslam wrote. "In practical terms Clifford and Altman coached Darwish extensively prior to his testimony, including times when I was present."

Aslam accompanied Darwaish to Washington. They were met at Dulles airport by Dildar Rizvi, one of Abedi's chief deputies, who was involved in orchestrating the takeover attempt. "When Darwish went

to Washington D.C. in the fall of 1978 for his deposition, I accompanied him and was with him during his entire stay there except during
the actual taking of the deposition," Aslam wrote.

There was additional coaching in Washington the week before the
deposition, according to Aslam. As a result, almost all of Darwaish's
"testimony in the FGB actions was a reflection of what Clifford and
Altman wanted it to be rather than what had occurred in Darwish's
knowledge," Aslam said. "I specifically recollect [Darwaish's] being
told to answer certain questions in a certain manner." He added, "It is
my belief and in my knowledge that such answers are not true and I
can isolate them if given access to his deposition transcript."

After his release from prison in 1990, Aslam saw a transcript of the
deposition and found numerous statements that he maintained were
false. Darwaish testified that he represented Mohammed and Sultan
separately, that he was Mohammed's legal guardian, and that FGB
stock was purchased with Mohammed's personal funds. All of this
was false, according to Aslam. Darwaish, he said, represented Mohammed only at Zayed's explicit instructions, Darwaish's only compensation was from Zayed, and Darwaish informed Mohammed
about the share purchases only after they had occurred. Darwaish also
stated falsely that Zayed did not have control over Mohammed's
spending.

During the Washington visit in 1978, Aslam found further evidence
of Zayed's prominent role in the takeover attempt. The UAE's ambassador to Washington, Hamad al-Midfa, talked about "attempting
to manage the situation with the press" with regard to the takeover.
In Aslam's view, the ambassador "could and would only have become involved with [the takeover attempt] at the direct instructions of
Zayed."

Sheikh Sultan refused to cooperate with Abedi's scheme, according
to Aslam; he was extremely upset that his name had been used in the
takeover. So, in the fall of 1978, it was arranged that Adham would
"buy" his Financial General stock. (Aslam believed that Clifford never
met Sultan or Mohammed, even though Clifford and Altman acted as
their attorneys.)

In his 1983 statement, Aslam said that throughout the takeover
battle, he had "strict instructions from Darwish" that the books of the
Department of Personal Affairs "should at no time reflect the purchase
of [Financial General] shares." As a result, the DPA ensured that the
$10 million used to purchase the stock — ostensibly for Sheikh Mo-

hammed — was recorded on the books as "a deposit with BCCI London."

An important character in the illegal takeover was Zafar Iqbal, according to Aslam. In 1978, he was the head of BCCE, the UAE affiliate of BCCI in which Zayed held a controlling interest. (Iqbal became BCCI's chief executive in 1990.) According to Aslam's 1983 statement, Iqbal doctored BCCI's accounts to disguise the fact that the ruler's office had supplied funds through BCCI to acquire Financial General stock. Aslam knew this from "discussions with Zafar Iqbal and Shafquat Bokhari of BCCI, Abu Dhabi as well as S. H. Naqui (on telephone only)." He said, "It is my recollection that certain fictitious entries were made in the books to show (specifically in the case of Sh Sultan's 'share purchase') that the source of funds were different, i.e. that he had provided the funds and not the D.P.A." He added, "It is my recollection that at least on two occasions Iqbal and/or Bokhari showed [me] the statements that purported to show account relationships between DPA/Sultan/Mohammed on the one hand and BCCI on the other. It is my specific recollection that such account statements were false and did not reflect the correct state of the account relationship."

Such account statements, of course, were created by BCCI to support the false statements made in the SEC filings and court pleadings in the United States. False money entries were even put through the accounts and the dates of transactions were changed, Aslam said. There were other reasons for the doctoring of accounts. BCCI wanted to show that the sheikhs who invested in Financial General were not indebted to BCCI. It also wanted to show that "the initial purchase of shares had come from the sheikhs' personal resources, whereas in fact it was provided by the bank initially."

In recent statements, Aslam has described how "the two sheikhs [Sultan and Mohammed] routinely ran an overdraft account at BCCE, under the approval of Zafar Iqbal and his deputy, Bokhari, which was paid down from time to time by the DPA at the direction of Darwish. Because of the questions about credit from BCCI and the need to present a 'clean slate' these routine credits were altered on the record presented."

BCCI's takeover of Financial General was completed in 1982 through nominees, according to Aslam. Discussing these front men, he stated recently that "the guys didn't have the money, most probably didn't know what was happening, and they just had their names used.

They probably didn't even know their names were being used." Although some of the shareholders were men of substance and wealth, Aslam believed "that they would be hard put to come up with this size of money for one investment, particularly as it had already been committed to the U.S. authorities that their role in running [First American] would have to remain strictly passive." Aslam also doubted that these investors had the expertise to make a judgment about acquiring a bank holding company in the United States.

Aslam pointed out another important anomaly in the takeover of First American. Darwaish, who was identified as one of the lead investors from 1978 to 1982, had been arrested months before the acquisition was consummated in the spring of 1982. U.S. regulators, particularly at the Federal Reserve, should have been aware of this. The ruler's investment committee, on which Abedi and Crown Prince Khalifa sat, had made serious accusations against Darwaish in December 1981, and he was soon arrested. In January 1982, the Abu Dhabi Investment Authority sent telexes to fifteen major international banks saying that Darwaish had been involved in a massive fraud against the ruler and that the banks should not do business with him. By March, Zayed had filed major lawsuits against Darwaish in Chicago and New York, alleging fraud totaling about $100 million. Yet it was only after the *Washington Post* reported Darwaish's incarceration in August of that year that the Fed's general counsel, Michael Bradfield, wrote to Clark Clifford to request information about the affair.

Clifford, Altman, and Sheikh Zayed have denied any wrongdoing in connection with the takeover of First American. The Washington lawyers say they were duped by BCCI. The ruler of Abu Dhabi claims he was a victim of the bank. Nevertheless, it is impossible to dismiss Aslam's allegations out of hand. Although he is clearly an interested party — having been jailed for several years by Zayed — he was a witness to the takeover, and his story is consistent with what is now known about it; much of it can also be corroborated with documents and statements by other witnesses. Aslam could be a powerful witness against Clifford, Altman, and other suspects in the BCCI affair.

The trauma of Clifford and Altman coincided almost exactly with the twentieth anniversary of the founding of BCCI. It was in the late summer of 1972 that Sheikh Zayed agreed to back this new banking venture. It was portrayed as an institution from the developing world that would rival the biggest banks in New York, London, Frankfurt, and Tokyo. Abedi's vision proved extremely seductive to Zayed and many others. For the Abu Dhabi ruler and other Arab potentates, BCCI could serve as a vehicle to extend their influence. For Abedi and his coterie of Pakistani financiers, it would provide an opportunity to enter the world of international finance. For Clifford and Altman, a relationship with BCCI meant millions of dollars and greater power in Washington. For these men and many others, BCCI had become a nightmare.

EPILOGUE

AGHA HASAN ABEDI seldom gave interviews to journalists, but he made an exception in late 1982, when he agreed to sit down with a writer for *Institutional Investor,* a New York financial magazine. Abedi's willingness to talk at that time is understandable, for 1982 had been a glorious year. In just ten years, BCCI had become a global financial empire, with offices in fifty-eight countries and assets of $8.5 billion. It was believed to be the fastest-growing bank in the world. That same year, Abedi had achieved an enormously impressive coup in the United States when he had secretly acquired control of First American Bankshares, which would soon become the largest banking company in Washington, D.C.

The interviewer began by noting that some critics of BCCI said it was "different" from other banks, and he asked Abedi about his "philosophy of banking." Abedi replied that BCCI's was "the age-old philosophy of banking; there is nothing new about it. Our greatest concern, and our greatest desire, is to protect the interests of our clients, the depositors." When the interviewer suggested that this didn't sound very different, Abedi became more expansive: "There have also been some more important objectives. We want to serve a useful purpose, not only for our shareholders, but for our clients and our staff, whom we call 'the BCCI family.' " He also spoke of BCCI's moral dimension. It was the belief of Abedi and his colleagues that "no material end can be achieved without a moral aspect behind it."

Abedi, of course, was neither a successful international banker nor a pillar of morality but one of the most successful con men in history. A master illusionist, he could make his audience see things that did not exist. In carrying out this deception, he paid an enormous amount of attention to physical appearances. Whenever BCCI opened a new office, Abedi showed little interest in its financial performance. Location and design were what mattered. BCCI's branches had to be sleek, modern, and tastefully appointed. When visiting one of his outposts, says a former official, Abedi would make sure every detail was correct. "He would go all the way to Zimbabwe and he would reprimand the manager, saying, 'I saw that chair in the reception area is broken.' "

Abedi was equally concerned about his own image. In order to be accepted as a successful international financier he had to look the part, so he purchased his suits at Bijan in New York, one of the most expensive clothing stores in the world. "He was always impeccably dressed," says a colleague.

In conversation, Abedi would discourse on subjects ranging from international trade and economics to world politics and Third World development. A Pakistani banker recalls meeting him for the first time in the 1970s, when there was widespread talk of establishing a "new world economic order" to help developing countries. Abedi, says this man, used all the right buzzwords: "He appeared to be more of a diplomat than a banker. I was totally impressed." Soon afterward he applied for a job with BCCI.

Within BCCI, the "Founding President" was the object of a personality cult. Outsiders were impressed as well. Abedi was a man of tremendous charm, which helps explain why so many powerful people were drawn to him. Jimmy Carter seems to have been mesmerized by Abedi, talking about him almost as if he were a religious figure.

Abedi's most important props, however, were not the fancy branches, expensive suits, or financial jargon, but wealthy Arab friends who pretended to be BCCI shareholders. In using these men, Abedi skillfully manipulated the expectations and beliefs of his audience. BCCI appeared on the financial stage at a time when hundreds of billions of petrodollars were beginning to flow to Arab nations. Newspapers, magazines, and television screens were filled with images of "oil sheikhs" in flowing robes, Midases of the desert who had accumulated wealth beyond the dreams of ordinary mortals. If men like this were behind BCCI, it had to be a solid institution. When the deception was exposed, BCCI turned out to be an artfully contrived fake, with front men posing as stockholders, nonexistent capital, and profits manufactured out of thin air. It was an optical illusion, a mirage in the desert. BCCI was the bank that never was.

When BCCI was seized in July 1991, Abedi was a pathetic figure. He was fragile physically and his mind appeared to be cloudy. But his decline had begun more than three years earlier, in early 1988, when he suffered severe health problems. His physical deterioration mirrored that of his bank. Without his ability to charm Sheikh Zayed and other longtime supporters, Abedi found it harder to perpetuate the BCCI illusion. The bank and its creator crumbled together.

The founder of BCCI has been living out his days in quiet seclusion behind the high walls of his compound in the wealthy Clifton section of Karachi, Pakistan. Crippled by a series of coronaries and kept alive with a transplanted heart, he has been confined to a wheelchair. His wife, Rabia, and a group of servants attend to his needs. Although Rabia has generally shielded him from media attention, she made a few remarks to reporters after the closure. "My husband has lost everything," she said. "He lost his health, his bank, his dream, everything he worked for. And now people say he is to be blamed."

When Abedi was asked to comment on the July 1991 indictment in New York, he insisted that he was innocent. Speaking through his wife, he said, "The truth will ultimately prevail. I have full faith in God. He's always guided me."

The cost of Abedi's deception has been enormous. Robert Morgenthau has called the BCCI affair the biggest bank fraud in history. At its height, BCCI had more than $20 billion in deposits, and all of that money had been collected fraudulently. Many customers, of course, pulled their money out before the seizure, causing BCCI's total liabilities to shrink by about half. Nevertheless, an incredible $9.5 billion was lost or stolen.

Not all of this money will be lost, however. After the liquidation of assets, contributions by Sheikh Zayed, and restitution by some of the culprits, depositors will get back a portion of their money — perhaps as much as a third. That will still leave enormous losses, however, that will be borne by depositors. BCCI had nearly a million customers when it was closed, many of them people of modest means from developing countries.

Indeed, one of the saddest aspects of the BCCI affair is that it was a hoax on thousands of people from impoverished countries who believed in the bank, including BCCI employees who had nothing to do with the bank's misconduct. It was a source of pride that an institution owned and run by people from the Third World could become a major force in international banking, an industry dominated by banks from industrial nations. Beyond that, BCCI managed to convince a great many people that it was a force for good because it supported such ventures as Global 2000 and the Third World Foundation. The reality, of course, is that BCCI ravaged developing countries by collecting flight capital, bolstering dictators, and fostering corruption. In Nigeria alone, BCCI drained hundreds of millions of dollars in hard currency out of the country through illegal dealings in the foreign exchange market.

In the industrial countries, depositors will suffer large losses in only a few places. Britain is one example, mainly because of the bank's heavy penetration of immigrant communities. In addition, several local government bodies in the UK had large deposits at BCCI.

In the United States, Federal Reserve officials have stressed that BCCI was forbidden to take retail deposits, implying that Americans have lost nothing. This is highly misleading. BCCI did take deposits at its foreign offices — and, in some cases, at domestic branches — from American individuals, companies, and government agencies. In addition, BCCI employees in the United States engaged in an illegal telemarketing scheme to collect retail deposits, some of which came from U.S. residents.

BCCI's victims also include American taxpayers. Two U.S. financial institutions in which BCCI invested through Ghaith Pharaon — CenTrust Savings Bank and Independence Bank — have collapsed, at a huge cost to taxpayers. The failure of CenTrust would not have been as catastrophic if the regulators had not been fooled by the CenTrust/BCCI bond-parking scheme into prolonging the life of the savings bank. BCCI, in short, contributed to one of the worst savings and loan failures in history.

Beyond the direct financial consequences are many other costs that are harder to quantify. Through its involvement in money laundering, BCCI promoted the trade in illegal drugs, which has been a scourge on the United States and other countries. BCCI was an accomplice in other forms of crime, including investment fraud, terrorism, and illegal arms trafficking. There is considerable evidence that its involvement in the arms trade extended to nuclear weapons technology.

Perhaps most important, BCCI's practice of coopting and corrupting public officials helped to undermine the institutions that are supposed to protect the public, including law enforcement agencies and central banks. Former BCCI officials have told investigators about payoffs to government officials in a long list of countries.

But corruption is not the only explanation for the failure of these institutions. The scandal exposed incredible negligence by those who should have been policing BCCI. Confidence in bank regulators had already been undermined by a series of shocks to the system, including the debt crisis of the early 1980s in developing countries and, later, the savings and loan scandals.

The credibility of audits and auditors has also been battered. Since late 1989, Price Waterhouse has played a vital role in helping the regulators and prosecutors expose BCCI's crimes. But why did it fail to detect the rampant fraud at BCCI for so many years before that? Why did the firm sign BCCI's unqualified financial statements for 1989 — after it learned of widespread misconduct? Is corruption part of the answer? The Manhattan district attorney and Britain's Serious Fraud Office are now investigating the possibility that former Price Waterhouse officials received payoffs from BCCI.

The bank's malevolent influence extended even to the interrelated worlds of foreign policy, espionage, and covert action. BCCI was involved in manipulating American foreign policy to benefit its political patrons in Pakistan and the Middle East. Western intelligence officials who could have exposed its political activities preferred instead to use the bank for their own purposes.

The collapse of BCCI is by no means the end of the story. The painful dénouement will continue for many more years. Some of the victims will be partially compensated and some of the villains will be punished. Although prosecutors, investigators, and journalists are struggling to understand what happened, many mysteries, inevitably, will never be solved.

Who is ultimately responsible for the scandal? Abedi, of course, was clearly the principal culprit. He conceived BCCI, founded it, recruited the nominee shareholders, built its international network, and presided over the institution when it began robbing its own depositors. But Abedi did not act alone.

A small group within the bank helped him siphon billions of dollars out of the institution through fraudulent loans and other schemes, then covered up the looting. Others assisted in the covert takeovers of companies and financial institutions. Still others specialized in cultivating rich and powerful people — using flattery, favors, bribes, prostitutes, and other inducements — in an effort to amass deposits and political power.

Outside the bank, Abedi was assisted by financial backers, front men, propagandists, and influence peddlers. Some of BCCI's most important allies were political figures and government officials. Officials of Arab nations were among the most important accomplices in the multibillion-dollar Ponzi scheme and the covert takeovers of U.S. financial institutions.

Sheikh Zayed and many of his associates — including relatives, members of the ruling families of other emirates, financial advisers, and UAE officials — have been accused of acting as front men in BCCI and several of its satellites. Although spokesmen for Zayed have denied that he was involved in wrongdoing, it is hard to accept these professions of innocence as long as Abu Dhabi authorities continue to withhold vital witnesses and documents from investigators. Until there is full cooperation from Abu Dhabi, it will be impossible to say whether Zayed was the biggest victim, as he claims, or one of the biggest villains.

There is also increasing evidence that members of the Saudi Arabian elite — including close associates of King Fahd — were involved in orchestrating BCCI's frauds and looting the bank. After all, two of the central figures in the scandal — Kamal Adham and Khalid Bin Mahfouz — are among the most powerful people in Saudi Arabia.

And there are strong indications that BCCI was just one of several financial institutions looted by associates of Abedi's. The Bin Mahfouz family's National Commercial Bank seems to have been undermined by fraud. In the BCCI Ponzi scheme, a large portion of the stolen deposits came from Feisal Islamic Bank in Cairo, a institution whose controlling shareholders include members of the Saudi royal family. New evidence has emerged linking BCCI to the BNL affair. In late 1992, investigators learned that Mohammed Hammoud, the BCCI front man, had borrowed millions from the Italian bank.

BCCI's most important allies in the United States were Clark Clifford and Robert Altman. Although they claim that they were deceived by the bank, they now stand accused of helping BCCI commit some of its most serious crimes.

The federal and state indictments of Clifford and Altman touched off a major legal battle in the summer and fall of 1992. Their lawyers at Skadden, Arps insisted on a speedy trial in Washington on the federal charges. Their preference for a federal trial was not surprising. The federal indictment was narrower than the New York State indictment that Robert Morgenthau had secured, and the federal prosecutors were much less prepared than Morgenthau's team. Moreover, if the federal trial occurred first, there might never be a trial in New York, since this could violate the New York law that forbids trying a person twice for the same crime.

Skadden, Arps seemed to get its way when, on July 31, a federal judge in Washington agreed to an October 26 trial date on the federal charges. Defense lawyers confidently told friends that the New York courts wouldn't be able to schedule a trial until 1993 at the earliest. They were in for a shock: on August 5, at a hearing in a New York court, Judge John A. K. Bradley set a trial date of October 22, 1992.

Defense lawyers and prosecutors traded barbs at Judge Bradley's hearing. John P. Cooney, Jr., an attorney from Davis, Polk & Wardwell who represented Clifford and Altman, told the judge that he would probably soon ask the court to dismiss much of the case on jurisdictional grounds. Morgenthau, he said, had overextended himself and his jurisdiction by bringing charges related to a worldwide fraud when his authority extended only to New York. John Moscow, the prosecutor who had headed Morgenthau's probe, accused the defense lawyers of trying to delay the state's case so that they could get to trial in federal court first. "Quite frankly, I think they are trying to maneuver this court and the court in Washington," he said, arguing that Clifford and Altman should face the broader state charges first.

Once again, it seemed, the Justice Department had fallen down on the job. There had been no need for the federal prosecutors to agree so hastily to a trial date. Was Justice really interested in getting to the bottom of the BCCI affair? Or did it simply want to dispose of this messy case quickly and quietly? The *Wall Street Journal* and the *Washington Post* ran editorials saying that Clifford and Altman should be tried in New York, by a prosecutor who was not part of the Washington establishment.

The Justice Department quickly reversed itself. On August 18, at a hearing in Washington before U.S. District Judge Joyce Hens Green, federal prosecutors appeared to concede that the New York case should be allowed to go first. Judge Green said she would rule on the issue the following month. The day after the hearing, lawyers for

Clifford and Altman tried a countermeasure at a hearing in New York. They said they had chosen new counsel for the New York trial* and that the lawyers could not possibly be ready by October 22. The clear implication was that the federal trial would have to come first. Judge Bradley did not appreciate the maneuvering; he said he thought the trial should still take place in New York and that he would discuss the matter with Judge Green.

On September 10, Clifford and Altman arrived at the federal courthouse in Washington to find out where they would be tried. After a brief introductory statement, Judge Green announced her decision: the trial would take place in New York, providing it began no later than March 1993.

This was a devastating blow to Clifford and Altman, and they were unable to conceal their shock. One year earlier, when they were grilled by the House Banking Committee, they seemed remarkably cool. No longer. Upon hearing the judge's ruling, Altman buried his face in his hands. When he left the courtroom with his wife, Lynda, they both appeared shaken. Clifford was more composed, perhaps because his health problems could enable him to avoid prosecution.

After the ruling, lawyers for Clifford and Altman tried to postpone the trial in New York, but Judge Bradley refused. In late October, Clifford's lawyers said they would ask the judge to dismiss the case, citing Clifford's heart condition. It seemed increasingly likely that Altman would stand trial alone.

As the trial date drew closer, investigators in Morgenthau's office, the Justice Department, and other agencies were continuing to gather evidence. New criminal charges seemed inevitable, as well as superseding indictments against some of the people who had already been charged with crimes. The names of some Bush administration officials had come up in grand jury testimony, raising the possibility that other powerful people would be engulfed by the BCCI scandal.

One mystery in the BCCI affair that may never be solved is where the money went. Some of BCCI's losses have been explained, but billions of dollars are still unaccounted for. Are there large caches of loot in secret bank accounts controlled by Abedi and his close associates? Did

---

*Charles A. Stillman of Stillman, Friedman & Shaw would represent Clifford. Gustave H. Newman of Newman & Schwartz was retained by Altman. (Both firms are in New York.)

a large portion of the missing money go to some of the political figures who helped the bank?

There is strong evidence that money was diverted to accounts controlled by Saudi and Abu Dhabi sheikhs. A New York grand jury has already accused Khalid Bin Mahfouz of stealing as much as $300 million from the bank. BCCI and Capcom documents show that more than $200 million went to accounts in the names of Kamal Adham and Abdul-Raouf Khalil. Abedi also benefited, according to former associates. A former BCCI official with ties to Pakistani intelligence says that information on Abedi's hidden wealth has been given to British investigators by Bashir Choudhury, a BCCI officer in Naqvi's special duties department who is now in Pakistan. Choudhury, according to this source, said that Abedi had salted away several hundred million dollars in Liechtenstein.

The whole issue of political corruption raises another set of questions. How successful was BCCI in buying its way into the power centers of the West? How did it use its influence? To what extent does corruption explain the blindness and lethargy of the regulators and law enforcement officials who failed to stop BCCI? It is already clear that the Justice Department, the Federal Reserve, several powerful members of Congress, and the CIA were reluctant to investigate this scandal, even after it was exposed as the biggest bank fraud of all time. President Bush has said little about the affair apart from criticizing Ed Rogers, the former White House aide who was hired by Kamal Adham. This silence is striking in view of Bush's supposed commitment to the war on drugs. After all, BCCI — which has been described as one of the world's biggest laundries of drug money — secretly owned a major financial institution based just a few blocks from the White House. The reluctance of powerful people to go after BCCI — or even to talk about it — has helped to fuel suspicions about political corruption.

The BCCI affair suggests that a criminal organization with enough money and connections can buy its way out of trouble. Sadly, there are few signs of reform. Influence peddlers like Clifford and Altman may be in disgrace, but other political fixers continue to thrive. Anyone who doubted that the system is intact had only to follow the 1992 presidential race. Both President Bush and his Democratic rival, Governor Bill Clinton of Arkansas, were surrounded by people with ties to BCCI.

One evening at the Democratic convention in July could well have been dubbed BCCI night. The speakers included Jimmy Carter and Jesse Jackson, both beneficiaries of BCCI's largesse. The convention was organized by Ronald Brown, the chairman of the Democratic National Committee. One of the most important clients of his law firm — Patton, Boggs & Blow — is Sheikh Zayed. Patton, Boggs also manages a U.S. real estate portfolio for Zayed that is valued at about $1 billion.* Clinton's campaign aides included at least two officials of Hill and Knowlton, the PR and lobbying firm that represented BCCI and First American.

For much of his political career, Clinton received substantial financial backing from Jackson Stephens, the Arkansas investment banker who helped to bring BCCI into the United States. In addition, Stephens's firm has given substantial legal work to the Little Rock law firm in which Hillary Clinton, the governor's wife, is a partner. Mrs. Clinton even represented one of Stephens's companies in a case related to BCCI; in 1978, she did legal work for Systematics Inc. when it was sued for its role in Abedi's scheme to collect stock in First American. In the 1992 campaign, Jackson Stephens himself was backing George Bush, but many of his employees were writing checks for Clinton. A study released in July found that employees of Stephens Inc. gave more money to Clinton than employees of all but two other firms in the entire country (Goldman, Sachs, a Wall Street investment banking house, and Wilkie, Farr & Gallagher, a New York law firm).

Clinton's ties to Stephens and the BCCI network attracted some media interest during the campaign. What reporters didn't discover, however, was that Clinton's association with Stephens was the subject of an FBI investigation in 1992, according to government sources. The purpose of the probe was, in part, to determine if Clinton was connected with BCCI. One investigator said he believed that the probe might be politically motivated, instigated by Republicans who wanted to undermine the Arkansas governor.

If Bush supporters were, in fact, behind the investigation, it would be extremely ironic, in view of the president's own ties to Stephens and other BCCI associates. Those familiar with the BCCI story were reminded of the bank's connections with Republicans during the GOP

---

*Brown plays down his links to the law firm. He told the *Wall Street Journal* that he has been "inactive" because of his commitments to the Democratic party, though he continues to draw a modest amount of partnership income. Yet when the city of Washington, D.C., selected Patton, Boggs as its new bond counsel in the summer of 1991, it made the choice on the basis of a proposal submitted under Brown's name.

convention in August. Before Ronald Reagan gave a speech, he was introduced by former Senator Paul Laxalt, whose law firm represented BCCI in the Tampa drug money case. The convention chairman, Craig Fuller, had until early 1992 been the number-two man in the Washington office of Hill and Knowlton. (Fuller joined the firm after the Tampa case was over, but he was there when Hill and Knowlton worked for First American.) Bush's campaign press spokesman was James Lake, who served simultaneously as a lobbyist and PR man for Sheikh Zayed. Lake was rewarded handsomely for portraying the sheikh as an innocent victim of the BCCI affair; in just two months in the fall of 1991, Lake's firm received more than $200,000 in fees.*

BCCI's powerful friends also include many people with connections to the intelligence world. Were intelligence agencies — including the CIA — involved in covering up BCCI's crimes or even committing them?

The CIA seems to have protected BCCI and its backers for well over a decade. When, for example, the Federal Reserve looked into the backgrounds of the BCCI clients who were seeking permission to buy First American, it received "no adverse information on the investors" from the CIA, according to J. Virgil Mattingly, Jr., the Fed's general counsel. The CIA, said Mattingly, did not inform the Fed that two of the investors — Kamal Adham and Abdul-Raouf Khalil — were foreign intelligence liaisons of the United States. Paul Volcker, the former chairman of the Fed, told a Senate committee in 1991 that when the takeover was approved, he "wasn't aware" of Adham's intelligence background.

In 1986 — four years after the takeover — the CIA issued a potentially explosive report stating that BCCI was involved in drug trafficking and that it secretly owned First American. This report was not given to the Federal Reserve, as we have seen, but it did go to other federal agencies, including the Treasury Department, where it apparently made no impression. Interestingly, the Treasury aide responsible for circulating the report, Douglas P. Mulholland, had come to the department in 1982 from the CIA — at the suggestion of its director,

---

*It would be impossible to list all of the direct or indirect ties, but one additional example is worth noting. The chairman of the Republican National Committee, Richard N. Bond, was a lobbyist for President Eric Arturo Delvalle of Panama from 1985 to 1988; Bond was paid $10,000 a month. BCCI's customer Manuel Noriega was, of course, the de facto ruler of Panama at the time, and he forced Delvalle out of office.

William Casey. In 1987, Mulholland left the government to work on Bush's presidential campaign. After the election, Bush appointed him assistant secretary of state for intelligence and research.

The CIA — and its allies — may even have assisted the bank in connection with the Tampa drug money case. Prosecutors who worked on the case say that they did not receive a single CIA report, even though some of the reports alleged that BCCI was involved in money laundering — the principal charge against the bank.

Various CIA allies have been involved in the campaign of lobbying and disinformation, aimed at squelching the investigations of the bank, after the Tampa indictment. BCCI was assisted by Hill and Knowlton, whose Washington office was headed by Robert Gray, a man with close ties to U.S. intelligence.

Larry Barcella, one of the lead defense lawyers in the Tampa case, was apparently quite sensitive to the interests of the U.S. intelligence community during his days as a federal prosecutor. Two of his cases could have been highly embarrassing to American intelligence agencies: his investigation into the murder of the Chilean dissident Orlando Letelier by agents of the Pinochet dictatorship and his probe of Edwin Wilson, the renegade CIA agent who sold arms to Libya's Qaddafi. One potential embarrassment in the Letelier case was that many of Pinochet's security agents had been trained by the Americans. In the Wilson case, there have been allegations that many of his activities were sanctioned by the U.S. government. Barcella even assisted in the Reagan administration's efforts to supply the Nicaraguan contras. In 1985, he gave a legal opinion relating to the sale of arms to the contras by private individuals. Barcella says he was asked by someone at the Pentagon to give the opinion, but he declines to identify the individual. His former boss, former U.S. Attorney Joseph diGenova, told a reporter that "Larry was sought out by a lot of people in intelligence" and law enforcement because he was "creative."*

Orrin Hatch, a forceful defender of the plea bargain, had served on the Senate Intelligence Committee. The Utah Republican has had intriguing ties to the CIA's biggest covert operation of the 1980s: aid to

---

*In early 1992, Barcella began working on a congressional investigation of "October Surprise." According to this conspiracy theory, Reagan campaign aides persuaded the Iranian government not to release American hostages before the November 1980 election because it would help Carter win. In exchange, the Reaganites supposedly agreed to sell arms to the Iranians. Several people linked to the alleged conspiracy had ties to U.S. intelligence, including William Casey.

the Afghan rebels. In 1986, Hatch visited China with senior Reagan administration and CIA officials to try to enlist the support of the Chinese government. BCCI, of course, was also involved in the operation.

Since mid-1991, the federal official with overall responsibility for the BCCI case has been Attorney General William P. Barr. Like so many other characters in the drama, he has connections with the intelligence world. Before becoming a lawyer, Barr spent four years as an employee in the general counsel's office of the CIA.

The cover-up of the CIA's involvement with BCCI has continued into 1992. When Senator Kerry's staff looked into the CIA's ties to the bank, the agency repeatedly stonewalled. First, it claimed that it had no information on BCCI. When it finally agreed to talk, it provided a briefing officer who specialized in narcotics issues and who had no special knowledge about the bank or the people behind it. When one of Kerry's staff members asked a question about Kamal Adham, the CIA officer replied, "Who's he?" In subsequent months, according to the Senate investigators, the agency provided misleading and, in some cases, patently false information.

The CIA's hostility to Kerry's inquiry is not at all surprising when one considers that BCCI was involved in some of the most sensitive intelligence operations of the Reagan-Bush years, including the secret sales of arms to Iran. When questions were raised about the CIA's ties to BCCI after the shutdown of the bank, spokesmen for the agency insisted that its hands were clean. "Any allegations of unlawful use of BCCI by the agency are without foundation," the CIA said in a press statement. Its inspector general carried out an investigation which, he said, cleared the CIA of misconduct.

Characteristically, these statements sidestep some of the most important questions. The issue is not merely how the CIA *used* the bank but what it knew about BCCI and its backers and why it failed to blow the whistle on this criminal organization. Why did the CIA fail to tell the Federal Reserve about Adham and Khalil — the Saudi intelligence officials — when they were taking over First American? Why was none of the CIA's information about BCCI passed on to the prosecutors in Tampa?

Adham and his associates were involved in other activities that the CIA should have known about. They were major shareholders in Capcom, which developed intimate ties to the men who control Tele-Communications Inc. (TCI), the giant cable TV company. Capcom was also an important vehicle for the looting of BCCI. It is hard to believe that the CIA knew nothing about these activities, in view of its close ties with the Saudis. Khalil, according to some sources, was even on the CIA payroll until 1990. Speaking through his lawyer, Khalil denies working for the CIA, but he wouldn't comment on whether he works with the agency.

Congressional investigators and others familiar with BCCI have their own theories about the CIA's conduct. There are strong suspicions that the agency wanted to protect an important intelligence asset. As Norman Bailey, the former National Security Council official, put it, the CIA was not interested in "blowing the BCCI cover." There is another alarming possibility: some investigators believe that a portion of the money stolen from BCCI's depositors was used to finance covert operations sponsored by the U.S. government. If BCCI's frauds were exposed, this source of funds would dry up.

There are even indications that CIA officials were involved in the founding of BCCI. One former officer of the bank recalls a conversation he had in the early 1980s with a close associate of Abedi's, a Pakistani who had worked for United Bank and then joined BCCI when it was established. The Pakistani said that Abedi had worked with the CIA during his United Bank days and that the CIA had encouraged him in his project to launch BCCI, since the agency realized that an international bank could provide valuable cover for intelligence operations. The Pakistani mentioned one U.S. intelligence official by name: Richard Helms, the director of the CIA until early 1973. Helms, as we have seen, later became a legal client of Clark Clifford's and a business partner of two BCCI insiders. "What I have been told," says this source, "is that it wasn't a Pakistani bank at all. The guys behind the bank weren't Pakistani at all. The whole thing was a front."

If the CIA was indeed involved in founding BCCI, covering up its frauds, and even using the stolen money, the implications are frightening. It would mean that an agency of the United States government not only failed to protect the public from BCCI but was a partner in crime.

The BCCI deception lasted for nearly two decades. Not until 1988 were serious efforts made to peel off Abedi's mask and reveal the true nature of the man and his bank. Even then, three more years would pass before the criminal organization known as the Bank of Credit and Commerce International was put out of business.

BCCI's crime wave lasted as long as it did because of an appalling breakdown in the systems of control that are supposed to protect the public. With few exceptions, board members, auditors, bank regulators, and law enforcement agencies behaved with extraordinary blindness, lethargy, naiveté, and timidity. In several cases, these watchdogs were not fools but knaves: in exchange for money, favors, jobs, and other forms of largesse, they looked the other way.

Abedi's skills as a corrupter were honed in countries like Pakistan and Abu Dhabi where rules, laws, and regulatory procedures are easily bypassed by those who are willing and able to make payoffs to the right people. Many people from "developed" countries like to believe that this sort of corruption rarely occurs in Western cultures. American schoolchildren, for example, have been taught that the United States is a nation of laws, not of men, and thus utterly different from autocracies like Abu Dhabi where all power flows from the ruler. Such sharp — and oversimplified — distinctions may provide comfort to Westerners, but they make it far too easy to put much of the blame for the BCCI affair on foreigners who come from "morally backward" societies. One man who has expressed that view is Paul Warnke, a partner in Clark Clifford's law firm. When Clifford was indicted, Warnke said, "The problem is that he was involved with a culture he did not understand. He had no background in the Middle East. He didn't recognize their values are different from ours."

But are Westerners really so different from people in developing nations — or just a bit more subtle? When Abedi wanted to expand in the United States, he did more or less what he would have done in Pakistan, Nigeria, or Indonesia: he linked up with the best friend of the head of state. When he ran into legal and regulatory problems, he hired politically connected lawyers to guide him through the governmental maze. When BCCI was charged with laundering drug money, Abedi's successors spent millions of dollars on lawyers, lobbyists, and PR men and managed to win a favorable settlement of the case. Even after the guilty plea, the bank was defended by prominent political figures — several of whom had profited financially from their ties to BCCI.

The sons of Sheikh Zayed engaged in highly suspect financial transactions with BCCI. But what about the sons of President Bush? George W. Bush and his brother Jeb were both associated with people in the BCCI network. George, of course, profited handsomely from an oil deal that involved a long list of people with ties to BCCI.

In Washington — just as in Karachi, Abu Dhabi, and Riyadh — money can buy influence. The most obvious manifestation of this, of course, is political campaign financing. It is instructive that when Senator Kerry's investigation posed a serious threat to BCCI, Clifford, Altman, and two of their law partners suddenly opened their checkbooks and contributed to Kerry's reelection campaign. Kerry has said that he did not solicit the donations, and there is no sign that he was influenced, but it is hard to believe that this was not the intention.

BCCI was eventually put out of business, but that does not mean that "the system worked," as the saying goes. The system failed to work for years. It was only through the efforts of a handful of dedicated people — including Robert Mazur, Jack Blum, and especially Robert Morgenthau — that BCCI's criminal rampage was finally ended. If it were not for these men, the bank might still be in business today, laundering criminal money, stealing deposits, and corrupting governments.

The day after the indictments of Clifford and Altman were announced, Senator Kerry's committee held a hearing on BCCI in which corruption was a recurrent theme. The senator began by criticizing the government of Abu Dhabi for withholding documents and witnesses from Western investigators and strongly suggested that Sheikh Zayed and other Abu Dhabi officials had failed to cooperate because they did not want their own role in the scandal exposed. Two bankers who had been convicted in the Tampa case testified that day. Akbar Bilgrami described how the bank made payoffs to African officials. Amjad Awan spoke of his dealings with Noriega.

After the hearing, Kerry returned to his office and talked with a visitor about the importance of political influence in the BCCI affair. Four years earlier, he said, Clifford came to his office and vouched for BCCI. "Clifford sat right on that sofa and said, 'BCCI's a good bank.' He said, 'We're anxious to be cooperative, we've never done anything wrong.'" Kerry also touched on the pernicious influence of campaign contributions. "The amount of money that floats around this city is grotesque," he said. When asked if anyone could be relied on to protect the public, he said, "Only good people — the Robert Morgenthaus — people who see their duty and do it."

The system in which BCCI flourished is intact. Many government officials are still for sale to the highest bidder, enabling monied criminal interests to buy what they want in Washington and other capitals. Unless there is serious reform, there will be more scandals like BCCI, perhaps with more devastating consequences.

.   .   .

Many aspects of the BCCI affair will remain shrouded in mystery forever. We will certainly never know the name of every government official corrupted by BCCI. Nor will we ever learn the full story of how BCCI's complicated frauds were committed. Many records were falsified or simply destroyed; in numerous cases cash transactions were never recorded.

There will, however, be fresh revelations in the months and years to come. Robert Morgenthau and other investigators are continuing their probes and may well seek further indictments. New information will also emerge in the trial of Robert Altman, scheduled to begin in early 1993.

Of one thing there is no doubt: amorality and contempt for the law were at the very core of Agha Hasan Abedi's empire. "The only laws that are permanent are the laws of nature," he used to tell his minions. "Everything else is flexible." For nearly twenty years, Abedi and his accomplices were able to live above the law. In the end, this essential lawlessness led only to destruction.

ACKNOWLEDGMENTS

We would like to thank our respective employers — Dow Jones & Company, publisher of the *Wall Street Journal;* and the Investigative Group Inc. (IGI) — for giving us time to pursue this project. Without their help and cooperation, this book would not have been possible.

In particular, we are grateful to the *Journal*'s current managing editor, Paul Steiger, his predecessor, Norman Pearlstine, and the Washington bureau chief, Albert Hunt, as well as the deputy managing editor, Byron Calame, all of whom gave their blessing and support to this book and generously granted Peter his leave of absence. We would also like to thank especially Peter's colleagues and friends Tom Petzinger and George Anders for their comments, suggestions, and editing. So many people at Dow Jones helped us that it would be impossible to name them all, but we particularly want to thank Jill Abramson, Marcus Brauchli, Nicholas Bray, Geraldine Brooks, John Bussey, William Carley, Bob Davis, Dave Dolinger, John Fialka, Craig Forman, William Hoover, Jonathan Moses, Walt Mossberg, Alan Murray, Tom Ricks, Johnnie Roberts, Allanna Sullivan, Clayton Wiggins, and Allison Wright.

At IGI, Terry Lenzner, the chairman, and Jim Mintz, the president, generously agreed to give Larry a leave of absence so that the book could be completed. Other colleagues were helpful and supportive in a variety of ways, including Ron Cesar, Mike Fellner, John Hanrahan, Bob Mason, and Jeff Nason. John and Jeff reshuffled the work to make the leave possible. Ron, Mike, and Bob took over cases. Thanks also go to Bill Regardie, who courageously resisted attempts to kill the First American article commissioned by his magazine, and Brian Kelly, the former editor of *Regardie's.* Bill Hogan, a former senior editor, provided invaluable assistance and moral support for both the article and this book.

We would like to thank the many people we have worked with at

Houghton Mifflin. John Sterling, the editor in chief of the trade books division, was unfailingly supportive throughout the project, providing us with valuable suggestions, enthusiasm, and even our title. Luise Erdmann, our manuscript editor, was always a joy to work with. We also appreciate the skills and efforts of Gordon Brumm, Anne Chalmers, Chris Coffin, Dan Maurer, Katya Rice, Becky Saikia-Wilson, Barbara Williams, and Irene Williams.

This book would not have been possible without the efforts of Rafe Sagalyn, our agent, who has sung our praises from Anaheim to Tokyo. We were further assisted by Alex Kramer, an able researcher, and Karen Huntt Mason, a skillful and patient picture editor. Thanks go to Jim Condon, Marco Herrera, and Dan Ion of the *Journal*'s graphics department for preparing the maps and chart. Several friends and colleagues helped in various ways, including Scott Armstrong, Tino Bakker, Bill Barnes, Stephen Ellis, Nick Fielding, Pascal Henry, Larry Lifschultz, Feruccio Petracco, and Steve Pizzo.

We have been helped by countless sources in our reporting on BCCI over the past several years and in the research for this book, as evidenced by our source notes. Many of these people — including several former BCCI officers — cannot be mentioned by name, but we thank them all.

We also want to thank Jacqueline Veldhuis, Larry's wife, who graciously let the book take over the Gurwin-Veldhuis home for days, weeks, and months.

October 1992
Washington, D.C.

APPENDIX

1922 Agha Hasan Abedi is born in Lucknow, India.

1945 Clark Clifford joins Truman's White House staff as a junior naval aide. In 1946, he becomes special counsel to the president, leaving in 1950 to establish a law firm in Washington.

1946 The rajah of Mahmudabad, India, recommends Abedi for a job with Habib Bank in Bombay. He is hired as a clerk.

1947 The Indian subcontinent is partitioned and Habib Bank transfers its headquarters to Karachi, in the new country of Pakistan. Abedi moves with the bank.

1959 Pakistan's Saigol family establishes United Bank and installs Abedi as president.

1963 Saudi Arabia's intelligence service is established, headed by Kamal Adham, a brother-in-law of Crown Prince Faisal, who becomes king the following year.

1966 Sheikh Zayed bin Sultan al-Nahyan overthrows his brother Sheikh Shakhbut to become the ruler of Abu Dhabi, the largest component of a British protectorate known as the Trucial States. Around this time, Abedi meets Zayed, and a close relationship soon develops.

Ghaith Rashad Pharaon, whose father is an adviser to King Faisal, establishes Saudi Research & Development Corporation (REDEC).

1968   In January, Clifford becomes secretary of defense in the Johnson administration and serves for one year.

1971   Robert A. Altman joins Clifford's firm after obtaining his law degree at George Washington University.

Zulfikar Ali Bhutto comes to power in Pakistan, nationalizes United Bank, and arrests Abedi and other bankers.

December: The Trucial States gain independence as the United Arab Emirates (UAE), with Sheikh Zayed as president.

1972   Abedi establishes BCCI. Its most important backers are Sheikh Zayed and Bank of America.

1973   BCCI opens its first branch, in London. London soon becomes the bank's de facto headquarters, although BCCI is incorporated in Luxembourg (and later establishes a holding company in the Cayman Islands).

BCCI and Bank of America establish a joint venture bank, National Bank of Oman.

October: Egypt and Syria attack Israel, starting the Yom Kippur War. Abu Dhabi soon becomes the first of several Arab nations to declare an embargo on oil exports to the U.S. as punishment for its support of Israel. Over the next few months, OPEC quadruples oil prices.

December 31: BCCI's total assets are $200 million.

1975   Robert M. Morgenthau takes office as Manhattan district attorney.

First Arabian Corporation, a company partly owned by Pharaon and Adham, takes over Detroit's Bank of the Commonwealth. They are assisted by the Houston law firm of John Connally, a former treasury secretary and a presidential aspirant. (Pharaon sells his stock in 1977.)

In January, T. Bertram ("Bert") Lance becomes president of National Bank of Georgia (NBG), a subsidiary of Financial General Bankshares (FGB), a bank holding company based in Washington, D.C. In June, Lance and other investors acquire control of the Atlanta bank from FGB.

1975–   Acting through Abbas Gokal, a Pakistani businessman, BCCI
1976   attempts to acquire Chelsea National Bank, in New York City.

The state banking department vetoes the deal because of concerns about BCCI's role.

1976   Altman becomes a partner in Clifford's law firm.

Bank of America, alarmed at BCCI's rapid growth and dubious practices, declines to invest new capital in the bank.

BCCI establishes ICIC (Overseas) Ltd. in the Cayman Islands.

Banque de Commerce et de Placements (BCP), a BCCI affiliate, opens in Geneva.

January: George Bush becomes director of the CIA and serves for one year. He strengthens the agency's ties with "friendly" Arab intelligence agencies.

Fall: General George Olmsted, who controls FGB through International Bank and other entities, begins looking for a buyer after the Federal Reserve rules that he must sell control of FGB. Lance is approached but declines, apparently because of his plans to join the Carter administration.

1977   *January:* Jimmy Carter takes office as president. Lance, who assisted in the campaign, is appointed director of the Office of Management and Budget. During Carter's presidency, Clifford serves as a special emissary to such countries as Turkey, Cyprus, and India.

March: Bhutto's party wins the general election. It is later alleged that Abedi channeled between $2 million and $3 million to Bhutto's party; the money is believed to have come from Sheikh Zayed. Bhutto's government allows investors close to BCCI to acquire a large stake in the Pakistani unit of Attock Oil.

April: A group of investors led by J. William Middendorf II acquires a large stake in FGB. Middendorf soon becomes chairman and president. Dissident members of his group soon begin scheming to oust him and to sell control of FGB to others. One member of the group is Jackson Stephens, an investment banker in Arkansas with ties to Lance and Carter.

May: The Carter administration proposes the sale of F-15 fighters to Saudi Arabia. The Senate approves the deal one year later.

July: General Mohammed Zia-ul-Haq overthrows Bhutto and becomes Pakistan's dictator. The Zia regime permits associates of BCCI to acquire a majority of Attock Oil's Pakistani unit. The investors, who are front men for BCCI, include Adham, Pharaon, Abdullah Darwaish (an adviser to Sheikh Zayed), and Faisal Saud al-Fulaij, a Kuwaiti businessman.

September: Adham steps down as Saudi intelligence chief; he is succeeded by his nephew Prince Turki bin Faisal al Saud. Both men are BCCI stockholders.

Connally invests in Houston's Main Bank with Pharaon and Khalid Bin Mahfouz, whose family controls National Commercial Bank, the largest bank in Saudi Arabia.

September 5: Carter asks Clifford to represent Lance in connection with the Senate's investigation into Lance's banking practices.

September 21: Carter announces Lance's resignation as budget director.

October–December: R. Eugene Holley, a Georgia politician, introduces Lance to Abedi, who retains Lance as an investment adviser. Abedi arranges for Pharaon to acquire Lance's stock in National Bank of Georgia. Lance and some of his associates then persuade Abedi to buy a large block of stock in Financial General Bankshares. Abedi agrees, and they assist him in acquiring the stock. One of those involved is Jackson Stephens. The ostensible purchasers are four BCCI clients: Adham, al-Fulaij, and two sons of Sheikh Zayed, Sultan and Mohammed, with the latter acting through Zayed's financial adviser Darwaish.

December 31: BCCI's total assets reach $2.2 billion. It touts itself as the fastest-growing bank in Britain and one of the fastest-growing in the world.

1978 *January 4:* Lance sells his controlling stake in NBG to Pharaon, who is acting as a front man for BCCI. Abedi arranges for the repayment of Lance's biggest debt, about $3.5 million owed to the First National Bank of Chicago.

Late January: Bank of America announces that it will be disposing of its BCCI stock over the next few years.

February 7: Lance informs FGB's chairman, B. F. Saul II, and its president, Middendorf, that he represents investors who own about 20 percent of FGB's stock.

February 17: FGB sues Lance, Abedi, BCCI, the Arab investors, and others, alleging an illegal takeover attempt.

February 27: Joseph E. Vaez, a bank examiner in the Office of the Comptroller of the Currency, submits a report on BCCI that highlights serious irregularities and potentially grave financial problems.

March 13: Abedi's Third World Foundation applies for registration as a charity in Britain.

March 17: The Securities and Exchange Commission (SEC) files suit against BCCI, Abedi, Lance, Stephens, and others, alleging securities law violations in the purchases of FGB stock. With Clifford's assistance, the suit is settled with a consent agreement the next day. The investors agree to make a tender offer for all outstanding stock. Clifford and Altman advise the investors during the ensuing takeover battle.

April: A federal judge finds that BCCI, Abedi, and the four Middle Eastern investors acted as a group when they collected stock in FGB, which means they should have filed disclosure statements with the SEC.

June 28 and July 31: The *Wall Street Journal* publishes articles on Boeing's questionable payments to Arab middlemen, including Adham. Sheikh Zayed was involved in one deal.

October 18: Sheikh Sultan, one of Zayed's sons, sells his FGB shares to Adham.

October 20: Richard Helms provides advice to the chairman of one of the dummy companies set up to acquire FGB.

1979 BCCI acquires Hong Kong Metropolitan Bank; it is later renamed Bank of Credit and Commerce (Hong Kong) Ltd.

BCCI establishes Bank of Credit and Commerce (Nigeria) Ltd.

January 19: King Khaled of Saudi Arabia announces the sacking of Adham from his post as a royal adviser for having supported the Carter administration's Camp David initiative.

February 11: The shah of Iran is overthrown by followers of the Ayatollah Khomeini.

February 16: The Fed rejects a bid by BCCI's clients to acquire FGB.

March: Israel and Egypt sign a peace treaty at the White House. Adham assisted the Carter administration in bringing Egypt to the negotiating table.

April: Bhutto is executed in spite of appeals to Zia from world leaders to spare his predecessor's life. The U.S. suspends economic and military aid to Pakistan; the reasons include the execution of Bhutto and Zia's refusal to halt efforts to build a nuclear bomb.

April 27: The *Wall Street Journal* reports that Fulaij was bribed by Boeing, according to U.S. investigators. (He denies it.)

May 23: Lance and three business associates are indicted by a federal grand jury in Atlanta on charges of violating banking laws. Lance pleads not guilty and is eventually acquitted.

November: Muslim fundamentalists seize the Grand Mosque in Mecca, Saudi Arabia.

December: The Soviet Union invades Afghanistan, prompting the Carter administration to channel substantial amounts of aid to Pakistan and to the Afghan resistance. BCCI later becomes involved in the CIA's efforts to assist the Afghan rebels.

1980 *January:* Clifford visits India as Carter's envoy.

April: The Bank of England tells BCCI that it does not merit the status of a "recognised bank" and can only call itself a licensed deposit taker.

April 11: Ernst & Whinney qualifies BCCI's 1979 accounts. The auditors were concerned about inadequate provisions against possible loan losses in Iran.

July: Bank of America completes the divestiture of its BCCI shares.

July 25: Adham and the other Arab investors win a definitive agreement with FGB's board that allows them to acquire the company. The takeover must be approved by bank regulators.

September 22: War breaks out between Iraq and Iran; it will last for eight years. During the war, BCCI finances arms purchases by both sides.

October: The first issue of *South* magazine is published. It is heavily subsidized by BCCI.

1981 Abedi sets up the BCC Foundation in Pakistan and names Zia's top adviser, Ghulam Ishaq Khan, as chairman.

January 20: Ronald Reagan takes office as president.

March 12: The Office of the Comptroller of the Currency says in a letter that if the FGB takeover goes through, "BCCI will have no involvement with the management and other affairs of Financial General."

April 23: The Fed holds an informal private hearing to review the proposed acquisition of FGB. Clifford and Altman represent the BCCI clients who want to buy it. Four of the investors — Adham, Fulaij, and two associates of Adham's (Abdul-Raouf Khalil and Sayed Jawhary) — testify at the hearing.

August 25: The Fed approves the application by BCCI's clients to acquire FGB.

October 16 and 23: Britain's *New Statesman* magazine publishes the first major exposé of BCCI. The writer, Tariq Ali, alleges political payoffs and other wrongdoing.

October 28: The Senate votes to allow the sale of AWACS to Saudi Arabia.

1982   The Panamanian strongman Manuel Antonio Noriega begins banking with BCCI/Panama.

March 2: The New York State Banking Board approves the BCCI clients' application to acquire New York banks owned by FGB, although one of the banks will have to be divested.

April 19: The Arab investors announce that their tender offer has been successful: they have acquired 96 percent of FGB's outstanding common stock.

Before and after the tender offer, top management positions and the composition of the board are reshuffled. Clifford is chairman, Stuart Symington is vice chairman, and Robert G. Stevens is president (serving until 1989). Altman is a board member of FGB as well as president of FGB Holding Company (later renamed First American Corporation), which owns all of Financial General's stock and is in turn owned by foreign dummy companies.

June: Fahd bin Abdel-Aziz al-Saud becomes king of Saudi Arabia.

August: FGB changes its name to First American Bankshares. Lance introduces Abedi to Carter. Soon afterward, Abedi donates $500,000 to the Carter Presidential Center. BCCI will later contribute millions to Carter's projects.

December 31: BCCI has grown to 262 offices in 58 countries. Total assets are $9.6 billion.

1983   David L. Paul acquires Miami's Dade Savings and Loan and renames it CenTrust Savings Bank. It soon becomes the biggest S&L
in the Southeast.

BCCI acquires Colombia's Banco Mercantíl and later renames it
Banco de Crédito y Comercio Colombia.

BCCI acquires Spain's Banco de Descuento and renames it Bank of
Credit and Commerce S.A. Española.

BCCI forms Bank of Credit and Commerce (Emirates), a locally
incorporated unit in the UAE, to evade a new law limiting to eight
the number of branches allowed foreign banks.

1984   Capcom, a commodity futures trading company, is founded in
London. Its controlling shareholders are close associates of BCCI,
including Adham, Khalil, and Jawhary. Other major shareholders
include Bob Magness, the chairman of Tele-Communications Inc.
(TCI), the biggest U.S. cable TV company, and his protégé, Larry
Romrell. Both join the board of directors, with Romrell as chairman. Capcom becomes a vehicle for the looting of BCCI.

January 29: Altman marries Lynda J. Carter, an actress who portrayed Wonder Woman on television.

October 4: Clifford tells the First American board that his goal is
for First American to become one of the twenty largest banking
companies in the country within ten years.

1985   *August:* The Comptroller of the Currency charges Lance with
check kiting, receiving the proceeds of nominee loans from Calhoun First National Bank, and obtaining money from the bank's
credit life insurance company.

October 1: Pharaon acquires Independence Bank of Los Angeles
for $23 million as a front man for BCCI.

November 29: The Nigerian government signs a secret agreement
with BCCI for a $1.25 billion financing. Interest and principal
payments are to be made in oil.

December: Pharaon's company REDEC declares a moratorium on
principal payments on its debts.

1985– BCCI claims it incurred losses of $225 million in options trading
1986   during this period. A purported capital infusion of $150 million
helps to calm the concerns of auditors and regulators. BCCI officers later say that the real losses totaled almost $440 million.

Syed Ziauddin Ali Akbar, the head of BCCI's treasury division, takes the blame and resigns to become managing director of Capcom in 1986.

BCCI helps Adnan Khashoggi finance sales of arms to Iran, which are part of the Reagan administration's Iran-contra dealings.

1986   Pharaon reportedly sells all of his BCCI stock.

Global 2000, a charitable organization, is founded by Carter. BCCI becomes the largest single donor.

February: Lance reaches a settlement with the Comptroller of the Currency, agrees to pay a $50,000 fine, and is barred from working for any federally insured bank without permission from the regulators.

March: Pharaon's company REDEC halts interest payments on its debts.

June 3: BCCI says its 1985 net income plunged by 21 percent, to $158 million, from $201 million the previous year. Ernst & Whinney, the auditor of BCCI Holdings (Luxembourg) S.A., later resigns after disagreements over the accounting for the bank's losses. Price Waterhouse, which previously audited BCCI's Cayman Islands holding company, takes over the whole BCCI audit.

June: Saudi Arabia's Bin Mahfouz family acquires large stakes in BCCI and First American. Khalid Bin Mahfouz joins BCCI's board of directors.

July: BCCI's Tokyo branch opens.

The U.S. Customs Service's Tampa office begins Operation C-Chase, an undercover investigation aimed at catching launderers of drug money.

September 30: The CIA circulates a report to the State, Treasury, and Commerce departments alleging that BCCI acquired control of First American in 1982. The report is not given to the Fed.

October 1: The Carter Presidential Center is dedicated in Atlanta. Among the major donors honored at the ceremony are Agha Hasan Abedi, King Fahd of Saudi Arabia, Armand Hammer, and Ted Turner.

November: First American's parent company signs an option to buy National Bank of Georgia.

1986– Clifford and Altman get nonrecourse loans from BCCI to buy
1988 stock in First American. They sell most of the stock after nineteen months, reaping millions of dollars in profits.

1987 Carter visits Pakistan with Abedi and meets with President Zia. In the spring, Carter and Abedi go on a world tour, with stops in London, Hong Kong, Tibet, Peking, and Moscow, and meet with the leaders of several countries.

TCI orchestrates a $560 million rescue of Turner Broadcasting (which operates Cable News Network), leaving TCI the largest single shareholder in Turner.

Abedi arranges for the Bin Mahfouz family to sell its BCCI stock.

February: An undercover Customs agent opens an account at BCCI/Tampa. He later begins laundering drug money with the help of BCCI officers.

March: First American agrees to acquire National Bank of Georgia from Pharaon for about $220 million.

July: Pharaon buys about one fourth of CenTrust Savings Bank as a front man for BCCI.

The Fed approves First American's takeover of NBG.

October 5: Pharaon's REDEC signs a $340 million debt rescheduling agreement with its Western and Arab creditor banks.

1988 *February 4:* Federal grand juries in Miami and Tampa indict Noriega for drug trafficking, laundering drug money, and providing assistance to major drug traffickers in exchange for millions of dollars in bribes. Around the time of the indictments, BCCI helps Noriega to hide $23 million in European bank accounts.

February 8: Leigh Bruce Ritch, a convicted drug trafficker, tells a Senate subcommittee chaired by John Kerry about his dealings with Noriega. He also states that he and Noriega both used BCCI. Ritch's testimony, together with other information received by the committee, prompts an investigation of Noriega's ties to BCCI. The probe is headed by Jack Blum of Kerry's staff.

February 9: Abedi suffers a heart attack and undergoes a heart transplant. Swaleh Naqvi takes over the running of BCCI.

May: The College of Supervisors — comprising bank regulators from Britain, Luxembourg, Spain, and Switzerland — holds its first meeting. The panel was established to improve the regulation of BCCI. Regulators from Hong Kong and the Cayman Islands join in 1989, the United Arab Emirates in 1990, and France in 1991. The Federal Reserve never becomes a member.

July: As part of the Kerry Committee's probe of Noriega and BCCI, the Senate Foreign Relations Committee issues subpoenas to the bank, demanding all records relating to Noriega. Clifford and Altman represent BCCI before the committee.

August 17: Pakistan's Zia dies when a bomb destroys his plane in midair.

September 9: Amjad Awan, one of the BCCI officers who is a target of Operation C-Chase, tells an undercover agent he suspects that BCCI secretly acquired control of First American and National Bank of Georgia.

October 4: A federal grand jury in Tampa indicts BCCI, Capcom, and ten current or former BCCI employees on charges of laundering drug money. These include Awan and the head of Capcom, S. Z. A. Akbar.

October 8: Customs agents arrest five of the indicted bankers in Tampa. Other defendants are arrested in Los Angeles, London, and Paris.

October 11: The BCCI indictment is announced by U.S. Attorney Robert Genzman and Customs Commissioner William von Raab at a press conference in Tampa. Shortly afterward, Clifford and Altman assemble a team of criminal lawyers to defend BCCI and the individual bankers.

October 14: BCCI retains the public relations firm of Hill and Knowlton to limit the damage to its image caused by the Tampa indictment.

November: The political party of Benazir Bhutto, the daughter of the late Pakistani leader, wins the national election. She soon becomes prime minister.

December: An agent of the Internal Revenue Service informs the Fed that BCCI secretly owns First American, according to one of the bankers indicted in the Tampa case. Further information is provided two months later. The Fed does little to check out the allegation.

December 31: BCCI has 417 offices in 73 countries and 1,300,000 customers, with total assets of $20.6 billion. It is the seventh-largest privately held bank in the world.

1989   *January 20:* George Bush takes office as president.

February: The Federal Reserve Bank of Richmond gives BCCI's relationship with First American a clean bill of health. The Fed approves First American's application to acquire Bank of Escambia of Pensacola, Florida.

March: Jack Blum persuades Amer Lodhi, a former employee of BCCI and Pharaon, to meet with federal prosecutors in Tampa. The informant says he believes that BCCI acquired control of First American, National Bank of Georgia, and Independence Bank through front men.

April: Blum, who had resigned from the Kerry Committee's staff at the end of March, meets with Manhattan D.A. Morgenthau. After he provides information about BCCI, Morgenthau opens his own investigation of the bank. A federal grand jury in Tampa returns a superseding indictment against BCCI, alleging that laundering drug money was part of BCCI's corporate strategy.

June 12: The Fed issues an order against BCCI, requiring it to implement better compliance procedures.

August: The FBI raids the Atlanta branch of Italy's Banca Nazionale del Lavoro (BNL) and discovers that the branch has illegally lent billions of dollars to Iraq. It is later discovered that BNL had close ties to BCCI.

August 21: Morgenthau's office tells the Fed that an informant has reported that BCCI owns or controls First American through nominees.

Fall: Bank regulators in Britain and Luxembourg ask Price Waterhouse to conduct a special audit of BCCI. Based on findings by the auditors, the Bank of England informs the Fed that several First American shareholders had substantial loans from BCCI, secured by First American stock.

December 13: The Fed asks Altman about BCCI's loans to First American's shareholders.

December 20: American troops invade Panama.

1990   *January 3:* Noriega surrenders to U.S. authorities. He is arraigned the next day in federal court in Miami.

January 16: BCCI agrees to plead guilty to money-laundering charges in Tampa.

January 30: Harken Energy, a company in which President Bush's son George W. Bush is a major shareholder and a board member, signs a highly coveted contract with the government of Bahrain. Several people with connections to BCCI also have ties to Harken or the Bahrain deal.

February 2: Federal regulators seize CenTrust Savings Bank, charging it with numerous violations of banking regulations. The failure of CenTrust will cost taxpayers an estimated $2 billion.

February 5: A federal judge in Tampa accepts BCCI's guilty plea, places the bank on probation for five years, and requires it to forfeit about $14 million. In a letter to the Fed, Altman asserts that he does not have access to information about BCCI's loans to First American's shareholders; he fails to mention the loans he and Clifford received.

February 22: Senator Orrin Hatch, a Utah Republican, delivers a speech on the Senate floor defending BCCI and the Tampa plea bargain.

April: As the centerpiece of a rescue scheme, Sheikh Zayed agrees to inject new capital into BCCI. Zayed and his associates increase their ownership to 77 percent. Naqvi is replaced as chief executive by Zafar Iqbal.

April 30: BCCI's 1989 annual report is released; it contains a clean opinion from Price Waterhouse, stating that the report gives a "true and fair view" of the bank's financial condition. The *Wall Street Journal* reports that BCCI is expected to announce a huge loss for 1989, about $500 million, and may move its headquarters to Abu Dhabi. The bank soon confirms the loss and the move.

May: *Regardie's* magazine publishes a cover story showing that BCCI has close ties to First American, National Bank of Georgia, and Independence Bank. On May 3, the *Wall Street Journal* publishes a front-page exposé of BCCI, characterizing it as a "rogue bank." On May 8, Altman meets with Fed officials and attempts to discredit the articles.

June 19: BCCI announces 4,000 layoffs from its international work force of 14,000.

July 29: A federal jury in Tampa finds five BCCI bankers guilty on charges of money laundering: Amjad Awan, Syed Aftab Hussain, Akbar Bilgrami, Sibte Hassan, and Ian Howard. (Guilty verdicts are later returned against S. Z. A. Akbar and Asif Baakza in London. Nazir Chinoy later pleads guilty in Tampa.)

August 2: Iraqi forces invade Kuwait.

August 6: A BCCI ally, President Ghulam Ishaq Khan of Pakistan, backed by the Pakistani military, dismisses Prime Minister Benazir Bhutto, dissolves the National Assembly, and declares a state of emergency.

September 20: BCCI moves its headquarters from London to the UAE after refusing to release six-month financial statements.

October: Abedi and Naqvi are forced to resign from BCCI.

November: Nawaz Sharif, a BCCI ally, becomes prime minister of Pakistan.

December: Morgenthau informs the Fed that an audit of BCCI showed $854 million in loans to First American's shareholders using that bank's stock as collateral.

1991   *January 4:* The Fed orders an investigation into BCCI's alleged control of First American. The Fed subsequently makes criminal referrals to the Justice Department.

February 27: Saddam Hussein agrees to give up all Iraqi claims to Kuwait. President Bush orders an end to the Gulf War.

February 28: The Justice Department announces the indictment of BNL's former Atlanta branch manager, Christopher Drogoul, and other defendants. Drogoul is charged with fraud in connection with BNL's lending to Iraq.

March 4: The Fed accuses BCCI of illegally acquiring control of First American, and BCCI agrees to give up its stake. The Bank of England asks Price Waterhouse to conduct a special investigation of BCCI, under Section 41 of Britain's Banking Act.

May: The Fed says BCCI illegally owns Independence Bank and orders it to sell its shares.

May 5: The *Washington Post* reports that Clifford and Altman earned millions of dollars on investments in First American stock that were arranged and financed by BCCI.

May 22: Pamela Harriman, a fund-raiser for the Democrats, holds a party in Georgetown to celebrate the publication of Clifford's memoirs, *Counsel to the President*. Several prominent Democrats attend.

May 23: Fed officials testify to the Senate Banking Committee that they were lied to for more than a decade about the ownership of First American.

June: Price Waterhouse provides the Bank of England with reports alleging widespread fraud at BCCI.

July 5: Regulators in the U.S., Britain, Luxembourg, the Cayman Islands, Spain, Switzerland, and France shut down BCCI. The depositors face potential losses of billions of dollars. During the next few weeks, reporters in various countries publish new revelations about BCCI, including information on its ties to intelligence agencies and links to terrorism.

July 8: A court in Luxembourg discloses that BCCI lost more than its entire net worth in 1990.

July 11: A retired Pakistani general, Inam ul-Haq, is arrested in Germany after allegations that he helped procure materials for his country's nuclear program. BCCI was implicated in the alleged scheme. He is later extradited to the United States and convicted in July 1992.

July 12: The Fed takes action against Abedi, Naqvi, Pharaon, and Kamal Shoaib, the BCCI officer who ran Independence Bank.

July 17: The *Wall Street Journal* reports that a few senior BCCI executives received $50 million in hush money.

July 22: British officials reveal that BCCI used First American's stock as collateral for loans used to cover up fraud at BCCI and that the bank probably never made a profit in its nineteen-year existence. The government of Britain's Prime Minister John Major asks Lord Justice Bingham to conduct a public inquiry of BCCI.

July 23: Robin Leigh-Pemberton, governor of the Bank of England, places the blame for the fraud at BCCI on its former executives and asks Sheikh Zayed to protect its depositors.

July 29: Morgenthau announces that a Manhattan grand jury has indicted BCCI, Abedi, and Naqvi. The Fed charges that BCCI violated banking laws and assesses a $200 million fine. (The Fed later lifts the fine so that BCCI will not be able to escape criminal prosecution on the ground of double jeopardy.)

August 13: Clifford and Altman resign from First American. Nicholas Katzenbach, a former U.S. attorney general and a friend of Clifford's, becomes chairman.

September 5: The Justice Department announces the indictment of Naqvi, five other BCCI officials, and Capcom on racketeering charges. Congressman Charles Schumer of New York issues a report criticizing the conduct of federal law enforcement agencies in the BCCI case.

September 9: Plainclothes policemen arrest Naqvi and several other BCCI officers at the bank's main office in Abu Dhabi.

September 11: Clifford and Altman testify before the House Banking Committee. They deny they knew about BCCI's ownership of First American.

September 13: The Fed's general counsel, J. Virgil Mattingly, Jr., testifies that investigators are probing loans from First American to former public officials.

September 17: BCCI board member Alfred Hartmann resigns from the chairmanship of BNL's Swiss subsidiary after the *Wall Street Journal* reports his ties to both BCCI and BNL.

November: News organizations begin reporting on Senator Hatch's intriguing ties to BCCI.

November 15: The Justice Department announces the indictment of BCCI, Abedi, Naqvi, and Pharaon. They are charged with engaging in a racketeering conspiracy involving the illegal ownership of Independence Bank and 25 percent of CenTrust Savings Bank.

December: BCCI's liquidator reveals that about $9.5 billion has been lost or stolen. (This is the difference between liabilities and realizable assets.)

1991– BCCI's liquidators plead guilty to all U.S. charges against the bank
1992 and agree to forfeit all the bank's U.S. assets, worth an estimated $550 million.

1992 *January 30:* The Federal Deposit Insurance Corporation seizes Independence Bank.

February 28: The Justice Department announces the indictment of CenTrust's David Paul on fraud charges. He is accused of concealing the savings bank's true financial condition by parking $25 million in CenTrust junk bonds with BCCI.

April: Noriega is convicted by a federal jury in Miami.

June: Harry W. Albright, Jr., is appointed trustee for a majority of the shares in First American. They were previously owned by BCCI and Sheikh Zayed's family.

June: BNL's former Atlanta branch manager, Christopher Drogoul, pleads guilty to multiple counts of bank fraud in the BNL-Iraq case. (In September, the plea agreement is canceled.)

July 1: A Manhattan grand jury indicts Khalid Bin Mahfouz on charges that he stole $300 million from BCCI; charged with him is his assistant Haroon Kahlon.

July 22: A Manhattan grand jury returns two sealed indictments in the BCCI case. One accuses Abedi, Naqvi, Pharaon, and Fulaij with participating in "enterprise corruption." The other accuses Abedi, Naqvi, Clifford, Altman, and Fulaij with participating in a scheme to defraud.

July 27: Adham and Jawhary plead guilty to New York charges and sign cooperation agreements with the Manhattan D.A.'s office and the Justice Department.

July 29: A federal grand jury in Washington returns a three-count indictment against Clifford and Altman. It is announced simultaneously with the Manhattan indictments returned seven days earlier. The Fed announces a detailed order alleging that Clifford and Altman violated numerous banking regulations. Clifford and Altman plead not guilty to all charges.

September 30: The Kerry Committee releases an extensive report on the BCCI affair.

October 22: A Luxembourg court approves a settlement of claims by BCCI's depositors. Zayed's government is committed to pay about $1.7 billion. Lord Justice Bingham releases his report on BCCI; it is critical of the Bank of England and Sheikh Zayed's government.

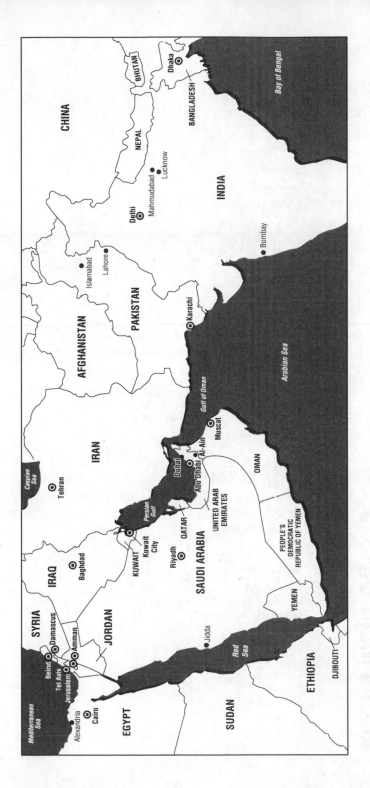

BCCI's Main Offices

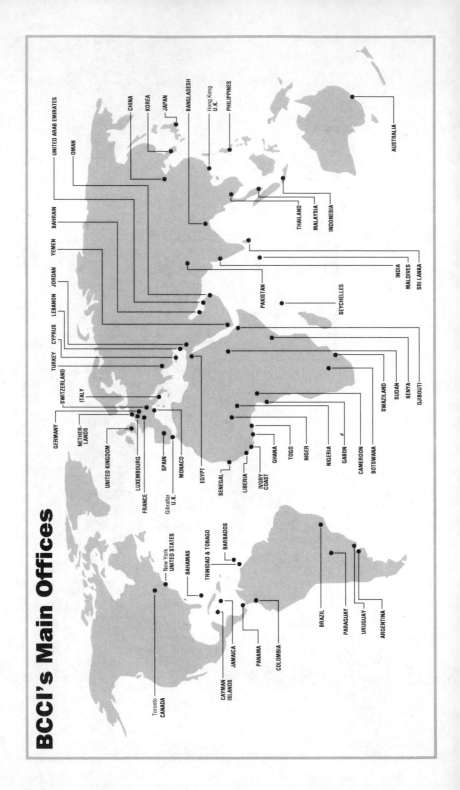

BCCI Corporate Organization

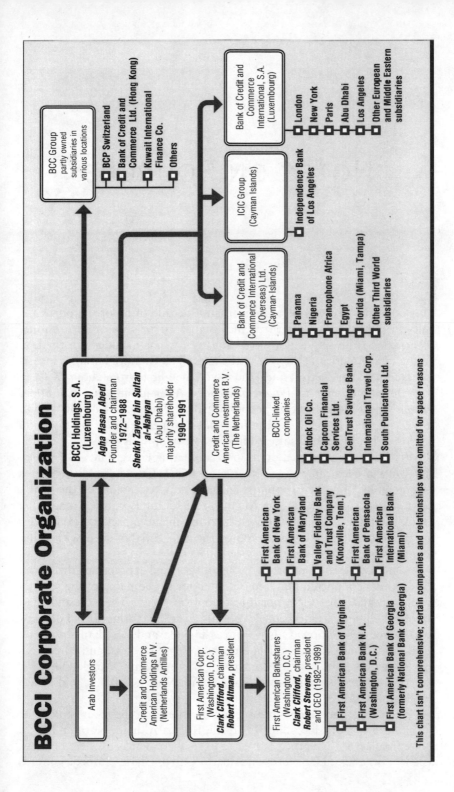

BCC Group partly owned subsidiaries in various locations
- BCP Switzerland
- Bank of Credit and Commerce Ltd. (Hong Kong)
- Kuwait International Finance Co.
- Others

BCCI Holdings, S. A. (Luxembourg)
Agha Hasan Abedi Founder and chairman 1972–1988
Sheikh Zayed bin Sultan al-Nahyan (Abu Dhabi) majority shareholder 1990–1991

Bank of Credit and Commerce International, S.A. (Luxembourg)
- London
- New York
- Paris
- Abu Dhabi
- Los Angeles
- Other European and Middle Eastern subsidiaries

ICIC Group (Cayman Islands)
- Independence Bank of Los Angeles

Bank of Credit and Commerce International (Overseas) Ltd. (Cayman Islands)
- Panama
- Nigeria
- Francophone Africa
- Egypt
- Florida (Miami, Tampa)
- Other Third World subsidiaries

Credit and Commerce American Investment B.V. (The Netherlands)

BCCI-linked companies
- Attock Oil Co.
- Capcom Financial Services Ltd.
- CenTrust Savings Bank
- International Travel Corp.
- South Publications Ltd.

Arab Investors

Credit and Commerce American Holdings N.V. (Netherlands Antilles)

First American Corp. (Washington, D.C.)
Clark Clifford, chairman
Robert Altman, president

First American Bankshares (Washington, D.C.)
Clark Clifford, chairman
Robert Stevens, president and CEO (1982–1989)
- First American Bank of New York
- First American Bank of Maryland
- Valley Fidelity Bank and Trust Company (Knoxville, Tenn.)
- First American Bank of Pensacola
- First American International Bank (Miami)
- First American Bank of Virginia
- First American Bank N.A. (Washington, D.C.)
- First American Bank of Georgia (formerly National Bank of Georgia)

This chart isn't comprehensive; certain companies and relationships were omitted for space reasons

NOTES ON SOURCES

This book has grown out of more than a decade of reporting on BCCI. Gurwin published an article in the August 1979 issue of *Institutional Investor* on Arab acquisitions of U.S. banks, which included information on the First American takeover battle as well as Ghaith Pharaon's investments in banks in Detroit and Houston. Truell first wrote about BCCI in 1981 for the *Economist Financial Report*. After joining the *Wall Street Journal* the following year, he published several stories on BCCI and related matters. An article in the *Journal*'s European edition in May 1986 disclosed that BCCI had suffered huge losses in options trading.

After BCCI was indicted on money-laundering charges in 1988, Truell and Gurwin began intensive research on BCCI. Gurwin published three articles on BCCI in the *Economist* and a lengthy cover story on the bank's ties to First American for the May 1990 issue of *Regardie's* magazine. Truell has published scores of BCCI stories, including several exclusives, for the *Wall Street Journal,* some of them in collaboration with other *Journal* reporters.

It is impossible to mention all of the sources used in preparing this book. The authors conducted hundreds of interviews, and many of the sources would speak only on a not-for-attribution basis. These confidential sources include law enforcement officials as well as former BCCI officials who feared retribution. Other sources include auditors, bankers, bank regulators, congressional staff members, defense lawyers, and employees of various companies connected to BCCI (including Attock Oil, First American, National Bank of Georgia, Independence Bank, and South Publications).

Many people mentioned in the book did speak on the record to one or both of the authors, including Tariq Ali, Robert Altman, Norman Bailey, Sidney Bailey, E. Lawrence Barcella, Jr., Robert Bench, Robert Bennett, Michael Bradfield, Hank Brown, Alberto Calvo, Clark Clifford, James F.

Dougherty II, Robert W. Genzman, Eddie George, Henry Gonzalez, John Heimann, Mike Hershman, Pierre Jaans, Laurent Kasper-Ansermet, John Kerry, Bert Lance, Frank Mankiewicz, Middleton A. ("Sandy") Martin III, J. Virgil Mattingly, Jr., David McKean, Robert Morgenthau, John Moscow, Ghaith Pharaon, Masihur Rahman, Abdur Sakhia, Charles Schumer, Jackson Stephens, the late William Taylor, William von Raab, Lawrence Wechsler, and Jonathan Winer.

Thousands of pages of documents have been gathered and reviewed. The most useful articles, broadcasts, and books are cited in the notes; books are usually identified by the surname of the author. The following abbreviations are used.

AP Associated Press

"BCCI Activities" "BCCI and Its Activities in the United States," *House Banking Committee Minority Staff Report,* September 10, 1991. Reprinted in the record of the committee's September 11, 1991, BCCI hearing.

Burris Affidavit An affidavit for a search warrant by David H. Burris of the Internal Revenue Service dated October 7, 1988. (Burris, who worked on Operation C-Chase, sought court permission to search BCCI's offices. This document contains a detailed summary of the evidence obtained in the investigation.)

Church Committee The Subcommittee on Multinational Corporations of the Senate Foreign Relations Committee was chaired by the late Frank Church, a Democrat from Idaho. In the mid-1970s, this committee conducted an investigation of the bribery of foreign officials by American companies.

Fed The Federal Reserve

FT *Financial Times*

House Banking Chronology This chronology of the BCCI affair was prepared by the majority staff of the House Banking Committee and released at a hearing on September 11, 1991.

Kerry Committee The Subcommittee on Terrorism, Narcotics, and International Operations of the Senate Foreign Relations Committee, chaired by John F. Kerry of Massachusetts.

Kerry Report *The BCCI Affair. A Report to the Senate Committee on Foreign Relations,* from Senators John Kerry and Hank Brown (a Colorado Republican), September 30, 1992.

LAT *Los Angeles Times*

L.G. Larry Gurwin

MEED *Middle East Economic Digest,* a magazine published in London

NYT *New York Times*

P.T. Peter Truell

PW Price Waterhouse

Schumer Report *Federal Law Enforcement's Handling of Allegations Involving the Bank of Credit and Commerce International,* a staff report issued on September 5, 1991, by the Subcommittee on Crime and Criminal Justice of the House Judiciary Committee. The report was prepared at the direction of the chairman, Charles E. Schumer of New York, and was not "reviewed or approved by other members of the subcommittee."

U.S. v. Awan et al. The money-laundering case against BCCI and several employees announced by the U.S. attorney in Tampa in October 1988.

U.S. v. Noriega et al. The drug case against the former Panamanian dictator and several other defendants. The indictment was announced in early 1988.

Vaez Report A report on BCCI submitted by Joseph E. Vaez of the Office of the Comptroller of the Currency on February 27, 1978, to Robert R. Bench, the associate deputy comptroller for international banking.

WP *Washington Post*

WSJ *Wall Street Journal*

PROLOGUE

The description of the arraignment of Clifford and Altman is based partly on reporting by Tom Petzinger and Jonathan Moses of the *WSJ.*

Abdur Sakhia's statements about Abedi are from his October 22, 1991, testimony to the Kerry Committee. Calvo provided his description of Abedi to the authors. The columnist William Safire compared Abedi to Moriarty.

1: THE COURTIER AND THE SHEIKH

The principal source for the fall 1972 gathering in Abu Dhabi is a written statement by Riaz Saleem Aslam, a Pakistani who served as a financial adviser to Sheikh Zayed. Information on Abedi's early life and career is drawn from interviews with former BCCI officials, press reports, and Abedi's March 8, 1978, deposition in *Financial General Bankshares, Inc., v. Lance et al.* Najam Sethi's article was in the *WSJ,* July 29, 1991. Also useful was a lengthy article on Abedi's background by Steve Coll on September 1, 1991, in the *WP.*

Sheikh Zayed is described in Kelly, Mosley, and Thesiger. (The Bousted quote is from Mosley.) Baldwin Tuttle, an attorney for the BCCI clients who took over First American, explained Zayed's control of Abu Dhabi's resources in a November 5, 1980, letter to the Fed. Sakhia's remark was made in an October 7, 1991, interview with Kerry's staff. Some of the information on Carlson's role in the founding of BCCI is from the *LAT,* September 3, 1991. Rahman's remarks are from his August 8, 1991, Kerry Committee testimony, a February 1992 article by Alan Friedman in *Vanity Fair,* and Rahman's August 7, 1991, interview with the Kerry staff. P.T. also conducted several interviews with Rahman.

2: THE NETWORK

Information on the early history of BCCI comes from former bank officers, an article in the July 1978 issue of *Euromoney,* and Tariq Ali's articles for the *New Statesman* on October 16 and 23, 1981. Most of the information on the branch network comes from BCCI's annual reports.

The remarks about Abedi by former colleagues come from several sources, including *Vanity Fair,* February 1992, P.T.'s interview with Calvo, and L.G.'s interview with Lozano.

Several people who attended BCCI's annual conferences (employees and others) described them in background interviews. Aslam, the former financial adviser to Zayed, provided some of the information on BCCI's role in managing the sheikh's investments. Bilgrami talked about Zayed in an interview with Kerry's staff on July 13, 1992, and in his July 30, 1992, Kerry Committee testimony.

Abedi's explanation of BCCI's ownership comes from his March 8, 1978, deposition in *Financial General Bankshares, Inc., v. Lance et al.* Sani Ahmed's remark about Abedi's ambitions appeared in *Newsweek* on August 26, 1991.

3: COMING TO AMERICA

Several of the characters mentioned in this chapter were interviewed by one or both of the authors, including Altman, Bailey, Clifford, Heimann, Lance, Pharaon, and Stephens. Saul was interviewed by Keith Girard, a writer for *Regardie's* when L.G. was preparing his article on First American. There were also off-the-record interviews, including one with a former BCCI official who was familiar with Eugene Holley's 1977 meeting with Abedi. Other confidential sources included bank regulators and an adviser to Financial General during the takeover battle.

Contemporaneous press reports were useful for the section on Lancegate, as was a profile of Altman by Harry Jaffe in the June 1991 issue of

Washingtonian. Lancegate was also mentioned in the memoirs of Carter, Clifford, and Lance.

The Financial General takeover battle was covered thoroughly by the *WP* and the (now defunct) *Washington Star.* Also useful were court papers from the takeover litigation, notably the SEC's complaint, Financial General's complaint, affidavits by Saul and Middendorf, and depositions of several of the defendants, including Abedi, Adham, and Lance. In response to requests filed under the Freedom of Information Act, the Federal Reserve released hundreds of pages of documents, including a transcript of the April 23, 1981, hearing at the Fed as well as internal memoranda.

New information about the takeover has emerged in recent years as a result of investigations by congressional committees and prosecutors. For example, the Kerry Committee and the House Banking Committee have released internal BCCI documents about the takeover battle. On September 11, 1991, House Banking released a detailed chronology of the BCCI affair, which lists many of the events in the takeover battle. Abbas Gokal's attempt to acquire Chelsea National Bank was described by Heimann in May 23, 1991, testimony to the Senate Banking Committee and by a confidential source to L.G.

Pharaon showed off the "Titian" during a meeting with P.T. in the spring of 1990.

Clifford's career as a "superlawyer" is described in Goulden, which also lists most of the clients mentioned in this chapter. Gailey's recollection of Clifford appeared on March 21, 1991.

Boeing's questionable payments were reported in the *WSJ* on June 28 and July 31, 1978, and April 27, 1979. The comment by Adham's lawyer appeared in a September 30, 1991, article by John Fialka in the *WSJ.* Regarding the PLO, the governments of Saudi Arabia and the UAE openly acknowledge that they have channeled substantial aid to the organization over the years. It was in a July 1989 interview with L.G. that Altman refused to comment on how such support jibed with his 1981 statement that none of the investors in First American had been involved in supporting terrorist groups. (The U.S. government continues to classify the PLO as a terrorist group.)

4: THE UNDERGROUND EMPIRE

Most of the facts and figures on the expansion of BCCI's network are from the annual reports. Information about BCCI's ties with its satellites is based largely on confidential interviews with BCCI officials, associates of Ghaith Pharaon's, and employees of Attock, National Bank of Georgia,

First American Bankshares, First American Bank of New York, Independence Bank, and South Publications.

REDEC's debt rescheduling was covered by P.T. for the *WSJ*. Former BCCI officials described in interviews in 1990 how BAII "fronted" for BCCI in the Independence Bank takeover; they provided supporting documents. (This transaction resulted in federal criminal charges against BCCI, some of its senior officers, and Pharaon in November 1991. BAII has not been accused of any wrongdoing.)

Altman said in a July 1989 interview with L.G. that First American's purchase of NBG was an "arm's-length" deal. Clifford's remarks appeared in *American Banker,* December 10, 1987. Pharaon's were published in *Atlanta Business Chronicle,* April 27, 1987. Altman's deposition was taken on June 23, 1988, in *Doris I. Sandberg et al. v. Virginia Bankshares, Inc., et al.,* a suit filed by former minority shareholders of First American Bank of Virginia in U.S. District Court in Alexandria, Virginia. The price paid for NBG is from the Fed's July 29, 1992, order.

Peter Becker's profile of David Paul was published in *M, Inc.* in March 1991. The $2 billion estimate was made by bank regulators. The bond-parking scheme was first reported in the *WSJ* on May 3, 1990, in a story by P.T. and John Fialka.

Clifford's assertion that BCCI exerted no control over First American was made at a September 11, 1991, hearing of the House Banking Committee. The remarks about the "so-called shareholders" were made by a top official of First American Bankshares, who spoke to L.G. on a not-for-attribution basis. At the House Banking hearing, Clifford said that in the thirteen years he and Altman represented BCCI, he made twenty-six trips to London. Abedi's role in hiring Richter was revealed in the *WP,* February 3, 1991; additional details are contained in the Fed order issued on July 29, 1992. Information on the extensive correspondent banking relationship is from "BCCI Activities."

The terms of Afridi's mortgage are contained in real estate records filed in Westchester County, New York. A government investigator confirmed that Elley was also granted a below-market rate on his mortgage. Altman's comments on the mortgages were made in a July 1989 interview with L.G. Invitation lists for the conferences contain the names of several employees of BCCI satellites. A number of these people have confirmed in interviews that they attended, including Altman.

5: Friends in High Places

Abedi's practice of supplying prostitutes to influential people has been confirmed in interviews by several former BCCI employees as well as others familiar with the bank. The detailed information about Begum Asghari Rahim comes mainly from the *Kerry Report*.

The allegation that Abedi provided cash to Bhutto's political party in 1977 is contained in a document entitled "White Paper on the Conduct of the General Elections in March 1977," issued in July 1978. The Attock takeover was described in Tariq Ali's October 16, 1981, story for the *New Statesman* and in confidential interviews with a former BCCI official.

The authors have a copy of the loan agreement for the $100 million financing of Pakistan's Rice Export Corporation. BCCI's role in helping Pakistan inflate its foreign currency reserves was described by Nazir Chinoy in his March 13, 1992, Kerry Committee testimony. Abedi's close relationship with Zia was confirmed by several former BCCI employees as well as other sources. Lawrence Lifschultz and Zahid Hussain, a Pakistani journalist, also assisted the authors.

The examples of Pakistani officials who went to work for BCCI were provided by Zahid Hussain and former BCCI officials. When BCCI was asked by L.G. in 1989 to confirm these examples, it declined to do so. A spokesman would only confirm in general terms that it had hired several former government officials.

Bert Lance's account of how he introduced Abedi to Carter is based on Lance's October 23, 1991, testimony to the Kerry Committee as well as interviews with the authors. Most of the information about donations to Carter's projects was provided by the Carter Center. Khashoggi's role in paying for a fund-raising event is described in Kessler. Sasakawa's unsavory background has been widely reported; the specific information in this chapter is from the book by Anderson and Anderson.

Carter's 1987 trip with Abedi was described by Kovach in the *Atlanta Constitution* on June 29 and 30, 1987. The description of the BCCI jet is from *Vanity Fair*, February 1992. The Kovach remarks quoted here appeared in the *LAT*, July 28, 1991.

Details of Young's relationship with BCCI come from interviews with a former BCCI official, press reports, and internal BCCI documents. The payment of expenses for Young's Middle Eastern trip is from Emerson, citing the *Atlanta Journal*, March 23, 1983. The *Kerry Report* states that the loan balance reached $197,000 and that Young's associate Stony Cooks maintains this was offset by travel expenses. The report then points out that Young would have to have traveled a tremendous amount for BCCI to incur such large expenses. Young declined to answer questions from the authors.

Pharaon's practice of entertaining VIPs in Savannah was described by a former associate of his and in press reports, notably an August 28, 1991, article in the *NYT*. The Pharaon-Paul visit and subsequent donation were described in the *LAT*, July 28, 1991.

Lord Callaghan mentioned his relationship with BCCI in a December 1, 1988, letter to a researcher for *Bandung File,* a program on Britain's Channel 4, which was preparing a feature on BCCI. It said, in part, that "Mr Abedi had kindly volunteered financial assistance in my travel and other arrangements." Rahman's quote on Callaghan is from *Vanity Fair,* February 1992. Ridsdale and Amery mentioned their financial ties to BCCI in their parliamentary disclosure statements.

Virani's relationship with BCCI has been widely reported in the British press. A former BCCI official described in an interview with the authors how Virani introduced bank officials to Conservative politicians.

Two former employees of South Publications provided information on Gauhar's activities, as did Lawrence Lifschultz in interviews with L.G. Other sources included interviews with former BCCI officials, the Third World Foundation's application for registration as a charity (dated March 13, 1978), a 1987 brochure on the Third World Prize, and back issues of *South* magazine and the *Third World Quarterly.* It was during a 1981 interview with L.G. that a BCCI official blamed the bank's poor image on racism and jealousy.

Abedi's efforts to ingratiate himself with Zimbabwean politicians were described by former BCCI officials in interviews with the authors, Bilgrami's July 30, 1992, testimony to the Kerry Committee, and Sakhia's October 22, 1991, testimony to the same committee.

BCCI's efforts to operate in Singapore were reported by Marcus W. Brauchli in the *Asian Wall Street Journal* on August 26, 1991.

BCCI's Florida connections were discussed in Aziz Rehman's October 24, 1988, deposition to the Kerry Committee. Sakhia provided additional information in his public testimony to the committee. The party to launch the regional office was described in the *Economist,* October 16, 1981, the *Miami Herald,* August 4, 1991, and the *Kerry Report.*

Information on the Washington representative office comes from interviews with former employees, press reports, and correspondence between BCCI and Clifford & Warnke. The $20 million figure is from a law enforcement source. Abedi's Third World bank scheme was described by a former BCCI official in an interview with the authors. Qureshi's 1991 interview was with P.T.

The estimate that nearly a third of Clifford & Warnke's lawyers did work for First American was contained in a *WSJ* article by Jill Abramson, October 4, 1988. The story was the first detailed discussion in the press of Clifford's multiple roles at First American. The *WP*'s profile of Altman appeared on October 8, 1984.

The remark that Abedi "wanted to be bigger than the bank" appeared in a September 4, 1991, report on BCCI by the Task Force on Terrorism and Unconventional Warfare of the House Republican Research Committee, entitled "BCCI — An Introduction." BCCI's relationship with Abu Nidal was first reported by London's *Sunday Times* in July 1991; the information here is mainly from Seale.

Roosevelt's meeting with Abdel-Aziz is described in Lacey's *Kingdom*. Other valuable sources on Saudi Arabia and U.S.-Saudi relations include *The House of Saud* by Holden and Johns and *The American House of Saud* by Emerson — a major source on Saudi Arabia's lobbyists.

Khashoggi's courtship of Nixon is described in Sampson's *Arms Bazaar* and Boulton. Boulton is the source for the rumors that Nixon used campaign money from Khashoggi and that Khashoggi financed a record of Nixon's speeches. Nixon's use of Khashoggi as a go-between emerged in a 1976 investigation by the Church Committee. The failure of Nixon administration officials to turn in gifts from foreign officials was disclosed by Maxine Cheshire of the *WP* in a series of stories in 1974.

Pharaon's investments in Bank of the Commonwealth and Main Bank were discussed in detail in L.G.'s August 1979 article for *Institutional Investor;* he interviewed several sources at that time, including Pharaon's U.S. representative, Frank Van Court. Information also came from Crowe and Levins. The Hunts' silver scheme is the subject of Fay's book.

Carter's 1983 speech was in Atlanta in May at a U.S.-Saudi conference; the source is Emerson. Yassin's role in collecting FGB stock for Prince Nawaf was reported in the *WP*, February 11, 1978, citing Fed documents. Carter's op-ed piece on Rushdie appeared in the *NYT*, March 5, 1989. The information on Dutton comes mainly from Emerson, based on various documents Emerson obtained.

Lance recalled his meeting with Zayed in his October 23, 1991, testimony to the Kerry Committee and in an interview with the authors. The UAE official who discussed Zayed's intentions for First American is Aslam, the former financial adviser to the sheikh; he made these remarks in written statements obtained by P.T.

The statement by Clifford about the creation of Israel is from the March 1991 issue of *M, Inc.;* he also discusses this in his memoirs. Clifford described his role as an envoy for Carter in September 1988 trial testimony in the suit against First American by former shareholders.

Symington's Church Committee vote is described in Levins. Information on DiBona, Lesher, and Battle comes mainly from Emerson. Information on Gray's lobbying activities comes mainly from Trento and Emerson.

The information on Avenel is based on real estate records, press reports, and interviews with investigators and real estate experts. Dan Moldea, a writer in Washington, D.C., provided valuable information on the Avenel project and the FBI investigation. Natelli's pardon file was obtained from the Justice Department through a Freedom of Information Act request.

Confidential sources with access to First American records provided the information on loans to Gray and other First American directors. Deaver and Novak commented on their real estate loans from First American in interviews with P.T. Gary Hart's loans from First American were reported in the press at the time. A former BCCI official described Abedi's trip to Washington to meet with Hart. *Newsweek* quoted the Hart campaign aide on August 26, 1991. Hart was interviewed by P.T.

The Libyan donation to Jesse Jackson was reported in *Newsweek,* February 13, 1984. The Arab League donation was mentioned in the *WP,* January 31, 1984. The Yamani dinner was described in the *WP* on October 22, 1979.

Dutton's op-ed piece appeared in the *LAT,* June 17, 1988. Clifford's praise of Jackson was quoted in *Newsweek* on April 11, 1988. Jackson's remark about Clifford is quoted in Colton. (She was Jackson's press secretary during the campaign.) Lance told the authors in an interview how he introduced Jackson to Abedi. Nazir Chinoy testified to the Kerry Committee on March 13, 1992, about BCCI's payment of travel expenses for Jackson.

6: COVERT OPERATIONS

Kermit Roosevelt's letter to Northrop was obtained by the Church Committee. The letter is quoted in Holden.

Adham talked about his background in a December 20, 1979, deposition in *Fulaij et al. v. Middendorf et al.* (a lawsuit stemming from the First American takeover battle) and during the April 23, 1981, hearing at the Fed. Other sources on Adham include Holden, Lacey, Halliday, Crowe, and Blandford. His role as an intermediary between Sadat and Kissinger is mentioned in Anderson, Holden, and Kissinger. Adham confirms through his lawyer his role as a liaison with foreign intelligence agencies but denies being trained by the CIA.

The Saudi attitude toward foreign banks was explained to P.T. in interviews with Saudi officials conducted in that country in the early 1980s. Adham's account of how he met Abedi is contained in the December 1979 deposition cited above.

The Camp David negotiations are discussed in detail in Carter's *Blood of Abraham.* Adham's role and subsequent dismissal are discussed in Holden, which also notes that Adham remained an influential figure.

Adham's role in Saudi intelligence and his ties with the CIA are mentioned in several places, notably Holden. Khalil's attorney, James Linn, confirmed in an interview that his client held a senior position in the Saudi government, related to communications and intelligence. Investigators for the Kerry Committee learned that Khalil was a frequent visitor to the CIA station in Saudi Arabia as recently as 1991. Through his lawyer, Khalil denies working for the CIA but declines to say if he worked *with* the CIA.

Nicholas Deak's services for the CIA were reported by Tad Szulc in a story for *Inquiry,* November 21, 1977. Information on Castle Bank, Mercantile, and Nugan Hand comes mainly from Kwitny and Lernoux. The Middendorf-Casey discussions were reported in Jack Anderson's column in the *WP,* July 30, 1984.

Prince Mahmood Reza Pahlavi was identified as a BCCI shareholder in the *Vaez Report.* The assistance Helms received from Clifford, Williams, and Symington is discussed in Thomas. Information on Helms's consulting business and his ties to Irvani and Carlson comes from documents released by the Kerry Committee. When the committee sought information from Carlson in 1992, he invoked his constitutional right against self-incrimination. Carlson declined to be interviewed by the authors.

Information on Gray's intelligence links is from Trento. Harr's career at the NSC is mentioned in Prados. Issan Kabbani is identified as a business associate of Close's in the *International Herald Tribune,* December 10, 1981 (from the NYT News Service). Bilgrami mentioned Kabbani in his July 30, 1992, Kerry Committee testimony. The information on Mazrui, Yassin, and Shaheen is from the *Kerry Report.*

Bush's tenure as CIA director is discussed in detail in "Company Man," by Scott Armstrong and Jeff Nason, in the November/December 1991 issue of *Mother Jones.* Rogers's ties to the shah are discussed in Crowe.

A former BCCI official is the main source for Abedi's assistance to Zia. The Afghan operation is in McCoy and Woodward as well as articles by Steve Coll of the *WP.* A July 19, 1992, story by Coll includes the $2 billion estimate; a September 1, 1991, story mentions Prince Turki's role.

BCCI's involvement in the Afghan operation was described by former officials of the bank. The sources for information on war matériel and pack animals include internal BCCI documents. Abedi's meetings in Washington with Casey were reported on NBC-TV's *Sunday Today* program on February 23, 1992. In interviews with the authors, a former BCCI official provided information on the content of their discussions as well as other details on the Abedi-Casey relationship. Kerry's staff members and the *Kerry Report* are the sources for the footnote on the CIA's denials.

The CIA has acknowledged publicly that it maintained accounts at BCCI for routine banking business. Altman said in October 24, 1991, testimony to the Kerry Committee that the CIA maintained accounts at First American.

The role of Khashoggi and Ghorbanifar in Iran-contra is discussed in Persico, the *Tower Commission Report,* and other sources. The incident in which Khashoggi told his colleagues about potential profits is based on June 8, 1987, testimony to the congressional Iran-Contra Committee by Emmanuel Floor, a former aide to Khashoggi. BCCI's Chinoy described the bank's role in Iran-contra in March 13, 1992, testimony to the Kerry Committee. Further details are contained in the *Kerry Report.*

Durrani discussed his use of BCCI in interviews with P.T. The Gokals' status as BCCI's biggest borrowers is confirmed in the *Vaez Report* and in audit reports by PW, issued in 1989, 1990, and 1991. The authors obtained internal BCCI documents and other company papers that pertain to the business of Banerjee and others. Yacoub Wadawalla's remark appeared in *New York Magazine* on December 16, 1991.

Iraq's $13 million debt is mentioned in an auditor's review of BCCI's foreign loans obtained by the Kerry Committee. The most important single source of information for the BNL affair is the House Banking Committee, which has released or quoted many relevant documents. Other sources include the *Kerry Report,* Timmerman, *FT* articles by Alan Friedman, and stories in the *WSJ* as well as the Italian and Swiss press.

Gonzalez criticized Scowcroft and Eagleburger during a May 21, 1992, hearing of the House Banking Committee. The role of Pakistani officials in the U.S. opening to China is described in Kissinger's memoirs. First City's lending to the Gokals was disclosed in legal documents in Switzerland. A source close to Abboud said that the banker discussed buying some of BCCI's offices. Abboud himself denies this, though he admits he planned to buy BAII's New York office.

Gonzalez's inquiry into the BNL affair turned up information on Stoga's trip to Iraq and Kissinger's consulting relationship with BNL. Kissinger's office provided the information on the resignation from the advisory board and the June 1991 speech.

Pakistan's efforts to obtain nuclear technology have been widely reported. The legal troubles of Inam ul-Haq and Arshad Pervez were reported in the U.S. and Canadian press. *Time's* interview with General Zia was published on March 30, 1987.

Aitken's ties to the Saudi royal family and the investment by Prince Mohammed were reported in the *Independent* on February 25, 1990.

The main sources for the section on TCI and Capcom include company documents and interviews with former BCCI officials and several investigators. An extensive *WSJ* article by Johnnie Roberts, on January 27, 1992, provided valuable background information on TCI. Investigators' notes and summaries as well as documents relating to TCI and its executives were also critical. Public TCI accounts and filings provided useful information. Articles by Christopher Byron of *New York Magazine* were helpful, particularly those on August 19, 1991, and August 10, 1992.

The Kerry Committee devoted part of its July 30, 1992, BCCI hearing to Capcom. During the hearing, it released hundreds of pages of documents, including the committee's correspondence with Carlson, Fox, Magness, Romrell, and TCI; some of Romrell's correspondence with Akbar, Khalil, Adham, and others; Peat Marwick's 1989 report for Britain's Securities and Investments Board with supporting documentation and exhibits; the Chicago Mercantile Exchange's 1989 report on Capcom Futures; memos to and from Romrell; portions of Romrell's personal notebooks; Capcom shareholder lists; Capital Fund documents; and Fox correspondence.

In reply to questions related to Capcom, Adham's Washington lawyer merely stated that the Saudi "invested in Capcom and [that] accounts were maintained there for his children, not for himself."

Khalil's lawyer, James Linn, responded to the authors' questions about Khalil's role in the BCCI affair by saying that the Saudi maintains he is innocent of wrongdoing. In late October 1992, Linn gave the authors an undated, four-and-a-half-page statement from Khalil, which was translated into English from Arabic. In the statement, Khalil says he worked in various positions in the Saudi government, that he became an employee of Adham's in 1962, and that he met Abedi through Adham. He says he asked BCCI to close his accounts and sell all his BCCI stock in the mid-1980s, after he learned that the bank had incurred large losses. Because the bank failed to carry out these instructions, Khalil says, he suffered "serious financial losses." He says that when he learned of problems at Capcom, he sold his stock in that company — at "a considerable financial loss" — to Akbar. The statement does not address in any detail the allegations that have been made against Khalil by prosecutors and bank regulators.

Robert Gray's relationships with the CIA and CNN are discussed at length in Trento. A former senior BCCI official told the authors about Turner's trip to China. Bailey's remarks were broadcast on the *NBC Nightly News* on February 21, 1992. North made the quoted remarks on July 10, 1987.

7: The Dirty Money Machine

Abedi's remarks about BCCI's serving a purpose appeared in an interview with *Institutional Investor* in January 1983. The comment on "purity and chastity" appeared in *Euromoney* in July 1978. Rahman's remark about the "moral balance sheet" is from an interview with P.T.

The account of BCCI's ties to Ershad is based on a November 2, 1991, article in the *LAT* and an interview by P.T. with Mike Hershman of the Fairfax Group of Falls Church, Virginia, which was retained by the Bangladesh government. Information on Kroll's investigation of Saddam Hussein's hidden wealth comes from press reports and interviews by P.T. with Kroll's investigators.

BCCI's role in handling dirty money in Pakistan has been described by former bank officials and government investigators. McCoy is an excellent source on the Golden Crescent drug trade. Valuable information was also provided by Lawrence Lifschultz. The 1988 State Department estimates are from that year's edition of the *International Narcotics Control Strategy Report*. McCoy is the source of the $8 billion–$10 billion figure; he said these were conservative estimates by economists. Fazle Haq's "blue murder" remark appeared in the *NYT Magazine*, January 15, 1989.

BCCI's ties to Nawaz Sharif were reported in the *WSJ*, October 23, 1991. The former associate cited in the article was Salmaan Taseer, who worked with Sharif in Dubai and is now a political opponent. The prime minister's praise of Fazle Haq was reported by Agence France Presse on October 3, 1991.

Nigeria's population was generally thought to be more than 100 million. In early 1992, the results of a new census were reported, and it put the total at 88.5 million. The quote on the evils of bribery appeared in Sandbrook. Tam David-West's $1 billion estimate appeared in *Time*, September 8, 1985.

A list of the shareholders of BCCI's Nigerian bank was provided to L.G. in March 1989 by Clement R. Gagné III, a Washington lawyer who represented BCCI. The relationship between Dasuki and Babangida was described in interviews with Nigerian sources. A major source on Dasuki's background was an article in the August 26, 1988, issue of *Africa Confidential*, a London-based newsletter. The problems faced by foreign banks in Nigeria were described to L.G. by several American and European bankers in interviews conducted in 1989. BCCI's foreign exchange fraud was reported in the *FT*, September 16, 1991. Former BCCI officials described to the authors how employees made money on the side.

Attock's cozy ties with the Nigerians were described by a former Attock employee. Additional information was provided by a former BCCI official familiar with the company. Early reports of Nigeria's barter deal appeared in *MEED* in May 1986 and *Platt's Oilgram* on June 16, 1986. BCCI's lawyer Gagné declined to provide any information. The terms were eventually published in the *FT*, November 26, 1991.

Blum's conversation with the Nigerian diplomat is from an interview with Blum and his August 1, 1991, testimony to the Kerry Committee.

The authors have a copy of the Suriname loan agreement. Goedschalk's remarks about the deal appeared in the *LAT*, March 1, 1992. BCCI's role as a depository for various governments and government agencies is documented in bank records obtained by the authors. The Jordanian army deposits were reported in the *WSJ*, July 28, 1991.

The evidence of bribes to central bankers has been obtained by investigators for Robert Morgenthau. In a July 29, 1991, press conference, he alleged that Peruvian central bankers were bribed. One year later, allegations of bribes to several other central bankers were made in a Morgenthau press conference and a New York State indictment of Abedi and other defendants. Sakhia recounted his experience in Seoul in his October 22, 1991, Kerry Committee testimony.

A former BCCI official told the authors about the half-billion-dollar deposit from a member of the al-Ibrahim family. The Price Waterhouse audits of 1989 and 1990 showed Ibrahim borrowings of close to $100 million. An investigation arising from a Los Angeles court case subsequently disclosed that the Ibrahims' deposits at BCCI of more than $100 million substantially exceeded their borrowings from the bank.

The information on formal charges that BCCI violated exchange controls comes mainly from a March 10, 1989, memo to L.G. from BCCI's lawyer Gagné. The Colombian charges were reported in *El Tiempo,* a Colombian newspaper, on May 25, 1989. The Brazilian charges appeared in *Jornal do Brasil,* June 8, 1989. Hershman of the Fairfax Group described his Indian investigation in a 1992 interview with P.T.

Several former BCCI officials described in confidential interviews how they were pressured to bring in deposits. Chinoy made his remark about the law in an interview with Ira Silverman, a producer for NBC News. (The interview, which was not broadcast, was conducted on March 13, 1992, the day Chinoy appeared before the Kerry Committee.)

Wallace Kemper's activities and his relationship with BCCI were described by a law enforcement source in Britain, who also provided documentation, including copies of correspondence between Kemper and victims. The description of his brochures appeared in the *Sunday Times* of London, September 27, 1987.

The account of Morris Miller's career is based on the indictment as well as interviews with a law enforcement source and some of the would-be borrowers. L.G. also attended part of the trial. Information on the proprietors of the phony Montserrat bank comes from law enforcement sources, a bank regulator, and victims.

Information on First American Currency and its relationship with BCCI comes from press reports, BCCI records, and an interview by L.G. with Jim Harbin, a U.S. postal inspector who worked on the case.

The estimate of penny-stock losses is contained in a report by the North American Securities Administrators Association (NASAA), released in September 1989. Details of the Quinn case and Quinn's use of BCCI come from various press reports, the NASAA report, and interviews with investigators, including Laurent Kasper-Ansermet, the Swiss magistrate.

Valuable information on First Commerce Securities was given to L.G. by a former employee, who also provided various documents. Other interviewees included Jan Koers, the prosecutor, and Jan van Apeldoorn, the bankruptcy trustee. Diane Francis wrote about First Commerce and other boiler rooms in *The Contrepreneurs.* Nazerali declined to respond to questions from the authors.

Bilbeisi's business activities have created a lengthy trail of paper. Some of the most important sources were court papers related to litigation against Bilbeisi by the Lloyd's of London syndicate. The lead plaintiff was a Lloyd's underwriter named Nicholas Collwyn Sturge, and the suit was filed on January 18, 1988, in the U.S. District Court for the Southern District of Florida. On December 28, 1990, the syndicate filed a civil RICO suit against Bilbeisi and other defendants. Other sources included Bilbeisi's deposition in a 1983 civil suit, *Interastra v. Teledyne,* filed in the Western District of Michigan. P.T. obtained a copy of an extensive report on Bilbeisi compiled by BCCI's Florida law firm, Holland & Knight, which sets out much of Bilbeisi's alleged wrongdoing while blaming BCCI's Miami office for running a rogue operation beyond the control of the bank's head office. On August 11, 1991, the *New York Daily News* broke the news of Bilbeisi's plans to go into business with alleged mobsters. Other sources included FBI documents, letters from Dougherty to Dexter Lehtinen (the former acting U.S. attorney in Miami), and photocopies of the porter's log at the Sanctuary.

8: FALSE PROFITS

Rahman's interviews with the Serious Fraud Office in London in 1991 and his August 1, 1991, testimony before the Kerry Committee were important in understanding BCCI's financial condition. Several other former BCCI officers, including one who was part of Naqvi's special duties team, were also helpful. Throughout this chapter, two reports prepared by PW were invaluable: its June 22, 1991, report on BCCI for the Bank of England and its report on ICIC of June 17, 1991. The *Vaez Report* contains critical information about BCCI's early years. Earlier Price Waterhouse reports and correspondence, much of which was released by the Kerry Committee, also provided useful background. Other important information came from P.T.'s interviews with Masihur Rahman and several other BCCI officials.

A former official of the Gulf Group explained some of its structure and its relationship with BCCI. Former BCCI and Bank of America officials also provided information about BCCI's tangled finances. A lawyer for the Gokals denies they were involved in wrongdoing.

Sakhia's remarks were made in testimony to the Kerry Committee on October 22, 1991. Abedi's remarks were made in his March 8, 1978, deposition in *Financial General Bankshares, Inc., v. Lance et al.* Interviews with past and present U.S. government investigators provided useful guidance for the analysis of BCCI's true financial condition.

The authors obtained several BCCI shareholder lists, some from its internal records, one from its 1983 offering of floating-rate notes, others from various published sources. Court documents were the principal source for Zayed's dispute with Darwaish and Aslam. Information also came from one of the lawyers involved.

Congressional sources and government investigators were particularly important sources on Capcom. Gil Miller's remarks were made in an interview with P.T. in the summer of 1991. P.T. obtained a copy of a report on Capcom prepared by accountants from Peat Marwick McLintock; it was submitted in 1989 to Britain's Securities and Investments Board. The destruction of a large number of Capcom records was reported by the London *Independent* on August 18, 1991.

9: EL DORADO

Kalish described his dealings with Noriega in January 28, 1988, testimony before the Permanent Subcommittee on Investigations of the Senate Committee on Governmental Affairs. His partner, Ritch, appeared before the Kerry Committee on February 8, 1988. Other useful sources were the biographies of Noriega by Dinges and Kempe.

BCCI's anomalous performance in Hong Kong was described in *Euromoney* in October 1986. The same magazine discussed its performance in the UAE in May of that year. Khun Sa's use of BCCI was reported in the *FT,* August 3, 1991, which credited Reuters.

Fafowora's ties with BCCI were mentioned to L.G. by a law enforcement source. Details are contained in court records, including a pleading called *Government's Response to Victor O. Adeniji's Petition for an Ancillary Hearing in U.S. v. Steve Fafowora et al.,* which was filed on July 14, 1988. Attached as an exhibit are the Articles of Association of Afro Caribbean Connections Limited.

Bilgrami discussed his background and his activities in Latin America in July 30, 1992, testimony to the Kerry Committee. Other former BCCI officials, including Alberto Calvo, have discussed the Latin American expansion in interviews with the authors.

A source involved in trying to broker the Peruvian jet deal discussed the transaction in interviews P.T. conducted in 1991. Members of the Peruvian congress, U.S. investigators, and lawyers for some of the participants also discussed the transaction.

Pharaon's activities in South America were described by former associates and in García Lupo's book. It was in a 1990 interview with P.T. that Pharaon blamed an employee for the mistake on his application for Argentine citizenship. The Yoma case was widely reported in the press.

Sakhia's remark on drug money was made in an October 7, 1991, interview with Kerry's staff. The use of BCCI by Rodríguez Gacha was described in the *WP,* August 19, 1991. Aziz Rehman recounted his experiences at BCCI to Jack Blum in a deposition on October 24, 1988. The IRS's lack of follow-up was described in the *Schumer Report.*

The footnote on the Shahid Riky case is based on a copy of the indictment, a story in the *Chicago Tribune* (September 5, 1986), and an interview with a law enforcement source involved in the case.

Anibal Zapata's use of BCCI was reported in the *London Observer* on February 12, 1989. The Iranian heroin trafficker was discussed in the *Schumer Report* as well as in an AP report on August 16, 1991. The Federal Reserve's 1987 criminal referral was mentioned in the House Banking Chronology and has also been mentioned in congressional testimony by Fed officials.

Patrick Anthony Good's use of BCCI was described to L.G. in 1989 by a Canadian law enforcement officer. Additional details come from a court document (an "information to obtain a search warrant"), *Equity — The Business of Vancouver,* September 1989, and the *Vancouver Sun,* August 26 and September 30, 1992.

Amjad Awan discussed his background and his dealings with Noriega in his September 30, 1988, deposition to the Kerry Committee, in his December 1991 testimony in *U.S. v. Noriega et al.,* and his July 30, 1992, testimony to the Kerry Committee. Some of the information on Noriega's financial dealings is based on BCCI records. Kempe is the source for CIA deposits through dummy companies. A former BCCI official who worked closely with Awan told L.G. about "sackfuls of money" and the rumored advice from the CIA.

The allegation that Noriega received $10 million in bribes was made by Assistant U.S. Attorney Myles Malman before Noriega's trial began in September 1991. The sources for Awan's relations with Rodríguez and Pretelt include Awan's September 30, 1988, deposition to the Kerry Committee and a September 24, 1988, memo to file by Jack Blum.

The backgrounds of Kalish and Ritch were described in their Senate testimony (cited above), in various press reports (notably *St. Petersburg Times,* February 22, 1988), and in Dinges and Kempe.

Awan discussed the loans he received from Noriega in his December 1991 testimony at the Noriega trial. Details of Awan's real estate investments emerged during bond hearings in late 1988, after his arrest in *U.S. v. Awan et al.* His practice of transferring money through First American is documented by a large number of BCCI records.

10: TROUBLE IN TAMPA

Several of the people mentioned in this chapter spoke on the record to the authors, as noted above. Many others spoke on a not-for-attribution basis, including current and former BCCI employees, Justice Department officials, sources at Customs, and defense lawyers.

Court records, of course, were extremely useful. Among the more important were the October 1988 indictment, the superseding indictment issued six months later, transcripts of bond hearings held in late 1988, and the Burris Affidavit. The authors also obtained transcripts of several of Mazur's conversations with Awan, Akbar, and other targets.

Several people involved in Operation C-Chase testified to the Kerry Committee in late 1991, including Robert W. Genzman, Greg Kehoe, and Mark Jackowski of the U.S. Attorney's Office in Tampa and Robert Mazur and William von Raab of Customs (although both had left Customs by that time). Jack Blum testified on August 1, 1991, about his experiences.

The statement about "deposit marketing" is from the notes of a BCCI marketing meeting held in New York on September 30, 1988. The role of Rackley in advising Abedi's doctors was reported by Douglas Frantz of the *LAT* on June 19, 1992; Frantz wrote a book on BCCI with James Ring Adams which contains a great deal of information on C-Chase.

Information on the clash between the Naqvi and Iqbal factions and the power struggle after Abedi's illness comes mainly from a background interview with a highly placed BCCI official. The *Forbes* report on the Lance rumor appeared on June 13, 1988; the *Times* of London column on August 25, 1988.

Reagan's call for a "national crusade" was quoted in *Newsweek* on February 9, 1987. Von Raab's assistance to the DEA after the Camarena abduction is described in Shannon.

Mazur explained the origin of the C-Chase name in his November 21, 1991, Kerry Committee testimony. Awan's boast about $10 million is mentioned in the October 1988 indictment. The amount of money channeled through First American is based on figures in the Burris Affidavit.

Awan's trip to Washington with Noriega was described in Awan's September 30, 1988, deposition to the Kerry Committee and his July 30, 1992, testimony to the same committee. The visits to Casey and North are mentioned in Dinges.

Awan's status as an unindicted co-conspirator in the Noriega case was revealed by Jackowski at a bond hearing on November 28, 1988. The conversation with Naqvi and Noriega's decision to transfer the money were described in Awan's testimony at the Noriega trial. The $23 million transfer is mentioned in the federal indictment of Naqvi and others announced in November 1991.

Blum described his background and his investigation in interviews with the authors and in his Kerry Committee testimony. The quote mentioning Hannah Arendt and others is from a profile of Blum in the *WP*, August 13, 1991. PW's allegation that Akbar was bribed is from a report for the Bank of England in 1991; it was reported in the *WSJ* on July 17, 1991.

The Alcaino anecdote is from a detailed article on C-Chase by Mike Weiss in the *San Francisco Examiner* on July 22, 1990.

Altman testified to the Kerry Committee on October 24, 1991, about his handling of Blum's investigation. Blum's statements about the conduct of Clifford and Altman are from interviews with Blum. His remarks about the destruction of records are from his Kerry Committee testimony. Additional information about the movement or destruction of records comes from the October 1988 indictment, Mazur's Kerry Committee testimony, and Sakhia's November 22, 1991, testimony to the same committee. Kerry's recollection of his meeting with Clifford appeared in the *NYT,* July 29, 1991; he provided other details in an interview with L.G.

Awan mentioned his plan in a taped conversation with Mazur and in his testimony at the Noriega trial. The Iacocca remark is from a transcript of the conversation.

Mazur talked about his desire to continue the investigation in his testimony to the Kerry Committee. Additional information on this point is contained in the *Schumer Report,* which also mentions Mazur's hope to meet Naqvi. The quote on BCCI's "moral dimension" is from the November 1988 issue of *BCC International.*

11: CONTAINMENT

The authors reported on most of the events dealt with in this chapter and interviewed several of the principals, including, as noted above, BCCI officials, Justice Department officials, and defense lawyers.

Cook's remark about the volume of documents is from a 1989 interview with L.G. The *FT* headline appeared on October 12, *Le Monde*'s the following day. Von Raab made his prediction in an October 1988 interview with L.G.

Information on trips to London by Clifford and Altman comes from invoices sent to BCCI by their law firm on December 13, 1988, and August 14, 1989. Their role in recruiting, paying, and overseeing the work of the criminal defense lawyers is undisputed.

Correa da Costa's role at Kissinger Associates is documented by records obtained by the Kerry Committee. The information on Stoga's dealings with Helmy is based on copies of the correspondence cited in the book. Information on William D. Rogers is from the *Kerry Report* and from copies of correspondence obtained by the authors.

Hill and Knowlton disclosed its fee when it registered with the Justice Department as a "foreign agent." Gray's extensive ties to Edwin Wilson are discussed in Maas and Trento.

Mankiewicz's remarks were reported in a story by Paul Starobin in the *National Journal,* July 9, 1991. The authors have copies of the Hill and

Knowlton documents mentioned in the chapter. One copy of the "plan of action" was forwarded to BCCI's Sakhia in New York by Donald C. Deaton, the managing director of Hill and Knowlton in New York. The remarks attributed to a Hill and Knowlton official are based on confidential interviews conducted by L.G. in early 1989.

Barcella's March 26, 1990, interview was with L.G. When asked to explain the apparent contradiction, Barcella said that BCCI improved its standards after the 1988 indictment. However, L.G.'s notes of the March 1990 interview indicate clearly that Barcella was referring to BCCI's conduct before the indictment. The account of Tariq Ali's experiences with BCCI is based on interviews with Ali and on British press reports. Blum described his trip to Pakistan in a June 1989 interview with L.G.

Jackowski's remarks were made at bond hearings on October 11 and 13, 1988.

Blum described the Customs investigation of the leak of the Noriega documents in interviews with L.G. The account of his meetings with informants in Florida is based on interviews with Blum, his August 1, 1991, testimony to the Kerry Committee, and Jackowski's November 21, 1991, testimony to the same committee.

The account of what the U.S. Attorney's office did to investigate the allegations regarding First American is based in part on "BCCI Activities" and interviews with federal prosecutors.

The information on the legal fees paid by BCCI is from the *Kerry Report*. Altman's discussions of the case with BCCI's board are mentioned in minutes of board meetings held on August 18 and November 27, 1989, by directors of BCCI Holdings (Luxembourg) S.A. Blum described his discussions with Barcella in an interview with L.G. in November 1989. Barcella confirms that he met with Blum but cannot recall talking about BCCI's attempts to get a plea bargain. He said plea negotiations did not begin until December. The prosecutors, however, say that BCCI's lawyers had been trying to make a deal for months, although they add that serious negotiations did not begin until about December. L.G. was in the audience when Thornburgh spoke at the money-laundering conference in Miami.

Kerry's and Tischler's remarks about the plea bargain were reported by the *NBC Nightly News* on January 16, 1992. The January 19, 1990, letter to Thornburgh was signed by Senators Kerry, Howard Metzenbaum of Ohio, Howell Heflin of Alabama, and Dennis DeConcini of Arizona. The February 1, 1990, letter to Judge Hodges was signed by Kerry, Metzenbaum, and Congressmen William Hughes of New Jersey, Mel Levine of California, Edward Feighan of Ohio, and Charles Rangel of New York. Von Raab's remarks about influence peddlers were made at an August 1, 1991, hearing of the Kerry Committee.

Clifford's statements about his contributions to Kerry appeared in the

WP on March 31, 1991. Mankiewicz was quoted in the *National Journal,* September 7, 1991; this story was also the source for the campaign contribution by Parvez. Kerry's remarks about the difficulty of lining up support for hearings come from "The Bank of Crooks and Criminals," a *Frontline* documentary on PBS-TV on April 21, 1992. The visit by Culver and Banoun to Kerry is mentioned in a letter from Kerry to the two lawyers dated July 18, 1989. Blum described his experience with Culver in an interview with L.G. All of Hatch's comments about his speech are from an interview with L.G. on February 27, 1990, with the exception of his remark about Wechsler and Barcella, which appeared in *Newsweek,* August 26, 1991.

Carter's 1988 remarks about Global 2000 were reported by UPI on October 13, 1988. His trip to Nigeria was reported by the *NBC Nightly News* on January 16, 1990. His *Atlanta Constitution* interview appeared on February 3, 1990.

Roma Theus's September 24, 1990, memo was released by the Kerry Committee at its October 24, 1991, hearing on BCCI. The information on campaign contributions is from various press reports and Federal Election Commission records.

Jackowski's comments about Blum's informants and related matters were made in his November 21, 1991, Kerry Committee testimony.

Naqvi's remark about his "clean conscience" appeared in *Newsweek,* August 12, 1991. His celebratory message to Clifford was in the form of a fax dated January 17, 1990. The Acoca-Shafi letter was provided to L.G. in 1990 by a BCCI employee; identically worded letters were sent to BCCI offices in several parts of the world.

Blum's reaction to the plea bargain is from a January 17, 1990, interview with L.G.

12: THE ENFORCERS

The *Harry F. Bauer* citation was issued by Navy Secretary John Sullivan on behalf of President Roosevelt. Much of the information on Morgenthau's background is from the family history by his brother, Henry Morgenthau III. The comments on Henry Morgenthau, Jr., by Clifford are from his memoirs.

The account of Blum's job application and his meeting with Morgenthau is based on interviews with Blum conducted by P.T. and L.G. Brian Rosner described Moscow in a 1990 interview with L.G.

Von Raab described his conversation with Gates and the CIA report he received from him in a 1991 interview with L.G. and in his August 1, 1991, Kerry Committee testimony.

Burris's experiences with the Fed were described in the House Banking Chronology, various press reports, and in the *Schumer Report*.

Morgenthau described his problems with the Justice Department in his May 23, 1991, testimony to the Senate Banking Committee. Federal prosecutors responded to the criticism in interviews with the authors. P.T. obtained a copy of the internal Fed memo that mentioned Morgenthau's August 1989 tip to the Fed.

Most of the information about PW's audits is based on copies of the audit reports, supplemented by interviews with bank regulators. The fact that the Bank of England informed the Fed about loans from BCCI to First American's shareholders was revealed by E. Gerald Corrigan, president of the New York Fed, in his September 13, 1991, testimony to the House Banking Committee. He said the information came from the chairman of the College of Supervisors; at that time, the panel was chaired by a Bank of England official. Separately, a Fed official confirmed to P.T. that Corrigan was referring to a Bank of England official.

The main source for Abedi's trip to Abu Dhabi in early 1990 is a former BCCI official. The information about the sale of Bin Mahfouz's stock was provided by A. Hafeez, a BCCI official, in a May 1, 1990, letter to William Rutledge, a vice president of the New York Fed. PW's explanation of its handling of BCCI's 1989 accounts appeared in the *WSJ*, June 24, 1991. Details of the layoffs and branch closures come from various press reports in the spring of 1990, including *WSJ* stories by P.T.

Altman's remarks are from two interviews with L.G., one in July 1989, the other in March 1990. The *WSJ*'s "rogue bank" story, co-authored by P.T., appeared on May 3, 1990. Altman described his May 8, 1990, meeting at the Fed in a memo. The authors have the minutes of First American's May 24, 1990, board meeting.

The account of Clifford's efforts to sell First American is based mainly on the correspondence cited in the chapter, which was released at the Kerry Committee's October 24, 1991, hearing. Clifford's statement to the board about the need for a bridge loan is mentioned in the House Banking Chronology.

Altman's September 27, 1990, letter to the *WP* was quoted in the newspaper on March 31, 1991. The Rahman quote is from his August 8, 1991, testimony to the Kerry Committee. Moscow's account of his conversation with Fiske and Cherkasky's remarks about Eddie George were reported in *Vanity Fair*, April 1992.

The authors have a copy of the McQueeney memo; they learned of the Manhattan D.A.'s provision of information to the Fed from interviews with government investigators and the Fed.

The *WP*'s story on the investments by Clifford and Altman in First American's stock appeared on May 5, 1991. According to a statement issued by Hill and Knowlton in May 1991, Clifford's pretax profit was

$6,557,319; Altman's was $3,271,109. Rahman described Hammoud as a flexible front man in testimony and in an interview with P.T.

The PW probe and the clash with the regulators are set out in documents and audits released by the Kerry Committee and in other BCCI documents obtained by the authors. The information on the abortive restructuring is based mostly on P.T.'s interviews with regulators and BCCI officials. The decision to close the bank was described in detail by Jaans and by two other participants in interviews with P.T.

13: THE SHUTDOWN

The account of the July 5, 1991, seizure of BCCI and the aftermath was covered by P.T. for the *WSJ*; he interviewed many of the principals. Useful information also came from press reports, notably stories by other *WSJ* reporters as well as *FT* and *NYT* writers. The estimate of more than $9 billion in losses is from the liquidator's report of December 1991. Choudary's remarks appeared in the *NYT*, August 29, 1991. The BCCI employee who said he was "buried" was interviewed by P.T.

Most of the information on deposits by British local authorities is from a report entitled *Banking Supervision and BCCI: The Role of Local Authorities,* issued on December 16, 1991, by the Treasury and Civil Service Committee of the House of Commons.

The effects of the BCCI closure on customers in Cameroon were described in the *WSJ*, August 6, 1991. Mohiuddin's remarks were quoted in the *WSJ*, July 26, 1991.

The account of Morgenthau's July 29, 1991, press conference is based on notes by P.T., who wrote about it for the *WSJ*. The Fed order issued that day is the main source for the allegations against Adham. The Fed order is also the source for information on the payments to Khalil, Jawhary, and Fulaij as well as the statement that the three men held stock in First American as nominees for BCCI.

Altman asserted on more than one occasion in interviews with P.T. in the first half of 1991 that First American was not a source of funds for BCCI. The information on Mathias's plan to install Volcker as trustee comes from P.T.'s interviews with the two men and with Michael Bradfield, the Fed's general counsel.

The main source for Abu Nidal's dealings with BCCI is Seale. *Time*'s "black network" story ran in its July 19, 1991, issue. Sartaj Asis's remarks appeared in the *FT*, July 24, 1991. Masihur Rahman described the threats he received in his August 8, 1991, Kerry Committee testimony and in interviews with P.T.

Jam Sadiq Ali's statement that Abedi would not be extradited was reported in the *WSJ* on August 1, 1991, based on an AP dispatch. The assistance Jam Sadiq Ali had received from Abedi was reported in an October 23, 1991, *WSJ* story by Tom Petzinger and P.T.

14: CLIFFORD AND ALTMAN

The description of Harriman's book party is from the *WP*, May 23, 1991, and an interview with one of the guests. Clifford made his remark about a "criminal conspiracy" in his October 24, 1991, testimony to the Kerry Committee. Kinsley's column appeared in the *New Republic*, April 4, 1991. The *Globe*'s story on the Altmans appeared on April 9, 1991.

P.T. and L.G. attended the September 11, 1991, hearing. The account of it is based on their notes and on a transcript. Wylie's remark about Clifford's abilities as a salesman appeared the next day in the *WP*.

Skadden's role in the Financial General case is made clear in documents and newspaper accounts concerning the takeover fight. The *WSJ*'s Jill Abramson and P.T. wrote about it on September 11, 1991. P.T. interviewed Robert Bennett and Peter Brown as well as sources at Skadden who requested anonymity.

Quesada's remark that he couldn't remember approving the Clifford-Altman stock deal appeared in the *WP*, May 5, 1991. The information on loans to board members comes from a list of insider loans supplied to the authors.

P.T. and L.G. attended the October 24, 1991, Kerry Committee hearing; the account of it is based on their notes and on a transcript. Many of the documents showing BCCI's close ties to First American Bank of New York were released at the hearing and reprinted in the hearing record.

The section on clues to BCCI's role is based on the following sources.

- Altman's statement that the Arab investors were not told about the buyout of the Virginia bank's minority shareholders is from a July 23, 1988, deposition. He was deposed in the shareholder suit.
- Altman described BCCI's pervasive influence at NBG in his October 24, 1991, Kerry Committee testimony.
- Abedi's role in the hiring of Stevens was first reported publicly in the *WP*, February 3, 1991. Several additional examples are contained in the Fed order of July 29, 1992.

The section on dubious statements by Clifford and Altman is based on the following sources.

- Helms's query to Clifford was a written question inserted into the record of Kerry's October 24, 1991, hearing.
- Clifford's letter to the Fed about the Darwaish affair is dated August

16, 1992. It was released by the Fed (along with other documents) in response to a Freedom of Information Act request. Clifford's affidavit to the Kerry Committee is dated February 7, 1992.

- Altman's statement that the law firm's relationship with Abedi stemmed from its "international practice" is from the *WP,* October 8, 1984. It was in their September 1991 House Banking testimony that Clifford and Altman said that Lance introduced them.
- Lawyers for First American described the company as foreign-owned on several occasions during the Virginia litigation. For example, during a pretrial hearing on September 16, 1988, one attorney, John Stump, described the owners as "non–United States citizens." When the U.S. magistrate, W. Harris Grimsley, asked if they were "majority shareholders," Stump replied, "They're 100 percent shareholders of the holding company." Stump, of course, was acting at the direction of Clifford and Altman.
- Altman said in a July 1989 interview with L.G. that he had been to only one of BCCI's annual management conferences. He amended his story in a March 1990 interview with L.G.
- First American's comment on the Noriega checks appeared in the *WSJ,* May 3, 1990.
- The Sami telex and the invoice from Clifford's firm were found by the Kerry Committee.
- The information on C-Chase money through First American is from the Burris affidavit.

The sources for some of the statements about BCCI's role vis-à-vis First American are cited in the text. The other sources are listed below.

- Altman's letter to the Richmond Fed was dated November 24, 1978.
- The April 1987 remark is from *MEED,* April 4, 1987.
- Altman's remark to the *WP* appeared on October 13, 1988.
- The July 1989 remark was made in an interview with L.G.
- The March 1990 remark was made in an interview with L.G.
- The *WP* story quoting Clifford appeared on February 3, 1991.

Sakhia made his comment about communicating with the shareholders in his October 22, 1991, Kerry Committee testimony. The Howrey & Simon partner was quoted in the *WP,* November 4, 1991.

15: THE WATCHDOGS

Schumer was quoted about the Justice Department's timing in the *WP,* September 6, 1991. The *Schumer Report* is the source for all of the examples of lack of follow-up; some details of the Iranian case come from an AP report dated August 16, 1991. Schumer's new findings were reported in the *NYT* on August 27, 1992. Mazur compared the C-Chase team to a reconnaissance squad when he testified to the Kerry Committee on November 21, 1991.

Dexter Lehtinen testified before the Kerry Committee on May 14, 1992. He was also interviewed by P.T., as was James Dougherty, the lawyer for the Lloyd's of London syndicate that sued Bilbeisi.

The Justice Department official mentioned his "three rules" in an interview with P.T. Ambassador Hussain was interviewed by P.T. in Washington in late 1991.

Gonzalez made his remark about a "stealth banking operation" in his opening statement at the September 11, 1991, hearing of the House Banking Committee. BCCI's illegal telemarketing program was reported in *Newsday* on July 31, 1991; the story was based partly on an AP dispatch. Bailey commented on the Fed's powers in his May 23, 1991, testimony to the Senate Banking Committee.

Beith's criticism and Leigh-Pemberton's response occurred at a July 23, 1991, hearing of the Treasury and Civil Service Select Committee of the House of Commons. Jaans's remarks are from an interview with P.T. Leigh-Pemberton's statement that BCCI was not viewed as "crooked" appeared in the *FT,* July 13, 1991.

Lewis's description of the favors offered by BCCI appeared in the *Miami Herald,* August 4, 1991. The information on his use of CenTrust's plane is from *M, Inc.,* March 1991. The "finder's fee" to Muriel Siebert was reported in a March 22, 1991, *WSJ* story by P.T. and Jill Abramson.

The examples of federal bank regulators joining law firms that did business with BCCI or First American are from a September 6, 1991, story in the *WSJ* by P.T.

Bench testified before the Kerry Committee on February 19, 1992, and his various roles at OCC and PW have been described in P.T.'s interviews with Bench, OCC officials, and former BCCI executives.

Morgenthau's allegation that BCCI bribed Peruvian central bankers was made in the July 29, 1991, press conference at which he announced the indictment of BCCI. One year later, allegations of bribes to several other central bankers were made in a Morgenthau press conference and in the "enterprise corruption" indictment announced at that time.

Bilgrami's account of his shopping trip with the Sudanese central banker is from Bilgrami's July 30, 1992, testimony to the Kerry Committee.

The allegation about BCCI's giving rugs to a Bank of England official is contained in notes made by an investigator during a 1991 interview with Jahavanger Masud in London. The investigator worked for a law firm that represented BCCI depositors.

Abedi's remark about the Bank of England and NatWest appeared in the *FT,* August 8, 1991.

The *WP*'s report on Thornburgh's position regarding corporate crime appeared on April 28, 1990. Blum talked about influence peddlers in his August 1, 1991, Kerry Committee testimony.

16: THE POLITICIANS

The information on Ed Rogers is taken mainly from the *Kerry Report;* one Kerry staff member told the authors that he thought Rogers's explanation was shallow and unconvincing. Additional information is from P.T.'s reporting for the *WSJ*. Safire's remark is from a November 28, 1991, column about Rogers.

President Bush's remarks are from the White House transcript of his press conference. The Adham interview was carried on Middle East News Network on January 18, 1992. The allegation that the CIA sold planes to Skyway was made by Charles ("Bill") White, the estranged business associate of Bath's.

Irvani's letter to Baker (and the cover note from Helms) were released by the Kerry Committee. Stephens's financial backing for Bush was reported in the *WSJ* by Tom Petzinger, P.T., and Jill Abramson on December 6, 1991. Stephens discussed the Riadys in an interview with P.T. in early 1992. Scowcroft's financial disclosure statements reveal that he is an investor in a partnership based in Washington, D.C.; P.T. was told by several sources that the partnership has done business in Pakistan.

Dillon, Read's work for Sonatrach was discussed in an article by L.G. for the October 1979 issue of *Institutional Investor.* Emerson described Clifford's work for Sonatrach. Von Raab made his remarks in a February 1991 interview with L.G.

A former BCCI official told P.T. about Jeb Bush's social ties with Sakhia. Bush confirmed to P.T. that he knew Sakhia but declined to discuss their social relationship. BCCI is identified as a lender to Duque in internal records. The Harken Energy deal was described at length in the *WSJ* story by Petzinger, P.T., and Abramson cited above.

Information on campaign money from Clifford, his law partners, and Lynda Carter is from press reports and Federal Election Commission records.

Dingell's mortgage is reported on his congressional disclosure form.

Nunn discussed his meetings with Pharaon in a telephone interview with P.T. in August 1991. A spokesman confirmed the friendship with Jones.

Both authors interviewed Senator Hatch, L.G. in 1990 and P.T. in 1991. The NBC report on Hatch's ties with Hammoud was broadcast on November 26, 1991. *WSJ* stories on Hatch appeared on November 21, November 27, and December 3, 1991. Pillsbury talked extensively with P.T.

Hatch's office provided his statement in reply to NBC's report on November 27, 1991. The authors obtained copies of Hatch's July 31, 1986, letter to Peter O. Stearns at the FSLIC. Hatch's financial disclosure statements contain the information on the apartment managed for him by Hourani. Tom Petzinger of the *WSJ* provided the notes of his December 3, 1991, interview with a spokesman for Hostler for the December 6, 1991, *WSJ* story on Harken. Details of Pillsbury's dealings with BCCI's representatives are contained in the *Kerry Report.*

Information about Hammoud's death comes from medical reports obtained or reviewed by P.T. and from interviews with a lawyer for a member of the family. Chinoy said in his March 13, 1992, Kerry Committee testimony that he didn't believe Hammoud was dead. A U.S. government investigator discussed Hammoud's activities in Washington, D.C., with P.T. Separately, another person involved with the Hammouds allowed P.T. to read Violette Hammoud's account of her husband's death. P.T. obtained the documents relating to the Altman-Pillsbury meeting at the Helmsley Palace. The Hammoud telephone intercept was reported in *Newsweek,* August 10, 1992; information consistent with that report was provided to P.T. by a law enforcement source.

Von Raab mentioned the CIA report to L.G. and in an interview on ABC-TV's *Nightline* broadcast on July 15, 1991. The 1986 CIA memo was obtained by the authors. There was extensive discussion of it in Mulholland's February 19, 1992, testimony before the Kerry Committee.

Gonzalez's remarks about the parallels between BCCI and BNL were made at the September 11, 1991, hearing of the House Banking Committee. P.T. reported on Hartmann's connections in the *WSJ* on September 13 and October 7, 1991.

Information on the possible whereabouts of the Gokal brothers was provided by former BCCI officials and sources in Switzerland. Seymour Glanzer, a lawyer for the Gulf Group and for Abbas Gokal, told the authors that he did not know how to reach them.

The awarding of banking licenses to Shoaib and Nawabi was reported in an October 23, 1991, story for the *WSJ* by Tom Petzinger and P.T. The SEC's suit was reported in the *WSJ,* May 7, 1992.

Much of the material for the rest of the chapter is from PW reports, the Fed's July 29, 1992, order, newspaper accounts, P.T.'s interviews with Elias (and other big creditors of BCCI), and P.T.'s reporting of the U.S. court developments for the *WSJ.*

17: ROUNDING UP THE SUSPECTS

P.T. talked with Albright and people who know him, including his lawyer, Sol Corbin. In interviews conducted by P.T., sources at the Fed and other regulatory agencies described the squabbling over the issue of the trustee for First American. The authors obtained Judge Green's order of June 23, 1992, from the court.

The details of the Bin Mahfouz investments in BCCI and First American are set out in the Fed's July 8, 1992, order against Khalid Bin Mahfouz. The PW report of June 22, 1991, on ICIC and *WSJ* stories based on it (published in February 1992) were also sources for the section on Bin Mahfouz.

The New York State indictment of Bin Mahfouz and Kahlon and P.T.'s reporting of the July 2, 1992, press conference to announce it were sources for this section of the chapter. An *NYT* story by Elaine Sciolino and Jeff Gerth on August 2, 1992, brought together many of the recent developments in U.S.-Saudi relations over banking matters in general and National Commercial Bank (NCB) in particular. P.T. also drew on his background knowledge of Saudi Arabia and its banks. (In the early 1980s, he conducted interviews with officials at NCB and other Saudi banks.)

Information about the raids in the Cayman Islands comes from separate interviews with a lawyer and an investigator who visited the colony around the time of the raids.

The section of the chapter on the events leading up to the July 1992 indictments was based mainly on reporting by P.T. and his *WSJ* colleagues, including Jonathan Moses. Most of the examples of evidence against Clifford and Altman are from the Fed order of July 29, 1992.

Information relating to the plea negotiations of Adham and Jawhary is from P.T.'s interviews with lawyers involved in the case.

P.T. attended Clifford's and Altman's meeting with the press and the subsequent hearing. Again, the authors are indebted to Moses for reporting on some of the events in New York.

Written statements by Aslam (with some supporting documentation) are the basis for the final section of this chapter.

EPILOGUE

Institutional Investor published its interview with Abedi in January 1983. Former BCCI officers described Abedi's preoccupation with appearances.

As noted in Chapter 5, Bill Kovach, formerly of the *Atlanta Constitution,* is the source for how Carter spoke of Abedi; Kovach was quoted in the *LAT* on July 28, 1991. Abedi's quotes are from a July 16, 1991, *WSJ* story by John Bussey, based on his reporting in Pakistan in the days after the seizure of BCCI; Abedi's remark on God is from the *WSJ,* July 30, 1991.

Information on Hammoud's borrowing from BNL is from congressional investigators.

P.T. reported on the legal problems of Clifford and Altman for the *WSJ* and attended Judge Green's September 10, 1992, hearing.

Brown's involvement with Patton, Boggs & Blow was discussed in a *WSJ* article by Jill Abramson on July 9, 1992. The information on the real estate portfolio is from a May 10, 1992, *WSJ* story by Tom Petzinger.

A study by the National Library on Money and Politics, reported in the *NYT* on July 27, 1992, is the source for campaign money from employees of Stephens Inc. and other firms. The Center for Public Integrity's report of February 1992 is the source for Hill and Knowlton's people working in the Clinton campaign. The section on Hillary Clinton's work for Stephens is based on a court filing; at that time Clinton used her maiden name (Hillary Rodham) professionally. The information on the FBI probe is from interviews conducted by P.T.

The Center for Public Integrity's report is the source for James Lake's various roles and his fees from the Abu Dhabi interests.

Mattingly's comment that he received no adverse information from the CIA is from his September 13, 1991, testimony to the House Banking Committee. He told the Kerry Committee staff that the Fed was not told about the liaison roles of Adham and Khalil. Volcker's comment is from the *Kerry Report,* which cites Volcker's March 1991 testimony to the Senate Banking Committee. Mulholland testified about the 1986 CIA report before the Kerry Committee on February 19, 1992.

Federal prosecutors in Tampa told L.G. and P.T. in interviews that the CIA provided no information about BCCI during the C-Chase case. Robert Gray's intelligence connections are discussed at length in Trento.

Barcella's role in giving a legal opinion related to an arms deal was disclosed in a story by Lyn Bixby for the *Hartford Courant* on May 29, 1992; the story is also the source for diGenova's comment. Barcella's comments are from an interview with L.G.

Hatch's trip to China is from a series on the Afghan operation by Steve Coll of the *WP,* published on July 19 and 20, 1992.

The CIA's possible role in encouraging the establishment of BCCI is from L.G.'s interviews with a former BCCI official in 1990 and 1992.

Warnke's comment on different values appeared in the *WP,* July 30, 1992. The quote on Abedi is from a Kerry staff interview conducted on October 9, 1991. Kerry's remarks are from an interview with L.G.

SELECTED BIBLIOGRAPHY

BOOKS

Aburish, Said K. *Payoff: Wheeling and Dealing in the Arab World*. London: André Deutsch, 1985.

Adams, James Ring, and Douglas Frantz. *A Full Service Bank*. New York: Pocket Books, 1992.

Ali, A. Yusuf, ed. *The Holy Qu'ran*. Lahore, Pakistan: Sh. Muhammad Ashraf, 1975.

Anderson, Jack, with James Boyd. *Fiasco: The Real Story Behind the Disastrous Worldwide Energy Crisis*. New York: Times Books, 1983.

Anderson, Scott, and Jon Lee Anderson. *Inside the League*. New York: Dodd, Mead, 1986.

Bhutto, Benazir. *Daughter of the East*. London: Hamish Hamilton, 1988.

Blandford, Linda. *Oil Sheikhs*. London: Star, 1977.

Boulton, David. *The Grease Machine: The Inside Story of Lockheed's Dollar Diplomacy*. New York: Harper & Row, 1978.

Carter, J. R. L. *Leading Merchant Families of Saudi Arabia*. London: Scorpion, 1979.

———. *Investors in Saudi Arabia*. London: Scorpion, 1981.

Carter, Jimmy. *The Blood of Abraham: Insights into the Middle East*. Boston: Houghton Mifflin, 1985.

———. *Keeping Faith: Memoirs of a President*. New York: Bantam, 1982.

Clifford, Clark, with Richard Holbrooke. *Counsel to the President: A Memoir*. New York: Random House, 1991.

Colton, Elizabeth O. *The Jackson Phenomenon*. New York: Doubleday, 1989.

Cooley, John K. *Payback. America's Long War in the Middle East*. New York: Brassey's, 1991.

Crowe, Kenneth C. *America for Sale.* New York: Anchor, 1980.

Dinges, John. *Our Man in Panama.* New York: Random House, 1990.

Emerson, Steven. *The American House of Saud.* New York: Franklin Watts, 1985.

Faith, Nicholas. *Safety in Numbers: The Mysterious World of Swiss Banking.* London: Hamish Hamilton, 1984.

Fay, Stephen. *The Great Silver Bubble.* London: Hodder and Stoughton, 1982.

Field, Michael. *The Merchants: The Big Business Families of Arabia.* London: John Murray, 1984.

Francis, Diane. *The Contrepreneurs.* Toronto: Macmillan of Canada, 1988.

García Lupo, Rogelio. *Paraguay de Stroessner.* Buenos Aires: Serie Reporter, 1989.

Gibb, H. A. R., and J. H. Kramers, eds. *Shorter Encyclopaedia of Islam.* Leiden, The Netherlands: E. J. Brill, 1974.

Glad, Betty. *Jimmy Carter: In Search of the Great White House.* New York: Norton, 1980.

Goulden, Joseph C. *The Superlawyers: The Small and Powerful World of the Great Washington Law Firms.* New York: Weybright and Talley, 1972.

Gurwin, Larry. *The Calvi Affair: Death of a Banker.* London: Macmillan, 1983.

Halberstam, David. *The Best and the Brightest.* New York: Fawcett Crest, 1973.

Halliday, Fred. *Arabia Without Sultans.* New York: Vintage Books, 1975.

Hirst, David, and Irene Beeson. *Sadat.* London: Faber & Faber, 1981.

Holden, David, and Richard Johns. *The House of Saud.* London: Sidgwick & Jackson, 1981.

Hourani, Albert. *A History of the Arab Peoples.* Cambridge: Belknap Press of Harvard University Press, 1991.

Howe, Russell Warren, and Sarah Hays Trott. *The Power Peddlers: How Lobbyists Mold America's Foreign Policy.* Garden City, N.Y.: Doubleday, 1977.

Kelly, J. B. *Arabia, the Gulf and the West.* New York: Basic Books, 1980.

Kempe, Frederick. *Divorcing the Dictator: America's Bungled Affair with Noriega.* New York: Putnam, 1990.

Kessler, Ronald. *Khashoggi.* London: Corgi, 1987.

Kindleberger, Charles P. *Manias, Panics, and Crashes: A History of Financial Crises.* New York: Basic Books, 1978.

Kissinger, Henry. *The White House Years.* Boston: Little, Brown, 1979.

Kochan, Nick, and Bob Whittington. *Bankrupt: The BCCI Fraud.* London: Gollancz, 1991. (The U.S. edition, which contains material added by Mark Potts of the *Washington Post,* is *Dirty Money: The Inside Story of the World's Sleaziest Bank.* Washington, D.C.: National Press Books, 1992.)

Kwitny, Jonathan. *The Crimes of Patriots.* New York: Touchstone, 1987.

Lacey, Robert. *The Kingdom: Arabia & the House of Sa'ud.* New York: Avon Books, 1981.

Lance, Bert. *The Truth of the Matter.* New York: Summit, 1991.

Lernoux, Penny. *In Banks We Trust.* Garden City, N.Y.: Anchor Press/Doubleday, 1984.

Levins, Hoag. *Arab Reach: The Secret War Against Israel.* Garden City, N.Y.: Doubleday, 1983.

Lilienthal, David E. *The Journals of David E. Lilienthal. Volume III, Venturesome Years, 1950–1955.* New York: Harper & Row, 1966.

Maas, Peter. *Manhunt.* New York: Random House, 1986.

Marchetti, Victor, and John D. Marks. *The CIA and the Cult of Intelligence.* New York: Dell, 1983.

Mayer, Martin. *The Bankers.* New York: Ballantine, 1976.

McCoy, Alfred W. *The Politics of Heroin: CIA Complicity in the Global Drug Trade.* New York: Lawrence Hill Books, 1991.

Mollenhoff, Clark R. *The President Who Failed: Carter out of Control.* New York: Macmillan, 1980.

Morgenthau, Henry, III. *Mostly Morgenthaus: A Family History.* New York: Ticknor & Fields, 1991.

Mosley, Leonard. *Power Play: Oil in the Middle East.* Baltimore: Penguin Books, 1974.

National Security Archive. *The Chronology: The Documented Day-by-Day Account of the Secret Military Assistance to Iran and to the Contras.* New York: Warner Books, 1987.

Naylor, R. T. *Hot Money.* New York: Linden Press/Simon & Schuster, 1987.

Persico, Joseph E. *Casey.* New York: Penguin, 1990.

Powers, Thomas. *The Man Who Kept the Secrets: Richard Helms and the CIA.* New York: Pocket Books, 1981.

Powis, Robert E. *The Money Launderers.* Chicago: Probus, 1992.

Prados, John. *Keepers of the Keys: A History of the National Security Council from Truman to Bush.* New York: Morrow, 1991.

Reston, James, Jr. *The Lone Star: The Life of John Connally.* New York: Harper & Row, 1989.

Rosner, Brian. *Swindle: How a Man Named John Grambling, Jr., Cheated Banks out of Millions.* Homewood, Ill.: Business One Irwin, 1990.

Sampson, Anthony. *The Arms Bazaar.* New York: Viking, 1977.

———. *The Seven Sisters: The Great Oil Companies and the World They Made.* London: Coronet, 1980.

Sandbrook, Richard. *The Politics of Africa's Economic Stagnation.* Cambridge: Cambridge University Press, 1985.

Seale, Patrick. *Abu Nidal: A Gun for Hire.* New York: Random House, 1992.

Shannon, Elaine. *Desperadoes.* New York: Viking, 1988.

Smith, Richard Harris. *OSS: The Secret History of America's First Central Intelligence Agency.* Berkeley, Calif.: University of California Press, 1981.

Thesiger, Wilfred. *Arabian Sands.* London: Penguin Books, 1984 (originally published in 1959).

Thomas, Evan. *The Man to See: Edward Bennett Williams.* New York: Simon & Schuster, 1991.

Timmerman, Kenneth R. *The Death Lobby: How the West Armed Iraq.* Boston: Houghton Mifflin, 1991.

Tosches, Nick. *Power on Earth: Michele Sindona's Explosive Story.* New York: Arbor House, 1986.

Tower Commission Report. New York: Times Books and Bantam Books, 1987.

Trento, Susan. *The Power House: Robert Keith Gray and the Selling of Access and Influence in Washington.* New York: St. Martin's Press, 1992.

Truman, Harry S. *Where the Buck Stops: The Personal and Private Writings of Harry S. Truman.* New York: Warner Books, 1989.

Wakefield, Mary Rose, ed. *UAE. A MEED Practical Guide.* London: Middle East Economic Digest (MEED), 1986.

Walter, Ingo. *Secret Money: The World of International Financial Secrecy.* London: George Allen & Unwin, 1985.

Wehr, Hans. *A Dictionary of Modern Written Arabic,* ed. J. Milton Cowan. Wiesbaden, Germany: Otto Harrassowitz, 1971.

Winter-Berger, Robert N. *The Washington Pay-off.* Secaucus, N.J.: Lyle Stuart, 1972.

Witcover, Jules. *Marathon: The Pursuit of the Presidency, 1972–1976.* New York: Viking, 1977.

Yergin, Daniel. *The Prize.* New York: Simon & Schuster, 1991.

Woodward, Bob. *Veil: The Secret Wars of the CIA, 1981–1987.* New York: Simon & Schuster, 1987.

DOCUMENTS

Banking Supervision and BCCI: International and National Regulation. The Treasury and Civil Service Committee Reports of the House of Commons, 1991 and 1992.

The BCCI Affair. Hearings before the Subcommittee on Terrorism, Narcotics, and International Operations of the Committee on Foreign Relations. U.S. Senate, 102nd Congress, first and second sessions. Part 1 (August 1, 2, 8, 1991), Part 2 (October 18, 22, 1991), Part 3 (October 23, 24, 25, November 21, 1991), Part 4 (February 19, March 18, 1992), Part 5 (May 14, 1992), Part 6 (July 30, 1992).

The BCCI Affair: A Report to the Senate Committee on Foreign Relations from Senator John Kerry, Chairman, and from Senator Hank Brown, Ranking Member, Subcommittee on Terrorism, Narcotics, and International Operations, at the Conclusion of an Investigation of Matters Pertaining to the Bank of Credit and Commerce International. 102nd Congress, second session, September 30, 1992.

Bank of Credit and Commerce International (BCCI) Investigation. Hearings before the Committee on Banking, Finance and Urban Affairs, U.S. House of Representatives, 102nd Congress, first session, Part 1 (September 11, 1991), Part 2 (September 13, 1991), and Part 3 (September 27, 1991).

The Bank of Credit and Commerce International and S. 1019. Hearing before the Subcommittee on Consumer and Regulatory Affairs of the Committee on Banking, Housing, and Urban Affairs. U.S. Senate, 102nd Congress, first session, May 23, 1991.

BCCI papers: various memos, accounts, and internal documents from the bank's offices, including Abu Dhabi, Grand Cayman, London, Los Angeles, Miami, New York, Paris, and Washington, D.C.

Drugs and Money Laundering in Panama. Hearing before the Permanent Subcommittee on Investigations of the Committee on Governmental Affairs. U.S. Senate, 100th Congress, second session, January 28, 1988.

Drugs, Law Enforcement, and Foreign Policy: Panama. Hearings before the Subcommittee on Terrorism, Narcotics, and International Operations of the Committee on Foreign Relations. U.S. Senate, 100th Congress, second session, Part 2 (February 8, 9, 10, 11, 1988) and Part 3 (April 4, 5, 6, 7, 1988).

Federal Reserve orders and papers relating to BCCI, First American, National Bank of Georgia and Independence Bank, including BCCI, July 29, 1991; Khalid Bin Mahfouz et al., July 2, 1992; and Clifford and Altman, July 29, 1992.

Price Waterhouse papers: various audits and memos, including BCCI Holdings (Luxembourg) S.A. Report to the Directors on ICIC Group S.A., June 17, 1991, and Report on BCCI S.A. under Section 41 of Britain's Banking Act, June 22, 1991.

Touche Ross: Provisional Liquidators' Report on BCCI, January 1992.

INDEX